OTHER BOOKS BY LEO ROSTEN

Dear "Herm"
Leo Rosten's Treasury of Jewish Quotations
People I Have Loved, Known or Admired
A Trumpet for Reason
Rome Wasn't Burned in a Day: The Mischief of Language
The Joys of Yiddish
A Most Private Intrigue
The Many Worlds of L°E°O R°O°S°T°E°N
Captain Newman, M.D.
Religions in America (ed.)
The Story Behind the Painting
The Return of H°Y°M°A°N K°A°P°L°A°N
A Guide to the Religions of America (ed.)
The Dark Corner
112 Gripes About the French (War Department)
Hollywood: The Movie Colony, the Movie Makers
Dateline: Europe
The Strangest Places
The Washington Correspondents
The Education of H°Y°M°A°N K°A°P°L°A°N

RELIGIONS OF AMERICA

FERMENT AND FAITH IN AN AGE OF CRISIS

A NEW GUIDE AND ALMANAC

Edited with Extensive Comments

and Essays, by LEO ROSTEN

A TOUCHSTONE BOOK
Published by Simon & Schuster
New York   London   Toronto   Sydney

To Gardner Cowles

Designed by Irving Perkins
Manufactured in the United States of America

40 39 38 37 36 35

Library of Congress Cataloging in Publication Data

Rosten, Leo Calvin, 1908–   comp.
Religions of America.

First published in 1955 under title: A guide to the religions of America,
1963 under title: Religions in America.
Includes index.
1.   Sects—United States.   2.   United States-
Religion.   I.   Title.
BR516.5.R67   1975   280'.0973   73-11703
ISBN 0-671-21970-7
ISBN 0-671-21971-5 pbk.

For research assistance, I thank Kathleen Mazzie and Angelika Wolff.

Grateful acknowledgment is made to the following for permission to reprint valuable material, in part or in whole, from their publications:

American Association for the Advancement of Science, Washington, D.C., for material from *Science,* copyright © 1973 by the American Association for the Advancement of Science.

The American Jewish Committee and the Jewish Publication Society of America, New York, for data from Alvin Chenkin, "Jewish Population in the United States, 1971," *American Jewish Year Book, 1972* [Vol. 73].

Geoffrey Chapman Publishers, London, for excerpts from *The Documents of Vatican II,* edited by Walter M. Abbott, S.J., and translated from the Latin by Msgr. Joseph Gallagher, 1966.

Continuum, Chicago, for material from *Anti-Semitism in the United States* by Oscar Cohen, © Justus George Lawler.

Doubleday & Co., Inc., New York, for excerpts from *Protestant—Catholic —Jew* by Will Herberg, copyright © 1955, 1960 by Will Herberg.

Encyclopaedia Britannica, Chicago, Illinois, for data from the 1972 *Britannica Book of the Year,* copyright © 1972 by Encyclopaedia Britannica.

The Editor of *The Jewish Journal of Sociology,* London, for material from "Intermarriage and Conversion: A Guide for Future Research" by Bernard Lazerwitz, first published in *The Jewish Journal of Sociology* (Vol. XIII, No. 1, June 1971, pp. 41–63).

Johnson Publishing Co., Chicago, for data from *The Negro Handbook,* copyright © 1966 by Johnson Publishing Co., and from *The Ebony Handbook,* copyright © 1974 by Johnson Publishing Co.

P.J. Kenedy & Sons, New York, for data from the General Summary of Statistics, supplement to the *Official Catholic Directory.*

New York *Post* for excerpts from an article by Barbara Trecker, March 14, 1972, © 1972, New York Post Corporation.

The New York Times for excerpts from articles by Dr. Alan F. Guttmacher, January 23, 1973; Edward B. Fiske, August 6, 1972; and Evan Jenkins, June 27, 1973, © 1972–73 by The New York Times Company.

Newspaper Enterprise Association, Inc., New York, for data from *The World Almanac, 1975,* published by Newspaper Enterprise Association, Inc.

Newsweek Magazine for opinion polls and extracts. Copyright Newsweek, Inc., 1967.

Our Sunday Visitor, Inc., Huntington, Indiana, for data from the *1968, 1970, 1971, 1972* and *1973 Catholic Almanacs,* copyright © 1967, 1969, 1970, 1971, 1972 by Our Sunday Visitor, Inc.

The Population Council, New York, for material from *Studies in Family Planning.*

CONTENTS

EDITOR'S PREFACE   17
    BY *Leo Rosten*

PART ONE / RELIGIOUS BELIEFS AND CREDOS
    —in question-and-answer form

WHAT IS A BAPTIST?   25
    BY *William B. Lipphard* AND *Frank A. Sharp*

WHAT IS A CATHOLIC?   39
    BY *Donald W. Hendricks*

WHAT IS THE CHRISTIAN CHURCH?
    See WHO ARE THE DISCIPLES OF CHRIST?.

WHAT IS A CHRISTIAN SCIENTIST?   69
    BY *J. Buroughs Stokes*

WHAT IS A CONGREGATIONALIST?
    See WHAT IS THE UNITED CHURCH OF CHRIST?

WHO ARE THE DISCIPLES OF CHRIST (*Christian Church*)?   83
    BY *James E. Craig* AND *Robert L. Friedly*

WHAT IS AN EPISCOPALIAN?   96
    BY *W. Norman Pittenger*

WHAT IS A GREEK ORTHODOX?   112
    BY *Arthur Douropulos*

WHO ARE JEHOVAH'S WITNESSES?   132
    BY *Milton G. Henschel*

WHAT IS A JEW?   142
    BY *Morris N. Kertzer*

WHAT IS A LUTHERAN?   156
    BY *G. Elson Ruff* AND *Albert P. Stauderman*

WHAT IS A METHODIST?   170
   BY *Ralph W. Sockman* AND *Paul A. Washburn*

WHAT IS A MORMON?   186
   BY *Richard L. Evans*

WHAT IS A PRESBYTERIAN?   200
   BY *John S. Bonnell*

WHAT IS A QUAKER?   213
   BY *Richmond P. Miller* AND *R. W. Tucker*

WHAT IS A SEVENTH-DAY ADVENTIST?   244
   BY *Arthur S. Maxwell*

THE "UNCHURCHED" AMERICANS:
WHAT DO THEY BELIEVE?   255
   BY *Edward L. Ericson*

WHAT IS A UNITARIAN UNIVERSALIST?   263
   BY *Karl M. Chworowsky* AND *Christopher Gist Raible*

WHAT IS THE UNITED CHURCH OF CHRIST?   277
   BY *The Church Office of Communication*

WHAT IS AN AGNOSTIC?   284
   BY *Bertrand Russell*

THE RELIGION OF A SCIENTIST   296
   BY *Warren Weaver*

PART TWO / ALMANAC
   A comprehensive collation of facts, events,
   opinion polls, statistics, analyses, and essays on
   the problems and crises confronting the churches
   today

   I. ABORTION   309
     *Supreme Court Decision, 1973: Highlights and Analysis
       of Effects,* 309
     American Attitudes Toward Abortion, 313
     *Response of Catholics Prior to the Supreme Court
       Decision,* 317
     *Analysis of 72,988 Abortions Performed in the United
       States: 1970–1971,* 320
     *Abortions Performed on Catholic Women: International
       Data,* 321

Abortion and Young Blacks, 321
Lutherans and Abortion, 322
Effects of Legalizing Abortion, 323

II. "ACTIVISM": THE GROWTH OR DECLINE OF
RELIGIOUS GROUPS RELATED TO THEIR SOCIAL
ACTIVISM IN THE 1960s AND 1970s   324
*Should the Churches Speak out on Social and Political
   Issues?* 324
Opinions of Priests, Ministers, and Rabbis, 325
Comparison of Attitudes, 325
*Are "Socially Oriented" and "Liberal" Churches Losing
   Members? Are "Conservative" Churches Gaining?* 326
Has the Catholic Church Gained or Lost Members? 327
Sunday Sermons: What Do They Say? 327

III. AFFIRMATIONS OF RELIGIOUS IDENTITY:
CATHOLICS, JEWS, PROTESTANTS, AGNOSTICS   329
What Is Your Religious Preference? 332
Is Religion a Relevant Part of Your Life? 332
U.S. Census Bureau Voluntary Survey, 333
AGNOSTICS IN THE UNITED STATES
See Part One, "The 'Unchurched' Americans: What Do
   They Believe?" by Edward L. Ericson; and Part
   Two, Chapters III and XXII
ANTI-SEMITISM IN THE UNITED STATES
See Part Two, Chapters XXV, "Jews," and XXX,
   "Prejudice and Religion"

IV. BELIEF IN GOD   337
"Do You Believe in a God?" 337
*Comparison of the United States with Ten Other
   Nations,* 339
Belief in God: Priests, Ministers, and Rabbis, 339

V. BELIEF IN HEAVEN, HELL, THE DEVIL, LIFE
AFTER DEATH   341
"Do You Believe in Heaven?" 341
*Comparison of United States with Ten Other
   Nations,* 342
"Do You Believe in Hell?" 342
"Do You Believe in the Devil?" 343
"Do You Believe in Life After Death?" 343
Belief of Clergy in Life After Death, 344

VI. THE BIBLE   345
The Ecumenical Bible: 1973, 345
Facts About the Bible: Editor's Summary in
     Question–Answer Form, 346
Chart of the English Bible: Its Origin and History, 348
Historical Highlights of the Bible, 350
Catholic Bibles, 352
Protestant Counterparts of Douay-Rheims Bible, 353
The New American Bible, 353

VII. BIBLE READING IN THE UNITED STATES   354
"Have You Yourself Read Any Part of the Bible at
     Home Within the Last Year?" 354
"Which Version of the Bible Did You Read . . . ?" 354

VIII. BIRTH CONTROL   356
U.S. National Statistics, 356
Roman Catholic Contraception and Fertility: An
     International Survey, 357
Use of Birth Control Devices by Catholic Women, 359
Statistical Tables on Birth Control Among U.S. Roman
     Catholic Women, 362
Trends in Attitudes Toward, and Use of, Birth Control
     Devices in the United States, 366
Family Planning, 368
Poll of Roman Catholics on Birth Control and the
     Pill, 369
Catholic Priests and Birth Control, 370
Pope Cautions United Nations on Birth Control as
     Means of Coping with World Population, 372

IX. BLACK AMERICANS AND THE CHURCHES   374
Black Militance, 374
Blacks and the Christian Church, 374
Statistics: Black Church Membership, 375
Intermarriage of Whites and Nonwhites: Current
     Statistics, 376
Black Roman Catholics, 377
Black Muslims, 380
Early Negro Churches in the United States, 385

X. CATHOLICS: FACTS, OPINIONS, TRENDS,
FERMENT, AND SCHISMS   386
Catholicism Today: An Essay, 386

Statistical Summary: Population, Clergy, Schools,
    Baptisms, Marriages, 388
Opinions of U.S. Roman Catholics on Key Issues, 392
Encyclical of Pope Paul VI: "Humanae Vitae," 394
Clergy and Orders: Problems, Defections, the Radical
    Nuns, the Jesuits, 397
Celibacy: The Problem, 402
Papal Authority and Papal Infallibility: Priests Versus
    Bishops, 415
On Vatican II, 418
Catholic–Jewish Relations, 419
Catholics and Blacks, 420
Vatican Policy Change on Communism, 421
Catholicism Today, 422
Catholic Holidays, Feasts, and Devotions, 424

XI. CHURCH ATTENDANCE IN THE UNITED
    STATES   431
Church Attendance, 431
Drop in Catholic Attendance at Mass, 434
The Clergy's Opinions on Churchgoing, 435
Comparison of Churchgoing in Seven Nations, 436

XII. CHURCH MEMBERSHIP: SEVENTY-NINE
    DENOMINATIONS   437
Census of Religious Groups in the United States, 437
Comparative Annual Figures, 441
Church Affiliation and Population Growth: Figures
    and Trends, 442
Census of World Religious Groups, 444
Comparison of Protestant and Catholic Membership
    Statistics, 445
Church Membership Statistics by States and
    Regions, 445
Sex and Race Composition, 448
Age Composition, 448
Education and Church Affiliation, 449
Occupation and Church Affiliation, 449
Income and Church Affiliation, 450
Composition by Regions, 450
Community Size and Church Affiliation, 451
Critical Evaluation of Statistics on Religion, 451

XIII. *THE CLERGY*   458
    Statistics for Forty Religious Groups, 458
    Income of Protestant Ministers, 460
    Clergymen's Estimate of Their Relation to the Laity, 462
    Clergymen's Criticism of Church Performance, 463
    Clergymen's Vote on the Role of the Church, 463
    Protestant Clergymen's Attitude: "Would You Enter the
        Clergy Today?" 464
    Women in the Protestant Ministry: Statistics, Attitudes,
        Problems, 465
    Catholics and the Ordination of Women, 469
    Jewish Women and the Rabbinate, 474
    Lutherans and the Role of Women, 476

XIV. *DENOMINATIONS AND THEIR "FAMILY"*
    GROUPS   477
    Church Groupings in the United States, 477
    Church Mergers, 483
    Lutheran Mergers, 485
    Clergymen's Preference on Protestant Church
        Merger, 487

XV. *DIVORCE AND RELIGION*   488
    Desertion as Divorce, 488
    National Divorce Figures and Projections, 489
    Catholic Divorce Rate and Trend, 489
    Catholic Attitudes Toward Divorce: 1967–1971, 491
    Catholic Law on Divorce, 492
    Catholic Theologians on Second Marriages, 492
    A Jesuit's View, 493
    Episcopalians Liberalize Divorce, 494

XVI. *ECUMENISM: HISTORY, HOPES, AND*
    DISAPPOINTMENTS   495
    Poll of Catholics and Protestants on Church
        Unification, 495
    The Ecumenical Movement: A Historical Summary, 496
    Less Optimistic Aspects, 505
    Papal Infallibility Reaffirmed, 506
    Obstacles to Ecumenism, 508
    Notable Studies—and Predictions, 510

XVII. *EDUCATION IN RELIGIOUS SCHOOLS IN THE*
    UNITED STATES   512

Religious Instruction (Denominations of 100,000 or
more), 512
Catholic Education in the United States, 513
Poll on Parochial Schools, 516
Parochial Schools and Racial Integration, 517
Crisis in Parochial School Financing, 517
Predictions: Parochial Schools, 518
Enrollment in Jewish Schools: 1969–1970, 519

XVIII. FAMILY SIZE AND PLANNING: POLLS AND
STATISTICS   522
Decline in Family Size and Birth Rate, 522
Poll Trend on Family Size, 523
Catholic Fertility and Birth Rates in Various
Countries, 523
Opinions on Fertility Control: Religious Groupings, 526
Fertility and Jews: A Special Problem, 528

XIX. FEDERAL AID TO EDUCATION   529
Supreme Court Rulings on Parochial Schools, 529
Federal Aid "Revoked," 529
Effects on Catholic Schools, 531

XX. HOLY DAYS AND RELIGIOUS OBSERVANCES:
ALL FAITHS   532
Calendar and Description, 532
Tables of Movable Holidays: Christian and Secular,
and Jewish: 1974–1982, 536
Extended Catholic Calendar: 1974–1999, 538

XXI. HOMOSEXUALITY: THE CHURCHES AND
PSYCHIATRY   540

XXII. HUMANISTS: MANIFESTO II   542

XXIII. INFLUENCE OF RELIGION: OPINION POLLS   545
Is Religion Losing Its Influence? 545
Confidence in and Respect for the Church as Compared
with Other Institutions, 546
Clergymen's Estimate of Religion's Influence, 546
Influence of Sermons: Sociologists' Views, 546
Optimism Regarding Future of Religion, 547

XXIV. INTERMARRIAGE–STATISTICS, OPINIONS, AND
CONVERSION DATA: CATHOLICS, PROTESTANTS,
AND JEWS   549
American Attitudes Toward Intermarriage, 549

Opinions on Intermarriage: 1969, 550
Attitudes Toward Marriages Between Christians and
Jews, 551
Attitudes of Jews Toward Intermarriage, 551
Catholics and Intermarriage: Apostolic Letter, 551
Opinions by Groups, 555
Intermarriage in a Denominational Society: Comparison
of Rates and Religious Groups, 555
Intermarriage and Conversion: Catholics, Protestants,
and Jews, 556
Research on Mixed Marriages, 560
"JESUS MOVEMENTS"
See Part Two, Chapter XXVII, "Pentecostal and
Charismatic Movements in the 1970s"

XXV. JEWS   564
Population Figures, 564
Faith and Religious Observance, 565
Education, 566
Changes in the Status of Jewish Women, 567
Jews and Intermarriage, 568
Jewish Women and the Rabbinate, 569
Opinions of Jews: Anti-Semitism, Pride, 570
Intermarriage: Opinions, 571
Storm Within the Rabbinate over Intermarriage, 573
Family Life and Judaism, 575
Jews and Politics, 577
Jewish Holidays, 580
Jewish Calendar, 586

XXVI. LUTHERANS: RECENT CRISES   587
Editor's Summary, 587
MARRIAGE AND RELIGION
See Part Two, Chapters XV, "Divorce and Religion,"
and XXIV, "Intermarriage"

XXVII. PENTECOSTAL AND CHARISMATIC MOVEMENTS
IN THE 1970s   590
Nature of the Movements, 590
How Large Are the Pentecostal Movements? 591
What Is Pentecostalism? 591
Church Responses, 592
Four Different Pentecostal Groups, 593
Psychology of Pentecostalism, 594
Drugs and Pentecostalism, 594

Historical Note, 595
Prediction, 596
A New Roman Catholic Mass, 596

XXVIII. POLITICS AND RELIGIOUS AFFILIATION   598

XXIX. PRAYER IN PUBLIC SCHOOLS   599

XXX. PREJUDICE AND RELIGION   600
*Attitudes Toward Other Faiths: Catholics, Protestants,
     Jews,* 600
*Religious Prejudice and Politics: Catholic, Jewish,
     Black, Woman President,* 601
Prejudice Among Teen-Agers, 604
Christian Faith and Anti-Semitism, 605
Catholics and Jews, 607
*Papal Declaration on Anti-Semitism and Historical
     Background,* 608
Summary: Catholic–Jewish Relations Since Vatican II, 612
Anti-Semitism Among Lutherans, 613

XXXI. RELIGION IN U.S. HISTORY   615
Chronology: Highlights, 615
Religious Affiliation of Presidents of the United States, 620
*Religious Affiliation of Justices of the Supreme
     Court,* 622
Religious Affiliation of Colonial Leaders, 622
WOMEN AND RELIGION
Data on women are included in various chapters of Part
     One; see Almanac above for polls, statistics, material
     on the clergy, different denominations, etc., especially
     Chapter XIII

XXXII. YOUTH AND RELIGION   625
College Students: Relevance of Religion, 625
College Students: Religion and Today's Problems, 626
College Students: Church Attendance, 628
Youth Attitudes: Birth Control, Abortion, Divorce, 628
High-School Response to "Right and Wrong," 629
Interpretation of Data on Youth and Religion, 629

REFERENCE AIDS   631
*Headquarters of Denominations with Membership of
     100,000 or More,* 633
Glossary of Religious Terms, 637

INDEX   645

EDITOR'S PREFACE

This book is divided into two parts. It is worth taking a moment to see why this is important.

PART ONE is in question-and-answer form. I asked the questions; the authors wrote the answers.

What I insisted upon was direct, simple, candid answers. What I rejected was theological jargon or sonorous cant. The question-and-answer form is the surest road I know to clarity, and the best way of avoiding those lofty ambiguities and irritating hairsplittings which, alas, characterize so much of the literature on religion.

I cheerfully admit to bluntness in my queries: about God, the Bible, sin, salvation, heaven, hell, divorce, the status of women and the status of black people, birth control, abortion, homosexuality, life after death, new "charismatic" movements, the defection of priests and nuns, attitudes toward other faiths, and so on.

Part One, therefore, presents the specific, detailed articles of faith of nineteen groups: the sixteen largest denominations in the United States, plus Bertrand Russell's classic analysis of agnostics, Warren Weaver's surprising portrayal of the religion of a scientist, and Edward L. Ericson's graceful exploration of "the Unchurched"—those millions of Americans (humanists, nonsectarians, deists, members of Ethical Culture) who do not identify themselves with any church, yet may consider themselves religious "in their own terms."

PART TWO is an Almanac: a massive compendium, more complete and far-ranging than any I know, of the statistics, public opinion polls, basic documents, sociological résumés, and psychological analyses of the role, conflicts, influence, and trends which characterize religion in the United States today—plus my own essays, summaries, and comments on material rarely subjected to critical examination.

It is no exaggeration to say that our churches are being as severely shaken as our political institutions. Both are forced to respond to a revolution in our moral and ethical codes. Anyone who thinks I exaggerate need only scan the findings in Part Two.

Consider these dramatic facts, chosen at random:

- About 75 percent of our people think "religion is losing its influence."
- Only 50 percent of Roman Catholics attended church during an average week—and only 37 percent of Protestants. (Ten years ago, 71 percent of Catholics and 38 percent of Protestants attended a church service each week.)
- Yet 98 percent of Americans (age 21 and over) say they believe in God, and 66 percent say they respect the church far more than they respect the Supreme Court (44 percent), Congress (37 percent), television (30 percent), trade unions (26 percent).
- An official commission of 26 Roman Catholic and Lutheran theologians has concluded that "papal primacy" need no longer be "a barrier to reconciliation" between their churches. This may prove to be the most historic event in Lutheranism since Martin Luther nailed his astounding manifesto to the door of the Castle church in Wittenberg.
- The southern branch of the Presbyterian Church elected a black Moderator, the Reverend Lawrence W. Bottoms—the first black to occupy the highest office in that denomination.
- A commission of Roman Catholic and Anglican churchmen reached an agreement in 1972 on the essential aspects of Holy Communion in a declaration which described the concord as "the most important statement since the Reformation." The report was approved by Pope Paul VI and the Archbishop of Canterbury. (The Episcopal Church in America is in "full communion" with the Anglican Church in England.)
- In Philadelphia, in August, 1974, four bishops of the Episcopal Church defied their superiors and were present when eleven women—the first in the history of the church—were ordained as Episcopal priests.
- The birth rate among Roman Catholics is rapidly declining, and will soon approach the birth rate for Protestants and Jews.
- Of the Catholic women polled, 83 percent opposed the Vatican's strict ban on the use of "artificial" birth-control devices; 37 percent stated that they used the contraceptive Pill; less than one-third used the rhythm method recommended by the Church. (In 1955, 43 percent of Catholic women in the United States had used no birth-control methods whatsoever; by 1970, that percentage had dropped to 18.)
- The Episcopal Church has so liberalized its position on divorce that excommunication is no longer imposed on those who ignore the church's earlier requirement that a remarriage must be judged and approved by a bishop; the one-year waiting period between a divorce and a second marriage has been revoked.
- The Rabbinical Assembly, representing the Conservative branch of Judaism, has voted to "count" women henceforth for a *minyan*—the

minimum number of adults (10) needed for communal worship. This is a revolutionary break with centuries of rabbinical teaching. One woman has already been ordained and serves as rabbi in a Reform congregation.

- The 40th International Eucharistic Congress, in Melbourne, Australia (1973), replaced solemn portions of the Roman Catholic Mass with ecstatic dances, songs, embraces, hand-clappings, stamping, and spontaneous shouting—one aspect of the pentecostal movement in Christian churches.
- Roman Catholics, asked if a divorced Catholic who remarries is "living in sin," responded: No—60 percent; Yes—28 percent; Don't know—12 percent.
- In 1972, 67 percent of the adult American public approved of marriages between Christians and Jews. (In 1968, only 59 percent held this view.)
- Deacons of the Roman Catholic Church may now be laymen—a revival of the ancient form of Christian ministry. Within the past year, 13 laymen in the New York archdiocese have been ordained as deacons, and have presided over weddings.
- Last year, Concordia College (St. Louis), the largest Lutheran seminary in the United States, was closed down by a boycott of faculty and students—because Concordia's president, the Reverend John H. Tietjen, had been suspended (on grounds of doctrinal error tantamount to heresy) by the conservative leaders of the Lutheran Church-Missouri Synod. A severe conflict on the interpretation of the Bible has split the orthodox and liberal wings of this denomination.

The ferment within Roman Catholicism is perhaps the most dramatic (and surely the most publicized) revelation of the rebellion agitating our religious orders. Consider these highlights from a survey (Chapter X) of American Catholics over 17:

- Over a third do not attend Sunday Mass regularly.
- Two-thirds had not gone to confession within the preceding two months.
- Over two-thirds predict that the Church will have to abandon its disapproval of divorce.
- One-half favor a relaxation of the Church's prohibition of abortions.
- Attendance in Catholic elementary schools has dropped from 4,566,809 in 1965 to 2,717,898 in 1974. The number of Catholic high schools in the United States has dropped from 304 in 1965 to 258 in 1974.
- Less than 10 percent of the Catholic laity think their children will "lose their souls" if they leave the Church.
- Sixty-four percent of the Roman Catholic *priests* under 40 disagree with the Vatican's ban on the use of "artificial devices" for birth control.

- A Gallup poll estimates that 2,500 Catholic priests are "dropping out" each year.
- Among *priests* 39 years old and under, 77 percent hold that priests should be allowed to marry; 52 percent of all the priests polled agreed.
- Almost 80 percent of the Roman Catholic laity polled by the National Opinion Research Center in 1974 favor allowing priests to marry.
- Almost a third of American Catholics would support the ordination of women as priests.
- "Should priests who marry be excommunicated?" The Catholic clergy responded: No, 60 percent—and 79 percent of those age 39 and under.
- In many Catholic churches, the Latin Mass, novenas, benedictions have been abandoned.
- Of white Catholics, only 21 percent said they would respect a "priest's exhortation" to integrate their neighborhoods; 46 percent would refuse Holy Communion from a black priest.
- When troubled, or when trying to decide what to believe, a majority of Catholics are more likely to consult their mate or friends, not their priest or the pronouncements of their bishops.
- A majority of Catholics in America no longer seem to "share the hierarchy's moral and spiritual vision."

The words of Monsignor John T. Ellis are as portentous as they are succinct: "This is not a time of change, but of revolution."

Among Jews, to sample another dramatic portion of the material in the Almanac:

- Only 19 percent attend a synagogue or temple regularly.
- Over half do not observe the dietary (kosher) laws.
- Almost one-third of the Jews who married within the past five years wed a non-Jewish spouse. Research by the National Opinion Research Center concludes that Jews are "least likely" (and Catholics "most likely") to marry members of other faiths.
- In 1964, 83 percent of the Jews polled opposed marriage with non-Jews; by 1971, this number had dropped to 41 percent.

. . . . .

However I interpret the mass of hard data in the Almanac, I cannot help concluding that the fortresses of faith are experiencing the most profound alterations in centuries. Church authority is being challenged on a dozen fronts. Traditional creeds are being drastically revised. Hallowed canons are being shelved. Religious practices are daily changed. Church leaders are beleaguered by new, bold, persistent demands—from their clergy no less than from their congregations.

It is not hyperbole to say that we are witnessing a remarkable erosion of consensus within the citadels of belief. What prophet, what theologian, what historian or scholar could have predicted such dramatic events as those I have listed above? Or the militant participation of clergymen in civil rights marches; the reverberations of the Second Vatican Council; the presence at Catholic altars of Protestant and Jewish clergymen during marriage ceremonies; the "God is Dead" debate; the rise of desegregated congregations; the opposition of Catholics to the doctrine of Papal infallibility; the open campaign of homosexuals against anathematization; the mounting skepticism about the validity or effectiveness of church teachings; the growth of "charismatic" groups and interfaith communes; the phenomenon of "jazz Masses" and rock-and-roll music in cathedrals . . . ?

All of these you will find—described and appraised—in the Almanac.

We are in the eye of a storm, as it were. The velocity and power of that storm has surprised the most sophisticated observers.

Finally, let me emphasize that this is a *new* book. Its predecessors (*A Guide to the Religions of America* and *Religions in America*) are wholly and hopelessly out of date. The mere titles of the 33 chapters in the Almanac make this point more forcefully than any words I can marshal.

To those who know the rewards of browsing, and the treasures of serendipity, I recommend the spacious pastures of my Almanac.

LEO ROSTEN

PART ONE

RELIGIOUS BELIEFS AND CREDOS

—in question-and-answer form

WHAT IS A BAPTIST?

NOTE TO THE READER: The original text of "What Is a Baptist?" was written by the late William B. Lipphard. Many new answers (to new or old questions) have been supplied for this new, revised edition by Dr. Frank A. Sharp.

Wherever the text has been supplied by Dr. Sharp, his initials appear in brackets.

WILLIAM B. LIPPHARD / Mr. Lipphard wrote from an editorial background of nearly fifty years of professional association with the American Baptist Convention, which consists of over 6,500 churches. He was president of the Associated Church Press from 1947 to 1949 and served for ten years as its executive secretary. He was for twenty years editor of the Baptist publication *Missions Magazine* and served as a delegate to Baptist World Congresses in Sweden, Canada, Germany, the United States, Denmark, and England.

Mr. Lipphard was born in Evansville, Indiana, and was educated at Yale University, from which he received a B.A. and M.A., and at Colgate-Rochester Divinity School, where he earned his B.D.

From 1940 to 1943, Mr. Lipphard was secretary of the World Relief Committee of the American Baptist Convention. He was a member of the Joint Commission on Missionary Education of the National Council of Churches of Christ and a member of the American Friends of the World Council of Churches and the Foreign Policy Association. Mr. Lipphard received an award from the Associated Church Press for eminence in editorial writing. He served as director of the Church Press at the 1954 second assembly of the World Council of Churches at Evanston, Illinois. He died in 1971.

FRANK A. SHARP / The Reverend Frank A. Sharp is director of the Department of Public Interpretation of the American Baptist Churches (Valley Forge, Pennsylvania). His weekly column in the American Baptist News Service is widely distributed throughout the United States.

A graduate of Colgate and the Colgate-Rochester Divinity School, he received his Ph.D. from the University of Pittsburgh in 1948 and served as pastor of several Baptist churches.

Dr. Sharp has traveled widely as a representative to, and reporter on, many Baptist and interdenominational conventions—in Europe and Latin America. In 1966 he attended the World Conference on Church and Society in Geneva; in 1968, the Fourth General Assembly of the World Council of Churches in Uppsala, Sweden; in 1970, the Baptist World Alliance Congress in Tokyo.

His writings have appeared in many journals on religion, including *Christian Century, Churchman,* and *International Journal of Religious Education.*

NOTE TO THE READER: It should be emphasized that neither the American Baptist Convention nor the Southern Baptist Convention has ever adopted an "official" statement of doctrine and faith; accordingly, minor differences among Baptists, on specific points of creed or practice, may be regarded as individual, not official, variations. [LR]

What Is a Baptist?

Baptists have never adopted one of the historic Christian creeds —because Baptists have been dedicated to a high degree of personal independence and to the right of the individual to interpret the New Testament for himself in matters of faith and practice. It is difficult, therefore, to present one fixed set of criteria by which to characterize a Baptist.

Among Baptists, there is a great deal of diversity because of their insistence on purity, on personal responsibility, and on freedom of belief and worship.

Any attempt to describe a Baptist would include the following points:

1. Belief in the supremacy of the Scriptures, rather than in the church or a hierarchy.
2. Belief in religious liberty, in the freedom to worship without any compulsion from or by the state.
3. Belief in the baptism of believers, rather than the baptism of infants.
4. Belief in the independence of the local church. [FAS]

Is There Then No Baptist Hierarchy or Central Authority?

Baptists have no hierarchy, no centralized control of religious activity, no headquarters that conduct an "oversight" of churches— or liturgies, practices, or regulations.

The local Baptist parish church is a law unto itself. Its relations with other Baptist churches, its compliance with recommendations from national church headquarters, its acceptance of any resolutions formulated at regional, national, or international conventions—all these are entirely voluntary on the part of the parish church, without the slightest degree of compulsion from any central or national or international body.

Indeed, Baptists are more properly called a denomination, not a church.

Why Do Baptists Call Themselves a Denomination Instead of a Church?

Most Baptists do not believe that they constitute a "church" because they are organized into independent, local "churches."

The local parish church is the *sovereign, all-powerful ecclesiastical unit.*

The term "Baptist Church" is used for convenience; "denomination" is preferred by most Baptists. In fact, a recent attempt to change the name to "American Baptist Church" was discarded in favor of the name "American Baptist Churches in the U.S.A."

Can Any Group of Believers in the Baptist Faith Form a Congregation or Church?

Yes.

A Baptist congregation needs no specific chain of historical events in order to be a true church. Any group of dedicated, regenerated, Bible-oriented people can form a Baptist church that can be an authentic part of the Body of Christ.

Such a church would not need a fully accredited, ordained pastor in apostolic succession—because originally Baptist churches were run by laymen, and even today pastors are ordained by local churches. [FAS]

Do Baptists Accept the Literal Interpretation of the Bible?

Some do; some don't.

All Baptists believe in the inspiration of the Bible and accept the Bible as infallible in religious teachings: as a trustworthy record of the progressive revelation of God, climaxed by the supreme revelation of Himself in Jesus Christ.

"Progressive" and "liberal" Baptists regard some sections of the Bible as written in the thought patterns of Biblical times—that is, as allegorical, figurative, and legendary yet conveying eternal religious truths.

"Fundamentalist" or "extreme" Baptists accept the Bible literally, regarding it as infallible and final in every detail.

But no official dogma prescribes how any individual Baptist shall interpret the Bible.

Do Baptists Have Sacraments?

No. What are known as sacraments are regarded by Baptists as simple, dignified ordinances with no supernatural significance and no sacramental value.

But Do Not Baptists Observe the Communion Service, or the Lord's Supper?

The Lord's Supper, or communion service, is usually observed on the first Sunday of the month. It is a reminder of the death of Christ and is observed in obedience to His command to commemorate the Supper on the night before He was crucified.

But whatever grace a Baptist derives from participating in the Lord's Supper depends on his own awareness of what the Supper signifies as a memorial service. No grace is supernaturally bequeathed to him—neither by the officiating clergyman nor by partaking of the bread and of the cup. Whatever blessing a Baptist receives comes through some new rededication, by him, in the communion service to a life of righteousness and service to his fellow men.

Why Do Baptists Baptize Only by Immersion?

For two reasons:

1. Immersion is the mode of baptism described in the New Testament; John the Baptist immersed his converts in the Jordan River; Christ Himself was so immersed.

2. Baptists regard baptism as a public confession of Christian

faith and as a symbol of the burial and resurrection of Christ, as stated by Paul in his Epistle to the Colossians. Hence, Baptists look upon immersion as realistic symbolism, through which the life of sin is buried in baptism and the new life of faith emerges.

Incidentally, "baptize" is a transliteration (not a translation) of the Greek word *baptizein,* meaning "to immerse." Therefore, to say that Baptists "baptize by immersion" is redundant; baptism originally was immersion.

Why Don't Baptists Baptize Infants?

Baptism is a voluntary public profession of Christian faith; therefore, Baptists believe, only persons old enough to understand its significance and its symbolism should be accepted for baptism.

Baptists give their children the right to decide for themselves whether or not they wish to be baptized as a public profession of Christian faith. We believe that such a decision makes the ceremony of baptism, and religion itself, more meaningful.

Is Baptism Mandatory for All Baptists?

There are differences of opinion among Baptists in regard to baptism. Some churches limit their membership to immersed believers only (closed membership); other churches admit members by letter from other Christian bodies—but limit the right to vote on certain issues (associate membership); and still other churches admit members on their profession of faith, leaving the question of baptism to the conscience of the believer (open membership).

There are also some Baptists who refuse to regard baptism as valid and call it "alien baptism" if it is or was administered by any other than a New Testament church, which is usually interpreted as being a Baptist church of like mind and theology.

Most Baptists do regard immersion as the New Testament mode, but some hesitate to make that mode a theological absolute, feeling that the confession of faith is more important than the symbolic rite. [FAS]

Do Baptists Accept the Doctrine of the Virgin Birth of Christ?

A great majority undoubtedly do. A substantial minority do not. For the majority, the doctrine of the Virgin Birth is essential to faith in the deity of Christ. The minority need no such support, since they find no reference to the Virgin Birth in the writings of Paul or in the Gospels of Mark and John.

Baptists pay no special homage to Mary but respect her as the noblest of women. They have never accepted the doctrine of her immaculate conception or the doctrine, announced in 1950 by Pope Pius XII, of the Assumption of Mary.

Since Baptists have no authoritarian creed to control their faith and practice, each local parish church has the right to decide whether or not to make acceptance of the doctrine of the Virgin Birth a condition of church membership.

Do Baptists Accept the Doctrine of the Trinity?

Most Baptists do.

This is a basic doctrine of Christianity. The trinitarian formula, "in the name of the Father, and of the Son, and of the Holy Ghost," is used at every baptism.

The sublime mystery of the Trinity, of the eternal and infinite essence of God manifested in three persons—these, the Baptist leaves to theologians to interpret. He accepts them.

What Do Baptists Believe About Sin and Salvation?

Baptists believe that every true believer in Christ as personal Savior is saved—without the intervention of preacher or church.

The confession of sin is a personal matter between the individual and God.

Each individual must give evidence of his personal redemption by faith, good works, and the Christian way of life. [FAS]

Do Baptists Believe in Heaven and Hell?

Most Baptists believe in some form of life beyond the grave. Ideas range from a nebulous, indefinable existence to a definite place, like a city of golden streets or a region of everlasting torment.

Some Baptists find it difficult to reconcile the fact of an all-merciful God with endless punishment for sins committed within the short span of a lifetime on earth. [FAS]

Do Baptists Approve of Divorce?

No, except when there has been adultery.

But there is no regulation among Baptist churches regarding divorce. Annual conventions of Baptists have often condemned the rising divorce rate in the United States. Each Baptist clergyman depends on his conscience in deciding whether or not to officiate at the marriage of divorced persons. No church law prescribes what he must do.

What Is the Baptist Attitude Toward Black People?

Our denomination has passed a resolution as follows:

We recognize the—
Failure of the white-dominated society to respect and rely on the voice of the poor citizens, and especially poor black men, in decisions affecting their welfare in white-owned, white-dominated and white-maintained ghettos.
We call our churches to—
Develop and support opportunities for all, especially the minority group poor, to participate in decisions by religious, governmental, industrial, commercial, welfare and other institutions affecting their lives.
Join with the victims of discrimination in securing legislation and business practices that insure open housing in established and new communities, and that improve opportunities for full participation in economic life by all citizens. [FAS]

What Is the Status/Role of Women Among Baptists?

At the Seattle, Washington, National Convention in 1969, a resolution was passed urging the American Baptist Convention, and its affiliated organizations and constituent churches, to:

1. Reverse the declining number of positions held by professionally trained women in local churches, states, cities, and regional and national staffs.
2. Establish policies and practices in electing and appointing persons to offices, committees, and boards to ensure more adequate opportunities for women.
3. Urge member churches to give equal status to women in positions of major responsibility (deacons, moderators, trustees, etc.) within the local church. [FAS]

Can Women Be Ordained?

The American Baptist Churches already have some fifty women ordained as ministers. Some of them serve in churches, others in executive positions. [FAS]

Do Baptists Sanction Birth Control?

No parish Baptist church and no ecclesiastical convention of Baptists has ever by resolution expressed approval or disapproval of birth control or planned parenthood.

Even if it had, such resolution would not be binding on any Baptist. Most Baptists would resent and repudiate any such resolution as an unwarranted intrusion into the private life of husband and wife.

What Is the Baptist Attitude Toward Abortion?

There is no official or single stand. Every Baptist is free to make up his own mind.

The nearest thing to "the" Baptist attitude may be found in the resolution adopted by our National Convention. (These resolutions, be it noted, express and reflect only the attitudes of the delegates, but many Baptists, no doubt, are influenced by the National Convention's deliberations and resolutions.)

With reference to abortion, the American Baptist Churches meeting in Boston, in 1968, passed a resolution asking that the termination of a pregnancy, prior to the end of the twelfth week of pregnancy, be at the request of the individual or individuals concerned and be regarded as an elective medical procedure, governed by the laws regulating medical practice and licensure.

The other part of the resolution stated that *after* the twelfth week of pregnancy, the termination of the pregnancy shall be performed only by a duly licensed physician, at the request of the individual or individuals concerned, in a regularly licensed hospital, for one of the following reasons—as suggested by the Model Penal Code of the American Law Institute:

1. When there is danger to the physical or mental health of the woman;
2. When there is documented evidence that the conceptus possesses a physical or mental defect;
3. When there is documented evidence that the pregnancy was the result of rape, incest, or other felonious acts. [FAS]

What Is the Baptist Attitude Toward Homosexuality?

Again, there is no official, single position.

No resolution pertaining to homosexuality has yet been presented before a national convention. [FAS]

How Do Baptists Propagate Their Faith?

The historic Baptist view holds that *every* church member and every professing Christian is an evangelist. By word, deed, and character, he is committed to proclaim his Christian faith and to seek to win others to its acceptance. Throughout their history, Baptists have engaged in very active missionary effort, at home and abroad. Baptist foreign missions have been successful on every continent.

Do Baptists Cooperate in the Ecumenical Movement?

Some do and some don't. Because of their cherished independence, many Baptist groups do not become involved in ecumenical movements on the national and world levels. (There may be more interdenominational activity on the local level because such action is nearer home and there is the feel of participation.)

Out of twenty-seven Baptist bodies in the United States, only ten belong to the Baptist World Alliance and five belong to the National Council of Churches. Out of 115 Baptist groups around the world, ten are members of the World Council of Churches.

But there are some notable exceptions. The American Baptist Convention has been a part of the ecumenical movement from its inception.

Baptists were active in the formation of the American Bible Society (1816), the American Sunday School Union (1824), the

Federal Council of Churches (1908), and the National and World Council of Churches.

A recent survey showed that the American Baptist Convention has provided more staff workers—in national, state, and local councils of churches—than any other major denomination. [FAS]

Are Baptists Active in Social Issues?

Once again, because of their sense of independence and their conservative outlook, most Baptists are inclined to emphasize the responsibility to evangelize *individuals,* in the hope that the individuals will in turn change society. A few Baptists attempt to apply Christian principles to the political and social issues of the day. Some Baptists would attempt to do both, seeing evangelism as the total witness of the Christian to all of his relationships in society.

The most activist group in the area of social concern is the American Baptist Convention. Written into its Articles of Incorporation, in 1910, were these words:

The objects of the corporation shall be to give expression to the opinions of its constituency upon moral, religious, and denominational matters, and to promote denominational unity and efficiency in efforts for the evangelization of the world. [FAS]

How Many Baptists Are There?

NOTE TO THE READER: Since membership is limited to baptized believers, all of these figures do not include young children. Most young people are ten to twelve years old when they join the Baptist church. [LR]

Baptists (as a family of denominations) constitute the largest Protestant group in the United States. *The World Almanac* for 1974 lists 21 different Baptist bodies with a total membership of 26,315,235.

The largest single Baptist body in the United States is the Southern Baptist Convention: 34,441 churches, with 11,826,463 members.

The next two largest Baptist denominations are Negro: the National Baptist Convention, U.S.A., with 27,396 churches and

6,487,003 members; and the National Baptist Convention of America, with 11,398 churches and 2,668,799 members. (In fact, 50 percent of all Negroes in the United States belong to some Baptist body.)

The fourth largest Baptist denomination in the United States is the American Baptist Convention, with 6,090 churches and a membership of approximately 1,472,478.

A full list of Baptists in the United States would also include many less commonly known groups, such as the General Six Principle Baptists, the Primitive Baptists, the Two-Seed-in-the-Spirit Predestinarian Baptists, the Duck River and Kindred Associations of Baptists, Free Will Baptists, Seventh Day Baptist General Conference—as well as Baptist groups established by immigrants from European countries—from Sweden, Germany, Norway, and Italy, for example.

According to the 1972 statistics released by the Baptist World Alliance there are Baptists in 115 countries around the world.

One of the largest Baptist bodies outside the United States is located in the USSR (about 550,000). Next in size are Baptists of Zaire, Africa, with 450,000 members, and Britain, with a membership of 215,000.

In all of Europe there are 1,161,606 Baptists; 1,079,471 in Asia; 808,266 in Africa; 442,859 in South America; 215,670 in Central America; and 145,412 in the Southwest Pacific. [FAS]

Where Did the Baptist Movement Begin?

Because of the independent character of Baptists, they are related to, and were a part of, the same spirit that brought about the Reformation—although Baptists are not directly related to Luther, Calvin, Zwingli, or Knox, the great reformers.

Baptists are spiritually related to those who wanted freedom from the established church: freedom to read and interpret the Scriptures according to the leading of the Holy Spirit, freedom from government interference, and freedom to hold a strong belief in an adult believer's baptism as opposed to infant baptism.

Most historians would place the historical roots of Baptists in England, growing out of the Puritan and Separatist movements. The early Baptists were those who wanted to reform, or who withdrew from, the established church in England, whether it was Roman Catholic or the Church of England.

In 1602, John Smyth, an Anglican preacher, renounced the episcopacy while speaking at Lincoln Cathedral. He was removed by the church authorities and became pastor of a small group of Separatists. This congregation, along with some others, moved to Holland in 1606. Smyth's convictions led him to the conclusion that a church did not have to be part of a historical succession and that its membership should be composed only of those who had repented of their sins, had confessed their faith in Jesus Christ, and were baptized.

In 1609, thirty-six men and women in Amsterdam formed the first Baptist church on record: Smyth poured water upon himself, first, and then upon the others. (Pouring was employed initially as the mode of baptism; by 1641, immersion was the established form.)

In 1611, Thomas Helwys and part of the Amsterdam congregation returned to England and established the first Baptist congregation there. This church and its descendent congregations were "General Baptists," so called because they believed that salvation was for everyone. Another branch came into existence in London in 1638 called Particular Baptists, because their Calvinist theology included predestination or the limitation of salvation to a particular group. In 1891, both groups of Baptists in Britain joined to form the Baptist Union for Great Britain and Ireland. [FAS]

When Did Baptists Originate in the United States?

When New England was settled by the English, they brought with them the same religious affiliations as they had had back home: There were Puritans, Pilgrims, Separatists, Congregationalists, and a few Baptists. To this day there is an argument whether the Newport Church of Rhode Island or the Providence Church was the first Baptist church in America. The reason is historically interesting.

In 1639, Roger Williams, a young Puritan minister, came to the Massachusetts Bay Colony seeking religious freedom. But the Puritan Congregationalists did not allow freedom of worship, and Williams was expelled by the authorities. In 1636, he founded the colony of Rhode Island—for the purpose of granting full religious freedom for all. In 1639, in Providence, he founded the First Baptist Church in America.

But Roger Williams remained a Baptist for only a short time (although he is listed as the founder of Baptists in America). An English physician, John Clarke, remained a Baptist leader all of his life. He spent twelve years in London until he secured the final charter, from Charles II, establishing Rhode Island as a colony in 1663. John Clarke became pastor of the Baptist Church at Newport, Rhode Island. [FAS]

How Do Local Congregations Work Together?

Although each local Baptist church is independent, soon after new churches began to spring up in New England and throughout the American colonies, the churches felt the need for mutual guidance and fellowship. So they organized themselves into voluntary groups, known as associations. In 1707, when five congregations formed the Philadelphia Baptist Association, the first association of Baptist churches in America was organized.

National Baptist work was also organized on a voluntary basis to support foreign missionary work. In 1814, the Triennial Baptist Convention came into being to support Ann and Adoniram Judson, the first foreign missionaries to leave American shores for service in India and Burma. This organization's descendant is known as the American Baptist Foreign Mission Society.

Other cooperative efforts were found to be necessary inasmuch as printed materials were needed to evangelize the Indians and to follow the trek westward on the frontier. In 1824 the General Tract Society was organized (today called the American Baptist Board of Education and Publication). In 1832 the American Baptist Home Mission Society was founded. Until 1845, practically all Baptists belonged to the same national body, the Triennial Convention.

When Did Baptists Separate from This Convention?

In 1845, a clash over the slavery issue—and a difference over the organizational structure (independent societies vs. related boards)—caused the withdrawal of those Southerners who formed the Southern Baptist Convention.

Baptists of the North continued to be related to all of the original societies and to the Triennial Convention, until 1907. Because of the need for a single financial appeal to the churches and for a stronger voice to speak out on social issues, the Northern Baptist Convention was created.

In 1950, the name was changed to the American Baptist Convention. In 1972, the name was changed to American Baptist Churches in the U.S.A.

WHAT IS A CATHOLIC?

DONALD W. HENDRICKS / The Reverend Donald W. Hendricks is professor and chairman of the Department of Classics in Cathedral College of the Immaculate Conception (Douglaston, New York).

He received his B.A. in philosophy at Cathedral College and entered Saint Joseph's Seminary. He was ordained to the priesthood in 1955. His priestly assignments have included the Church of Saint Mary in Newburgh, the Church of the Good Shepherd in Rhinebeck, the Church of Saint Eugene in Yonkers, and the Church of Saint Anastasia in Harriman, New York.

Father Hendricks undertook full-time graduate studies at Columbia University, where he received an M.A. and completed the course requirements for his Ph.D. In 1968, he joined the faculty of Cathedral College of the Immaculate Conception.

NOTE TO THE READER: The historic second Vatican council (1962–1965), known as Vatican II, and papal declarations and encyclicals since then on such critical questions as birth control, abortion, and celibacy have provided extremely important "advances in Catholic thought." Hence, much of the text by John Cogley in previous editions of this book required new formulation.

The Archdiocese of New York kindly assigned Father Donald W. Hendricks to write a new article on Catholicism "in terms of the newer vocabulary," retaining portions of Cogley's text.

I have provided the significant highlights of recent papal declarations in Part Two, which contains a great deal of arresting material for clergymen or laymen of all faiths. [LR]

What Was the Second Vatican Council?

It was the Twenty-first General Council of the Church,* a meeting of 2,860 voting bishops, lasting from 1962 to 1965. It was called by Pope John XXIII with the following purpose:

* See page 498 for a complete list.

In this assembly, under the guidance of the Holy Spirit, we wish to inquire how we ought to renew ourselves, so that we may be found increasingly faithful to the gospel of Christ. We shall take pains so to present to the men of this age God's truth in its integrity and purity that they may understand it and gladly assent to it.

How Does the Second Vatican Council Define the Catholic Church?

In the thirteenth chapter of the Constitution on the Church, it describes it as "the one People of God, which takes its citizens from every race . . . Taking to herself, insofar as they are good, the ability, resources, and customs of each people, she purifies, strengthens, and ennobles them."

The term "Catholic," therefore, does not refer to mere geographic universality; it conveys the vision that "all men are called to be part of this catholic unity of the People of God . . . And there belong to it or are related to it in various ways, the Catholic faithful as well as all who believe in Christ, and indeed the whole of mankind. For all men are called to salvation by the grace of God."

Do Catholics Believe Theirs Is the Only True Religion?

As the last answer indicates, the emphasis of Vatican II was on situating the role of the Catholic Church in the context of the full workings of the will of God that all men be saved. The Church does not give up the claim that God has decided to extend the fullness of salvation to men through a visible structure, the Roman Catholic Church, but it also affirms that "many elements of sanctification can be found outside that structure." Instead of merely saying that the Roman Catholic Church is the Church of Christ, it used the formula that the Church of Christ "subsists in" the Catholic Church. In the following paragraphs, some quotations may indicate what elements of truth it sees in other religions and how they aid in the salvation of all men.

Concerning religions such as Buddhism and Hinduism, it acknowledges that "the Catholic Church rejects nothing which is true and holy in these religions . . . which often reflect a ray of that Truth which enlightens all men" (Declaration on the Relationship of the Church to Non-Christian Religions, para. 3).

Speaking of Islam, whose teaching reflects the Biblical revelation, and Judaism, which contains it in part, it acknowledges with increasing respect the amount of truth to be found in them.

Of other Christian communities it says, "The Spirit of Christ has not refrained from using them as means of salvation which draw their efficacy from the very fullness of grace and truth entrusted to the Catholic Church" (Decree on Ecumenism, para. 3).

However, after saying all this, it remains true that "it is through Christ's Catholic Church alone, which is the all-embracing means of salvation, that the fullness of the means of salvation can be obtained."

What Are the Chief Differences Between the Roman Catholic and Protestant Faiths?

Protestantism embraces a variety of doctrines. Some Protestants are closer to Catholic belief than others. Two of the chief differences seem to be these:

THE BIBLE

Protestants believe in private interpretation. Catholics believe that the Church is the divinely appointed custodian of the Bible and has the final word on what is meant in any specific passage. The Church guards orthodoxy (including interpretation of the Scriptures) and passes down essential Christian tradition from one generation to another.

UNIVERSAL PRIESTHOOD

Most Protestants affirm the "priesthood of all believers," in opposition to the Catholic idea of a specially ordained priesthood. Vatican II speaks rather of the priesthood of Christ, transmitted to all Christians by baptism, giving all believers a mission to the world. Instead of speaking of some Christians as subordinated to others by the sacrament of Holy Orders, it sees the ministerial priesthood as a ministry of service, different in kind and not degree from the ministries exercised by each member of the Church.

The Catholic Mass is not the same as a Protestant Communion Service—not only in ceremony but in what each congregation believes is taking place. Protestantism provides for a greater variety of opinion on such matters as divorce and birth control, which the

Catholic accepts as settled by the teaching authority of the Church.

The average Protestant thinks of "the Church" as a broad spiritual unity; the Catholic using the same words has a precise institution—the Roman Catholic Church—in mind.

What Are the Chief Differences Between the Catholic and Jewish Faiths?*

The Catholic Church claims four distinctive marks: it is *one* (in doctrine, authority and worship), *holy* (perfect observance of its teachings leads inevitably to sanctity), *catholic* (it is unchanging in its essential teachings and preaches the same gospel and administers the same sacraments to men of all times in all places), and *apostolic* (it traces its ancestry back to the apostles and, like them, carries the message of Christ to all, regardless of race, nationality, station or class).

On Judaism, Pope Pius XI at the time of the Hitler persecutions wrote: "Spiritually, we are Semites." In the Mass, reference is made to "our father Abraham."

The Catholic recognizes the unique religious role of the Jewish people before Christ. He shares their belief in God the Father, in the brotherhood of man, and in the moral teachings handed down by the patriarchs and prophets. Christianity, as he sees it, is the fulfillment of Judaism. "I came not to destroy the law but to fulfill it," Christ said.

The big difference is that Catholics believe that Jesus Christ was the promised Messiah, true God and true Man. They believe that mankind was redeemed by Christ's atonement, though individual men must still work out their own personal salvation by faith and good works. Catholics accept the New Testament with its "new law" of charity—by which is meant the love of God for His own sake and of all men (even of enemies) because they too are children of God. The Catholic believes that with the coming of Christ, all races and nations became "chosen people."

* For the historic "Declaration on the Relationship of the Church to Non-Christian Religions," issued by Vatican II, which relieves the Jews of the century-old charge of deicide, see Part Two, Chapter XXX, p. 608.

Do Catholics Believe the Pope Can Do No Wrong?
Must Catholics Accept Everything the Pope Says?

Catholics do not believe the Pope can do no wrong. Nor does the Pope. He confesses regularly to a simple priest, like the humblest peasant in the Church. Catholics admit freely that there were popes who were wicked men (I first learned of them in parochial schools), though their number and the enormity of their sins have often been exaggerated.

Catholics do believe that the Pope, be he saint or sinner, is preserved by God from leading the Church into doctrinal error. This is referred to as his infallibility.

More exactly, the Catholic Church claims to speak in matters of faith and morals through her bishops, and in a special way through the Pope, with an authority that demands respect. The exact degree of respect differs with the circumstances. On some occasions, that authority must be adhered to with the submission of faith in the promise of Christ that He would be with His Church until the end of time, since the official leaders whom He appointed would be leading His Church into error and thus voiding that promise. On such occasions, the Pope or the body of bishops with him are held to pronounce their judgment in accord with Christ's revelation, not proposing a new revelation.

These occasions would be when the bishops of the world concur with the Pope and each other that some matter of faith or morals must be held conclusively, either at a general council or even while scattered around the world. The Pope is therefore exercising the infallibility of the Church since, when he acts in this fashion, he is acting as teacher of the whole Church.

Catholics are free to disagree with the Pope outside of the rather narrow range of issues that have been definitely settled in this fashion, although there are restrictions flowing from the respect that they must pay even to his ordinary teaching with which they do not lightly disagree.*

* See Part Two, Chapter X for data on the attitudes of Roman Catholics toward papal infallibility and related topics. [LR]

What Actually Happens in Confession? Can a Catholic Gain Absolution for a Sin, Repeat the Same Sin, and Receive Absolution Repeatedly?

Confessions are usually heard in the boxlike "confessionals" found in every Catholic Church. It is dark inside. Sometimes you can see the priest dimly, but often a white cloth is tacked to the grille separating priest and penitent. Before you enter the confessional, you prepare yourself by examining your conscience.

Inside, you kneel and whisper to the priest on the other side of the grille. You tell him how long it has been since your last confession. Then, as completely as you can, you name your sins, giving their number and such details as are necessary to supply a clear idea of what you did that was wrong.

When you finish, the priest usually says a few words of spiritual counsel and encouragement. Then he gives you your "penance." This is a certain number of prayers or prayerful acts that you must perform to signify your genuine sorrow and your resolution to do better. You say the Act of Contrition, a formal prayer that expresses love for God, sorrow for sin, and "purpose of amendment." You recite this prayer before or after the priest absolves you so that you can hear the priest's words of absolution. The priest sends you out with a "God bless you" and usually asks you to pray for him, a sinner like yourself.

Like other people, Catholics find themselves repeating the same old sins. But no one sins *because* he goes to confession regularly. If one does not intend to make a sincere effort to break sinful habits, there is no point in going to confession. A "bad confession" (where sins are withheld or where genuine sorrow or the "purpose of amendment" are not present) is considered invalid and sacrilegious.

What Changes Have Been Made in Confession Procedure Since Vatican II?

Among the reforms initiated by the second Vatican council are attempts to achieve more fully the purposes of the sacraments by renewal of the ceremonies by which they are administered. The renewal of the sacrament of Penance in February 1974 is an example of how this has been accomplished. The Catholic Church understands the original grant of authority by Christ to Saint Peter as including the power to forgive sins. But implied in the words "Whatever you declare bound on earth shall be bound in heaven; whatever you declare loosed on earth shall be loosed in heaven" (Matthew, 16:19) is an obligation to discern the sincerity of the penitent, so that forgiveness will not be frivolously granted or denied. In the Catholic tradition, this exercise of judgment takes place through confession of sin to a priest wherever this is possible.

Until recently, confession took place in a private ceremony in a confessional whose darkened atmosphere of anonymity made it easier for most penitents to unburden their consciences. Absolution was granted without confession only in emergencies, and on the understanding that a full confession take place as soon as possible.

There are two main results of the present reform by the Vatican Congregation for Divine Worship: first, the penitent is to regard the occasion not as a mere recitation of past sins but as an encounter with a loving God; second, the benefits of the sacrament are given to the greatest number of people possible.

In practice, this means many Catholics will still enter a confessional, a small booth with a curtained entrance, kneel, and confess their sins to a priest, who will ask any questions needed to resolve any ambiguities in the confession, or to aid him in counseling the penitent to avoid future sins. He will then assign a penance: prayers or other works by which the penitent may in some way atone for his sins and strengthen himself for the future.

The new rite offers three approaches to the administration of the sacrament. In each, the basic ceremony has become more of an experience of reconciliation, designed to deepen sorrow for sin and heighten awareness of God's mercy.

1. For those who still wish to make individual confessions, there are, besides some new prayer formulas, various options for satisfying particular needs, such as the chance to sit (instead of kneeling) while speaking to the confessor (for those who prefer this as well as those who simply need more time for counseling).

2. For many, this experience of reconciliation comes more easily in a group. In this case, the ceremony of private confession takes place in the context of a group prayer.

3. There is now a new version of confession to meet a new need. In certain places, owing to the shortage of priests, many

Catholics in a state of sin would be denied the graces of the Holy Eucharist if they had to make a full confession in order to receive the sacrament. These penitents may now take part in a ceremony like the one just described. However, they do not confess their sins at this time. Instead, the priest absolves all present—on the understanding that each penitent will later make a full private confession.

The obvious point of this last stipulation is to make sure that the sacrament not be seen as a chance for "automatic" forgiveness, with a license to repeat the same sins, granted to one who merely recounts his past transgressions. The new changes are meant to make each confession an encounter with a loving Master. Catholics do not find it strange that One Who ordered His disciples to forgive their brothers "seven times seventy times" would be willing to forgive His brothers again and again when they are truly contrite, even though their wounded human nature has yielded to weakness.

What Is the Real Meaning of the Mass?

The Constitution on the Sacred Liturgy of Vatican II speaks of the Mass in these terms: "At the Last Supper, on the night when He was betrayed, our Savior instituted the Eucharist Sacrifice of His Body and Blood. He did this in order to perpetuate the sacrifice of the Cross throughout the centuries until He should come again, and so to entrust to His beloved spouse, the Church, a memorial of His death and resurrection: a sacrament of love, a sign of unity, a bond of charity, a paschal banquet in which Christ is consumed, the mind is filled with grace, and a pledge of future glory is given to us" (Chap. 11, No. 47).

Hence, the Mass is understood to be: (1) a sacrifice in which the Sacrifice of the Cross is perpetuated; (2) a memorial of the death and resurrection of the Lord; (3) a sacred banquet in which the congregation, the People of God, receive the body and blood of Christ under the sacramental signs of consecrated bread and wine.

Through the Holy Communion the People of God share the benefits of the Paschal Sacrifice, renew the New Covenant with God in Christ, and enjoy a foreshadowing of everlasting life.

The Mass structure consists of the Introductory Rite, which incorporates a brief penitential rite; the Liturgy of the Word (scripture readings and responses); the Liturgy of the Eucharist (as outlined above); and the Dismissal Rite.

Mass can only be celebrated by a Christian man in Holy Orders (priest or bishop). As of the liturgical renewal pursuant to Vatican II, Mass is celebrated in many languages in the new edition of the Roman Missal promulgated in 1969 by Pope Paul VI.

What Is Purgatory?

Like "heaven" or "hell," the word "purgatory" refers to a place and a state. Catholics believe that purgatory exists to *purge* those souls who are not yet pure enough for heaven and its vision of God but who have not died in a state of serious (mortal) sin. Such near-saints must undergo the pain of intense longing for God until they have paid the debt of temporal punishment due them because of their sins on earth.

In a word, purgatory exists to make saints who will be ready for the purity of God's presence. If one does not succeed in becoming a saint on earth but yet escapes eternal hell, he is purified in purgatory.

After the Last Judgment, when all men have achieved their final state, purgatory will cease to be.

What Do Catholics Believe About the Virgin Mary?
Does the Doctrine of the Assumption, Defined in 1950,
Mean That Mary Is Now in an Actual Place?

Catholics believe that from the moment of her conception in *her* mother's womb, the mother of Jesus Christ was preserved free from original sin. This is what is known as the Immaculate Conception, often confused with the Virgin Birth—which, of course, refers to the birth of Christ. Mary remained a virgin throughout her life (Catholic Biblical scholars hold that the mention of Jesus' brethren in the scriptures is to be interpreted as referring to His cousins and kinfolk). Because of her stainless life and vast dignity as the Mother of the God-Man, Catholics believe, Mary is the greatest of the saints. Catholics pray *to* God *through* Mary because they believe she is a powerful intercessor and that, in keeping with what Christ said on Calvary—"Behold thy mother!"—she is the mother of mankind. In order to avoid the impression that Catholics see Mary as somehow separate from the rest of the pattern of salvation, Vatican II spoke of her "role in the mystery of Christ and the Church" and Pope Paul VI declared her Mother of the Church.

The Assumption (the belief that Mary's body was preserved from corruption and taken to heaven and reunited to her soul) is not a new belief. Fifteen hundred years ago, the feast was celebrated. What took place during 1950 was this: Pope Pius XII solemnly declared that the ancient belief was now a formal doctrine, to which all Catholics must give assent. The Pope made this solemn declaration in answer to a widespread popular request by clergy and laity.

The word "heaven" is used to mean both a place and a state of being. Of the state, Catholics believe that it consists essentially in seeing God "face to face" (I Corinthians 13, 12). Of the place, we have no knowledge beyond the fact that it *exists*. "Eye hath not seen, ear hath not heard, nor hath it entered into the heart of man what God hath prepared for those who love Him" (I Corinthians 2,9).

Do Catholics Believe That Unbaptized Babies Cannot Go to Heaven Because of "Original Sin"?

Strictly speaking, Catholics do not *believe* anything on this point, since Revelation describes the ordinary dealings of God with men. It is silent on the type of reward given by a merciful Father to infants who have died without Baptism. On a similar matter, Vatican II has given a fresh point of view. It emphasizes that the Gospel must be preached to all men and then, in speaking of the fate of those who have not heard it through no fault of their own, it says, "God in ways known to Himself can lead [them] to that faith without which it is impossible to please Him (Hebrews 11:6)" (Decree on the Missions, para. 7). There are thus three possible answers. Some would rely on this general will of God to save all men and feel that here also there are ways known to Himself to save these unbaptized children.

Though there are Catholic theologians who hold that such babies may achieve salvation through the desire of parents and *their* bond with the Church, the more general belief is that unbaptized babies are forever cut off from heaven.

This belief is not as harsh as it is sometimes understood to be. It is Catholic teaching that no one by nature has a "right" to heaven. Man, just because he is a man, does not have a claim on the *supernatural* happiness he enjoys in seeing God "face to face." That is a free gift of God.

The loss of supernatural life—generally called the fall from grace—was incurred by Adam at the time of his rebellion against God. Because Adam was head of the human race, all mankind was involved in the historic sin of disobedience by which the first man rejected the gifts God had given him that were above and beyond the needs of human nature.

Since the redemption by Christ ("the new Adam"), it has been possible for men to regain the life of grace. Baptism restores supernatural life. Without that life, man simply does not have the capacity to enjoy heaven. In the case of adults, the life of grace may be gained by an act of perfect contrition or pure love of God ("baptism of desire"). Infants are incapable of such an act of the will.

Unbaptized babies (in "limbo"—the poetic designation for an eternal state of purely natural happiness) do not suffer in any way; even from a sense of loss. Saint Thomas Aquinas taught that they, too, have a knowledge of God—but according to a "natural' capacity. Their happiness is greater than any known by man on earth, however limited it may be as compared with that of the saints in heaven.

How Do Catholics Look upon the Devil?

Catholics believe that Satan (the leader of the fallen angels) and his cohorts are pure spirits with an intelligence of a very high order and a will that is now obstinately bent on evil. The Devil and the other fallen angels can tempt and torment men, though all temptations are not directly attributable to them. Many religious thinkers have said that the Devil's greatest triumph lies in convincing the world that he doesn't exist.

Hell, to Catholics, means two things: a place and a state of punishment. The Devil is not confined to hell as a place, and will not be until the last day; but he exists "in hell"—as a state of eternal punishment.

Why Do Catholics Worship "Graven Images"?

They don't. Like any religion, Catholicism uses symbols to heighten the meaning of spiritual truth.

The Council of Trent summed up the Catholic position on images four hundred years ago: The images of Christ and the Virgin Mother of God, and of the other saints, are to be had and to be kept, especially in the churches, and due honor and veneration are to be given to them; *not that any divinity or virtue is believed to be in them, on account of which they are to be worshiped, or that anything is to be asked of them, or that trust is to be put in images,* as was done of old by the Gentiles, who placed their hopes in idols; but because *the honor which is shown them is referred to the prototypes which these images represent.* [My italics.]

Why Do Catholics Sprinkle Holy Water on Such Things as Buildings and Farm Implements?

Water is an ancient symbol of spiritual purification. Holy water in the Church is an adaptation of an old Jewish custom. Catholics do not believe that the water has any power in itself. When it is sprinkled, with appropriate prayers, on buildings, farm implements, and the like, the ceremony signifies that the Church is humbly calling upon God to drive away the forces of Satan and accept for His own glory the uses to which the thing blessed will be put. Man is a unity of body and spirit, and the Church has never hesitated to recognize this by using material objects to signify spiritual realities.

Must All Catholics Abstain from Eating Meat on Fridays?

No. The obligation to abstain bound Catholics who are fourteen or older (see below). And the obligation to fast (which means limiting oneself to one full meal a day and two lighter meals) bound Catholics who are twenty-one to fifty-nine years of age.

On February 23, 1966, the Pope issued an apostolic constitution (*Poenitemini:* "do penance") that authorized the substitution of other works of penance for the previous observances of abstinence and fast on various days of the year.

In the United States, the Roman Catholic bishops (in a pastoral statement of November 18, 1966) specified this for their people as follows: Catholics are obliged to abstain from the eating of meat on Ash Wednesday and all Fridays during Lent; they are also obliged to fast on Ash Wednesday and Good Friday.

While Catholics are conscience bound to the observance of fast and abstinence on these days and must never lightly excuse themselves from this responsibility, nevertheless the obligation is not binding in sin.

Why Does the Church Forbid Catholics to Read or See Certain Books, Plays, and Movies?

What a Catholic believes by faith, he believes absolutely. He is ready to take the Church's word on what constitutes a danger to this faith.

Catholics regard their Church as a moral teacher. When books, plays, movies, and such are forbidden, it is because it is the Church's judgment that, for the ordinary person, they may provide either a temptation to sin, a false religious understanding, or a challenge to faith that he is not equipped to handle.

Is a Catholic Permitted to Get a Divorce?

Catholics believe that marriage, by its nature, must be a contract "till death do us part." The Church does not recognize any absolute divorce between a couple who are linked in a sacramental consummated bond, where one or the other would be free to marry again. In the cases of some nonsacramental bonds or in nonconsummated sacramental bonds, a dissolution may take place by the "Power of the Keys" for a serious spiritual reason. For good reasons (infidelity, cruelty) the Church may approve separation from bed and board. In such cases, a Catholic may be permitted to get a civil divorce in order to satisfy some legal requirement. He may not, however, remarry during the lifetime of the other party. In cases where the Church has decreed nullity—where, according to Church law, there was no marriage in the first place—a civil annulment or divorce may sometimes be necessary.*

* The number of annulments has risen dramatically: from around 650 in 1970 to more than 3,000 in 1972. (See *Time*, Nov. 12, 1973, p. 56.) [LR]

What Does the Catholic Church Teach About Birth Control?

"Birth control" can have several meanings, some acceptable, some not. The Church encourages responsible family planning, using morally acceptable means—for example, continence, calendar rhythm method, symptothermic rhythm method, ovulation method.

It does teach, however, that artificial contraception (using mechanical or chemical means) and direct sterilization are immoral methods, because they are directly contrary to the nature of conjugal intercourse, which "must remain open to the transmission of life," or direct abortion, which is a "direct interruption of the generative processes already begun."

Pope Paul VI, in the encyclical *Humanae Vitae,* acknowledged that "married couples faced with conflicting duties are often caught in agonizing crises of conscience," finding it "difficult to harmonize the sexual expression of conjugal love with respect for the life-giving powers of sexual union and the demands of responsible parenthood."

He further noted, "The honest practice of regulation of birth demands first of all that husband and wife acquire and possess solid convictions concerning the true values of life and of the family, and that they tend towards securing perfect self-mastery. To dominate instinct by means of one's reason and free will undoubtedly requires ascetical practices, so that the affective manifestations of conjugal life may observe the correct order, in particular with regard to the observance of periodic continence."

Are Catholics Conscientiously Obliged to Support Anti-Birth Control Laws?*

This question is retained from an earlier edition even though decisions of the Federal courts have rendered the point a moot question by declaring that such laws violate the rights of the individual to privacy. The same issue is raised in many ways and is probably the most fertile source of anti-Catholic feeling in this country.

* For the important, most recent papal declarations on birth control and fertility, see Part Two, Chapters VIII and X. [LR]

What follows is an attempt to show why there will always be a tension in the Catholic community over the wisdom of such legislation and why this tension is a healthy one.

We may begin by quoting a modern Catholic thinker, Norman St. John-Stevas:

The proposition that an act is contrary to the natural law does not imply that the act should be forbidden by the law of the state. Whether legislation is desirable is a jurisprudential rather than a theological question, which must be decided in relation to the conditions prevailing in a given community. While Roman Catholics in a democracy have every right to work for legislation outlawing the sale and distribution of contraceptives . . . the total Catholic community would be wise not to attempt to secure a total legislative ban on contraceptives, but should limit its efforts to securing a policy of state neutrality on the issue and the passing of measures to protect public morality that command the general support of the community.

In the first place, this merely establishes the right of an individual Catholic to have his own opinion on the wisdom of a particular legislation; it does not say that such legislation is always undesirable. Secondly, the experience of the last fifteen years may illustrate why this is so. Reread the last sentence in the quotation and, wherever the phrase "sale and distribution of contraceptives" occurs, substitute the words "discrimination against human rights" or "unjust treatment of farm workers." A church whose members pursued a policy of benign neglect in these areas would not be true to its prophetic mission.

The current controversy over amnesty for those whose consciences obliged them to oppose the war in Viet Nam is one of many instances where we can see that to trust always in "general support of the community" can lead to moral problems for individuals.

Finally, there are matters about which the State does not really remain neutral. Twenty years ago, the case against birth control legislation was that it was the exclusive right of the parents to decide how many children they should have. Today, the discussion at conferences on population control is how to pass the legislation needed to keep parents from having too many children. There will, therefore, be occasions when the Catholic Church must be involved in the drafting of legislation precisely to maintain the individual freedom of its members.

Do Catholics Regard the Human Body and the Act of Love as Shameful?

The Church puts great stress on modesty—precisely because it disapproves so strongly of any cheapening of sex, which it regards as a sacred trust.

How could a Church that teaches the Son of God became flesh and blood regard the human body as shameful? Far from looking upon the act of love as unclean, the Church teaches that it is the means by which husband and wife intimately express their love and share in the creation of life.

Is It True That Catholics Consider All Non-Catholic Children as Illegitimate?

No. The Church recognizes the sacredness and binding nature of all ceremonies that mark "the conjugal union of man and woman, contracted between two qualified persons, which obliges them to live together throughout life."

Ordinarily a Catholic must be married in the presence of a priest and two witnesses.

Does the Church Forbid Interfaith Marriages?

"The Church discourages interfaith marriages since she wishes married Catholics to attain to perfect union of mind and full communion of life." She relaxes her rules, however, in particular cases, provided the Catholic promises to have the children baptized and reared as Catholics. The non-Catholic must be informed of this promise but is no longer required to make a formal statement.*

In a Case Where Doctors Agree That a Mother May Die During Childbirth, Must Catholic Doctors Save the Child Rather Than the Mother?

No. The Catholic doctor is bound to make every effort to save *both*. Both the mother and the child have an inherent right to life. *Neither may be killed so the other can live.*

* See Part Two, Chapter XXIV for figures on interfaith marriages. [LR]

Modern advances in medical science have, in fact, rendered the question academic. Doctors agree that proper medical care can save both mother and child.

Why Does the Catholic Church Oppose Direct Abortion?*

Human life begins at the moment of conception. We know that from that moment the child is a complex and rapidly growing individual, uniquely different from all other humans. Although dependent on the privileged environment of the womb for development, the unborn child has a life of his own.

The child in the womb is human. Direct abortion is the unjust destruction of that human life. Society has no right to destroy such a life. Even the expectant mother has no such right; her unborn child is dependent on her but distinct from her.

Every decision to abort, no matter how early in pregnancy the decision is made, is a decision to kill an individual, unique human baby.

Along with a vast number of other religious bodies, the Catholic Church teaches that innocent human life may never deliberately be taken. This teaching applies to all innocent human life along the whole continuum of existence; from conception through infancy, into childhood and adolescence, to maturity and old age. No circumstances ever justify any deliberate taking of innocent human life. It is unjust. It is murder.

Why Doesn't the Catholic Church Ordain Women?

It has been the tradition in the Catholic Church, uncontested until recently, that women not be ordained. No doubt part of the reason why it was not contested for so long was that the position of women in society was such that no one thought of giving them any position of leadership. Further, it is not certain that there is an intrinsic theological reason why women should not be ordained.

This does not necessarily mean that women will be ordained, now that the question has been raised. The development of the

---

* For the important text of the most recent papal declaration on abortion, see Part Two, Chapter X. [LR]

Catholic tradition has not been hostile to the role and dignity of women in the Church. In his essay on the Papacy, Macaulay, a non-Catholic historian, pointed out that one of the strengths of the Roman Church was its almost unique willingness to employ the talents of women. Again, devotion to Mary not only engendered greater respect for women but demonstrates that the Catholic tradition on women allowed one, Mary, such a high rank that to some non-Catholics it seemed a deification.

Granted that today women enjoy greater respect in civil society, this should no more affect the theological question of their ordination than a diminution in that respect should cause us to bar them from ordination. It is a misuse of a sacrament to use it as a means to an end.

Further, since Vatican II, Catholic theology has stressed that the priesthood is not a rank in the Church but a service to the Church. It is to be hoped that women will receive all the respect due them and that the Church receive all the benefits which will flow from their emancipation.

The question for Catholic theology is not whether women should be ordained or not but will the growth in our understanding of the role of women be an organic one that takes account of the richness of our tradition.*

Why Don't Priests and Nuns Marry?

There are really two questions here, one about the clergy, the other about what are technically called "religious" Christians who have handed over their entire lives to God's service in acts of special consecration, such as priests, "brothers," "sisters," monks, or nuns. As a manifestation of their baptismal consecration, these people further commit themselves by vows of poverty, chastity, and obedience.

Nuns and monks take a vow of chastity not because they despise marriage and human love, but in order to consecrate themselves wholly to the service of God in a religious order. As long as they choose to remain in a religious order, they are obliged to keep these vows, but the proper Church authority can dispense them from their vows if there is sufficient reason. They would then be free to

---

* Also see Part Two, Chapter XIII. [LR]

marry with the Church's blessing. Such self-chosen celibacy is quite in keeping with the teaching of Saint Paul on the superiority in the spiritual order of virginity.

The situation of the clergy is complicated by the fact that there are two different traditions, one in the Western Church keeping married men from the priesthood (with the rarest of exceptions) and that of the Eastern Church, which has allowed the ordination of married men. In both cases, once a man is committed to the priestly life, he is no longer free to marry. Thus, when Vatican II revived the order of deacon as a permanent rank, it followed the rule for priests of the Eastern Churches: single men would have to promise celibacy, and men already married would lose the right to remarry if their wives die.

In both Eastern and Western Churches, only unmarried men can be bishops. In the Eastern Church, this is done by choosing only monks who have made a vow of chastity. The rule of the Western Church that a married man cannot become a priest and that permission to marry is only granted where one is dispensed from the exercise of his ministry is a matter of long-standing custom.

Could this custom be changed? Any simple answer is misleading. Since married men have been ordained in the Eastern Churches, there is obviously no necessary connection of priesthood and celibacy. On the other hand, both Eastern and Western Churches have a long tradition of preferring celibate ministers, where possible.

After Vatican II, there was some discussion of change but the Synod of Bishops of 1971, held in Rome, decided against it. This was no mere pro forma endorsement, since there were strong pressures to relax the requirement.

Celibacy has been questioned for centuries and yet has been retained after all the questioning; thus, it does not appear likely that this policy will be changed.*

How Many Priests and Nuns Have Changed Their Commitment in Recent Years?

It is difficult to give any reliable answer since until 1969 there was no single published source on Catholic religious statistics. The

---

* For the important and most recent papal declaration on celibacy, see Part Two, Chapter X. [LR]

figures published that year show a drop between 1964 and 1970 in the number of priests (from causes other than death) of 13,440, or roughly 7 percent of the total.

Several comments are in order. In the first place, the rate of departures varies across the world, the number being larger in Europe and North America than on other continents. Second, in many of these cases, there was no departure from the Church. Instead it was decided that, for the better good of the Church as a whole, priests and nuns would be relieved from their commitments who had, in many cases, done valuable service up to that point.

Finally, these figures reflect final decisions: They do not cover those who have asked for leave to consider their future. This last point applies with greater force to religious sisters. In the first place, there are still no complete statistics on their numbers that are useful. Many of them were only bound by temporary vows, hence their departure could be for several reasons. Others have found new ways of service that make it difficult to ascertain whether they have left the convent to serve better or after abandoning their commitment, while for others, the time outside the convent is an opportunity to reconsider their future form of service.°

May Catholic Priests Take Part in Interreligious Services?

Yes. Since the issuance of the Decree on Ecumenism of Vatican II, both priests and laity can participate in interreligious (ecumenical) prayer services. They may also participate in the official worship service of other faiths, both Christian and non-Christian, without performing a specific role in the service (reading scripture, preaching, etc.).

Receiving the Eucharist is never permitted except at orthodox services under extraordinary circumstances.

What Is the Position of the Catholic Church on Black People?

The statement of Vatican II quoted in the second answer shows that the Church would not be Catholic if it did not seek to develop

° For figures and attitudes, from Catholic and non-Catholic sources, see the data in Part Two, Chapter X. [LR]

the special gifts that black people have to contribute to the building of the people of God. (In fact, with the decline in the Church in Europe and North America, she may become less European as the decline of the Roman Empire made her less Mediterranean.)

As different groups of people in history have suffered special difficulties, the Church and its members have always sought justice and relief for them. So Catholics, individually and through their institutions, never approved of slavery—and tried to relieve the worst miseries of the enslaved.

The Church joins others in demanding equality of opportunity and the full implementation of civil rights where they have been denied. Today, the main problems of black and Third World peoples involve eradicating the structural injustices that still affect society after the theoretical liberation of individuals. This issue was raised in Rome at the Synod of Bishops in 1974 as part of the total problem of the spread of the Gospel and the freeing of men from the effects of sins. Of the 209 bishops at the synod, 17 were from North America and 73 were from Europe; on the other hand, 39 were from Africa, 32 from Asia, 42 from Latin America, and 6 from Australia and Oceania.

Thus, when we speak of the attitude of the Church, we can no longer think of merely the white European part of the Church but must take into account the many flourishing Third World communities whose leaders spoke for them at the synod.*

What Is the Catholic Church's Attitude Toward Homosexuality?

The Catholic Church has always considered homosexual practice an unnatural vice. By its spiritual resources of prayer and the sacraments, it stands ready to show its pastoral concern and desire to help.

The *tendency* toward homosexuality is not a sin but a psychological disorder that needs treatment and deserves our sympathy.

The widespread acceptance of a homosexual style of life has generally been offensive to Catholic culture and family life.

* Also see Part Two, Chapters IX and X. [LR]

Do Catholics Believe in Religious Tolerance?

Vatican II in its Declaration on Religious Freedom (para. 2) says:

This Vatican Synod declares that the human person has a right to religious freedom. This freedom means that all men are to be immune from coercion on the part of individuals or of social groups and of any human power, in such wise that in matters religious no one is to be forced to act in a manner contrary to his firm beliefs. Nor is anyone to be restrained from acting in accordance with his own beliefs, whether privately or publicly, whether alone or in association with others, within due limits.

The Catholic Church Is an Authoritarian Institution. Does This Contradict Democratic Principle?

Insofar as the Church speaks for a Master Who "taught with authority," there will be times when to "neglect to speak the message both in and out of season" would be to fail "one's whole duty" (II Timothy 4:2, 5). The New Testament shows that preaching with authority and discerning where the Spirit is truly speaking are genuine forms of service in the Church (Romans 12:9, 10).

However, one of the great fruits of Vatican II is the emphasis on the reciprocal forms of service offered—for example, by the layman when he is permitted and even obliged to express his opinions on matters that concern the good of the Church. There is clearly stated the duty of pastors to "willingly use this advice and . . . acknowledge that just freedom which belongs to everyone in this earthly city" (Constitution on the Church, para. 37).

In order to carry this out, there have been developed new organs to promote this sort of dialogue: parish, diocesan, and national councils of laity and clergy; senates of priests inside a diocese; national conferences of bishops; an international theological commission; and the Synod of Bishops. Through these it is hoped that we will better hear what "the Spirit has to say to the Church."

The Church *is* authoritarian. So are the family, the school, the army, and various other institutions that thrive in democracies. But the central point is that the Church is a religious, not a political, society.

Democracy is a system of government in which each man is free to serve God—that is, to acknowledge the authority of God—according to his own conscience. The Catholic is convinced that his Church is a divinely founded institution with the right to speak with God-given authority on matters of faith and morals. How, then, can he "contradict democratic principle" by following the religious dictates of his conscience? Wouldn't it, rather, "contradict democratic principle" to demand that Americans act, not in accordance with their own consciences, but in accordance with some standard of religious orthodoxy derived from a political, not a theological, principle?

Have Not the Changes of the Second Vatican Council Weakened the Authority of the Papacy by Destroying the Monolithic Structure of the Church?

Pope Gregory the Great said of his relations with his brother bishops: "My honor is the honor of the universal Church. My honor is the stout energy of my brothers. When each is accorded the honor due to him, then I am honored." The Catholic Church, then, is not supposed to be a monolith; it is an organic unity where each Christian must aid in the constant growth of the Church.

Most people see the Catholic Church as dedicated to teaching what has been held "everywhere, always, and by all," in the phrase of Vincent of Lerins. They tend to overlook the fact, stressed by the same fifth-century French theologian, that as a body grows it changes in accord with its nature.

The authority of the Pope would be diminished if he merely checked the rephrasing of a few pat formulas. When Pius XII wrote his encyclical on biblical studies, *Divino Afflante Spiritu* (September 30, 1943), he was acting in an old tradition in directing the Catholic faithful to be more charitable toward the efforts of Catholic biblical scholars because he knew that any mistakes they might make would be compensated for by the truth they would uncover.

Theologians today make public their ideas more freely than before, and some of these ideas cause controversy. There are open disagreements between priests and their bishops, between bishops themselves, and even between bishops and the Pope. To an outsider, this may seem like the recipe for chaos. But Catholics can be more serene, knowing that discussion, even controversy, can be healthy, as a sign of a growth which will never degenerate into cancer—precisely because above and beyond the controversy stands the authority of the Pope, harnessing the "stout energy of his brothers."*

Is the Catholic Church Any Closer to Intercommunion with Other Churches?

One part of the answer is to say that we are all finding out that we were not as widely divided as we had thought. Since Vatican II, groups of theologians from the Catholic and non-Catholic churches have determined that some of their differences in the past were due to misunderstanding; and so, for instance, the reciprocal anathemas between the Catholic and Greek [Eastern] Orthodox were lifted in December 1965.

This still leaves the real differences between churches; so other groups of theologians have been commissioned to develop new formulas for further reconciliation in the future. Among these, we could list the Windsor Agreement of September 1971 between Catholic and Anglican theologians on the Eucharist. If this were accepted by the churches that these theologians represent, a further narrowing of differences would result.

While all this is going on, the Catholic Church has said that she is willing, on certain occasions, to allow certain non-Catholics to receive her sacraments. For example, a Catholic priest might administer the last rites to an Eastern Orthodox who is dying far from one of his own priests. The question arises whether the groups to which these non-Catholics belong would wish their members to take advantage of this offer. On this point, there have been meetings of Catholic theologians in this country and representatives of the Episcopalian and Eastern Orthodox churches.†

Can a Catholic Be a Pentecostal?††

Since Vatican II, there has taken place in the Catholic Church an increased interest in prayer, especially among small groups of the

---

* See also Part Two, Chapters X, XVI.
† For further data, see Part Two, Chapters X, XVI.
†† For a survey of Pentecostal and Charismatic movements, see Part Two, Chapter XXVII. [LR]

faithful. One form of this is described as the Charismatic Renewal. As with non-Catholic Pentecostals, there are Catholics who enjoy the power of glossolalia, a "gift of tongues." This movement has received sympathetic approval from the hierarchy, and there are, in fact, bishops among its members. There are also, however, differences, and these are noted by non-Catholic Pentecostals. Catholics who possess a gift of tongues regard it as a charism or grace which they hope all might achieve, rather than a necessity for Christian life. Catholic Charismatics do not put the same stress as non-Catholic Pentecostals on "holiness" of life as a condition for this gift, if that holiness is defined in terms such as abstinence from tobacco or alcohol.

What Is the Attitude of the Church Toward Drinking and Gambling?

Neither is considered evil in itself, though both may become sinful by excess or abuse. The Church approves total abstinence in the same way that it puts its approval upon voluntary celibacy. Both sex and alcoholic drinks are the creation of God; they may be forsworn but must not be condemned as intrinsically evil.

Gambling is regarded as an innocent pastime unless one or all of the following conditions are present: (1) the subject matter of the bet is sinful; (2) one party is *forced* to play; (3) one party is certain of the outcome; (4) one party is left in ignorance of the real terms of the gamble; (5) cheating and fraud are present; (6) the money staked is needed to pay debts or for the support of oneself or family; or (7) the gambling game is forbidden by legitimate public authority.

Why Do Catholics Have Their Own Schools?

Religious schools antedate the public school system in the United States (which did not get under way until, in 1805, the Free School Society was founded in New York "for the education of such poor children as do not belong to, or are not provided for by any religious society"). Until 1825, American religious schools received help from public funds. In that year, New York City's share of the state school fund went exclusively to the Free School Society, which was renamed the Public School Society.

Catholic schools had existed since colonial times—the earliest was founded by Maryland Jesuits at Saint Mary's City in about 1640— but the first parish school was established by Mother Elizabeth Seton at Emmetsburg, Maryland, in 1810. Her system was endorsed by the American bishops in 1843, when they ordered that all pastors were "to provide a Catholic school in every parish or congregation subject to them, where this can be done."

This step was taken mainly because the public schools of the time were in effect "Protestant" schools. Even Horace Mann, who fought against "sectarian" indoctrination, held that the public school system "found its morals on the basis of religion" and welcomed the Bible into the schools "enshielded from harm, by the great Protestant doctrine of the inviolability of conscience, the right and sanctity of private judgment, without note or interpreter." Catholic pupils were required to join in reading the Protestant Bible, reciting Protestant prayers, and singing Protestant hymns, in accordance with custom. Moreover, the textbooks used, according to the bishops, were biased against Catholicism. "The schoolboy can scarcely find a book," they protested, "in which one or more of our institutions or practices is not exhibited for otherwise than it really is, and greatly to our disadvantage." The Catholic hierarchy of the time were convinced that the Presbyterian clergyman who wrote in the *Freeman's Journal* (July 11, 1840) that "the Bible and the Common Schools [were] two stones that [would] grind Catholicity out of Catholics" knew whereof he spoke.

Later, after the parochial school system was well established, religion and religious practices were gradually removed from public school classrooms. Most Catholics, concerned about the religious education of their children and with a heavy investment in their own schools, found this even less satisfactory. Hence, at great sacrifice, over the years the American Catholic community has built, staffed, and supported an ever-growing parochial school system, while continuing to meet in full its obligations to the public schools.

These sacrifices have been made because Catholics believe that no ignorance is as tragic as religious ignorance and that imparting a religious attitude related to life and learning is a seven-day-a-week, not merely a Sunday-morning, task.*

How Many Students in the United States Attend Catholic Schools?

The Catholic school effort in the United States is unique in the universal Church. In the 1973–1974 school year there were 10,585 elementary and secondary schools, educating almost 4 million students. (This represents a drop of 1.8 million from the peak enrollment of the 1964–1965 school year.) The enrollment is concentrated in New York, Pennsylvania, Illinois, California, Ohio, New Jersey, Michigan, and Massachusetts.

The enrollment in Catholic schools is overwhelming in metropolitan areas, and as these urban areas have deteriorated in the United States the Catholic schools have remained to serve the urban poor.

What Is the Position of Catholics on Public Aid to Nonpublic Schools?

Most Catholics feel that it is legitimate and just for the government to assist parents in the exercise of their constitutional right to choose nonpublic schools for the education of their children.

In the 1960s, the cost of all education in the United States rose rapidly due to inflation, the increased sophistication of education, the need for increased teacher training, and the recognition of the legitimate salary demands of teachers. All of these factors obviously affected Catholic schools as well as public schools. In addition, after 1965, a gradual change in the staffing pattern of Catholic schools took place so that many religious sisters and brothers, who had previously made great contributions in their services, were replaced by lay teachers. This added significantly to the cost of education.

In the public sectors of American life, there has been recognition that local property taxes are not sufficient to provide the support necessary for quality education; increased reliance on state and federal funds has become recognized as the only answer in the public sector. Parents of most nonpublic school children, facing the

* For the current crisis in parochial schools, see Part Two, Chapter XVII. [LR]

greatly increased cost of education, also look to the state and federal governments for assistance.

How Has Federal Legislation Affected Catholic Schools?*

In 1965, after many years of debate, the Congress passed a most significant piece of legislation, which provided federal aid to education in the Elementary and Secondary School Act. Children in nonpublic schools benefited from this legislation by becoming eligible for services and materials that would be provided through the local public school. (While the funds did not go to the nonpublic school, the children enrolled in such schools did benefit.)

To meet the mounting crisis facing the elementary and secondary schools, involving over 5 million children, many state legislators passed laws providing teacher salary assistance, payment for secular services, grants to parents of low income, grants to insure health and safety. (The Supreme Court of the United States in 1971 ruled that laws passed by the Rhode Island and Pennsylvania legislators were unconstitutional since they involved the State in an "excessive entanglement" with the Church. Following this decision, lower federal courts ruled that other programs were unconstitutional for the same reason.)

Does Not Federal Aid or Tax Relief to Parochial Schools Violate the First Amendment?

No. The Supreme Court established a clear precedent for providing tax relief for a parish school when it held that tax exemption for a parish church does not offend the First Amendment. *The Court has recognized the secular purpose, as well as the religious purpose of the school.*

The Supreme Court in its various rulings has pointed out that to be constitutional the following must be true: (1) the legislation must have a secular legislative purpose; (2) it must have a primary effect that neither advances nor inhibits religion; (3) it must not bring about an excessive entanglement of the State in religious affairs.

* For the Supreme Court decision on federal aid to education see Part Two, Chapter XIX. [LR]

Catholics Often Claim That Parochial Schools Help, Rather Than Hinder, American Education. How?

Catholics feel their schools serve the national interest (and therefore Catholics feel justified in asking for assistance for parents who choose these schools for their children) because:

1. Catholic schools provide quality education in secular subjects, equipping the millions of students with knowledge and skills that enable them to contribute to the nation's economic, political, cultural, and political life. As Justice Byron White of the Supreme Court said: ". . . a wide segment of informed opinion, legislative and otherwise, has found that those [parochial] schools do an acceptable job of providing secular education to their students . . ."

2. Catholic schools render a significant service in education to the poor and disadvantaged.

3. In major urban areas, Catholic schools help to promote population stabilization, as well as neighborhood and school integration.

4. The continued existence of Catholic schools helps *contain the rising cost for providing public education.* It has been estimated that the cost to the taxpayer that would result from transferring all nonpublic school students to public schools could be in the area of $7.4 billion.

5. The pluralism that is evidenced by the existence of Catholic schools contributes to the total educational enterprise in the United States. The freedom to innovate and the spirit of competition that is present when a monopoly is avoided assist all education.

6. Catholic schools make it possible for 2 million parents to exercise their right of parental freedom of choice in education.

7. Training of youth in sound moral principles is highly beneficial to the civic community and should be encouraged and promoted for the common good.

WHAT IS THE CHRISTIAN CHURCH?

See WHO ARE THE DISCIPLES OF CHRIST?

WHAT IS A CHRISTIAN SCIENTIST?

NOTE TO THE READER: The original text for "What Is a Christian Scientist?" was written by the late George Channing.

For the new, wholly revised volume, Dr. J. Buroughs Stokes (see below) undertook to rewrite and simplify the answers to many questions. "This is in line with our church's increasing [effort] to making discussions of metaphysical points intelligible to readers or hearers who may be unacquainted with our general conceptual framework."

J. BUROUGHS STOKES / Dr. J. Buroughs Stokes is manager of the Christian Science Committees on Publication for The First Church of Christ, Scientist, in Boston.

A graduate of Temple University, he holds the degrees of Master of Education and Doctor of Education from Harvard University.

During World War II he served as a commander in the United States Naval Reserve. He was educational adviser to the superintendent of the United States Naval Academy in Annapolis for five years, and after the war served as special assistant to the secretary of the Navy.

He is a Christian Science practitioner.

NOTE TO THE READER: The views expressed in this article were officially approved by The Mother Church, The First Church of Christ, Scientist, Boston, Massachusetts.

What Is a Christian Scientist?

The Church of Christ, Scientist, has been defined by its founder, Mary Baker Eddy, as "a church designed to commemorate the word and works of our Master, which should reinstate primitive Christianity and its lost element of healing."

A Christian Scientist is one who accepts and practices the teaching of this church as it is found in the Bible and the Christian Science textbook, *Science and Health with Key to the Scriptures* by Mrs. Eddy.

Why Do You Consider It Christian?

Because it is based squarely on the life and teachings of Christ Jesus, including his promise that his followers through all time should heal the sick in his name.

Why Do You Consider It Scientific?

Because it reveals God as the divine Principle of all that really is and shows how His infinite goodness, power, and love may be demonstrated in every phase of human life.

This demonstration rests on the understanding of divine law and is not the product of mere faith in the unknown.

What Is the Basic Premise of Christian Science?

That God is divine Mind, the source and substance of man's true being. Mind, or Spirit, is cause; man and the universe are effect. When seen as Mind sees them, both man and the universe are found to be as perfect, spiritual, and immortal as their divine cause.

Imperfection of every sort belongs to a mortal, material sense of existence. Matter itself is only a false sense of substance.

In proportion as the individual understands his true selfhood to be spiritual rather than material, he is able to follow the example of Christ Jesus in overcoming the ills and evils of the flesh.

This is the process described by Saint Paul as putting off the old man and putting on the new, "which after God is created in righteousness and true holiness" (Ephesians 4:24). It is the process of finding and demonstrating reality to be wholly spiritual and evil to be illusory and unreal.

What Is the Relation of Man to God?

Man is the manifestation of Mind, Spirit, Soul, Principle, Life, Truth, Love—all of which, when capitalized, are terms used in Christian Science as synonymns for God.

Man is created in the image and the likeness of his divine Father-Mother, as the first chapter of Genesis makes clear. Man is the object and evidence of Mind's infinite care for its creation.

The sick, sinful, erring mortal commonly called "man" is not in fact man but only a misconception or a lie about man. This lie is the product of the mortal or carnal mind, which the Bible describes as "enmity against God."

By claiming our true spiritual identity, we are able to correct the false evidence of the lie in human experience.

What Does Health Mean to a Christian Scientist?

Health is a spiritual reality, not a physical condition; therefore true health is eternal.

Disease is an aspect of falsehood—a delusion of the carnal mind that can be destroyed by the prayer of spiritual understanding.

Is the Church of Christ, Scientist, a "Church of Laymen"?

Yes.

The Church of Christ, Scientist, is a church of laymen—a church without clergy or priesthood. The Bible and *Science and Health*, by Mary Baker Eddy, are the only "pastors" of the denomination.

What Happens at a Christian Science Service?

A "lesson sermon" each Sunday consists of a reading, aloud, from the Bible and from *Science and Health*. This is the chief part of the service in all Christian Science churches.

The readings are done by a first and second reader, who are elected by the local members and serve in that capacity for a three-year term.

Who Was Mary Baker Eddy?

Mary Baker Eddy (1821–1910) was the discoverer and founder of Christian Science. As a lifelong student of the Bible, she discovered in the scriptures what she felt to be a divine Science, the Science of Christ; and she saw this as the Comforter foretold by Jesus.

From a background of Congregationalism, she became the founder of a new denomination, which has as its first tenet: "As adherents of Truth, we take the inspired Word of the Bible as our sufficient guide to eternal Life."

Christian Scientists see in Mrs. Eddy the revelator to this age of the universal applicability of the Christ-power revealed in the Gospel records.

What Do Christian Scientists Believe About Jesus?

"The divinity of the Christ was made manifest in the humanity of Jesus" (*Science and Health*). Christ is the true idea of God, or Son of God, eternally present to redeem humanity from sin, disease, and death.

Jesus is the highest human expression of the Christ. Through his virgin birth, healing works, crucifixion, resurrection, and final ascension above all materiality, he has brought to light man's true spiritual nature.

The great works of Christ Jesus are regarded by Christian Scientists *not as miracles or exceptions to law* but as the natural effect of the Christly understanding of divine law, demonstrating man's inseparability from God. As illustrated in the life of the Savior, man is not God—but bears witness to God's ever-presence and infinite power.

How Do Christian Scientists Feel About the Sacraments?

Baptism to Christian Scientists means the spiritual purification of daily life; baptism is not a special or material rite.

The Eucharist is spiritual communion with God, celebrated in silence and without visible elements.

Salvation, to a Christian Scientist, means the present demonstration of Life, Truth, and Love and includes a rescue from every form of materiality that would try to alienate one from God.

What Is the Attitude of Christian Scientists Toward the Trinity?

By the Trinity, Christian Scientists mean the unity of Father, Son, and Holy Spirit—not as three persons in one but as Life, Truth, and Love, or three offices of one divine Principle.

What Role Does Prayer Play in Christian Science?

An all-important role. The desire to live rightly is basically prayer. "Men ought always to pray" (Luke 18:1). The understanding of God and the demonstration of man's true being are reached through prayer.

The prayer toward which Christian Scientists strive is not merely one of devout petition or blind faith; it is the prayer of spiritual understanding. Real devotion and experience are needed to attain this perfect prayer, but results may follow from it that seem miraculous to others.

Do Christian Scientists Hold That Praying Actually Heals Physical Ailments?

Healing is accomplished by spiritual understanding.

Faith, if it rests on blind belief, may be shaken by the evidence of the senses; but the prayer of real understanding lays hold on spiritual reality with such assurance as to change the evidence before the senses.

What Is a Christian Science Practitioner?

A practitioner is one who prays for those who ask his prayers in their behalf.

To be listed as a full-time public practitioner, one must be approved by The Mother Church, The First Church of Christ, Scientist, in Boston, Massachusetts. To be a practitioner requires study, prayer, consecration, as well as instruction under an authorized teacher and satisfactory evidence of successful healing work. Candidates must demonstrate a capacity to apply spiritual understanding to the destruction of human ills and discords.

Can a Practitioner Treat a Patient Hundreds of Miles Away?

Yes. False beliefs are destroyed by spiritual truth, through prayer, regardless of the geographical location of the person who entertains such false beliefs.

Jesus healed the centurion's servant (Matthew 8:5–13) and the daughter of the Greek woman (Mark 7:25–30) while not physically present with them.

Do Christian Scientists Deny That Some Diseases Are Caused by Germs, Microbes, and Viruses?

Regardless of what may seem to be the material cause of a disease, Christian Science teaches that all disease is a phase of the basic false belief that man is mortal and material. In the realm of belief, disease theories are modified and changed, new "causes" and treatments are found, competing therapies operate with greater or lesser success.

But the Christian Scientist knows from experience that the understanding of man's life as wholly derived from God, Spirit, brings to bodily ills of every description a healing that has nothing to do with current medical theories.

How Can Christian Science Maintain Its Attitude Toward Disease in View of Modern Medical Knowledge?

The Christian Scientist sees his attitude to disease as supported by revelation, reason, and demonstration. Christ Jesus demonstrated, as did his followers for 200 or 300 years, what healing and health really mean. Christian Scientists during the past hundred years have found this reasoned faith supported by the accumulating proofs of healing in their own experience.

The psychosomatic nature of an increasing number of diseases has been widely recognized in this century. The experience of Christian Scientists points to the fact that not some but all bodily ills are mental in origin. Christian Scientists feel they have incontestable evidence that in proportion as the Christ-power is brought to bear on the hatreds, lusts, fears, doubts, and frustrations of the human mind, bodily ills are dispelled.

The objective of Christian Science is not primarily to heal physical disease but to regenerate human thought and character. Healing is the effect of attaining this spiritual regeneration in some degree. The achievements of medical research do not change the situation for the Christian Scientist, since they do not change the substance and permanency of spiritual truth. It should be added, however, that Christian Scientists have only a feeling of deep appreciation for the devoted efforts of medical men and women in serving the needs of those who turn to them for help.

Do Christian Scientists Go to Hospitals?

The faith and experience of Christian Scientists confirm the fact that God's power surpasses human skills. This being so, they would not normally seek hospitalization. Christian Science sanatoriums and Christian Science nurses exist for those needing expert care during the course of a healing, but this care does not include medication.

Do Christian Scientists Refuse Medical Attention When Their Own Children Are Sick?

Christian Scientists love their children just as deeply as do other parents. When their children are ill, they want them to have the most effective help possible. From their own experience they have found wholehearted, systematic reliance on God to be superior to any other method of healing, and they turn to it naturally and confidently. But it would be contrary to their teaching to force Christian Science treatment on anyone who did not want it.

Christian Scientists in many schools and colleges ask for and receive exemption from medical requirements, yet investigation has shown their health to be at least as good as the group average, and often better.

Why Do Christian Science Students Request Exemptions from Certain Examinations—in Bacteriology, for Instance?

The only instruction to which Christian Scientists object is that which tends to set up the method of material medicine as the *only* healing method or system. They also object to picturing the processes of disease in ways that tend to produce the very fear that begets disease.

Would Christian Scientists Abolish Sanitation and Public Health Measures?

By no means. Christian Scientists advocate sanitation because they value cleanliness—inner and outer. They fully respect the right of the community to take such measures as the community considers essential—so long as these measures do not impose compulsory medication on those who seriously rely on the practice of spiritual healing.

Do Christian Scientists Call in a Doctor at Childbirth?

Yes. The Christian Scientist makes sure that someone who possesses the necessary skills is present at childbirth. The Christian Scientist does not presume to do what he is neither trained nor licensed to do.

Have Not Christian Scientists Died Because They Refused Medical Attention or Relied Entirely on Faith and Prayer or Called in a Doctor Too Late?

One might as readily ask, without intending to give offense, "Have not many persons died *who might have been healed* if they had tried the spiritual method of Christian Science?"

We know that thousands of men and women who were pronounced "incurable" and who spent years in invalidism and suffering have turned to Christian Science and have been healed. Such persons are numerous among the members of the Church of Christ, Scientist.

Of course, the ideal possibilities of any system of healing may sometimes be limited by personal factors in the situation. Even an exact science can be demonstrated only to the extent that it is correctly understood and faithfully applied by the human practitioner of it, and there must be a willingness on the patient's part to abide by the rules. In the Gospel of Matthew we read that when he came into his own country, Jesus "did not many mighty works there because of their unbelief."

It is worth adding that the vast majority of insurance companies recognize Christian Science in lieu of medical treatment, and the same is true of many federal and state laws, regulations, and agencies.

There are today families that have relied on Christian Science for their health needs through four generations. After a hundred years of demonstrated effectiveness, it is clear that Christian Science healing is an established fact, not a wishful fancy.

Do Christian Scientists Refuse Medical Attention in the Case of Fractures or Accidents?

There are innumerable instances of bone fractures that have been set and healed perfectly under Christian Science treatment—without medical or surgical aid. Results depend upon honest effort, correct understanding, and constancy in Christian Science practice.

A Christian Scientist does not surrender his status as a free man or woman under God. He works out his own salvation by following the course that wisdom dictates to him.

Science and Health itself makes provision for a Christian Scientist to employ a surgeon to set a bone if the Christian Scientist has not reached the degree of understanding needed for healing by spiritual means alone.

Such a person does not undergo condemnation for this, nor does he assume any burden of guilt. He is always free to improve his spiritual understanding and employ it exclusively, thus demonstrating a higher degree of integrity and consistency in his practice of Christian Science.

If God Is Infinite and Good, How Does Evil Exist?

A lie may seem very powerful, but it "exists" only insofar as it is accepted. It has no logical necessity, no real legitimacy, no structure of ultimate truth to support it. In somewhat the same way, the false suggestion that evil has an inevitable and even overwhelming place in our affairs is basically a lie about God and the universe. The whole mortal, material sense of things is based on this lie, and we escape from it as we escape from a terrible nightmare—by waking up.

This is a gradual process, however, for the false claim of a power opposed to God takes many forms and is not banished by a simple declaration. Yet each awakening from the despairing suggestion that evil has power to defeat good brings healing and undermines the basic lie that infinite good permits evil any power whatever. The process is rather like letting the sunlight into a series of dark rooms, one by one.

Christ Jesus, who spoke of the devil as a liar and the father of lies, also said, "Ye shall know the truth, and the truth shall make you free" (John 8:32). Paul likewise sent forth a clarion call to reject the lie when he wrote, "Awake, thou that sleepest, and arise from the dead, and Christ shall give thee light" (Ephesians 5:14).

Does Christian Science Believe in Sin?

The fundamental sin is the belief in a life apart from God. All the sins of the flesh, all material-mindedness, and self-centeredness are rooted in this fundamental error. It claims that man has a finite, fallible mind of his own that can set itself in opposition to the one divine Mind.

This is the lie that Christ Jesus came to destroy. In proportion as one understandingly obeys the biblical injunction to "let this mind be in you, which was also in Christ Jesus" (Philippians 2:5), one demonstrates man's true nature as the sinless child of God, the unerring manifestation of divine Mind.

Do Christian Scientists Believe in Heaven or Hell?

Yes, but as present states of thought rather than as future dwelling places. As Mrs. Eddy said, "The sinner makes his own hell by doing evil, and the saint his own heaven by doing right."

Why Don't Christian Scientists Use the Word "Death" or the Word "Died"?

They do use both words. Mrs. Eddy used them hundreds of times in her own writings, whenever the context demanded.

But the term "passed on" is used to designate the fact that what is called death does not mark the termination of individual life.

The Christian Scientist sees death as only one more phase of the belief that life is material. The changing conditions of mortal existence leave untouched man's immortal spiritual life.

Do Christian Scientists Oppose Vaccination?

Christian Scientists do not oppose vaccination for those who want it and believe in it. They do oppose compulsory vaccination for those who are proving the preventive as well as the curative power of divine law.

Mrs. Eddy specifically instructed Christian Scientists to obey the laws of the land but to seek legal exemption from those requirements that violate their religious rights or the rights of conscience. To exempt Christian Scientists from vaccination does no harm to others—especially if vaccination is as effective as it is claimed to be for those who believe in it.

Incidentally, Christian Scientists and their children obey all quarantine regulations. They sincerely want to avoid giving their neighbors cause to feel fearful of their safety.

What Is the Attitude of Christian Science to Black People?

Christian Science makes no discrimination between one race and another. It aims at the healing of racial divisions.

What Is the Status of Women in the Church?

Women occupy a position of complete equality in our church.

May Women Be Ordained as Ministers?

We have no ordained ministers, but the elected readers who conduct our church services on Sunday are normally composed of a man and a woman.

What Is the Attitude of Christian Science Toward Birth Control?

While *Science and Health* puts strong emphasis on the spiritual and moral responsibilities of marriage and the home, married couples are free to follow their own judgment as to having children and as to the number they will have.

What Is the Christian Science Attitude to Abortion?

Matters of family planning are left to individual judgment. But methods that involve operations or drugs would normally be considered incompatible with Christian Science.

What Is the Attitude of Christian Science Toward Homosexuality—by Males or Females?

Christian Science sees all forms of random or deviant sexuality as calling for specific healing rather than for condemnation, on the one hand, or mere permissiveness, on the other.

We see God's grace expressed most clearly in Jesus' liberating words to the adulterous woman, "Neither do I condemn thee: go, and sin no more."

What Is the Attitude of Christian Science Toward Psychiatry and Psychoanalysis?

There is no similarity between medical psychiatry and Christian Science. Christian Science is religion. It treats all ills by prayer. As Mrs. Eddy said: "To heal . . . is to base your practice on immortal Mind, the divine Principle of man's being; and this requires a preparation of the heart and an answer of the lips from the Lord."

Psychiatrists and psychoanalysts investigate the *human* mind, or psyche; Christian Science is based on the understanding of the divine Mind, or Soul. Its answer to the ills and wants of the human mind is the Christian answer of a "new birth"—the discovery of the "new man," or real man, revealed through Christ.

To start with God as the divine Principle of all real being is to bring the grace of infinite Love to the healing of human woes.

Does Christian Science Maintain That Death Itself Can Be Eliminated?

It holds that, in Paul's words, Christ Jesus himself has "abolished death, and . . . brought life and immortality to light" (II Timothy 1:10). His victory over the grave foretells the final conquest over all death.

Christian Science holds that God is our Life and that death is simply a phase of the mortal dream of life in matter.

Sooner or later, either on this side of the grave or on the other, each individual must awaken from this dream to the full recognition of his immortal life in God.

Do Christian Scientists Hold Funeral Services?

Some do; some choose not to. In the former case, the family selects a Christian Scientist to conduct the service and read passages from the Bible and from Mrs. Eddy's writings. These passages will normally bring out the comforting fact of man's immortal being as the expression of God—of Life, Spirit, Love.

Do Christian Scientists Consider Themselves Protestants?

Yes, in a general sense, but with some crucial differences.

Christian Science holds that God's creation is entirely spiritual and that evil, in all its aspects, belongs only to a mistaken, material sense of creation.

Christian Science maintains that healing is a *religious* function.

What Is the Attitude of Christian Science Toward Other Religions?

Christian Scientists feel spiritual fellowship with all sincere seekers for truth and with all who worship a just and merciful God.

Mrs. Eddy has defined Christian Science as "the law of God, the law of good, interpreting and demonstrating the divine Principle and rule of universal harmony." This definition reaches beyond denominational boundaries to unite in some measure all who respond to "the law of good" in their hearts.

This attitude is summed up in Mrs. Eddy's further statement: "A genuine Christian Scientist loves Protestant and Catholic, D.D. and M.D.—loves all who love God, good; and he loves his enemies."

WHAT IS A CONGREGATIONALIST?

See WHAT IS THE UNITED CHURCH OF CHRIST?

WHO ARE THE DISCIPLES OF CHRIST (*Christian Church*)?

NOTE TO THE READER: The original article on the Disciples of Christ was written by the late James E. Craig. New material has been contributed by Robert L. Friedly, and such material is identified by initials [RLF] immediately following a passage.

JAMES E. CRAIG / James E. Craig, honorary elder for life of the Park Avenue Christian Church, New York City, had a distinguished career in journalism. He was chief editorial writer for the New York *Sun,* editor of its editorial page, and managing editor of *The Protestant World.*

Mr. Craig was born in Norborne, Missouri, in 1881. He was baptized into the Disciples of Christ by his father, a Disciples minister. Mr. Craig studied at the University of Missouri. As reporter, feature writer, and editor, he worked on the Kansas City *Journal, Star,* and *Post,* and the St. Louis *Post-Dispatch.* He was city editor of the St. Louis *Globe-Democrat* and the New York *Evening Mail,* and was managing editor of the Brownsville, Texas, *Herald.* He wrote an authoritative history of the Freemasons and won the *Masonic Outlook* prize essay contest in 1925.

ROBERT L. FRIEDLY / Robert L. Friedly, director of the Office of Communications for the Christian Church (Disciples of Christ), was born in 1933 in Moundsville, West Virginia, and received his B.A. in journalism from Marshall University, Huntington, West Virginia.

He has served as president of the Association of Christian Churches of Greater New Orleans and is a past elder and member of the board of directors of the Eastgate Christian Church in Indianapolis, where he resides.

He has been active in ecumenical activities: as a member of the board of directors of *Religion in American Life* and as a member of the Communications Committee of the National Council of Churches.

Mr. Friedly has had extensive experience in newspaper work, has written widely for *The Christian,* and has contributed to the *Encyclopaedia Britannica.*

NOTE TO THE READER: Local congregations of this church generally use the name "Christian Church." However, some add "(Disciples of Christ)," and others even use "Church of Christ." [LR]

The official name is "Christian Church (Disciples of Christ)."
The headquarters of most general units of the church are in Indianapolis, Indiana. [RLF]

Who Are the Disciples of Christ?

The Christian Church (Disciples of Christ) is one of the largest religious bodies that had its origins on American soil. The church got its start on the American frontier, at the beginning of the nineteenth century, as a movement to unify Christians who were divided mainly over issues that developed in Europe and had little relevance on the frontier. The Disciples had almost 200,000 members by 1860 and more than 1 million by 1900. The church currently has leveled off to about 1.3 million in the United States and Canada.

Spreading from western Pennsylvania and northern Kentucky, moving as the American frontier developed westward, the church's strength numerically grew and remains concentrated in the eight-state arc that runs from Ohio and Kentucky through the Middle West and down into the Southwest states of Oklahoma and Texas. [RLF]

How Did the Church Come by Its Name?

The name "Christian Church (Disciples of Christ)" stems from its frontier origin, when similar movements to restore New Testament simplicity and church unity grew almost simultaneously in Pennsylvania and Kentucky.

Barton W. Stone, a former Presbyterian, chose simply the name "Christian" for the Kentucky branch, to emphasize the putting away of denominational divisiveness and the blending into the body of Christ at large. Alexander Campbell, also of Presbyterian background, preferred the name "Disciples" for his western Pennsylvania movement, since he felt it less presumptuous than calling oneself "Christian." The two groups joined forces in 1832. [RLF]

Is the Church Related to the "Churches of Christ"?

Many people are confused by the similarity in the names of the three present-day groups that grew from the same frontier roots.

The three are the "Christian Church (Disciples of Christ)," "Churches of Christ," and the so-called "independent" Christian Churches. Of the three, the Disciples are more likely to be involved in the ecumenical movement in its various forms—councils of churches, union conversations, and the like.

The Churches of Christ were listed separately for the first time in the 1906 Federal Religious Census and are distinguished by their opposition to the use of musical instruments in worship and to church organization beyond the local congregation. The independent Christian Churches pulled away gradually in more recent years and now list themselves separately in the Yearbook of American Churches. [RLF]

What Are the Basic Beliefs of Your Creed?

The church professes no doctrine or dogma beyond belief in Jesus Christ; all other matters are therefore open to individual interpretation, even the characteristics mentioned here as being distinctively Disciple.

The Disciples reject the use of creeds when applied as tests to determine "rightness of belief."

Disciples, from the very beginning of the movement, have objected to matters that tend to divide Christianity. They have therefore rejected creeds and dogma with vehemence. They have opted strongly for the right of every Christian to read the scriptures for himself or herself and to decide on matters of opinion.

There is no church authority that fixes a position on doctrine. [RLF]

What Authority Does the General Assembly Exercise?

The General Assembly of the church does not hesitate to speak out on issues, but congregations and regions and individuals have only a moral compunction to listen and respond (see below). [RLF]

Do You Believe in the "Priesthood of the Laity"?

Yes. The Disciples have a well-trained clergy, of course, but retains from its frontier-born origins a commitment to the priesthood of the laity as well. [RLF]

What Are the Requirements for Membership in the Christian Church (Disciples of Christ)?

The church has been very careful to require only a confession of faith, using a simple statement such as: "I believe that Jesus is the Christ and I accept him as my Lord and personal Savior," followed by baptism by immersion as sole requirement for membership. [RLF]

Do You Observe Sacraments?

The Disciples of Christ believe strongly in Christian unity and always have observed a Lord's Supper, or Communion, open to all Christians. Lay elders preside over the Lord's Supper and may perform all other pastoral functions except those regulated by civil law. Disciples celebrate the Lord's Supper each Sunday as a central part of worship. [RLF]

What Is the Church Service Like?

With minor variations, Sunday morning service in Disciple churches follows pretty much the same pattern. With or without processions, and with or without organ, the worship begins with the singing of hymns. This is followed by responsive readings, recitation of the Lord's Prayer, reading of the scriptures, pastoral prayer, an anthem or two, the sermon, an invitation to fellowship, gathering of tithes and offerings, Communion service, benediction, and final hymn or recessional.

Sometimes Communion precedes the sermon. On occasion, the sermon may be omitted, but seldom ever Communion.

Do the Disciples Baptize?

We baptize only those who are adult enough to know what they are doing when they stand up to confess Christ.

We baptize by immersion, believing it to have been the New Testament way—an act of obedience and surrender, a symbol of the death, burial, and resurrection of the Lord Jesus.

Do the Disciples Accept Nonbaptized Members?

Nonimmersed persons are accepted as transfers from their churches.

How Do the Disciples Differ from Other Protestants?

Disciples have no catechism and no prescribed rituals of worship.

Disciples do not concern themselves with the doctrine of apostolic succession. Hence, they have no archbishops or bishops or hierarchy of ecclesiastical authority.

Disciples believe that a confession of faith in Jesus as the Christ requires no added metaphysical doctrine.

They regard conversion as a voluntary, rational act that does not require special personal revelation. In receiving a new member, they take the applicant's simple statement of faith at face value. They employ no formula of interrogation or board of inquiry.

Disciples believe that a Christian's right to Holy Communion is entirely a matter for his own conscience. They admit to the Lord's Supper any baptized person, without regard to his sectarian affiliations.

Disciples base their whole case and their whole appeal on a simple outline of faith and a democratic system of church government. They hold that as long as a member accepts the simple faith and the idea of democratic government in the church, he may believe what his mind dictates about many of the tenets of other Christian bodies.

Disciples observe with joy that the differences among Protestants are receiving less and less attention today, while the many things they have in common receive more and more. Disciples have been in the forefront of almost every important Protestant cooperative and ecumenical movement. Thirty-nine Disciples were active in establishing the old Federal Council of Churches; about eighty are enrolled in the National Council of Churches of Christ in America; about twenty Disciple leaders serve the World Council of Churches.

What Do the Disciples Believe About the Bible?

The Disciples share the common Protestant belief that the Bible (except for the Apocryphal Books) is the inspired Word of God, written by different persons at different times under the inspiration of the Holy Spirit. They use the Old Testament for meditation and instruction, a schoolmaster bringing the faithful to Christ.

In common with other Christian bodies, the Disciples have their fundamentalists and their liberals. The literalists, or fundamentalists, accept every word of the Bible as a final and infallible word of God. The liberals believe that a book of faith is not meant to be taken literally, that it is God's effort to explain his works to a people learning in the faith.

There is nothing to prevent literalists and liberals from sitting down together around the Table of the Lord's Supper, each responsible for his own belief and each serving God according to the dictates of his own conscience.

Do the Disciples Believe in the Virgin Birth?

It is probable that a majority of them do. It is certain that many have doubts on the subject. But there is no ecclesiastical or denominational authority that can declare one belief to be orthodox and reject the other as heretical.

Do the Disciples Believe in the Holy Trinity?

The Disciples have had little trouble in discarding most of the dogmas that sprang up between the first century and the nineteenth. Hence, speculation about the Holy Trinity and the nature of a triune God has bothered them little or not at all. They baptize in the name of the Father, Son, and Holy Spirit, as Christ commanded. They believe that the Holy Spirit is the Comforter promised in the New Testament, but they do not worry over its constitution or the nature of its operations. They accept its guidance as constantly enlarging the horizons of Christian thought. They are not concerned about such matters as original sin or predestination.

Do the Disciples Believe in Heaven and Hell?

Here again it is difficult to give an answer that will prove satisfactory to all members of this great fellowship. Many doubtless believe in a literal paradise and a literal hell. Most are content to leave the details of future rewards and punishments in the hands of Divine Mercy, without troubling themselves over theories elaborated in medieval theology. Disciple faith in general is a matter of deep personal conviction, rooted in serene confidence that the Kingdom of God will prove invincible in this world and in the life to come.

What Do the Disciples Believe About Sin and Salvation?

No answer covering all the congregations is possible. The Disciples as a rule reject the doctrine of original sin, but most of them believe that we are all sinful creatures unless and until redeemed by the saving sacrifice of the Lord Jesus.

Early in the history of the movement, the conception gained ground that a reasonable God would not leave His creatures without a rational plan of salvation that any person could understand and follow. Walter Scott was perhaps the first notable exponent of this idea. He suggested a fivefold plan: faith, repentance, baptism, newness of life, gift of the Holy Spirit. By faith he meant a sincere belief in the power and goodness of God, accompanied by complete surrender to His holy will. By repentance he mant not merely sorrow for past misdeeds, but perfect contrition, coupled with resolution not to sin again. By baptism he meant obedience to a command of the Savior and emulation of the example of the apostles. By newness of life he meant such conduct thereafter as would be void of further offense to God and scandal to the Church. By the gift of the Holy Spirit he meant the coming of the indwelling Comforter promised in the Gospels.

It was Walter Scott's belief that when a sinner honestly fulfilled these requirements he had no need to look for some mystical and emotional inner manifestation of saving grace. If you do what God has told you to do, he argued, you may be sure that God will reward you accordingly. Although the accent and terminology may have shifted, the essentials of this plan are still widely accepted among the Disciples.

What Is the Position of Your Church on Black People?

The Christian Church (Disciples of Christ) has about 50,000 black members, or about 4 percent of the total membership of the

church in the United States and Canada. There are 550 essentially
black congregations, most of them in North Carolina.

Our church has a long record of civil rights activity; its General
Assembly has always been integrated, even though blacks have had
a convention of their own as well. The church raised $2 million in
the four-year period that ended July 1972, in over-and-above funds
for dealing with race, poverty, education, housing, and community
organization—with the preponderant emphasis black. It also resolved in its 1969 assembly that even though the church membership is but 4 percent black, denominational boards and committees
by 1975 should have 20 percent minority representation.

The Moderator of the Christian Church for the term that ended
in October 1973 was a black pastor from Louisville, Kentucky: Dr.
Walter D. Bingham. The forty-five-member Administrative Committee of the Church, which is the key leadership body, contains ten
black members currently. The 1971 General Assembly of the church
established at the national level a holiday commemo. *ting the
birthday of Martin Luther King, Jr., and urged federal legislation
declaring a holiday.

Though the practice has not always been as good as the word, our
church strongly supports equal employment opportunities, both
within the church and without, assistance to persons in poverty, and
welfare measures—all particularly important to black people.

What Is the Status of Women in the Christian Church?

Women serve in a great number of capacities: as elders and
chairpersons of committees of local congregations; as first vice-
moderator of the General Assembly; as members of the Commission
on Budget Evaluation, General Board, division boards; as chairpersons of key committees.

Women have served on delegations to ecumenical organizations,
including the general board of the National Council of Churches
and the Consultation on Church Union.

There are some women pastors but not many. Dr. Jean Wool
Folk of Little Rock, Arkansas, an insurance executive, served as
moderator of the church in the United States and Canada, 1973–1975.

Can Women Be Ordained in Your Ministry?

Yes. Women have been ordained as *missionaries* since the late 1880s. There is no record on the date of the ordination of the first woman minister; it apparently came as a natural outgrowth of women's involvement.

As professionals in the ministry, women are chaplains, ministers of congregations, Christian education directors, missionaries, regional executives. [RLF]

What Are the Disciples' Views on Divorce?

There is no central authority on this subject.

In practice, ministers and congregations of the Disciples of Christ differ in their attitudes to divorce. Some believe that the questions propounded to Jesus by the Pharisees on this subject were "trick" questions concerned with then-current Jewish law and that what Jesus answered must be viewed in that light. Some ministers and congregations take the Master's answer as binding to this day and therefore oppose any remarriage of divorced persons. Others are willing to consent to the remarriage of any innocent party to a divorce obtained on the ground of adultery. Most believe that divorce has become a legal function of the state and do not hesitate to remarry any person to whom the civil government has accorded the right of remarriage.

What Are the Disciples' Views on Birth Control?

The old Disciple rule is that where the scriptures speak, we speak; where they are silent, we are silent.

For most Disciple ministers, birth control and family planning are keys to the solution of world population and hunger problems. The church is heavily involved in family-planning efforts in India and other places.

By the terms of ordination, each minister considers himself or herself empowered, as were the Prophets of old, to denounce whatever is amiss in the life of the people—and silence seems to give at least a modified consent.

In general, Disciples are content to leave matters such as birth control to the individual consciences of husband and wife.

What Is Your Position on Abortion?

The church does not hold an official position on abortion at this time, although a number of regional organizations, and the General Assembly, have urged study of the issue, the consequences, and alternatives.

As in other areas of our church, individual members are free to hold a variety of opinions. [RLF]

What Is Your Position on Homosexuality?

The church holds no formal position on homosexuality at this time. Members are free to have a variety of opinions. [RLF]

Do the Disciples of Christ Proselytize?

No Sunday morning service closes without an offering of fellowship to any adult who cares to take his stand by the Cross of the Risen Lord. But because of the close ecumenical ties of the Disciples and the sincere conviction that Disciples represent only a part of the Christian family, there is little effort any more to "steal sheep from someone else's fold."

How Do Disciples Feel About Roman Catholics?

Although, like most Protestants in years gone by, there was great suspicion of the Roman Catholic Church, Disciples now have strong relationships to the Roman Catholics including bilateral conversations that have gone on since 1967 on such subjects as the Lord's Supper and marriage. Roman Catholics and Disciples have seen similarities in each other at the point of emphasis on the Lord's Supper or Mass as central to worship. [RLF]

Are Disciples Involved with Other Denominations?

Most definitely. Although they certainly have not realized all their Christian unity objectives, they have made strong contributions to the ecumenical movement.

The Christian Church helped form the old Federal Council of Churches, and participates actively now in the leadership of the National Council of Churches, the World Council of Churches, and in many state and local councils. Dr. Paul A. Crow, Jr., a young Disciples seminary professor, was called to be the first general secretary of the nine-denomination Consultation on Church Union. [RLF]

Is the Christian Church Involved Overseas?

About 150 overseas staff (no longer called missionaries) serve in some 22 countries, though the number belies the extent of involvement of the church abroad. The Disciples long have encouraged united Protestant churches abroad, have sought to turn control of "missions" over to foreign leaders, and have participated financially in ecumenical work in all parts of the world. The largest national body of Disciples outside North America has been the church in the Republic of Zaire (formerly Congo), where I. B. Bokeleale, a member of the Disciples of Christ, now leads a broadly inter-denominational Church of Christ in Zaire. [RLF]

What Are the Church's Involvements at Home?

The Disciples of Christ operate seven children's homes around the country and fourteen homes for the aging and have special mission activities among the Yakima Indians in Washington, Appalachians in Kentucky, and Spanish-Americans and Negroes in a number of places.

There are thirty-two institutions of higher education related to the church, the largest being Butler University (Indianapolis), Drake University (Des Moines), and Texas Christian University (Fort Worth). [RLF]

How Are the Disciples of Christ Organized?

The Christian Church, historically a congregationally governed church, has a rather unique structure—operating at three distinct levels: congregational, regional, and general. It is unique in that there is no pyramid of authority running from the congregation up to the international, or general, level.

In our church, each level is on a par with the other levels, each owning its own property, managing the available finances, and organizing programs. The levels are bound together by moral covenant rather than legal agreement. Local congregations participate financially in the regional and general work as they see fit. Both congregations and regions send representatives directly to the General Assembly.

Prior to 1968, when this structure was adopted, the Disciples had done all of their work beyond the local congregation through societies organized by individuals who saw particular needs that should be met. The myriad agencies that grew up independently of each other—sometimes with overlapping responsibility—reported to a "convention of churches" but were not bound by the convention's actions. These agencies, by their own consent, are gradually making changes in their operations that bring them under the General Assembly as divisions and councils of the church. [RLF]

What Is the General Assembly?

The General Assembly meets every two years and has roughly 8,000 to 10,000 persons in attendance, about half of them voting representatives, either as the church's ordained ministers or as lay representatives from congregations and regions. A 222-member General Board, at least half of its members lay people, meets annually; and a 45-member Administrative Committee of the board gathers three times each year.

The General Assembly elects a moderator and two vice-moderators every two years to preside over the general gathering. There are thirty-six regions of the church, each of which developed like the other former "agencies" of the church in an unidentifiable pattern, independent of each other. They vary widely in size, both by membership and geography. They have played a prominent role, headed up by their "regional minister," in certifying the standing of ministers in the Christian Church, development of new congregations, assistance to troubled congregations, provision for a sharing of ideas and programs, education as to the broader mission of the church, and provision of counsel in pastor-congregation relationships. [RLF]

Are Disciples of Christ Social Activists?

As in most major denominations, members are sharply divided over church involvements in civil rights, war and peace, and other social action. The General Assembly of the church listed as its primary concerns for the 1970s and beyond these five areas: evangelism and renewal; reconciliation in the urban crisis; world order, justice, and peace; leadership; and ecumenical involvement.

The assembly has adopted such resolutions as one favoring amnesty for draft evaders and another favoring guaranteed family income, but, on the other side, has turned down a designation of the Disciples as a "peace church" and issued one of the stronger rejections of the rhetoric of the Black Manifesto, which demanded reparations from churches for blacks. (It followed up the latter by raising $2 million for black and other minority projects.) [RLF]

Do the Disciples Believe That Theirs Is the Only True Religion?

Certainly not. They believe theirs to be most nearly in accord with the practices of the early Christian churches. They also believe that their greatest mission in life is to bring Christians of all faiths into one Church of Christ.

Their ancient retort to an ancient gibe about their name was to say: "We are not the only Christians, but are Christians only."

WHAT IS AN EPISCOPALIAN?

NOTE TO THE READER: The original article, written by Dr.
W. Norman Pittenger, has been read and revised at the General
Theological Seminary in New York, under the direction of the Right
Reverend Stephen F. Bayne. The seminary supplied new material in
answering new questions that have come into importance since
Dr. Pittenger's article was written.

Where text is new, and not Dr. Pittenger's, the initials of the General
Theological Seminary [GTS] or of the Executive Council of the Episcopal
Church [ECEC] identify the material.

Where part of the text is Dr. Pittenger's and part of the text was
provided by the General Theological Seminary, the appropriate initials,
after different passages, identify the source.

W. NORMAN PITTENGER / W. Norman Pittenger was professor of
Christian Apologetics at General Theological Seminary in New York until
1970. He is now a resident and member of the divinity faculty at King's
College, Cambridge (England). He was vice-chairman of the Commission
on Christ and the Church, appointed under the World Council of Churches.

Dr. Pittenger was born in Bogota, New Jersey, in 1905, and studied at
Columbia University, Ripon Hall, Oxford (England), Union Theological
Seminary, and the General Theological Seminary, from which he was
graduated in 1936. He was made a deacon in the Episcopal Church in
1936 and was ordained a priest the following year.

Dr. Pittenger has served as an examining chaplain in the Diocese of
New Jersey and as president of the American Theological Society.
He was for many years American editor of *Theology*, an English monthly
journal, and served on the editorial boards of *The Anglican Theological
Review* and *Religion in Life*.

Dr. Pittenger has written more than twenty-five books. He is the coauthor
(with the late Right Reverend James A. Pike, Episcopal Bishop of
California) of *The Faith of the Church*, the authoritative and quasi-official
statement of the Episcopal point of view. His most recent books are
The Word Incarnate (1959), *Pathway to Believing* (1960), *Proclaiming
Christ Today* (1962), *Life in Christ* (1972), and *Trying to Be a Christian*
(1972).

What Is an Episcopalian?

An Episcopalian is a member of the Protestant Episcopal Church in the United States, which is one of the twenty self-governing national (or regional) churches within the Anglican Communion. These churches, with some 47 million members in all, are found on every continent.

They are called "Anglican" because the Church of England was, directly or indirectly, the mother of them all, and the Archbishop of Canterbury holds a primacy of honor among all the bishops. The unity among these very diverse churches is rooted in their common ancestry; their full communion with the Archbishop of Canterbury and with one another; their prayer books, which establish the body of common faith; and their increasing common action in many relationships.

They are also called "Episcopalian" (officially so only in Scotland and the United States) because they place emphasis on bishops as the chief symbols of unity and continuity with the church of all ages, and as the chief pastors. (The Greek word *episkopos* means "overseer" and has become "bishop" in English.)

Is the Episcopal Church Catholic or Protestant?

It is both. As with all churches of the Anglican Communion, it has maintained the ancient Catholic sacraments, creeds, and orders of the church. (This was the intention of the English reformers in the sixteenth century.)

It is also "reformed" because, in that reformation, the authority of the Pope was rejected, the services were translated into English and much simplified, and the authority of the Bible was strongly re-emphasized.

But in no sense were these attempts to deny the truth of Catholic faith and order.

The title of the church in the United States—"Protestant Episcopal"—was adopted in 1789, to signify that the church was a nonpapal or non-Roman body.

In England, the church is called simply the Church of England.

Do Episcopalians Believe That Theirs Is the Only True Faith?

No. We hold that all who are baptized (whether by Episcopalian or other rites, provided it is with water and in the name of the Holy Trinity) are members of the Church of Christ. Christ is the "head" of His Church (called in the New Testament "The Body of Christ") and those who belong to Him by baptism are His "members."

Confirmation by the bishop is necessary to communicant status, but it is not believed to be "joining the Church." It is a sacramental rite by which, Episcopalians believe, the gift of the Holy Spirit at baptism is sealed, fulfilled, confirmed, when the baptized person comes to maturity.

Even those who are not actually baptized, but by intention would be baptized if they were able, are believed by many to be supplied by God with the gifts of baptism.

The Church is Christ's instrument for fulfilling His purpose in the world and the means by which His continuing presence is made available. Of that one Church, Episcopalians believe they are a part; they have never claimed they are the *only* part.

What Is the Episcopalian Attitude Toward Roman Catholicism?

The Episcopal Church has no official position in regard to present-day Roman Catholicism. It believes that the Anglican Communion possesses all the essential marks of historical Catholicism—the Holy Scriptures, the apostolic faith, sacraments, and ministry.

Most Episcopalians would seriously question Roman Catholic centralization of power in the Bishop of Rome and would regard with disfavor what they conceive to be the Roman Church's suppression of freedom in many intellectual areas, as well as in the understanding of the relation of Church to civil government and education. [WNP]

However, such questions are rapidly losing force—what with the changing patterns within the Roman Catholic Church; and significant new discoveries are being made in bilateral dialogues between the Roman and Anglican churches, both nationally and internationally. [GTS]°

° See Part Two, Chapter XVI, p. 506, for the historic report of the Anglican-Roman Catholic International Commission, which reached "basic agreement" on "the nature of the priesthood" and certain aspects of Holy Communion. [LR]

What Are the Basic Beliefs of Episcopalians?

They are affirmed in the Apostles' Creed and the Nicene Creed. The Apostles' Creed is the ancient baptismal statement of faith. As used in Episcopalian services, it runs:

I believe in God the Father Almighty, Maker of heaven and earth:
And in Jesus Christ his only Son our Lord: Who was conceived by the Holy Ghost, Born of the Virgin Mary: Suffered under Pontius Pilate, Was crucified, dead, and buried: He descended into hell; The third day he rose again from the dead: He ascended into heaven, And sitteth on the right hand of God the Father Almighty: From thence he shall come to judge the quick and the dead.
I believe in the Holy Ghost: the holy Catholic Church; The Communion of Saints: The Forgiveness of Sins: The Resurrection of the body: And the Life everlasting. Amen.

The Nicene Creed, used at the service of Holy Communion, is an expanded statement of the Christian faith, essentially the same as the Apostles' Creed.

Both creeds state the main points of Christian belief in a pictorial and dramatic form. Some of the phrases are clearly "symbolic" (as, "sitteth on the right hand of God the Father," which of course could not be *literally* true); some parts are historical in intention (as "born," "crucified," "dead," "buried," "rose again"); and some parts are theological such as "of one substance," in the Nicene Creed, although more often the theological affirmations are phrased in the pictorial language that the early Church took over from its Jewish background.

What Is the Book of Common Prayer?

At the time of the English reforms, the old service books of the Church were translated into English. Some of the services were combined and edited; many were shortened and simplified. The result was the Book of Common Prayer, completed in 1549.

All later prayer books, including that used in America today, are reeditings of the 1549 book, whose beautiful, stately language, simplicity, and dignity are unparalleled. The regular services, like the Holy Communion or Holy Eucharist, Morning and Evening Prayer, the Litany, are all taken from the Prayer Book. Episcopalians believe that a prescribed form of service with parts assigned to clergy and people is the most fitting way to adore God.

Frequent revisions are made to meet the needs of succeeding ages; but the principle of ordered worship remains at the heart of Anglicanism. The Episcopal Church is currently using and studying a series of trial rites, looking toward another revision of the Prayer Book, the first since 1929. [WNP and GTS]

What Is Meant by "High," "Low," and "Broad" Church?

These words, once commonly used of congregations or individuals, are now becoming obsolete.

A "high" parish was one that emphasized sacramental worship, the supreme value of the "Catholic tradition," and a rather elaborate service of worship. A "low" parish was one in which the services were simpler and a stronger emphasis was placed on the Gospel and on personal religion. In a "broad" parish, which might have been either "high" or "low," the importance of a rational understanding of the Christian tradition was stressed, with a concern for "liberal values."

But all such relative emphases met, and similar ones still do, in the proclamation of the Gospel, sacramental worship, and the reasonable presentation of Christianity. Episcopalians appeal to Scriptures, to tradition, and to personal experience, as well as to reason, for vindication of the truth of the Christian faith.

Differences in emphasis are welcomed in the Episcopal Church, as long as the central affirmations are maintained. [WNP and GTS]

Did Henry VIII Found the Episcopal Church?

No. Under Henry, the freedom of the English Church from the authority of the Bishop of Rome was achieved; but that was the end of a long period of protest and agitation against what were conceived to be the Pope's unwarranted usurpations of authority. Henry's desire for an annulment provided the occasion but was not the *cause* of the independence of the Church of England.

It is unfortunate that in many textbooks the mistake of identifying occasion and cause has led to the propagation of what is in fact an untruth.

What Do Episcopalians Believe About Jesus Christ?

They believe that He is "truly God and truly man, united in one person" for the salvation of mankind. There are different ways of understanding and teaching this doctrine, but it is central and unchangeable for all Episcopalians.

What Is the Episcopal View of the Virgin Birth?

The creeds and the liturgy of the Episcopal Church assert the traditional belief that Jesus was born of Mary without human father. There is no disagreement within the Church on the *theological* meaning of the Virgin Birth. There has been, and still is, disagreement about the Virgin Birth in its biological detail.

Most Episcopalians probably accept it as literally true; some regard it as symbolic in character. The Episcopal Church is able to contain both types of thinking within it, since all Episcopalians accept the Incarnation—the true deity and humanity of Jesus—as the central truth about Christ.

What Is the Episcopal Position About the Trinity?

The Trinity is the Christian teaching about God. In the light of man's experience of God's working in the world, Christians have been driven to assert that God *is* as He *reveals* Himself. He is Creative Reality (God the Father); He is Expressive Act (God the Son); He is Responsive Power (God the Holy Spirit). Yet He is *one* God. This is "theology."

What matters most, in the Book of Common Prayer, about the Trinity is that we worship God and experience Him in a "trinitarian" fashion.

What Does the Episcopal Church Believe About the Lord's Supper?

Holy Communion, sometimes called the Lord's Supper or Holy Eucharist (from an ancient Christian word for the service), is the chief service of worship in the Episcopal Church, although it does not always occupy the chief place in the Sunday schedule.

The teaching of the Church about this sacrament is expressed in these words: "The Sacrament of the Lord's Supper was ordained for the continual remembrance of the sacrifice of the death of Christ, and of the benefits which we receive thereby"; and the Offices of Instruction (Prayer Book, page 293), from which these words are quoted, goes on to say that "the . . . thing signified" in the sacrament "is the Body and Blood of Christ, which are spiritually taken and received by the faithful."

Do Episcopalians Practice Private Confession?

They may, since provision is made in the Prayer Book for private confession of sins to a priest, with the declaration of absolution by him. However, this is not enforced, as in the Roman Catholic Church; it is entirely optional.

Many Episcopalians avail themselves of the privilege, some frequently, some occasionally. Many do not desire to use this "means of grace" and find satisfaction in the *general* confessions and absolutions provided in the regular services of the Church.

How Do Episcopalians Regard the Bible?

The Holy Scriptures are, for Episcopalians, the great source and testing ground of Christian doctrine. Nothing may be taught "as necessary to eternal salvation" except what can be "proved" (the Elizabethan word for "tested") by Holy Scripture.

But the Episcopal Church does not hold to the literal inerrancy of Scripture. The Bible is considered sacred for its general inspiration, as the record of God's revelation.

The Episcopal Church maintains a balance between Gospel and tradition, on the one hand, and the use of reason on the other. Freedom of investigation, restatements of the Christian faith, and incorporation of scientific truths are possible *without* creating violent fundamentalist-modernist controversies.

Does the Episcopal Church Accept the Theory of Evolution?

The Episcopal Church has accepted the theory of evolution as an account of man's origin, as well as other new scientific discoveries, without disturbing its central beliefs.

In both freedom of inquiry and Biblical criticism, the Episcopal Church's position has been liberal and has left a place for a "modérnist" school of thought among its members, as well as a "catholic" and an "evangelical" emphasis.

Do Episcopalians Believe in Heaven and Hell?

The teachings of the Episcopal Church about death, judgment, heaven, and hell are stated plainly in the Book of Common Prayer. Death marks the end of this period of man's life. He is judged in terms of his real character, by a God "unto whom all hearts are open, all desires known, and from whom no secrets are hid." Heaven is a state in which the vision of God is enjoyed in a "life of perfect service" of God. Hell is alienation from God, and therefore the loss of that goal to which man's whole existence is directed.

Episcopalians do not believe in a *physical* heaven or hell; these are "states of being." The departed in whom there is some possibility of goodness are prepared for the full enjoyment of God by such cleansing and purifying as they may require—in a way, this resembles the idea of "purgatory." But Episcopalians do not use the term in their official teaching, because they feel that it is often associated with crude ideas of payment of penalty and the like.

Do Episcopalians Believe in the Resurrection?

By the "resurrection," the Episcopal Church means not the raising of the physical body we now possess but the re-creation by God of the total personality of man with a "spiritual body"—that is, with an instrument of self-expression and a means for continuing fellowship, appropriate to a heavenly life.

What Then Is Meant by Salvation?

Modern Episcopalians tend to understand by this term "health or wholeness of life." Salvation means that one is given the wholeness that is God's will for man and is delivered from arrogance and selfishness.

Salvation has to do not only with the "hereafter" but also with man's present earthly existence. In man, sinner because he is ridiculously proud and self-centered, there is no real "health"; by fellowship with God in Christ, he is brought into the sphere of healthy and whole life.

Does the Episcopal Church Have a Priesthood?

It does. There are three "orders of ministry" included in "Holy Orders": bishops, priests, deacons.

The Offices of Instruction state that the bishop's office is "to be a chief pastor in the Church; to confer Holy Orders; and to administer confirmation." A priest's office is "to minister to the people committed to his care; to preach the Word of God; to baptize; to celebrate the Holy Communion; and to pronounce absolution and blessing in God's name." The deacon assists the priest in divine service and other ministrations; he is a minister in the real sense of the word, but without such "higher" privileges as priest and bishop.

The priest is the "ministerial representative" for Christ in his church; he also represents the priesthood of the laity, which is shared by all who are baptized.

An Episcopal minister is never called a "preacher," since that is only one aspect of his office; he is also celebrant of the Holy Communion—absolver, teacher, shepherd of his flock.

May Episcopalian Ministers Marry?

The ministers of the Episcopal Church may marry or not marry as they see fit, "as they shall judge the same to serve better to godliness." (But see next question.)

Are There Monks and Nuns in the Episcopal Church?

Yes. There are many communities of Episcopal monks and nuns, both in the United States and elsewhere. Some are purely "contemplative"—that is, engaged in prayer; others are "mixed"—that is, engaged both in prayer and in teaching, writing, preaching.

These men and women take the vows of poverty, chastity, and obedience. They do not marry. They live in communities established for the purpose of sharing a common life of work and prayer.

Does the Episcopal Church Permit Divorce?

In America, the "canons" (or church law) do not recognize divorce, but do provide a number of grounds for annulment—the ecclesiastical declaration that no marriage has in fact existed because of some factor that made such impossible.

A bishop may permit a divorced person to remarry if certain conditions are met. He may also admit to Holy Communion persons who have been divorced and remarried—if they can prove that they are in good faith, are struggling to live a Christian life, and have demonstrated their stability and repentance.*

What Is the Status/Role of Women in the Episcopal Church?

Women can be "declared to be within the Diaconate," according to one of the resolutions adopted by the Episcopal General Convention of 1970.

This order embraces the following duties as set forth in the Book of Common Prayer:

. . . to assist the Priest in Divine Service, and specially when he ministereth the Holy Communion, and to help him in the distribution thereof; to read Holy Scriptures and Homilies in the Church; and to instruct the youth in the Catechism; in the absence of the Priest, to baptize infants; and to preach, if he be admitted thereto by the Bishop. And furthermore,

---

* On October 9, 1973, at its sixty-fourth general convention, the Episcopal Church of America issued an historic agreement, between its House of Deputies and its House of Bishops, which
1. recognized civil divorce,
2. liberalized rules for divorce,
3. liberalized rules for remarriage,
4. eliminated the waiting period between divorce and remarriage.
Thus the Episcopal Church deleted from its canons previous threats of excommunication against those who ignored the church's prior requirements that remarriage be judged by a bishop and that either bride or groom be "a member in good standing" of the church.
Before the Convention, permission for a second marriage had to be acquired from a bishop; now it may be obtained from a parish priest—but at least one partner must have "received holy Baptism."
These important changes in the canons were accompanied by a warning from the bishops to their diocesan priests to guard against extreme interpretations of the new rules which could lead to an excessive number of permissions for remarriage. [LR]

it is his Office, where provision is so made, to search for the sick, poor, and impotent people of the Parish, that they may be relieved with the alms of the Parishioners, or others. [ECEC]

Can Women Be Ordained to the Priesthood? To the Episcopate?

In November 1972, the House of Bishops, meeting in New Orleans, issued the following official statement:

It is the mind of this House that it endorses the principle of the Ordination of Women to the Priesthood and of the Ordination and Consecration of Women to the Episcopate.

However, the General Convention of September 1973 refused to authorize the ordination of women as presbyters and bishops. The question continues to be a matter of concern and debate among Episcopalians. [RF]*

What Is the Church Attitude Toward Drinking and Gambling?

The Episcopal Church has been nonpuritanical in most respects; it believes that God intends men to enjoy life—if they can do so without such excesses as will harm them and spoil their potentialities as children of God.

The Episcopal Church's primary concern has been with abuses. It has not taken an official stand on gambling and drinking, although

---

* On July 29, 1974, in Philadelphia, eleven Episcopalian women were ordained as priests by four bishops of the church—but without the permission or approval of the Bishop of Pennsylvania. Since the four bishops who presided held no ecclesiastical authority in or over the Pennsylvania Diocese, the ordinations were declared invalid by a special meeting of the House of Bishops, held in Chicago, on the ground that the canon laws of the Episcopal Church had not been followed.

On October 18, 1974, the House of Bishops endorsed the principle that women may be ordained to the priesthood—and urged that "well-informed action" be taken at the 1976 General Convention. The General Convention is the only body within the church which can change church canons.

The General Convention consists of the House of Bishops and the House of Deputies—more than nine hundred priests and laymen. It is worth noting that the House of Bishops, which carried the resolution for women's ordination by 97 votes to 35 (with six abstentions) did not call for a special convention to debate this issue. The House of Bishops did urge that no further attempts be made to ordain women as Episcopalian priests until the laws of the church had been reformed by a general convention. [LR] there have been some quasi-official condemnations of the gambling evil and the perils to character that it involves.

As to drinking—like card-playing, dancing, and the like, the Episcopal Church has on the whole been "liberal" in attitude, feeling that the evils come when the activities are abused.

What Is the Lambeth Conference?

Every ten years, more than 300 bishops of the Anglican Communion meet at Lambeth in London, under the presidency of the Archbishop of Canterbury. This assembly has no legal power; its decisions have moral authority only.

The meetings are the great symbol of the unity of the whole communion. The presidency of the Archbishop of Canterbury indicates that all the churches in the world-wide Anglican fellowship are at one in their common loyalty and in their communion with the see of Canterbury.

What Is the Episcopalian Attitude Toward Birth Control?

The Lambeth Conference of 1958, in a resolution later adopted by the Episcopal Church, expressed this attitude toward birth control:

The Conference believes that the responsibility for deciding upon the number and frequency of children has been laid by God upon the consciences of parents everywhere: that this planning, in such ways as are mutually acceptable to husband and wife in Christian conscience, is a right and important factor in Christian family life and should be the result of positive choice before God. Such responsible parenthood, built on obedience to all the duties of marriage, requires a wise stewardship of the resources and abilities of the family as well as a thoughtful consideration of the varying population needs and problems of society and the claims of future generations. [GTS]

What Is the Episcopalian Attitude Toward Abortion?

The Thirty-third Women's Triennial Meeting, held in 1970, stated that the debate over whether a human fetus is "a life" and whether abortion therefore constitutes the taking of a life are questions that simply "cannot be resolved to the satisfaction of all individuals and/or religious faiths." Since liberal "model" abortion laws have failed in several states to achieve a significant decrease in the number of illegal abortions and have proved to be discriminatory against women from the lower economic strata, the Triennial Meeting adopted a resolution to "support efforts to repeal all laws concerning abortion which deny women the free and responsible exercise of their conscience."

The resolution went on to urge support of "efforts to make generously available to all women and men, regardless of economic or marital status, other methods of birth control—including birth control for men—which are more acceptable than abortion to many individuals of Christian conscience."

There has been no statement on abortion by or from the General Convention of the Church as of the date this present volume went to press. [ECEC]

What Is the Episcopalian Attitude Toward Homosexuality?

The Episcopal Church has taken no official position on homosexuality. [ECEC]

What Is the Attitude of the Episcopal Church to Black People?

The Episcopal Church is predominantly white and shows all the marks and strains of that condition.

There have been some significant changes in our procedures, so as to require the inclusion of representatives of the black and other minorities in the Church's central bodies. Additionally, in 1967 the Episcopal Church launched a special program in which as much as 40 percent of the church's national budget was expended in grants to ghetto organizations—mostly black.

However, such responses do not represent any radical change in the inherited racism that still characterizes American society and many of America's churches. [GTS]

What Role Do Black People Play in the Episcopal Church?

Small though the number still is, black people play a significant part in the affairs of the Episcopal Church, probably disproportionately large in respect of the numbers. For example, of the thirty-nine members of the Church's Executive Council, eight are from minorities, five of them black. In many diocesan and parish bodies, a somewhat similar ratio would probably be in effect.

The number of black candidates for the ministry remains discouragingly small, despite the election of black bishops in four of the largest dioceses. [GTS]

How Is the Episcopal Church Governed?

In different countries the Anglican Communion has different kinds of government.

In the United States, the local organization is usually in the form of a "parish," an incorporated body governed by a group usually called the "rector, churchwardens, and vestrymen," the lay persons being elected by all the members annually.

The diocese includes all the congregations within its area. It is governed by a "convention" consisting of all the resident clergy and elected lay representatives of the congregations.

Nationally, the General Convention is the bicameral governing body, consisting of all the bishops in one house and four priests and four lay persons representing each diocese in the second house. [GTS]

Does the Episcopal Church Own Schools and Colleges?

Nine colleges in the United States are owned by or closely related to the Episcopal Church, including the University of the South, Hobart and Kenyon. A large number of schools are Episcopalian, both preparatory schools such as St. Paul's or Groton and an increasing number of parochial schools.

There are eleven accredited theological seminaries, as well as three others that are diocesan in character.

Overseas the church supports four seminaries and two colleges, as well as a number of schools. [GTS]

Does the Episcopal Church Believe in Missionary Work?

The Episcopal Church has maintained an overseas missionary program since the early years of the nineteenth century, in areas not served by another church of the Anglican Communion.

Currently, eighteen of its dioceses are outside the fifty states, including thirteen in Latin America and the Caribbean, Liberia in Africa, and the Philippines and Taiwan in the western Pacific. Almost all of these are in the final stages of autonomous indigenous life.

In addition, Episcopalian clergymen and lay persons serve in other Anglican and non-Anglican churches around the world and financial and other support is given from the Episcopal Church. [GTS]

What Role Has the Episcopal Church Played in American History?

Services of the Anglican Communion were held in North Carolina, on San Francisco Bay, and perhaps elsewhere, before the first regular worship of the Church was inaugurated at Jamestown, Virginia, in 1607.

For many years, the Episcopalians in the American colonies were under the jurisdiction of the Bishop of London; with the War of Independence, they became self-governing.

Episcopalians constituted probably the largest single group among the leaders in the founding of the United States, including George Washington, Alexander Hamilton, James Madison, James Monroe, John Marshall, and John Jay. From that time to the present, Episcopalians have played a significant part in our national life.

Though closely linked in history and communion with the Church of England and the other Anglican churches, it is thoroughly American and deeply involved in the ecumenical fellowship of this country. [GTS]

How Many Episcopalians Are There in the United States Today? In the World?

In 1973, when last reported, there were 3.2 million recorded baptized members of the Episcopal Church in the fifty states, and an additional 135,000 in areas related to the Episcopal Church overseas.

The church is one of the twenty-five regional or national churches related closely with one another in the Anglican Communion. This family of churches, all stemming directly or indirectly from the Church of England, has a total membership of 65 million—about half of whom live in the British Isles.

In most areas, members are known as "Anglicans" rather than "Episcopalians," but this is simply a matter of nomenclature. [GTS]

WHAT IS A GREEK ORTHODOX?

ARTHUR DOUROPULOS / Arthur Douropulos is a consultant to the Greek Orthodox Archdiocese of North and South America, where he also served as director of Information and Inter-Church Relations.

He was born in Baltimore, Maryland, and obtained his A.B. (*cum laude*) and M.A. from Harvard. From 1938 to 1942 he taught English at Pennsylvania State College; from 1942 to 1948, he was a member of the English Department of Harvard College.

Mr. Douropulos was the representative of the Archdiocese in the first official pilgrimage of the Greek Orthodox Ecumenical Patriarchate of Constantinople in Istanbul in 1964.

He is a member of the General Board of the National Council of Churches of Christ in the U.S.A. and is on the board of directors of Religion in American Life.

What Is the Greek Orthodox Church?

The Greek Orthodox Church considers itself to be the one, holy, catholic, and apostolic Church, founded by Jesus Christ in the year of His death, A.D. 33.

It is holy because its founder, Jesus Christ, is holy. It is catholic because the whole world is considered its province and because it is universal in time and place. It is apostolic because it was established on earth by the apostles of Christ.

"Orthodox" means "true belief," from the Greek words *orthe* and *doxa.*

Is the Greek Orthodox Church the Same as the Eastern Orthodox Church?

Yes. The term "Greek Orthodox" is historically correct; the early Scriptures were written in Greek, and Christianity originated and spread largely through Greek culture and traditions.

For centuries the various national bodies of the Orthodox Church retained the word "Greek" as part of their titles; some still do. But with the rise of nationalism, the tendency has been to use the national name, as in the Albanian Orthodox Church, the Bulgarian Orthodox Church, and so on.

As a *group,* the Orthodox Churches are now generally known as the Eastern Orthodox Church. All Eastern Orthodox bodies are in full communion with each other; they hold the same beliefs and observe the same rituals.

How Were the Various Branches of the Eastern Orthodox Church Established?

In two ways: (1) by the apostles of Jesus Christ; and (2) by missionaries of these first churches. The four original Patriarchates of the Church are in Constantinople (Istanbul), in Alexandria, in Antioch, and in Jerusalem. These churches were established by the apostles Andrew, Mark, Paul, and Peter and James, respectively. The Church of Cyprus, established by the apostles Paul and Barnabas, is also considered an original church.

To the second class belong the national churches of Albania, Bulgaria, Finland, Poland, Rumania, Russia, and others.

There are three leading Russian branches, totaling over 800,000 members. By far the largest of these is the Russian Orthodox Greek Catholic Church of America, also known as "the Metropolia." It was independently established here after the Russian Revolution and has over 700,000 worshipers. Since 1970, following an agreement with the Russian Patriarchate of Moscow, it has assumed the name of the Orthodox Church in America and claims "autocephalous" status on the grounds that this was conferred upon it by the Patriarchate of Moscow. However, such status has not been recognized, up to now, by the other Eastern Orthodox Patriarchates or by the Church of Greece, which claim that autocephaly can be granted only by a Pan-Orthodox Synod, after a thorough study, and not by the Russian Patriarchate alone.

Does the Eastern Orthodox Church as a Whole Have One Head?

No, not in the sense that the Pope is the head of the Roman Catholic Church. Each Orthodox Church is independently administered by a Council of Bishops, called a synod.

The Patriarch of Constantinople, oldest of the Patriarchates, is known as "the first among equals" and is generally regarded as the spiritual leader of world Orthodoxy. He bears the title "Archbishop of Constantinople, the New Rome, and Ecumenical Patriarch."

The late Athenagoras I, who died on July 6, 1972, ascended to the ecumenical throne in 1948. (He had served as Greek Orthodox Archbishop of the Americas from 1931 to 1948.)

On July 16, 1972, the Holy Synod of the Church of Constantinople elected Demetrios I, fifty-eight, formerly Metropolitan of Imbros and Tenedos, as the 263rd Ecumenical Patriarch.

Statements made by the new Patriarch after his election indicate that he will follow the ecumenical line of his predecessor, seeking good relations with other ecclesiastical bodies.

When the papacy was first founded, the Pope was in effect another patriarch. He still retains the title "Patriarch of the West."

Was the Eastern Orthodox Church Ever the Same as the Roman Catholic Church?

Yes, for over 1,000 years. In A.D. 1054 the united Church of Christ finally divided into Eastern and Western segments. This break, known as the great schism, had been building up for centuries; it contained both political and ecclesiastical roots.

Politically, the Eastern emperors had for centuries supported the Patriarchs, while the emperors of Rome gave support to the Popes. Gradually, ecclesiastical differences also arose as the Patriarchs of the East exercised a growing independence that denied the authority of the Pope. The Western Church of Rome became known as Roman Catholic. The Church of Constantinople, the site of ancient Byzantium, has since been called the Greek or Eastern Orthodox Church.

The Eastern Church has always maintained that it was the Roman Catholic Church that drew apart from the original Christian Church. The Eastern Orthodox Church considers itself the continuation of the original and true Church of Christ. The Roman Catholic Church, on the other hand, considers that the Eastern Church separated from it. (Catholicism considers Orthodoxy as "separated," not "heretical.")

Are Roman Catholicism and Eastern Orthodoxy More Alike Than Different in Their Beliefs?

Yes. Actually, the basic tenets of both bear the sanction of the same seven ecumenical councils, the last of which took place in A.D. 787, when the Eastern and Western branches of Christianity were still united.

What, Then, Are the Main Differences Today Between the Eastern Orthodox Church and the Roman Catholic Church?

There are differences of administration, of doctrine, and of practice. Most important in the first category is the refusal of the Eastern Orthodox Church to accept the concentration of the church in one person—a person, moreover, considered infallible, as Roman Catholics consider the Pope, when he speaks "ex cathedra" on religious matters. The Orthodox Church considers as infallible only the Church as a whole. In doctrine, the Eastern Orthodox Church differs from Roman Catholicism in the following:

1. The Roman Catholic Church holds that the holy spirit proceeds "and from the Son" (a doctrine known as the "filioque" clause), as well as from the Father. Eastern Orthodoxy believes that the holy spirit proceeds only "from the Father."

2. Roman Catholicism affirms the existence of a purgatory, in addition to a heaven and a hell. Eastern Orthodoxy does not accept the idea of a purgatory, though it does believe in an intermediate state between heaven and hell where souls experience a foretaste of the bliss or the punishment that will eventually be theirs.

3. The Roman Catholic Church believes in the Immaculate Conception of the Virgin, a doctrine that Eastern Orthodoxy does not accept. Eastern Orthodoxy holds that only Christ was conceived and born without original sin, that the Virgin Mary was cleansed of it on Annunciation Day.

4. The Roman Catholic dogma that the body of the Virgin Mary "was taken up into heaven" (declared by Pope Piux XII) is not subscribed to by Eastern Orthodoxy, which does not believe in such a physical assumption.

5. Eastern Orthodoxy does not recognize the saints canonized by the Catholic Church after the schism of 1054, unless these saints have also been proclaimed by Eastern Orthodox synods.

In ritual and practices, the following differences exist between the Eastern Orthodox and the Roman Catholic churches:

1. The Eastern Orthodox Church does not subscribe to the custom, traditionally practiced by the popes, of granting indulgences on the grounds that the head of the church has authority to transfer to others the surplus good works of Christ, the Blessed Virgin, and the saints.

2. Roman Catholicism does not grant divorce. Eastern Orthodoxy issues ecclesiastical divorces under certain circumstances, described later in this article.

3. In the Roman Catholic Church, Holy Communion is not given until the "age of reason" (usually about twelve). In the Eastern Orthodox Church, the Holy Eucharist may be partaken after baptism.

4. In the Roman Catholic Church, confirmation is usually practiced from the ages of seven to eleven. The Eastern Orthodox Church gives chrismation (the equivalent of confirmation, or anointing with Holy oil) at the baptismal ceremony.

5. Celibacy is obligatory for Roman Catholic deacons, priests, and bishops (though there are certain exceptions). Orthodoxy requires celibacy among bishops only.

6. Roman Catholics celebrate the sacrament of baptism by pouring water on the head of the baptized person. In the Orthodox Church, the baptismal rite is performed by a triple immersion into water.

7. The Roman Catholic Church uses unleavened bread in Holy Communion. The Holy Eucharist of the Eastern Orthodox Church is given with a leavened bread, as occurred in the Last Supper.

8. The Roman Catholic Church serves the holy bread and the holy wine, symbolizing the body and blood of Christ, to the clergy only. In the Eastern Orthodox Church, both clergy and laity partake of both.

9. A Roman Catholic priest may receive permission to celebrate several Masses on the same day and on the same altar. An Eastern Orthodox priest may celebrate only one liturgy (which is the equivalent, in Orthodoxy, of a Mass) on one day.

What Are the Main Doctrines of the Eastern Orthodox Church?

Orthodoxy believes that God is one in substance and a Trinity in persons. Orthodoxy worships one God in the Trinity and the Trinity in unity, neither confusing the persons nor dividing the substance.

Orthodoxy holds the creation to be the work of the blessed Trinity and believes the world is neither self-created nor has it existed from eternity; it is the product of the wisdom, the power, and the will of one God in Trinity. God the Father is the prime cause of the creation, God the Son perfected the creation, and God the Holy Ghost gives it life.

The Orthodox believe that our Lord Jesus Christ, while truly God, begotten of the same substance as the Father and consubstantial with Him, is also truly a man in every respect except sin. The denial of His humanity would constitute a denial of His incarnation and of our salvation.

What Is the Basic Creed of the Orthodox Church?

The official creed accepted by Orthodoxy, formulated and adopted by the First Ecumenical Council of Nicaea (A.D. 325) and the Second Ecumenical Council of Constantinople (A.D. 381), is generally known as the Nicaean Creed. It reads as follows:

I believe in one God, the Father Almighty, maker of heaven and earth and of all things visible and invisible; and in one Lord Jesus Christ, the only begotten Son of God, begotten of His Father before all ages: light of light, very God of very God, begotten, not made, consubstantial with the Father, by Whom all things were made, Who for all men and for our salvation came down from heaven, and was incarnate by the Holy Ghost of the Virgin Mary, and was made man; and was crucified also for us under Pontius Pilate. He suffered and was buried; and the third day He arose again according to the Scriptures, and ascended into heaven, and sitteth on the right hand of the Father. And He shall come again with glory to judge both the quick and the dead, whose kingdom shall have no end.

And I believe in the Holy Ghost, the Lord and giver of life, who proceedeth from the Father, who with the Father and Son together is worshiped and glorified, and who spoke by the prophets.

I believe in one, holy, catholic and apostolic church; I acknowledge one baptism for the remission of sins. I look for the resurrection of the dead, and for the life of the ages to come.

What Are the Sacraments or "Mysteria" Recognized by the Orthodox Church?

Orthodoxy recognizes seven sacraments: baptism, chrismation, holy eucharist (or communion), confession, ordination, marriage, and holy unction. All but holy unction, ordination, and marriage are obligatory. Chrismation is the anointment of the baptized with holy oils. It symbolizes a confirmation in the faith. In the Orthodox Church, chrismation is administered immediately following the traditional baptism of infants, children, or, in rare cases, adults.

May Greek Orthodox Priests Participate in Interreligious Services?

Orthodox priests cannot take part in interreligious services without violating church doctrine.

What Language Is Used in Orthodox Church Services?

Originally, the language of the Orthodox liturgy was the Greek of the Gospels, a form closer to modern than to classical Greek; later, the early church fathers made translations of the Gospels for ethnic Orthodox groups.

Today, each Eastern body uses the national language in the services and rites of the church. In the United States, there is a growing tendency to substitute English translations, in part, for ethnic languages.

Do Eastern Orthodox Make the Sign of the Cross Differently from Roman Catholics?

Roman Catholics make the sign of the cross with open palm from left to right. Eastern Orthodox communicants cross themselves from right to left with the thumb, forefinger and middle finger closed together (to represent the Holy Trinity).

How Is the Divine Liturgy Performed?

The Divine Liturgy is performed so as to rise to a climax. The main rituals are:

1. The Little Entrance, which includes the litany of peace, the secret prayer, the apostle reading, and the sermon of the preacher. The Little Entrance is climaxed by the priest, accompanied by choir boys, descending the altar steps from the sanctuary, holding the Bible, and chanting the Gospel of the day.

2. The Great Entrance, which begins with the supplication within the sanctuary and the censing of the holy icons and the faithful. The priest with his choir boys comes out of the altar, holding in each hand a square veil, the "aer," which symbolizes the holy gifts offered to God, and in honor of which a prayer is then recited.

3. The "Anaphora," which is the offering of the special prayer to the Almighty. The Nicaean Creed is recited, as are other hymns and prayers.

4. The Communion, which includes a prayer for worthiness to receive the Holy Eucharist. With heads inclined, the congregation recites the Lord's Prayer, followed by the chant "holy things to the holy." The priest, who now has come forth alone from the altar bearing the communion chalice, then says to those who are about to receive communion, "With fear of God, with faith and with love, draw near." After the communicants have received the Holy Eucharist, the priest intones the benediction: "We have seen the light."

5. The Dismissal, in which is chanted the thanksgiving "Arise . . . let us give due thanks." The Divine Liturgy ends with the prayer "Be the Lord's name blessed," addressed to the icon of Christ at the gate of the altar, and with the final benediction by the celebrant. The Divine Liturgy is traditionally preceded by the morning prayer, during which the priest comes forth from the altar with his altar boys, holding the gold-encased Bible used in Orthodox churches. Anyone in the congregation may come forth to kiss the Bible. When a bishop, archbishop, or patriarch officiates at a Divine Liturgy, he is usually assisted by several priests and at the end of the service ascends the episcopal throne to address the congregation.

Do the Orthodox Stand Throughout the Service?

Until very recent times, Eastern churches contained no seats or pews; the worshipers remained standing throughout the long service (two or more hours). Now, in America, the communicants may sit throughout most of the liturgy but stand or kneel at the more sacred moments. In the Old World, the men occupy the right portion of the church, the women the left, and all stand throughout the service.

Is There More Than One Orthodox Divine Liturgy?

There are five Orthodox liturgies: the one named after Saint James of Jerusalem, performed on October 23; the one of Saint Mark, celebrated on April 25, in Alexandria; Saint Basil's, which is used on Christmas and Epiphany eves, on the first five Sundays of Easter Lent, on Holy Thursday, Holy Saturday, and January 1; the fourth, and most widely used, is that of Saint Chrysostom, traditionally celebrated every Sunday and on saints' days; the fifth is the liturgy of the presanctified gifts, the oldest and most mystical, which is celebrated every Wednesday and Friday of Easter Lent, and on Holy Monday, Tuesday, and Wednesday of Easter Week.

When Should the Orthodox Receive Holy Communion?

Each communicant may decide for himself when he is worthy. Communion may be received every Sunday and on every day that the liturgy is celebrated.

Custom holds that every member of the church should have communion at least four times a year, after proper fasting and adequate spiritual preparation: on Christmas, Easter, the Commemoration of the Apostles on June 30, and the Assumption of the Virgin Mary on August 15.

Does Confession Precede Communion in the Orthodox Church?

Strictly speaking, yes. Confession (together with repentance) is a sacrament, through which the sinful man is cleansed and by which the regeneration of the human soul is achieved.

Most Orthodox priests, however, will not refuse communion to those who have not confessed—if the communicant himself feels that his conscience allows him to be worthy of the Holy Eucharist. But confession at least once a year is considered a prerequisite to communion in most Orthodox churches.

How Does Orthodox Confession Differ from Roman Catholic?

The practice of confession in Orthodoxy is more personal. The communicant is encouraged to choose a confessor-priest who knows him personally, even intimately, and who is acquainted with, and sympathetic to, his problems.

The confessional is held in the open, not in a confessional booth, usually facing the altar of the church. If the communicant wishes more privacy for his confession, he may ask the priest to receive him in private.

How Do the Orthodox Regard the Virgin Mary?

The Orthodox honor her most of all the saints but do not consider her a deity. They venerate her especially for her supreme grace and the call she received from God. Though not exempt from original sin, from which she was cleansed at the time of the Annunciation, it is believed that by the Grace of God she committed no actual sin.

Do the Orthodox Venerate Icons and Relics?

Yes. Veneration of sacred icons and relics is a part of the Orthodox tradition. But in accordance with the decree of the Seventh Ecumenical Council of Nicaea, in A.D. 787, this veneration is directed not to the images, as such, but to the holy persons whom they represent.

The Orthodox, therefore, venerate flat, two-dimensional icons; they do not pray to three-dimensional statues, as do other religious groups, because these representations may be too realistic and may become in themselves idols of veneration.

What Are the Orders of Ministry in the Eastern Orthodox Church?

There are three orders of ministry: deacon, priest, and bishop. Those holding the higher ranks—metropolitans, archbishops, and patriarchs—are, in effect, bishops.

A metropolitan is the head of an ecclesiastical district; an archbishop is the head of a church; a patriarch is the head of a see, which may also be a separate church. Metropolitans, archibishops, and patriarchs are elected by a holy synod of a church and assume office by enthronement.

Are There Monks and Nuns in the Eastern Church?

Yes. Monasteries and convents are widespread within the old Eastern churches, but are few in America (and wherever Orthodoxy has spread in modern times) mainly because priests are urgently needed for the active ministry.

Orthodox monasticism has three main divisions: (1) the robe wearers (*rasofori*), who are on trial, can leave at any time, and can even marry, if they are not already ordained; (2) the small-gowned (*mikroschema*), who are ordained; and (3) the large-gowned (*megaloschema*), who can enter the final step of monkhood only after thirty years of pious service.

Orthodox nuns are also divided into ordained and lay groups, the latter active in philanthropy and charitable deeds.

What Vestments Do Orthodox Priests Wear?

In the old countries, Orthodox clergymen wear a full-length, cassocklike robe, black or deep blue, which is known as the "rasso." In the United States and in modern cities, priests often adopt the usual clerical garb and collar for street wear. Metropolitans, archbishops, and patriarchs never use modern dress.

The traditional headgear of the Orthodox clergy for service is the "kalimafki," a cylinder-like hat, about six inches high, with a protruding flat top. Over this those of episcopal rank, as well as celibate archimandrite priests, wear a black veil, attached to the "kalimafki," which falls backward over the shoulders.

When officiating at liturgical services, hierarchs wear a golden miter, often glittering with jewels. They also wear the "engolpion," a relicarium with representations of the saints, suspended from a gold chain. In the celebration of the liturgy, Orthodox priests and bishops wear multicolored vestments, embroidered in gold and silver.

Are All Orthodox Priests Bearded?

Until very modern times, all Orthodox priests wore beards, to emulate Christ and the fathers of the church. This tradition still persists in old Orthodox centers. But in America, most priests are cleanshaven. However, hierarchs of the church, as well as monastics, remain bearded.

Are Orthodox Priests Allowed to Marry?

An Orthodox clergyman is permitted to marry *before* ordination into priesthood. Married clergymen may not become bishops. Unmarried priests may attain the rank of archimandrite, a high order of priesthood that observes life-long celibacy. Bishops are usually chosen from the archimandrites.

Do the Orthodox Churches Allow Mixed Marriages?

Marriages within the faith are preferred and encouraged, but mixed marriages are permitted—if the non-Orthodox has been baptized in the name of the Holy Trinity (even in another Christian denomination), and if he or she agrees to baptize the children of the marriage in the Orthodox church.

An Orthodox who marries outside the church is denied participation in the sacraments and is not allowed to be a sponsor at an Orthodox wedding or baptism.

What Is the Position of Your Church on Black People?

The Greek and Eastern Orthodox churches believe in the continuation and acceleration of equality for black people—in all aspects of society and employment. We hope this will be achieved without the violence and lawlessness that has characterized some extreme, militant black groups.

Archbishop Iakovos, Greek Orthodox Primate of North and South America, has repeatedly made statements and pronouncements to this effect—and himself participated in the demonstration in Selma, Alabama (March 1965), marching in the forefront with Martin Luther King, Jr.

Our church maintains close ties with the Church of Abyssinia, one of the oldest of Christianity, though it is not listed among the Orthodox churches.*

Although Greek and Eastern Orthodox churches have but a few black members in the Americas, marriages between blacks and whites are performed in Orthodox churches.

The Greek Orthodox Church in New York maintains a mission in Uganda and has sent several seminarians from South African countries to study at the Holy Cross Orthodox Theological School of Hellenic College (Brookline, Massachusetts).

What Is the Status of Women in the Eastern Orthodox Church?

Greek Orthodox women exercise great influence on the church. They may become members of the Clergy-Laity Council, which is the governing body of the church, and they perform many auxiliary tasks: teaching in Sunday schools, organizing social and fund-raising events, directing choirs, chanting the responses to the liturgies. The largest body of women are members of the "Philoptohos" (friends of the poor), and there are also several youth auxiliaries.

Can a Woman Be Ordained as a Member of the Greek Orthodox Clergy?

Greek Orthodox women have no clerical function in the church and they have no right of ordination.

There are, however, monastic orders of women, in which they serve and participate in the usual functions of nuns: teaching, nursing, meditating, creating beautiful handicrafts, and producing ecclesiastical garments. Most monasteries for nuns are located in Greece, although we have one or two in the United States and a scattering of nuns in various Orthodox jurisdictions.

* The Church of Abyssinia is "monophysite," believing that Jesus had only a divine (but not a human) nature; otherwise, its beliefs and services correspond closely to those of acknowledged Eastern Orthodox churches. [LR]

Do the Orthodox Churches Permit Divorce?

Though Orthodox churches believe in the essential indissolubility of marriage, divorce is permitted as a last resort, in certain cases, and after all attempts for reconciliation by the clergy have failed.

Typical are the canons of the Patriarchate of Constantinople, which allows divorce only for the following reasons: adultery, fornication, or immoral acts; treacherous actions and threats against life by either of the spouses; abortion without the consent of the husband; impotence, existing prior to marriage and continuing for two years; abandonment of a wife or husband for more than two years; apostasy and the falling into heresy; or incurable insanity, lasting four years after marriage.

Remarriage of the innocent party is permitted, though not more than three marriages are allowed. In addition to the civil divorce of the land, a church separation, granted by an ecclesiastical court of an archdiocese, is required.

What Is the View of Orthodoxy on Birth Control?

Though birth control is not mentioned in the binding seven ecumenical councils, it has been repeatedly disapproved of by Orthodox synodical and patriarchal pronouncements and encyclicals. The question of birth control is on the agenda for discussion at a Pan-Orthodox Synod to be held in the future.

What Is the Position of Orthodoxy on Abortion?

The Greek Orthododx Church is strictly opposed to abortion, but the church gives tacit approval to it when responsible medical advice holds that the life of the mother will be endangered by childbirth.

The subject of abortion is included in the agenda for discussion at a Pan-Orthodox Synod to be held soon.

What Is the Position of the Eastern Orthodox Church on Homosexuality?

Homosexuality in any form is strictly opposed by the Greek Orthodox Church.

However, there is a growing tendency to regard it as a disease that may be helped by priestly and medical counseling. No "Gay Liberation" movements are tolerated by the church.

The question of homosexuality is on the agenda for discussion at a Pan-Orthodox Synod to be held in the future.

How Have Recent Ecumenical Activities Affected the Relationship Between the Eastern Orthodox Church and the Roman Catholic Church?

As a result of the new ecumenical climate of the 1960s, and particularly because of Vatican II (1962–1965), to which the Ecumenical Patriarchate sent observers, an unprecedented spirit of amity arose between Roman Catholicism and Eastern Orthodoxy, enhanced by the initiatives taken by the late Ecumenical Patriarch Athenagoras I and Pope Paul VI.

Their first historic meeting, on January 5 and 6, 1964, took place in Jerusalem. Later, in 1967, the two ecclesiastical leaders exchanged visits to the Ecumenical Patriarchate, in July, and to the Vatican, in October. And most significant was the milestone reached on December 6, 1965, the last day of Vatican II, when Paul VI at the Vatican and Athenagoras I in Istanbul presided over special ceremonies to nullify the mutual excommunications of 1054, which had caused the great schism between the churches of Constantinople and Rome.

Anticipating these developments, the late Ecumenical Patriarch convened several Pan-Orthodox Conferences, beginning with the first on the Greek Island of Rhodes in the fall of 1961, in order to discuss the problems of Christian unity and to prepare agendas for inter-Orthodox concerns to be dealt with at a full-scale Pan-Orthodox Synod that is yet to come.

Does the Orthodox Church Conduct Missionary Activities?

Eastern Orthodoxy was, from its beginnings, a missionary church. Its highest level of missionary activity was reached in the ninth century, when the Christian faith was brought to the Slavic and other ethnic groups in central and northern Europe.

When Constantinople came under Ottoman rule in 1453, Greek

Orthodoxy was faced with the question of survival. It could no longer send out missions. The Russian Church, however, continued missionary activities in Japan, Korea, and the Far East. Recently, the Greek Orthodox Church has initiated missionary activities in Africa and Asia.

Orthodoxy does not approve of the practice of proselytizing other Christian denominations. But genuine converts are accepted and welcomed.

How Are the Orthodox Saints Canonized?

An Orthodox saint is canonized by the holy synod of a patriarchate, or an autonomous church, *after he or she has been accepted as such by the people.* It is the Orthodox faithful who, in fact, make the saints of their churches; the ruling ecclesiastical bodies later verify the sainthood by official decree.

Why Do Eastern Orthodox Churches Celebrate Christmas and Saints' Days on Dates Different from Those in the West?

Because they retain the Julian calendar, instead of the newer Gregorian calendar used by the Western churches. (The Gregorian calendar has been adopted by some of the Eastern churches, including the Ecumenical Patriarchate, the Church of Greece, and the Church in the Americas, which is under the Ecumenical Patriarchate.) The holidays of the Julian calendar occur thirteen days later than those of the Gregorian calendar: thus, Christmas is celebrated on January 7 and New Year on January 14.

Is That Why the Orthodox Easter Is Celebrated on a Different Date from the Western Easter?

Differences concerning the date of Easter arose between the East and the West as early as the second century. The date of the Orthodox Easter was finally fixed by the Council of Nicaea in A.D. 325, which decreed that Easter should be celebrated on the Sunday immediately following the first full moon after the vernal equinox (the first day of spring), but always after the Hebrew Passover. This maintains consistency with the Biblical sequence of events.

The Easter of the Western churches is not necessarily preceded by the Hebrew Passover.

Once every few years, Eastern and Western Easters coincide, though not in a fixed pattern. When they do not fall on the same date, the Eastern always follows the Western. The dates of the two Easters through the year 1980 are as follows:

	Eastern	*Western*
1974	April 14	April 14
1975	May 4	March 30
1976	April 25	April 18
1977	April 10	April 10
1978	April 30	March 26
1979	April 22	April 15
1980	April 6	April 6

Is There a Distinctive Architectural Form for an Orthodox Church?

Yes. Orthodox churches follow the form of the cross, with a dome over the center. The interior of an Orthodox church is divided into three main parts: the sanctuary, or altar; the main church; and the narthex, or entrance. The sanctuary should be at the eastern end of the church building. The altar, "the holy of holies," is divided from the main church, which is occupied by the congregation, by a screen, called the "iconostasion," where icons (two-dimensional paintings) are placed, often with metal adornments, of Jesus Christ, the Virgin Mary, Saint John the Baptist, and other saints and martyrs.

The sanctuary is reached by three entrances, the central one of which is known as the royal or holy gate (when the Eucharist is celebrated, the holy gifts are brought forth through it). Though unordained men may go into the sanctuary, they are not permitted to enter it through the holy gate. No women, except girls less than six years of age, are permitted to enter the altar, which closes by two wooden leaves or panels, representing the entrance into heaven. These are closed off, at solemn moments during the Divine Liturgy, by a curtain of silken material.

The openings to the left and right of the congregation are called the northern door and the southern door. On these doors are painted the archangels Michael and Gabriel, the guardians of paradise.

Over the holy gate is placed a painting of the Last Supper, to symbolize the preparation of the Holy Eucharist on the holy table. The holy table is covered, first, with a cloth of fine linen, symbolizing the swaddling clothes that wrapped Jesus after His birth, and the winding sheet that enveloped the body of Jesus in the tomb. Over this cloth, a rich material is spread, to reflect the glory of the king of heavens. Under and in the holy table, relics of saints are placed to honor the holy fathers and martyrs. A light, signifying the eternity of the faith, always burns above the holy table.

Are There Eastern Churches Which Are Not Orthodox Churches?

Strictly speaking, yes. Autonomous churches, among the oldest of Christianity, which differ from Orthodoxy only in minor respects, are known as the ancient Oriental churches. The more important are the Armenian, the Coptic and the Abyssinian of Africa, the Church of Malabar in South India, and certain Syrian groups. Their communicants are called "monophysites" (from Greek words meaning "a single nature") since they reject the dual nature of Christ, which Orthodoxy accepts, and believe that He was divine at all times, rather than mortal on earth. The ancient Oriental churches are not bound by all the seven ecumenical councils. Some of them recognize only the first and the second.

These Eastern churches, however, are not Roman Catholic churches. They should not be confused with other churches of the East that do owe allegiance to the Vatican, such as the Greek Catholic Church (also known as the Byzantine Rite or the Uniate Church).

Does the Orthodox Church Participate in the Ecumenical Movement?

"Ecumenical," from the Greek word *oikoumene*, means "for all the world." In this movement, a hope and plan for the eventual union for all Christian churches, Orthodoxy has long played a leading part. Dr. Francis House, associate secretary of the World Council of Churches, has written as follows:

The Ecumenical Patriarchate of Constantinople has behind it many centuries of concern . . . for unity among Christians. A thousand years ago the patriarchs were already distinguished for their concern for unity and their missionary zeal. In spite of the excommunication of the Patriarch by the Pope in 1054, and of the terrible injuries caused to the relations between Eastern Orthodox and Western Christians by the sack of Constantinople by the Crusaders in 1204, the Ecumenical Patriarchs made many friendly contacts with Western Christians, especially after the Reformation . . .

During the last hundred years these contacts became increasingly frequent.

In 1920, the church of the Patriarchate of Constantinople issued a call "to the churches of Christ everywhere" to create a union of the different denominations. The detailed proposals correspond closely to the World Council of Churches, established in 1948, which includes Eastern Orthodox churches. The late Ecumenical Patriarch Athenagoras I, a great champion of the unity of the Christian Churches, established a permanent representative at the Geneva headquarters of the World Council of Churches.

What Types of Ecumenical Activity Do the Orthodox Churches Engage In?

Most Orthodox churches in America are members of the World Council of Churches and the National Council of the Churches of Christ in the U.S.A. Under the auspices of the Ecumenical Commission of the Standing Conference of Orthodox Bishops in the Americas, dialogues are held regularly with other Christian bodies.

These bilateral conversations are currently in progress with the Anglican (Episcopal), Lutheran, Reformed and Roman Catholic churches. Also, the first Greek Orthodox–Jewish theological colloquium was held in New York in January 1972.

What Efforts Have Been Made in Recent Years for Inter-Orthodox Cooperation and Unity in America?

In 1960, the Standing Conference of Orthodox Bishops in the Americas (SCOBA) was organized as an inter-Orthodox agency to achieve cooperation among the various Eastern Orthodox churches, to act as a body to centralize and coordinate the mission of the church, and to better enable it to make its contribution to the American religious scene. Since its inception, Archbishop Iakovos, the Primate of the Greek Orthodox Church of North and South America, under whose initiative it was formed, has been its chairman. Special departments of SCOBA are devoted to campus work, military and other chaplaincies, regional clergy fellowships, and ecumenical relations.

In 1967 the Orthodox Theological Society in America was founded, under the sponsorship of SCOBA, to promote Orthodox theology and to provide an outlet for the work of Orthodox theologians in America. In September 1970 the society held the first international congress of Orthodox theology at the Holy Cross Orthodox Theological School of Hellenic College in Brookline, Massachusetts.

How Many Eastern Orthodox Branches Are There in America?

There are some fifteen Orthodox groups represented in America. Most of them are under old-country ecclesiastical jurisdictions, although a few are independent of foreign ties. Their communicants total about 4.5 million.

The Greek Orthodox Church of North and South America is the largest of the American bodies, with almost 2 million members (1.5 million of them in the United States).

There are three leading Russian branches, totaling over 800,000. (By far the largest of these is the Russian Orthodox Greek Catholic Church of America with over 700,000 worshipers, which was independently established here after the Russian Revolution. Since 1970, after an agreement with the Russian Patriarchate of Moscow, it calls itself the American Orthodox Church.)

Other Orthodox bodies include the Serbian (200,000), Ukrainian (130,000), Carpatho-Russian (100,000), Syrian (80,000), Rumanian (50,000), and smaller branches of national extractions including the Bulgarian, Estonian, Latvian, Lithuanian, and others.

WHO ARE JEHOVAH'S WITNESSES?

MILTON G. HENSCHEL / Milton G. Henschel is a director of the Watch Tower Bible and Tract Society of Pennsylvania and is a member of the governing body of Jehovah's Witnesses.

A third-generation Witness, Mr. Henschel was born in Pomona, New Jersey, in 1920. He began house-to-house preaching at the age of eight. By the time he was fourteen, he was devoting himself entirely to the work of the ministry.

Mr. Henschel is an ordained minister of Jehovah's Witnesses and has traveled to 120 countries in his official duties as executive aide to the president of the Watch Tower Bible and Tract Society.

What Is the Basic Creed Professed by Jehovah's Witnesses?

The Witnesses have no creed. They follow the Bible all the way, not halfway. They feel the Bible is entirely consistent—both the Hebrew and the Greek Scriptures—and practical for our day.

Where Did the Name Come From?

The name "Jehovah's Witnesses" is found in the Bible in Isaiah 43:12: "Ye are my witnesses, saith Jehovah, and I am God." A history of Jehovah's Witnesses and their service to God takes us back 6,000 years. Abel and other men of faith before Christ are called "witnesses" in Hebrews 11 and 12:1. Christ is "the faithful and true witness" in Revelation 3:14. He designated others to continue the testimony, saying, "Ye shall be witnesses unto me . . . unto the uttermost part of the earth"—Acts 1:8.

Jehovah's Christian Witnesses today are merely the last of a long line of servants of God. They are not an incorporated body. They use the nonprofit Watch Tower Bible and Tract Society, which was incorporated in Pennsylvania by Charles Taze Russell and associated Christians in 1884, as the legal agency.

What Are the Teachings of Jehovah's Witnesses?

That Jehovah is the only true God. His sovereignty has been challenged by Satan, who caused the rebellion in Eden and who puts the integrity of all men to the test. God's primary purpose is the vindication of this sovereignty. In carrying out this purpose, God sent Jesus to earth to provide the ransom sacrifice and to lay the foundation for God's new system of things.

Jehovah will not tolerate wickedness on earth forever. The beginning of the end for Satan came when Christ took power in heaven as King. This happened in 1914. Christ's first act was casting Satan out of heaven, and this was followed by great troubles on earth.

In the coming "great tribulation," God will destroy the entire wicked system of things, and then the Devil himself will be completely put out of action. This is the vindication of Jehovah's name and the beginning of the thousand-year reign of Christ. Then all that breathe will praise Jehovah.

Christ is now invisibly present. He will aways remain invisible to humans; but his presence is proved by world events since 1914, which fulfill all the predictions of Matthew 24.

Now the Christian's duty is to keep integrity to Jehovah, to announce the King's reign, and to help neighbors find the way to godly service and everlasting life.

Do Jehovah's Witnesses Believe in the Virgin Birth?

Jesus was born miraculously, a virgin birth in fulfillment of the prophecy of Isaiah 7:14. He died a ransom to relieve man from sin inherited from the first parents in the Garden of Eden. As I Corinthians 15 shows, Christ died a human body but was resurrected as a mighty spirit creature.

Do Witnesses Believe in the Holy Trinity?

Jehovah's Witnesses believe that Jehovah God and Christ Jesus are two distinct persons and are not combined with a so-called "Holy Ghost" in one godhead called a Trinity. The "Holy Spirit" is not a person. It is God's active force.

Do Witnesses Salute the Flag?

Saluting a flag, of any nation, is regarded by Jehovah's Witnesses as unchristian image worship. Any national flag is a symbol of sovereign power, regarded by people as sacred.

Jehovah's Witnesses cannot conscientiously participate in an act that ascribes salvation to the national emblem and to the nation for which it stands, for, in the Ten Commandments, it says: "Thou shalt not make unto thee any graven image, or any likeness of any thing that is in heaven above, or that is in the earth beneath, or that is in the water under the earth: thou shalt not bow down thyself to them, nor serve them."

Jehovah's Witnesses do not wish to incur the wrath of God by acts of worship contrary to his commands. They do not oppose anyone's desire or right to salute the flag. Each must decide for himself what he will do. That is true freedom of worship. The Supreme Court of the United States has so declared in a case involving Jehovah's Witnesses: Its decision was that there is no requirement of the conscientious to salute the flag of the United States.

Do the Witnesses Deny Government Authority?

No. Without governments, anarchy and chaos would reign. Earthly governments have the right to make laws to regulate morals, protect persons and property, and maintain public order. Jehovah's Witnesses obey all such laws, *if* they are in accord with God's laws. When there is direct conflict between God's law and that of a government, they obey the supreme law of God as set forth in the Bible.

Why Do the Witnesses Claim Service Exemption?

Because they have conscientious objections, based on the commandments of God, against taking part in the *world's* wars. Wars between nations today are not the same as Israel's wars in ancient times. Israel was Jehovah's theocratic nation, and the Israelites were fighters in God's wars. No political nation today can properly claim that status.

Though not pacifists, Jehovah's Witnesses fight only when God commands them to do so. Since the days of ancient Israel, God has not commanded men to fight in wars between nations. That is why Christians of the first century refused to serve in the imperial armies of Rome. Besides, ministers of religion are exempted from military service by law in many countries. Because the vocation of each Jehovah's Witness is the ministry, all Witnesses claim exemption under such laws.

They do not oppose the desire of any person to serve in the armed forces of any nation. Nor do they oppose the efforts of any nation to raise an army by conscripting its manpower. They merely keep their own neutrality, refusing to break their allegiance to their God and Savior. Their position is that of neutral ambassadors for Christ the King.

Having a good conscience toward God does not make a person a weakling or a coward. Fear of death does not cause the Witnesses to take this position; in some lands, they are executed by firing squads because of it. It takes more courage to stand up for unpopular principles than it does to go along with the majority.

What Bible Do Jehovah's Witnesses Use?

In our publications and in our public preaching we use many Bible translations, including all the most popular Protestant, Catholic, Jewish and Orthodox Bibles. And since we preach in more than two hundred lands, we use Bibles in hundreds of languages.

In 1961, the Watchtower Society published in one volume *The New World Translation of the Holy Scriptures*. Rendered from the original Bible languages, this translation is available in English, Dutch, French, German, Italian, Portuguese, and Spanish. This Bible is widely used by Jehovah's Witnesses (though not exclusively) where it is available in the language of their country.

What Do the Witnesses Believe About Hell?

Hell is the grave; it is *not* a place of fiery, eternal torment. Hell is a place of rest, in hope of resurrection, not a place of torture from which one can never escape. Peter said Jesus was in hell after his death. Death and hell will both be destroyed at the end of the thousand-year rule of Christ. Purgatory is not mentioned once in the Bible. It is an invention of men. There is no "intermediate" state of the dead. Such ideas are found in the ancient pagan religions, not in the Bible.

What Do Witnesses Believe About Heaven?

Heaven is the habitation of spirit creatures; it is the place of God's throne. The reward of spiritual life with Christ Jesus in heaven for men on earth is limited to those who inherit the Kingdom of God. In Revelation 7:4, the number of these is given as exactly 144,000.

What Will Become of the Billions of People Who Have Lived on the Earth?

After mentioning the 144,000 who will go to heaven, Revelation 7 tells of "a great multitude, which no man could number, of all nations," standing before the throne. These are destined to live forever on the earth.

The apostle Peter said: "We, according to his promise, look for new heavens and a new earth." This means the removal of the wicked and oppressive system under Satan and the ushering in of the righteous rule of Christ.

Then the earth will be made a paradise. "There shall be no more death, neither sorrow, nor crying, neither shall there be any more pain"—Revelation 21:4. Jehovah will provide all things needed by the human family, and animals now ferocious will be at peace with man—Isaiah 65. There will be no more national boundaries, no political divisions and no war—Micah 4. It is to such a world that those in the graves will be resurrected, with the opportunity of living forever if they prove themselves obedient to God.

Do Witnesses Believe in Baptism?

Yes. Baptism is a symbol of dedication to the will of Jehovah. We consider baptism to be complete submersion, not just sprinkling. The baptism that started with Jesus is not meant for cleansing from sin, because Jesus was no sinner—Hebrews 7. Matthew 28 shows that the baptized ones must first be taught. This, with Jesus' baptism at the age of thirty, shows that baptism is not for infants but for persons of responsible age who have the ability to learn.

Can Any Witness Be an Ordained Minister?

Yes, for true ordination comes from God. Jehovah, through Christ, ordains his witnesses to serve as ministers—John 15:16. Jesus chose fishermen, tax collectors, and other untrained men, as well as the learned Paul. Similar men may become ordained ministers today. Jehovah's Christian Witnesses are, indeed, a society or body of ministers.

The public ceremony of water immersion identifies one as a minister of God. It marks him as a person who has dedicated his entire life to the service of Jehovah; it implies acceptance of the obligations that the ministry imposes. Jesus set the example by his baptism in the River Jordan, after which he devoted his life to the ministry. We believe that titles like "Reverend" and "Father" are not properly applied to ministers but belong to God alone—Matthew 23:9. Clerical garb is never used.

Are Boys and Girls Allowed to Preach?

Yes. Youths are not only permitted to preach, but they are invited to do so—just as Samuel, Jeremiah, and Timothy did in their youth. Jesus was only twelve when he was about his "Father's business," discussing the Scriptures.

Are Ministers and Workers Paid?

Ministers at our international headquarters in Brooklyn, New York, and in the field are voluntary workers. All officers of the Watch Tower Bible and Tract Society and others at headquarters receive a $14 allowance per month for personal needs. They are given free room and board. As a means of support, most of the Witnesses do secular work.

What Is Your Position on Black People?

Jehovah's Witnesses practice no discrimination, nor show any partial distinctions toward people of any race, color, or nationality.

The Bible (Acts 17:26, 27) says: "He [God] made out of one [man] every nation of men, to dwell upon the entire surface of the earth, and he decreed the appointed times and the set limits of the dwelling of [men], for them to seek God."

It is also written (Acts 10:34, 35): "God is not partial, but in every nation the man that fears him and works righteousness is acceptable to him."

Jehovah's Witnesses hold this Bible view and look upon people of all colors and races as equals, descendants of the one man Adam.

What Is the Nature and Status of Women in the Congregation?

Under inspiration of the holy spirit, the apostle Paul wrote that "the head of a woman is the man" (I Corinthians 11:3). This is God's arrangement. It is shown in the order of creation, in that Adam was created first and the woman was created as a complement of the man (Genesis 2:20–23).

This does not allow for a man to lord it over the woman, as in a master-slave relationship. Rather, the apostle Paul shows us that in the marriage relationship the husband is to love his wife as he does himself. The two are one flesh (Ephesians 5:28, 29, 31).

May Women Be Ordained as Ministers?

As for the ordination of women as ministers, the Bible Book of Acts (2) shows that on the day of Pentecost, fifty days after the death of Jesus, the holy spirit from God was poured out upon 120 persons gathered in Jerusalem—and women were included among that group.

However, there are some limits on the ministerial activity of women, based upon the Bible: for example, Phoebe serving the congregation at Cenchreae, as a helper of many; and the four daughters of Philip, who spoke God's Word to others (Romans 16:1, 2; Acts 21:9).

Women did not *preside* over a congregation of men and teach them; for Paul, under inspiration, instructed us: "I do not permit a woman to teach or to exercise authority over a man" (I Timothy 2:12; see also I Corinthians 14:34).

Women may share in our congregational Bible studies and meetings, but they would never enter into debates with men in the congregation, challenging them.

Christian women do have a large share in ministerial activity outside of congregational meetings—explaining God's Word to others, as did the daughters of Philip.

What Is Your Attitude Toward Divorce?

Divorces may be obtained only on the ground of marital unfaithfulness: that is, when there have been sexual relations, whether natural or unnatural, outside the marriage relationship.

If a Witness obtains a divorce on other grounds and remarries, he must be expelled from the congregation.

What Is the Attitude of the Witnesses Toward Birth Control?

The purpose of marriage is the rearing of children. Jehovah's Witnesses regard birth control as an entirely personal matter.

Do Jehovah's Witnesses Practice Abortion?

No. According to God's law, given through Moses, the human embryo or fetus is considered as a life, and anyone causing a miscarriage or abortion was to be put to death (Exodus 21:22, 23).

Jehovah's Witnesses believe that God's Word thus condemns abortion, and it is viewed as taking away life, directly contrary to the Bible's teaching on the sacredness of human life.

Why Do Witnesses Refuse Blood Transfusions?

Leviticus 17:10 says: "Whatsoever man . . . eateth any manner of blood; I will . . . cut him off from among his people." And Acts 15:20: "Abstain from . . . things strangled, and from blood." This is explicit.

Jehovah's Witnesses see no difference between being fed blood through the mouth or nose or intravenously. In emergencies, blood substitutes may be used. The Witnesses would risk "temporary" death rather than accept a blood transfusion and incur God's disapproval.

We do not condemn medical practice; there are many physicians and dentists among Jehovah's Witnesses.

Some people defend transfusions because they save lives and refer to Jesus as the greatest example of giving a blood transfusion. This is shallow reasoning: Christ Jesus' blood was not drained off and preserved. What little of his blood was literally shed, fell to the ground. None of his blood was used to put into the veins of someone else.

Why Do Witnesses Enter People's Homes to Try to Convert Them?

Jehovah's Witnesses preach at the homes of the people because Christ Jesus did and they are to take him as their example and follow in his footsteps. Paul said that he taught "publicly and from house to house."

We believe we have the most urgent message of all time and should follow the example in the Bible and take it to people's homes.

Do Jehovah's Witnesses Consider Homosexuality a Sin?

Although governments may legalize homosexuality between consenting adults, this is not the criterion for establishing whether homosexuality is right or wrong.

The Creator of men gives the answer that can be relied upon as accurate and true: God's Word (Leviticus 18:22) plainly says: "And you must not lie down with a male the same as you lie down with a woman. It is a detestable thing."

Under the law of Moses such an act was punishable by death. The law of Christ, as found in the writings of the Christian Greek Scriptures, is just as explicit. I Corinthians 6:9, 10 says this: "Do not be misled. Neither fornicators, nor idolaters, nor adulterers, nor men kept for unnatural purposes, nor men who lie with men . . . will inherit God's kingdom."

Romans (1:26, 27, 32) shows that in God's sight those who practice Lesbianism or sodomy are deserving of death.

No homosexuals are permitted to be members of the congregations of Jehovah's Witnesses.

Why Do Witnesses Distribute Literature on Street Corners?

Many people cannot be reached at their residences. Jehovah's Witnesses believe they must preach to people around the world before this generation passes away, and they use all possible ways of doing it. Preaching in the streets is one way. The apostle Paul preached in the marketplaces. Jesus taught on the streets of the people. Hence this method has its foundation in the Bible.

Why Are Witnesses Persecuted?

The Bible says, "All that will live godly in Christ Jesus shall suffer persecution"—II Timothy 3:12. Jehovah's Witnesses believe their work is of God. They know their real persecutor is the Devil. They have been arrested, beaten, and jailed in many countries, including communist countries where they are banned.

Do Jehovah's Witnesses Believe Theirs Is the Only True Faith?

Certainly. If they thought someone else had the true faith, they would preach that. There is only "one faith," said Paul.

Jehovah's Witnesses do not believe that there is more than one way to gain salvation or that the majority of people will meet the strict requirements of true faith. Jesus showed that only a minority would be right: "Narrow is the way which leadeth unto life, and few there be that find it."

How Are Jehovah's Witnesses Governed?

All of Jehovah's Witnesses govern their activities in accord with God's Word, the Bible, and thus look to Jehovah God to guide them. They recognize and submit themselves to the Lord Jesus Christ, and no man, as the one whom Jehovah has appointed to be Head of the congregation.

A governing body made up of ten ordained ministers oversees our preaching and teaching activity.

On legal matters, Jehovah's Witnesses use the Watch Tower Bible and Tract Society of Pennsylvania, a nonprofit religious corporation, and similar corporations, worldwide, as agencies in their preaching—and for publishing Bibles and religious periodicals.

WHAT IS A JEW?

MORRIS N. KERTZER / Morris N. Kertzer, who has served as rabbi of the Larchmont and the Riverdale Temples in the state of New York, is a former president of the National Association of Jewish Chaplains in the Armed Forces. In World War II, he received the Bronze Star Medal for "meritorious achievement" as chaplain on the Anzio beachhead.

Dr. Kertzer was formerly director of interreligious activities for the American Jewish Committee. He has addressed the World Conference of Christian Education in Kobe, Japan; has conferred with religious leaders in Italy, Turkey, India, Thailand, Brazil, Rumania, Austria, and Hungary; and has made eighteen visits to Israel.

He led a delegation of rabbis to the Soviet Union in 1956—the first of its kind. His analysis of Soviet anti-Semitism won him the George Washington Medal of the Freedoms Foundation. He received the *Pro Deo* gold medal from the International University in Rome for his work in furthering Catholic-Jewish understanding.

Dr. Kertzer was born in 1910 in the "bush country" of northern Ontario, Canada, where his father was a pioneer. A graduate of the University of Toronto, he was ordained at the Jewish Theological Seminary in New York and pursued graduate studies at three American universities: Columbia, Illinois, and Michigan. He spent seven years as associate professor in the School of Religion at the University of Iowa.

He has served as chairman of the Social Action Commission of the Synagogue Council of America, as chairman of the Church-State Commission of the Central Conference of American Rabbis, and as a member of the executive committee of the New York Board of Rabbis.

Dr. Kertzer is the author of *With an "H" on My Dog Tag*, based on his experiences as a chaplain during World War II, *A Faith to Live By*, a booklet designed for men in the American army, *What Is a Jew?*, a work that has gone through thirty-three printings, and *Today's American Jew*.

What Is a Jew?

It is difficult to find a single definition. The most puzzling aspect of Jewish identity, as an eminent scholar has suggested, is that we are not sure whether being a Jew is a matter of condition or conviction.

A Jew is one who accepts the faith of Judaism. That is the *religious* definition. A Jew is one who, without formal religious affiliation, regards the teachings of Judaism—its ethics, its folkways, its literature—as his own. That is the *cultural* definition of a Jew. A Jew is one who considers himself a Jew or is so regarded by his community. That is the *practical* definition of a Jew. In other words, being a Jew may be a matter of belonging, believing, or behaving.

Professor Mordecai Kaplan calls Judaism "a civilization." Jews share a common history, common prayer, a vast literature, and, above all, a common moral and spiritual purpose. Judaism is really a way of life.

In modern Israel, the 1952 "Law of Return," which permits all Jews automatic admission to the country, places a new burden on the matter of definition. Generally, Israeli law declares that a Jew is one born of a Jewish mother who has not embraced another faith.

What Are the Principal Tenets of Judaism?

Judaism holds that man can most genuinely worship God by imitating those qualities that are godly: As God is merciful, so must we be compassionate; as God is just, so must we deal justly with our neighbor; as God is slow to anger, so must we be tolerant.

Some 1,800 years ago, one of our sages taught: "He who is beloved of his fellow men is beloved of God." To worship God is to love the works of His hands.

The Jewish prayer book speaks of three basic principles of faith:

1. *The love of learning.* As long ago as the first century, Jews had a system of compulsory education. The education of the poor and the fatherless was a responsibility of the Jewish community, as well as of the family. And the ancient rabbis knew something about the psychology of learning. On the first day of school, youngsters were fed honey cakes shaped in the letters of the alphabet so that they would associate learning with sweetness.

2. *The worship of God.* From their earliest childhood, Jews are taught that He is to be worshiped out of love, not out of fear.

3. *Good deeds*—deeds that stem from the heart. The Hebrew word for charity, *tzdakah,* means justice or righteousness. It is the *obligation* of those who have to those who do not have.

According to the ancient rabbis: "We are *required* to feed the poor of the gentiles as well as our Jewish brethren . . ."

No one is exempt from obligations to his fellow men. The Talmud informs us that "even one whom the community supports must give to the poor."

It is interesting to note that, in Jewish tradition, kindness to animals is the purest form of goodness because it is done without any hope of reward.

Do Jews Believe That Judaism Is the Only True Religion?

Jews do not presume to judge the honest worshiper of any faith. Our prayer book tells us: "The righteous of *all* nations are worthy of immortality."

We Jews know that there are many mountain tops—and all of them reach for the stars.

Do Christianity and Judaism Agree on Anything?
On What Points Do They Differ?

Christians and Jews share the same rich heritage of the Old Testament, with its timeless truths and its unchanging values. They share their belief in the fatherhood of one God—all-knowing, all-powerful, ever-merciful, the God of Abraham, Isaac, and Jacob. They share their faith in the sanctity of the Ten Commandments, the wisdom of the prophets, and the brotherhood of man.

Central to both faiths is the firm belief in the spirit of man; in the pursuit of peace and the hatred of war; in the democratic ideal as a guide to the political and social order; and, above all, in the imperishable nature of man's soul.

These are the points of agreement—the broad common ground of Judaism and Christianity that makes up the Judeo-Christian heritage.

The chief areas of disagreement between the two religions are these: Jews do not accept the divinity of Jesus as the "only begotten Son" of God. Jews recognize Jesus as a child of God in the sense that we are all God's children. The ancient rabbis taught us that God's greatest gift is the knowledge that we are made in His image.

Jews also cannot accept the principle of incarnation—God becoming flesh. It is a cardinal tenet of our faith that God is purely spiritual; He admits of no human attributes.

Nor can Judaism accept the principle of vicarious atonement—the idea of salvation *through* Christ. It is our belief that every man is responsible for his own salvation.

We believe that no one can serve as an intermediary between man and God, even in a symbolic sense. We approach God—each man after his own fashion—without a mediator.

Judaism does not interpret the principle of original sin as meaning that man is inherently evil. We do not interpret the story of Adam and Eve as reflecting man's fall from grace.

Nor do we consider our bodies and their appetites as sinful. We look upon them as natural functions of life itself, for God created them.

Are Jews Forbidden to Read the New Testament?

No. Jews cannot conceive of being "forbidden" to read anything.

There has certainly never been a ban against reading the New Testament or any other Christian writings. I have seen pious Jews poring over the contents of missionary literature; and many Jewish scholars know the Gospels as intimately as the Old Testament, which is the basis of our creed.

In Israel, be it noted, Christian clergymen are permitted to reach out to the Jewish community for converts.

Do Jews Try to Convert Gentiles?

No. Modern Judaism is not a proselytizing creed. There has been no active missionary effort in Jewish religious life for many centuries.

Jews have always welcomed converts who embraced Judaism out of true conviction. Our tradition makes no distinction between Jews born in or out of the faith.

Conversion to Judaism is not uncommon today. I have participated in the conversion of a number of Protestants and Catholics to the Jewish faith.

In recent years, there has been a considerable growth in conversions to Judaism. Some rabbis have tried to revive the ancient practice of proselytizing as an indication of a new openness of the faith.

Do Jews Believe in Heaven and Hell?

Jews believe in the immortality of the soul—an immortality whose nature is known only to God—but they no longer accept the literal idea of a heaven and a hell.

There was a time when heaven and hell were accepted in Jewish theology but, even then, rarely as physical entities. A soul tormented with remorse for misdeeds was "in hell"; a soul delighting in a life well lived was "in heaven."

The great twelfth-century philosopher Maimonides opposed the idea of rewards and punishments for behavior; the reward for virtuous living, he said, is simply the good life itself. (Maimonides makes this point in his *later* writings. He gives a more literal interpretation of the hereafter in his "Thirteen Principles," written when he was twenty. Thus, Judaism can be said to have two concepts of the hereafter—one sophisticated and philosophical, the other relatively simple.)

Does Judaism Oppose Intermarriage?

Practically all religions are opposed to marriage outside their faith. Religious Jews oppose intermarriage for the same reasons. When a husband and wife disagree on an issue as basic as their religious creed, the prospect for a lasting and harmonious relationship may be harmed.

In the past decade, a significant number of Reform rabbis (see below) have officiated at interfaith marriages.[*]

---

[*] See Part Two, Chapters XXIV and XXV for statistics on intermarriage by Jews; almost one-third of American Jews who married during the period 1966–1971 chose a spouse who was not a Jew. This figure is more than 400 percent above what it was in 1960. Part II, Chapter XXV also contains a lengthy survey: "Storm Within the Rabbinate over Intermarriage." [LR]

Are There Various Creeds and Sects Among Jews?

American Judaism contains three religious groupings: the Orthodox, the Conservative, and the Reform (sometimes called the Liberal).

The *Orthodox* Jew regards his faith as the mainstream of a tradition that has been unaltered for the past 3,000 years. He accepts the Bible as the revealed Will of God. He does not change with each new "wind of doctrine." He says that his way of life yields neither to expediency nor to comfort.

Orthodox Jews observe the Sabbath strictly (no work, no travel, no writing, no business dealings, no carrying of money). They observe every detail of the dietary laws. They maintain separate pews for women in the synagogue. They use only Hebrew in prayer and ceremonial services.

Reform Judaism differs sharply from Orthodoxy on the matter of Revelation. A Reform Jew accepts as binding only the *moral* laws of the Bible and those ceremonies that "elevate and sanctify our lives." He does not follow customs he believes "not adapted to the views and habits of modern civilization."

Reform Jews feel that faith must be rational and capable of withstanding the careful scrutiny of reason and science.

The worship of Reform Judaism departs from traditional forms. There is complete equality of the sexes in the temple. Prayer is largely in English (or the prevailing vernacular). There is greater flexibility in the choice of prayers. Instrumental music is permitted in the temple. The prayer shawl (*tallith*) is not worn by the male worshipers.

Conservative Jews follow the pattern of traditional Judaism, by and large, but regard Judaism as an evolving and ever-growing religion. They feel that change should be the result of natural growth and in consonance with the spirit of Jewish law. They regard Reform Judaism as too sharp a break with the past.

The Conservative Jew follows the dietary laws, with only minor relaxations. He observes the Sabbath, high holidays, and festivals in traditional ways. But he has borrowed many of the forms of Reform Judaism—such as the late-Friday-evening service and the use of English in prayers.

Among all three, there has been a trend back to tradition. Liberal Judaism has incorporated many of the customs of the past that had been abandoned as irrelevant.

Exactly What Is a Rabbi and What Does He Do?

Literally, "rabbi" means "teacher." The authority of a rabbi is based not on his position but upon his learning. He has no special privileges. He is in no sense an intermediary between man and God.

In Orthodox Jewish practice, the rabbi *rarely* leads in the services: it is the cantor who conducts worship. And any well-informed layman may rise to the pulpit to lead the congregation in prayer.

There is no religious hierarchy in the Jewish faith. The influence of an individual rabbi is determined solely by his ability to keep the respect of laymen and colleagues as an interpreter of Jewish law.

The modern rabbi, like the minister, is responsible for religious education, for worship in the synagogue, for ceremonials surrounding birth, confirmation, marriage, and death, and for pastoral guidance.

Is It True That in Judaism the Home Is More Important Than the Synagogue?

Yes. Many times in history, Jews have been forbidden to worship publicly: synagogues and temples have been closed by law. Yet Jewish religious life has continued intact. The center of Judaism resides in the family and the home.

Jews regard the home as a fitting place of worship—just as they regard marriage as a three-way partnership between husband, wife, and God. Our religion is essentially a family religion. The mother, lighting the Sabbath candles; the father, blessing his children at the table; the many happy rituals that surround holidays; the scroll (*mezuzah*) on the doorpost, which signifies that God is in the home—each of these is an integral part of Jewish life.

The Catholic weekly *America* observed that "the disproportionately small number of Jewish children requiring public care is a tribute to Jewish family life." Juvenile delinquency is rare among Jews and alcoholism almost unheard of.

Though divorce is permitted by the laws of the Talmud, the divorce rate among Jews is far below the community average. (See Part Two, Chapters XV and XXV.)

Do All Jews Wear Hats When They Pray?

No. *Orthodox* Jews wear a hat or skullcap (*yarmulke*) at all times—not only during prayer. *Conservative* Jews cover the head only during acts of worship. *Reform* Jews generally pray without hats.

In ancient times, Jews covered their heads during worship by lifting their prayer shawls over their heads in order to cover their eyes. This removed all distraction from prayer and made it possible for the worshiper to attain the greatest concentration during worship. The hat or skullcap is the symbolic descendant of the prayer-shawl covering.

With an upsurge of traditionalism in liberal ranks, many more Reform temples have now reinstituted the use of the skullcap.

What Are the "Kosher" Laws?

The Old Testament (Leviticus) sets down certain definite dietary restrictions:

1. It is forbidden to eat the meat of certain animals (such as the pig and horse) and certain sea foods (shrimp, lobster, crab, oyster).

2. Meats must be slaughtered according to ritual, and must meet specific health standards.

3. Meat products and dairy products may not be eaten together. (The Bible says that meat must not be boiled in milk. This was a pre-Biblical, pagan custom.)

Maimonides, who was a distinguished physician as well as philosopher, said that "kosher" food restrictions were health measures—particularly in the case of pork, which deteriorates rapidly in warm climates. He also saw important moral values in applying restraint to eating habits—for if we practice discrimination in satisfying our appetite, we may be more self-controlled with the other temptations of life.

Many of the laws concerning kosher food deal with the *method* of slaughtering the animal: it must be done without pain to the beast, with the greatest possible speed, and by a God-fearing man.

Jews who follow the dietary laws do not feel a sense of deprivation. They regard kosher practices as a symbol of their heritage, a daily lesson in self-discipline, and a constant reminder that human beings must feel pity for all living things.

How many Jews obey the dietary laws today? No one can answer authoritatively. In recent years, after a period of considerable decline, there has been a marked upturn in the use of kosher food.

Incidentally, Jews are forbidden to hunt animals for sport.

What Is the Torah?

The word "Torah" is used in two ways. Broadly, "Torah" means a way of life. It is synonymous with learning, wisdom, love of God. Without this, life has neither meaning nor value. More narrowly, the Torah is the beautiful, hand-printed scroll of the Five Books of Moses (the Bible from Genesis to Deuteronomy), which is housed in the Ark of the synagogue.

A portion of the Torah is read aloud every Sabbath during worship. The worshiper stands when the Torah is taken out of the Ark. A pious Jew kisses the Torah by placing his prayer shawl on the parchment (so his fingers will not touch the scroll), then lifting the fringes of the shawl to his lips.

The Torah is the most sacred *object* in Jewish worship. Throughout history, men have bled and died and endured terrible persecution and torture to save the revered scroll from desecration.

What Is the Talmud?

The Talmud consists of sixty-three books (or "orders") of legal, philosophical, ethical, and historical writings of the ancient rabbis. It was edited five centuries after the birth of Jesus.

The Talmud is a compendium of law and lore. It is the legal code that forms the basis of Jewish religious law. It is the textbook used in the training of rabbis.

Interlaced with the Talmud's intricate legal discussions by scholars are thousands of wonderful parables, biographical sketches, historical notes, humorous anecdotes and epigrams—a storehouse of wisdom that is as real today as it was many centuries ago.

Many of the moral maxims of the Talmud have become household phrases: "Give every man the benefit of the doubt." "An ignorant man cannot be a pious one." "Don't look at the flask but at what it contains." "All's well that ends well." "Words without deeds are like a tree without roots—a puff of wind, and it collapses." "Why are we born into the world with clenched fists and leave it with outstretched fingers? . . . To remind us that we take nothing with us."

What Is the Jewish Attitude Toward Black People?

It is forbidden to discriminate against a Jew on the ground of his color. The prophet Amos depicted the God of Israel as saying to His people: "Are you not like the Ethiopians unto Me?"

Since Jewish identity is a matter of faith, and not of color, there have been black Jews for many centuries. The Falashas, a tribe in Ethiopia, are Jews who trace their ancestry back to King Solomon: they still observe all the essentials of the Jewish religion.

In the United States, there are several thousand black Jews and more than ten synagogues whose rabbis are black.

What Is the Status of Women in Judaism?

The extension of women's rights, and the enhancement of women's status, in the contemporary world have had their impact on Jews.

Reform Judaism, for example, has granted women equal status in all synagogue affairs, and in many temples today women hold high office.

Conservative Judaism has also enlarged the scope of women's activities in the religious life of the congregation.*

The election of a woman, Golda Meir, to Israel's highest office obviously has dramatized the new role of women in Jewish communal and religious affairs.

Any ancient faith will tend to embody some historical bias against

---

* Among Conservatives, a movement is growing to accept women in *minyans*. See Part Two, Chapter XXV. [LR]

women in its traditions. Yet even Biblical Judaism—and certainly rabbinic Judaism, in the first centuries of the Common Era—granted rights to its women that were simply unknown in other or surrounding cultures. (For example, Jewish law dictates that the sexual needs of the wife are as basic as those of the husband.)

The best perspective, vis-à-vis the status of the Jewish woman, is obtained by separating the private from the public realm. Jewish religious requirements in *personal* relations are the same for a woman as they are for a man. But the responsibilities for *communal* affairs are placed upon the shoulders of the men, who are free from domestic obligations (running the home, the rearing of children, and so on).

An excellent illustration is "the law of hospitality," a basic principle of the Jewish faith, based upon mandatory compassion and concern for the disadvantaged. The *mitzvah* (or command) of hospitality impels any male worshiper, on the Sabbath, to bring home a poor guest for the Sabbath meal. The wife's obligation is to treat him well and, indeed, to urge her husband to make certain that no hungry worshiper be left uninvited after the Sabbath service.

The administration of the machinery of philanthropy, as the operation of the synagogue, is in male hands; but the personal obligations of kindness and concern are not only extended to the wife and mother but are often best fulfilled under her guidance and inspiration.

Can a Woman Be Ordained as a Rabbi?

Only Reform Judaism permits the ordination of women.

Sally J. Preisand was ordained at Hebrew Union College—Jewish Institute of Religion, the seminary of Reform Judaism, on September 19, 1972. Rabbi Preisand, age twenty-five, preached her first Yom Kippur sermon at the Stephen Wise Free Synagogue in New York City. Rabbi Preisand serves as assistant to the senior rabbi of the synagogue.

What Is the Attitude of Jews Toward Divorce?

Jewish tradition has always regarded the integrity of the family as the basic element in the preservation of the faith. Divorce is therefore regarded as a calamity, a blow to the perpetuation of the Jewish community. The prophet Malachi once said that "the very altar [of God] sheds tears for the man who divorces his wife."

Yet humane Jewish law would regard a home without love and without harmony as worse than a home broken by divorce. Jewish law permits divorce on the basis of mutual consent. The termination of a marriage is a relatively simple procedure, but it was nevertheless rare in the Jewish community. Statistics indicate that the divorce rate is very low among observant Jews.

Some of the social factors that led to a disintegration of the home have been notably absent among Jews. Alcoholism, for instance, was (and is) a rarity—so also wife beating.

Jewish law and tradition strongly stressed the obligation of family support. And the presence of the extended family—grandparents, aunts, uncles, cousins—has been a stabilizing influence in preserving those marriages in which minor difficulties are encountered.

The rights of the divorced Jewish woman are actually embodied in the marriage document, the *ketubah,* itself. Alimony was instituted among Jews in the first century of the Christian Era. And eleven centuries later, Maimonides ruled that "a woman is not like a captive, compelled to consort with a man against her will." If a husband was sexually repulsive to his wife or could not satisfy her conjugal needs, the wife could obtain a divorce from a rabbinical court.

In our day, both Orthodox and Conservative Jews turn to a rabbinical court for a *religious* divorce. After a civil, secular divorce is obtained, neither the man nor the woman may remarry until they have obtained a *Get,* a Jewish declaration that the marriage has been terminated.

What Is the Attitude of Judaism to Abortion?

Orthodox Judaism permits abortion to save the life of the mother. Among more liberal Orthodox Jews, this principle is extended to take into consideration the mental health of the mother.

Reform and Conservative Judaism permit abortion if it is undertaken for unselfish reasons.

What Is the Position of Judaism on Homosexuality?

Homosexuality is forbidden in all the branches of Judaism, whether between males or females.

What Is Yom Kippur?

Yom Kippur means "Day of Atonement," the last of the Ten Days of Penitence. It is marked by twenty-four hours of prayer and fasting, during which the worshiper (and the congregation collectively) recounts the catalog of human transgressions—pride, greed, jealousy, vanity, lust, and so on.

Throughout this day runs the prayer: "Father, *we* have sinned before Thee."

Judaism stresses that prayer is not the sole avenue to God's grace. Equally important in God's eyes are deeds of love and compassion.

A lovely story is told of Rabbi Israel Salanter, who failed to appear for worship one Yom Kippur eve. His congregation was frantic, for it was inconceivable that their beloved rabbi would be absent on this holiest night. After a long search, they found him in the barn of a Christian neighbor. On his way to the synagogue, the rabbi had found his neighbor's calf, lost and tangled in the brush. He had freed the calf and brought it back to its stall. The rabbi's prayer was his act of mercy.

What Is Rosh Hashanah?

Rosh Hashanah means New Year. It ushers in the Ten Days of Penitence, during which mankind "passes in judgment before the heavenly throne." It is the season when Jews also sit in judgment on themselves—by comparing their aspirations to their conduct during the year that has just ended.

The Rosh Hashanah of 1974 marks the Jewish year 5735.

Among the Rosh Hashanah prayers is one that asks the Lord to hasten the day when "all men shall come to serve Thee"—when mankind will be joined in universal brotherhood under the Fatherhood of God.

Is an American Jew's First Loyalty to Israel or America?

The only loyalty of an American Jew is to the United States of America—without any ifs, ands, or buts.

To the Jew, the state of Israel is the ancestral home of his forefathers, the birthplace of his faith and his Bible. It is the haven for almost 3 million Jews—after the agonies and nightmares and murders of the Nazi holocaust, which destroyed 40 percent of world Jewry.

Surely, it is not surprising that Israel has great and special meaning for Jews all over the world. Nor is it surprising that the courage and the pioneering of the people of Israel have won the respect of men of every religious faith. But spiritual bonds and emotional ties are quite different from political loyalty.

Many Americans retain strong attachments to the land of their fathers. But their political loyalty—whether they be Irish or German or Italian; Catholic, Protestant, or Jew—is and will always be to America alone.

A considerable number of American Jews have chosen to emigrate to Israel. The right to leave the United States is as precious as the right to remain in it.

Does Israel's New Status as a Modern State Weaken Its Biblical Role?

The creation of a modern state, with all its apparatus of government, may seem quite remote from the prophetic vision of a land destined as "a light unto the nations." Yet, the forces of contemporary history have lent a measure of reality to the dreams of Isaiah and Ezekiel.

Already there is a generous flow of technical help from Israel to the even younger states of Ghana, Burma, and Nigeria, offering infant countries the benefits of Israel's experience in government, in health and welfare, and in scientific education.

"Out of Zion shall go forth the Law, and the word of the Lord from Jerusalem," said the prophets.

WHAT IS A LUTHERAN?

NOTE TO THE READER: The original article was written by the late G. Elson Ruff. Additional new material, and certain revisions, have been supplied by Dr. Albert P. Stauderman—and such material has been identified by the initials [APS].

Where no initials are employed, the text is Dr. Ruff's.

Where the answer to a question combines material by the two authors, separate sets of initials clearly identify which author wrote which portion.

G. ELSON RUFF / G. Elson Ruff was editor of *The Lutheran* for twenty-six years until his death early in 1972. He had served as president of the Associated Church Press, an organization of 180 church periodicals, mostly Protestant, and of the National Lutheran Editors Association. Under his leadership, *The Lutheran* reached a circulation of 590,000, second among all nationally circulated Protestant publications. It has several times won awards for excellence in reporting religious news.

Dr. Ruff was born in Dunkirk, New York, in 1904. He studied at Thiel College and the Philadelphia Lutheran Theological Seminary. He received an A.M. degree from the University of Pennsylvania and honorary doctorates from Thiel and from Wagner College. He was ordained to the ministry of the Lutheran Church in 1926 and served for fourteen years as a pastor in Pennsylvania.

ALBERT P. STAUDERMAN / The Reverend Albert P. Stauderman, D.D., is editor of *The Lutheran*, biweekly national magazine of the Lutheran Church in America, and director of the LCA Commission on Church Papers.

A native of Mount Vernon, New York, Dr. Stauderman was graduated from Wagner College and from Hartwick Lutheran Theological Seminary.

Dr. Stauderman served for sixteen years as pastor of St. Paul's Church in Teaneck, New Jersey. He was one of the organizers of the New Jersey Synod and was the first president of its Northern Conference. He has been a member of many synodical, national boards, and committees of the Lutheran Church. He has been president of the National Lutheran Editors Association and a director of the Associated Church Press.

Dr. Stauderman is the author of many magazine articles and of five books, including *Earth Has No Sorrow*, *Facts About Lutherans*, and *Our New Church*.

NOTE TO THE READER: Church mergers within the past fifteen years have placed 95 percent of the 9 million Lutherans in North America within three major bodies:

The Lutheran Church in America (LCA): about 3.2 million members
The Lutheran Church–Missouri Synod (LC–MS): around 2.8 million members
The American Lutheran Church (ALC): around 2.5 million members

1. *The Lutheran Church in America,* whose history traces back to early settlers in the New World, was formed in 1962 by a merger of the United Lutheran Church, the Augustana (Swedish) Lutheran Church, and smaller bodies with Finnish and Danish backgrounds. The LCA, the most ecumenical of the Lutheran groups, is a member of the World Council of Churches, the National Council of Churches, and the Lutheran World Federation.

Within the framework of the Lutheran confessions, the LCA permits broad theological freedom to its constituent churches. It is headquartered in New York, has 7,800 clergy, and contains 6,200 congregations.

2. *The Lutheran Church–Missouri Synod* may fairly be called the most conservative of the three major Lutheran groups. It conducts a vigorous parochial school system. Headquartered in St. Louis, the LC–MS does not belong to any ecumenical organization, although it cooperates in social service and mission work. It has 7,328 ministers and 6,084 congregations.

3. *The American Lutheran Church* was formed in 1960 by a merger of churches of Norwegian, German, and Danish background. It belongs to the World Council of Churches and the Lutheran World Federation. It cooperates closely in several areas (parish education and missions) with the LCA and holds a similar theological outlook. The ALC has 6,412 ministers and 5,141 congregations.

In 1965 these three major bodies—LCA, LC–MS, and ALC—organized the Lutheran Council in the U.S.A. to act as a common agency for them in various cooperative endeavors that did not compromise their respective theological positions: service to military personnel, campus ministries, refugee and relief work. (A similar agency serves the Canadian branches of the churches.)

The remainder of the Lutherans in the United States are scattered in nine small bodies. The largest is the Wisconsin Evangelical Lutheran Synod (976 ministers, 980 congregations, 380,000 members). Like most of the smaller Lutheran groups, it may be said to be marked by conservatism.

Lutheran policy places ultimate authority in its separate congregations—which, in turn, transfer some of this authority to the larger bodies.

Regional Lutheran groups are known as districts or synods. They elect delegates to national conventions, which then act as "the church."

It should be emphasized that despite organizational variances, all Lutheran bodies hold a similar doctrinal basis: They accept the Bible as the Word of God and their creeds and confessions as a proper explanation of that Word.

The chief "confessional documents" are the Augsburg Confession and Martin Luther's catechisms. These and six other "confessions" are collected into the Book of Concord.

Variations in the practices of different Lutheran groupings are indicated, when important, in the article that follows. [APS]

How Did Lutheranism Originate?

On October 31, 1517, there was only one Protestant—Martin Luther.* A few years later, there were millions. The violent explosion known as the Reformation split the church of the sixteenth century into a number of segments, of which the Lutheran Church is one.

Luther had been a Roman Catholic priest who loved the church and had no intention of separating from it. But he ventured to protest in 1517 against the church's sales of certificates, called indulgences, which were said to reduce the time a soul must stay in purgatory.

Luther had learned from Scripture that full forgiveness of sin is promised through faith in the merciful God revealed in Christ. This central idea led Luther to criticize many Roman Catholic teachings and practices. Soon the break was beyond repair.

What Are the Basic Tenets of the Lutheran Creed?

Lutherans don't claim any doctrines different from the common Christian faith described in the New Testament and first summarized in the Apostles' Creed. We are created by God, but we employ the freedom given us by God to disobey our Creator. The

---

* "Protestant," as a term describing the followers of Luther, was not actually used until 1529, when it was applied to the princes at the Diet of Spires, who protested against the edict decreed by the majority. Of course, there were many before Luther who protested against abuses in the church in the Middle Ages; but Lutherans were the first to be called "Protestants." [APS]

result is continual tragedy in human life. But God does not abandon us in our tragedy. He shares it with us.

In Christ, He reveals Himself as the Savior God, suffering punishment and death so we may share with Him in the resurrection from death. Through faith in Christ, a new life begins in us. It is nourished by God's gifts through His Word and sacraments. The Word is recorded in the Bible, but the Word itself is a living, active thing through which the Holy Spirit stirs us to growth in understanding and obedience to God's will.

What Distinguishes Lutherans from Other Protestant Groups?

You don't hear Lutherans say, "It doesn't matter what you believe, just so you live right." Lutherans think that a way of living is a by-product of a way of believing.

Since Lutheranism developed from Luther's intense experience of salvation through faith, it has been marked by concern for faith as the essential part of religion. So Lutherans, more than most of the other Protestants, emphasize doctrine. They insist on unusually thorough education of their pastors and require young people to engage in a long period of study of the Lutheran Catechism before being admitted to full church membership.

Lutherans do not stress prohibitions or blue laws. They think of the Christian life as a grateful response to a loving Father rather than as obedience to a stern monarch. Such life should achieve a high ethical level without emphasis on rules and regulations. In this, Lutheranism is sharply different from some other forms of Protestantism.

Since Luther had been an ardent Roman Catholic before his excommunication, he was less drastic than some later reformers in abandoning Catholic forms of worship. These are retained among Lutherans in a simplified form.

Lutherans observe the festivals and seasons of the historic church year. In their churches, they have the altar, cross, candles, vestments, and other equipment of worship that most other Protestants discarded as "too Catholic." Lutherans believe that these forms of liturgy are not required but are valuable because of their beauty and because, through them, we share in the experiences of the family of Christian worshipers of all the ages. Lutheran music is world-famous, especially the compositions of Johann Sebastian Bach.

Do Lutherans Worship Martin Luther?

Luther had faults. He was of a violent temperament and sometimes scalded his opponents with intemperate abuse. When driven into a corner, in the turbulent events of his career, he made several unfortunate compromises, which nobody defends today.

Luther asked his followers not to call themselves "Lutherans." The name was given to them by their opponents as a mark of contempt. They called themselves "Evangelicals"—believers in the Gospel.

Yet Lutherans deeply respect Martin Luther as one of the greatest teachers and liberators of the church. His ideas still stimulate fresh thinking. Every year, Lutheran scholars write many books exploring his thoughts. But nobody worships him.

Do Lutherans Worship Any Saints?

Every Christian is a saint. In the Apostles' Creed, the church is called "the communion of saints." A saint is not a perfect person but one who, by Gods' grace, is progressing toward holiness.

Every Christian is also a sinner until the day he dies, even such great Christians as Peter and Paul. Lutherans worship God alone. They do not pray to the Virgin Mary or to anyone but God.

What Is the Lutheran Concept of Sin?

Sin is the word describing the situation of all people as disobedient to God. Sin is not specific wrongdoing (this is the *result* of sin) but the basic condition of our personality. It is our nature to try to make ourselves the center of our lives.

Sin means trying to pretend that we are God. It is refusal to accept the restriction on our freedom that is the inescapable consequence of the fact that we are created beings and that the only reason for our existence is doing the will of our Creator. This is portrayed in the old story of Adam and Eve in the garden, who were not satisfied to accept the one limitation placed on them—that they must not eat the fruit of a certain tree.

How Do Lutherans Believe Mortals Are Saved?

We can no more escape by our own efforts from our condition as sinners than we could swim to shore if we fell off a ship in mid-Atlantic. Our only hope is to be rescued. Salvation is a *gift* from God. The only thing we can do about it is to want it. Even this desire comes from God.

In other words, when we recognize our fatal human weakness and are thoroughly dissatisfied with it, we are prepared to let God come to us with His gift of faith. This was Luther's situation during his long "dark night of the soul," when, as a monk, he was trying to do all the things that were supposed to result in salvation. He discovered, when he got through trying to save himself, that the merciful and loving God was waiting to save him through faith in Christ.

If people could be saved by obeying laws or fulfilling ritual requirements, they would be saving themselves. Lutherans believe that only God can save us.

How Do Lutheran Sacraments Differ from Roman Catholic Sacraments?

Luther came to the conviction that the complete sacrifice for man's sin had already been made in our Lord's crucifixion. So the Roman teaching of the Mass as a sacrifice no longer had meaning for Luther. The Lord's Supper, in Lutheran teaching, is an encounter of the believer with the living Lord, Who is truly present in the Holy Communion to forgive sins and renew the spiritual life of believers. But no physical change takes place in the bread and wine of the Communion.

This teaching was perhaps the most radical part of the Reformation. It attacked the whole Roman Catholic idea of the church as a treasury of merit stored up through saying masses and of the priesthood as divinely ordained to celebrate the sacrifice of the Mass. In the "priesthood of all believers," of which Luther often spoke, each Christian directly encounters God and receives His saving grace.

Lutherans believe that, in baptism, a person is born into the Kingdom of God and becomes an heir of salvation. It is the beginning of the life of faith in which each day our human nature "should be drowned through daily repentance; and that day after day a new self should arise to live with God in righteousness and purity forever" (*The Small Catechism*, by Martin Luther).

The remaining five of the seven sacraments of the Roman Catholic Church were discarded by Luther, and by all Protestants since his day, as not true sacraments because they were not established by Christ. Confirmation, marriage, and ordination of the clergy are rites of the church to which no unique promise of divine grace is attached. Penance is not necessary because God promises complete forgiveness to all who ask for it in faith. There is no guilt "left over" that penance can erase or for which one must make amends in purgatory. Anointing of the sick with oil, with prayers for their recovery, is good Christian therapy but not a Scriptural requirement.

Do Lutherans Believe in the Holy Trinity?

They do, along with orthodox Christians of all ages. God the Father is our Creator. God the Son is our Redeemer. God the Holy Ghost is the Sanctifier and Nourisher of our souls. Yet there is one God in three personalities.

It is not possible to make any essential Christian teaching—such as how God could be a man, how the dead can live eternally, how one God can be three personalities—conform to mathematical formulas or submit to scientific proof. Such things are beyond the range of human reasoning and are matters of faith.

Are There Any Special Rituals in Lutheran Worship?

There is no requirement that Lutheran congregations should all worship in the same way. There is wide variation between the ritual of a cathedral of the Church of Sweden, for instance, and of a small country parish in Saskatchewan.

A service of confirmation at which young people reaffirm their baptismal vows is a rite that has a distinctive form in Lutheran churches. Preceding each celebration of the Lord's Supper there is a service of public confession, which is characteristically Lutheran.

Private confession is practiced by Lutherans in some places but is not required.

In the Lord's Supper, communicants receive both the bread and the wine. In most churches, they kneel at the altar rail, but in recent years experimental new forms have been tried (with communicants seated around a large table, for instance). [APS]

Do Lutherans Believe in Heaven and Hell?

The goal of the Christian life is the perfect existence that will finally be ours when we can be completely obedient to our Creator. Lutherans do not believe this Kingdom of God will come through gradual improvement of human nature. Fulfillment of God's purposes lies beyond the limits of our present life. Those who live and die in faith in Christ will live with Him eternally, freed from the limitations of time and space. Predictions about this eternal life must necessarily be in some sort of picture language, for it is beyond the range of finite minds. Naïve descriptions of heaven and hell, which were common in old times, are obviously inadequate. But victory over death is the certain destiny of God's people.

What Is the Attitude of the Lutheran Church to the Pope? To the Roman Catholic Church? To Roman Catholics?

We are more moderate in speaking of the Pope than Luther was. For one thing, the papacy has been drastically reformed since Luther's time. However, Lutherans absolutely reject any teaching that God has delegated supreme authority over the souls of His people to any man.*

There is only one church, we believe, but it is not any visible institution, such as the Roman Catholic Church or the Lutheran Church. It consists of all the congregations of believers "among

* See Part Two, Chapter XVI ("Papal Infallibility Reaffirmed") for the historic report by a joint commission of Roman Catholic and Lutheran theologians ("Ministry and the Church Universal") on Papal primacy, Papal infallibility, the "Petrine function," and other important issues—which were held not to be "a barrier to reconciliation" between the two churches. [LR]

whom the gospel is preached in its purity and the holy sacraments are administered according to the gospel" (*Augsburg Confession*, Article 7). [GER]

Theological discussions have been conducted in recent years, between the Lutheran World Federation and the Vatican Secretariat for Promoting Christian Unity on an international level, and between the U.S. Committee of the Lutheran World Federation and representatives of the Roman Catholic Church in the United States. Basic understandings have been reached on the mutual validity of baptism and of the ministry.

Lutherans know that their personal attitude toward Roman Catholics should be to love them as Christian brothers, even though we may disagree in our understanding of the Gospel. The Pope and bishops of the Roman Catholic Church often make profound statements of Christian truth and peace. Lutherans know that among Roman Catholics are many of the finest Christians on earth. [APS]

Do Lutherans Believe in the Separation of Church and State?

In America, they emphatically do. Luther taught that church and state are both ordained by God and that each has separate, clear-cut functions. Church-state separation is a logical application of the Lutheran principle of resistance to the attempts of human authorities to rule men's souls.

In the Scandinavian countries and Finland, the Lutheran Church is the state church, under nominal control of Parliament (as is the Anglican Church in England).

There has usually been some connection between the Lutheran Church and the government in other European countries, due to the historical development of the churches. Yet, in Norway under the wartime Quisling government, the Lutheran Church rebelled against the authority of the state. All bishops and most pastors refused to obey its orders. In Germany also, some pastors were strong leaders in the opposition to Hitler. They quoted Luther, who wrote, "If your worldly master is wrong, and you know for certain he is wrong, then fear God more than man and do not serve him." [GER]

Lutherans in the United States have affirmed the right of citizens to "selective conscientious objection," refusing to serve in a particular war that they consider immoral. However, such objectors are warned that they must pay whatever penalty their action entails.

In matters of public health, social welfare, and education, Lutherans recognize the need for government involvement. They have, however, called for "functional interaction" in such areas, with the government and church agencies working side by side without either interfering with the rights of the other. In regard to prayers and devotions in public schools, Lutherans have been cool to proposed legislation or constitutional amendments. Religious freedom means that government has no right either to prohibit prayer or to require it, they hold. [APS]

Do Lutherans Believe Theirs Is the Only True Religion?

Yes, but they don't believe they are the only ones who have it. There are true Christian believers in a vast majority of the churches, perhaps in all.

Lutherans are among the leaders in interchurch assemblies, such as the World Council of Churches, because they are eager for better understanding and cooperation among Christians everywhere.

Does the Lutheran Church Permit Its Pastors to Marry?

Luther taught that enforced celibacy of the priesthood was a mistake. Eight years after the beginning of the Reformation, he himself married a nun who had left her convent as a result of Luther's teaching. (The date is important because enemies of Luther often assert that "he left the church to get married.")

How Is the Lutheran Church Governed?

Lutherans believe that church government is a practical concern without doctrinal significance. Lutheran churches in Europe generally have bishops and an authoritarian structure because of their history and their ties to the government. In American churches, and in those of developing nations, a more democratic structure is maintained. Church conventions elect presidents or bishops, but these have limited terms and constitutional authority. [APS]

The foundation of this authority is in the congregations themselves, because in them the free people of God exercise their right to hear the Gospel and receive the sacraments. They cannot be held in obedience to an earthly hierarchy.

Each Lutheran congregation owns its church building or other property and is self-governing in all of its local affairs. Men are called to the office of the ministry by God through the congregations, and if they cease to perform the functions of their office they cease to be ministers. [GER]*

What Is the Position of Lutherans in Regard to the Status of Women?

The predecessor bodies of the Lutheran Church in America granted full suffrage to women as early as 1936. The American Lutheran Church took similar action in 1960.

The Lutheran Church–Missouri Synod granted women the right to serve on local church councils in 1968, and at its 1973 convention only 22 women were among the 1,020 voting delegates. This compares to 123 women among the 340 lay delegates at the LCA convention in Baltimore in July 1974. [APS]

Can a Woman Be Ordained as a Lutheran Minister?

The ordination of women to the ministry was approved in 1970 by the Lutheran Church in America and by the American Lutheran Church.

The LCA now has fourteen ordained women pastors; the ALC has two.

A proposal for ordination of women was presented at the 1971 Missouri Synod convention, but was defeated 674–194. [APS]

What Is the Lutheran Position on Divorce?

Christian faith affirms marriage as a covenant of fidelity—a dynamic lifelong commitment of one man and one woman in a personal and sexual union. It is also a structure in God's created order, providing an intimate community in which parents and children may nurture and strengthen one another in love.

* For an extended survey of recent conflicts within the Lutheran Church–Missouri Synod, see Part Two, Chapter XXVI. [LR]

But human sinfulness crops up in the marriage relation just as everywhere else. Some marriages become so badly eroded by infidelity and selfishness that to end them is less evil than to try to keep them going. Although divorce often brings anguish to all those concerned, there may be situations in which securing a divorce is more responsible than trying to stay together.

The Lutheran Church in America in 1970 adopted a statement that called on the church "to continue to minister to all persons involved" in the dissolution of a marriage. The aim should be to assist them to see their problems more clearly and to avoid future errors. "When the question of the remarriage of a divorced man or woman arises, the church and the individuals themselves will do well to concentrate upon the potential of the new rather than the collapse of the former marriage." [APS]

Do Lutherans Believe in Birth Control?

Few official statements have been made by Lutheran churches on this question, but there has been no general objection to the fact that countless Lutherans practice birth control. The statement of 1970 cited above adds:

[Use] of any medically approved contraceptive method within the covenant of marital fidelity depends upon the motivation of the users. A responsible decision for or against having a child will include evaluation of such factors as the health of the potential mother . . . number and spacing of children . . . economic circumstances . . . population growth.

People have a right not to have children without being accused of selfishness or a betrayal of the divine plan; and every child has a right to be a wanted child. All persons are entitled to receive from governmental and voluntary agencies information about conception control.

Another portion of the LCA statement cites similar factors as a reason why "a woman or couple may decide responsibly to seek an abortion." Medical advice and spiritual counsel should be sought by those "who conscientiously make decisions about abortion," the statement says.

The guarded wording of this statement indicates the Lutheran Church's hesitation about legislating on moral or ethical questions. The church is not a law-making society but an agency through which the Holy Spirit shapes and directs Christian lives so they may have the freedom and strength to grow toward holiness. [APS]

What Is the Position of Lutherans on Abortion?

The Lutheran Church in America in 1970 adopted a statement on "Sex, Marriage and Family Life," which states, among other things:

On the basis of the evangelical ethic, a woman or a couple may decide responsibly to seek an abortion. Earnest consideration should be given to the life and total health of the mother, her responsibilities to others in her family, the stage of development of the fetus, the economic and psychological stability of the home, the laws of the land, and the consequences for society as a whole.

Neither the American Lutheran Church nor the Missouri Synod has adopted a statement on the subject. [APS]*

What Is Your Position on Black People?

In regard to the Lutheran churches, there has never been any official segregation or racial separation.

Black people have been members of congregations for centuries and the Lutheran tradition in the Virgin Islands goes back to the middle of the seventeenth century. [APS]

What Is the Position of Lutherans Regarding Homosexuality?

The 1970 statement of the Lutheran Church in America states that "homosexuality is viewed biblically as a departure from the heterosexual structure of God's creation. Persons who engage in homosexual behavior are sinners only as are all other persons—alienated from God and neighbor. . . . It is essential to see such persons as entitled to understanding and justice in church and community."

An earlier version had listed homosexuality as a "deviation from the norm."

Neither the ALC nor the Lutheran Church–Missouri Synod has a similar statement, so far as I know. [APS]

* For an important modification of the Lutheran attitude toward abortion, see Part Two, Chapter I. [LR]

Is Lutheranism International?

Lutheranism includes almost the entire population of Denmark, Finland, Iceland, Norway, and Sweden; a majority of the Germans, Latvians, Estonians, and minorities in most other European countries. Mission work has resulted in Lutheran churches in South America, Africa, Asia, and Australia.

How Many Lutherans Are There in the United States? In the World?

Lutheran membership in the United States at the end of 1973 was 8,703,252. Membership in Canada was 301,961. An additional 4 or 5 million persons give "Lutheran" as their church preference when they fill out questionnaires. The same is true in all Iron Curtain countries. Perhaps 70 million would be a reasonable guess at the present world total.

WHAT IS A METHODIST?

NOTE TO THE READER: The Methodist Church and the Evangelical United Brethren Church became the United Methodist Church on April 22, 1968.

For purposes of clarity and simplicity, the name "Methodist" is retained in the late Dr. Sockman's text—even though "United Methodist" would today be more accurate.

In bringing this article up to date, considerable new material and a more contemporary interpretation of many questions have kindly been supplied by Bishop Paul A. Washburn.

Wherever the text is not Dr. Sockman's, the initials [PAW] identify Bishop Paul Washburn's valued contribution.

RALPH W. SOCKMAN / The late Ralph W. Sockman, who had been selected in various nondenominational surveys as "one of the greatest religious leaders in America," retired in 1961, after forty-four years as minister of Christ Church, Methodist (formerly Madison Avenue Methodist Episcopal Church), in New York City. Dr. Sockman was known as the "Dean of Religious Broadcasters" because of his thirty-four seasons as minister of the Sunday morning *National Radio Pulpit*, the oldest Protestant broadcast in America. He also wrote a nationally syndicated column entitled "Lift for Living."

Born in 1889 in Mt. Vernon, Ohio, Dr. Sockman studied at Ohio Wesleyan University and received an M.A. in 1913 from Columbia University. He was graduated from Union Theological Seminary in 1916 and received his Ph.D. from Columbia University.

Dr. Sockman received twenty-one honorary degrees from prominent institutions, delivered the Lyman Beecher lectures at Yale, and served as visiting professor of homiletics at Yale Divinity School.

In 1949, Dr. Sockman was elected director, for his lifetime, of the Hall of Fame for Great Americans. He was president of the Council on Religion and International Affairs (Church Peace Union), and president of the Board of World Peace of the Methodist Church from 1928 to 1960. A member of the Central Committee of the World Council of Churches, he was twice president of the Protestant Council of the City of New York.

Dr. Sockman was the author of twenty books, including *The Higher Happiness, The Whole Armor of God, How to Believe, The Paradoxes of Jesus,* and the most recent, *The Meaning of Suffering.*

PAUL A. WASHBURN / Paul Arthur Washburn, who has supplied additional and new material to Dr. Ralph W. Sockman's text, is a bishop of the United Methodist Church.

He served as executive secretary of the union movement that brought the United Methodist Church into being and is the author of *The United Methodist Primer*.

What Is a United Methodist?

The Methodist Church is "a unique blend of New Testament Christianity, the Protestant Reformation and the influence of John Wesley." Wesley himself was fond of saying: "A Methodist is one who has the love of God shed abroad in his heart by the Holy Ghost given unto him, one who loves the Lord his God, with all his soul, with all his mind, and with all his strength."

Methodism began in England as a movement within the existing Protestant church, not as a new sect.

What Are the Roots of the United Methodist Church?

The United Methodist Church, at first glance, seems to be the confluence of two churches, the Methodist Church and the Evangelical United Brethren Church, which on April 22, 1968, became the United Methodist Church. When seen more deeply, this union is the result of the divisions, reunions, and unions of ten churches. The most recent of the unions were those of the Methodist Episcopal Church, the Methodist Episcopal Church South, and the Methodist Protestant Church in 1939, and the union of the Church of the United Brethren in Christ and the Evangelical Church in 1946.

Within the celebration of the most recent union, in 1968, one phrase was reiterated again and again: "Lord of the church, we are united in thee, in thy church, and in the United Methodist Church."

This unity is a unity in Christ that encompasses different stances of belief and styles of ministering. [PAW]

How Do Methodists Regard the Bible?

United Methodists are persuaded that the Bible "contains all truth required for eternal salvation through faith in Jesus Christ." Their doctrinal standard statement of 1972 identifies the Scriptures as the first among four sources and guidelines for Christian theologizing. The other three sources and guidelines are tradition, experience, and reason. [PAW]

How Did the Methodist Church Begin?

The Methodist Church was born in the Church of England through the work of John Wesley. Educated at Oxford and ordained to the Anglican priesthood, the young Wesley sought in vain for religious satisfaction by the strict observance of religious rules and the ordinances of the church. The turning point in his life came at a prayer meeting in London on May 24, 1738. There he learned what Saint Paul had discovered—that it is not by rules and our own efforts at self-perfection that man may enter upon life and peace but only by faith in God's mercy.

When Wesley went forth to preach his new, heart-warming experience, the people who had been unreached by the church flocked to hear him. Multitudes came asking Wesley to teach and direct them. He gathered these people into societies "in order to pray together, to receive the word of exhortation, and to watch over one another in love, that they might help each other to work out their own salvation."

He appointed leaders, assigned them to various fields of labor, and supervised their work. The movement spread rapidly over England, then to Ireland and America. Wesley's intention was not to form a new sect but only to organize societies within the Church of England. The preachers were not ordained, and the members were supposed to receive the sacraments in the Anglican Church. But the Bishop of London, to whose diocese Wesley belonged, would not ordain ministers to serve the Methodist societies. Nor would he consecrate their meeting places. If Wesley's work was to expand, he had to take the irregular steps of ordination and consecration.

Furthermore, Wesley was confronted with the care of his followers in America, where the Anglican clergy had nearly all returned to England as Tories during the Revolution. The 15,000 American Methodists at the close of the Revolutionary War clamored for clerical leadership. Wesley responded to their demand by asking the Bishop of London to ordain some ministers for America. Failing in his request, Wesley himself ordained two men to "preside over the flock in America."

Under their leadership, the Methodist Episcopal Church in America was organized at Baltimore on December 24, 1784.

Where Did the Name "Methodist" Come From?

It arose from the methodical habits of the "Holy Club," which John and Charles Wesley founded at Oxford University. The members arranged a daily schedule of duties, setting hours for visiting the sick and those in prison, conducting schools among the poor, and observing the religious offices of the church. They prayed aloud three times each day and stopped for silent prayer every hour.

These strict rules of conduct aroused the ridicule of the student body. "Methodists" was almost the mildest epithet hurled at the Holy Club. The name clung to the followers of Wesley because he continued to stress rules of conduct and religious observance.

What Are the Source Books of Your Church?

United Methodists are people of three books: the Bible, which is primary; the Book of Hymns, which is salted and peppered with the hymns of John and Charles Wesley; and the Book of Discipline, a gathering of the covenants agreed upon by United Methodists. These covenants suggest that United Methodists intend to be devout, sincere, and disciplined to giving God's love through their effective witness in word, work, mission, and life. [PAW]

What Is the United Methodist Attitude Toward the Trinity?

To United Methodists the doctrine of the Trinity is one of the most important ways of thinking about God. It describes God as creator, savior, and divine presence and power in history. Within

United Methodist liturgies, there are many references to trinitarian theology. [PAW]

How Do United Methodists Regard the Virgin Birth?

United Methodists regard the doctrine of the virgin birth as one of the attempts to explain the unexplainable mystery of God's presence, power, and action in the person of Jesus of Nazareth. This explanation is one of at least three explanations included in the four Gospels, with the Gospel according to Mark writing of God's spirit descending upon Jesus at his baptism, and with the Gospel according to John using a more philosophical approach. [PAW]

Do Methodists Pray to Saints?

No. They believe God is directly accessible to each of his children. Since God is Love, no intermediary is needed to intercede for his children. Methodists, like other Protestants, believe in the "individual priesthood of all believers."

Do Methodist Ministers Hear Confessions?

United Methodists do not hear confessions in the sense of a priest listening to statements of penitence on the part of the faithful; but the practice of pastoral counseling, in which clergy and laity consult with persons about their needs for revision of their ways of thinking and acting, is a common practice among United Methodists. [PAW]

Do Methodists Believe in Heaven and Hell?

The concepts of heaven and hell vary widely, according to the educational and religious background of the believers. Some have very concrete ideas of golden streets in heaven and fiery furnaces in hell.

But the majority of Methodists are emancipated from the pre-scientific view of a physical heaven "up there" and a physical hell "down there." They trust the promise of Christ: "I go to prepare a place for you." Heaven is the realm of mind and spirit where the redeemed keep company with God and His Risen Son, Jesus Christ. Hell is the state where such fellowship is absent.

Do Methodists Believe in Purgatory?

No. Methodists find no scriptural warrant for the Roman Catholic belief in purgatory. They do not presume to peer behind the veil of death or departmentalize the processes of divine judgment. Many Methodists believe that God's punishments are redemptive rather than punitive. They trust the justice and love of God to care for the departed.

What Sacraments Do Methodists Recognize?

Methodists held only two sacraments as ordained of God: baptism and the Lord's Supper (Holy Communion). Baptism is a sign not only of profession but also of regeneration, or a new birth. The Supper of the Lord is the sacrament of our redemption by Christ's death and a sign of the love that Christians ought to have among themselves.

Methodists maintain the general Protestant position of only two sacraments because, according to the Gospel record, only two have the direct touch of Jesus. This does not mean that the Methodists have a weakened conception of other rites, such as marriage and confirmation. These are held in high reverence, but Methodists still limit the word "sacrament" to the two ordinances that Christ Himself performed.

Do Methodists Believe in the "Real Presence" of Christ in the Sacrament of the Lord's Supper?

In the sacrament of the Lord's Supper United Methodists celebrate the real presence of Christ but do not think of that presence as confined within the bread and wine. They would be more apt to think of that presence in the community of the faithful as the bond of unity. [PAW]

What Do United Methodists Mean by Salvation?

United Methodists believe that it is the nature of God to bestow His grace in the form of liberations, healings, and reconciliations upon all of His children. This nature of God is revealed and made available to humanity through the birth, life, death, and resurrection of Jesus Christ. As persons respond to the grace of God in Christ through repentance, faith, and going on toward perfection, such persons find themselves in the way of salvation.

Within the way of salvation, the United Methodists believe that the Gospel applies both to individuals and to societies. In their understanding the whole Gospel is both personal and social. This explains why United Methodists will be found cooperating in both evangelistic and social action programs. [PAW]

What Is the United Methodist Practice Concerning Baptism?

Baptism is seen by United Methodists as a recognition of the entrance of a person into the Church of Jesus Christ (the family of God), with such entrance including a symbolic washing of the person through sprinkling, pouring, or immersing that person with or in water.

It is understood that the rite of baptism is the beginning of a process that must be nurtured throughout the person's life within the Christian community. [PAW]

Do Methodists Have to Accept a Creed?

They are not required to sign any formal creed. Those joining the church are asked to answer affirmatively two questions:

"Do you confess Jesus Christ as your Savior and Lord and pledge your allegiance to His Kingdom?"

"Do you receive and profess the Christian faith as contained in the New Testament of Our Lord, Jesus Christ?"

Wesley, the founder, once declared: "I believe the merciful God regards the lives and tempers of men more than their ideas." One of his basic principles was "Think and let think." With its emphasis on life rather than creed, Methodism has been relatively free from heresy trials.

Are Methodists Stricter Than Others in Matters of Personal Conduct, Especially as to Amusements?

Methodists today are about as broad and liberal in their codes of behavior as are other leading Protestants. Methodists traditionally have fought against intemperance, gambling, and licentious indulgence. John Wesley formulated a list of general rules for the members of his societies because he believed they needed concrete standards as well as ideals.

For many years, the church had a provision forbidding diversions such as card playing and dancing. This provision was changed nearly thirty years ago to read, "not taking such diversions as cannot be used in the name of the Lord Jesus."

What Is the Methodist Position on Birth Control?

The General Conference of the Methodist Church has stated: "Parenthood is a Christian privilege and responsibility; and the highest ideals of the Christian family can be achieved when children are wanted, anticipated and welcomed into the home. We believe that planned parenthood practiced in Christian conscience fulfills rather than violates the will of God."

The justifying motive must be unselfish. The children we bring into the world have a right to a wholesome home life. Toward that end, the spacing of children, the health of parents, and adequate economic support are factors to be considered. The Discipline recommends courses of instruction for young married couples on "life adjustments and personality problems."

What Is the Methodist Position on Divorce?

Methodists regret the prevalence of divorce and seek to preserve the marriage bond by every means humanly possible. However, they recognize that situations do arise where the sanctity of individual personality requires the severance of a marital relationship. They hold that those who have been wronged have the right to a second chance.

No Methodist minister should solemnize the marriage of a divorced person whose wife or husband is living and unmarried: but this rule shall not apply (1) to the innocent person, when it is clearly established by competent testimony that the true cause for divorce was adultery or other vicious conditions that, through cruelty or physical peril, invalidated the marriage vow; nor (2) to divorced persons who seek to be reunited in marriage. [RWS]

The following is taken from the 1968 Book of Discipline:

Divorce—Since marriage is of divine appointment and the union of one man and one woman entered into mutually, it is sacred and morally binding so long as both shall live and ought not be dissolved at will. When human failure results in placing the marriage in jeopardy, the Church strongly urges the persons involved to seek counsel with their minister in order to effect reconciliation so that the marriage may be preserved. *The Church does not sanction nor condone divorce except on the ground of adultery.* [Italics added—LR]

Ministers of the Church shall not solemnize any marriage without first counseling earnestly with the couple. Whenever divorced persons seek marriage through the Church, ministers may solemnize such marriages *only* after having ascertained the circumstances through counsel with those persons involved, and after they are satisfied that the divorced persons have sought for and received forgiveness and are seeking a genuine Christian relationship not only in marriage but with God. Ministers may, if it seems desirable, consult with fellow ministers and/or local church officials. [PAW]

What Distinguishes Methodists from Other Protestant Denominations?

It is difficult to say, because modern practices and the growing spirit of church unity tend to draw the leading Protestant denominations ever closer together.

The Methodist Church retains, in general, the theology of the Anglican Church, from which it sprang. Some Methodist parishes preserve much of the Protestant Episcopal liturgy. On the other hand, in some Methodist churches, the services of worship are very informal. Within the 40,000 American Methodist churches, there is probably as wide variation in types of thought and worship as there is between Methodists, Presbyterians, Congregationalists, and others.

Of course, Methodists do have some differences from the other branches of the Protestant church. For instance, the Protestant Episcopal Church believes that divine grace is imparted through apostolic succession. Methodists do not hold to this doctrine. Hence, a Methodist minister cannot administer the sacraments in an Episcopal church. And the confirmation of members in the Methodist Church is an office not limited to bishops, as in the Protestant Episcopal Church, but can be given by all ordained ministers.

Also, the Methodist Church differs from the Baptist and some others in the matter of baptism. Not only do Methodists believe in infant baptism, which the Baptists do not, but also they baptize usually by sprinkling rather than by immersion. Other differences might be cited if space permitted consideration of the various denominations.

The two most marked Methodist emphases are the inner experience of religion and the social applications of conscience. John Wesley stressed "the witness of the spirit," "an inward impression on the soul whereby the spirit of God immediately and directly witnesses to my spirit that I am a child of God . . . that all my sins are blotted out and I am reconciled to God." Holding this emphasis, Methodism has made much of conversion, revivals, and testimonies of religious experience.

The Methodist social conscience has kept the church in the forefront of reform movements, such as the improvement of labor conditions, the inculcation of temperance, and the abolition of war. In the number of missions, hospitals, and colleges, Methodism leads in Protestantism.

The Methodist Church also emphasizes the democratic principle in its organization and government. Laymen are increasingly given leadership in the church councils. [RWS]

Some of the distinctive marks of the United Methodist Church are:

1. Strong tendencies toward catholicity through positions like John Wesley's insistence: "The world is my parish."
2. Seeking the truth of the faith in Scripture, tradition, experience, and reason.
3. Trying to hold within its life both the unity and the diversity of the church, while seeking to project the wholeness of the Gospel.
4. A strongly "connectional" form, which is both vertical and horizontal in its connectionalism. [PAW]

What Is the Position of Your Church on Black People?

About 4 percent of the members of the United Methodist Church are black, but blacks are not the only minority group of the church. Continuing efforts are being made within this church to give minority groups both voice and decision-making power within the life of the denomination.

The House of God must be open to the whole family of God. If we discriminate against any persons, we deny the essential nature of the church as a fellowship in Christ.

This message of the 1959 Dallas Conference on Human Relations is quoted (paragraph 2026) in our 1960 Book of Discipline. Further:

With respect to race, the aim of the United Methodist Church is nothing less than an inclusive church in an inclusive society. The United Methodist Church therefore calls upon all its people to perform those faithful deeds of love and justice in both church and community as will bring this aim into full reality.

Our Social Principles, adopted by the 1972 General Conference, includes this statement on racism vis-à-vis all ethnic minorities:

We affirm all persons as equally valuable in the sight of God. We therefore work toward societies in which each person's value is recognized, maintained, and strengthened.
A. Rights of Ethnic Minorities. Racism plagues and cripples our growth in Christ, inasmuch as it is antithetical to the gospel itself. Therefore, we reject racism in every form, and affirm the ultimate and temporal worth of all persons. We rejoice in the gifts which particular ethnic histories and cultures bring to our total life. We commend and encourage the self-awareness of all ethnic minorities and oppressed people which leads them to demand their just and equal rights as members of society. We assert the obligation of society, and groups within the society, to implement compensatory programs that redress long-standing systematic social deprivation of ethnic minorities. We further assert the right of members of ethnic minorities to equal opportunities in employment and promotion; to education and training of the highest quality; to non-discrimination in voting, in access to public accommodations, and in housing purchase or rental; and to positions of leadership and power in all elements of our life together. [PAW]

What Is the United Methodist Attitude to Anti-Semitism?

Religious persecution has been common in the history of civilization. We urge policies and practices that ensure the right of every religious group to exercise its faith free from legal, political, or economic restrictions. In particular, we condemn anti-Semitism in both its overt and its covert forms and assert the right of all religions and their adherents to freedom from legal, economic, and social discrimination. [PAW]

What Is the Status of Women in Your Faith?

Some 54 percent of the members of the United Methodist Church are women, but women have not had 54 percent of the decision-making power of the church.

In the 1970s there are strong movements toward giving women their due place in the administrative and missional life of the church. A commission on the Role and Status of Women is the Church's newest, and one of its most effective, general agencies. [PAW]

Can Women Become Ordained as Ministers?

Yes. [PAW]

What Is the United Methodist Attitude Toward Abortion?

The beginning of life and the ending of life are the God-given boundaries of human existence. While individuals have always had some degree of control over when they would die, they now have the awesome power to determine when and even whether new individuals will be born.

Our belief in the sanctity of unborn human life makes us reluctant to approve abortion. But we are equally bound to respect the sacredness of the life and well-being of the mother, for whom devastating damage may result from an unacceptable pregnancy. In continuity with past Christian teaching, we recognize tragic conflicts of life with life that may justify abortion.

We call all Christians to a searching and prayerful inquiry into the sorts of conditions that may warrant abortion. We support removal of abortion from the criminal code, placing it instead under laws relating to other procedures of medical practice. A decision concerning abortion should be made after thorough and thoughtful consideration by the parties involved, with medical and pastoral counsel. [PAW]

What Is the Position of Your Church on Homosexuality?

We search for a greater understanding of sex and sexual development, and we have called upon our local churches to extend to all persons, including homosexuals, the redemptive life of the church community.

We have also urged local churches to: (1) provide understanding and support to those who face crises in sexual identity; (2) work for the removal of laws that define as a crime acts of sex that are privately committed, by consenting adults—excluding prostitution; (3) work to enact civil rights legislation that prohibits discrimination—in employment or housing or public accommodations—because of a person's sexual orientation.

We strongly affirm that this deep concern for civil rights does not relieve the church, on all levels, from teaching Christian values, behavior, and attitudes to sex.

The Social Principles adopted at our General Conference in 1972 contains this passage:

We reject all sexual expressions which damage or destroy the humanity God has given us as birthright, and we affirm only that sexual expression which enhances that same humanity, in the midst of diverse opinion as to what constitutes that enhancement. Homosexuals no less than heterosexuals are persons of sacred worth, who need the ministry and guidance of the church in their struggles for human fulfillment, as well as the spiritual and emotional care of a fellowship which enables reconciling relationships with God, with others and with self. Further we insist that all persons are entitled to have their human and civil rights insured, though we do not condone the practice of homosexuality and consider this practice incompatible with Christian teaching. [PAW]

How Do United Methodists "Theologize"?

The 1972 General Conference of this church adopted a significant, newly worded statement on Doctrine and Doctrinal Standards. The conference agreed that Articles of Religion and Confession of Faith "are not to be regarded as positive, juridical norms for doctrine, demanding unqualified assent on pain of excommunication." They are, rather, landmarks in the church's theological journey.

The conference also said: "The recovery and updating of our distinctive doctrinal heritage—'truly Catholic, truly evangelical and truly reformed'—takes on a high priority."

How, then, do United Methodists have their most fruitful, fulfilling theological experiences? By free inquiry within the boundaries of four main, interdependent sources and guidelines: Scripture, tradition, experience, and reason.

The 1972 conference said: "Doctrine and Doctrinal Standards are never an end in themselves, nor even a resting place along the way. They must be a springboard from which we are propelled into creative living and our tasks as agents of reconciliation in the name of the loving God." [PAW]

What About the Social Creed of the United Methodists?

The 1972 General Conference adopted a new and important statement of Social Principles, which embraces the responsibilities of United Methodists in the natural world, the nurturing community, the social community, the economic community, the political community, and the world community. The statement concludes with the following social creed—to be used liturgically:

VII. OUR SOCIAL CREED

We believe in God, the Creator of humanity, the natural world, and society; and in Jesus Christ, the Redeemer of creation. We believe in the Holy Spirit, through whom we receive God's gifts, and we repent of our sin in perverting those gifts to idolatrous ends.

We affirm the natural world as God's handiwork and dedicate ourselves to its preservation, enhancement, and faithful use by mankind.

We joyfully receive, for ourselves and others, the gifts of community, sex, marriage, and the family.

We commit ourselves to the rights of women, children, youth, and the aging; to improvement of the quality of life; and to the rights and dignity of ethnic and religious minorities.

We believe in the right and duty of persons to work for the good of themselves and others, and in the protection of their welfare in so doing; in the rights to property, collective bargaining, and responsible consumption; and in the elimination of economic and social distress.

We dedicate ourselves to peace throughout the world and to the rule of law among nations.

We believe in the present and final triumph of God's Word in human affairs and gladly assume His commission to live the Gospel in the world. Amen. [PAW]

How Is the Methodist Church Governed?

Since British Methodism differs in its organization from that of the American church, we shall speak only of the United States and the main body of Methodists here.

Organized at about the time the United States Constitution was adopted, the Methodist Church parallels rather uniquely the pattern of American government. The executive branch of the church consists of a Council of Bishops, whose members are elected by jurisdictional conferences composed of ministers and laymen. A bishop presides over a geographical "Area" (comprising one or more Annual Conferences); there are forty-four Areas in the United States and sixteen in mission fields abroad. The bishops appoint the ministers of individual parishes.

The legislative power of the Methodist Church is vested in a General Conference, which meets every four years and is composed of both clergy and laymen—in equal numbers. The delegates to the General Conference are democratically elected by annual conferences and on a proportional basis.

The supreme judicial power of the church rests in a Judicial Council, whose members and qualifications are determined by the General Conference of the church.

Is the United Methodist Church Ecumenical?

This church participates, in every way possible, in the World Council of Churches, the World Methodist Council, the Regional Councils of Churches, the National Council of Churches of Christ in the U.S.A., the Consultation on Church Union, and bilateral consultations, including one with the Roman Catholic Church.

This church believes that the fullness of the mind of Christ can be discovered fully only in a common search, in a common acceptance, in a common active acknowledgment, in common Christian love with all those who call upon the one God to whom we desire to remain open. [PAW]

Is This a World Church?

In recent years, many Christian communities that formerly were Methodist mission outposts either have entered into union with churches in their own lands or have become autonomous.

The United Methodist Church does not make decisions either for or with Christians in many parts of the world where once the Methodist Church did. But in a traditional, fellowship sense, the

United Methodist Church is genuinely related to churches in the whole world; and in a constitutional sense, it is one with United Methodist Churches in Africa, Europe, and southern Asia.

Through the World Methodist Council, this church meets Wesleyan Christians from all the world in fellowship and joins with them in evangelism and mission. [PAW]

How Many United Methodists Are There in the United States?

The most recent figures on the number of members of the United Methodist Church is 10,334,521, not including preparatory members.

WHAT IS A MORMON?

**RICHARD L. EVANS / ** Richard L. Evans (1906–1971) was a member
of the Council of Twelve of the Church of Jesus Christ of Latter-day Saints
until his death on November 1, 1971. From 1930 until his passing, he
wrote and narrated the famed CBS broadcast of *Music and the Spoken
Word,* with the Salt Lake Mormon Tabernacle Choir and organ from
Temple Square.

Mr. Evans was born in Salt Lake City. Following three years of church
and editorial work in Europe, he received B.A., M.A., and later LL.D.
degrees from the University of Utah. He was a member of the board of
trustees of Brigham Young University and was director of Temple Square,
Salt Lake City. He was married, the father of four sons, and traveled and
lectured extensively.

For some years Mr. Evans wrote a widely circulated newspaper column
for King Features Syndicate. He was the author of thirteen books, including
Unto the Hills, This Day—and Always, The Spoken Word, and *The Everlasting Things.*

NOTE TO THE READER: For this new edition, Dr. Evans' article
was submitted to the Church of Jesus Christ of Latter-day Saints, for
such changes or corrections as might be thought appropriate.

A few such changes, approved by the First Presidency of the Church,
have been included in this version. Where the text is not that of
Dr. Evans, the initials [TFP] (The First Presidency) identify it.

This article presents the doctrines and practices of the Church of
Jesus Christ of Latter-day Saints, Salt Lake City, Utah, the largest
Mormon body in the world (3,321,556 members in 1974).

The position of other Latter-day Saints bodies should be noted: The
Reorganized Church of Jesus Christ of Latter-day Saints, with headquarters in Independence, Missouri (205,484 members in 1974) claims
to be the legal successor of the church founded by Joseph Smith; it refers
to an Ohio court decision (1880) to substantiate this claim. In 1860, some
sixteen years after Joseph Smith's martyrdom, the son of the founder
became president of the Reorganized Church, which denied the leadership
of Brigham Young and has always condemned polygamy.

The Church of Christ, Temple Lot, with headquarters in Independence,

Missouri (3,000 members in 1956), and several groups with memberships under 2,500 (Cutlerites, Bickertonites, Strangites), hold different views on questions concerning succession to the presidency of the Church, the use of temples, and certain matters of organization and procedure. [LR]

What Is a Mormon?

Strictly speaking, there is no such thing as a Mormon, and there is no Mormon Church. "Mormon" is merely a nickname for a member of the Church of Jesus Christ of Latter-day Saints.

Are Mormons Christians?

Unequivocally yes—both as to the name of the Church and in unqualified acceptance and worship of Jesus the Christ.

Are Mormons Protestants?

No. Joseph Smith (*see below*) never belonged to any other church. He claimed no authority by succession from any other church or sect. He inferred no authority from the Bible. He and his associates testified that they received their authority by direct divine bestowal.

When and How Was the Church of Jesus Christ of Latter-day Saints Founded?

The Latter-day Saint believes that the Gospel of Jesus Christ was proclaimed in the heavens before the world was; that it was on earth anciently, and known to Adam and others; but that mankind has repeatedly departed from it (as in the days of Noah); and that is has had to be "restored" in various "dispensations" (as through Abraham, Moses, and others). He believes that the last such "restoration" occurred in the early nineteenth century, beginning "the dispensation of the fullness of times" (Ephesians 1:10).

In 1820, near Palmyra, in western New York, in a period of religious unrest and "revival," Joseph Smith (then in his fifteenth year) related how (prompted by an impression from reading James 1:5) he retired one morning to a grove near the family farm to petition

the Lord in prayer. What he saw and experienced is recorded in a
widely published pamphlet (*Joseph Smith's Testimony*), including
the appearance of "two Personages, whose brightness and glory
defy all description . . . One of them spake unto me . . . and
said, pointing to the other—'This is my Beloved Son. Hear Him!'"
(*See also* Matthew 3:17 and 17:5.) The declarations that followed
indicated the need for a "restoration" of the Gospel of Jesus Christ
(which many among the religious "reformers" had long recognized).

As a legal entity, the "restored Church" was organized at Fayette,
Seneca County, New York, April 6, 1830. Membership quickly
increased, and so did opposition. The main body first moved to
Ohio, then to Missouri, then to Illinois. After Joseph Smith was
martyred by an armed mob at Carthage, Illinois, in 1844, the Latter-
day Saints moved westward under the leadership of the senior
member of the Twelve Apostles, Brigham Young, into the valley of
the Great Salt Lake (1847), into "a land that nobody wanted."

In each move they made, they left behind them homes and
prosperous farms and other possessions—including Nauvoo (population 20,000), which they had built from a swampland on the
Mississippi and which was then (1846) the largest city in Illinois.

In the two following decades, some 80,000 Mormon pioneers
traversed the thousand miles of plains and Rocky Mountains, from
the Missouri River to the Great Basin. Some rode in wagons; some
pushed all their possessions in handcarts; some walked—and more
than 6,000 died along the way.

It was no passing persuasion that enabled them to do what they
did or that induced them, time after time, to leave what they left.

How Do the Mormons Look Upon Joseph Smith?

They look upon him as one who was commissioned of God to
effect a "restoration" of the Gospel of Jesus Christ and to open a
new Gospel "dispensation." They look upon him as a prophet of
God, in the same literal sense as they look upon other prophets of
the Old and New Testament.

Joseph Smith was born in Sharon, Vermont, in 1805. His progeni-
tors were early New England settlers, the first arriving in 1638. His
forebears fought with the Colonial forces.

Do Mormons Believe in the Holy Trinity?

Yes. The Latter-day Saint accepts the Godhead as three literal, distinct personalities: God the Father; His Son, Jesus the Christ (who is one with the Father in purpose and in thought, but separate from Him in physical fact); and the Holy Ghost, a Personage of spirit (Acts 7:55, etc.). Here, the Mormon points to literal scriptural language. He believes in a loving, understanding Father who made his children "in His own image" (Genesis 1:27), and Jesus His Son is said to be in "the express image of his person" (Hebrews 1:3).

What Do the Mormons Believe About Jesus Christ?

They believe Him to be the Son of God, "the only begotten of the Father" in the flesh. They believe in His atoning sacrifice and literal resurrection. They accept Him as the Savior and Redeemer of mankind. They look to Him as the "one mediator between God and men" (I Timothy 2:5), and pray to the Father in His name. They believe that He will come again and reign on earth (Acts 1:9–11).

Do Mormons Believe in the Virgin Birth?

Yes. The Latter-day Saint accepts the miraculous conception of Jesus the Christ.

What Do Mormons Believe About the Bible?

The Bible is basic to Mormon belief. The King James Version is officially used and is believed "to be the word of God as far as it is translated correctly" (8th Article of Faith).

What Is the Book of Mormon?

The Book of Mormon is not the "Mormon Bible," as is sometimes supposed. It is one of the complementary works that the Mormon accepts as scripture. The Mormon does not believe that the revelations of God were confined to ancient Israel. He does not believe that a loving Father would restrict his communication to one part of His family, to one time of history, or to one land. He believes "all that God has revealed, all that He does now reveal, and . . . that

He will yet reveal many great and important things pertaining to the Kingdom of God" (9th Article of Faith).

The Book of Mormon is part of a record, both sacred and secular, of prophets and peoples who (with supplementary groups) were among the ancestors of the American Indians. It covers principally the peoples of the period from about 600 B.C. to A.D. 421. These peoples were of Asiatic origin, of the House of Israel, and left Jerusalem during the reign of King Zedekiah, eventually to cross the sea to the Western world, where they built great cities and civilizations. Ultimately, they all but destroyed themselves in warring with one another.

They brought with them certain records of the Old Testament. In addition, their historians, statesmen, and prophets kept records of important events of their own civilization, some of which were engraved on gold plates. It was from such plates "preserved by the gift and power of God" that Joseph Smith translated the Book of Mormon (first published in 1830).

The book takes its title from a man whose name was Mormon, who was one of the later prophets of the thousand-year period, and who was not greatly different from the prophets of Old and New Testament times, except that he lived in the Western Hemisphere among some of the Savior's "other sheep" (John 10:16). The Book of Mormon witnesses that Jesus the Christ visited the inhabitants of this hemisphere after His ascension.

What Does the Mormon Believe About Man's Immortality?

Energy, matter, and "intelligence" exist eternally and are indestructible. And man himself has existed from the premortal past and will continue, with his individual identity, into the endless eternal future.

At an appointed time, after the change called death, man will emerge as a resurrected being with a deathless union of spirit and body, literally following the promise and pattern set by the Savior.

Do Mormons Practice Polygamy?

No. For any Church member, the penalty for plural marriage today is excommunication.

Polygamy or plural marriage was at one time practiced by a small part of the Mormon people. Federal laws prohibiting this practice were passed but were questioned by the Church as an unconstitutional infringement of religious liberty. In 1890, after the constitutionality of these laws had been reaffirmed by the Supreme Court of the United States, Wilford Woodruff, then president of the Church, issued a manifesto that, upon acceptance by the Church, proscribed the further practice of polygamy.

Polygamy was practiced at certain periods in Biblical times, righteously and with divine sanction. And those who entered into polygamy in the nineteenth century did so with a conviction that it was also for them so sanctioned. They honored their wives and families.

The practice of polygamy was revoked by the same authority by which it had been sanctioned.

Do Mormons Believe in Baptism? Confirmation? Holy Communion?

As to baptism—yes—by immersion, and by those having authority, according to the pattern set by the Savior, who was baptized by John in the River Jordan. The Mormon believes that the symbolism of being "buried with Him in baptism" (Colossians 2:12) is not found in any other form but by immersion.

The Latter-day Saint does not believe in baptizing infants but only those who have become "accountable" for their actions, at the age of eight years and over. He believes "that men will be punished for their own sins, and not for Adam's transgression" (2nd Article of Faith). Infants are innocent and will not be held accountable here or in heaven for the actions or errors of others, "for of such is the Kingdom of God" (Mark 10:14).

A simple confirmation immediately follows baptism, "by the laying on of hands for the gift of the Holy Ghost."

As to communion: The sacrament of the Lord's Supper is administered in a simple manner. Bread and water are blessed and partaken of by all the congregation "in remembrance" of the Savior and as a witness that "they are willing to keep His commandments."

Do Mormons Believe in Heaven and Hell?

The "heaven" the Mormon looks to and lives for is a real place of eternal progress, with endless association with loved ones, with families and friends. For those who are willfully indifferent to their opportunities on earth, the knowledge that they have fallen short of their highest possible happiness will be part of the penalty of the "hell" of hereafter.

Who Will Be "Saved"?

The Latter-day Saint believes in universal "salvation"—"For as in Adam all die, even so in Christ shall all be made alive. *But every man in his own order* . . ." (I Corinthians 15:22–23.)

The Savior referred to "many mansions" (John 14:2). Paul speaks of the man "caught up to the third heaven" (II Corinthians 12:2), and further observed (I Corinthians 15:40, 41, 42) that there are different "degrees of glory." While "salvation" is universal, "exaltation" (with the highest eternal opportunities) must be earned by obedience to laws, ordinances, and commandments of the Kingdom.

What Is the Mormon Attitude on Liquor and Tobacco?

A code of health and conduct given in 1833 and known as the "Word of Wisdom" disapproves the use of tobacco, alcoholic beverages, and "hot drinks" (specifically tea and coffee). The spirit of the "Word of Wisdom" requires abstinence from all injurious substances and suggests that man should enjoy all the wholesome things of the earth "with prudence and thanksgiving" (Doctrine and Covenants, 89).

Do the Mormons Have Ministers?

Among the Latter-day Saints, there is no "professional" clergy. The Church offers opportunity for participation and responsibility for everyone. Any worthy priesthood holder may be called to be a bishop or to fill any other priesthood office for an unspecified time and without financial compensation. For his livelihood, he would usually continue his lay profession or occupation.

A boy or girl of eight or ten may occupy a pulpit for a short talk. Boys beginning at the age of twelve are ordained to an office in the priesthood. There are organizations within the Church that provide for study, for service, and for the cultural and recreational activities of every man, woman, and child of all ages. All are expected to participate and to perform some service.

The Mormon is proud of his "practical" religion, which takes into account the "wholeness" of man and teaches that "men are that they might have joy" (Book of Mormon, II Nephi 2:25), and touches upon the needs and activities of every day, as well as the hereafter.

What Is the Mormon Concept of Marriage?

The Mormon believes that there can be no heaven for him without his family, and if he fully conforms to the teachings of his Church, he enters into a marriage covenant that lasts not only until "death do us part" but continues "for time and eternity." "Neither is the man without the woman, neither the woman without the man, in the Lord" (I Corinthians 11:11).

Such marriages are performed in Mormon temples. Marriages performed outside of temples, by civil ceremony alone, are not believed to be binding beyond death unless they are later solemnized for "eternity."

Marriages with non-Mormons are contrary to counsel and are not solemnized in the temples.

Do Mormons Permit Divorce?

Divorce is deplored and discouraged. "Temple divorces" (as distinguished from civil divorces) may be granted only by the president of the Church, for serious cause, including infidelity.

What Is the Mormon Attitude Toward Birth Control?

The Church has always advocated the rearing of large families, and birth control, as commonly understood, is contrary to its teachings.

What Is the Position of the Church on Abortion?

The Church is unalterably opposed to all forms of abortion—except in those cases where medical advice dictates that a mother's life would be in jeopardy. [TFP]

What Is the Status of Women in the Church of Jesus Christ of Latter-day Saints?

In the teachings of the Church, women have traditionally held an honored place. Woman's principal role, the Church teaches, is in the home, with the family. The family is the basic unit of the Church and of society. The Church stresses family solidarity, teaching that the family that is properly sealed continues after earth-life.

While a woman's first responsibility is in and to the home, she may hold positions of leadership in the functioning of the Church. For example, the women's organization of the Church, Relief Society (a partnership organization with the Priesthood), is presided over by women.

Women also serve as the sole officers and teachers of the Primary Association of the Church, providing weekday Gospel instruction for children, both boys and girls under twelve years of age. [TFP]

Can Women Be Ordained as Ministers?

Women, on occasions, occupy the pulpit in our Church meetings. In the Church of Jesus Christ of Latter-day Saints, women do not hold the priesthood, but they share its blessings with its bearers. [TFP]

What Is the Attitude of the Mormon Church to Black People?

Blacks are welcomed into Church membership, and their numbers are growing.

The former world leader of the Church of Jesus Christ of Latter-day Saints, President Harold B. Lee, said:

There is no church in the world which offers more to all minorities. Many of our black members are called to positions of trust in the church.

They also participate in certain ordinances in the temple. Faithful church members of all races, including black, have the right to the saving ordinances of the gospel which qualify them for a place in the celestial kingdom after death. [The celestial kingdom is the highest of three degrees of glory, according to doctrine of the Church of Jesus Christ of Latter-day Saints.] Among our black membership are some of our most devoted members and my dearest friends. [TFP]

Can a Black Mormon Be Ordained as a Minister?

Black male members of the Church and many white male members, for various reasons, do not now hold priesthood in our church.

In a message issued by the First Presidency of the Church on December 15, 1969, this statement was made:

From the beginning of this dispensation, Joseph Smith and all succeeding presidents of the church have taught that Negroes, while spirit children of a common Father, and the progeny of our earthly parents, Adam and Eve, were not yet to receive the priesthood for reasons which we believe are known to God, but which He has not made fully known to man.

President Harold B. Lee reaffirmed the statement of his predecessor presidents of the Church that "sometime in God's eternal plan the Negro will be given the right to hold the priesthood."

The Lord directs the affairs of His Church through continuing revelation. To those who do not believe in revelation, there is no satisfactory answer; to those who believe in revelation, there should be no question.

Priesthood, historically, has always been held by only a small minority of people on the earth. The Holy Bible teaches that only one of the twelve tribes of Israel, the tribe of Levi, held the priesthood. There is no suggestion in the Bible, and our Church has never taught, that members of the other eleven tribes were or are "inferior."

On the contrary, the very core of Church doctrine is that all persons in the world are literally spirit sons and daughters of the same Heavenly Father, which makes all men brothers. Those who do not hold the priesthood are as precious in the sight of God as those who do.

A black member of the Mormon Church, Darius Gray, holding a position in the Sunday school presidency in his ward (parish), has said:

I was born black, I am black now, and I will die black. I am proud of my black heritage and I am proud of being a member of the Mormon Church. There is no conflict between the color of my skin and my religion. [TFP]

What Is the Position of the Church on Homosexuality?

The Church strongly opposes premarital sex relations or infidelity after marriage—and homosexuality is viewed as an equally grievous sin with adultery, considered second only to murder in seriousness. [TFP]

What Are Mormon Temples Used For?

All men are welcome to worship in Mormon chapels and meeting places throughout the world. But Mormon temples (of which there are sixteen in use today) are not places of public worship. Temples are used for solemnizing marriages and for other sacred ordinances.

God (who is a God of law and order) has set certain requirements for citizenship in the highest "Kingdom" of the hereafter. But obviously all men have not known the laws and commandments and requirements of the "Kingdom." Yet the Mormon believes that a just God will give to all those who have ever lived an adequate opportunity to hear and accept the Gospel and its required earthly ordinances. In the words of Peter: "For this cause was the gospel preached also to them that are dead . . ." (I Peter 4:6). Thus these essential ordinances—including baptism—are "vicariously" performed in the temples for those who have died without adequate opportunity to receive these ordinances for themselves. Ancient knowledge of this principle and practice is suggested by Paul: ". . . if the dead rise not at all? Why are they then baptized for the dead?" (I Corinthians 15:29).

The principle of doing for others what they cannot do for themselves is not new. The Savior performed a "vicarious" service for all of us (I Peter 3:18).

Do the Mormons Proselyte Other People?

Yes. Missionaries have gone out since the 1830s in an earnest endeavor to carry the message of the "Restoration" "to every nation, and kindred, and tongue, and people" (Revelation 14:6).

This work is done principally by young men about twenty years of age (supplemented by young women and older people also), taken from all walks of life. During their missionary service, they are ordained ministers. They pay their own expenses (assisted by families or friends) and give usually two or more years of their time.

How Is the Church Governed?

The 6th Article of Faith affirms that the offices and organization of the Church of Jesus Christ should follow the plan and pattern set by the Savior: "We believe in the same organization that existed in the Primitive Church, *viz.*, apostles, prophets, pastors, teachers, evangelists, etc.," including high priests, seventies, elders, bishops, priests, and deacons, as named in the New Testament.

The Church has a strong central organization, with a First Presidency of three presiding high priests ("after the order of Melchisedec"—Hebrews 5:10), followed in order by the Council of the Twelve Apostles (with assistants); a Patriarch; the First Council of the Seventy; also a Presiding Bishopric who preside over the Aaronic Priesthood.

Geographically, the Church is divided into "stakes" and "wards" (somewhat resembling the diocese and parishes) and "missions."

How Is the Church Financed?

Principally by tithing—the scriptural tenth (Malachi 3:8–11).

Work, thrift, and industry are taught as the best cure for want. Acceptance of government "dole" or any "unearned" public aid is discouraged. Through the voluntary spare-time labors of men of many occupations and professions, a church welfare program provides means to rehabilitate those in need and to see that no one goes without the necessities of life.

Why Do the Mormons Emphasize Education?

This can best be answered by quoting three significant sentences:
"The glory of God is intelligence, or . . . light and truth" (Doctrine and Covenants 93:36).

"It is impossible for a man to be saved in ignorance" (*Ibid.* 131:6).

"Whatever principle of intelligence we attain unto in this life, it will rise with us in the resurrection" (*Ibid.* 130:18).

Brigham Young said: "Our religion is simply the truth. It is all said in this one expression—it embraces all truth, wherever found in all the works of God and man . . ."

Since the Latter-day Saint believes that the intelligence each man attains will remain forever with him, his search for knowledge, for truth, for light is not only a permissible privilege but also an inescapable obligation.

What Is the Mormon Philosophy of Freedom?

When Joseph Smith was asked how he governed his people, he replied: ". . . teach them correct principles, and let them govern themselves."

The Mormon loves freedom as he loves life. He believes that there is no principle more basic to the Gospel of Jesus Christ than the God-given free agency of every man. He believes that a war in heaven was fought for freedom; that the right of choice is essential to the soul's salvation; and that anyone who seeks to enslave men in any sense is essentially in league with Satan himself.

Further, as to freedom, he cites these Articles of Faith:

We claim the privilege of worshiping almighty God according to the dictates of our own conscience, and allow all men the same privilege, let them worship how, where, or what they may.

We believe in being honest, true, chaste, benevolent, virtuous, and in doing good to all men. . . . If there is anything virtuous, lovely or of good report or praiseworthy, we seek after these things.

With these convictions, the Mormon stands willing to leave all things and all men in the hands of a just Judge and loving Father.

Do Mormons Believe There Is Conflict Between Science and Religion?

To the Latter-day Saint, truth is an eternal whole, and if there are seeming discrepancies between science and religion, it is simply because men do not know enough. And where there is doubt and controversy, the Mormon feels that he can afford to wait for final answers—for truth and intelligence and life are everlasting.

How Many Mormons Are There?

The Church of Jesus Christ of Latter-day Saints (with head-quarters in Salt Lake City, Utah) numbers 3,321,556 (January 1, 1974), with some 6,856 congregations throughout the world. There are also some schismatic groups with historical and doctrinal differences. The Reorganized Church of Jesus Christ of Latter-day Saints, Independence, Missouri, numbers 200,113 (January 1, 1970).

WHAT IS A PRESBYTERIAN?

JOHN S. BONNELL / John Sutherland Bonnell is minister emeritus of the Fifth Avenue Presbyterian Church. In January 1962 he resigned as senior minister, after more than twenty-six years of service. After his retirement, he served for three years as president of the New York Theological Seminary.

Mr. Bonnell was born on Prince Edward Island, Canada, in 1893. He received his B.A. degree from Dalhousie University, Halifax, Nova Scotia, and his B.D. degree from Pine Hill Divinity Hall in the same city. He was ordained in 1922 and served as minister of Saint Andrew's Presbyterian Church, Saint John, N.B., and Westminster United Church, Winnipeg, Manitoba. In 1927 he undertook postgraduate studies in London, England, and New York City. He has since received nine honorary doctorates.

Mr. Bonnell served in World War I with the Canadian Artillery in France. He was twice wounded. In World War II, he lectured extensively in military camps on psychology and religion, and counseled with chaplains and military personnel.

Mr. Bonnell has traveled widely in Europe and the Soviet Union. For his wartime mission to Britain in 1941, he was awarded the King's Medal for Service in the Cause of Freedom.

For twenty-three years, while minister of the Fifth Avenue Presbyterian Church, Mr. Bonnell conducted coast-to-coast radio programs, among which was the well-known *National Vespers*.

He is the author of thirteen books including *Pastoral Psychiatry*, *Psychology for Pastor and People*, *I Believe in Immortality*, and his most recent work, *Presidential Profiles*.

What Is a Presbyterian?

A Presbyterian is a Protestant who belongs to a particular form of church government. The word "Presbyterian" refers not to a special system of doctrine or worship but to a representative form of church government. In Greek, *presbyteros* means "elder."

The Presbyterian Church is governed by elders: teaching elders, who are ordained ministers or pastors, and ruling elders elected from the ranks of the Church. In each congregation these elders, with a minister at their head as moderator, form the session with supreme authority in all spiritual matters in the local church.

There are two additional boards in each congregation: the deacons have responsibility for distributing charity and in some congregations other duties have been allocated to them, and the trustees hold the property for the congregation and are entrusted with its upkeep. They are also charged with responsibility for the finances of the church. In some Presbyterian churches the responsibilities of the board of trustees are performed by the board of deacons.

What Is the Basis of the Presbyterian Creed?

In 1643 the Parliament of England appointed 151 laymen, clergymen, and church scholars to draw up a system of Reformation doctrine and government. They labored for six years, holding 1,163 sessions, and produced among other important theological works the Westminster Confession of Faith, which is recognized as the creed of English-speaking Presbyterians.

Most Presbyterians accept also the creeds of the early undivided Christian Church—the Nicene and the Apostles' Creeds.

What Do Presbyterians Believe About the Bible?

Presbyterians believe that the Scriptures of the Old and New Testaments are the Word of God and "the only infallible rule of faith and practice" and that they are the source of those truths by which men live. They believe in the "inspiration" of the Scriptures: that God spoke through men whose minds and hearts He had touched. They therefore emphasize inspired men, not inspired words.

Most Presbyterians have rejected the view of inspiration, held by pre-Christian pagan writers, that the personalities of inspired men were "possessed" or entranced by a spirit so that they became "pens of God" or wrote down what Deity had dictated. Rather they believe that God employed the personalities of chosen men in making His Divine revelation.

Presbyterians do not equate tradition with the Bible. Tradition plays a decidedly inferior role in Presbyterian thinking.

Do Presbyterians Believe in Heaven and Hell?

Yes. The Bible and human experience teach that we are living in a moral universe where sin carries its own appropriate penalty and righteousness its own reward, including the vision of God. The New Testament emphasizes the dread nature of the punishment that sin inevitably incurs, the severest of which is separation from God.

It is understandable that men should think of the spiritual world in material terms: heaven as streets of gold and gates of pearl. Similarly, hell has been pictured in such material imagery as fire and brimstone. While these are symbols, it must not be forgotten that they represent a spiritual reality.

All thoughtful Christians will, however, reject as immoral and un-Christian the teaching once proclaimed that the bliss of the redeemed will be heightened by watching the sufferings of the damned.

Heaven and hell are not only places; they are also states of mind and character. They have their commencement in the here and now. An utterly selfish, godless man could find no happiness in the Christian heaven because he carries hell in his heart.

What Sacraments Do Presbyterians Observe?

Only two: Holy Communion (the Lord's Supper) and baptism. With the vast majority of Protestants, Presbyterians believe that Jesus instituted only these two sacraments.

Do Presbyterians Believe That Christ Is Physically Present in the Sacrament of Holy Communion?

No. Presbyterians believe that Christ is *spiritually* present in the Lord's Supper. Presbyterians do not believe that Christ is offered up in the sacrament to the Father or that any real sacrifice is made. The sacrament is a *commemoration* of the sacrifice of Christ once offered for all men.

The Westminster Confession of Faith expresses the doctrine in this way: "Worthy receivers outwardly partaking of the visible elements of this sacrament do then inwardly by faith, really and indeed, yet not carnally and corporally, but spiritually receive and feed upon Christ crucified, and all the benefits of His death, the body and blood of Christ . . . really but spiritually present to the faith of believers . . ."

Do Presbyterians Believe That Baptism Is Necessary to Salvation?

No. Presbyterians believe that Christ is *spiritually* present in the water on the person, as a holy sign or seal of the Covenant of Grace—an outward symbol of inward regeneration.

While baptism is urgently recommended in the Presbyterian Church, and while its omission is regarded as a grave fault, it is not held to be necessary for salvation. The Confession of Faith declares: "Grace and salvation are not so inseparably annexed unto it that no person can be regenerated or saved without it."

Do Presbyterians Baptize Children?

Yes—to signify that they, too, are received as members of the Church and are in union with Christ. When these children have reached the age of discretion, they will assume the obligation taken on their behalf by their parents.

Presbyterians do not believe that children dying without baptism are excluded from the bliss of heaven or the vision of God.

Do Presbyterians Believe That Jesus Christ Is the Son of God?

Yes. This belief is central in Presbyterian doctrine, which teaches that Jesus Christ, the Eternal Son of God, for us and for our salvation became man. Therefore, He is true God and true man: at once the Revealer of God and the Savior of men.

Do Presbyterians Believe in the Trinity?

Yes. The Trinity is frequently invoked in worship, at every baptism, and in the benediction at the close of each service. When God is spoken of as three Persons—Father, Son, and Holy Spirit—Presbyterians do not think of Him as three individuals. That is tritheism. One God reveals Himself in three manifestations.

The word "Persons" used of the Godhead is employed in the same sense as "persona." It signifies a character or a representation. Various analogies have been employed by theologians to explain this doctrine but most Presbyterians accept it by faith.

Do Presbyterians Accept the Virgin Birth?

Yes. A majority of Presbyterians undoubtedly believe that the entrance of Jesus into our world was by a miraculous birth as related by Saint Matthew and Saint Luke. This doctrine is set forth in the Apostles' Creed, the Westminster Confession of Faith, and the Doctrinal Statement of the Basis of Union of Presbyterian Churches. All Presbyterians believe in the Incarnation—that God was made flesh and came to man in Jesus Christ.

Some find a symbolic rather than a physical meaning in the accounts of the birth of Jesus. They base their views on the contention that the physical details of His birth were not taught by Paul or Jesus Himself.

Presbyterians honor and revere Mary as the Mother of our Lord. But they reject the traditions that have grown up through the centuries concerning her. These have resulted in such dogmas as the Immaculate Conception and the Assumption, which, Presbyterians hold, have no foundation in the Scriptures.

Do Presbyterians Employ the Confessional?

Not in the same sense as Roman Catholics or High Church Episcopalians. Believing in "the priesthood of all believers," Presbyterians make their confession directly to God—without a human intermediary.

The great increase of spiritual counseling has taught Presbyterians that confession is sometimes more searching and thoroughgoing when it is made to God in the presence of a pastor. Such confession is voluntary, never compulsory; and the confession is made to God, not the pastor.

What Do Presbyterians Believe About Salvation?

They believe that salvation is not earned by good works but is the gift of God. Good works are the *fruits* of salvation, evidence that we are growing in grace and in the knowledge of Christ.

Presbyterians believe that salvation is found only through a complete commitment and surrender to God as He is revealed in Christ. God pardons our sins and accepts us, not for any merit of our own but because of our faith in the perfect obedience of Christ and His sacrificial death.

Forgiveness, grace, and salvation are obtained through a direct personal relationship to God—without the mediation of ministers or priests. Presbyterians accept the New Testament witness: "For there is one God, and one mediator between God and men, the man Christ Jesus."

Do Presbyterians Believe in the Resurrection?

Yes. With a few exceptions, Presbyterians do not interpret the phrase in the Apostles' Creed "the resurrection of the body" as meaning the *physical* body. Saint Paul writes: "Flesh and blood cannot inherit the kingdom of God; neither doth corruption inherit incorruption." They understand "the resurrection of the body" as a reference to the *spiritual* body of the resurrection. Paul writes: "It is sown a natural body; it is raised a spiritual body" (I Corinthians 15:44).

Presbyterians believe in the Resurrection of Jesus Christ. Our Lord's sinless body did not see corruption. It was transformed into a spiritual body. Saint John in his Gospel suggests that the resurrected body of Jesus for evidential purposes retained certain physical properties.

According to the New Testament and especially Saint Paul, man's body, unlike that of Jesus, will experience corruption. But the body of believers will be transformed into a spiritual body that will be the body of the resurrection.

Do Presbyterians Employ Symbolism in Worship?

Yes. There was a time when Presbyterian churches were largely devoid of religious symbols and noted for their austere appearance. This was due to the desire of Scottish reformers to avoid everything that might suggest the veneration of religious objects and relics. Such practices were regarded as idolatrous.

The descendants of these reformers, however, came to see that a legitimate use may be made of symbolism in worship and that holiness and beauty are not contradictory, that there is indeed a "beauty of holiness." This change of emphasis brought a return to Gothic architecture, the construction of chancels, the use of organs and choirs, and the employment of candelabra and the cross.

When a cross is used as a religious symbol in Presbyterian churches, it is the cross of the Resurrection—the empty cross—symbolizing the risen, victorious Christ. The crucifix is never employed.

Can Presbyterians Alter Their Confession of Faith?

Yes. Presbyterians, believing the promise that God's Holy Spirit will lead us constantly into larger truth, have never adopted a slavish attitude toward the Westminster Confession of Faith. While ministers, ruling elders, and deacons at their ordination are required to "sincerely receive and adopt the Confession of Faith as containing the system of doctrine taught in the Holy Scriptures," the Presbyterian Church, both in Scotland and in America, has constantly maintained its right to say in what sense the declarations of this Confession are to be understood.

The Presbyterian Church of the United States, the United Presbyterian Church of North America, and the Presbyterian Church in the United States of America have all from time to time amended the Confession of Faith or adopted Declaratory Statements as "permissible and legitimate interpretations" of the doctrines set forth in this Confession. Such statements have been adopted by the United Presbyterian Church, U.S.A., in recent years.

Do Presbyterians Believe in Predestination?

Presbyterians believe that God alone determines man's salvation. Salvation is not a human achievement.

The wording of the Westminster Confession leads some to believe that predestination deprived man of all freedom of choice—that his fate was "sealed" at birth. But the Declaratory Statement adopted by the Presbyterian Church in the United States in 1903 states: "Men are fully responsible for their treatment of God's gracious offer [of salvation] and . . . no man is hindered from accepting it and . . . no man is condemned except on the ground of his sin."

Do Presbyterians Permit Divorced Persons to Remarry?

Yes, but with important safeguards. Divorce is permitted to the innocent party on Scriptural grounds (adultery) and such innocent party may remarry. It is also permitted in case of "such willful desertion as can in no way be remedied by the Church or civil magistrate."

In other circumstances if the Presbyterian minister is in doubt as to what ought to be done to avoid injustice, he may consult his Presbytery's Committee on Divorce.

Presbyterian churches are seeking to curb divorce by a more careful examination of persons presenting themselves for marriage and by organizing groups of young people in "Preparation for Marriage" classes.

Does the Presbyterian Church Forbid Birth Control?

The Presbyterian Church does not legislate for its people on personal moral issues.

Nothing in the Church's teaching, however, can be construed as forbidding an intelligent, conservative, and unselfish employment of birth control. The commandment of God to our first parents, "Be fruitful and multiply," was given at a time when the world was underpopulated. Presbyterians do not believe this precept is relevant today when overpopulation in many areas produces hunger and disease.

Who Was the Founder of Presbyterianism?

John Calvin, who broke with the Church of Rome at the age of twenty-four, did more than any other man to set forth the principles upon which modern Presbyterianism is built. But it is questionable whether the term "founder" is appropriate.

Calvin summoned Christians to return to a form of government which was prevalent in the first century A.D. John Knox, during his exile from Britain, lived in Geneva, where he studied Calvin's teaching. Knox was the most powerful single force in establishing Presbyterianism in Scotland, where it is the dominant creed.

Do Presbyterians Believe That Theirs is the Only Form of Church Government Authorized by the New Testament?

No. While they find ample evidence in the Gospels and the Epistles of their type of government, Presbyterians believe that church polity varied from place to place and time to time.

Presbyterians, in agreement with many able New Testament scholars, believe that no Christian church today can claim exclusive possession of a system of church government authorized by Christ.

After the second century A.D., the bishop came to be the chief official of the Church, supplanting the authority of the elders. This new development gave rise to an autocratic form of church government that in the Middle Ages became corrupt, making inevitable the Protestant Reformation.

What Is the Presbyterian Attitude Toward Education?

From the time of John Calvin, the denomination has always stressed the importance of education for the laity as well as the ministry.

In Scotland, from John Knox to this day, the public schoolhouse has stood beside the kirk. On the mantelpiece of many a crofter's tiny home in the highlands of Scotland, where Presbyterianism is deeply rooted, may be seen the pictures of a son or daughter in academic robes.

The fact that the Presbyterian Church has always put the Bible into the hands of its people, printed in their mother tongue, has been a powerful incentive to public education and has raised the standard of literacy in Scotland.

How Is the Presbyterian Church Governed?

The Presbyterian system of church government is itself a representative democracy. The people govern the Church through elected representatives.

The layman has a prominent role in the Presbyterian Church. All property is vested in laymen—not in ministers or bishops.

In the larger courts of the Church, the vote of every minister is balanced by the vote of a layman. Laymen are eligible for the highest office (moderator) in each court.

What Are the Courts of the Presbyterian Church?

There are four: the Session, with which we have already dealt; the Presbytery; the Synod; the General Assembly. Each has its own function.

The Presbytery, made up of ministers and elders, has oversight of all congregations within its prescribed area. The Synod is composed of ministers and representative elders from congregations within a specified number of Presbyteries. The General Assembly is the court of final appeal. It is representative of the whole Church and is attended by delegates—ministers and elders—from all the Presbyteries. An equal number of elders and ministers are appointed as delegates to the three highest courts of Presbyterianism.

How Many Presbyterians Are There Throughout the World?

Only an approximate answer can be given to this question. There is general agreement, however, that Presbyterians—in the broadest sense—number more than 20 million, constituting one of the largest and most influential Protestant groups in the world.

We know that Presbyterian churches are found even behind the Iron Curtain. There are, for instance, more than 2 million Presbyterians in communist Hungary, 600,000 in Rumania, and between one-third and one-half million in Czechoslovakia. In the United States there are over 4 million communicant members of Presbyterian churches. The Presbyterian form of church government is strong in the Netherlands, and by far the greater part of the population of Scotland is affiliated with the Presbyterian Church.

What Role Did Presbyterians Play in the Establishment of American Democracy?

So great was the participation of Presbyterians in the Revolutionary War that it was described in the British House of Commons as this "Presbyterian rebellion." A historian writing in the *Encyclopaedia Britannica* says: "The Presbyterians exerted a great influence in the construction of the Constitution of the United States, and the government of the Church was assimilated in no slight degree to the civil government of the country."

Presbyterians are proud of the fact that the Reverend John Witherspoon was the only clergyman who signed the Declaration of Independence. At least thirteen other signers of this historic document can be identified as Presbyterians.

Having suffered greatly from persecution in the Old World, Presbyterians had an immense fear of political and religious oppression in the New. The words of John Knox to Mary, Queen of Scots, the Roman Catholic sovereign of Scotland, were frequently quoted during the Revolutionary War in America: "If princes exceed their bounds, Madam, they may be resisted and even deposed."

What Is the Status of Women in Your Church?

Women of all races in the United Presbyterian Church have full membership rights and privileges with respect to office bearing, including ordination to the ministry and offices in the local church and higher governing bodies.

Can Women Be Ordained as Ministers?

There are 185 ordained women Presbyterian ministers.

What Is the Position of Your Church on Black People?

Black people in the United Presbyterian Church have full membership rights and privileges with respect to office bearing, including ordination to the ministry and positions in local church and higher governing bodies.*

What Is the Position of Your Church on Abortion?

"Women should have full freedom of personal choice concerning the completion or termination of their pregnancies and . . . the

---

* In June 1974, the Reverend Dr. Lawrence W. Bottoms, a black, was elected a moderator of the Presbyterian Church in the United States. [LR]

artificial or induced termination of pregnancies therefore should not be restricted by law, except that it be performed under the direction and control of properly licensed physicians." (Excerpted from the statement on "Freedom of Personal Choice in Problem Pregnancies" adopted by the 184th General Assembly, 1972.)

What Is the Position of Your Church on Homosexuality?

We, the 182nd General Assembly (1970), reaffirm our adherence to the moral law of God as revealed in the Old and New Testaments, that adultery, prostitution, fornication and/or the practice of homosexuality is sin. We further affirm our belief in the extension Jesus gave to the law, that the attitude of lust in a man's heart is likewise sin. Also, we affirm that any self-righteous attitude of others who would condemn persons who have so sinned is also sin. The widespread presence of the practice of these sins gives credence to the Biblical view that men have a fallen nature and are in need of the reconciliating work of Jesus Christ which is adequate for all the sins of men. [Minutes, 1970, Part 1, Journal, page 889.]

In determining the attitude of the United Presbyterian Church, U.S.A., on the subject of homosexuality, it is important to note that the above resolution was not a part of the original paper on "Sexuality and the Human Community" (presented to the Assembly after prolonged study), but was proposed from the floor of the Assembly in the form of an amendment. It passed by a small majority: 356 affirmative, 347 negative.

In "Sexuality and the Human Community" we read: "Since the state of knowledge about homosexuality is far from fully developed in our society, we urge the Church to support further and more adequate research into this phase of human sexual behavior and to participate actively in the theological and ethical reflection on the matter which may be prompted by the insights resulting from such research."

Thus it will be seen that the United Presbyterian Church of the U.S.A. has not adopted a rigid and inflexible position with respect to homosexuality but is earnestly seeking to know the will of God and the duty of man in regard to the whole realm of human sexuality.

What Is the Membership of the United Presbyterian Church?

The membership of the United Presbyterian Church of the U.S.A., as reported to the 1974 General Assembly, is 2,817,052 persons. This is 99,705 less than reported to the General Assembly of 1973.

Is the United Presbyterian Church Ecumenically Inclined?

Yes. It has held negotiations with several large Protestant bodies, including the Protestant Episcopal Church. The 186th General Assembly of the United Presbyterian Church in 1974 voted enthusiastically for a Church-wide study to be made of the Second Draft Plan for Union with the Presbyterian Church in the United States, commonly called "The Southern Presbyterian Church," which came into being during the Civil War and is the second largest Presbyterian Church in the United States.

No formal steps toward union are likely to be taken before 1976.

WHAT IS A QUAKER?*

NOTE TO THE READER: The original article, by the late Richmond P. Miller, was intended by him to be representative of the so-called "liberal" branch of Quakerism. It was therefore subject to certain criticisms by the "conservative," "evangelical," and "independent" groups, even though he made no attempt to speak for those groups.

To provide updating and another viewpoint on the broad front of the beliefs and practices of the Religious Society of Friends, material has kindly been supplied by R. W. Tucker. He was asked to undertake this task by the Friends General Conference in Philadelphia, partly because he does not share that body's prevailing viewpoint.

Readers will find lively points of difference between the answers of Friends Miller and Tucker on certain critical points. The differences, of course, reflect schisms and controversy—over practices, "activism," creed, goals—which are by no means limited to Friends. No part of contemporary society seems exempt from vigorous challenge and debate.

Text by the late Richmond P. Miller is identified by his initials: [RPM]. New text by R. W. Tucker is identified by his initials: [RWT].

**RICHMOND P. MILLER / ** Richmond P. Miller was for many years Secretary of the Central Philadelphia Monthly Meeting, and of the Philadelphia Yearly Meeting of the Religious Society of Friends. He was a vice-president of the Historical Society of Pennsylvania and president of the Friends Social Union. An active officer of the Greater Philadelphia Council of Churches, he also served on the boards of the National Council of Churches and the World Council of Churches.

Mr. Miller was born in Reading, Pennsylvania, and studied at Swarthmore College, Harvard College, and Woodbrooke Graduate School (England). He was a member of the faculty of Swarthmore College and was director of Religious Interests at the George School. He was a fellow of the National Council on Religion in Higher Education and a member of many Quaker boards and committees, including the American Friends Service Committee and the Friends Committee on National Legislation.

As secretary of the Friends William Penn Committee, Mr. Miller visited many Friends centers abroad. In 1952, he was a leader of the Friends

---

* "Quaker" is the common name for a member of the Religious Society of Friends.

214 / RELIGIONS OF AMERICA

World Conference at Oxford, which commemorated the 300th anniversary of the founding of the Quaker movement.

His writings appeared in numerous magazines, newspapers, and anthologies, and he was the editor of *The Quaker Persuasion*. He wrote *The Messenger* magazine for the Philadelphia Yearly Meeting of Friends. He died in 1972.

R. W. TUCKER / Rob Tucker is a member of the historic Arch Street Friends Meeting in Philadelphia and of its Preparative Meeting on Worship and Ministry.

He is a graduate of Harvard College and describes himself as a "Quaker polemicist." He is best known outside of Quaker circles for his political writings. One major essay, "Revolutionary Faithfulness," has been anthologized several times. Among Friends he is known as a controversial writer and speaker.

Friend Tucker is a member of the steering committee of the Quaker Theological Discussion Group and of its quarterly journal, *Quaker Religious Thought*. This keeps him in touch with Friends of all varieties and with counterpart Mennonite and Brethren groups.

Besides occasional "agitational" work (he devoted 1957–1961 to writing and debating on behalf of socialized medicine, in the employ of Norman Thomas), Rob Tucker has been a magazine editor and lexicographer. He is now a schoolmaster and reading specialist.

What Is a Quaker?

A Quaker is a member of the Religious Society of Friends, a worldwide fellowship of those who believe that there is "that of God in everyone."

Quakers hold that the worship of God is the primary purpose of the religious life. For non-Friends, this is accomplished by receiving sacraments, performing rituals, listening to sermons, reading from the Scriptures, singing sacred music. For Friends, group worship is a fellowship of the spirit—based on silent communion without any program, yet resulting in vocal prayer, "witness," testimony or exhortation.

Quakers believe that God speaks to all men and women through the still, small inner voice. This was true not only in the past; God speaks also in the present; his revelation is continuing. That is the Quaker contribution to religious experience. [RPM]

Corporate worship is enormously precious; but it is *not* the "primary purpose of the religious life," in the view of many Friends. Such a statement borders on "sensationalism"—i.e., that what religion is all about is feeling good.

The primary purpose of the religious life, of life in general, and of human history itself, is hearing and obeying the Lord, after the model of the relation of the original disciples to Jesus. For the community of discipleship, it is the task of conforming the entire world (starting with its own members) to the mind of Christ. God has a purpose in gathering people together into visible fellowship, and that purpose is to bring the entire world under his dominion.

The answer to "What is a Quaker?" is, therefore, "Somebody who has transferred his allegiance from the kingdoms of this world to the Lamb's Kingdom and has enlisted in the Lamb's War against the many dissents and treasons from God's dominion." Friends, so understood, are not dissenters, but loyalists. [RWT]

What Does "Quaker" Mean?

"Quaker" was the nickname given to the followers of George Fox in seventeenth-century England when, at a magistrate's trial in Derby, he told the magistrate to tremble at the word of God. Early Quakers called themselves "Children of the Light" and "Friends in the Truth." [RPM]

There are several explanations of the origin of the word "Quaker," none of them definitive. It was a term of contempt. Friends finally adopted it themselves, informally, because "Quakerism" was the only alternative to the word "Truth"—which had been used, until modern sensibilities made it seem unacceptable.

Early Friends insisted that they had been "Seekers" but now were "Finders."

"Friends" and "Religious Society of Friends" is, of course, a reference to John 15:6–16. [RWT]

How Did the Quaker Movement Begin?

A schoolboy once wrote: "The Quakers are a peculiar people invented by Oliver Cromwell. They are a quiet people, do not fight, and never answer back. My father is a Quaker. My mother is not!" This is amusing but not true.

Quakerism sprang up in England's Lake District during the turbulent seventeenth century. It spread quickly after 1652. There were several sects, which protested against the religious hierarchy, the domination of the church by the state, excessive formalism in religious doctrine, and elaborate rituals in religious ceremonies. Friends suffered imprisonment, mob violence, loss of property, and severe persecution. (In Massachusetts, they were banished or put to death.) Yet all this only fired them into a remarkable band of "publishers of Truth." It was a heroic period similar to the days of early Christian persecution by the Romans.

The great American philosopher William James wrote:

The Quaker religion which George Fox founded is something which it is impossible to overpraise. In a day of shams, it was a religion of veracity rooted in spiritual inwardness, and a return to something more like the original gospel truth than men had ever known in England. So far as our Christian sects today are evolving, they are simply reverting in essence to the position which Fox and the early Quakers so long ago assumed. [RPM]

Quakerism arose in England and America about 1650, was persecuted bitterly, responded zealously, thrived and spread, largely sank back into respectability, and today is a world-wide communion.

Friends have always justified their differing interpretations of Quaker identity with differing interpretations of Quaker origins. In recent years, scholars of Quakerism from all branches have reached consensus on a "Reconstructionist view" of what Quakerism originally was. At the moment, there is a gap between the understanding shared by most Friends and the understanding of scholars.

Reconstructionist scholarship essentially confirms the conservative view that Quakerism was a new, prophetic outburst that owed few debts to prior religious movements. Older views, relating Quaker origins to the radical Puritan reformation (or to the centuries of Christian "mystical" offshoots on the European continent) have been rejected.

One-by-one study of the very earliest Friends (where they came from, geographically and socially) shows that Quakerism arose first in the most backward and feudal part of northern England, the area cruelly repressed a century earlier, following the "Pilgrimage of Grace." In 1650, the Reformation had not significantly reached that area. George Fox and his companions had only minimal contact with Puritanism, and indeed were most successful where Puritanism was weakest. They had known Anglicanism only in its poorest form, for they came from the area where incompetent Anglican priests were deliberately sent to be "out of the way."

Quakerism was entirely spontaneous where it first arose, and it *was* the Reformation.

Early Friends gathered their following among the dissidents of the Puritan left—"Seeker" groups in England and the followers of Anne Hutchinson in Rhode Island. They moved into head-on, bitter confrontation with Puritanism, although they adopted much Puritan vocabulary for religious discourse. All this happened so rapidly as to obscure the independence of their origins.

Very soon the Friends also made contact with dissident grouplets on the continent of Europe, at first by recruiting them. Through this route, "Quietism" came to influence Quakerism after 1700.

The second generation of Friends, seeking respectability, repressed some records, such as George Fox's *Book of Miracles,* and freely expurgated many early documents. It has taken a great deal of scholarly work to undo the Puritan and Mystical theories of Quaker origins and to see early Quakerism in its own frame of reference.

Are There Sects in American Quakerism That Vary in Their Belief and Forms of Worship?

Yes. The variety of beliefs and forms of worship can bewilder the inquirer. American Quakerism suffered a series of schisms over issues of Quaker identity, starting in the 1820s. Both the vitality and the numbers of Quakers declined for over a century.

A reunion movement gained momentum in the 1930s. Today, "reunionism" may be called the chief influence within Quakerism.

The reunions did not resolve ancient differences. They are organizational ("Let's all live together anyway") or political ("We can agree on social ethics, if not on our reasons for a given opinion") and/or liturgical ("We agree on the form of worship on the basis of silence, though not on what we are worshiping, nor why, nor to what end").

The chief effects of reunionism are:

1. A slow rise in silent-Meeting membership over the past forty years, with a growing edge, first in college towns, then in related second-wave new Meetings within upper-income suburbs
2. Organizationalism, politicization, and liturgicalism as increasingly important in Quaker self-understanding
3. Dialogue between Friends of different viewpoints and the emergence of scholarly consensus on a "reconstructionist" view of what Quakerism originally was (if not what it should now be). [RWT]

Do Quakers Consider Themselves Protestants?

Quakers consider themselves a "third way" of Christians, emphasizing fundamentals differently from Roman Catholics and Protestants. Roman Catholics emphasize Church authority, the hierarchy, and an absolute creed. Protestant denominations emphasize one or another interpretation of religion as found in the Holy Bible.

But the Society of Friends puts its mark on religion as a fellowship of the Spirit, a movement that can and does grow, develop, and change because it has within it the inward power of expansion. To Friends, all those who do the will of the Father are brethren of Jesus in the Spirit. [RPM]

Some don't. Some do. Some say, "Define Protestantism." And this writer, who affirms that Quakerism is the Church, feels impartially and good-naturedly "hostile" to all other forms of Christianity. [RWT]

What Are the Basic Tenets of Quaker Faith?

The faith of a Friend is simple and rests on absolute sincerity. Quakers believe that God can be approached and experienced by the individual directly—without any intermediary priest or preacher. God is experienced through the "Inward Light," which is the spirit of "Christ Within." From this contact, God's will is determined, direction is given for all human affairs, and the power to live the abundant life is shared. This is a universal grace.

"The Quakers, of all Christian bodies, have remained nearest to the teaching and example of Christ," wrote the Anglican prelate Dean William Ralph Inge. Many Friends are embarrassed when such praise is poured upon them. After all, they are human followers of the "Way of Christ" and know they are fallible and weak in performance. But Friends know what kind of Christians they *ought* to be. [RPM]

The central Quaker belief is in immediate and continuous revelation, available to all who seriously seek it, in all times and places. All other sources of religious authority are secondary.

George Fox, the founder of the Society of Friends, reported that after long religious seeking and repeated disappointments with the answer offered him by clergymen of many persuasions, "Then, oh then, I heard a voice which said, 'There is one, even Christ Jesus, that can speak to thy condition.' And when I heard it my heart did leap for joy."

Friends from the beginning insisted that the word of God has been offered to all men in all generations, and cited evidence in the pagan philosophers, or in the religious beliefs of American Indians. At the same time, the particular Christian orthodoxy of Quakers was beyond question.

Later, some Friends began emphasizing universal revelation at the expense of Christian tradition; and other Friends reacted by emphasizing Christian tradition at the expense of universal revelation. This led to the separation of 1827–1828, when the two bodies of Quakers moved slowly further apart.

The Conservative separations, from 1845 to 1905, at their best were attempts to retain Christian orthodoxy and the belief in universal revelation in a single outlook. In practice, Conservative Friends tended to try to do this by preserving original Quaker viewpoints and opposing "innovationism." [RWT]

How Many Major Groups or Sects Are There in the American Quaker Fellowship?

American Friends today can be fitted into four groupings, but it must be emphasized that *each group is actually a spectrum,* and there is overlapping of many kinds.

1. The Friends General Conference includes mainly silent-Meeting, "liberal" Friends—who understand Quaker identity in

terms of mysticism, rationalism, and humanism. Many Friends of this type think of themselves as having more in common with, say, Zen Buddhists and other non-Christian mystics than with nonmystical Christians or even with most Friends.

2. The Friends United Meeting includes Friends with liberal-to-conservative Protestant conceptions of Quaker identity. These Friends are likely to feel more at home with "mainstream" Protestants than with most other Friends. FUM takes in unprogramed silent Meetings, fully programed "Friends Churches" with pastors, and every imaginable point between these extremes.

3. The Evangelical Friends Alliance includes Friends with a pentecostal understanding of Quaker identity, who feel more at home with other pentecostalists than with most Friends. Their form of worship runs the same gamut as is found in FUM Meetings, but is probably more participatory and more enthusiastic.

4. "Conservative" Friends include several independent Yearly Meetings, many local Meetings (with various affiliations), and an unknown number of individuals in still other Meetings. They do not maintain a central organization. They are not "conservative" in the usual political or religious sense but in that they hold to some viewpoints and practices that other Friends tend to see as archaic, narrow, or both. They worship on the basis of silence.

The scholarly reconstructionist viewpoint (mentioned above) belongs, broadly speaking, in the Conservative category. These Friends are likely to feel more at home with (some) Mennonites. [RWT]

How Do Quakers Worship?

The "Meeting for Worship" is a form of church service that has no fixed, prearranged character. It is held without ritual or an ordained minister, and with no outward sacraments or formalized program. It takes place in a Meeting house without a steeple, stained-glass windows, altar, reredos, or organ.

Friends gather at the appointed time "on the basis of silence." Out of their silent waiting may flow spiritual messages, vocal prayer, Bible reading, or ministry—from anyone who feels called to participate. After about an hour of worship, the Meeting is broken by everyone shaking hands with the neighbor who sits beside him, following the lead of those Friends who have been appointed to have oversight of the Meeting and who sit on the benches facing the Meeting.

It should be emphasized that the form of Quaker worship and ministry is not prescribed or uniform. In some parts of the United States, Meetings for Worship differ from the description given above. Where Quaker Meetings follow a programed system, they are called "Pastoral Meetings." [RPM]

Worship on the basis of silence is normally presented as the most distinctive Quaker practice. Actually, it incorporates many variants, and there are drastic departures from it.*

Worship is under the direct guidance of the Holy Spirit, and therefore cannot be preprogramed. Worship is held on the basis of silent expectancy.

Persons rise to speak, or kneel to pray, spontaneously—when they strongly feel their utterances will contribute comfort or add to the corporate understanding of God's will—and the capacity to obey it. [RWT]

Do the Quakers Have a Formal Creed?

No, not a written or spoken formal creed. They do have deep and strong beliefs. The Society never requires of its members the acceptance of any formula of belief. Friends hold that the basis of religious fellowship is an inward, personal experience.

The essentials of Quaker unity are the love of God and the love of man, conceived and practiced in the spirit of Jesus Christ. George Macaulay Trevelyan put it this way:

The finer essence of George Fox's queer teaching was surely this—that Christian qualities matter much more than Christian dogmas. No church

---

* For a number of reasons, many Meetings have abandoned the silent Meeting in part or in whole. They are likely to have pastors, who may be only one of several recorded ministers speaking or not speaking in the silent part of the Meeting or who may be clergymen presiding over fully programed Protestant-type services. Recording has in some measure become a substitute for ordination. This pattern came in after the Civil War; in recent years, Meetings of this type have slowly lost ground to unprogramed silent Meetings or to pentecostalist Meetings in which there may be a pastor, but there is also much participation and enthusiasm. Such Meetings often label themselves "Friends Churches." They predominate in the Midwest. [RWT]

or sect had ever made that its living rule before. To maintain the Christian quality in the world of business and domestic life, and to maintain it without hypocrisy, was the great achievement of these extraordinary people. [RPM]

Do the Quakers Have Any Substitute for a Creed?

Yes—the "Queries." Originally, the Queries were a set of questions designed to encourage the faithfulness of the members in their religious life. It is the practice to answer one of the Queries in Meeting each month and to report on all twelve at the annual Yearly Meeting.

Typical Queries are: Do your Meetings give evidence that Friends come to them with hearts and minds prepared for worship? Are love and unity maintained among you? Do you manifest a forgiving spirit and a care for the reputation of others?

What are you doing as individuals or as a Meeting: To aid those in need of material help? To ensure equal opportunities in social and economic life for those who suffer discrimination because of race, creed, or social class? To understand and remove the causes of war? To develop the conditions and institutions of peace? To assure freedom of speech and of religion, and equal educational opportunities for all?

Do you frequently and reverently read the Bible and other religious literature? Are you punctual in keeping promises, just in the payment of debts, and honorable in all your dealings? In all your relations with others, do you treat them as brothers and equals? [RPM]

What Is Meant by the Quaker "Witness"?

An essential part of the Quaker tradition is that all members bear individual and group witness to their principles by the simplicity, integrity, uprightness, and directness they exhibit in personal life and in their dealing with all peoples.

The outward expression of Quaker beliefs is found in group testimonies against war, for penal reform, against capital punishment; in opposition to slavery and all forms of discrimination and segregation; in efforts for better intercultural relations, a more Christian economic and social order, intelligent treatment of the mentally ill, equality for women; and in opposition to the use of alcohol and gambling. [RPM]

What Is the "Inward Light"?

The "Inward Light" is not conscience. It is what Quakers call "that of God" in everyone. It instructs and transforms the conscience as the true guide of life. Most often it is termed the "Inner Light" or the "Light Within." It exists in all men and women. It resembles the doctrine of the Holy Spirit.

But to Quakers, it is known directly, without any mediation by any prophet or priest. For Friends, it is the source of all reality in religion, leading immediately to the experience of God. [RPM]

What Bearing Does the "Inward Light" Have on Quaker Conceptions of Sin and Grace?

Early Friends had a strong sense of man's sinful nature, except for God's mercy. But they also believed that the Holy Spirit makes God immediately accessible to all, that God helps us all accept the gift of His love, and that all may be perfectly freed from sin. (Universal perfectibility, incidentally, was the most offensive Quaker doctrine to the Calvinist enemies of the early Friends.)

Seeking new, vivid language to describe the inward sense of one's response to God's initiatives, George Fox coined the term "Inward Light." He spoke of "inward grace" just as frequently.

Different Quaker viewpoints have made these phrases doctrinal. One belief holds that man is innately good and that the Inward Light, or That of God in Everyone (Fox meant that in everyone that is owned by God), is intrinsic in human nature.

Other Quakers believe that the world, or for that matter the Society of Friends, is chock-full of evidences of God's mercy to those who do not deserve it. One sees providences everywhere, and one is struck with awe and thankfulness. One's own spiritual growth is seen as happening despite one's resistance and is undeserved. One's sense of grace is a sense of something imposed from without.

To Friends with such views (or, with such perceptions of their inward experience of the Lord), the notion of innate human goodness is an abomination.

Other Friends object just as strongly to a ministry that even mentions sin or affirms the "outsideness" of God's grace.

This whole area is one of active, ongoing controversy. [RWT]

What Is the "Meeting for Business"?

The affairs connected with organization are discussed at a "Meeting for Business," at another time than on First-day (Sunday) morning. Pure democracy is practiced in all decisions, which are recorded in minutes written by the clerk of the meeting. There is no vote. The clerk takes down "the sense of the meeting" after full discussion has reached agreement.

The local meeting is the Monthly Meeting; groups in a particular district form a Quarterly Meeting; the Yearly Meeting is the inclusive body for all meetings in a region. In the United States and Canada, there are thirty Yearly Meetings, comprising over 1,000 Monthly Meetings. [RPM]

Friends assemble for business on the basis of prayerful silence, with the intention of discovering the Lord's will in respect to items on the agenda or to matters brought up spontaneously. Individuals with specific concerns may bring them before the Meeting for endorsement; this may carry financial support as a corollary.

There is no voting; compromise is also deemed inappropriate. The purpose of the Meeting is not to find a majority view, nor a halfway point between my opinion and thine, but to discover who has the most light as to the Lord's will and to unite around the view thus elicited.

The truth of a given view or proposal is tested not only against the prayerful understanding of others but also against Scripture and Quaker precedent. This method of business procedure is designed literally to let Christ be the charismatic leader. Its justification is found in Matthew 18. It is a major basis for the claim made by some Friends that Quakerism is "the church."

Business Meetings often sink into discussion-groupism, committeeism, preoccupation with property matters, and so on. The search for consensus is slow, often involves long postponements, and is frequently a bore. Nevertheless, it works.

Despite grumblings, especially from younger Friends, Quaker

groups, gathering to seek the Lord's will, consistently manage to surprise themselves by uniting around views more advanced than could have been expected—views sometimes more difficult than acceptable to the bulk of those present.

To this writer, Quaker business Meetings, despite their faults, are the primary evidence that the Lord still wants to use the Society of Friends. [RWT]

How Do Quakers Regard the Bible?

Friends have always believed that the truth is found in the Bible, rather than holding that what has been written is true *because* it is in the Bible. Quakers have always been students of the Bible, placing strong emphasis on its value and use.

A Quaker scholar was a member of the committee that issued the American Standard Version of the Bible, and another Quaker, a New Testament scholar, served on the group that translated the new Revised Standard Version of the Bible, published in 1952. Another Friend was a member of the Joint Committee on the New Translation of the Bible that resulted in The New English Bible publication of the New Testament in 1962. [RPM]

The Bible is central in the religious life of virtually all Friends. The classic Quaker position asserts that the source of religious truth and authority is the Holy Spirit, that the Bible was written under the inspiration of that spirit and may be understood only by the power of that same spirit.

Robert Barclay, the greatest early Quaker theologian, further advocated using the Bible as a negative check of truth that is inwardly perceived: If an individual or a group "leading" is clearly contrary to Scripture, then it cannot be a true leading, since the Holy Spirit is not changeable; God does not teach one truth now, an opposite truth later.

Friends incline to see the Sermon on the Mount as catechetical. Early Friends, and some Friends today, also see the Bible as a unified whole, in that it is a record of God's covenant-making activities and shows the pattern of how God chooses to work with people.

The Book of Revelation is centrally important to the belief that one starts living in the kingdom now; passages such as 21:1–5 and 22:3–5 are taken as close descriptions of the immediate situation of those who have entered into the new dispensation.

Historically, this was the source of "advanced" Quaker views on the work ethic, the status of women, oppressed peoples (see below). The promise of Revelation that "there shall be no more curse" was taken by early Friends as applying to them, and potentially to all.

The curse upon Adam was that by the sweat of his brow he should earn his bread, and Puritan thinking used this to justify long, hard, thankless work. Friends asserted that work *in proportion* is part of the fullness of life and that work out of proportion is a social evil to be stamped out.

Incidentally, the curse upon Eve was that woman shall be subject to man; Friends from the start rejected this as not applicable to them, nor to the social order. [RWT]

What Is the Attitude of Friends Toward Jesus?

Quakers have a common belief in the revelation of God in Christ. There is a variety of points of view among Friends, but there is a universal witness (a common faith) that God expressed His love historically in Jesus of Nazareth and eternally through the Spirit of Christ. To many Friends, these are two experiences of the same reality—the historical Jesus and the risen Christ within. [RPM]

There is general agreement among Quakers that the teachings of Jesus should be obeyed, that the example of Jesus should be emulated, that the Sermon on the Mount should be taken literally, and that a religious community doing these things ought to be too busy to argue over speculative matters.

Christianity has to do with accepting Jesus as leader and example, and with doing what he commands. It does not have to do with speculations as to his metaphysical nature.

Friends, in their private opinions, run the gamut from Christian orthodoxy to extreme unorthodoxy. Yet even those Friends who refuse to label themselves Christians are likely to cite their disillusionment with forms of Christianity that seem preoccupied with making up doctrines about Jesus instead of following his message and example. [RWT]

Do Quakers Believe Jesus Was Divine?

This is a difficult question to answer categorically for all Friends. Friends refer to the "Seed," the "Light of Christ," the "Inner Guide," the "Inner Light" as the external creative power of God, expressed supremely and uniquely in the supreme gift of God to man—Jesus Christ. [RPM]

Many Friends believe this an inappropriate question (see preceding question on Jesus). [RWT]

How Do Friends Feel About the Trinity?

Again, there is wide freedom for personal opinion. It must be remembered that Quakerism is based on a religious way of life rather than accepted dogmas. The Quaker faith is a religion of experience. Whatever is known experimentally about God, the Holy Spirit, the Christ Within, becomes the true guide. Friends tend to believe in the immanence of God rather than His transcendence. [RPM]

"Trinity" is a term not found in Scripture and is an example of unnecessary speculation—of turning Christianity into a religion about Jesus instead of the religion of following Jesus. [RWT]

Do Quakers Believe in the Virgin Birth?

The question of the Virgin Birth does not seem as important a problem for Quakers as the meaning and teaching of Christ's life on earth and His continuing power to reveal Himself at all times and to all seekers. [RPM]

The Scriptural witness is confused on the subject of the Virgin Birth. Friends who find it spiritually useful to believe in it, of course, may do so, but there is no corporate affirmation of this doctrine. [RWT]

Do Quakers Believe in the Sacraments?

For Friends, there is no necessity for any ritual to establish relationship between man and God. Friends believe in all the sacraments but only in their inward and spiritual revelation of the Divine presence. All life is sacramental. At all times, and to all men and women, God is available to those who reverently wait upon Him. [RPM]

Friends oppose baptizing with water and outward rituals of communion. Friends initially were not gathered from one cult into another, but away from all cults.

Sacramental rituals are apostacies, because they lead people to mistake outward form for inward substance, and because they treat ongoing spiritual processes as "events."

The Scriptural arguments for outward sacraments are readily balanced by Scriptural arguments against them.

It is inward baptism and inward communion that are central to the spiritual life. [RWT]

How Do Quakers Try to Convert Others to Their Faith?

Friends are always alert to discover those who are in unity with them and nurture them until they are accorded full membership—following a written request of the applicant to become a member.

New members are called "convinced." Those whose parents are Friends acquire membership by right of birth and are called "birthright" members. [RPM]

In an abrupt recent trend, "birthright" membership is rapidly dying out. (Among other things, this makes membership statistics difficult to compare.) A majority of Friends today may be "convinced"—the first time this has been so since 1827.

Urbanization, nomadism, and reunionism have made it more difficult for Meetings to avoid being assemblies of strangers and have added to the trend toward unity on a rather shallow basis. Yet people normally join a Meeting out of a feeling that "this is a community I want to be part of."

Consequently, other recent trends are: (1) very large Meetings are either subdividing or losing membership rapidly; (2) groups within Meetings, seeking deeper community, are forming communes.

Communes were never part of the Quaker heritage, but they are nowadays proliferating.

Quakerism initially was a religion of and for the poor and the unlettered, and there is wide concern over Quakerism's weakness in black ghettos and "blue-collar" neighborhoods—where it should be strongest. Only sporadically successful attempts have been made to organize Meetings in such milieus. [RWT]

Are All Quakers Pacifists? Must They Be?

No. Some Quakers have given up their pacifism and gone to war. But Quakers as a group hold that nonviolent forms of peacemaking are the only ways to solve international strife. William Penn maintained that it was "not fighting but suffering" to which Friends were called. The witness for peace is one of the most universal of all Quaker testimonies.

Quakers have always been among the conscientious objectors to war. When Oliver Cromwell asked George Fox to fight with him in 1650, Fox wrote in his *Journal:* "I told him I knew from whence all wars arose and that I lived in the virtue of that life and power that took away the occasion of all wars."

During World War I, the right of conscientious objectors was not recognized and many Friends went to jail. Selective Service legislation today establishes the right of conscientious objectors to be assigned to civilian service of national importance, in lieu of military service. [RPM]

No Quaker body has ever departed from or watered down the Declaration to Charles II in 1661:

We utterly deny all outward wars and strife and fightings with outward weapons, for any end or under any pretense whatsoever . . . The spirit of Christ, which leads us into all Truth, will never move us to fight and war against any man with outward weapons, neither for the kingdom of Christ nor for the kingdoms of this world.

Those who join the Society of Friends are normally expected to accept the "Peace Testimony" of Friends. However, there is great tolerance toward individual variations in practice.

Friends who go to war are not normally disowned from membership on that account (although this may be taken as reason for inquiring as to whether a member wishes to remain in membership). Refusal to pay war taxes is an ancient Quaker testimony; but there is disagreement among Quakers as to whether it applies to general taxes, such as the income tax, as opposed to explicit war taxes.

In practice, Friends who get in trouble over the Peace Testimony must have violated it in an outrageous degree—as by war profiteering, being members of draft boards, or becoming professional soldiers.

Corporate attitudes toward war vary with the war. It was difficult to oppose World War II, except on the argument that Christians are always obliged to choose to suffer rather than to inflict suffering. By contrast, the Vietnam war led many Friends into strong opposition.

The recent shift in Quaker emphasis from conscientious objection to political resistance and draft refusal is a product of the changing times, as well as a sign of renewed zeal in the form of rejection of special sectarian privileges. [RWT]

What Is the "Plain" Dress?

The early Friends refused to doff their hats, as a sign of either honor or respect, except in prayer to God. For both of these customs, they suffered bitter ridicule and persecution. When William Penn, whose father was an admiral, a general, and a courtier, first visited the court after his conversion to Quakerism, he advanced to meet Charles II with his conscience dictating that he keep his hat upon his head. The King, with a smile, removed his own hat. Whereupon Penn asked with surprise, "Friend Charles, wherefore dost thou uncover thyself?" "Friend Penn," King Charles replied, "it is the custom of this place for only one man to wear a hat at a time."

"Hat honor" no longer prevails; Friends today follow custom in tipping their hats. But there are still some Friends who wear hats into Meeting and take them off only when they rise to pray in the presence of the Lord.

In like manner, Quaker simplicity in dress and color (gray for the women and black for the men) has largely disappeared—because of the disappearance of the trimmings and foppery that separated the plain people of God from "the world's people" in the seventeenth century. Some women Friends still wear plain dresses and sugarscoop bonnets, while their men use plain gray suits, without lapels or useless buttons, no neckties and broad-brimmed plain hats. [RPM]

The wearing of "plain dress" is a custom that had almost died out, but now some younger Friends are reviving it (essentially to assert a "countercultural" identity). Plain dress was an early protest against conspicuous consumption: "The trimmings of the vain world would clothe the naked one" (William Penn, *Fruits of Solitude*).

The unnecessary use of cloth in the pre-ready-made era was understood as creating extra work to vain ends—at the cost of resources that other people lacked and at the wider social cost of forcing some people to labor too much.

"Hat honor" has also been revived in a sense. This writer and quite a few other Friends, especially younger Friends, feel strongly that "isms" are the idolatries, the brazen images, of our times, and that "nationalism" is the most pernicious of them. We also feel our allegiance is to the Lamb's Kingdom, not to those of man. We therefore refuse to honor the rituals of nationalism, such as rising for flags or anthems or magistrates, insisting (with early Friends) that we reserve such postures of deference for God. [RWT]

Do Friends Baptize?

No. They do believe in the baptism of the Spirit but practice no form of baptism. [RPM]

What Is Meant by the "Plain" Language?

A characteristic of early Friends that has persisted through three centuries is the "plain" language—which means refusing to use "you," the plural form, in addressing one person. (This differentiated plain people from those of noble status in the seventeenth century.) Quakers went back to Biblical Christianity and used "thee" and "thou."

Friends also replaced the customary names of the months and days of the week because of their pagan origins. Even today, they use "First-day" for Sunday or "Fourth-day" for Wednesday, "First month" for January or "Third month" for March.

Use of the plain language is now generally confined to conversations among members of the Society of Friends and in intimate family life. [RPM]

Plain speech today, other than as a custom, is justified mainly in terms of asserting a countercultural identity. Many Friends oppose "plain" language as an "in-language." Of these, some therefore do not use it at all, while others (an increasing number of younger Friends) have returned to using it to everybody.

Older Friends who have given up practices of plainness say it impedes communication. Younger Friends who have taken up practices of plainness say it helps communication. Both views seem to be true for those who think that way.

Younger Friends also believe increasingly that their elders actually abandoned plainness not for the reasons cited but out of sheer embarrassment, which in turn reflected a loss of the sense of revolutionary "otherness" that ought to characterize a Christian. [RWT]

What Do Quakers Believe About Sin?

For over 300 years, the Quakers have pointed to the inherent goodness in men and women, instead of emphasizing the inheritance of sin from the fall of Adam and Eve as recorded in the Bible. In this, Friends oppose the views of both Catholics and the majority of Protestants. Roman Catholics hold that it is the high calling of the Church, through its sacraments, to save its members from sin. The majority of Protestants regard sin as the fundamental fact of man's life on earth and hold that the will of God is discovered through faith, not reason.

Quakers believe that while sin is a fact in life, it is best described as existing in a universe like a checkerboard of black (sin) and white (goodness) squares. But the black squares are imposed on the basic white squares, not the reverse. There is an "ocean of light over the ocean of darkness," George Fox said.

To Friends, the term "original sin" overemphasizes the power of evil. Even when he is fallen, man still belongs to God, who continues to appeal to the goodness within him. [RPM]

What Do Friends Feel About Atonement?

Our views on the atonement are summed up in the Quaker phrase "No Cross, No Crown."

We think it is the common human experience that man's hard-heartedness to the condition of others is the greatest impediment to his spiritual growth and equates with hard-heartedness to God. We all need to practice an open, naked vulnerability to the joys and sufferings of others.

Jesus totally identified with the sufferings of others, and therefore with the joys of others, including us, and we are summoned to attempt to do the same.

Atonement is not a matter of legalistic sacrifice but of spiritual growth. Christ's cross is Christ's path—and ours—to Christ's crown. [RWT]

What Is the Quaker Conception of Heaven, Hell, and Purgatory?

Quakers consider these matters for individual interpretation. The Book of Discipline, Faith and Practice does not deal with these theological issues. [RPM]

While there is a spectrum of private beliefs on these matters, Friends of most kinds emphasize that "the kingdom is now"—a doctrine of "realized eschatology."

This makes questions of an afterlife appear unnecessary, an inappropriate basis for religious belief, and fruitlessly speculative. [RWT]

What Then Is the Solution to Evil in the World?

The Quakers believe that evil is destroyed by "concern." Everywhere Quakers "have a concern"—to eliminate war, to make for righteousness in economic and political life, to treat all humans as equals on the basis of freedom, to stimulate education, to bear witness to the testimonies of integrity, simplicity, sincerity in every walk of life.

One of the first committees established by the Society was called the "Meeting for Sufferings." One of the prayers most often used by Quakers (written by John Wilhelm Rowntree) is this:

Thou, O Christ, convince us by Thy spirit; thrill us with Thy divine passion; drown our selfishness in Thy invading love; lay on us the burden of the world's sufferings; drive us forth with the apostolic fervor of the early church. So only can our message be delivered. Speak to the children of Israel that they go forward. [RPM]

Evil is denial of God's sovereignty and the consequences thereof. "Divine history" is the record of God's "Mighty Acts" of intervention into history for the purpose of bringing all the world into faith-fulness.

History is the history of God's covenant-making activities, first in the old covenant of laws with the Jews, then in the new covenant of love through Jesus, which was predicted and prefigured and prepared for by the old covenant.

"Covenant making" consists of God's initiatives in gathering a faithful people of God to himself through whom he chooses to work. The purpose of the church, in short, is to bring the world under God's sovereignty. Christian community therefore exists for what, from the world's viewpoint, must always look like "revolutionary" purposes; from the community's viewpoint, it exists to do God's bidding in the struggle against evil. [RWT]

Do the Friends Have an Ordained Clergy?

From the beginning, Friends have believed that everyone has the potentiality to become a minister. Among Friends, there is no division between clergy and laity. The vocation of every Friend is to be a lay minister and to practice the free ministry of all laymen. (That includes women.) Overseers, and sometimes elders, are appointed to serve each meeting on suggestions by a nominating committee.

Individual Friends are given the "oversight" of the religious Meetings for worship, for marriage, and for memorial services at the time of death. All Meetings have a recorder who is responsible for the careful keeping of all vital statistics. Overseers look after the pastoral care of the membership.

When a minister is found to be gifted in the ministry, then he or she is recommended in some Meetings to be recorded (as it were, in the ministry), and a record kept of these names. [RPM]

Persons (of either sex) with spiritual gifts pertaining to public worship are recorded as ministers or are acknowledged as elders. This is in no way equivalent to ordination; there is no meaningful distinction among Friends between clergy and laity.

A recorded minister is not expected to speak in Meeting; others are advised not to come to Meeting intending not to speak.

The point of a corporate recognition of a gift in the ministry is, first, to tell the person possessing it that his or her gift is acceptable to the Meeting; and such a person should make ministry the central study of his or her life.

Ministry in Meeting for Worship is a general obligation for Friends, but in practice the universal ministry depends on several members having a concern in the ministry and nurturing it in others. [RWT]

Since the late nineteenth century some groups of Quakers have adopted the practice of employing a recorded minister to carry out pastoral duties. Now, approximately half of the Meetings in the United States follow this pattern. It is the predominant practice among Friends in Africa and South America.

Why Do Quakers Object to Taking the Oath in Courts?

Instead of swearing to the truth, Quakers affirm that they are telling the truth. The Quaker stand against judicial oaths has caused them great trouble throughout their history. The objections to swearing an oath was once the one way to catch Quakers and persecute them legally. Objection to swearing is in conformity with Biblical injunctions to "Swear not at all" and "Above all things my brethren, swear not."

Besides, swearing to the truth implies a double standard of truth: If one tells the truth *only* when under oath, then obviously a man's word is not good unless he is under oath. Quakers believe in telling the truth at all times. Today, laws permit affirmations in court, instead of the conventional oath. [RPM]

How Do Quakers Get Married?

Friends practice a simple wedding ceremony without music or ritual, held in connection with a Meeting for Worship. The bride and the groom "marry each other" in the presence of God. Their families and their friends are witnesses. Permission is obtained from the Meeting to secure "oversight" of the marriage, called "passing Meeting." In many states, a special marriage-license form certifies to a legal marriage. This form is signed by witnesses, rather than an ordained minister or official.

After the legal license has been obtained, the couple go to the Meeting house on the appointed wedding day. The bride and groom repeat their vows to each other. The certificate of marriage is read publicly. The certificate is signed by all who witnessed the marriage. The whole ceremony is in the form of a Meeting for Worship. Prayer may be offered, poetry recited, or a message given suitable to the occasion. Silent waiting bathes all those present. After the Meeting, there is a reception for the newly married couple. [RPM]

The bride and groom, after submitting their proposal of marriage to Meeting and being found "clear" to marry, appear in a Meeting for Worship and exchange promises to be loving and faithful to one another for as long as they both shall live. Wedding guests sign a certificate, attesting that this happened, as witnesses. Otherwise, the procedure is that of a regular Meeting for Worship. Simplicity is commended as to dress, receptions, and so forth.

The bride and groom customarily enter together. This is an ancient Quaker protest against the custom that women are "given" in marriage, as chattel, by the father to the husband.

Love has always been understood by Friends as the only appropriate basis for marriage among Christians (as, indeed, for all other activities). The bride and groom give themselves to each other, in the presence of God and their friends.

Exchanging promises before witnesses is an ancient Scottish form of marriage whose origins are lost in the mists of Celtic antiquity. Early Friends adopted and adapted it as particularly appropriate to their understanding of marriage.

In most states, a special wedding certificate is required, or one annotated with citations from statutes. In Pennsylvania, however, the early Quaker legislature simply provided that there are two forms of marriage and two marriage certificates: one for the exchanging of promises before witnesses, one for use with a magistrate or clergyman. Anybody may use either form.

This provision of the law in Pennsylvania recently came under attack by judicial interpretations. The first reaction of Philadelphia Friends was to respond in terms of protecting sectarian privilege—specifically, the right of a Meeting to marry anyone, whether members or not. But, typically, on further deliberation, Friends felt that what they needed to protect was not a special privilege for Friends but a right for all people, and attorneys were so instructed.

Marriage is understood to be a partnership of equals. [RWT]

Do Quakers Permit Divorce?

Divorce is contrary to the "Discipline of Friends." Marriages are promises to love, cherish, and obey until death. Since divorce is legal, however, there *are* divorces within the Society—but not nearly as frequently as would be expected statistically.

Quakers have committees on family relationships and offer marriage counsel to deal constructively with family problems and prevent family breakdown. Marriage study, education, advice, and Friendly interest apply to the entire membership—not only to those in marital difficulties. [RPM]

Divorce historically was very strongly opposed by Friends. This position has been watered down lately, for two opposite reasons. The negative reason is a surrender to the norms of the surrounding world. The positive reason is growing sensitivity to the processual character of all human relationships and growing distaste for across-the-board flat rules. [RWT]

What Is the Quaker Position on Birth Control?

This is a matter for the individual conscience. Friends, like other Christians, have always regarded marriage as a continuing religious sacrament, not merely a civil contract.

Education for marriage and parenthood has long been a concern of Quakers, particularly as part of their stand for the equality of women and the religious basis of all family relationships. [RPM]

What Is the Status of Women Among Quakers?

From the earliest days, women enjoyed full equality in all Quaker internal affairs. Women enjoyed equal right to preach in Meeting for Worship and to hold all offices. They have an equal right to be recorded as ministers.

Until modern times, in recognition of the legal, social, and educational disadvantages under which women labored, Friends' business Meetings were conducted under a system of sexual bicameralism—to assure that women's views would get equal attention with men's and that women, less experienced in the affairs of the world, would not sit mute while men dominated the discussions.

Many Quaker women were pioneer suffrage leaders. The current Women's liberation movement is supported by many Friends, though it is seen by many as rather "old hat."

The practice of addressing women as "Ms." runs up against the old Quaker discarding of all honorifics; formal address among Friends uses first and last names, unadorned. [RWT]

What Do Friends Believe About Abortion?

Among silent-Meeting Friends, the views seem to favor liberalization of abortion laws, at the very least to put an end to "back-alley" abortions. Many also feel that women should have control over what happens to their own bodies.

But because of the Quaker bias against corporate positions on speculative topics, there is no formal agreement on when human life begins. Now that this has become a practical issue, Friends discover a variety of opinion among themselves: Some Friends relate this issue to historic views on women's rights, others to historic views on peace and against killing.

Historically, Friends have gotten along better with Catholics than with Protestants. We are half-hearted about ecumenical activities that exclude Catholics, and we hesitate to seem critical of Catholics. Still, there is a good deal of feeling that the Catholic position on abortion, if it is to be credible, ought to be equally strong against killing in warfare. [RWT]

What Is the Quaker Attitude Toward Black People?

From 1688 until about 1760, Friends increasingly opposed slavery. They finally made slave holding a disownable offense—the first Christian body to take this position.

Friends pioneered in early abolitionism. They formally withdrew from political abolitionism in the middle of the nineteenth century on the grounds that it was becoming violent and became intensely involved in the Underground Railroad. (This involved clandestine activities and created a major controversy about ends and means: Should Christians lie and sneak, even on behalf of so great a cause as liberty from bondage?)

Many Friends were open and public about their work for the Underground Railroad and were jailed or fined into poverty.

In Philadelphia, Friends pioneered in the education of black people from colonial days. Anthony Benezet's early School for Colored Children produced a great many black leaders. The idea of this school, and the chain of schools it grew into, was to demonstrate that blacks are educable; at that time, this was highly controversial.

Yet for all that, black membership in the Society of Friends has been virtually nil until recently. It still is negligible, despite continuing strong Quaker corporate positions on the rights of black people and unceasing involvement. (One reason for this may be that because of the position of Friends on slavery, Quakerism was wiped out in most of the South; most Southern Friends were forced to emigrate to the Midwest.) [RWT]

What Do Friends Believe About Homosexuality?

In recent years, at least three Yearly Meetings have formally come out for an end to laws relating to the sexual conduct of consenting adults; this view seems to be gaining strength rapidly.

Friends are likely to feel that American culture in general puts far too much emphasis on sex, whether "straight" or "gay."

Quaker opinions about homosexuality otherwise appear to mirror those of Americans as a whole: that is, there is disagreement, and no consensus. [RWT]

How Is Quaker Influence Felt?

Service is the Quaker word that represents for many Friends what missionary activity does for the churches. It grows out of spiritual conviction. In social service, foreign relief, reconciliation and mediation—both at home and abroad—Quakers carry on an enormous amount of activities around the globe. The American Friends Service Committee and Friends Service Council, London, won the Nobel Peace Award for 1947 and Friends enjoy consultative status in the United Nations. The eight-pointed star of the American Friends Service Committee is known all over Europe and in Israel, India, China, Japan, Korea, and Africa. [RPM]

During the Vietnam war, Friends maintained a center in South Vietnam for making and fitting people with prosthetic limbs and for training Vietnamese in making prosthetics. In order to reassert traditional Quaker neutrality in wars, it was felt essential that medical help should also be given to North Vietnam; and after much internal controversy, a number of Yearly Meetings formally and officially practiced civil disobedience by raising moneys for medicines and illegally taking money and medicine out of the country.

While war opponents hailed this act as political, Friends saw it in terms of proclaiming their belief that love and brotherhood must be practiced toward everyone, without exception, and without regard to the changings of political opinion. [RWT]

What Do Friends Believe About the Mission of the Church?

The Good News of Quakerism is that any group of ordinary people can come together and be the church. They do not need ritual. They do not need successions, either episcopal or presbyterian. They do not need a creed or a book. They do not need a learned clergy—nor, indeed, any clergy at all.

What they do need is the sincere intention of practicing, as best they can, faithfulness to Christ as their direct and immediate prophet, priest, and king. The relationship of the original disciples to one another and with Jesus is the Friends' model.

The validity of our churches requires our community of discipleship to follow the duties of mutual counsel, admonition, and encouragement; to be mutually supportive in the search for truth—and corporate in all decision making; and to be mutually supportive as to spiritual, financial, and other needs.

In relating to the world at large, the Quaker community must be faithful to God's reason for having a church, namely the task of "saving the world." The world is the whole world, governments and institutions as well as individuals.

Socially, the Christian task is to conform the world to the mind of Christ. This is a "revolutionary" task in every generation and in every place.

PROBLEMS

The above statement is acceptable to many "liberal" Friends. But Conservative/Reconstructionist Friends part company with most Friends, and agree with Mennonites, over their additional understanding of the authority of the church. They have a "high church" opinion, set forth by Robert Barclay, the seventeenth-century theologian, which emphasizes the authority granted by Jesus to his disciples (Matthew 18:15–20) corporately to bind and to loose, to forgive sins, and to proclaim truth in God's name. These Friends understand the promise of "the presence in the midst," with which that Scriptural passage ends, as referring to decision making and not to worship.

Meetings with this understanding of apostolic authority are intensely interested in "right ordering" (being extremely careful about the procedures used in corporate decision making) and believe that unity within a Meeting must be doctrinal, on a deep level, and worked for exhaustively. Such Meetings stress the primacy of corporate over individual witness. Such Meetings find "umbrella-type reunionism" very hard to live with.

The difference described here, between types of Meetings, leads to significant practical problems that may not be at first visible to the inquirer.

VARIANTS

1. Some Friends believe that the only true church is the inward "church mystical." Persons who are "inwardly converted" and gathered to Christ find it convenient to gather outwardly, for purposes of corporate worship, and for mutuality in seeking and doing the Lord's will.

2. Some Friends believe that Quakerism can be the "syncretist faith" that can bring into one fold mystics of the Western and Eastern religions, if only it can escape its inherited attachment to Christianity. This view was encouraged by the life of Gandhi.

3. Some Friends believe that Quakerism is the purest form of Protestantism, having carried to their logical extreme such great Protestant reforms as "the priesthood of all believers" or the Protestant view of the sacraments. Friends emphasize the role of the Holy

Spirit. Each Protestant group needs to learn from the others in order to bring the true church into being.

4. Some Friends believe that George Fox invented pentecostalism and that no one has yet managed to reinvent it better. Salvation is individual, though it also has social implications. [RWT]

What Message Do Friends Offer the World Today?

When the Friends commemorated their 300th anniversary as a religious movement with a World Conference at Oxford, England (1952) they dedicated themselves anew to God's will and purpose and to the "Way of Jesus Christ."

At the conclusion of ten days of conference, 900 Quakers from 22 countries issued this message to persons everywhere:

The Christian faith, which we believe is the hope of our troubled world, is a revolutionary faith. It is rooted in inward experience, but, wherever it is genuine, it leads to radical changes in the ways in which men live and act. We rejoice in the movements, appearing in many parts of the world at once, which are inspired by the desire for social justice, equal rights for all races and the dignity of the individual person. These changes can neither be achieved nor prevented by war. War leads to a vicious circle of hatred, oppression, subversive movements, false propaganda, rearmament and new wars. An armaments race cannot bring peace, freedom or security. We call upon peoples everywhere to break this vicious circle, to behave as nations with the same decency as they would behave as men and brothers, to substitute the institutions of peace for the institutions of war.

Let us join together throughout the world to grow more food, to heal and prevent disease, to conserve and develop the resources of the good earth to the glory of God and the comfort of man's distress. These are among the tasks to which in humility for our share in the world's shame, and in faith in the power of love, we call our own Society and all men and nations everywhere. [RPM]

Since 1952, this rededication has been taken more seriously than its authors may have anticipated, with some interesting changes. The new historical scholarship emphasizes the revolutionary character of early Quakerism and such concepts as "the Lamb's War"; and many younger Friends (many older ones, too) seriously work at "living the kingdom now" in explicit understanding that this is revolutionary and an affront to social norms.

The organizationalism of the 1952 statement has been balanced by an emphasis on mutual support in just living a Christian life, as the most revolutionary and socially "offensive" thing one can do. [RWT]

How Large Is the Quaker Movement?

There are 195,664 members of the Society of Friends all over the world, according to the latest count from the Friends World Committee for Consultation offices (located at Woodbrooke, Selly Oak, Birmingham, 29, England).

There are 124,581 Friends in the United States, including Alaska and Hawaii, with an additional 822 in Canada and Mexico, and 5,871 in Central and South America.

The membership in Great Britain and Ireland totals 23,226.

There are fifty-two Yearly Meetings in the world-wide movement, which is now found on every continent.

WHAT IS A SEVENTH-DAY ADVENTIST?

ARTHUR S. MAXWELL / Until his death, in 1970, Arthur S. Maxwell was editor of *Signs of the Times,* the leading evangelistic journal of the Seventh-day Adventists, for over thirty-five years. He was the author of more than ninety books, some of which (stories for children) have been translated into twenty-three languages.

Mr. Maxwell was born in London in 1896. He attended Stanborough College in England, was manager of the Stanborough Press from 1925 to 1932, and served as editor of *Present Truth* from 1920 to 1936. Four of his children are ordained ministers in the Seventh-day Adventist Church.

Among Mr. Maxwell's writings are *This Mighty Hour, Our Wonderful Bible, Great Prophecies for Our Time, Your Bible and You, Courage for the Crisis,* and *The Bible Story.*

NOTE TO THE READER: New answers to new questions have been provided by Wayne A. Martin, communication director of the Ohio Conference of the Seventh-day Adventist Church. Wherever the text is not Mr. Maxwell's but was provided by Mr. Martin, identifying initials [WAM] are used.

What Is a Seventh-day Adventist?

A Seventh-day Adventist is one who, having accepted Christ as his personal Savior, walks in humble obedience to the will of God as revealed in the Holy Scriptures. A Bible-loving Christian, he seeks to pattern his life according to the teachings of this book, while looking for the imminent return of his Lord.

He lives under a sense of destiny, believing it his duty to warn mankind that the end of the world is at hand.

Are Seventh-day Adventists Protestants?

Yes. Like the reformers of the sixteenth century, Seventh-day Adventists believe that every individual may have immediate access to

God by prayer—without the intervention of any priest, saint, or other ecclesiastical functionary.

They believe that their Church constitutes the nucleus of a twentieth-century Reformation, a world-wide revival of New Testament Christianity.

How Do Seventh-day Adventists Differ from Other Protestants?

Most noticeably to their observance of Saturday, not Sunday, as the Sabbath. But they also differ from many (but not all) Protestants in their teachings concerning the nature of man, the state of the dead, and the manner of Christ's second coming.

Seventh-day Adventists claim that they are not inventors of new doctrines but recoverers of old truths—truths long eclipsed by the infiltration of pagan traditions and superstitions into the Christian Church.

Why Do Seventh-day Adventists Observe Saturday as the Sabbath?

Because God, in the beginning, set apart the seventh day of creation week as a perpetual memorial of His creative power. Saturday is the seventh day of the week. Sunday is the *first* day of the week.

In Exodus 20:8–11, it is written: "Remember the Sabbath day, to keep it holy. Six days shalt thou labor, and do all thy work: but the seventh day is the Sabbath of the Lord thy God: in it thou shalt not do any work, thou, nor thy son, nor thy daughter, thy manservant, nor thy maidservant, nor thy cattle, nor the stranger that is within thy gates: for in six days the Lord made heaven and earth, the sea, and all that in them is, and rested the seventh day: wherefore the Lord blessed the Sabbath day, and hallowed it."

It is distinctly stated of Christ that it was His "custom" to attend the synagogue on "the Sabbath day" (Luke 4:16). And after His crucifixion, His closest disciples were so loyal to His teaching and example they would not even embalm His body on the holy seventh day. Instead, "they . . . rested the Sabbath day, according to the commandment" (Luke 23:56).

As Seventh-day Adventists have never been able to find a single text in the Bible suggesting that Christ authorized a change of the

Sabbath from the seventh day of the week to the first, they say, "What else can a true Christian do but follow the clear teaching of the Word?"

How Do Seventh-day Adventists Know Saturday Is the Seventh Day?

Two unquestionable pieces of evidence confirm Saturday as the seventh day. First, the fact that Orthodox Jews, from time immemorial, have observed the seventh-day Sabbath on Saturday; and, second, millions of Christians, for many centuries, have observed Sunday because Christ *rose* on the first day of the week.

Do Seventh-day Adventists Accept the Bible Literally?

Yes. They believe that the original authors were inspired by God. As the apostle Peter said, "Holy men of God spake as they were moved by the Holy Ghost."

Seventh-day Adventists, of course, know that there have been many translations of the Bible but hold that the original intent of the inspired authors has come down unimpaired through the centuries. Because words change in meaning with the passage of time, occasional revisions of translations are desirable, but through them all the original message is clearly discernible and "the word of the Lord endureth forever."

What Do Seventh-day Adventists Teach About the Beginning of the World?

They believe God created the world by divine fiat, in six literal days.

They believe that the record of creation in the first chapter of Genesis is not fable but fact. They consider that if the omnipotent Creator could make billions of suns (which astronomers claim to have seen circling through the immensities of space), it was no great problem for Him to call this one planet into existence.

The evidence to which geologists and paleontologists point, to support their theory that the earth is millions of years old, is regarded by Seventh-day Adventists as substantiating the Bible story of the Flood. That global catastrophe, they hold, affords a completely satisfactory explanation of all the fossils, buried coal beds, and oil-bearing strata.

Do Adventists Believe in Life After Death?

Yes. But they hold that life comes only from Christ, the source of life. No one, they assert, can have eternal life apart from Christ. Man by himself is mortal, subject to death. Only Christ can make him immortal. And immortality, says the Bible, will not be conferred until the resurrection at the second coming of Christ in glory.

How Do Adventists Feel About the Existence of Heaven and Hell?

Seventh-day Adventists hold that the ancient supposition that people go to heaven or hell immediately upon death is an infiltration of pagan mythology into Christian theology.

Bible teaching on this subject, they claim, is as clear as day—that the dead are asleep until the glorious return of Jesus Christ as King of Kings and Lord of Lords. Then, but not till then, when the resurrection occurs, will final rewards and punishments be meted out.

Do Seventh-day Adventists Believe in the Trinity?

They do. Reverently they worship Father, Son, and Holy Spirit, "three Persons in one God." And they do so because they believe this to be the teaching of the Bible concerning God in His relation to this world and the human race.

Do Seventh-day Adventists Believe in the Virgin Birth?

Most definitely. They hold that it is one of the vital truths of the Christian faith, foretold in the Old Testament and confirmed in the New.

Do Adventists Believe in Baptism?

Yes. Heeding Christ's teaching that "he that believeth and is baptized shall be saved" (Mark 16:16), they require all who would enter the Church to be baptized by *immersion*, the method followed by the Church of New Testament times.

How Did the Seventh-day Adventist Movement Start?

It grew out of the world-wide discussion, in the early decades of the nineteenth century, concerning the second advent of Christ. At that time, many godly scholars, in many countries and of many denominations, simultaneously came to the conclusion, from their study of Bible prophecy, that the coming of Christ was near. Between 1820 and 1830, more than 300 clergymen of the Church of England, and twice that number of Nonconformists, were advocating this belief.

In America, a similar advent movement began, supported by 200 leading clergymen—including Presbyterians, Baptists, Congregationalists, Episcopalians, and Methodists. Led by William Miller, a farmer, they stirred America with the message that Christ would come in 1844. When He failed to come, the movement melted away.

One of the smaller groups decided to restudy the prophecies and search for clearer light. In doing so, they caught the vision of a world to be *warned* before Christ could come again. Penniless, but full of faith, this group set out to accomplish the task. Accepting the Sabbath truth from the Seventh-day Baptists, they became the nucleus of the Seventh-day Adventist movement, which now claims over 2 million members around the globe.

Do Adventists Teach That People Must Obey the Ten Commandments in Order to Be Saved?

No. Salvation is by grace alone. There is only one way of salvation. That is faith in the atoning death of Jesus Christ.

No one can "work his way" into the kingdom of God. No degree of obedience, no works of penance, no amount of money entitles anyone to any divine favor. Nevertheless, "faith without works is dead."

Keeping the commandments is the result, the evidence, of salvation. It is a matter of love, not legal duty. "If ye love me," said Jesus, "keep my commandments" (John 14:15).

What Do Adventists Believe About Christ's Return?

The word "Adventist" indicates their special concern for this phase of Christian teaching. From their study of the Bible, they have become convinced not only that Christ is coming but that He is coming soon. They believe He will come personally, exactly as He went away (Acts 1:11).

Christ's second coming will climax a sequence of stupendous events—political and religious—which will involve the entire population of the globe and mark the end of the world, or age, as we know it today. In that day, when "the Lord Himself shall descend from heaven with a shout, with the voice of the Archangel and with the trump of God," the graves of all God's children will be opened, the "dead in Christ" shall rise, and all true Christians alive at that moment will be "caught up together with them in the clouds, to meet the Lord in the air" (I Thessalonians 4:16–17).

The effect of Christ's coming upon unbelievers is described, Seventh-day Adventists believe, in Revelation 6, where they are pictured as fleeing from His presence, only to be destroyed by "the brightness of his coming" (II Thessalonians 2:8).

Do Seventh-day Adventists Believe in a Millennium?

Yes. They believe that the followers of Christ who are raised, or translated, at His second coming will live and reign "with Christ a thousand years" (Revelation 20:4). However, they believe this reign will take place in heaven, not on earth, which will remain a desolated, depopulated wilderness throughout this period.

At the close of the millennium, the earth will again become a scene of great activity, with the resurrection of the wicked, the return of the righteous from heaven, the setting up of the New Jerusalem on earth, and the execution of final judgment upon the unrepentant (Revelation 20).

After that, Seventh-day Adventists believe, the earth will be purified by fire and re-created at the command of Christ into the eternal home of His redeemed. "The eyes of the blind shall be opened, and the ears of the deaf shall be unstopped" (Isaiah 35:5). "And there shall be no more death, neither sorrow nor crying, neither shall there be any more pain" (Revelation 21:4). Then all sorrows will be over, and all man's brightest hopes will be realized. This will be "heaven on earth" at last, not only for Seventh-day Adventists but for all who love the Lord Jesus Christ in sincerity.

What Makes Adventists Think Christ Is Coming Soon?

The signs of the times. Notably, certain developments among the nations and in the social, economic, and religious life of the masses —including the invention of the hydrogen bomb. As never before, a great fear grips the nations—fear of war, fear of inflation, fear of atomic annihilation. And this fear is driving men, in their search for security, to combine into massive confederacies, as foreshadowed in Bible prophecies.

This tragic situation, Seventh-day Adventists believe, was predicted by Christ Himself when, enumerating the signs of His second coming, He said, "There shall be . . . upon the earth distress of nations, with perplexity; . . . men's hearts failing them for fear, and for looking after those things which are coming on the earth: for the powers of heaven shall be shaken. And then shall they see the Son of Man coming in a cloud with power and great glory" (Luke 21:25–27).

Seventh-day Adventists believe another striking sign is the amazing multiplication of inventions that have changed man's whole way of life. This unprecedented increase of knowledge, with multitudes running to and fro, was prophesied to occur in the "time of the end" (Daniel 12:4).

Still another sign is the moral collapse so evident in social and political life today. Everybody admits that the moral underpinnings of Western civilization are giving way. And while there is still much outward show of religion, there is little inward piety or spiritual power. This too, Seventh-day Adventists believe, was forecast by the apostle Paul to happen in "the last days" (II Timothy 3).

Do Seventh-day Adventists Set a Time for Christ to Come?

No. Nor have they ever done so. They accept Christ's statement "Of that day and hour knoweth no man, no, not the angels of heaven, but my Father only" (Matthew 24:36). However, they give special force to His declaration "When ye shall see these things come to pass, know that it is nigh, even at the doors" (Mark 13:29).

What Is the Attitude of Adventists Toward Drinking and Smoking?

No Seventh-day Adventist drinks alcoholic beverages or smokes tobacco. They accept at face value Paul's statement that man's body is the "temple of the Holy Spirit." Believing this, they refrain from all harmful indulgences that might weaken their efficiency and the sincerity of their witness, as workers for God.

They are also motivated by a regard for the example that true Christians should set before others who do not acknowledge Christ and, in particular, before children and youth.

What Is Your Position Regarding Black People?

In all areas of the United States and, of course, overseas, black people attend the same church as white people, though black churches still exist.

Adventist schools are integrated in every part of the United States.

Wherever the Church holds conferences, councils, or conventions, no distinction is made between white and black, for the teaching of the Church is that "all are brethren under God."

Although black "regional conferences" exist, these conferences continue because the black constituency wants them. In addition, black people as well as white serve on conference staffs, in institutions, and in the world headquarters. One of the vice-presidents of the General Conference of Seventh-day Adventists is black.

Special programs have been designed to provide scholarships for young people of minority groups who wish to secure a professional education.

An annual appropriation (around $250,000) is assigned to inner-city projects. This fund is supervised by a departmental secretary of the General Conference who is black. [WAM]

What Is the Status of Women Among Seventh-day Adventists?

The status of women in the Seventh-day Adventist organization has never been a problem. For many years, women have held responsible posts on various levels of our organization.

At the present time, four members of the General Conference committee, which is the highest governing body of the Church, are women. Women are also assistant secretaries of departments at the world headquarters in Washington.

The Church closely follows government regulations in the matter of job remuneration. [WAM]

Can Women Be Ordained as Ministers?

Women teach in our schools and universities on a par with men. They have served as Bible instructors. Some few have served as ministers of churches without ordination. The Church feels it cannot move ahead in the matter of ordination of women to the ministry until it can do so in every part of the world.

What Is the Adventist Position Regarding Divorce?

Briefly, it is the Biblical position, enunciated by Jesus Christ when He said, "Whosoever shall put away his wife, except it be for fornication, and shall marry another, committeth adultery; and whoso marrieth her which is put away doth commit adultery" (Matthew 19:9).

Seventh-day Adventists believe that this counsel is very clear and that members who knowingly depart from it should not continue in the fellowship of the Church.

What Is the Adventist Position on Abortion?

The Seventh-day Adventist Church has taken no formal position on the subject of abortion. However, some guidelines for Adventist physicians and medical institutions have been suggested:

It is believed that therapeutic abortions may be performed for the following established indications:
1. When continuation of the pregnancy may threaten the life of the woman or seriously impair her health.
2. When continuation of the pregnancy is likely to result in the birth of a child with grave physical deformities or mental retardation.
3. When conception has occurred as a result of rape or incest.
When indicated therapeutic abortions are done, they should be per-

formed during the first trimester of pregnancy, and only after two licensed physicians other than the one who is to perform the procedure have agreed.

What Is the Adventist Position Regarding Homosexuality?

Homosexuality is included along with adultery and fornication, both of which are grounds for disfellowshipping from the Church. Anyone practicing it would not be admitted to the Church, and any member in the Church who practices it would be subject to Church discipline. [WAM]

Do Seventh-day Adventists Have Missionaries?

Yes—all over the world. There are 38,953 full-time workers outside North America. (Each year, more than 300 new missionaries leave for overseas posts.) They work now in 189 countries and 528 languages.

Seventh-day Adventists carry on large-scale health and medical work alongside their evangelistic activities. They have a chain of hospitals and clinics in all the principal countries of the world. Patients treated annually total some 4.2 million.

Are Adventists Interested in Welfare Work?

Very much. Most churches have a Dorcas Society, which is active in caring for the local needy and in projects of wider significance. At strategically located welfare centers, at home and overseas, Seventh-day Adventists stockpile quantities of clothing and bedding, which are kept ready for instant shipment to disaster areas.

The Church has a disaster and famine relief organization known as Seventh-day Adventist World Service (SAWS), which directs emergency relief operations of the Church, funneling relief materials to areas wherever disaster strikes in all parts of the world. More than 9 million people receive assistance from the Church annually through its mobile aid units, community service centers, and SAWS.

Special attention is given the inner cities and their needs through such programs as Day Care Centers, Better Living Centers, tutoring, adult education classes, and clinics. An Inner Cities Committee gives guidance in this area.

Do Adventists Believe in Religious Liberty?

They certainly do. As champions of religious liberty, they fought —and helped to defeat—the calendar reformers before the League of Nations in 1931 and later.

They are opposed to all religious legislation such as "blue" laws. They are ardent supporters of the principle of separation of church and state. They publish the bimonthly *Liberty* magazine, devoted exclusively to the preservation and extension of religious liberty.

How Many Seventh-day Adventists Are There?

As of 1974, the total number of baptized members in North America was 486,601; the world total was 2,390,124. In addition, more than 3.5 million attend Sabbath school weekly. Many thousands who have accepted the teachings of the Church are awaiting baptism.

THE "UNCHURCHED" AMERICANS: WHAT DO THEY BELIEVE?

EDWARD L. ERICSON / Edward L. Ericson is past president of the American Ethical Union, a national federation of Ethical Societies, and currently serves on the Board of Leaders of the New York Society for Ethical Culture. For twelve years (1959–1971) he was Leader of the Washington, D.C., Ethical Society. During that period, he organized the Council for Humanist and Ethical Concerns—now part of the Joint Washington Office for Social Concerns, which represents the social conscience and governmental concerns of Ethical Culturists, humanists, and other religious liberals.

A native of Florida, the son of Southern Baptist and Methodist parents, Mr. Ericson received his B.A. and M.A. at Stetson College, and his M.Div. at the King Starr School in Berkeley, California.

After five years in the Unitarian ministry, he came into the Ethical Culture movement. He has been a member of the American Humanist Association, which—like the Ethical movement—advocates the position of many of America's "unchurched."

Mr. Ericson has frequently testified before Congressional committees and consulted with administrative agencies on such problems as freedom of conscience for religious nonconformists, equal treatment for agnostic and "unchurched" conscientious objectors, and issues involving the relationship between church and state.

Who Are the Unchurched?

The "unchurched" are those millions of Americans who choose not to identify themselves with any of the organized religions.

We should distinguish between those people who are merely indifferent or inactive and *those who decline to join a church out of conviction.* It is this latter group—those who do not join a church out of principle—whom we shall consider here.

How Many Such Unchurched Americans Are There?

This is difficult to establish. There is no official religious census in the United States, and the various denominations vary greatly in their methods of counting members.

Probably a third of the adult population in the United States are not members of any church.

While some of these may nominally support one of the existing religions, millions of others are truly "unchurched"—considering themselves totally independent of church affiliation or practice.

With the recent decline in church influence, and with church membership falling behind population growth, the unchurched portion of the population becomes more prominent and socially important.

Are These Unchurched Millions Antireligious, or at Least Nonreligious?

Not necessarily. Over the years a number of public opinion polls have shown that roughly 4 to 5 percent of the population are agnostic or atheist—and some of these would profess to be religious in their own terms.

The number of explicitly antireligious people in America is quite small, smaller than the percentage in many other developed nations. This may be the result of the tradition of religious freedom in America, which means that there is no formally established state religion to combat.

Are the Unchurched Purely Negative in Their Beliefs?

Emphatically not. As I have suggested, many—perhaps most—consider themselves religious in their own terms.

For the unchurched, religion is a personal and nonsectarian matter rather than a question of church affiliation or formal ritual. Still others completely reject the concept of religion, viewing it as a relic of ancient superstition and authoritarian tradition. Some will admit that they experience familiar "religious" feelings, such as awe and wonder, but experience difficulty even with the word "religion"—because it has so many associations with sectarian strife, bigotry, and repression.

It is hard to generalize about the variety of ideas and attitudes that are common among the unchurched.

What Is a Secularist, or a Humanist?

Many of the unchurched would describe themselves as secularists or humanists. Unfortunately, these are terms that have very imprecise meanings.

In general usage, a secularist is one who rejects religion completely. A humanist, who may also be a secularist, believes that man must look to human experience for moral and spiritual guidance, without believing that there is a supernatural God or divine power to support him.

Many humanists, however, define humanism as a religious movement in its own right—a religion without revelation or God.

How Can You Claim to Be Religious and Not Believe in God?

This is a matter of definition, of course. But the question itself reveals an interesting cultural bias.

Jewish and Christian religious beliefs, which have so profoundly shaped Western ideas, have assumed that man's moral and spiritual life is derived from God and is dependent upon God. But if we look to other spiritual traditions—the teachings of early Buddhism, for example—we find a deeply religious attitude that does not draw from a claim of divine authority.

Buddha taught: Be ye lamps unto yourselves. Work out your own salvation. Do not accept any man's authority. These are precepts that appeal to many contemporary humanists as an early expression of the scientific, experimental attitude.

Whether one prefers to think of humanism as religious or not, most humanists regard their belief as a deeply satisfying moral commitment to the best in human experience—and consider humanism a practical faith for modern men and women.

Do Humanists Reject All Forms of Religious and Ethical Organization, or Only Traditional Churches?

The overwhelming percentage of avowed humanists belong to no organization to promote their distinctive religious or ethical beliefs.

Some humanists, on the other hand, cherish religion for its cultural and moral value and see nothing inconsistent in joining religious bodies that interpret religion in liberal, humanistic terms.

Liberal churches, Reform and Reconstructionist Jewish congregations, and Quaker meetings—all are fellowships that have attracted many who hold humanistic interpretations of religion. So, strictly speaking, not all people of humanistic belief are "unchurched." Moreover, the Ethical Culture Societies (American Ethical Union) and the American Humanist Association offer a distinctive form of humanistic organization.

With nonsectarian wedding ceremonies, naming ceremonies for children, memorial services, and ethical education and counseling functions, Ethical Culture and humanist groups often serve as a "church" for the unchurched.

Do the Leaders of Ethical Culture or Humanist Groups Consider Themselves "Ministers"? What Is Their Legal Status?

It is important to note that under federal and state legal practice, leaders and counselors in Ethical Culture and humanist groups are legally qualified to function as ministers of religion.

Why Should One Live a Moral Life If There Are No Rewards and Punishments Hereafter?

Would you commit a murder if you thought no one was looking, or if you thought you would never be found out? That, I think, is the basic question.

A human being is "born" morally when he recognizes his kinship to other life and cares for others as for himself. One of the weaknesses of authoritarian religion, from the standpoint of the humanist or secularist, is that it so often deprives people of a sense of their own moral capacity. Thus, there is the danger that when outmoded theologies or dogmas are discarded, moral restraint will also be abandoned.

A humanistic ethical education begins with the person himself, with his sense of moral relationship to other living beings. Once a person awakens to the value of human life, so that he reverences the humanity of others above all other values, he cannot be easily swayed by passion or cruelty. People will go to their death before they betray the values they prize most highly. All of history is witness to that.

Without Faith in God or an Afterlife, How Does One Face Death?

As an Ethical Culture Leader (counselor), I have ministered to many people of humanistic belief who knew they were dying.

I remember especially a retired law school teacher who was radiant as he expressed the memories that had made his life a rich experience. A bachelor with no children, he followed the careers of his former students with a fatherly interest, delighting that those who were reaching positions of influence were making an impact for social justice and constitutional rights—which had been the passion of his life and teaching.

Humanists find their immortality in the human community, in the endurance of the qualities that we most admire and respect.

Who Are the Deists?

Deists are people who believe in a Supreme Being or Creator but reject the idea of divine revelation, sacred scriptures, or miracles. They believe in a Deity who established an orderly universe but does not interfere in the working of nature's laws.

Many of the unchurched, of course, hold such beliefs. They may respect Jesus and other religious sages as wise teachers, but they deny that such figures were supernaturally inspired.

Deism rose to prominence in America about the time of the Revolutionary War. A number of the founding fathers, including Washington, Jefferson, and Paine, held deistic beliefs.

As a prominent landowner, George Washington served as a legal trustee (vestryman) of the established church of colonial Virginia; but he never took communion or became a full member. His beliefs came from ancient Stoic philosophy, a forerunner of deism, and not from Christianity.

Thomas Jefferson helped separate church from state, both in Virginia and with respect to the newly established federal government. He never joined a church.

The same was true of Abraham Lincoln, who was an atheist

through much of his adult life but came to a simple belief in a Supreme Being during his final years.

What Is a Pantheist?

Pantheism is the belief that there is no God except nature or the universe itself. Nature is an impersonal creative unity or whole, the pantheist believes.

Although the word "pantheist" has come to sound old-fashioned and is seldom used any more, many of the unchurched have a deep sense of awe and reverence for nature or the cosmos, which they accept as self-existing.

Why Are Many Young People Turning to Oriental Religions and the Occult?

There are many reasons. Some feel that the conventional churches do not speak to their needs. They find churches formal and remote from the problems and interests of youth. Some, no doubt, turn to unfamiliar and exotic paths as a form of rebellion against the older generation and the commercialism of American culture.

However, while there is much that is faddish and irrational in the revival of interest in fortune telling, astrology, other occult "sciences"—and even a revival of belief in witchcraft—we must admit a lack of moral and spiritual vitality in contemporary life that produces a hunger among the young for more adequate ways of living.

Zen Buddhism, Yoga, and Taoist philosophy represent profound spiritual traditions that developed in the cultural soil of the Asian nations. They cannot be lumped together; they represent a variety of faiths as rich as those found in Western thought.

Many Eastern philosophers, like Japan's widely respected D. T. Suzuki, have cautioned Westerners against the superficial adoption of these ancient ways without an understanding of their necessary disciplines and cultural roots.

Any meaningful way of life requires inner preparation and dedication. But we must remember that from the days of Emerson and Thoreau, who drew heavily upon the teachings of the Hindu Upanishads, American faith and philosophy have been enriched by the influence of India and the Far East. We can expect to see more of this interchange as a result of greater communication and global awareness.

Has the Ecumenical Movement Affected the Unchurched?

Emphatically. Humanist and secularist teachers and philosophers have frequently experienced a changed attitude of openness on the part of traditional churchmen, so that for the first time it is possible to meet together for discussion or "dialogue" in a mood of mutual respect.

The Vatican Commission for Nonbelievers and the International Humanist and Ethical Union (which includes the American Humanist Association and the American Ethical Union) have jointly sponsored a series of Catholic-Humanist dialogues in both Europe and the United States.

Other working relationships involving humanists have developed with Jewish and Protestant groups as well—sometimes to clarify ideas, but more often to consider practical social and ethical work in the community.

Many of the unchurched, unfortunately, have no mechanism to become engaged in these proceedings; but both Ethical Culture Societies and Humanist Chapters try to reach out beyond their formal membership to involve academic leaders, community figures, and social activists in these and similar developments.

How Do the Unchurched Express Their Moral and Social Ideals?

In addition to the ways I have mentioned, one will find that people with no formal religion are often leaders in efforts to make the world a better place to live: The civil rights movement, efforts to build peace and a sense of human fellowship among nations, reform efforts in politics and community life—all claim the selfless devotion of millions of the unchurched.

One might say that humanity is their religion and the great, wide world is their temple.

Do the Unchurched Hope to See Organized Religion Decline?

Perhaps some do, reflecting early bitter experiences in Sunday school or guilt-ridden fears. Certainly, most of the unchurched resent the heavy hand of religious hierarchies when they attempt to impose their beliefs and doctrines by law or political pressure.

Many of the unchurched reject as psychologically unsound those teachings that exaggerate human fears of death or divine punishment hereafter.

Many young people especially are turning away today from organized religion for such reasons—as well as for religion's lack of a clear social purpose, thus producing something of an institutional crisis in the churches. On the other hand, many of the unchurched appreciate the positive and constructive work of the churches and recognize the importance of preserving a wide variety of religious beliefs and associations.

Religion has played a profound and often creative role in the making of American democracy; and the unchurched struggle too vigorously for their own freedom and individuality to want to destroy the roots of spiritual diversity in our national life.

By and large, what the unchurched want is what organized religionists also want—a chance for personal choice and mutual respect in a free society.

While churches may lose some of their historic dominance—and many thoughtful theologians are among those who would like to see the churches lose such power—the unchurched are generally wise and generous enough to sympathize with sincere religious fellowship and practice.

It all comes down to a desire to live and let live—and a desire to bring out the best in one another.

WHAT IS A UNITARIAN UNIVERSALIST?

NOTE TO THE READER: This article was prepared by Christopher Gist Raible. It is partly based on the original material, written for this series by the late Karl M. Chworowsky, in the article entitled "What Is a Unitarian?"

KARL M. CHWOROWSKY / Dr. Chworowsky was, at the time of his death, minister emeritus of the First Unitarian Church of Fairfield County, Westport, Connecticut. His father was a Lutheran minister. Dr. Karl Chworowsky studied at Wartburg Seminary in Iowa and the University of Wisconsin. He served as minister in the Evangelical Synod (now part of the United Church of Christ) in Wisconsin and Illinois.

Thirty-one years after his ordination he became a Unitarian. He served churches in Newburgh, Brooklyn, New York, and Westport, Connecticut. He was active in such organizations as the United World Federalists and the American Civil Liberties Union. He was the author of many articles and sermons reprinted in journals throughout the world.

CHRISTOPHER GIST RAIBLE / Christopher Gist Raible, a lifelong Unitarian, is Director of Extension of the Unitarian Universalist Association. He is the son of a Unitarian Universalist minister, brother of another, and brother-in-law of a third.

Dr. Raible was born in New England, later lived in Texas, and was educated at the University of Chicago, the University of Manchester (England), and the King Starr School for the Ministry in Berkeley, California.

As a minister in New York and Wisconsin, he has given leadership to organizations working for mental health, better housing, civil rights, planned parenthood, and welfare reform. He has taught at three colleges and universities and has written numerous articles and pamphlets.

What Is a Unitarian Universalist?

A Unitarian Universalist is one of a community of religious persons whose beliefs and ethics are freely chosen and constantly evolving throughout the experience of their lives.

In general, Unitarian Universalists believe in the oneness of reality and think of God as a unity rather than a trinity. They honor the ethical leadership of Jesus without considering him to be their final religious authority. They rely upon their own reason and personal understanding, while they seek the guidance and inspiration of the great pioneers of religious insight of many cultures and various traditions.

Unitarian Universalists believe in the worth of all human beings and recognize their responsibility to help create a just and peaceful social order for all peoples. They believe that significant meaning and value can be discovered in life on earth without necessarily affirming a life after death.

They believe in the principles of freedom, trusting that a free society provides the maximum opportunity for all persons to find and enjoy the good life.

They have organized their churches as free religious communities in which they can unite for the celebration of life, for sharing values, for service, and for comfort—without being required to accept a dogmatic creed.

What Do the Names "Unitarian" and "Universalist" Mean?

"Unitarian" was a theological term, applied in the sixteenth century, to those who denied the doctrine of the trinity. Unitarians thought that the idea of equating Christ with God was unscriptural, illogical, and unnecessary.

"Universalist" stood for the teaching that salvation was not for a limited few—the "elect"—but was a gift of God for all. The joys of a final reconciliation with God were ultimately available to all men, regardless of their errors or doubts. No God of love, the Universalists declared, could eternally damn anyone.

Both Unitarians and Universalists, although focusing on different doctrines, were thus affirming the importance of human beings as not separated from God, and their natural ability to know and do what is right.

When Did the Unitarians and Universalists Unite?

The two separate but similar religious traditions gradually drew closer during this century and became one with the formation of the Unitarian Universalist Association in 1961. (A brief history of each movement is given below.)

Do Unitarian Universalists Believe in God?

Unitarian Universalists believe that all persons must decide about God for themselves.

In their churches are agnostics, humanists, even atheists—as well as nature worshipers, pantheists, and those who affirm a personal God. All recognize, however, that the word "God" is a stumbling block to religious communication for many people because it has so many meanings. All know also that there is no special virtue in being able to declare, "I believe in God."

Do Unitarian Universalists Believe in Prayer?

Many do, though it is frequently called "meditation."

For Unitarian Universalists, prayer is less a matter of who is listening and more a concern with the aspirations expressed. Whether spoken or silent, prayer is an expression of feelings of gratitude, regret, hope, and rededication. Its purpose is not to influence a God but to discipline the human mind or spirit.

Do Unitarian Universalists Consider Themselves Christians?

Unitarian Universalists are Christian in the same way that Christians are Jews; that is, they cherish the tradition from which they emerged (Christianity) without being completely limited to it.

Some Unitarian Universalists prefer to be called "liberal Christians," others simply "religious liberals." All know that morality and decency are not the exclusive possessions of Christians.

The religion of Jesus, so simply and beautifully expressed in the Sermon on the Mount, remains an ethical ideal for most Unitarian Universalists.

Do Other Christian Churches Consider Unitarian Universalists to Be Christian?

Many Christian churches refuse to accept them as Christians because they cannot pass the theological "test" of acknowledging Jesus Christ as "Lord and Savior."

For this reason, Unitarian Universalists have not been permitted to join the National Council of Churches of Christ, although they work amicably with the council and other religious groups on many common concerns.

How Do Unitarian Universalists Regard the Bible?

The Bible is a library of books written by many different men over a period of about a thousand years. It is inspired in the sense that it presents their most profound insights. But it also represents the changing and conflicting ideas of those who wrote, amended, edited, and compiled the Scriptures. Today, some portions are distinctly more valuable than others—and all are subject to interpretation in the light of modern knowledge and personal experience.

Many Unitarian Universalists have a concept of a "loose-leaf" Bible, that is, they find inspiration in many writings—the scriptures of many religions, the philosophers of many times, the literatures of many cultures.

Do Unitarian Universalist Churches Observe Any Sacraments?

Unitarian Universalists know that the significant events of life—birth, maturation, marriage, death—are vital to the individual and important to the whole community and should be celebrated. So they have services to dedicate children, to recognize coming-of-age, to join in marriage, and to remember the dead.

None of these services is required for personal "salvation" or to "wash away" sin.

Nor do Unitarian Universalists feel that God is especially present in such acts or ceremonies. Instead, they see all of life as a sacrament and feel that the fundamental goodness of life is always present.

Do Any Unitarian Universalists Observe Communion?

The sharing of food and drink in the context of the community is an ancient religious practice—indicating trust, gratitude, mutual dependence, and fellowship. Unitarian Universalists usually do this informally, through coffee hours following services and other social occasions.

Formalized as services, in some Unitarian Universalist churches, such observances are symbolic expressions of the importance of community. They also may express appreciation for the continued importance of the life and the teachings of Jesus.

Do Unitarian Universalists Believe in Heaven and Hell?

Heaven and hell are states of mind, created by human beings. Hell is created in injustice, violence, tyranny, and war. Heaven is created in compassion, mercy, liberty, and love.

As one Unitarian stated many years ago, "Our task is not to get men into Heaven; it is to get Heaven into men."

Do Unitarian Universalists Think That Jesus Christ Was Divine?

In a sense they think that every person is divine—that is, that there is goodness and worth in everyone. Some call it a "divine spark," others simply "human dignity."

However, Unitarian Universalists see no need for the concept of a special divinity in Christ, and they clearly reject any notion of God's requiring the sacrifice of "His Son" to atone for human "sin."

Nor do they see the need for a Messiah of the Jewish hope or the Savior of Christian belief. But they are inspired by the life and teachings of Jesus as an extraordinary fellow human being.

How Do Unitarian Universalists View the Virgin Birth? The Resurrection?

The modern Unitarian Universalist finds much of the old terminology no longer pertinent to the religious needs of people today. Concepts such as the virgin birth and the resurrection are of this nature. Unitarian Universalists emphatically reject them as contrary to both scientific and historical evidence.

What Do Unitarian Universalists Teach About Sin? About Salvation?

Unitarian Universalists reject the traditional Christian idea that the original sin of disobedience of Adam is inherited by all and can only be eliminated by God's "grace," operating through a church.

Unitarian Universalists recognize that there are cruel and destructive attributes of human nature, just as there are compassionate and creative attributes. They recognize also that evil is often a twisting or perverting of normal healthy human drives.

Human beings have a responsibility not only for their own personal behavior but to help create a society that does not breed crime, corruption, and brutality.

Unitarian Universalists reject the idea that God sacrificed Jesus, "His Son," to "atone" for human "sin." They believe in the importance of virtue and virtuous living and doing—for its own sake, and not out of some hypothetical "salvation" or "reward" in the future or the "hereafter."

What Do Unitarian Universalists Teach Their Children?

Unitarian Universalists believe that children must themselves discover and develop religious ideals to fit their own lives. They teach their children by helping them to experience the wonder and mystery of life, by sharing with them the best insights of the great religions, and by encouraging them to understand the consequences of their own choices.

The church school curriculum makes use of the arts and of such sciences as biology, anthropology, and psychology.

Do Unitarian Universalists Try to Make Converts?

No, Unitarian Universalists do not proselytize; they do not send out missionaries. They consider religion a private and personal matter. Of course, they do try to let others know about their principles and welcome all who are interested to participate in their activities.

Do Unitarian Universalist Services Differ from Those in Other Churches?

Some Unitarian Universalist worship services resemble typical Protestant services, although they are usually simpler and the readings are not taken exclusively from the Bible. Other services may make extensive use of drama, dance, music, and poetry to create services of celebration. Many services are very informal and include opportunities for discussion by anyone present.

Each congregation develops its own services to serve the needs of its own people.

What Kind of Sermons Do Your Ministers Preach?

Unitarian Universalist ministers cherish the tradition of the free pulpit and frequently preach on a wide range of topics, including controversial social and political subjects. Ministers are expected to express the truth as they see it, understanding full well that those attending the sermon are free themselves to make up their own minds.

What Is the Unitarian Universalist Attitude Toward Sex?

Sex is a most profound and beautiful aspect of being a human being. It ought to be joyfully and responsibly experienced.

Unitarian Universalists are agreed that sexual activity performed privately by consenting adults should not be subject to legal sanctions.

One of the church school curriculum units is entitled "About Your Sexuality." It provides opportunities for full and explicit discussion of many aspects of sexuality, so that young people may know the range of choices available to them and can learn to make their own responsible decision for their own lives.

What Is the Position of Your Church on Black People?

Absolutely no distinction is made in the church because of "race, color, sex, or national origin," to quote the Bylaws.

Unitarian Universalists are deeply sympathetic with efforts toward the empowerment of black people and other minority peoples, even though there has been disagreement among members over the tactics and militancy of some groups, both within and without the denomination, who are working for such empowerment.

What Is Your Attitude Toward Divorce?

Unitarian Universalists hold that divorce is entirely a matter for conscientious decision on the part of the persons involved.

What Is the Unitarian Universalist Position on Birth Control?

Unitarian Universalists have long pioneered in movements to eliminate restrictive laws in this area.

Unitarian Universalists are strong advocates of responsible parenthood—that is, in conceiving only those children who will enter the world wanted, loved, and cared for. Birth control information and devices ought to be readily accessible to all adults, so that they can make their own responsible decisions about whether and when to have children.

What Is the Status of Women in Your Church?

Unitarian Universalists make no distinction in their church life between women and men. Both may hold any position in the organizational structure.

There have been women in their ministry for over 100 years. One of the first American women ordained to the ministry was the Universalist Olympia Brown, in 1863. While less than 5 percent of Unitarian Universalist ministers are women, there is evidence of greater acceptance of women in the ministry in recent years.

The 1970 General Assembly passed a special resolution, which:

1. Urges special concern for improving the image, aspirations, and opportunities of women so that they may work together with men toward creating a more fully human society for both; and to that end changes are called for in the education and counseling of girls and boys;

2. Asks for greater efforts to prevent discrimination against women in employment and to encourage the utilization of women in significant levels in business, education, and government;

3. Calls upon the United States and Provinces of Canada to enact Fair Employment legislation prohibiting discrimination on account of sex, where such laws do not now exist;

4. Requests that a special effort be made in the Unitarian Universalist Association . . . to place greater numbers of qualified young and mature women in policy-making-positions, and to secure equal opportunities and

pay for women in the ministry, religious education, and administration;

5. Calls upon the United States Congress to pass the Equal Rights Amendent without delay and supports its ratification by the States.

What Is the Unitarian Universalist Attitude Toward Abortion?

Unitarian Universalists have pioneered in movements to eliminate restrictive laws regarding abortion. Abortion is a matter for the personal ethical choice of the pregnant woman. The law ought only to ensure that abortions are performed by qualified medical personnel.

By more than a two-thirds vote, the 1968 General Assembly passed a resolution urging "that efforts be made to abolish existing abortion laws, except to prohibit performance of an abortion by a person who is not a duly licensed physician, leaving the decision as to an abortion to the doctor and his patient."

A 1963 resolution had supported the enactment of a uniform statute to make abortion legal in cases where:

1. The pregnancy resulted from rape or from incest;
2. The mother's health, physical or mental, would be gravely impaired by a delivery;
3. The child would be born seriously defective, physically or mentally;
4. Other "compelling reasons"—physical, psychological, economic—exist.

What Is the Unitarian Universalist Attitude Toward Homosexuality?

Unitarian Universalists are opposed to all discrimination against homosexuals and bisexuals. They are agreed that sexual activity performed privately, between consenting adults, should not be subject to legal sanctions.

They have developed a course, for adolescents and adults, entitled, "The Invisible Minority: The Homosexuals in Our Society," whose emphasis is on understanding and accepting all people as human beings of worth and dignity.

The 1970 General Assembly passed a resolution (VII) concerning homosexual and bisexual persons, which stated that:

1. A significant minority in this country are either homosexual or bisexual in their feelings and/or behavior;
2. Homosexuality has been the target of severe discrimination by society, and in particular by the police and other arms of government;

3. A growing number of authorities on the subject now see homosexuality as an inevitable sociological phenomenon and not as a mental illness;

4. There are Unitarian Universalists, clergy and laity, who are homosexuals or bisexuals;

Therefore be it resolved: That the 1970 General Assembly of the Unitarian Universalist Association:

1. Urges all peoples immediately to bring an end to all discrimination against homosexuals, homosexuality, bisexuals, and bisexuality, with specific immediate attention to the following issues:

a. Private consensual behavior between persons over the age of consent shall be the business only of those persons and not subject to legal regulations.

b. A person's sexual orientation or practice shall not be a factor in the granting or renewing of Federal security clearance, visas, and the granting of citizenship or employment.

2. Calls upon the UUA and its member churches, fellowships, and organizations immediately to end all discrimination against homosexuals in employment practices, expending special effort to assist homosexuals to find employment in our midst consistent with their abilities and desires.

3. Urges all churches and fellowships, in keeping with our changing social patterns, to initiate meaningful programs of sex education . . . with the particular aim to end all discrimination against homosexuals and bisexuals.

What Is the Attitude of Unitarian Universalists Toward Other Religions?

Unitarian Universalists believe that no religion—including their own—has exclusive possession of the truth. All ought to be honored and respected for the truths in them. The following of almost any religion can help a dedicated individual find a better and more meaningful life.

Unitarian Universalists have always favored the study of world religions and have been influential in attempts to bring religious leaders together for dialogue and cooperation.

What Is Their Position on the Role of Church and State?

The Unitarian Universalist Association at its 1963 General Assembly reaffirmed its support of religious freedom based on the principle of separation of church and state and urged its members to:

uphold the principle of nonsectarian public education; oppose Bible readings and religious observances in public schools; oppose released time for religious education; refrain, if possible, from holding religious services or classes on public property; refrain from use of public school property for such purposes without payment of a fair rental.

Do Unitarian Universalists Engage in Political Activity?

Unitarian Universalists have always felt that an active concern for society is an essential part of their religious life. Religion is to them more a matter of deeds than creeds.

They have been among the leaders in every American movement for social justice—abolition of slavery, education, women's suffrage, peace, civil rights. Although they are members of a religious minority, they have never withdrawn from the larger society; they have identified themselves with it and worked for its betterment.

They do not as a denomination endorse particular candidates or political parties but are often outspoken in their defense of civil liberties and their insistence on racial justice. They have consistently advocated international cooperation and the principles of the United States.

Are Unitarian Universalists "Conscientious Objectors" to Military Service?

Although many Unitarian Universalists are conscientious objectors to participating personally in military service, many are not—and have served in the armed forces with distinction.

They all agree, however, that war represents a failure to solve international disputes by more moral means.

Does Your Denomination Engage in Many Humanitarian Activities?

The Unitarian Universalist Service Committee engages in humanitarian service in many countries. Its projects are completely nonsectarian and are designed to help empower those who are prevented from exercising their own free choices in their lives—because of sickness, poverty, ignorance, or lack of organizational resources.

How Did the Unitarian and Universalist Movements Arise?

The sources of both movements go back to those Jewish, Greek, and early Christian traditions that emphasized human creativity, the use of reason, monotheism, and ethical living. Their histories are more directly traced to the early Protestant Reformation in Europe.

Michael Servetus was burned at the stake, in 1553, in John Calvin's Geneva for his Unitarian "heresy." A Unitarian king, John Sigismund of Transylvania (now part of Hungary and Rumania), in 1568 issued the first edict of religious freedom—which affirmed the loyalty of citizens without their having to accept the king's religion. Unitarian churches still exist in that region.

Unitarianism as an idea spread to England and later to America, where Joseph Priestley, a refugee from England because of his ideas, formed the first American church specifically called "Unitarian." Already in Boston, historic Kings Chapel had altered its Anglican prayer book and embraced Unitarian ideas as early as 1785.

A trend toward the liberalization of doctrine in many New England congregational churches, begun in the eighteenth century, culminated in the "Unitarian Controversy" early in the nineteenth century. William Ellery Channing voiced the liberal view in his 1819 sermon "Unitarian Christianity," and many old established parish churches became Unitarian by congregational decision.

Meanwhile, outside these established churches the Universalists were challenging some of the main tenets of Calvinism. John Murray formed the first church of that denomination in Gloucester, Massachusetts, in 1779. Under the influence of Hosea Ballou, the message of Universal Salvation spread throughout New England and other parts of the country.

Rather than taking over existing churches and property (like the Unitarians), Universalists created their own independent congregations in the same democratic congregational tradition as the Unitarians. During the nineteenth century Universalist ideas were carried south and west by circuit-riding preachers who organized churches, helped found colleges, and joined in social reform movements.

From their beginnings in America, both Unitarianism and Universalism were in harmony with the democratic ideals of freedom, individualism, and social progress.

What Role Have Unitarian Universalists Played in American History?

Five presidents, including Jefferson and both Adamses, were Unitarians; and many "founding fathers"—Benjamin Franklin, Thomas Paine, James Madison, Benjamin Rush, and others—indicated their sympathy with Unitarian Universalist principles.

Many great literary figures of the last century—Emerson, Hawthorne, Longfellow, Thoreau, Holmes, Bryant, Lowell, Alcott—were Unitarians or Universalists. So were many social reformers, including Horace Mann, Susan B. Anthony, Henry Berg, and Clara Barton.

Today, many prominent persons in science, education, government, and the arts identify themselves with this religious movement.

How Is the Unitarian Universalist Church Organized?

Each local congregation is autonomous and enjoys full self-determination. It completely governs itself, including the employing and discharging of its minister (if it has one).

Of the more than 1,000 congregations in North America, approximately half have ministers. Those which do not (many are called fellowships rather than churches) tend to be smaller and more informal in their services. These congregations are members of a continental organization, the Unitarian Universalist Association, and elect its officers and trustees. They also express their combined views by votes of delegates at the denomination's General Assembly.

The denomination sponsors a publishing arm, Beacon Press, which has produced many notable books, and a Church of the Larger Fellowship, which serves isolated religious liberals.

How Do You Become a Unitarian Universalist?

You may already be one without knowing it. You are if you: (1) believe in the dignity and worth of all persons; (2) cherish full freedom of belief for yourself and for all others; (3) insist that religious ideas must be tested by personal thought and experience; (4) remain actively open to new knowledge and greater understanding; (5) honor the teachings of all great religions, while continuing to exercise personal judgment; and (6) welcome the mutual support of others in a free religious community.

Formally, you can become a Unitarian Universalist by joining a church or fellowship. Such joining requires no baptism, confirmation, or acceptance of a creed; it requires simply a commitment to follow the group's principles and promote its program.

What Does Unitarian Universalism Stress in the World Today?

To a world that is often cold, cruel, and impersonal, Unitarian Universalists offer warmth, compassion, and fellowship. They offer a religious outlook that reveres the past but remains open to fresh insight; that accepts diversity of opinion while it seeks a unity of spirit; that promotes social justice while it emphasizes personal responsibility; that defends individual liberty while it encourages effective organization; that has a vision of a better life on earth while it appreciates the beauty and joy that are continuously present.

They know they often miss living up to these ideals, both personally and organizationally. Their hopes are not always fulfilled. Satisfaction is not guaranteed. But they believe they are part of a noble experiment, and they invite all who are in sympathy to join and help to make it work.

WHAT IS THE UNITED
CHURCH OF CHRIST?

**THE CHURCH OFFICE OF COMMUNICATION / The United Church
of Christ, with 6,635 local churches and approximately 1,895,016
members, was formed in 1957 by union of the Evangelical and Reformed
and Congregational Christian churches. It was the first union in the
United States of denominations with different ethnic backgrounds and
forms of church government.**

What Constitutes Membership in the United Church of Christ?

Membership is in a local church. In accordance with the custom
and usage of the individual church, persons become members by
(1) baptism and either confirmation or profession of faith; (2)
reaffirmation or reprofession of faith; or (3) letter of transfer or
certification from other Christian churches. All persons who are
members of a local church affiliated with the United Church of
Christ are members of the United Church of Christ.

What Is the United Church of Christ Creed?

Traditionally the Congregational Christian churches were non-
creedal, although many individual churches adopted their own
statements of faith. The Evangelical and Reformed Church had a
statement of faith for the whole denomination. An important aspect
of the negotiations toward union was agreement upon a Statement
of Faith to be regarded "as a testimony, not a test of faith." In the
Preamble to the Constitution accepted by the uniting churches there
is this affirmation: "[The United Church of Christ] claims as its
own the faith of the historic Church expressed in the ancient creeds
and reclaimed in the basic insights of the Protestant Reformers. It
affirms the responsibility of the Church in each generation to make
this faith its own in reality of worship, in honesty of thought and
expression, and in purity of heart before God."

What Sacraments Does the United Church of Christ Recognize?

Two: Baptism and the Lord's Supper, or Holy Communion.

Infants are presented for baptism by their parents and/or sponsors. Baptism may also be administered to believers at the time of confirmation and reception into membership. Sprinkling is the usual mode of baptism. In most churches, the elements of communion are brought to the people in the pews.

Do Members of the United Church of Christ Believe in the Virgin Birth?

Probably the majority do not. There is no reference to the manner of Christ's birth in the Statement of Faith. It is his life and resurrection that the church celebrates.

Do You Believe in the Holy Trinity?

Yes. The Statement of Faith begins: "We believe in God, the Eternal Spirit, Father of our Lord Jesus Christ . . ." The Holy Spirit is referred to separately as "creating and renewing the Church of Jesus Christ, binding in covenant faithful people of all ages, tongues and races."

Who Is the Head of the United Church of Christ?

"The United Church of Christ acknowledges as its sole Head, Jesus Christ, the son of God and the Saviour of men" (Preamble to the Constitution of the United Church of Christ).

What Is Your View of Sin and Salvation?

As most Christians, members of the United Church of Christ believe that sin is opposition or indifference to the will of God. Most members accept the declaration in the Statement of Faith that God "seeks in holy love to save all people from aimlessness and sin [and] promises to all who trust him forgiveness of sins and fullness of grace . . ."

Do Your Members Believe in Heaven and Hell?

Many do not believe that there are specific places of eternal bliss or punishment after death. But they do tend to believe that God judges men and nations by his righteous will and that he promises eternal life.

What Is the Attitude Toward the Bible?

The United Church of Christ looks to the Word of God in the Scriptures as inspiration for its work in the world. Passages from the Bible are used for reading in worship and for interpretation through preaching, so that "the people of God relive what he had done in the past and participate in what he is doing now" (UCC Commission on Worship). Members are not charged to believe literally any version of the Scripture.

What Is the United Church of Christ Attitude Toward Abortion?

The Eighth General Synod of the United Church of Christ in 1971 adopted a resolution calling for repeal of all legal prohibitions of physician-performed abortions. The General Synod, while broadly representative of the church, speaks only for itself, not for the whole fellowship. Individual members differ widely on their attitudes toward abortion.

What Is the Attitude Toward Birth Control?

The United Church Board for World Ministries has supported the dissemination of birth control information and materials overseas, especially in India. Scientific research on various methods of birth control was supported by the United Church Board for Homeland Ministries and conducted in church-related hospitals. It would be safe to say that most United Church members do not regard birth control as a "religious" issue.

What Is the Attitude Toward Homosexuality?

There is no church policy on homosexuality per se. The question of the ordination of a homosexual to the ministry has been raised, and the Council for Church and Ministry of the denomination decided that it could not give a categorical endorsement, stating that each situation should be judged on its merits. Ordination is given by the local association in cooperation with the local church. In 1972 a stated homosexual was ordained to the United Church ministry by the Golden Gate Association of California.

What Is the Attitude of the Church to Black People?

Between 700 and 800 of the 6,635 churches of the denomination are predominantly black, about 2.5 percent of the total membership. Such figures do not, however, properly describe the role and influence of blacks in the church. Historically the Congregational churches were involved in the abolitionist movement, and during and after the Civil War supported the founding of schools and colleges for freed slaves by the American Missionary Association—now part of the United Church Board for Homeland Ministries. The institutions of higher education for blacks have contributed outstanding leaders, men and women who serve the church in high elective office not only as representatives of their race but of the best qualified among the membership. The Commission for Racial Justice was established by the General Synod to implement the concern of the church that minorities be brought into the mainstream of life both in the church and in society. Black clergy and laity of the denomination have organized around common concerns.

What Is the Attitude of the United Church of Christ Toward Women?

In theory, there is no distinction in church status between men and women. Women have been ordained in the Congregational churches for over a century. Boards of directors of church agencies and the General Synod itself are made up of one-third ordained ministers, one-third lay men and one-third lay women. There are 280 women clergy, and about 70 of these are pastors of local churches. The General Synod of 1971 established a Task Force on Women in Church and Society to inquire into and take steps toward ending any discrimination because of sex.

What Distinguishes the United Church of Christ from Other Protestant Communions?

The emphasis upon the congregation. The basic unit of life and organization of the denomination is the autonomous local church. The congregations maintain "free and voluntary relationships" with each other and with local associations, regional and national bodies. No higher body has the power to interfere in the local church's management of its own affairs.

What Type of Worship Is Used in the United Church of Christ?

At the heart of the corporate life of the church is the Service of Word and Sacrament. Since the churches generally accept the priesthood of all believers, congregational worship requires the full involvement of the people. There is no single style of liturgy required. The development of liturgical forms and materials is regarded as an ongoing task. The usual Lord's Day Service expresses adoration of God, confession of sin, assurance of pardon, thanksgiving, and dedication to God's will.

How Is the United Church of Christ Organized?

Local churches are banded together in associations (usually county-wide)—and all ministers have standing in their associations—and in conferences (often state-wide).

Conferences elect delegates to the biennial General Synod, which carries on the national and international work of the church and provides for its financial support. The work is done through the Executive Council, mission boards, and other instrumentalities. The Synod elects the full-time officers of the church: president, secretary, director of finance, and treasurer. According to the UCC Constitution, "Actions by or decisions or advice emanating from the General Synod, a Conference or an Association should be held in highest regard by every local church."

What Is the United Church of Christ Attitude Toward Social Problems?

The desire for liberation of human beings from both spiritual and physical bondage is frequently expressed in words and actions in the United Church of Christ. Resolutions have called for special administrative or legislative action, and church leaders have testified before national and state legislative bodies on social and economic issues. Current priorities of the church are the extension of racial justice and the use of United States power to serve humane ends and contribute to world peace.

In the United Church of Christ, What Is Seen as the Purpose of the Church?

This is expressed in the Statement of Faith: "He calls us into his Church to accept the cost and joy of discipleship, to be his servants in the service of men, to proclaim the gospel to all the world and resist the powers of evil, to share in Christ's baptism and eat at his table, to join him in his passion and victory."

What Is the Attitude Toward Cooperation With Other Denominations?

It has been called a "uniting church." The Constitution empowers the General Synod "to encourage conversations with other communions and when appropriate to authorize and guide negotiations with them looking toward formal union." The denomination was a founder and is still a member of the Consultation on Church Union. It is an active participant in ecumenical and interfaith bodies, including the National Council of Churches and the World Council of Churches. It is also active in world confessional bodies related to the Congregational and Reformed churches, now united in the World Alliance of Reformed Churches (Presbyterian and Congregational).

What Role Have the Fathers of the United Church Played in American History?

The Pilgrim fathers who landed on Plymouth Rock were the first Congregationalists to reach the New World from England. These Puritans and those who followed to settle throughout New England gave birth to constitutional liberty in this country. Their belief in an educated ministry and laity led them to found institutions of higher learning across the country.

The Reformed wing of the denomination was founded in the eighteenth century by German settlers who fled oppression in Europe and participated actively in the American Revolution. The Evangelical wing derives from German and Swiss refugees from political oppression and enforced military service who settled in the Mississippi Valley in the nineteenth century. Their style of religious life led to the foundation of hundreds of institutions for the poor and sick, hospitals, and homes for children and the aged.

WHAT IS AN AGNOSTIC?

BERTRAND RUSSELL / Bertrand Russell (1872–1970), winner of the Nobel Prize in literature, was one of the most original, incisive and significant minds of the twentieth century. Through more than forty books, Lord Russell has made lasting contributions to philosophy, mathematics, logic, political thought, theories of education, social problems. His Nobel Prize citation called him one who has "constantly figured as a defender of humanity and freedom of thought."

Bertrand Arthur William Russell was born in 1872 at Ravenscroft, England, in a family that has played an important role in English history since the sixteenth century. (His grandfather was twice prime minister.) He became the third Earl Russell in 1931, when his older brother died.

Bertrand Russell's first intellectual loves were mathematics (he studied Euclid when he was eleven) and philosophy. He received an M.A. from Trinity College, Cambridge, and won international attention with *The Principles of Mathematics* (1903), in which he explored the relationship between mathematics, logic, and symbols. With Alfred North Whitehead, he wrote the monumental and historic three-volume *Principia Mathematica*.

Russell was active in political affairs for seven decades. He was a member of the Fabian Society, was an early advocate of women's suffrage, and once decided to stand for Parliament. (He was turned down by the Liberal party because he was an avowed freethinker.) A pacifist and conscientious objector, he spent four months in an English prison during World War I—and used the time to write his admirable *Introduction to Mathematical Philosophy*.

Mr. Russell traveled widely and made many lecture tours throughout the United States. He taught at Harvard University, the University of Chicago, the National University in Peking (China), the University of California at Los Angeles, and the College of the City of New York— where, it will be remembered, a storm of public protest revolved around him as an advocate of "free love" and "an enemy of religion and morality."

In recent years, Lord Russell devoted his prodigious energy to the campaign for disarmament and against nuclear testing. He was the leader and spokesman for the Committee of 100, a militant group within the Campaign for Nuclear Disarmament in England, which reinforces its arguments with a policy of civil disobedience.

During 1961, the year of his ninetieth birthday, Russell served a week in prison—in the same jail where he had been imprisoned in World War I—

for refusing to call off a massive sit-down protest against the British government's nuclear weapons policy. He was a fervent and persistent pacifist (although he once urged the United States to drop an A-bomb on Moscow if the Russians persisted in refusing to accept then-current conciliatory offers vis-à-vis nuclear weapons and stabilizing the peace) and was an eloquent opponent of American intervention in Vietnam.

The insight, power, and originality of Bertrand Russell's mind are suggested by a listing of a few of the books for which he is famed: *The Principles of Mathematics, Our Knowledge of the External World, The Problems of China, Education and the Social Order, Mysticism and Logic, Marriage and Morals, The Conquest of Happiness, The Scientific Outlook, The ABC of Relativity, A Free Man's Worship, Human Knowledge: Its Scope and Limits, A History of Western Philosophy, Why I Am Not a Christian,* and *Unpopular Essays.* His three-volume *Autobiography* contains a wealth of intimate revelations about both his public and his private life. His *Portraits from Memory* contains fascinating information and insights about some of the most celebrated figures of his time.

Among the many honors Lord Russell received during his lifetime are the Order of Merit, the Nicholas Murray Butler Medal of Columbia University, the Sylvester Medal of the Royal Society, and the de Morgan Medal of the London Mathematical Society.

Lord Russell's literary style, celebrated for clarity and precision, has earned him a high place among the masters of English prose. When he was awarded the Nobel Prize in 1950, the Swedish Academy cited him as "one of our times' most brilliant spokesmen of rationality and hunmanity, and a fearless champion of free speech and free thought in the West." That, he certainly was.

He died at the age of ninety-seven. [LR]

Are Agnostics Atheists?

No. An atheist, like a Christian, holds that we *can* know whether or not there is a God. The Christian holds that we can know there is a God; the atheist, that we can know there is not. The agnostic suspends judgment, saying that there are not sufficient grounds either for affirmation or for denial.

At the same time, an agnostic may hold that the existence of God, though not impossible, is very improbable; he may even hold it so improbable that it is not worth considering in practice. In that case, he is not far removed from atheism. His attitude may be that which a careful philosopher would have toward the gods of ancient Greece. If I were asked to *prove* that Zeus and Poseidon and Hera and the rest of the Olympians do not exist, I should be at a loss to find conclusive arguments.

An agnostic may think the Christian God as improbable as the Olympians; in that case, he is, for practical purposes, at one with the atheists.

Since You Deny "God's Law," What Authority Do You Accept as a Guide to Conduct?

An agnostic does not accept any "authority" in the sense in which religious people do. He holds that a man should think out questions of conduct for himself. Of course, he will seek to profit by the wisdom of others, but he will have to select for himself the people he is to consider wise, and he will not regard even what they say as unquestionable. He will observe that what passes as "God's law" varies from time to time.

The Bible says both that a woman must not marry her deceased husband's brother, and that, in certain circumstances, she must do so. If you have the misfortune to be a childless widow with an unmarried brother-in-law, it is logically impossible for you to avoid disobeying "God's law."

How Do You Know What Is Good and What Is Evil? What Does an Agnostic Consider a Sin?

The agnostic is not quite so certain as some Christians are as to what is good and what is evil. He does not hold, as most Christians in the past held, that people who disagree with the government on abstruse points of theology ought to suffer a painful death. He is against persecution, and rather chary of moral condemnation.

As for "sin," he thinks it not a useful notion.

He admits, of course, that some kinds of conduct are desirable and some undesirable, but he holds that the punishment of undesirable kinds is only to be commended when it is deterrent or reformatory, not when it is inflicted because it is thought a good thing on its own account that the wicked should suffer.

It was this belief in vindictive punishment that made men accept hell. This is part of the harm done by the notion of "sin."

Does an Agnostic Do Whatever He Pleases?

In one sense, no; in another sense, everyone does whatever he pleases.

Suppose, for example, you hate someone so much that you would like to murder him. Why do you not do so? You may reply: "Because religion tells me that murder is a sin." But as a statistical fact, agnostics are not more prone to murder than other people, in fact, rather less so. They have the same motives for abstaining from murder as other people have.

Far and away the most powerful of these motives is the fear of punishment. In lawless conditions, such as a gold rush, all sorts of people will commit crimes, although in ordinary circumstances they would have been law-abiding. There is not only actual legal punishment; there is the discomfort of dreading discovery, and the loneliness of knowing that, to avoid being hated, you must wear a mask even with your closest intimates.

And there is also what may be called "conscience": If you ever contemplated a murder, you would dread the horrible memory of your victim's last moments or lifeless corpse. All this, it is true, depends upon your living in a law-abiding community, but there are abundant secular reasons for creating and preserving such a community.

I said that there is another sense in which every man does as he pleases. No one but a fool indulges every impulse, but what holds a desire in check is always some other desire. A man's antisocial wishes may be restrained by a wish to please God, but they may also be restrained by a wish to please his friends, or to win the respect of his community, or to be able to contemplate himself without disgust. But if he has no such wishes, the mere abstract precepts of morality will not keep him straight.

How Does an Agnostic Regard the Bible?

An agnostic regards the Bible exactly as enlightened clerics regard it. He does not think that it is divinely inspired; he thinks its early history legendary, and no more exactly true than that in Homer; he thinks its moral teaching sometimes good, but sometimes very bad. For example: Samuel ordered Saul, in a war, to kill not only every man, woman, and child of the enemy, but also all the sheep and cattle. Saul, however, let the sheep and cattle live, and for this we are told to condemn him.

I have never been able to admire Elisha for cursing the children who laughed at him, or to believe (what the Bible asserts) that a benevolent Deity would send two she-bears to kill the children.

How Does an Agnostic Regard Jesus, the Virgin Birth, and the Holy Trinity?

Since an agnostic does not believe in God, he cannot think that Jesus was God. Most agnostics admire the life and moral teachings of Jesus as told in the Gospels, but not necessarily more than those of certain other men. Some would place him on a level with Buddha, some with Socrates, and some with Abraham Lincoln.

Nor do they think that what He said is not open to question, since they do not accept any authority as absolute.

They regard the Virgin Birth as a doctrine taken over from pagan mythology, where such births were not uncommon. (Zoroaster was said to have been born of a virgin; Ishtar, the Babylonian goddess, is called the Holy Virgin.) They cannot give credence to it or to the doctrine of the Trinity, since neither is possible without belief in God.

Can an Agnostic Be a Christian?

The word "Christian" has had various different meanings at different times. Throughout most of the centuries since the time of Christ, it has meant a person who believed in God and immortality and held that Christ was God. But Unitarians call themselves Christians, although they do not believe in the divinity of Christ, and many people nowadays use the word "God" in a much less precise sense than that which it used to bear.

Many people who say they believe in God no longer mean a person, or a trinity of persons, but only a vague tendency or power or purpose immanent in evolution. Others, going still further, mean by "Christianity" merely a system of ethics that, since they are ignorant of history, they imagine to be characteristic of Christians only.

When, in a recent book, I said that what the world needs is "love, Christian love, or compassion," many people thought this showed some change in my views, although, in fact, I might have said the same thing at any time.

If you mean by a "Christian" a man who loves his neighbor, who has wide sympathy with suffering, and who ardently desires a world freed from the cruelties and abominations that at present disfigure it, then, certainly, you will be justified in calling me a Christian. And, in this sense, I think you will find more "Christians" among agnostics than among the orthodox.

But, for my part, I cannot accept such a definition. Apart from other objections to it, it seems rude to Jews, Buddhists, Mohammedans, and other non-Christians, who, so far as history shows, have been at least as apt as Christians to practice the virtues that some modern Christians arrogantly claim as distinctive of their own religion.

I think also that all who called themselves Christians in an earlier time, and a great majority of those who do so at the present day, would consider that belief in God and immortality is essential to a Christian. On these grounds, I should not call myself a Christian, and I should say that an agnostic cannot be a Christian.

But, if the word "Christianity" comes to be generally used to mean merely a kind of morality, then it will certainly be possible for an agnostic to be a Christian.

Does an Agnostic Deny That Man Has a Soul?

This question has no precise meaning unless we are given a definition of the word "soul."

I suppose what is meant is, roughly, something nonmaterial that persists throughout a person's life and even, for those who believe in immortality, throughout all future time. If this is what is meant, an agnostic is not likely to believe that man has a soul.

But I must hasten to add that this does not mean that an agnostic must be a materialist. Many agnostics (including myself) are quite as doubtful of the body as they are of the soul, but this is a long story taking one into difficult metaphysics.

Mind and matter alike, I should say, are only convenient symbols in discourse, not actually existing things.

Does an Agnostic Believe in a Hereafter, in Heaven or Hell?

The question whether people survive death is one as to which evidence is possible. Psychical research and spiritualism are thought by many to supply such evidence.

An agnostic, as such, does not take a view about survival unless he thinks that there is evidence one way or the other.

For my part, I do not think there is any good reason to believe that we survive death, but I am open to conviction if adequate evidence should appear.

Heaven and hell are a different matter. Belief in hell is bound up with the belief that the vindictive punishment of sin is a good thing, quite independently of any reformative or deterrent effect that it may have. Hardly any agnostic believes this.

As for heaven, there might conceivably someday be evidence of its existence through spiritualism, but most agnostics do not think that there is such evidence and therefore do not believe in heaven.

Are You Never Afraid of God's Judgment in Denying Him?

Most certainly not. I also deny Zeus and Jupiter and Odin and Brahma, but this causes me no qualms.

I observe that a very large portion of the human race does not believe in God and suffers no visible punishment in consequence.

And if there were a God, I think it very unlikely that He would have such an uneasy vanity as to be offended by those who doubt His existence.

How Do Agnostics Explain the Beauty and Harmony of Nature?

I do not understand where this "beauty" and "harmony" are supposed to be found. Throughout the animal kingdom, animals ruthlessly prey upon each other. Most of them are either cruelly killed by other animals or slowly die of hunger. For my part, I am unable to see any very great beauty or harmony in the tapeworm. Let it not be said that this creature is sent as a punishment for our sins, for it is more prevalent among animals than among humans.

I suppose the questioner is thinking of such things as the beauty of the starry heavens. But one should remember that stars every now and again explode and reduce everything in their neighborhood to a vague mist. Beauty, in any case, is subjective and exists only in the eye of the beholder.

How Do Agnostics Explain Miracles and Other Revelations of God's Omnipotence?

Agnostics do not think that there is any evidence of "miracles" in the sense of happenings contrary to natural law. We know that faith healing occurs and is in no sense miraculous. At Lourdes, certain diseases can be cured and others cannot. Those that can be cured at Lourdes can probably be cured by any doctor in whom the patient has faith.

As for the records of other miracles, such as Joshua commanding the sun to stand still, the agnostic dismisses them as legends and points to the fact that all religions are plentifully supplied with such legends. There is just as much miraculous evidence for the Greek gods in Homer as for the Christian God in the Bible.

There Have Been Base and Cruel Passions, Which Religion Opposes. If You Abandon Religious Principles, Could Mankind Exist?

The existence of base and cruel passions is undeniable, but I find no evidence in history that religion has opposed these passions. On the contrary, it has sanctified them and enabled people to indulge them without remorse. Cruel persecutions have been commoner in Christendom than anywhere else.

What appears to justify persecution is dogmatic belief. Kindliness and tolerance only prevail in proportion as dogmatic belief decays. In our day, a new dogmatic religion, namely, communism, has arisen. To this, as to other systems of dogma, the agnostic is opposed.

The persecuting character of present-day communism is exactly like the persecuting character of Christianity in earlier centuries. Insofar as Christianity has become less persecuting, this is mainly due to the work of freethinkers who have made dogmatists rather less dogmatic. If they were as dogmatic now as in former times, they would still think it right to burn heretics at the stake.

The spirit of tolerance that some modern Christians regard as essentially Christian is, in fact, a product of the temper that allows doubt and is suspicious of absolute certainties.

I think that anybody who surveys past history in an impartial manner will be driven to the conclusion that religion has caused more suffering than it has prevented.

What Is the Meaning of Life to the Agnostic?

I feel inclined to answer by another question: What is the meaning of "the meaning of life"? I suppose what is intended is some general purpose.

I do not think that life in general has any purpose. It just happened. But individual human beings have purposes, and there is nothing in agnosticism to cause them to abandon these purposes. They cannot, of course, be certain of achieving the results at which they aim; but you would think ill of a soldier who refused to fight unless victory was certain.

The person who needs religion to bolster up his own purposes is a timorous person, and I cannot think as well of him as of the man who takes his chances while admitting that defeat is not impossible.

Does Not the Denial of Religion Mean the Denial of Marriage and Chastity?

Here again, one must reply by another question: Does the man who asks this question believe that marriage and chastity contribute to earthly happiness here below, or does he think that, while they cause misery here below, they are to be advocated as means of getting to heaven?

The man who takes the latter view will no doubt expect agnosticism to lead to a decay of what he calls virtue, but he will have to admit that what he calls virtue is not what ministers to the happiness of the human race while on earth. If, on the other hand, he takes the former view, namely, that there are terrestrial arguments in favor of marriage and chastity, he must also hold that these arguments are such as should appeal to an agnostic.

Agnostics, as such, have no distinctive views about sexual morality. But most of them would admit that there are valid arguments against the unbridled indulgence of sexual desires. They would derive these arguments, however, from terrestrial sources and not from supposed divine commands.

Is Not Faith in Reason Alone a Dangerous Creed? Is Not Reason Imperfect and Inadequate Without Spiritual and Moral Law?

No sensible man, however agnostic, has "faith in reason alone." Reason is concerned with matters of fact, some observed, some inferred.

The question whether there is a future life and the question whether there is a God concern matters of fact, and the agnostic will hold that they should be investigated in the same way as the question "Will there be an eclipse of the moon tomorrow?" But matters of fact alone are not sufficient to determine action, since they do not tell us what ends we ought to pursue. In the realm of ends, we need something other than reason.

The agnostic will find his ends in his own heart and not in an external command. Let us take an illustration: Suppose you wish to travel by train from New York to Chicago; you will use reason to discover when the trains run, and a person who thought that there was some faculty of insight or intuition enabling him to dispense with the timetable would be thought rather silly. But no timetable will tell him that it is wise to travel to Chicago.

No doubt, in deciding that it is wise, he will have to take account of further matters of fact; but behind all the matters of fact, there will be the ends that he thinks fitting to pursue, and these, for an agnostic as for other men, belong to a realm which is not that of reason, though it should be in no degree contrary to it.

The realm I mean is that of emotion and feeling and desire.

Do You Regard All Religions as Forms of Superstition or Dogma? Which of the Existing Religions Do You Most Respect, and Why?

All the great organized religions that have dominated large populations have involved a greater or less amount of dogma, but "religion" is a word of which the meaning is not very definite.

Confucianism, for instance, might be called a religion, although it involves no dogma. And in some forms of liberal Christianity, the element of dogma is reduced to a minimum.

Of the great religions of history, I prefer Buddhism, especially in its earliest forms, because it has had the smallest element of persecution.

Communism, Like Agnosticism, Opposes Religion. Are Agnostics Communists?

Communism does not oppose religion. It merely opposes the Christian religion, just as Mohammedanism does.

Communism, at least in the form advocated by the Soviet government and the Communist party, is a new system of dogma of a peculiarly virulent and persecuting sort. Every genuine agnostic must therefore be opposed to it.

Do Agnostics Think That Science and Religion Are Impossible to Reconcile?

The answer turns upon what is meant by "religion." If it means merely a system of ethics, it can be reconciled with science. If it means a system of dogma, regarded as unquestionably true, it is incompatible with the scientific spirit, which refuses to accept matters of fact without evidence and also holds that complete certainty is hardly ever attainable.

What Kind of Evidence Could Convince You That God Exists?

I think that if I heard a voice from the sky predicting all that was going to happen to me during the next twenty-four hours, including events that would have seemed highly improbable, and if all these events then proceeded to happen, I might perhaps be convinced at least of the existence of some superhuman intelligence.

I can imagine other evidence of the same sort that might convince me, but so far as I know, no such evidence exists.

ADDENDUM:
An anecdote Bertrand Russell told me during my conversations with him, in London, about the article above, may interest readers.

It involved his entrance into prison, during World War I, which he publicly and passionately opposed—and for which he was convicted:

"When I reported to the warder," Russell said (his eyes for the first time changed their objective gravity to a twinkle), "he asked me the customary questions—name, age, place of residence. Then he inquired, 'Religious affiliation?' "

"Agnostic," Russell replied.

The poor man looked up. "How do you spell that?"

Russell spelled "agnostic" for him.

The warder wrote the word carefully on the prison admission form, then sighed, "Oh, well; there are a great many sects, but I suppose they all worship the same God."

. . .

THE RELIGION OF A SCIENTIST

WARREN WEAVER / Warren Weaver, scientist, mathematician, and educator, was vice-president for the natural and medical sciences of the Rockefeller Foundation until 1959; since then he has been vice-president of the Alfred P. Sloan Foundation.

He was born in Reedsburg, Wisconsin, in 1894 and received his Ph.D. at the University of Wisconsin, where he was chairman of the Mathematics Department. He has been awarded an honorary LL.D. from his alma mater, and a D.S. from the University of São Paulo, Brazil.

Dr. Weaver has had a distinguished career in government service. During World War II, he was chief of the Applied Mathematics Panel of the National Research Defense Committee of the Office of Scientific Research and Development. He has served as a member of the War Department's Research Advisory Panel and was chairman of the Naval Research Advisory Committee. He is a member of the Board of Scientific Consultants of the Sloan-Kettering Institute for Cancer Research.

He has been president and chairman of the board of the American Association for the Advancement of Science, vice-president of the board of trustees of the Academy of Religion and Mental Health, and chairman of the board of the Salk Institute for Biological Studies. In 1969 he was elected a member of the National Academy of Sciences.

Dr. Weaver has received the U.S. Medal for Merit, is an officer of the Legion of Honor, and was awarded the King's Medal for Service in the Cause of Freedom. His publications include an autobiography, *Scene of Change,* a compilation entitled *The Scientists Speak, The Electromagnetic Field* (with Max Mason), *Elementary Mathematical Analysis,* and the pioneering *The Mathematical Theory of Communication* (with Claude Shannon).

Throughout my life—and since I am now in my early eighties I am speaking of a considerable span of years—I have had two dominant interests and concerns: science and religion.

My interest in science was originally stimulated when, as a small boy, I was given two fascinating toys—a small electric motor and a gyroscope. I was determined that eventually I would be able to understand these. I took the motor apart, removed the windings from the field coil and the armature, and was thrilled indeed when, reassembled by me, the motor again ran. Having been told that the name of this activity was "engineering," I decided to obtain training in that discipline. Midway through college I corrected what had really been only an error in terminology and began to study physics and mathematics rather than engineering.

After a happy period as a teacher of mathematics and theoretical physics, I joined the staff of the Rockefeller Foundation, where for nearly thirty years I was privileged to exercise the primary responsibility for the activities in science of that great organization. Later, I served the Sloan Foundation as a consultant on scientific affairs. Then and subsequently, it was my fortunate lot to participate in a rather wide range of scientific activities in many organizations in New York City, Washington, and elsewhere. In the early 1950s I was elected president of the American Association for the Advancement of Science; in 1969 I was elected a member of the National Academy of Sciences.

Now, I mention these activities not pridefully but with a sense of humbleness for the opportunities I have had—and to establish my scientific credentials with the readers of this book, most of whom are unlikely to have heard of me. When I express my ideas about religion, I am anxious that the reader accept these as coming from a person who has, in fact, had extensive opportunity to work in, and think about, science.

If my interest in science began when I was a young boy, my contacts with religion began earlier than that: for I was a member of a family in Wisconsin that regularly attended Sunday school and church—even including, when I was very young, dull and sparsely attended prayer meeting services.

There has never been any disturbing crisis in my religious life. Until some twenty years ago, it did not really occur to me to worry as to whether my confidence in scientific thought posed a challenge or difficulty to my religious faith.

But then I began to realize that I could no longer neglect to face honestly such questions as "Is the Bible account of creation, of miracles, and of a life after death scientifically acceptable?" "Do I really believe in God?"

In retrospect, I feel thankful that I began to ponder such questions at a time when science had moved far away from that arrogant confidence in its unlimited power and "infallibility" that characterized the thinking of many scientists in the nineteenth century.

In contrasting the state of scientific ideas that existed prior to 1900 with the situation after that date, it is crucial to recognize the distinction between *macroscience,* which deals with objects large enough to be seen by the unaided eye, and *submicroscopic* science, which deals with objects too small to be seen even with a microscope.

Familiar examples of macro-objects include grains of sand, billiard balls, comets, and stars. Examples of submicro-objects are individual atoms, electrons, and the other so-called "elementary particles" of modern physics.

The great scientific advances prior to 1900 were, for the most part, concerned with macroscopic objects. (The laws of dynamics, as largely originated by Galileo early in the seventeenth century and as perfected by Sir Isaac Newton a half-century later, were strikingly successful in analyzing the motions of macro-objects.) The power of the large-scale laws of dynamics was dramatically demonstrated in 1758 by the appearance in the skies, on schedule, of "Halley's comet"—after its three-quarters-of-a-century-old journey, in a narrowly elliptical path, extending over 3,000 million miles out into space. Certainly a science that could chart such an excursion and could forecast accurately the comet's reappearance was capable of dealing with almost any conceivable problem; and scientific pronouncements surely seemed to deserve acceptance as having complete validity.

There were comparable successes during the nineteenth century in various other fields of physics.* Indeed, the wide variety and the dramatic success of science in the nineteenth century quite naturally led to the conclusion that science would go on formulating precise and fully deterministic theories for one after another of nature's previously mysterious phenomena. There was little reason to doubt

---

* A sound basis for static electrical phenomena and currents of electricity was laid by Coulomb, Ampere, and Ohm late in the eighteenth and early nineteenth century. Oersted and Faraday formulated laws for the interaction of electric currents and magnetic fields and made possible the whole modern development of electric power. Shortly after the Civil War, Maxwell formulated his elegant and amazing equations for the components of electromagnetic fields, providing the tools for the invention of wireless telegraphy and for the analysis and control of countless other electromagnetic phenomena.

the unlimited scope and perfection of scientific advance. Science, late in the nineteenth century, was rather smugly proud of itself (not without justification, to be sure) and was confident that it would continue, in all directions, its majestic advance, its pronouncements safe from any serious challenge.

And then the lightning struck. In 1895, X-rays were discovered. Two years later, the new era in science was initiated by J. J. Thompson's discovery of the electron. Previous theories in physics had largely dealt with objects whose dimensions were of the order of centimeters or larger; but with the electron, whose diameter was of the order of one ten-thousand-billionth of a centimeter, science entered the world of submicroscopic phenomena—and wholly unexpected ideas began to be a necessary and essential part of science.

In 1900, Max Planck advanced the revolutionary concept that energy is not a smooth, continuously divisible entity, capable of existing in any amount, but rather that energy exists in small but discrete and indivisible bits. This strange new idea was confirmed theoretically by Einstein and experimentally by Millikan; and "quantum" theory was the inevitable result.

The theory of relativity was announced, in a restricted form, by Einstein in 1905 and in its full generality in 1916.

In 1913, Niels Bohr published the first of a series of epoch-making papers on atomic structure, and the new world of modern physics was revealed.

In all this dazzling array of novel and shocking ideas, there are two that I judge to be of central significance in any discussion of the relation between science and religion. If I am to advance with any persuasiveness my ideas concerning religion, I must deal briefly with these two important principles of quantum theory.

The Uncertainty Principle

In order to predict where an object will be at some future moment (and the power to predict is the very essence of scientific procedure), one must know where the object is now and how it is moving. In 1927, the young German physicist Heisenberg enunciated the principle that when one seeks to measure the *location* and, at the same time, the *velocity* of an elementary particle (such as an electron), then as one of these measurements is made with greater and greater accuracy, the simultaneous measurement of the other quantity is necessarily less and less accurate. A joint uncertainty exists in the two measurements, an uncertainty that *cannot be avoided*. Heisenberg's theory specified quantitatively the minimum size of that joint and inevitable discrepancy.

It is not difficult to see why a joint uncertainty must exist in the simultaneous measurements of location and velocity. The experimenter might reflect (from the particle being observed) a more and more energetic pulse of radiant energy in order to measure *position* more and more precisely. But as this pulse is increased in intensity, it has a greater and greater disturbing effect on the *velocity* of the particle.

To put it roughly, if you bounce off enough energy to tell you accurately where a particle is, the rebound imparts so much unknown velocity to the particle that you don't know much about how it is moving.

It is essential to realize that the point here is not that it is *difficult* simultaneously to measure position and velocity with more and more accuracy, but that it is *impossible*.

The recognition of the uncertainty principle made it clear that science *cannot furnish us with a rigidly deterministic theory of events*. A precise forecast of the future is excluded if we can have only an inaccurate measurement of present circumstances.

Please remember that all previous theories of nature had been based on the assumption that one *can* successfully distinguish between the behavior of objects and the means used to observe that behavior. But in dealing with atomic (and other very fine-scale) processes, it became clear to scientists that the measuring and observing procedures themselves may exercise a significant influence on the thing being observed. The influence is not of significant size when we are observing objects of large size and mass; but the effect became important—very important—when physics began to concentrate on the world of submicroscopic objects.

The Principle of Complementarity

Such considerations led the great physicist Bohr to conclude that the information we can obtain about an object by using one set of experimental conditions of observation should not be expected to be the same as, or necessarily consistent with, the information we obtain when using a different set of observational procedures. (If the second set of observational conditions excludes the first set, then the information obtained by using either set must be viewed as *complementary* to the information obtained by using the other observational procedure.) However contradictory the two sets of information may appear to be, they must be accepted as equally valid.

This dualistic viewpoint, now referred to as the *principle of complementarity,* permitted physics to escape from a most embarrassing dilemma. Under some experimental conditions, electrons (and also photons, which are the quantum units of light) behaved as though they were *particles,* like exceedingly small bullets moving at very high speeds. But under other experimental conditions, electrons and photons behaved as though they were *wavelike* in character, producing diffraction patterns, just as waves do.

To an old-fashioned physicist, all this sounded like nonsense! What is an electron—a particle or a wave? It cannot be both: yet that, in fact, is precisely the answer! It can be both. Bohr's principle of complementarity indicated that under one set of observational circumstances, electrons must be considered to be particles, whereas under other observational circumstances, they must be considered to be wavelike. By accepting the two contradictory descriptions, and by using each under appropriate circumstances, we have a richer, more satisfying total concept than is furnished by either description alone.

The idea of the valid use of two contradictory viewpoints is by no means restricted to physics. As Bohr emphasized, there are numerous pairs of contradictory concepts (*love* and *hate,* for example; *practical* and *ideal; intuitive* and *logical*) that, when held jointly and used appropriately, give us a more complete and satisfying description than can be achieved otherwise.*

* It may be helpful for the reader to look at a simple example that further illustrates the concept of complementarity. If a person is interested in "positive numbers" and asks "What is the square root of +4?" the answer is of course +2. If another person is interested in "negative numbers," and asks the same question, the answer is −2. But if a third person takes a more embracing view, the answer is that *both +2 and −2 are square roots of +4,* since either of these numbers, when multiplied by itself, gives +4. The third person has a richer and more rewarding total reply, even though the two parts of it are completely inconsistent.

To summarize: quantum theory, and particularly the uncertainty principle and the principle of complementarity, have made it clear to us that:

1. The observations of the scientist are never strictly objective but depend upon the observer and upon the circumstances of observation.
2. The measurements of science are necessarily subject to some imprecision.
3. Scientific theories cannot be rigidly deterministic.
4. Science accepts, and in fact views as desirable, the sort of contradiction that is recognized and utilized in the principle of complementarity.

My Religious Belief

Let me now turn to a statement of my religious belief. I have no qualifications for attempting any philosophical analysis of the general relation between science and religion; I can only state, as simply as possible, what are my own religious views.

Throughout my discussion, I will be sustained—and liberated—by the concept of complementarity. For if I ask a question from one point of view, I will have one answer. But if I ask the same question from another, and quite different, point of view, I may very well have a second answer. The second may be inconsistent with the first, but it can be viewed as complementary. And the two answers taken together will provide a richer, truer picture than either separately.

In general, I take a very liberal position in religion. I think that this great body of thought has changed and grown over the years, from the primitive ideas held many centuries ago to the principles of Christianity as interpreted and understood today—a good deal the way atomic theory advanced and changed from Democritus to Bohr.

But I believe there is an important and abiding difference between religion and science. In religion there is little likelihood, as I see it, of a need developing for important changes in the basic, central concepts—although there will surely be great change in the more superficial aspects: forms of worship, specific dogmas defining moral behavior in modern situations, and so on. For example, in the church my wife and I now attend, the young people take part in informally structured services, playing musical instruments popular with them, and celebrating with dance as well as with music and words. This doubtless disturbs some of the conservative members. That is a pity, for the young people are simply returning to forms of worship that existed long ago, using modes of expression that are natural and appealing to them.

In contrast with religion, I think science is unlikely to alter its outward manifestations (the laws for gross matter, for example) but will almost surely have to change, significantly, its inner ideas.

This different situation with respect to change, in religion and in science, means, I believe, that in religion certitude is characteristic of the very core of the ideas, whereas confusion and uncertainty may characterize the superficial aspects. In science, certainty lies near the surface, but uncertainty and confusion lie near the very core.

I do not believe, for instance, that Western man will ever have to change the basic principles that Moses or Jesus enunciated, although we will surely have to reinterpret them, to make them applicable to changing modern problems.

Science and religion, then, *both change, but in very different ways,* because of the contrasting levels at which uncertainty and confusion exist.

It seems to me especially unfortunate and objectionable to repeat aloud, even if only formally, certain religious ideas that are neither understood nor believed by the speaker. I, for one, never recite the Apostles' Creed when it is part of the church service. For this creed asserts numerous beliefs that, in fact, I do not hold, and their acceptance does not seem to me to be at all necessary to an honestly held religious faith.

Some of the traditional dogmas of the Christian religion seem to me essentially unintelligible—the doctrine of the Trinity and the divinity of Christ, for example. These doctrines are phrased in words that I simply do not understand and to which I am unable to assign a reasonable and useful meaning. And the nonacceptance of these formal doctrines does not seem to me to weaken or disturb the essential truth and beauty of the Christian religion.

As to the Bible: I consider most of it to be a marvelous, beautiful human record of divine thought. In view of the historical facts about the various codices, their centuries-long wanderings through a number of languages, I am neither surprised nor disturbed at the wide range of quality in the Bible, nor at the textual inconsistencies. The infiltrations of folklore, myth, and poetry add much to the interest and charm—without, for me at least, affecting the validity.

There are many earnest, devoted Christians who, I realize, seem to think that God dictated the Bible in 1611, word for word, in English, including punctuation, to the committee of churchmen selected by King James. In contrast, I believe that there is some of the Bible that God would approve of eliminating.

I think that God could cause miracles to occur if, in his wisdom, that seemed sensible or useful. Indeed, modern science does not exclude miraculous happenings, for it can calculate the probability that a pan of water, placed on the fire, will freeze rather than boil. (I know that this sounds absurd, but it *is* possible.)

I do not accept—nor feel myself under any pressure to accept—all of the Bible's accounts of miracles. I think that these accounts are to be interpreted figuratively or poetically, and possibly as instances of overzealous exaggeration.

The magnificent orderliness that God incorporated into his complex universe seems to me more impressive than any miracle could be; and the God who created that supremely impressive order would not, I think, find it necessary or desirable to interrupt that order by causing miracles.

Indeed, the complex orderliness of the universe, as revealed by science, seems to me to constitute a compelling argument that God exists.

I am well aware that the philosophers are very skeptical about the "Here is a watch—there must be a watchmaker" argument. But I cannot study the incredibly detailed and poetic description that modern physics gives us of the construction and behavior of elementary particles (of which all matter is composed) without being convinced that this did not happen by chance but by virtue of a truly noble plan, conceived by an intellect infinitely superior to that possessed by men.

Therefore, when I ask myself what I believe about the nature of God, and when I do this within an impersonal, intellectual framework, I find it satisfying to say that God represents the moral purpose of the universe and that He is the author of the great, grand design.

On the other hand, when I am in trouble or frightened about the safety of those I love, or when I am wrestling with very personal problems, or when I hear the cry of a child in the night, or when I am moved by a well-remembered hymn, then my view of God is paradoxically different. Then He is the ever-dependable friend, the loving and protecting Father.

If these two concepts—the abstract, impersonal one and the emotional and very personal one—seem inconsistent and contradictory, then I repeat that they arise under mutually exclusive circumstances and can strictly be viewed as complementary.*

I cannot do better than repeat Tolstoy's affirmation: "I believe in God, who for me is Spirit, Love, the Principle of all things. I believe that He is in me, and I in Him."

---

* The latter part of the present statement is, in part, a rewording of portions of Chapter 11 of my autobiography, *Scene of Change* (New York: Charles Scribner's Sons, 1970).

PART TWO

ALMANAC

A Comprehensive Collation of Facts,
Events, Opinion Polls, Statistics, Analyses,
and Essays on the Problems
and Crises Confronting the Churches Today

I / ABORTION

SUPREME COURT DECISION, 1973: HIGHLIGHTS AND ANALYSIS OF EFFECTS

Digest and Analysis: Jane Roe v. Henry Wade (U.S. Reports, No. 70-18, January 22, 1973)

EDITOR'S NOTE:

The case came to the Supreme Court to test the laws of Texas pertaining to the legality of abortions.

The Supreme Court's decision runs over 100 pages. The Court voted, 7 to 2, to overrule all laws in the fifty states of the union that either prohibited or restricted the right of a woman to undergo an abortion *during the first three months of her pregnancy* (I italicize the time period, which is often overlooked in discussions of the historic ruling). The decision extended the period to the first six months of pregnancy.

The decision voided laws in thirty-one states that were permitting abortions *only* in certain cases: to save the mother's life; where the pregnancy was the result of rape; where malformed babies would be born.

It is important to note that the decision of the Court nowhere gives a pregnant woman a right to abortion *solely upon her demand*. The decision gives pregnant women the right to *request* an abortion—and since doctors are no longer restricted by law from performing abortions, this means that most women seeking abortions can find a consenting doctor. But no doctor is compelled by law to perform an abortion on any woman requesting one.

The Supreme Count decision, incidentally, placed the United States among a great many nations where abortions are legal, freely available, and frequently performed: for example, most countries in Eastern Europe, the USSR, India, Japan, and China.

Finally, it may be remarked that the decision of the Supreme Court can be overturned—by amendment to the Constitution. This seems unlikely, especially since the attitudes of the Catholic laity in the United States have so dramatically changed in favor of liberalized abortion laws (see below). [LR]

Excerpts From Text of Decision: Majority and Dissent

The majority opinion was written by Justice Harry A. Blackmun. The dissent was written by Justice Byron R. White.

I offer highlights, for the layman, of both the majority decision and the dissent. [LR]

MAJORITY OPINION: JUSTICE HARRY A. BLACKMUN

When most criminal abortion laws were first enacted, the procedure was a hazardous one for the woman.

The Constitution does not explicitly mention any right of privacy. In a line of decisions, however, the Court has recognized that a right of personal privacy, or a guarantee of certain areas or zones of privacy, does exist under the Constitution.

. . .

The detriment that the state would impose upon the pregnant woman by denying this choice [abortion] altogether is apparent. Specific and direct harm medically diagnosable even in early pregnancy may be involved. Maternity, or additional offspring, may force upon the woman a distressful life and future. Psychological harm may be imminent. Mental and physical health may be taxed by child care.

There is also the distress, for all concerned, associated with the unwanted child, and there is the problem of bringing a child into a family already unable, psychologically and otherwise, to care for it.

On the basis of elements such as these, appellants and some amici argue that the woman's right is absolute and that she is entitled to terminate her pregnancy at whatever time, in whatever way, and for whatever reason she alone chooses. With this we do not agree.

. . .

The appellee and certain amici argue that the fetus is a "person" within the language and meaning of the 14th Amendment. In support of this they outline at length and in detail the well-known facts of fetal development. If this suggestion of parenthood is established, the appellant's case, of course, collapses, for the fetus' right to life is then guaranteed specifically by the amendment.

The Constitution does not define "person" in so many words. The use of the word is such that it has application only postnatally. . . . The word "person," as used in the 14th Amendment, does not include the unborn.

. . .

It follows that, from and after this point, a state may regulate the abortion procedure to the extent that the regulation reasonably relates to the preservation and protection of maternal health.

With respect to the state's important and legitimate interest in potential life, the "compelling" point is at viability. This is so because the fetus then presumably has the capability of meaningful life outside the mother's womb. If the state is interested in protecting fetal life after viability, it may go so far as to proscribe abortion during that period except when it is necessary to preserve the life or health of the mother.

. . .

We need not resolve the difficult question of when life begins. When those trained in the respective disciplines of medicine, philosophy and theology are unable to arrive at any consensus, the judiciary, at this point in the development of man's knowledge, is not in a position to speculate as to the answer.

The unborn have never been recognized in the law as persons in the whole sense.

With respect to the state's important and legitimate interest in the health of the mother, the "compelling" point, in the light of present medical knowledge, is at approximately the end of the first trimester. This is so because of the now established medical fact that until the end of the first trimester mortality in abortion is less than mortality in normal child-birth.

. . .

Art. 1196 of the Texas Penal Code, in restricting legal abortions to those "procured or attempted by medical advice for the purpose of saving the life of the mother," sweeps too broadly. The statute makes no distinction between abortions performed early in pregnancy and those performed later, and it limits to a single reason, "saving" the mother's life, the legal justification for the procedure. The statute, therefore, cannot survive the constitutional attack made upon it here.

. . .

To summarize and to repeat:

1. A state criminal abortion statute . . . that excepts from criminality only a *life saving* procedure on behalf of the mother, without regard to pregnancy stage and without recognition of the other interests involved, is violative of the Due Process Clause of the Fourteenth Amendment.

(a) For the stage prior to approximately the end of the first trimester, the abortion decision and its effectuation must be left to the medical judgment of the pregnant woman's attending physician.

(b) For the stage subsequent to approximately the end of the first trimester, the State, in promoting its interest in the health of the mother, may, if it chooses, regulate the abortion procedure in ways that are reasonably related to maternal health.

(c) For the stage subsequent to viability the State, in promoting its interest in the potentiality of human life, may, if it chooses, regulate, and even proscribe, abortion except where it is necessary, in appropriate medical judgment, for the preservation of the life or health of the mother.

2. The State may define the term "physician," as it has been employed in the preceding numbered paragraphs of this Part XI of this opinion, to mean only a physician currently licensed by the State, and may proscribe any abortion by a person who is not a physician as so defined.

. . . The decision leaves the State free to place increasing restrictions on abortion as the period of pregnancy lengthens, so long as those restrictions are tailored to the recognized state interests. The decision vindicates the right of the physician to administer medical treatment according to his professional judgment up to the points where important state interests provide compelling justifications for intervention. Up to those points the abortion decision in all its aspects is inherently, and primarily, a medical decision, and basic responsibility for it must rest with the physician.

DISSENTING OPINION: JUSTICE BYRON R. WHITE

At the heart of the controversy in these cases are those recurring pregnancies that pose no danger whatsoever to the life or health of the mother but are nevertheless unwanted for any one or more of a variety of reasons—convenience, family planning, economics, dislike of children, the embarrassment of illegitimacy, etc.

The common claim before us is that for any one of such reasons, or for no reason at all, and without asserting or claiming any threat to life or health, any woman is entitled to an abortion at her request if she is able to find a medical adviser willing to undertake the procedure.

The Court for the most part sustains this position: during the period prior to the time the fetus becomes viable, the Constitution of the United States values the convenience, whim or caprice of the putative mother more than life or potential life of the fetus.

The upshot is that the people and the legislatures of the 50 states are constitutionally disentitled to weigh the relative importance of the continued existence and development of the fetus on the one hand against a spectrum of possible impacts on the mother on the other hand.

. . . In my view [the Court's] judgment is an improvident and extravagant exercise of the power of judicial review which the constitution extends to this court.

I find no constitutional warrant for imposing such an order of priorities on the people and legislatures of the states. . . . I cannot accept the Court's exercise of its clear power of choice by interposing a constitutional barrier to state efforts to protect human life and by investing mothers and doctors with the constitutionally protected right to exterminate it. This issue, for the most part, should be left with the people and to the political processes the people have devised to govern their affairs.

Effects on Fifty State Laws

The decision of the Supreme Court on abortion (January 22, 1973) affected different states differently. Three types of effects are given below. [LR]

States not affected (because they already had laws making abortion legal):

Alaska   New York
Hawaii   Washington

States that, despite existing laws permitting abortion in certain circumstances, would have to make substantial revisions in their statutes:

Alabama	Florida	New Mexico
Arkansas	Georgia	North Carolina
California	Kansas	Oregon
Colorado	Maryland	South Carolina
Delaware	Mississippi	Virginia

States whose antiabortion laws, made invalid, would have to pass new laws:

Arizona	Minnesota	Pennsylvania
Connecticut	Missouri	Rhode Island
Idaho	Montana	South Dakota
Illinois	Nebraska	Tennessee
Indiana	Nevada	Texas
Iowa	New Hampshire	Utah
Kentucky	New Jersey	Vermont
Louisiana	North Dakota	West Virginia
Maine	Ohio	Wisconsin
Massachusetts	Oklahoma	Wyoming
Michigan		

AMERICAN ATTITUDES TOWARD ABORTION

EDITOR'S NOTE:

A 1973 survey by the Institute of Social Research, University of Michigan, disclosed that 67 percent of the Roman Catholics polled opposed abortion (when the mother's life is not endangered; some of the 67 percent reject abortion under any circumstances); 59 percent of the Protestants polled opposed abortion; 82 percent of the Jews polled approved of the right of a woman to have an abortion. (See *Time*, May 28, 1973, p. 62.)

But a survey by Andrew M. Greeley and William McCready for the *National Catholic Reporter* shows that where the mother's life and/or health is in danger: 88 percent of the Catholics polled approved of abortion, as did 91 percent of the Protestants and 100 percent of the Jews.

In case of rape, the report continues: 75 percent of the Catholics favored abortion, as did 81 percent of the Protestants and 98 percent of the Jews.

Where a defective child is likely, 77 percent of the Catholics, 83 percent of the Protestants, and 100 percent of the Jews approved of abortion. [LR]

Harris Survey
Copyright: 1973, Chicago *Tribune*

A survey by Lou Harris and Associates reported, on April 19, 1973, that 52 percent of a nation-wide cross-section of 1,500 households now favor the legalization of abortion "up to three months of pregnancy," supporting the decision of the Supreme Court.

A comparison of public attitudes in similar polls conducted in June and August 1972 (when both President Nixon and his opponent for election, Senator George McGovern, opposed the legalizing of abortion) is revealing.

LEGALIZING ABORTIONS UP TO THREE MONTHS OF PREGNANCY

Position	1973	Aug. 1972	June 1972
Favor	52%	42%	48%
Oppose	41	46	43
Not sure	7	12	9

The Supreme Court decision seems to have influenced public approval by a full ten-point margin.

The Harris survey posed the following: "Let me read you some statements which have been made about legalizing abortions up to three months of pregnancy. For each, tell me if you tend to agree or disagree."

PRO AND CON ON LEGAL ABORTIONS

Position	Agree	Disagree	Not Sure
PRO LEGAL ABORTIONS			
Unless abortions are legalized, many women will die from having illegal and badly done abortions	76%	16%	8%
So long as a doctor has to be consulted, the matter of an abortion is only a question of a woman's decision with her doctor's professional advice	68	23	9
Many mothers have unwanted babies, and it is better to have abortions that are safe and legal	57	36	7
ANTI LEGAL ABORTIONS			
It is against God's will to destroy any human life, especially that of an unborn baby	63	28	9
No one's life should be taken without permission of the individual, and an unborn obviously cannot give his permission	55	35	10
By legalizing abortions promiscuity will be encouraged, and that is wrong	45	44	11

The Harris Survey report analyzes the results:

The most troubling argument for the public to overcome in condoning legalized abortions is the concept that an abortion is in effect "taking a human life," once the infant is conceived and the fetus is alive. On the other hand, the arguments in favor of the court decision are essentially pragmatic, running along the lines that women will have abortions whether legal or illegal and that it is better to have them performed safely than to risk the life of the mother. *Basically, however, the safeguard of the mother consulting with a doctor, with a final decision arrived at from such discussion, appears to be the decisive argument now tipping the balance in favor of legalizing abortions.* [Italics added.]

A closer breakdown of the findings is interpreted by the Harris Survey:

- Catholics are still opposed to legal abortions by a substantial 56–40 percent margin.
- Women leave the abortion decision to the mother and her doctor by a

narrow 48–45 percent. (Eight months earlier, women were opposed 53–37 percent.)
· Men favor legalized abortion by 56–36 percent.
· But the sharpest differences, as in previous Harris Surveys on abortion, were displayed not according to either religion or sex—but by the age of the respondents:

In August, young people favored legalizing abortions by 52–39 percent, while those over 50 opposed such a move by 54–32 percent. In the latest survey, the young are better than 2 to 1 in support of the Supreme Court decision, 63–31 percent, but older people still are opposed by 49–44 percent.

Gallup Poll Findings

EDITOR'S NOTE:

A Gallup Poll, conducted in June 1972, found that 73 percent of the public believe that the decision to undergo an abortion is a matter that should be left solely to the woman and her physician.

This opinion was shared by 56 percent of the Roman Catholics surveyed.

The change in attitudes is all the more striking when placed against 1968 opinion polls, only four years earlier, in which less than 15 percent of those polled approved of liberalizing the abortion laws.

By November 1969, this percentage had climbed to 40 percent.

By October 1971, a survey for the President's Commission on Population Growth showed that 50 percent of the public favored the liberalization of abortion laws.

A *Newsweek* survey of American Catholics (March 20, 1967) revealed that 59 percent supported their Church's opposition to abortion—but an equal number approved of abortion if a young mother's life were endangered by another pregnancy.

The Gallup Poll published on August 24, 1972, revealed that the only group that did *not* give at least majority support for liberalized abortion laws were those who had not completed high school. [LR]

Support of Supreme Court Decision

Among the positive reactions to the Supreme Court decision, several are worth noting here:

. . . a wise and courageous stroke for the right to privacy, and for the protection of a woman's physical and emotional health.

. . . By this act, hundreds of thousands of American women every year will be spared the medical risks and emotional horrors of back-street and self-induced abortions. And as a nation, we shall be a step further toward assuring the birthright of every child to be welcomed by its parents at the time of its birth. [Dr. Alan F. Guttmacher, president, Planned Parenthood Federation of America (January 23, 1973, *The New York Times*, pp. 1, 20)]

The decision is historic not only in terms of women's individual rights but also in terms of the relationships of church and state. . . . The doctrine of one religious group is not imposed by legal fiat or enforced by criminal sanction on the rest of American society. [Rev. Howard E. Spragg, of the United Church of Christ (*ibid.*)]

We trust that this is the beginning of the end for state efforts to interfere with the rights of women to secure medical abortions. [American Civil Liberties Union (*ibid.*)]

RESPONSE OF CATHOLICS PRIOR TO THE SUPREME COURT DECISION

Catholic Laity

The majority of Catholics, according to the available studies, believe that the position of the Catholic Church on contraception should be changed. Moreover, the proportion of Catholics, including the more devout Catholics, holding this opinion appears to be increasing over time. [*Studies in Family Planning* (Population Council, New York, October 1968).]

A Gallup Poll, published August 24, 1972 (for a survey conducted in June 1972) revealed that 56 percent of the Roman Catholics polled supported the view that the decision to undergo an abortion is a matter that should be left entirely to the woman and her doctor. [LR]

From 1973 *Catholic Almanac* (Huntington, Ind.: Our Sunday Visitor, Inc., 1973), p. 101

A Gallup survey showed that 56 percent of Catholics believed that the decision to have an abortion should be left solely to the woman and her doctor, and that 68 percent favored birth control information for teenagers. The survey also disclosed that 64 percent of Americans were in favor of liberalized abortion and that 73 percent believed that birth control services should be available to sexually active teenagers.

Msgr. James McHugh, spokesman on family life for the US Catholic Conference, charged that the survey was misleading and "raises more questions than it settles."

Response of Catholic Bishops

EDITOR'S NOTE:

On February 14, 1973, an unprecedented pastoral message to the Roman Catholic hierarchy, from the Administrative Committee of the National Council of Catholic Bishops, warned all American Roman Catholics

1. To disobey any civil law that may require abortion;
2. That excommunication would be pronounced upon any Catholics "who undergo or perform an abortion."

The pastoral message made it plain that "those who obtain an abortion, those who persuade others to have an abortion, and [those] who perform the abortion are guilty of breaking God's law."

The bishops called the Supreme Court decision on the permissibility of abortions "wrong and entirely contrary to the fundamental principles of morality," and therefore condoned civil disobedience of the law. "We reject the opinion of the U.S. Supreme Court as erroneous, unjust and immoral."

John Cardinal Cody of Chicago announced that Catholics who "place themselves in a state of excommunication" could not receive the sacraments.

Cardinal Cody and other leading Roman Catholic prelates have expressed their determination to persuade the Supreme Court to reverse its position. [LR]

CARDINAL COOKE OF NEW YORK (JANUARY 23, 1973)

How many millions of children prior to their birth will never live to see the light of day because of the shocking action of the majority of the United States Supreme Court today? . . . Seven men have made a tragic utilitarian judgment regarding who shall live and who shall die. They have made themselves a "super legislature." They have gone against the will of those American people who spoke their minds in favor of life as recently as last November in referendums in Michigan and North Dakota.

They have usurped the powers and responsibilities of the legislatures of 50 states to protect human life.

I remind all Americans, however, that judicial decisions are not necessarily sound moral decisions.

In spite of this horrifying decision, the American people must rededicate themselves to the protection of the sacredness of all human life. I hope and pray that our citizens will do all in their power to reverse this injustice to the rights of the unborn child.

CARDINAL KROL, ARCHBISHOP OF PHILADELPHIA, PRESIDENT OF THE NATIONAL CONFERENCE OF CATHOLIC BISHOPS (JANUARY 23, 1973)

The Supreme Court's decision today is an unspeakable tragedy for this nation. . . . The ruling drastically diminishes the constitutional guaranty of the right to life and in doing so sets in motion developments which are terrifying to contemplate.

The ruling represents bad logic and bad law. There is no rational justification for allowing unrestricted abortion up to the third month of pregnancy. The development of life before and after birth is a continuous process and in making the three-month point the cutoff for unrestricted abortion, the Court seems more impressed by magic than by scientific evidence regarding fetal development. The child in the womb has the right to life, to the life he already possesses, and this is a right no court has the authority to deny. . . .

No court and no legislature in the land can make something evil become something good. Abortion at any stage of pregnancy is evil. This is not a question of sectarian morality but instead concerns the law of God and the basis of civilized society. One trusts in the decency and good sense of the American people not to let an illogical court decision dictate to them on the subject of morality and human life.

CONNECTICUT BISHOP WARNS CATHOLICS

On February 9, 1973, the Roman Catholic Bishop of Connecticut reminded all Catholics that any direct involvement in abortion meant that they faced excommunication. A nine-point statement was issued—in the face of a general expectation that Connecticut would soon legalize abortions. [LR]

CLEVELAND BISHOP WARNS CATHOLICS

On February 25, 1973, the Bishop of the Cleveland Diocese warned 880,000 Roman Catholics in "greater Cleveland" that members of the Church who participated in abortions—as either doctors or patients—would be excommunicated.

The Bishop, the Most Reverend Dr. Clarence Issenman, called for special prayers "against abortions by the faithful," as part of all Masses in his diocese, until further notice. [LR]

Catholic Education and Its Effect on Attitudes Toward Abortion
Excerpt from *Studies in Family Planning* (Population Council, New York, October 1968)

The importance of a Catholic education in instilling traditional beliefs and attitudes has been pointed up in a number of studies. It is best documented for the United States, but among the urban elite in Ghana and among whites in Johannesburg also, contrary to normal expectation, practice of contraception is less for Catholics who have at least a high-school education than for those who have progressed less far through the parochial school system.

ANALYSIS OF 72,988 ABORTIONS PERFORMED IN THE UNITED STATES: 1970–1971

The classes of women undergoing abortions, types of abortion, complications, health risks, and results are depicted in Christopher Tietze, M.D., and Sarah Lewit, "Joint Program for the Study of Abortion (JPSA): Early Medical Complications of Legal Abortion," *Studies in Family Planning* (Population Council, New York, June 1972), Vol. 3, No. 6, pp. 98 ff.

SUMMARY AND CONCLUSIONS

A total of 72,988 abortions, performed from 1 July 1970 to 30 June 1971, about one-seventh of all legal abortions in the United States during that period, was reported by 66 institutions participating in the Joint Program for the Study of Abortion (JPSA), sponsored by the Population Council.

The major findings and conclusions are:

1. Although the type of patient most frequently seen in JPSA institutions was a young, single, white woman, pregnant for the first time and aborted as a private patient, the proportions of married black, parous, and nonprivate patients increased significantly in the course of one year, with little change in the age distribution of the women . . .

2. About three out of four abortions were performed in the first trimester (12 weeks) of pregnancy; the proportion of early abortions increased substantially over the year . . .

3. Late abortions were most frequent among women under 18 years of age, nonprivate patients, black women, and mothers who had had six or more children . . .

4. Most abortions in the first trimester were performed by suction (vacuum aspiration) and most abortions at 17 weeks or later, by saline. Classical dilatation and curettage (D & C) accounted for 4.5 percent of all abortions and hysterotomy and hysterectomy together, for 2.4 percent. Over the year, the share of the last three procedures was almost halved . . .

5. The incidence of early medical complications, including minor complaints, during the first trimester of pregnancy was on the order of one in 20 abortions; the incidence of major complications, as defined in this report, was one in 200 abortions . . .

6. The risk to health associated with abortions was three to four times as high in the second trimester of pregnancy as in the first trimester . . .

7. Complication rates were higher for abortions performed at six weeks' gestation or less, than at seven to ten weeks' gestation, especially for major complications. However, the complication rates were far lower for the earliest abortions than for abortions in the second trimester . . .

8. As might be expected, the risk of postabortal complications, and particularly major complications, was higher for women with known pre-existing complications than for apparently healthy women . . .

9. Nonprivate patients had significantly higher complication rates than private patients, especially for abortions in the second trimester . . .

ABORTIONS PERFORMED ON CATHOLIC WOMEN: INTERNATIONAL DATA

Excerpts from "Roman Catholic Fertility and Family Planning: A Comparative Review of the Literature," Studies in Family Planning (Population Council, New York, October 1968), No. 34

A surprisingly high proportion of Catholics in Latin American cities (apparently as many as half in most cities) have used forbidden methods of contraception, and the inclusion of those who have practiced induced abortion would raise this proportion even higher. *Resort to abortion by Catholics in Latin America, Eastern Europe and Korea appears to be remarkably high in view of the clear condemnation of the practice by the Church's Magisterium. Questions on attitudes to abortion are rarely included in surveys, but a clear majority of U.S. Catholics, and approximately half the Catholics of Australia, are willing to condone abortion for "hard" reasons.* [Italics added.]

In the developing countries, contraceptive practice among both Catholics and non-Catholics in rural (and some urban) areas is limited, partly because knowledge of contraceptive methods is also limited. Nevertheless, the few available studies suggest that half or more of Catholic city-dwellers in these countries may be willing to use or support family planning.

ABORTION AND YOUNG BLACKS

Excerpts from Frank F. Furstenburg, Jr., "Attitudes Toward Abortion Among Young Blacks," Studies in Family Planning (Population Council, New York, April 1972), p. 69

. . . it is clear from current opinion that the availability of safe, inexpensive and easily accessible abortion facilities would significantly decrease the number of unwanted pregnancies among young, low-income blacks. *Our findings suggest that nearly a third of the respondents who had reached their desired fertility goal would consider an abortion.* Nulliparas* experiencing an unwanted premarital pregnancy would be less likely to take advantage of increased availability, though even among that group, abortion reform would have some immediate impact. Nevertheless, if our data provide any indication, well-designed contraceptive programs are likely to be—at least for the present—an indispensable means of helping these young women to avoid unwanted pregnancies. [Italics added.]

LUTHERANS AND ABORTION

EDITOR'S NOTE:

On October 15, 1974, the American Lutheran Church voted (500 to 379) to modify church policy by permitting abortions "in compelling individual circumstances." The resolution reaffirmed church policy concerning an unborn child's right to live; but the resolution went on to remind Lutherans that all Christians bear "a responsibility to make the best possible decision" when considering the possible termination of a pregnancy. That decision must be based "on the situation" and must consider "accountability for God, self and neighbor."

The position of the American Lutheran Church theretofore permitted abortions only in those cases where the mother's health was clearly endangered, and official statements (in 1966 and in 1970) held: "there are times and circumstances when interruption of the pregnancy is necessary for therapeutic reasons."

The 1974 resolution permitted church members to make the judgment that "the developing life may be terminated to defend the health and wholeness" of those making the decision, but rejected "induced abortion" as an easy solution for pregnancies which present a problem to the parents.

The 1974 resolution rejected voluntary sterilization to prevent pregnancies but held that contraception is an alternative which may prevent the problem of unwanted unborn infants. Church counseling was recommended to parents who might be considering

---

* Females who have never given birth. [LR]

abortion; such counseling would clarify "the possible effects" of either an abortion or the decision to permit the pregnancy to continue. [LR]

EFFECTS OF LEGALIZING ABORTION

EDITOR'S NOTE:

Analyses made since July 1970, when the New York State law legalizing abortions went into effect, reveal a striking decline in the city of New York's (1) birth rate, (2) number of illegitimate births, and (3) number of illegal abortions.

From July 1970 to July 1971, the number of legal abortions performed on resident New York women was 67,400.

This number rose, in the 1971–1972 period, to 75,100.

In 1971, New York City recorded an 11.6% drop in births (17,300 fewer births than in 1970).

In 1972, New York City statistics showed a fall in births of yet another 16,400.

Legal abortions accounted for perhaps one-half of the 25% decline in births in New York City; the remainder of the decline is probably due to changes in attitude about family size—plus improved contraception.

Analysis of the figures on birth, fertility, and abortion was made by Dr. Christopher Tietze, noted biostatistician and expert on contraception and abortion, for the Population Council of New York's *Family Planning Perspectives*, March 1973.

In an interview Dr. Tietze (1) estimated that legal abortions in New York City had probably replaced around 100,000 illegal abortions in 1970–1972; (2) predicted that if the Supreme Court's 1973 ruling on abortions made them more easily and safely available, the drop in births might reach an additional 300,000–400,000 annually. (See *The New York Times*, February 21, 1973, p. 31.)

Population experts call such a decline in births greater than any in fifteen years and foresee the possibility of a drop in the *national* fertility and birth rate that may be well below "the replacement level." "Replacement level" is the average number of births per woman, over her lifetime, which would make the population eventually read "zero population growth."[LR]

II / "ACTIVISM": THE GROWTH OR DECLINE OF RELIGIOUS GROUPS RELATED TO THEIR SOCIAL ACTIVISM IN THE 1960s AND 1970s

SHOULD THE CHURCHES SPEAK OUT ON SOCIAL AND POLITICAL ISSUES?

Quoted from the American Institute of Public Opinion (Gallup Poll), release of April 12, 1968

The highly controversial nature of the issue is seen in the fact that 53 percent of all persons interviewed in a national survey in 1968 say churches should "keep out," while not far fewer, 40 percent, say churches should "speak out."

The latest findings [1968] mark a sharp change from a comparable survey in the spring of 1957 when opinion was slightly on the side that churches should express their views on social and political questions. Here are the latest results compared with those recorded in 1957:

SHOULD CHURCHES KEEP OUT OF OR SPEAK OUT ON SOCIAL AND POLITICAL MATTERS

Year	Keep Out	Express Views	No Opinion
1957	44%	47%	9%
1968	53	40	7

The results by key groups (1968):

Group	Keep Out	Express Views	No Opinion
Men	58%	36%	6%
Women	49	44	7
Protestants	52	42	6
Catholics	57	35	8
21–29 years	47	49	4
30–49 years	51	42	7
50 and over	58	35	7

Reasons given by those who think churches should not speak out on issues of the day fall into three general categories: (1) the first duty of churches is to comfort the individual; (2) ministers and priests do not have the kind of background or training needed to deal with social and political problems; and (3) churches should concentrate on raising the levels of religious belief and practice.

Reasons given by those who think churches should speak out on issues of the day also fall into three general categories: (1) churches are morally obligated to take a stand; (2) religion pervades all of life; and (3) churches have as much right to speak out as any other group in this country.

OPINIONS OF PRIESTS, MINISTERS, AND RABBIS

Source: The Gallup Opinion Index, *Religion in America 1971*, April 1971, Report No. 70, p. 19

A national survey by mail of 2,517 clergymen, conducted in February–March 1971, asked this question, among others: "In your opinion should churches keep out of political and social matters or should churches express their views on day-to-day social and political questions?" [LR]

Group	Keep Out	Express Views	No Opinion
Protestant ministers	21%	74%	5%
Catholic priests	6	90	4
Jewish rabbis	5	91	4

COMPARISON OF ATTITUDES

A comparison of the findings above may be made with earlier studies, in 1965 and 1952, by Martin Marty, Stuart E. Rosenberg, and Andrew M. Greeley. See *What Do We Believe?* (New York: Meredith Press, 1968), pp. 318–320. [LR]

ARE "SOCIALLY ORIENTED" AND "LIBERAL" CHURCHES
LOSING MEMBERS? ARE "CONSERVATIVE" CHURCHES GAINING?
Excerpts from Edward B. Fiske, in *The New York Times*, August 6, 1972, section 4, p. 1

In a new book called "Why Conservative Churches Are Growing," Dean M. Kelley, the resident church-state expert for the liberal National Council of Churches, offers one explanation.

The churches that are gaining members, he observes, are generally those that have held on to old-time beliefs, shunned compromising contact with other churches or secular causes and made clear their belief that they alone have the truth. They are strong on discipline, missionary zeal, absolutism, conformity and even fanaticism.

The churches that are losing members, on the other hand, Mr. Kelley reports, are those that profess tolerance of diversity and openness to dialogue with others. Efforts to foster interfaith cooperation may be conducive to brotherhood, peace, justice, freedom and compassion, but "they are not conducive to conserving or increasing the social strength of the religious groups involved."

Mr. Kelley, who is a Methodist, argues that the main reason his and other mainline churches are losing members is that they have diluted the principal product religion has to offer: providing meaning in personal life. "Man is an inveterate meaning-monger," he writes. "When churches get sidetracked into noble but nevertheless extraneous goals such as changing social structures, then allegiance falters."

Others have different theories. The Right Rev. Roger W. Blanchard, executive vice-president of the Episcopal Church, is among those who see the religious trend as a retreat from the social turmoil of the 1960's. "Many people today are looking for a kind of security that fundamentalist churches can provide," he says.

George E. Sweazey, a former moderator of the United Presbyterian Church who now teaches at Princeton Theological Seminary, takes the position that theological confusion is the major problem. "If professional theologians can't even say what to believe," he says, "what about the average person?"

Dean Dinwoodey, representative of Mormons in Washington, said that his church is thriving because "we remain committed to the family and put a lot of effort into youth work."

Porter W. Routh, executive secretary of the executive committee of the Southern Baptist Convention, said that his theologically conservative denomination has "benefited by the resurgence of interest in Jesus among young people."

Some officials in the so-called liberal churches, worrying about the effect on financial needs, church building and Sunday school attendance, are trying to reverse the trend. Bishop Blanchard said members of the

Episcopal executive council will soon visit every area of the country to "hear what people are saying at the grass roots."

But some argue that all these efforts are not needed; they see the decline in membership as a healthy sign, a sort of purification. "It may be a sign of the faithfulness of the church," said Mr. Fallart.

HAS THE CATHOLIC CHURCH GAINED OR LOST MEMBERS?

EDITOR'S NOTE:

In the 1960s, in the United States, many Catholic priests, nuns, and laity (especially in the colleges) became "activists" in social causes—the civil rights movement, antiwar protests, and so on—and pressed for a liberalization of Catholic practices in everything from liturgy to celibacy for priests and nuns.

An analysis of the 1970 figures published by the National Council of Churches, plus data from other sources, demonstrates that:

· National membership in the Catholic Church leveled off (did not rise with population increases).
· In 1970, the Catholic Church experienced its first actual *decrease* in membership in the United States since it first appeared in our nation.
· There appears to have been a recovery, albeit slight, in 1971–1972.

These data should not by any means be interpreted as the sole consequence of clerical activism; reasons for the decline in attendance at Mass, the decrease in parochial schools, and so on are explored more fully in Part Two, Chapter X: "Catholics: Facts, Opinions, Trends, Ferment and Schisms." [LR]

SUNDAY SERMONS: WHAT DO THEY SAY?

EDITOR'S NOTE:

The preceding portions deal with the effect on churches of social activism but do not address themselves to a central question: How many clergymen said what, in their sermons, during the feverish 1960s and early 1970s? How many "spoke out" on the war in Vietnam, racial problems, black power, birth control, poverty, juvenile delinquency, drugs, sex mores, abortion or abortion laws?

The only study I have found is one made in 1968 of a representative sample of Protestant ministers of nine major denominations in California: two-thirds of these ministers were sent an extensive questionnaire; 1,580 completed and returned them (63%, a remarkably high return rate).

I offer below the highlights of Rodney Stark *et al., Wayward Shepherds: Prejudice and the Protestant Clergy* (New York: Harper & Row, 1970). [LR]

• Most of the sermons in Christian congregations rarely dealt with controversial issues of any sort: social, moral, ethical—to say nothing of political.

• Over one-third of the clergy who responded stated that they had never, throughout their careers in the ministry, taken a stand, from the pulpit, on any political problem—including school prayers, drug legislation, pornography, racial conflicts, divorce.

• Only 25% of the clergy had given five sermons, within the preceding year, that involved "controversial" issues: *i.e.*, racial violence in a dozen cities, the war in the Middle East, the assassination of Martin Luther King.

• A third of the Protestant clergy had never devoted even part of a sermon to the war in Vietnam.

• On four issues, the Protestant clergy in California did "speak out": juvenile delinquency, drugs, alcoholism, sexual misconduct.

• Only 54% said that they had discussed "public affairs" with members of their congregation.

• Yet 68% agreed with the poll's statement: "Clergymen have great potential to influence the political and social beliefs of their parishioners."

• But 8% agreed that most of the members of their congregation would approve of a stand from their pulpit on a political issue.

• About two-thirds of the clergy reporting thought that their colleagues would approve of their preaching "socially relevant" sermons.

• The ministers' opinions about the role of the church were related to their allegiance to traditional doctrines: 44% agreed with the statement, "If enough men were brought to Christ, social ills would take care of themselves." But the division is significant: 77% of the conservative clergy agreed as against only 7% of the liberals.

III / AFFIRMATIONS OF RELIGIOUS IDENTITY: CATHOLICS, JEWS, PROTESTANTS, AGNOSTICS

EDITOR'S SUMMARY:

Figures on church membership are usually based on reports from church organizations. Such statistics are open to considerable criticism (see Part Two, Chapter X).

How do Americans identify themselves, with respect to religion, regardless of whether or not they belong to, or attend, any church?

From *Religion in America 1971,* Gallup Opinion Index, April 1971, Report No. 70, p. 70. Data based on 10 national surveys, totaling 16,523 personal interviews, in 1970.

A 1971 report of the American Institute of Public Opinion (Gallup Poll), below, using an exceptionally large sample (16,523 *adults*) of the total population, for personal interviews in 10 national surveys, during 1970, reveals how people classify themselves when asked, "What is your religious preference—Protestant, Roman Catholic or Jewish?" The results:

· Protestants account for about two-thirds (65%) of the total national population.
· 26% of adults are Roman Catholic.
· 3% are Jews.
· Another 2% reported they belonged to other religious faiths.
· 4% replied they had "no formal" religion.

The quite large sample of this Gallup study permits meaningful analysis by subgroups:

Of nonwhites in the United States, for example, 83% are Protestant, 9% are Roman Catholics, 1% are Jewish.

Most of the Southern population (84%) is Protestant.

In the Eastern states, 44% of the population is Protestant; 42% are Catholic.

The greatest proportion acknowledging "no formal religion" was found in the West: 7%.

HOW DO AMERICANS IDENTIFY THEMSELVES?

Group	Population Distribution	Protestants	Roman Catholics	Jews	All Others°	No Formal Religion
SEX						
Male	48%	47%	47%	49%	47%	69%
Female	52	53	53	51	53	31
RACE						
White	90	87	97	99	83	91
Nonwhite	10	13	3	1	17	9
EDUCATION						
College	23	22	21	42	34	44
High school	52	52	57	42	44	38
Grade school	25	26	23	16	21	18
OCCUPATION						
Prof. & bus.	22	20	22	40	34	35
Clerical & sales	12	11	12	22	9	12
Farmers	6	8	3	1	4	3
Manual	40	40	45	16	34	34
AGE						
21–29 years	20	16	22	19	27	39
30–49 years	38	37	41	31	34	33
50 & over	42	45	36	47	37	26

POLITICS						
Republican	28	33	19	6	24	16
Democrat	43	39	52	63	30	32
Independent	28	26	27	29	37	49
REGION						
East	30	20	47	82	31	28
Midwest	28	30	28	5	16	20
South	26	34	11	5	16	20
West	16	16	13	8	37	32
INCOME						
$15,000 & over	14	12	15	30	17	17
$10,000–14,999	23	22	27	26	21	24
$ 7,000– 9,999	21	20	23	16	20	20
$ 5,000– 6,999	16	17	5	11	16	15
$ 3,000– 4,999	13	15	10	9	11	13
Under $3,000	12	13	9	7	14	10
COMMUNITY SIZE						
1,000,000 & over	20	12	31	66	32	29
500,000–999,999	13	10	18	18	14	19
50,000–499,999	23	22	26	14	25	23
2,500–49,999	15	18	10	3	9	12
Under 2,500 rural	29	37	14	1	21	18

From *Religions in America 1971*, Gallup Opinion Index, April 1971, Report No. 70, p. 57, based on total national sample of 16,523 adults

* Includes Eastern Orthodox.

The large sample also offers meaningful generalizations about ethnic and geographical groups.

WHAT IS YOUR RELIGIOUS PREFERENCE?

The findings of the 1971 Gallup Poll may be compared with a similar poll Gallup conducted in 1965. See Marty, Rosenberg, and Greeley, *What Do We Believe?* (New York: Meredith Press, 1968), pp. 28 ff.

IS RELIGION A RELEVANT PART OF YOUR LIFE?
From *Religion in America 1971*, Gallup Opinion Index, April 1971, Report No. 70, p. 52

VIEWS OF COLLEGE STUDENTS

Group	Yes	No
NATIONAL	42%	58%
SEX		
Men	38	62
Women	50	50
AGE		
18 years & under	51	49
19 years	43	57
20 years	39	61
21–23 years	38	62
24 years & over	41	59
REGION OF COLLEGE		
East	38	62
Midwest	39	61
South	50	50
West	41	59
POLITICAL AFFILIATION		
Republican	56	44
Democrat	56	44
Independent	30	70

Group	Yes	No
PARENTS' INCOME		
$15,000 & over	32	68
$10,000–$14,999	42	58
$ 7,000–$ 9,999	49	51
Under $7,000	56	44
CLASS IN SCHOOL		
Freshman	46	54
Sophomore	44	56
Junior	37	63
Senior	38	62
Graduate	41	59
TYPE OF COLLEGE		
Public	39	61
Private	38	62
Denominational	69	31
RELIGIOUS PREFERENCE		
Protestant	51	49
Catholic	57	43

U.S. CENSUS BUREAU VOLUNTARY SURVEY

From U.S. Bureau of the Census, "Religion Reported by the Civilian Population of the United States: March 1957," *Current Population Reports*, February 2, 1958, Series P-20, No. 79, p. 1, Figure 1, and p. 6, Tables 1 and 2

EDITOR'S NOTE:

A historic survey of approximately 35,000 households in the United States was made (for the last time) by the Bureau of the Census in March 1957. The Bureau explained the survey as follows:

The answers to the question "What is your religion?" were obtained on a voluntary basis.

This survey was the first in which the Bureau asked a nationwide sample of persons a question on their religion, although the Bureau had obtained membership data from religious organizations in several Censuses of Religious Bodies.

The question did not relate to church membership, attendance at church services or gatherings, or religious belief.

The results are not directly comparable with the reports on membership issued by religious organizations. In replying to the question as asked, many persons, in addition to those who maintain formal affiliation with a religious organization, associated themselves with such a group and reported its name.

The original data from this survey have been destroyed, but extensive analysis of this information had been completed before it was decided to release no further reports (derived from the survey). Those tables that had been drawn were, in fact, preserved, but they were not published until the passage of the Freedom of Information Act in 1967. They contain valuable tabulations on intermarriage and socioeconomic patterns; their principal findings are reported in a later section of the book.

Although conducted nearly twenty years ago, the Census survey remains the most comprehensive national sample available on the demography of American religion. (The "civilian population" includes about 809,000 members of the armed forces living off post, or with their families on post, but excludes all other members of the armed forces.) [LR]

RELIGION REPORTED BY PERSONS FOURTEEN YEARS OLD AND OVER: CIVILIAN POPULATION, MARCH 1957

Religion	Total	WHITE		NONWHITE	
		Male	Female	Male	Female
PROTESTANT	66.2%	62.4%	65.1%	85.4%	89.4%
Baptist	19.7	15.1	15.2	59.1	62.0
Lutheran	7.1	7.9	7.7	0.3	0.2
Methodist	14.0	13.1	14.1	17.0	17.5
Presbyterian	5.6	5.8	6.4	1.0	0.8
Other Protestant	19.8	20.5	21.7	8.0	8.9
ROMAN CATHOLIC	25.7	27.8	27.9	6.4	6.6
JEWISH	3.2	3.6	3.6	—	0.1
OTHER RELIGION	1.3	1.3	1.2	1.5	1.5
NO RELIGION	2.7	4.0	1.3	5.4	1.7
RELIGION NOT REPORTED	0.9	0.9	0.9	1.3	0.7

AGNOSTICS IN THE UNITED STATES

See Part One, "The 'Unchurched' Americans:
What Do They Believe?" by Edward L. Ericson;
and Part Two, Chapters III and XXII.

ANTI-SEMITISM IN THE UNITED STATES

See Part Two, Chapters XXV, "Jews," and XXX, "Prejudice and Religion."

IV / BELIEF IN GOD

EDITOR'S NOTE:

There is a striking discrepancy between (1) professions of belief in God (or "a God"), (2) formal membership in a church, and (3) attendance at church services.

Consider this paradox: interest in religion appears to be growing in the United States, according to all the polls data I have seen, while formal membership in churches or actual attendance at any religious service clearly appears to be declining.

It is worth noting that 98 percent of the Americans questioned by the Gallup Poll in 1971 expressed a belief in "a God," and that only 2 percent of those cited in other polls, in *What Do We Believe?* (*op. cit.*), said they did not believe in a God.

I find especially interesting the beliefs expressed by priests, ministers, and rabbis (below). [LR]

"DO YOU BELIEVE IN A GOD?"
From *Religion in America 1971*, Gallup Opinion Index, April 1971, Report No. 70

Group	DATA FOR 1968	
	Yes	No
NATIONAL	98%	2%
SEX		
Men	98	2
Women	99	1
RACE		
White	98	2
Nonwhite	—	–
EDUCATION		
College	95	5
High school	99	1
Grade school	99	1

| Group | DATA FOR 1968 | |
	Yes	No
OCCUPATION		
Prof. & bus.	96	4
White Collar	97	3
Farmers	99	1
Manual	99	1
AGE		
21–29 years	97	3
30–49 years	98	2
50 & over	99	1
RELIGION		
Protestant	99	1
Catholic	99	1
Jewish	—	–
POLITICS		
Republican	99	1
Democrat	98	2
Independent	98	2
REGION		
East	96	4
Midwest	99	1
South	99	1
West	98	2
INCOME		
$10,000 & over	97	3
$ 7,000–$9,999	97	3
$ 5,000–$6,999	99	1
$ 3,000–$4,999	99	1
Under $3,000	99	1
COMMUNITY SIZE		
1,000,000 & over	96	4
500,000–999,999	99	1
50,000–499,999	99	1
2,500–49,999	99	1
Under 2,500, rural	99	1

COMPARISON OF THE UNITED STATES WITH TEN OTHER NATIONS

EDITOR'S NOTE:

The reader may be interested in comparing the responses of Americans with those of people in other countries—polled, at the same time, by Gallup International. [LR]

From *Religion in America 1971*, Gallup Opinion Index, April 1971, Report No. 70

"DO YOU BELIEVE IN A GOD?" (1968)

Nation	Yes	No
United States	98%	2%
Greece	96	2
Austria	85	10
Switzerland	84	11
Finland	83	7
West Germany	81	10
Netherlands	79	13
Great Britain	77	11
France	73	21
Norway	73	12
Sweden	60	26

BELIEF IN GOD: PRIESTS, MINISTERS, AND RABBIS
From *Religion in America 1971*, Gallup Opinion Index, April 1971, Report No. 70, p. 20

This poll was based on a mail survey of 2,517 clergymen in February–March 1971. The question was formulated as: " 'Which of these statements comes closest to your beliefs?' There is a personal God. There is some sort of spirit or vital force which controls life. I'm not sure that there is a God of any kind. There is no God of any kind." [LR]

BELIEFS OF PRIESTS, MINISTERS, RABBIS (1971)

Clergy	Personal God	Vital Force	Not Sure	No God	No Answer
Protestant ministers	93%	7%	1%	*	1%
Catholic priests	99	1	*	0	*
Jewish rabbis	55	43	3	1	3

* Less than 0.5%.

V / BELIEF IN HEAVEN, HELL, THE DEVIL, LIFE AFTER DEATH

"DO YOU BELIEVE IN HEAVEN?"
From Gallup Opinion Index, February 1969

BELIEF (JULY 1968)

Group	Yes	No	No Opinion
NATIONAL	85%	11%	4%
SEX			
Men	83	13	4
Women	87	9	4
RACE			
White	85	11	4
Nonwhite	—	—	–
EDUCATION			
College	72	23	5
High school	86	10	4
Grade school	94	4	2
OCCUPATION			
Prof. & bus.	77	17	6
White collar	81	14	5
Farmers	93	5	2
Manual	89	8	3
AGE			
21–29 years	84	13	3
30–49 years	84	11	5
50 & over	88	10	2
RELIGION			
Protestant	90	7	3
Catholic	89	7	4
Jewish	—	—	–
POLITICS			
Republican	86	10	4
Democrat	85	12	3
Independent	83	12	5

Group	Yes	No	No Opinion
REGION			
East	75	17	8
Midwest	90	7	3
South	96	2	2
West	77	20	4
INCOME			
$10,000 & over	77	19	4
$ 7,000 & over	80	16	4
$ 5,000–$6,999	87	8	5
$ 3,000–$4,999	94	4	2
Under $3,000	90	8	2
CHURCH ATTENDANCE			
Regular churchgoers	95	3	2
Infrequent churchgoers	84	12	4
Nonchurchgoers	66	26	8

COMPARISON OF UNITED STATES WITH TEN OTHER NATIONS
From Gallup Opinion Index, February 1969

"DO YOU BELIEVE IN HEAVEN?" (JULY 1968)

Nation	Yes	No	No Opinion
United States	85%	11%	4%
Greece	65	23	12
Finland	62	20	18
Norway	60	20	20
Great Britain	54	27	19
Netherlands	54	31	15
Switzerland	50	41	9
Austria	44	49	7
Sweden	43	42	15
West Germany	43	42	15
France	39	52	9

"DO YOU BELIEVE IN HELL?"

	Yes	No	No Opinion
Total	65%	29%	6%

The relations between members of the various subclasses was approximately the same as what was recorded in the first question.

Some 73 percent expressed a belief in life after death, which was a higher percentage than that reported in seven other countries tested. There was somewhat greater doubt about this basic Christian tenet found in men, the college-trained, younger adults, and among Catholics. [LR]

"DO YOU BELIEVE IN THE DEVIL?" (APRIL 1974)

A Louis Harris survey of Americans eighteen years and older (made public on April 29, 1974) asked: *"Do you believe in the existence of the Devil or not?"* The results: 53 percent of the respondents answered in the affirmative; 30 percent said they did not believe in the existence of the Devil; 12 percent replied that their answers would depend on how "the Devil" is defined; and 5 percent said they were not sure. (See Chicago *Tribune*, April 29, 1974.)

When asked *"Can people be possessed by a demon or a devil?,"* 36 percent of the respondents answered in the affirmative; 52 percent said they did not so believe; and 12 percent said they were not certain. A higher proportion of the eighteen-to-thirty-year-olds believed in "possession" than those fifty and over; more women than men believed in demon/devil "possession"; more blacks than whites answered "Yes." [LR]

"DO YOU BELIEVE IN LIFE AFTER DEATH?"
From Gallup Opinion Index, February 1969

Nation	Yes	No	No Opinion
United States	73%	19%	8%
Greece	57	28	15
Finland	55	23	22
Norway	54	25	21
Netherlands	50	35	15
Switzerland	50	41	9
West Germany	41	45	14
Great Britain	38	35	27

A poll of Lutherans (*A Study of Generation*, Minneapolis: Augsburg House, 1972), in answer to the question "Do you believe in a life after death?" reported that 70% answered yes. [LR]

BELIEF OF CLERGY IN LIFE AFTER DEATH

From *Religion in America 1971*, Gallup Opinion Index, April 1971, Report No. 70, p. 21, based on a national mail survey of 2,517 clergymen

"DO YOU THINK SOULS LIVE ON AFTER DEATH?"

Clergy	Yes	No	Don't Know
Protestant ministers	86%	9%	5%
Catholic priests	98	*	2
Jewish rabbis	68	19	13

* Less than 0.5%.

VI / THE BIBLE

THE ECUMENICAL BIBLE: 1973

EDITOR'S NOTE:
A remarkable new edition of the Bible, the Revised Standard Version Bible, was published in the United States on April 2, 1973— remarkable because it is the first version to be approved officially by Roman Catholics, Protestants, and the Eastern Orthodox churches.

The title page calls this "An Ecumenical Edition."

The text is similar to that of the 1952 editions of the Revised Standard Version of the Old and New Testaments.

Old Testament material that was not usually considered authoritative or "canonical" by Protestants (although found in Latin or Greek manuscripts/texts) is included, but the Apocrypha or "deuterocanonical" books are grouped together and appear after the Old Testament text (as in the Hebrew canon) and before the New Testament. This satisfied former objections of some Protestants and Roman Catholics, who had long disagreed.

The new Revised Standard Version Bible, published by the National Council of Churches, has been praised by the Vatican Secretariat for Christian Unity, the Archbishop of Canterbury, the president of the National Conference of Catholic Bishops (U.S.), the Episcopal Bishop of New York, and the primate of the Greek Orthodox Archdiocese of North and South America.

I cannot resist quoting the following passage from "A Belt of Bibles," unsigned, in the *Economist* (London) for January 20, 1973 (p. 101):

The particular achievement of the Common Bible is merely that it should have wrung a public blessing out of the English Catholic church even though the Deuterocanonical books are not interspersed through the Old Testament but lumped together in the middle.

Such are the milestones of ecumenical progress. But perhaps one should report that Agag, who walks delicately to David in the King James Bible, fat and trembling in the Douay Bible, and with faltering step in the NEB, actually walks cheerfully in the Common Bible. Surely that is worth a church controversy or two?

The history of the Bible, and its various editions in various vernaculars, is sketched below. To facilitate reading or quick reference, I have used the question-and-answer form. [LR]

FACTS ABOUT THE BIBLE: EDITOR'S SUMMARY IN QUESTION-ANSWER FORM

In What Languages Was the Bible First Written?

The Old Testament was written in Hebrew (a small part of it in Aramaic); the New Testament was written in Greek.

How Many Verses, Chapters, and Books Are There in the Bible?

	Old Testament	New Testament	Total
Verses	23,214	7,959	31,173
Chapters	929	260	1,189
Books	39	27	66

The Bible was divided into *chapters* by Cardinal Hugo de Sancto-Caro about 1250.

The Greek New Testament was divided into *verses* by Robert Stephens, a French printer, in 1551.

The first English Bible to carry both chapters and verse numbers was the Geneva Bible (1560).

The Bibles published today still use the same divisions for chapters and verses.

Where Are the Original Copies of the Bible?

The original manuscripts of the Hebrew Old Testament and of the Greek Gospels and Epistles, etc., were long thought to have been worn out or discarded. Copies were made by hand and were copied and discarded over and over again.

But in 1947 the entire book of Isaiah, with the exception of two very small breaks, was discovered in a cave northwest of the Dead Sea. The parchment had been hidden in an earthenware jar, wrapped in yards of cloth, and covered with pitch. This book is considered by experts to have been written during the first century B.C., fully 1,000 years before the oldest previously known Hebrew manuscript of a book of the Bible. The evidence points to the fact that this manuscript was in use while Christ was living.

A few manuscripts discovered since 1947 may be even older than the Dead Sea Scrolls.

The oldest Greek manuscripts of larger parts of the Bible are the *Codex Sinaiticus*, now in the British Museum, and the *Codex Vaticanus*, now in the Vatican. These were probably written in the fourth century. They contain the Greek text of nearly the whole Bible.

Older papyrus fragments exist in Greek.

What Were the Date and Place of the First Printed Bible?

The Bible was first printed between 1450 and 1456 at Mainz, Germany, from type devised by Johann Gutenberg. It was printed in Latin, from a contemporary manuscript of the Vulgate. Between forty and fifty copies of this Bible are known to be in existence. One copy, owned by the Library of Congress, Washington, D.C., is said to be one of only three perfect copies.

When Was the First Bible Printed in America?

The first Bible was printed in America in 1663 for the Indians of Massachusetts, in their language (translated by John Eliot, a missionary).

When Was the First English Bible Printed in the United States?

An English Bible was first printed in this country in 1782 by Robert Aitken, in Philadelphia, with the approval and recommendation of the Congress.

Is Any Translation Work Being Done Now?

Every year, portions of the Bible are translated afresh, or into new languages.

In 1970, complete Bibles were published for the first time in Igala (Nigeria), Lingala (Congo), and Setswana (South Africa). In 1970, first New Testaments were published in Cuna (Panama), Chuj (Guatemala), Fore (Papua and New Guinea), Idoma (Nigeria), Isoko (Nigeria), Kayan (Malaysia), and Maquiritare (Venezuela, Brazil).

New language translations are being added at the rate of about ten a year.

The Scriptures were published for the first time in 1970 in the following languages:

Language	Country
Agarabi	Papua and New Guinea
Gagou	Ivory Coast
Halia	Papua and New Guinea
Kalingua	Philippines
Konkani	India
Muyuw	Papua and New Guinea
Nasioi	Papua and New Guinea
Urubú	Brazil
Yucuna	Colombia

In How Many Languages Is the Bible Printed?

Some part of the Bible has been published in 1,431 languages according to the records of the American Bible Society. *This figure represents languages spoken by 97% of the world's population.*

Languages in which the whole Bible has been published	249
Languages in which the whole New Testament has been published	329
Languages in which at least a complete Gospel or other book has been published	853
Total languages in which some part of the Bible has been published	1,431

CHART OF THE ENGLISH BIBLE*

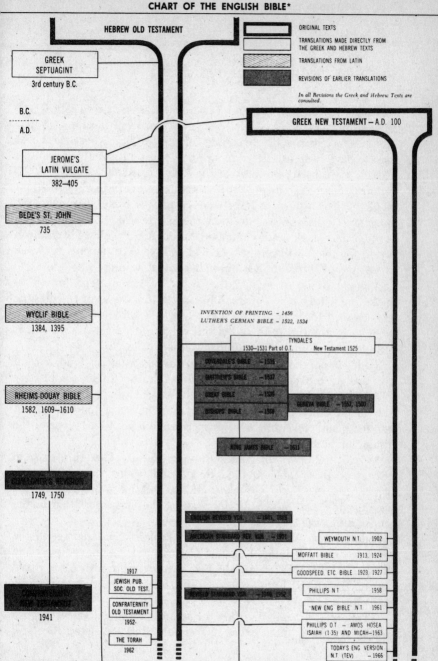

HISTORICAL HIGHLIGHTS OF THE BIBLE

Greek Septuagint: The Old Testament was translated into Greek in the third century B.C. for those Jews who lived outside of Palestine. Called Septuagint (meaning "of the seventy") because it was said to have been translated by seventy elders in seventy sessions in Egypt, it was used constantly by the early Christians.

Greek New Testament: Paul wrote his letters for early Christians in Greek. The sayings of Jesus were perhaps written in Aramaic, the language Jesus spoke, but soon the whole New Testament was written in Greek and circulated throughout the Mediterranean world. By the fourth century the Old and New Testaments in Greek were used by the Church as one collection of writings.

Vulgate Bible: About 382 the Bishop of Rome asked Jerome to make a new translation of the Bible into Latin. He went to Palestine and worked for twenty-five years to make a Bible for the common people. It was therefore called the vulgar or Vulgate Bible and is still the official Bible of the Roman Catholic Church.

Bede: Bede, the great historian of Anglo-Saxon England, started to translate the Vulgate (Latin) Bible into the English of his day because only the scholars could understand Latin. Legend says he died as he finished the translation of the Gospel of John in 735. In the tenth and eleventh centuries there were other translations of the Psalms and the Gospels.

Wyclif: John Wyclif sent out poor priests, called Lollards, to preach to the people in their own language instead of in Latin, which was used in the churches. He realized that a Bible in English was needed, and, under his inspiration, the first translation of the entire Bible was made from Latin in 1384.

Luther: The Reformation needed a Bible in the language of the people, so Luther himself made a German translation, completed in the years 1522–1534. It was the first Western European Bible based not on the official Latin Vulgate Bible but on the original Hebrew and Greek.

Tyndale: Church authorities in England prohibited a new English translation, so Tyndale went to Germany and translated the New

Testament from the original Greek. This was the first printed English New Testament, 1525. Copies were smuggled into England in shipments of grain and cloth, even though many of them were confiscated. He also translated parts of the Old Testament. Soon after, Tyndale was betrayed, strangled, and burned near Brussels. But so excellent was his work that almost every English version since is indebted to it.

Coverdale: Coverdale, like Tyndale, fled to Germany to complete the translation of the Bible. He used Latin and German versions and Tyndale's New Testament, Pentateuch, and Jonah. This was the first English Bible, 1535. Matthew's Bible, 1537, containing additional sections of Tyndale's work on the Old Testament, was revised by Coverdale. The result was known as the Great Bible, 1539. Its Psalms are still in the Book of Common Prayer. The Bishops' Bible, 1568, was a revision of the Great Bible, and the King James (see below) was ordered as a revision of the Bishops' Bible. The Geneva Bible, 1560, also a revision of the Great Bible, was produced by English Puritans in Geneva and strongly influenced the King James Bible also.

Roman Catholic Versions: The New Testament published in Rheims in 1582, followed in 1609–1610 by the Old Testament at Douay, was a translation from the Latin Vulgate. This was revised by Bishop Challoner in 1749 and 1750. The Confraternity New Testament, 1941, although strongly influenced by contemporary Greek scholarship, was based on the Vulgate, but the Confraternity Old Testament, 1952, on the Hebrew text.

King James: The various versions of the Bible aroused so many arguments that James I, after the Hampton Court Conference, appointed fifty-four scholars to produce a new version. It took about seven years, for all the known copies of oldest manuscripts and later translations were studied. Despite the great variety of men who worked on it, the book was harmonious in style and beauty. It was first published in 1611 and became the most popular English Bible.

Later Revisions: For more than 250 years, the King James Bible was supreme among English-speaking people. But during the last hundred years, knowledge from newly discovered manuscripts, archaeological discoveries, and recent scholarship led to considerable revision.

The first Revised Version was published in England, 1881–1888; a modification of this, the American Standard Revised Version, was issued in 1901. The most recent is the Revised Standard Version, 1946–1952.

There have also been many translations by individual and groups of scholars: Weymouth, Moffatt, Goodspeed, Phillips, for example. A new English-language edition of the Torah (Amos, Hosea, Isaiah 1–35, and Mica) was published in 1963 under the title "Four Prophets." The New Jerusalem Bible, a translation into English based on both the standard Paris text of *Le Bible de Jerusalem* and ancient texts, was published in 1968.

New American Bible: One of two new translations of the Bible to be published in English in 1970, the New American Bible was written by fifty-one scholars under the auspices of the Roman Catholic Church. It is translated from the original Hebrew, Aramaic, and Greek texts and was issued previously (in part) as the Confraternity Old Testament. Written in modern English, this version of the Bible is the first major English translation to drop the use of "thee" and "thou," even when addressing the Diety.

New English Bible: This new translation from original sources was the result of twenty-four years of scholarship sponsored by eleven British Protestant churches and religious societies. The New Testament section was published separately in 1961; the Old Testament and Apocrypha translations were completed in 1970. The full work then was published in March of that year.

New Ecumenical Bible (See above, opening of this chapter.) [LR]

CATHOLIC BIBLES
From 1973 Catholic Almanac (Huntington, Ind.: Our Sunday Visitor, Inc., 1973), p. 226

The English translation of the Bible in general use among Catholics until recent years was the *Douay-Rheims*, so called because of the places where it was prepared and published, the New Testament at Rheims in 1582 and the Old Testament at Douay in 1609. The translation was made from the Vulgate text.

As revised and issued by Bishop Richard Challoner in 1749 and 1750, it became the standard Catholic English version for about 200 years.

THE BIBLE / 353

Versions of the Bible approved for use in the Catholic liturgy are the *Douay-Rheims*, the *New American Bible*, *A New Translation from the Latin Vulgate* by Ronald A. Knox, the Catholic edition of the *Revised Standard Version*, and the *Jerusalem Bible*.

The Jerusalem Bible is an English translation of a French version based on the original languages. It was published by Doubleday & Co., Inc., which is also working toward completion of the *Anchor Bible*.

PROTESTANT COUNTERPARTS OF DOUAY-RHEIMS BIBLE

From 1973 *Catholic Almanac* (Huntington, Ind.: Our Sunday Visitor, Inc.. 1973), p. 226

The Protestant counterpart of the *Douay-Rheims Bible* was the *King James Bible*, called the *Authorized Version* in England. Originally published in 1611, it was in general use for more than three centuries. Its modern revisions include the *English Revised Version*, published between 1881 and 1885; the *American Revised Version*, 1901, and revisions of the New Testament (1946) and the Old Testament (1952) published in 1957 in the United States as the *Revised Standard Version*.

The latest revision, a translation in the language of the present day made from Greek and Hebrew sources, is the *New English Bible*, published March 16, 1970. Its New Testament portion was originally published in 1961.

THE NEW AMERICAN BIBLE

From 1973 *Catholic Almanac* (Huntington, Ind.: Our Sunday Visitor, Inc., 1973), p. 226

A new tanslation of the entire Bible, the first ever made directly into English from the original languages under Catholic auspices, was projected in 1944 and completed in the fall of 1970 with publication of the *New American Bible*.

The Episcopal Committee of the Confraternity of Christian Doctrine sponsored the NAB. The translators were members of the Catholic Biblical Association of America and several fellow scholars of other faiths. The typical edition was produced by St. Anthony Guild Press, Paterson, N.J.

VII / BIBLE READING IN THE UNITED STATES

Quoted from *Religion in America 1971*, Gallup Opinion Index, Report No. 70, April 1971, pp. 49, 50

"HAVE YOU YOURSELF READ ANY PART OF THE BIBLE AT HOME WITHIN THE LAST YEAR?"

THE VOTE (ADULT PROTESTANTS)

Yes	No
73%	27%

The survey showed that women were more likely to read the Bible than were men—81 percent compared to 64 percent; and that the South, with 81 percent reporting that they had read the Bible in the last year, led the rest of the nation by a considerable margin.

Little difference in response was noted by race, education, or even age (though young adults between 21 and 29 years of age scored somewhat lower than all others).

When those persons who said that they had read the Bible within the last year were next asked *which version* they had read, most replied King James (62 percent).

"WHICH VERSION OF THE BIBLE DID YOU READ AT HOME— THE OLDER KING JAMES VERSION OR SOME MORE RECENT VERSION OF THE BIBLE?"

THE VOTE (PROTESTANTS)

King James	More Recent	Both	Don't Remember
62%	21%	16%	1%

The King James version of the Bible continues to be the favorite of Americans. However, the figure representing Bible choice for all Americans may not be as high as the 62 percent recorded. This is because the survey was conducted before the publication later in 1970 of two widely heralded new translations of the Bible—*The New American Bible* and *The New English Bible*.

In addition, *Jews and Catholics were not polled;* and the fact that one of the two new translations was completed under the sponsorship of the Catholic Church may be of special importance in influencing Catholic selection. [All italics added. LR]

VIII / BIRTH CONTROL*

U.S. NATIONAL STATISTICS

EDITOR'S NOTE:

The National Fertility Study, a federally financed survey conducted by Norman F. Ryder and Charles F. Westoff of Princeton University, submitted its first report for 1970 to the Presidential Commission on Population Growth.

The study used a national sample of married women under forty-five—to measure the number of children women have borne without wanting them, and the number of children women want.

The highlights of the study may be summarized:

1. The goal of stabilizing the size of the population of the United States (known, among demographers, as "zero growth") was within reach.
2. Within all religious, age, and income groups, there was a downward trend in expectations of birth.
3. Among Catholic parents, the decrease in birth expectations for the future was far greater than for any other group; for Catholic women between twenty and twenty-four, the decline was over twice as large as among Protestant women the same age.
4. Roman Catholic couples had reduced dramatically the number of children they both were having or expected to have.
5. The birth expectations of Roman Catholics in the United States were rapidly approaching the birth expectations of non-Catholics.
6. Young Catholic women (20–24) reported that they wanted 20% fewer children than a similar group and survey finding in 1965 (falling from 3.45 to 2.75 children).
7. Non-Catholic women (20–24) reported that they wanted 9% fewer children than a similar group in 1965 (from 2.57 to 2.35 children).
8. The closing of the gap between Catholic and non-Catholic groups led the surveyors to report "a convergence of wanted fertility" between the groups.
9. Unwanted births among non-Catholic women dropped about one-third from 1965 to 1970; but among Catholics, this decline in birth rate reached almost one-half.
10. The findings strongly indicate the degree to which (despite Vatican

* See also "Fertility," Part Two, Chapter X.

opposition to, and severe strictures against, using "artificial" birth control methods) Catholic women in the United States were and are using contraceptive devices. [LR]

ROMAN CATHOLIC CONTRACEPTION AND FERTILITY: AN INTERNATIONAL SURVEY

From "Roman Catholic Fertility and Family Planning: A Comparative Review of the Literature," *Studies in Family Planning* (Population Council, New York, October 1968), No. 34

CONTRACEPTIVE KNOWLEDGE AND PRACTICE

In view of the current ferment with regard to methods of contraception, great interest attaches to the means whereby Catholic couples limit their family size. It has already been noted that in developed countries, Catholic fertility, while generally higher than non-Catholic, is nevertheless well below the physiological capacity to reproduce. How do Catholics achieve this fertility control? Are their knowledge and methods different from non-Catholics?

Developed Countries. The data for developed countries generally indicate that a higher percentage of Protestant than Catholic women have ever used any method of contraception. . . . (Use among Jewish women is almost universal, at least in the U.S. and Johannesburg, for which the data are available.) Nevertheless, despite their lower incidence of use compared with other religious groups, substantial proportions of Catholic women report ever using contraception; some 70 percent in the U.S., Johannesburg and France, over 60 percent in Canada. . . . Sixty-two percent for all Catholics in Canada; 78 percent for native-born Catholics, and 48 percent in Great Britain.

The pertinent question for this section is whether Catholic women use methods inconsistent with traditional Church doctrine. Data from the U.S. national fertility study show an increasing tendency in this direction. The proportion of married Catholic women (aged 18 to 39, including non-users) who had at least some experience with unapproved methods increased from 30 percent in 1955 to 38 percent in 1960 to 53 percent in 1965. Comparable figures for Great Britain were 39 percent for 1959–60 (ranging from 27 percent for devout Catholics to 69 percent among Catholics characterized as indifferent); for Grenoble, France, about 55 percent in 1959–62; and 67 percent in Johannesburg, South Africa in 1957–58. It should be noted that these proportions are considerably higher if expressed as percent of users rather than all women (users plus non-users). *As of 1965, more than two-thirds (68 percent) of U.S. Catholics who ever did anything to limit births had at some time used an unapproved method.* [Italics added. LR]

SUMMARY

Developed Countries

1. Although Catholics use contraception less than do Protestants and Jews, the majority do practice family limitation.
2. Many Catholics use methods of contraception that are inconsistent with traditional church doctrine. (Over 50 percent in three of the five available studies, and 44 percent in a fourth.)
3. Devout Catholics adhere more closely to the Church's teachings on contraception than do more nominal Catholics, although a substantial proportion of the more devout Catholics nevertheless use non-approved methods.
4. Among Catholics who practice contraception in the U.S. and Johannesburg, the college educated rely more heavily on Church-approved methods than do women of lower educational status.
5. Use of "non-approved" methods by Catholics, including more devout Catholics, is increasing over time in the U.S. and Britain.
6. In all studies, *a third or fewer of the Catholics using contraception rely on rhythm.* [Italics added. LR]

Developing Countries

1. In some developing countries, the restricted knowledge of contraceptive methods is a sufficient explanation for very limited practice.
2. However, *in urban areas of Latin America, Catholics practice contraception almost as widely as in the developed countries.* [Italics added. LR]
3. In most, but not all, studies, Protestants use contraception more widely than Catholics.
4. A quarter to a half of the women in Latin American cities who have ever used contraception have ever used rhythm. The more devout Catholics have a greater tendency to use rhythm, and a lesser tendency to use mechanical and chemical methods than the less devout.
5. In Latin America and the Philippines, studies show that contraceptive practice increases with education.

. . .

The fertility, ideal family size, and contraceptive practice of Catholics across the world depend on the milieu in which they live more than on doctrine as such. [Italics added.] There is an enormous cross-sectional "spread" in these variables, and with regard to each of them, *Catholics in developed countries are closer to non-Catholics in the same countries than they are to Catholics in under-developed countries.* [Italics added.] For example, even the more devout Catholics in Western countries have and desire smaller families than do marginal Catholics or non-Catholics in less developed countries. (Given the better health and nutritional status in

Western countries, we can rule out fecundability as an explanation for the difference. LR)

In underdeveloped countries, the almost universal high fertility norms preclude substantial Catholic–non-Catholic differentials. *Within developed areas, however, the pro-fertility impact of Catholicism is evident in the consistent margin of Catholic over Protestant fertility and family size ideals.* [Italics added. LR]

Catholics in developed countries practice contraception very widely, and although they rely to a greater extent than non-Catholics on the rhythm method, the majority of Catholic contraceptors have used methods inconsistent with traditional Catholic doctrine. As a result of widespread use of contraception, together with a somewhat lighter family size ideal, unwanted births are little more common for Catholics than for non-Catholics.

USE OF BIRTH CONTROL DEVICES BY CATHOLIC WOMEN
Extracts from Charles F. Westoff and Larry Bumpass, "The Revolution in Birth Control: Practices of U.S. Roman Catholics," *Science,* Vol. 179 (January 5, 1973), pp. 41–44

Ever since the 1968 papal encyclical ended the period of ambiguity and speculation about the Roman Catholic Church's position on birth control, there has been considerable interest in how American Catholics would respond to the reaffirmation of the traditional ban on methods of contraception other than the rhythm method.

• • •

The concept of "conformity" is defined here as following the traditional teaching of the Roman Catholic Church, reaffirmed by the encyclical, which prohibits the use of any method of fertility control other than periodic continence, the so-called rhythm method. There are two categories of Catholic women who are classified as conforming to Church doctrine: those who have never used any method of contraception and those whose most recent practice was the rhythm method.

• • •

The proportion of Catholic women between the ages of 18 and 39 who use methods of contraception other than rhythm has increased from 30 percent in 1955 to 68 percent in 1970, with the greatest changes occurring in the last 5 years.

Between 1965 and 1970, the percentage of Catholic women deviating from official teaching on birth control has risen from 51 to 68 percent. It seems clear that the papal encyclical has not retarded the increasing defection of Catholic women from this teaching.

• • •

There has been a spectacular increase in nonconformity among Catholic women in the youngest age groups.

Among women aged 20 to 24 in the year of each study, the proportion not conforming was 30 percent in 1955, 43 percent 5 years later, 51 percent by 1965, and 78 percent by 1970.

The increase from 1955 to 1970 was almost as great for the next two age groups: from 37 to 74 percent for ages 25 to 29 and from 30 to 68 percent for ages 30 to 34.

• • •

The increase in nonconformity . . . occurs as women grow older. . . . For example, of Catholic women born between 1936 and 1940, 43 percent were deviating from Church teaching by age 20 to 24 in 1960, 54 percent by age 25 to 29 in 1965, and 68 percent were not conforming by the time this cohort had reached 30 to 34 years of age in 1970.

• • •

EDUCATION AND CONFORMITY
Ibid

In 1965, nonconformity was greatest (57 percent) among Catholic women who had not completed high school and least (40 percent) among those who had attended or graduated from college. . . . By 1970, this relationship had reversed among younger Catholics, with college women deviating from Church teaching slightly more than women who had not completed high school.

These changes are due to a dramatic increase in nonconformity among the more educated Catholic women, an increase that has taken the form of a marked reduction in reliance on rhythm and a corresponding increase in the use of the pill.

. . . The rhythm method is least popular among the least educated women, but the largest proportion of women who have never used contraception are still found in this group.

• • •

There has been a decrease in the proportion of Catholic women who receive Communion at least monthly, from 52 percent in 1965 to 44 percent in 1970. Most of this change has been concentrated among the younger women, for whom the proportion receiving Communion monthly or more frequently declined from 52 to 37 percent.

Overall, nonconformity to teachings on birth control increased 16 percent between 1965 and 1970 (from 49 to 65 percent).

• • •

In 1970, the majority (53 percent) of the more committed Catholic women were deviating from the official position on birth control, a remarkable increase from the 33 percent so classified in 1965. . . . Even more remarkable, and perhaps an indication of changes yet to come, is the increase in nonconformity among the younger, more committed Catholic women: from 38 percent in 1965 to 67 percent by 1970. The increase among older, more committed Catholic women was from 30 to 44 percent.

. . .

The pill has played a major role in the decreasing conformity of the more committed Catholic women. Among women under 30, its use increased from 20 percent in 1965 to 37 percent in 1970. Almost exactly the reverse obtained for the rhythm method, which declined in use from 38 percent in 1965 to 18 percent in 1970.

. . .

SUMMARY AND CONCLUSIONS
Ibid

There has been a wide and increasing defection of Roman Catholic women from the traditional teaching of their Church on the subject of birth control over the past two decades and a resulting convergence of Catholic and non-Catholic contraceptive practices.

By 1970, two-thirds of all Catholic women were using methods disapproved by their Church; this figure reached three-quarters for women under age 30. Considering the fact that most of the one-quarter of young Catholic women conforming to Church teaching had never used any method, the percentage of those deviating may well reach 90 as these women grow older and the problem of fertility control becomes more important.

. . .

Perhaps the most significant finding is that the defection has been most pronounced among the women who receive Communion at least once a month. Even among this group, the majority now deviates from Church teaching on birth control; among the younger women in this group, the proportion not conforming reaches two-thirds.

It seems abundantly clear that U.S. Catholics have rejected the 1968 papal encyclical's statement on birth control and that there exists a wide gulf between the behavior of most Catholic women, on the one hand, and the position of the more conservative clergy and the official stand of the Church itself, on the other. That many Catholics can continue in their other religious practices and simultaneously deviate on the issue of birth control is an interesting commentary on the process of social change.

Ultimately this crisis of authority will probably be resolved by a change in official teaching, since it seems doubtful that such a major discrepancy can continue indefinitely without other repercussions. At a minimum, the cost to the Roman Catholic Church will be a loss of authority in a major area of life: that of sex and reproduction.

STATISTICAL TABLES ON BIRTH CONTROL AMONG
U.S. ROMAN CATHOLIC WOMEN

From Charles F. Westoff and Larry Bumpass, "The Revolution in Birth Control: Practices of U.S. Roman Catholics," *Science*, Vol. 179 (January 5, 1973), pp. 41–44

Table 1. Percentage of white, married Catholic women age 18 to 39 who have never used any method of contraception or who most recently used rhythm or some other method. . . . Data for 1965 differ from earlier data because "sterilization for contraceptive reasons" was not previously included as a form of contraception.

TABLE 1

MOST	YEAR			
	1955	*1960*	*1965*	*1970*
RECENT	NUMBER OF WOMEN			
METHOD	787	668	846	1,035
None	43%	30%	21%	18%
Rhythm	27	31	28	14
Other	30	38	51	68

Table 2. Percentage of white, married Catholic women not conforming to Church teaching on birth control. In the 1955 and 1960 studies (on the top and second diagonals, respectively), a woman is classified as not conforming to Church teaching if she had *ever* used any method of contraception other than rhythm. In the 1965 and 1970 data (third and bottom diagonals, respectively) the classification relates to the method *most recently* used.

TABLE 2

YEAR OF BIRTH	AGE OF WOMEN (YEARS)				
	20–24	*25–29*	*30–34*	*35–39*	*40–44*
1916–1920				28%	45%
1921–1925			30%	46	43
1926–1930		37%	40	52	50
1931–1935	30%	40	50	50	
1936–1940	43	54	68		
1941–1945	51	74			
1946–1950	78				

Table 3. Percentage of white, married Catholic women, by age and education, who have never used any method of contraception or whose most recent method was rhythm or the pill ("College" refers to women who attended or graduated from college).

TABLE 3

	AGE OF WOMEN (YEARS)					
	UNDER 45		UNDER 30		30–44	
Education	1965	1970	1965	1970	1965	1970
NOT CONFORMING						
College	40%	65%	42%	78%	38%	53%
Grade 12	47	67	51	76	45	58
Less than grade 12	57	63	57	73	57	55
Total	49	65	51	76	48	56
PILL						
College	13	29	24	42	6	16
Grade 12	13	29	24	38	6	20
Less than grade 12	11	25	23	35	5	17
Total	12	28	24	38	6	19
OTHER						
College	27	36	19	35	32	36
Grade 12	34	38	26	38	39	38
Less than grade 12	45	38	34	37	52	38
Total	37	37	28	37	42	37
RHYTHM						
College	39	19	36	10	41	27
Grade 12	34	16	31	12	36	20
Less than grade 12	13	7	11	4	14	9
Total	28	14	25	10	29	19
NONE						
College	21	16	22	12	21	21
Grade 12	19	17	18	12	19	22
Less than grade 12	30	30	31	23	29	35
Total	23	19	23	14	23	24
SIZE OF SAMPLE (NO.)						
College	166	262	59	127	107	135
Grade 12	548	701	211	351	337	350
Less than grade 12	369	287	131	121	238	166
Total	1083	1250	401	599	682	651

Table 4. Percentage of white, married Catholic women, by age and frequency of receiving Holy Communion, who have never used any method or who most recently used rhythm, the pill, or other methods.

TABLE 4

AGE OF WOMEN (YEARS)

MOST RECENT METHOD	RECEIVE COMMUNION AT LEAST MONTHLY						RECEIVE COMMUNION LESS THAN MONTHLY					
	Under 45		Under 30		30–44		Under 45		Under 30		30–44	
	1965 (N=558)	1970 (N=554)	1965 (N=207)	1970 (N=221)	1965 (N=351)	1970 (N=323)	1965 (N=525)	1970 (N=706)	1965 (N=199)	1970 (N=378)	1965 (N=331)	1970 (N=328)
None	25%	23%	24%	15%	25%	29%	21%	17%	22%	14%	20%	21%
Rhythm	42	23	38	18	45	27	12	8	12	5	12	11
Pill	11	26	20	37	5	18	14	30	28	39	6	19
Other	22	27	18	30	25	26	53	45	39	41	61	48
Total not conforming	33	53	38	67	30	44	67	75	67	80	67	67

Table 5. Method of contraception used most recently by married, white non-Catholic (NC) and Catholic (C) women, by age.

TABLE 5

	AGE OF WOMEN (YEARS)											
	UNDER 45				UNDER 30				30-44			
	1965		1970		1965		1970		1965		1970	
MOST RECENT METHOD	NC (N= 2,666)	C (N= 1,090)	NC (N= 3,708)	C (N= 1,255)	NC (N= 1,038)	C (N= 403)	NC (N= 1,723)	C (N= 602)	NC (N= 1,628)	C (N= 687)	NC (N= 1,985)	C (N= 653)
Sterilized†	10%	4%	12%	5%	5%	2%	5%	2%	12%	5%	19%	8%
Pill‡	21	12	33	28	37	24	49	38	11	6	19	19
IUD§	1	*	5	6	1	*	6	7	1	*	4	4
Diaphragm‖	12	4	7	4	8	1	3	3	15	5	10	5
Condom‖	20	14	12	10	17	11	10	10	22	15	15	11
Withdrawal	4	6	2	2	3	2	1	1	5	9	2	3
Foam	3	1	6	5	5	2	8	8	2	1	3	3
Rhythm	4	28	3	14	3	25	2	10	5	29	4	19
Douche	5	3	4	3	4	3	2	3	6	3	5	3
Other#	6	5	4	3	6	5	3	4	6	4	4	2
None	13	23	12	19	12	23	9	14	15	23	15	24

* Less than 1%. † Surgical procedures undertaken at least partly for contraceptive reasons. ‡ Includes combinations with any other method. § Includes combinations with any method other than the pill. ‖ Includes combinations with any method other than the pill or IUD. ‖ Includes combinations with any method other than the pill, IUD, or diaphragm. # Includes other multiple, as well as single, methods and a small percentage of unreported methods.

TRENDS IN ATTITUDES TOWARD, AND USE OF, BIRTH CONTROL DEVICES IN THE UNITED STATES

For the attitudes of Roman Catholic priests, in 1971, see p. 370.
[LR]

From *The Gallup Report,* September 1, 1968, published by the American Institute of Public Opinion (Gallup Poll)

Few issues over the last decade have caused such immediate and widespread interest both in the United States and abroad as Pope Paul VI's [1968] encyclical reaffirming the Catholic Church's traditional ban on artificial birth control methods.

A majority (60 percent) of all Americans who were polled disagreed with the Pope's position, while only 17 percent agreed. Even more significant is that 54 percent of the Catholics queried opposed the ban, with 28 percent in favor of it, and 18 percent having no opinion.

Even among Catholics who attended Mass once a week or more, criticism is nearly as strong as among those who don't. Almost 80 percent of young Catholics (those in their twenties) disagree with the encyclical. Catholics interviewed in the survey gave three reasons primarily for their opposition to the encyclical:

1. Catholics should be allowed to follow their conscience in family planning (24 percent).
2. The world is becoming overpopulated, causing poverty and starvation (13 percent).
3. Families should raise only those children they can properly care for (11 percent).

"DID YOU HAPPEN TO HEAR OR READ ABOUT POPE PAUL'S RECENT STATEMENT BANNING ARTIFICIAL METHODS OF BIRTH CONTROL?

	Yes	No
Catholic	93%	7%
Protestant	86	14

[NOTE: A poll published January 11, 1975, by the National Opinion Research Center showed that 83 percent of Roman Catholics now approve of artificial contraception. LR]

"DO YOU FAVOR OR OPPOSE HIS POSITION ON THIS MATTER?"
(ASKED OF THOSE WHO SAID THEY HAD READ ABOUT
THE POPE'S STATEMENT.)

	Favor	Oppose	No Opinion
Catholic	28%	54%	18%
Protestant	13	62	25

Further insight into changing attitudes on birth control was provided from responses to another question in this same series. When asked "Do you think it is possible to practice artificial methods of birth control and still be a good Catholic, or not?," almost two out of every three Catholics (65 percent) said that they did think it was possible.

In addition, fully as many Catholics as Protestants favor making birth control information available to anyone who requests it. Protestant opinion on this question has changed little during the 1960's, but Catholic opinion grew from 53 percent in 1965 who thought birth control information should be made available, to 76 percent in 1968.

"CAN A GOOD CATHOLIC IGNORE THE BAN ON ARTIFICIAL METHODS OF BIRTH CONTROL?"

Yes	No	No Opinion
65%	25%	10%

"SHOULD BIRTH CONTROL INFORMATION BE AVAILABLE TO ANYONE WHO WANTS IT?"

	Yes	No	No Opinion
Catholic	76%	17%	7%
Protestant	75	19	6

FAMILY PLANNING

Data from unpublished 1967 Gallup Poll, printed in *Studies in Family Planning* (Population Council, October 1968), No. 34, p. 20

AMERICAN ATTITUDES TOWARD FAMILY PLANNING

Question, Sample (N)	Yes or Approve	No or Disapprove	No Opinion
Q. "Do you feel the U.S. population growth rate is a serious problem?"			
Roman Catholic (1,565)	52%	43%	5%
Protestant (4,403)	56	38	6
Jewish (168)	41	51	8
Q. "Do you feel the world population growth rate is a serious problem?"			
Roman Catholic (1,564)	66	28	6
Protestant (4,395)	71	20	9
Jewish (168)	74	19	7
Q. "Should birth control information be made available to any married person who wants it?"			
Roman Catholic (1,568)	83	12	5
Protestant (4,372)	88	8	4
Jewish (168)	98	1	1
Q. "Should birth control information be made available to any single person who wants it?"			
Roman Catholic (1,563)	46	48	6
Protestant (4,388)	51	43	6
Jewish (168)	82	15	3
Q. "If requested, should U.S. Gov't. give birth control aid to states and cities?"			
Roman Catholic (1,569)	57	36	7
Protestant (4,396)	64	30	7
Jewish (168)	89	7	4
Q. "If requested, should U.S. Gov't. give birth control aid to other countries?"			
Roman Catholic (1,572)	56	38	6
Protestant (4,410)	65	29	6
Jewish (168)	86	10	4

Question, Sample (N)	Yes or Approve	No or Disapprove	No Opinion
Q. "If yes, does this include supplies?"			
Roman Catholic (868)	69	26	4
Protestant (2,818)	66	30	5
Jewish (142)	82	18	0
Q. "Should the Roman Catholic Church change its position on birth control methods?"			
(1965) Roman Catholic	56	33	11
Non-Catholic	53	22	25
(1967) Roman Catholic (1,568)	61	29	10
Protestant (4,366)	64	16	20
Jewish (167)	92	1	7
Q. "Would it be all right for a woman to have pregnancy interrupted:			
(a) If the pregnancy seriously endangered the woman's health			
Roman Catholic (1,561)	75	19	6
Protestant (4,411)	89	7	4
Jewish (168)	98	1	1
(b) If the woman had been raped			
Roman Catholic (1,561)	62	27	11
Protestant (4,398)	74	18	7
Jewish (168)	93	3	4
(c) If the couple could not afford another child			
Roman Catholic (1,557)	18	77	5
Protestant (4,405)	25	70	5
Jewish (168)	52	41	7

POLL OF ROMAN CATHOLICS ON BIRTH CONTROL AND THE PILL

EDITOR'S NOTE:

The range and rapidity of Catholics' changed attitudes to contraceptive (or "artificial") devices prohibited by the Church may be seen by comparing the previous data with polls taken for *Newsweek* and published in its March 20, 1967, issue, pp. 71, 72, as below. [LR]

HOW MANY CATHOLICS USE BIRTH CONTROL?

Method	Total	BY AGE			BY EDUCATION		
		Under 35	35–49	50 and Over	8th Grade or less	High School	College
Percentage using artificial device or birth-control pill	38%	60%	38%	12%	18%	42%	45%
Percentage using rhythm method only	35	38	43	18	13	36	44
Percentage using nothing	27	2	19	70	69	22	11

CATHOLIC PRIESTS AND BIRTH CONTROL

EDITOR'S NOTE:

One of the most surprising and possibly meaningful aspects of a 1971 poll of Roman Catholic priests in the United States was the

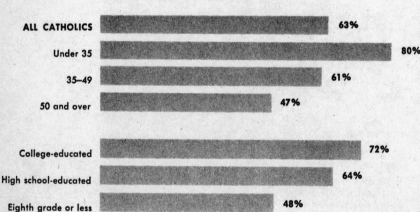

HOW MANY FAVOR THE PILL?

ALL CATHOLICS	63%
Under 35	80%
35–49	61%
50 and over	47%
College-educated	72%
High school-educated	64%
Eighth grade or less	48%

response to questions about birth control—and admitted permissions given to Catholic women to use "artificial methods" (not the Church-approved rhythm method). [LR]

From *Religion in America 1971*, Gallup Opinion Index, April 1971, Report No. 70, pp. 39–40. The data are taken from questionnaires in a national mail survey of 2,517 clergymen—of whom 845 Roman Catholic priests responded

Priests' Opinions on Birth Control

"DO YOU AGREE OR DISAGREE WITH THE CATHOLIC CHURCH'S BAN ON THE USE OF ARTIFICIAL METHODS OF BIRTH CONTROL?"

Catholic Priests	Agree	Disagree	No Opinion
All priests	52%	41%	7%
39 years & under	27	64	9
40 years & over	67	28	5

(The differences in the age groups seem especially notable—and, perhaps, prophetic. [LR])

Priests' Permission to Use Artificial Methods of Birth Control

"HAVE YOU, YOURSELF, GIVEN PERMISSION TO A PERSON TO USE ARTIFICIAL METHODS OF BIRTH CONTROL, OR NOT?"

Catholic Priests	Yes	No	Qualified, No Opinion
All priests	31%	58%	11%
39 years & under	45	41	14
40 years & over	23	69	8

Priests' Predictions of Church Attitude

"DO YOU THINK THE CATHOLIC CHURCH WILL SOMEDAY OFFICIALLY APPROVE THE USE OF ARTIFICIAL METHODS OF BIRTH CONTROL, OR NOT?"

Catholic Priests	Yes, Will	No, Won't	No Opinion
All priests	37%	50%	13%
39 years & under	52	31	17
40 years & over	29	61	10

POPE CAUTIONS UNITED NATIONS ON BIRTH CONTROL AS MEANS OF COPING WITH WORLD POPULATION

EDITOR'S NOTE:

On March 29, 1974, Pope Paul VI issued a message to UN officials that reaffirmed his firm, unyielding stand against birth control. The Vatican issued texts of the statement in English, French, and Italian. Here are the central points, extracted from the document (see *The New York Times*, March 30, 1974, p. 5):

No pressure must cause the church to deviate toward doctrinal compromises or short-term solutions. . . .

We are aware that the growing number of people, in the world taken as a whole and in certain countries in particular, presents a challenge to the human community and governments. . . . The problems of hunger, health, education, housing and employment become more difficult to solve when the population increases more rapidly than the available resources. . . .

For some people, there is a great temptation to believe that there is no solution and to wish to put a brake on population growth by the use of radical measures, measures which are not seldom in contrast with the laws implanted by God in man's nature, and which fall short of due respect for the dignity of human life and man's just liberty. Such measures are, in some cases, based upon a materialistic view of man's destiny.

After citing the historic and controversial encyclical *Humanae Vitae* ("Of Human Life")° proclaimed in July 1968, an encyclical that flatly condemned all physical or chemical contraceptive devices, the Pope continued:

The Church's teaching on population matters is both firm and carefully enunciated . . . . human in its pastoral approach.

The New York Times reporter Paul Hoffman, writing from Rome, stated that Pope Paul "clearly was putting the Church—and the United Nations—on their guard against liberal Catholics who were attempting to play down this veto on artificial contraception."

His Holiness advised the United Nations to search for a solution to the population problem of the world through means other than population control:

A fully human life, one endowed with freedom and dignity, will be assured to all men and all peoples when the earth's resources have been

° See Part Two, Chapter X.

shared more equitably, when the needs of the less privileged have been given effective priority in the distribution of the riches of our planet, when the rich—individuals as well as groups—seriously undertake a fresh effort of aid and investment in favor of the most deprived . . .

The public authorities, within the limits of their competence, can certainly intervene by favoring the availability of appropriate information, and especially by adopting suitable measures for economic development and social progress, provided that these measures respect and promote true human values. . . .

It is not of course for the Church to propose solutions of the purely technical order. [The decision as to how many children a couple wanted to have] depends upon their right judgment, and cannot be left to the discretion of the public authorities. [Excerpts selected by LR]

IX / BLACK AMERICANS AND THE CHURCHES

BLACK MILITANCE

From A. P. Klauser, "Religion," *Britannica Book of the Year* (Chicago: Encyclopaedia Britannica, 1972)

Black assertiveness manifested itself to an increasing degree on the U.S. religious scene. There were calls for a black Roman Catholic archbishop in Washington, D.C., where the population was predominantly black, and there was growing black participation and influence in high-echelon Protestant councils.

The rise of black Catholic militancy was accompanied by the charge that the Roman Catholic Church had a "racist history" in America. Similarly, black Protestant church leaders declared that American blacks had been "scarred" by the failure to end discrimination and injustice. At a caucus in Cincinnati, black Christians agreed to make every effort to establish black Christian identity.

Black voices were being heard in international church circles as well, one indication being the rising criticism of racial policies in southern Africa. The World Council of Churches Program to Combat Racism allocated funds to some groups that the South African government, among others, claimed were fostering guerrilla activities. The council pointed out, however, that none of the money would be spent for military purposes.

BLACKS AND THE CHRISTIAN CHURCH

From Alex Poinsett, article in *The Negro Handbook* (Chicago: Johnson Publishing Company, 1966), p. 307

The Negro's "place" in U.S. Christian churches almost mirrors his role in the rest of American society. *While all major church bodies have some Negro members, most Negro Christians are concentrated in six separate and predominantly-Negro denominations with a combined 11-million membership constituting, in effect, a colored division of the general church.*

Largest among them, in fact the world's largest single group of Negro Christians, are the 8.6 million members of the National Baptist Convention, U.S.A., the National Baptist Convention of America and the Progres-. sive National Baptist Convention, Inc. Another 2.4 million members are divided among the African Methodist Episcopal Church, the African Methodist Episcopal Zion Church and the Christian (formerly Colored) Methodist Episcopal Church. . . .

Meanwhile, the estimated 1.6 million Negroes "integrated" into pre- dominantly white congregations are less than one per cent of the 123.3 million total U.S. church membership, thus supporting a charge once made by former Yale Divinity School Dean Liston Pope that the church is "the most segregated major institution in American society." *In numerical terms the greatest amount of integration has occurred in the Roman Catholic Church* which in the last 25 years tripled its Negro membership to 722,609 and thus surpassed the totals of three all-Negro denominations. Its nearest rival, the Methodist Church, has some 373,327 Negro mem- bers, including about 225,000 in the gradually disbanding, all-Negro Central Jurisdiction. Another 200,000 Negroes are members of the American Baptist Convention, northern counterpart of the near lily-white Southern Baptist Convention. [Italics added. LR]

STATISTICS: BLACK CHURCH MEMBERSHIP

From *The Ebony Handbook,* compiled by the editors of *Ebony* (Chicago: Johnson Publishing Company, 1974), p. 355d

MAJOR DENOMINATIONS

Denomination	Number of Members	Number of Churches	Number of Pastors
National Baptist Convention, U.S.A., Inc.	5,500,000 (1958)	26,000	27,500
National Baptist Convention of America	2,668,000 (1956)	11,398	7,598
African Methodist Episcopal Church	1,166,000 (1951)	5,878	7,089
African Methodist Episcopal Zion Church	770,000 (1959)	4,083	2,480
National Primitive Baptist Convention, Inc.	1,645,000 (1971)	2,198	601
Progressive National Baptist Convention, Inc.	505,000 (1965)	411	450
Christian Methodist Episco- pal Church	444,493 (1961)	2,523	1,914

NEGRO MEMBERSHIP IN PREDOMINANTLY WHITE DENOMINATIONS

Denomination	Membership Total	Membership Negro
Roman Catholic Church	45,640,619 (1964)	722,609 (1963)
The Methodist Church	10,304,184 (1964)	373,327 (1964)
American Baptist Convention	1,559,103 (1963)	200,000 (1963)
Christian Churches (Disciples of Christ)	1,920,760 (1964)	80,000 (1964)
Protestant Episcopal Church	3,340,759 (1963)	73,867 (1963)
Seventh-day Adventists	370,688 (1964)	167,892 (1964)
Congregational Christian Churches	110,000 (1964)	38,000 (1964)
United Church of Christ	2,056,696 (1964)	21,859 (1962)
United Presbyterian Church in the United States of America	3,302,839 (1964)	6,000 (1964)

INTERMARRIAGE OF WHITES AND NONWHITES: CURRENT STATISTICS

EDITOR'S NOTE:

Marriages between racial groups are, of course, a phenomenon separate from religious intermarriages. But they reflect part of the broad sweep of social change—and therefore of the possible loosening of religious bonds and taboos that heretofore kept such marriages far below their current levels. [LR]

From "Marital Status," Vol. II, Subject Report Series PC (2)-4C (Washington, D.C.: U.S. Bureau of the Census, 1973)

The highlights of this special report of the Bureau of the Census may be summarized:

· Marriages between whites and nonwhites increased by 63% in the decade 1960–1970.
· The present rate is, nevertheless, a tiny fraction: of 44,597,574 marriages (1970), "interracial" unions accounted for 0.7% (a rise from the 1960 figure: 0.44%).
· Marriages between white men and black women declined—from 25,913 in 1960, to 23,566 in 1970 (or 2.1% of the black married population).
· But marriages between black men and white women rose from 25,496 in 1960 to 41,223 in 1970.

BLACK ROMAN CATHOLICS

From 1972 Catholic Almanac (Huntington, Ind.: Our Sunday Visitor, Inc., 1972), p. 116

Black Catholic leaders took their cause directly to the Vatican in the fall of 1971, with the presentation to Archbishop Giovanni Benelli of requests for a black rite and the appointment of a black prelate as the next archbishop of Washington.

Coupled with the presentation to the second highest official of the Vatican Secretariat of State was a statement in which the six leaders charged that the Church in The United States is racist. They said they had gone to the Vatican because "neither the white American hierarchy, representing white American Catholics, nor the apostolic delegation seem willing to deal with the situation nor present it honestly to the Holy See."

EDITOR'S NOTE:

On October 16, 1972, the Catholic bishops' Ad Hoc Committee for Priestly Life and Ministry issued a thirty-one-page report. Among the six major recommendations was one that declared that the inclusion in the hierarchy of more blacks and Spanish-speaking Catholics is "of utmost and immediate concern" (1973 Catholic Almanac, p. 145). [LR]

From 1973 Catholic Almanac (Huntington, Ind.: Our Sunday Visitor, Inc., 1973), p. 135

The National Office for Black Catholics originated from the first meeting of the Black Catholic Clergy Caucus in April, 1968, in Detroit.

According to executive director Brother Joseph Davis, S.M., "The NOBC is an effort to revitalize the Church in the black community as an institution for and about black people. It will be devoted to the liberation of people, black and white. In short, it will give black Catholics—especially black priests and religious—a chance to be about our Father's business." . . .

Establishment of the office was approved by the U.S. bishops in November, 1969. To date they have allocated nearly $250,000 for support of the office, which conducted its own fund raising campaign in 1972.

Sharing the aims and purposes of the NOBC are the Black Catholic Clergy Caucus, organized in 1968, the National Black Sisters' Conference . . . the National Black Lay Caucus, their affiliates and other groups.

Black Catholic Clergy

From 1972 Catholic Almanac (Huntington, Ind.: Our Sunday Visitor, Inc., 1972), pp. 116–117

The Black Catholic Clergy Caucus at its organizational meeting in April, 1968, in Detroit, sketched the outlines of a program to solve problems experienced by the black community in the Church and American society at large. Key demands in the program were for:

- black priests in decision-making positions;
- redistribution and more effective utilization of black priests and religious;
- institution of the permanent diaconate for blacks;
- reappraisal and redirection of clergy recruitment efforts in the black community;
- development of a black-directed department of social change within the U.S. Catholic Conference;
- allocation of substantial funds in each diocese for black leadership training programs.

Similar demands were made by delegates attending the first meeting of the national Black Catholic Lay Caucus Aug. 21 to 23, 1970, in Washington, D.C.

The clergy caucus has spearheaded efforts to gain recognition of black identity and black claims for positions of leadership in the Church. The organization, according to Father Lawrence E. Lucas, its president, "is prepared to take whatever means necessary to liberate black people from the system of oppression" in the Church and in society at large.

The caucus reports that it represents about 70 percent of the approximately 200 black priests in the country.

BLACK SISTERS' CONFERENCE

The female counterpart of the clergy caucus is the National Black Sisters' Conference, which was organized in August, 1968. . . .

Sister Martin de Porres calls the conference a radical movement seeking basic changes in the religious life of black women to conform with their distinctive identity and life style. Other objectives are to sensitize white religious and the Church, as well as society in general, to the aspirations of black sisters and the black community to control their own affairs.

BLACK PAROCHIAL SCHOOL CRISIS

On the school front, the conference wants black-controlled community schools. As a first step toward getting them, conference officials have urged black nuns to resign from teaching positions in predominantly white Catholic schools to accept similar positions in predominantly black Catholic schools.

The board of directors, meeting in April in Baltimore, called for "sweeping reform in the nature of parochial schools in the black community," opting for community-controlled schools as "the most viable survival strategy presently operative in the black community."

First Black Bishop in Episcopal Diocese of New York

On February 2, 1974, in the Episcopal Diocese of New York, the Reverend Harold Louis Wright was consecrated to the rank of bishop. There are now six black bishops in the Episcopal Church in the United States, which contains 140 active bishops (see *The New York Times,* February 3, 1974, p. 45). [LR]

Black Students in Parochial Schools
From Newsweek, October 12, 1971, p. 54

Joseph Dulin, principal of an all-black Detroit high school (St. Martin de Porres), has stated "most black people join the Catholic church so their kids can attend parochial schools." [LR]

Black Lay Catholic Caucus
From 1972 Catholic Almanac (Huntington, Ind.: Our Sunday Visitor, Inc., 1972), p. 101

More than 600 delegates to the third annual convention of the National Black Lay Catholic Caucus pledged to continue to work for "a black archbishop for Washington, D.C., and other dioceses as a means of obtaining black input in policy-making decisions as they affect the lives of black people." Delegates also said: "We have by no means exonerated the American hierarchy of racism in the Catholic Church, but we are appealing to them to support us in our struggle for total liberation and survival here in America."

Black Moderator Elected to Presbyterian Church

On June 17, 1974, the Reverend Lawrence W. Bottoms was elected a moderator of the Presbyterian Church in the United States. He is the first black in the 113-year history of the church to occupy this position. (Of the 900,000 members today, about 7,000 are black.)

Black Moderator Elected to United Church of Christ

EDITOR'S NOTE:
On June 23, 1973, Margaret A. Haywood, a black woman, was elected moderator of the United Church of Christ, the thirteenth largest denomination in the United States (about 2 million members), an amalgamation of the former Congregational Christian Church and the Evangelical and Reformed Church.

Mrs. Haywood, an associate justice of the Superior Court of the District of Columbia, was the first black woman to be appointed or elected to a leading post in any American (biracial) denomination. [LR]

BLACK MUSLIMS

EDITOR'S NOTE:

The Black Muslim movement is self-identified as "The Lost Found Nation of Islam in the Wilderness of North America." It claims a small but extremely fervent (critics call it "fanatical") membership among black people in, chiefly, the largest cities in the United States.

Below, I offer my text, or extracts from the best sources I could find, on the origins, purposes, creed, and practices of the Black Muslims in the United States. I thank the Library Research Service of the Encyclopaedia Britannica for contributing an excellent survey and supplementary data. [LR]

History

The Black Muslims were founded in 1930 by one W. D. Fard, who disappeared quite mysteriously in 1934. Orthodox Black Muslims regarded him as Allah Himself, in human form. To other Muslims (not Black) this was blasphemy.

Elijah Muhammad (Elijah Poole) became head of the Black Muslims in the 1930s, in Detroit, and preached a dogma in which hatred of all whites as "devils" aroused some attention. But it was the writings and the oratory of "Malcolm X" (Malcolm Little), an ex-convict, that brought the Black Muslims many new members and national attention.

Malcolm X made a pilgrimage to Mecca, in 1964, and upon returning announced that he had been converted to Sunni Muslim, the largest of the sects within the Muslim faith. The open break with Elijah Muhammad apparently cost Malcolm X his life: he was shot in 1965.

Since there are at least four sects within the Sunni Muslims

(Hanafi, Shafii, Hanbali, and Maliki), each stressing a different aspect of the Koran and of Muslim faith and practice, considerable intramural strife has characterized the movement for the past decade. [LR]

Creed and Church Services

Black Muslims revere Allah as God and the Koran as sacred scripture. They believe in "the divine guidance of Elijah Muhammad."

They adhere, if orthodox, to strict disciplines concerning food (no pork), tobacco, liquor, fasting, and cohabitation.

The orthodox regard Elijah Muhammad as the Messenger of Allah and accept his emphatic preachments against the "devils" of the white race. (Islam, outside of this Black Muslim group, has always preached total equality of the races. Yet the ancient idea of the *jihad*, or "holy war" against infidels, has driven the followers of Muhammad, down the centuries, to somewhat bloody action.)

Only black people can join the sect.

"The Way of the Messenger" imposes a strict regimen upon those who accept it—not only as a faith or creed but as an all-embracing code of daily living.

Asceticism is an ideal. The devout eat but one meal a day, in the evening, after a full day's work. The recreation of Black Muslims usually entails temple-centered work, proselytizing (aggressively) in the streets, selling the newspaper *Muhammad Speaks,* or—at home—reading the Koran.

Plays and pageants emphasize white hypocrisy, injustice, and brutality.

The ideology reinforces what social scientists call "self-fulfilling prophecies": If, for instance, some piece of legislation favorable to blacks is defeated, this "proves" white subjugation; and if the bill is passed, this "proves" white duplicity in erecting a false legal façade behind which to practice racist viciousness. [LR]

Abass Rassoull, national secretary of "The Nation of Islam," wrote to a reporter (see *Christian Science Monitor,* February 7, 1973, pp. 1 ff):

Every black child on earth is a born Muslim. One cannot become a Muslim unless he is born a Muslim. In order for one to accept his own and be himself, he must submit to Allah (God) and follow his last and greatest messenger, the Honorable Elijah Muhammad.

The Muslims will acquire and develop vast areas of the country known as the United States of America . . . by the will and promise of Allah. . . .

Any black brother or sister is welcome at Muhammad's Temple of Islam as long as he or she comes in peace to learn and do righteousness.

All persons are searched before entering. . . . Members of the Fruit of Islam search the men, and women search the women. . . . Sisters must dress modestly [no miniskirts].

As in all Muslim mosques and temples, men and women are separated while in the service.

No one is allowed in Muslim services under the influence of alcohol or drugs of any kind.

Membership Figures

According to the Islamic Center (Washington, D.C.) no one really knows how many Muslims there are in the United States: about 110,000 are non-Black (*Newsweek*, February 5, 1973, p. 61).

Black Muslim headquarters claim 100,000 to 200,000 members.

Federal authorities believe the number "registered" is 7,000 or so (see *Newsweek, ibid.*).

According to Jack Anderson, United Feature Syndicate, a classified Secret Service report estimates the total number of Black Muslims at 6,000–6,500. [LR]

Sects

There are perhaps seventy separate Muslim sects in the United States. Many are quite small and extremely secretive.

A sharp rift developed within the larger Black Muslim ranks as younger members, critical of their leadership (partly because of alleged "expensive living and wheeler-dealer spending"), resorted to violence. This violence was directed not only against Black Muslim hierarchs but—in consequence of shootings and bombings—against the police and civil authorities.

A group of young Black Muslims organized a fundamentalist Hanafi Mussulman sect. This sect claims to have 1,000 members.

They interpret the Koran literally and criticize the Black Muslims for totally excluding whites from conversion or membership.

The leader of the Hanafis, at this writing, is Hamaas Abdul Khaalis, who attacks Elijah Muhammad for preaching "false doctrines" and wrote to the leaders of fifty-eight Black Muslim mosques denouncing the revered leader, "Messenger of Allah," as a "lying deceiver" who is purveying a false brand of Islam—and hatred of whites. [LR]

Church Holdings

The Black Muslims are believed to own real estate (chiefly in urban ghettos), businesses, shops, and farms worth around $75 million (*Newsweek, ibid.*).

In Chicago, for example, the sect operates its own "University of Islam," which is a public school, and owns restaurants, a clothing factory, a grocery store, a cleaning establishment, and the official newspaper, *Muhammad Speaks*. All are operated under "the divine guidance of the Honorable Elijah Muhammad." [LR]

Recruitment

Usually, at the end of a Black Muslim sermon, the minister asks any who are "interested in learning more about Islam" to step to the back of the temple. Those who do so are handed three blank sheets of paper, plus a form-letter, addressed to Elijah Muhammad:

Dear Savior Allah, Our Deliverer:
I have attended the Teachings of Islam, two or three times, as taught by one of your ministers. I believe in it. I bear witness that there is no God but Thee. And, that Muhammad is Thy servant and apostle. I desire to reclaim my Own. Please give me my original name. My slave name is as follows . . .

"Slave name," of course, means legal or present name.

The applicant for membership is told to copy the letter above on each of the three blank sheets of paper. If he does not copy the letter perfectly, he must repeat the task. (No explanation is offered for these requirements.)

A letter of acceptance into Black Muslim membership formally inducts a new member. [LR]

Violence: A Note of Caution

It should be stated that despite the public reputation of the Black Muslims, they have on the whole been pious, peaceful middle-class blacks.

The murder of Malcolm X was the most dramatic exception to the pacifism; and federal intelligence sources believe that at least nine other deaths, in 1972, were the work of dissident members (*Newsweek, ibid.*).

The violence between and among Black Muslims has included the murder of a Muslim in Atlanta, the execution of another in Los Angeles, the massacre of seven (five of them children) in Washington, D.C., and the two-day seizure of a sporting goods shop in Brooklyn. [LR]

Motivations and Characteristics

From J. H. Blake, "Black Nationalism," *Annals of the American Academy of Political and Social Science* (March 1969), pp. 19–20

"The Lost Found Nation of Islam" is an unequivocal rejection of white America and a turn inward to the black man and the black community as the only source of hope for resolving racial problems. . . .

The rejection of white America involves a rejection of Christianity as the religion of the black man, English as the mother tongue of the black man, and the Stars and Stripes as the flag of the black man.

Muslims also refuse to use the term "Negro," their family names, and traditional Southern foods, which are all taken as remnants of the slave condition and a reaffirmation of that condition so long as they are used.

The Nation of Islam places great emphasis upon black consciousness and racial pride, claiming that a man cannot know another man until he knows himself. This search for black identity is conducted through the study of the religious teachings of Islam, as interpreted by Elijah Muhammad, and through the study of Afro-American and African history. . . .

Muslims also follow a strong program of economic nationalism, with their emphasis upon independent black businesses. Muslim enterprises, mostly of the service variety, have been established across the country and have been quite successful. . . .

From *Newsweek*, February 5, 1973, p. 61

"When blacks accept Islam, they feel they are returning to the roots of their African ancestors," says Dr. Muhammad Abdul Rauf, the Egyptian director of Washington's Islamic Center. "At the same time, it is a way of getting rid of what they regard as a not very honorable past. It is like becoming newly born into another whole life, in which they can have dignity and pride."

EARLY NEGRO CHURCHES IN THE UNITED STATES
From Will Herberg, *Protestant—Catholic—Jew* (Garden City, N.Y.: Doubleday Anchor Books, 1960), pp. 112–113

Before the Civil War, Negro slaves, as they became Christians, found themselves in the same churches as the whites, though of course segregated from them. Such was the case, too, with most of the free Negroes in the North. Considerations of Christian unity in Christ and the patriarchal responsibility of master for slave, combined with a natural reluctance to allow Negro slaves to develop independent institutions, helped bring about a very limited kind of fellowship in worship. The revival movement reached the Negroes in large numbers and swept them into the Methodist and Baptist churches as these spread in the South and Southwest.

Even before the Civil War, however, there were here and there beginnings of separate Negro churches, usually the result of resentment of free Negroes in the North at segregation and other discriminatory practices. But it was not until after the war that independent Negro churches emerged on a large scale. The Civil War and Emancipation removed restrictions which had fettered independent Negro organization and released the energies of the former slaves. At the same time, the war and postwar conflicts exacerbated the bitterness between the races and intensified the "color" consciousness of the whites. The newly emancipated Negroes carried out the work of separation and independent organization with astounding energy and success. The colored members of the Methodist Espicopal Church, South, left in vast numbers to join the African M.E. and African M.E. Zion churches, which had been formed as small groups in the North in 1816 and 1821 respectively. Of the 208,000 Negro members of the Southern Methodist Church in 1860, only 49,000 remained in 1866, and these soon departed to form the Colored Methodist Episcopal Church. Another Negro church came into being with the division of the Presbyterians, and still another with the separation of the Baptists, both in the decade and a half after the Civil War. The Northern Methodist Church and the Episcopal Church resisted division but could not avoid a great measure of inner segregation.

X / CATHOLICS: FACTS, OPINIONS, TRENDS, FERMENT, AND SCHISMS

CATHOLICISM TODAY: AN ESSAY

EDITOR'S NOTE:

Not since the Reformation, it is safe to say, have the Vatican and the Roman Catholic Church—its bishops and clergy and laymen—faced challenges so profound, or undergone changes so dramatic, as those within the past decade. Readers who may regard this assessment as exaggerated might ponder the following passage from the *1973 Catholic Almanac* (Huntington, Ind.: Our Sunday Visitor, Inc., 1973, p. 52):

Looking back across the past 10 years there is little doubt that Vatican II contained the seeds of a modern revolution within the Church . . .

In the nine years that he has been Pope, Paul VI has had an unequaled view from that "window of the council, opened wide to the world," as he described that event at the beginning of the council's second session in 1963.

There have been times when the winds blowing through that window have been cold and chilling, so biting that it once caused the Pope to weep when talking to a group of Latin American bishops of disaffection and strife within the Church.

Or consider the judgment of a Jesuit father and teacher (Canisius College, Buffalo), David S. Toolan, writing in *Commonweal* (February 22, 1974, p. 504):

I [am] aware of the psychic havoc wreaked upon so many sincere Catholics by the fiats of change issuing in the wake of Vatican II. Our people and our clergy were caught utterly unprepared by these changes, and the damage has been incalculable. I would hope we have learned something from the trauma—and now recognize that any transition from former custom must be preceded by a massive reorientation involving the adult education that the Vatican repeatedly calls for, and given our bishops' obsession with parochial schools, calls for to date in vain.

The Roman Catholic Church—at least in the United States—today faces pressures and resistances from within its ranks that promise to alter Catholicism on a dozen fronts within the next decade: birth control, abortion, divorce, an optionally celibate clergy, greater participation by priests in hierarchical decisions, a greater role for women . . .

By 1975, weekly confession at the Mass had declined to 50 percent (from 71 percent in 1964) and 38 percent of the Catholics polled said they "never" or "practically never" go to confession, as against 18 percent a decade earlier. (The figures are from the National Opinion Research Center report published January 11, 1975.)

Compare these facts with a 1971 survey of Roman Catholics over seventeen years old in the United States (*Newsweek*, October 4, 1971, pp. 78–81); the findings are more illuminating and eloquent than commentary by an editor:

· Over two-thirds of the Catholics in the United States expect that their Church will have to abandon its disapproval of divorce.
· One-half of the Catholics favor a relaxation of the Church's adamant opposition to abortion.
· Less than 10 percent of American Catholics think their children will "lose their souls" if they leave the Church entirely.
· Almost two-thirds of American Catholics no longer believe that Catholics who divorce and remarry are "living in sin."
· Over a third of the Catholics in the United States no longer attend Sunday Mass regularly.
· Two-thirds of the Catholics admit they have not gone to confession within the two months prior to being polled.
· Three-fourths of the American Catholic population does not belong to any secular Catholic organization (such as parish societies, Knights of Columbus, parochial school organizations).
· When troubled, or when trying to decide what to believe, a majority of American Catholics say they are more likely to consult Catholic friends, or their wife or husband, or resort to earnest prayer, than seek guidance from their priest or the pronouncements of Catholic bishops.
· Nine out of ten American Catholics could not name a single episcopal decision of the National Conference of Catholic Bishops that the respondents felt to be important in the conduct of their life or the content of their faith.
· A majority of Catholics in America simply no longer "share the hierarchy's moral and spiritual vision."

That pliant consensus which long characterized American Catholics has apparently been broken—and intense debate, conflict, pressures for (or against) further "liberalization" of the Church, the clergy, and Catholic doctrine itself seem certain to continue for years. "The church is in disarray," said Bishop Joseph Bernardin in 1971, "[but] we are experiencing a creative tension, a sign of the church's vitality. Out of the disarray, something good will come" (*Newsweek*, October 4, 1971, p. 80).

In the pages that follow, I offer what I believe to be the most significant aspects of problems that appear to be besieging the Vatican—and, more particularly, the Roman Catholic hierarchy in the United States today.

Vatican II was, clearly, more than a watershed in the history of the Church: it swept aside ancient and awesome rigidities. It was more than a wind of change, said one Monsignor: "It was a hurricane."

The editors of *Newsweek* concluded:

The "soul" of the U.S. Church—an integral Catholic substructure with its own distinctive blend of rituals and rules, mystery and manners—has vanished from the American scene. And the hurt of private loss is clearly discernible in the personal responses that were part of the . . . survey.

Largely because of Vatican Council II and the turmoil that has followed, there is now as much diversity in theology and life-style among Catholics as there is among U.S. Protestants. A Catholic, in effect, is anyone who says he is, and his attitude toward the church is likely to be shaped essentially by his income, education and where he floats in America's still bubbling melting pot [*ibid.*, p. 81]. [LR]

STATISTICAL SUMMARY: POPULATION, CLERGY, SCHOOLS, BAPTISMS, MARRIAGES*

From *1973 Catholic Almanac* (Huntington, Ind.: Our Sunday Visitor, Inc., 1973), p. 485

(Principal source: *The Official Catholic Directory, 1974.* Comparisons are with figures reported in the previous edition.)

Catholic Population: 48,465,438; 22.95 per cent of total population; increase, 5,011.

Jurisdictions: 32 archdioceses; 133 dioceses (including Guam); 1 exarchate; 1 prelacy; 1 abbacy; the military ordinariate.

Cardinals: 10.

Archbishops: 38.

Bishops: 249.

Abbots: 61.

Priests: 56,712. Includes: diocesan or secular priests, 36,058 (decrease, 165); religious order priests, 20,654 (decrease, 92).

* See also Part Two, Chapter XII, church membership figures in the United States.

Brothers: 9,233; decrease, 32.

Sisters: 139,963; decrease, 3,091.

Seminarians: 19,348; decrease, 2,432. Includes: diocesan seminarians, 11,765 (decrease, 1,160); religious, 7,583 (decrease, 1,272).

Infant Baptisms: 916,564; decrease, 58,507.

Converts: 74,741; increase, 816. Second lowest number since 1939, when the total was 73,677.

Marriages: 406,908; decrease, 8,579.

Deaths: 415,412; decrease, 10,928.

Parishes: 18,433; increase, 49.

Seminaries, Diocesan: 109; increase, 2.

Religious Seminaries, Novitiates, Scholasticates: 293; decrease, 11.

Colleges and Universities: 258; decrease, 4. Students, 407,081; decrease, 11,002.

High Schools: 1,702. Students, 911,730; decrease, 17,944.

Elementary Schools: 8,647. Students, 2,717,898; decrease, 156,353.

From the General Summary of Statistics, supplement to *Official Catholic Directory* (New York: P. J. Kenedy & Sons, 1971)

HIERARCHY AND CLERGY OF THE CATHOLIC CHURCH BY STATES

State	Cardinals	Archbishops	Bishops	Abbots	Diocesan Priests	Religious Priests
Alabama	—	1	2	1	153	171
Alaska	—	2	4	—	31	52
Arizona	—	—	2	—	163	175
Arkansas	—	—	2	—	120	67
California (Los Angeles)	1	2	18	—	2,150	1,825
Colorado	—	1	3	2	285	238
Connecticut	—	1	5	—	958	389
Delaware	—	—	1	—	124	89
District of Columbia	1	1	2	1	386	774
Florida	—	1	6	2	529	329
Georgia	—	1	1	1	136	90
Hawaii	—	—	1	—	34	125
Idaho	—	—	1	—	91	21
Illinois (Chicago)	1	—	12	2	2,356	1,622
Indiana	—	2	6	1	798	689
Iowa	—	1	5	3	999	123
Kansas	—	1	4	1	464	266
Kentucky	—	1	3	2	564	164
Louisiana	—	1	6	2	640	586
Maine	—	—	2	—	253	96
Maryland (Baltimore)	1	—	2	—	375	455

State	Cardi-nals	Arch-bishops	Bishops	Abbots	Dioce-san Priests	Reli-gious Priests
Massachusetts	—	1	9	1	2,293	1,509
Michigan (Detroit)	1	—	8	—	1,647	577
Minnesota	—	2	9	1	1,098	371
Mississippi	—	—	2	—	134	76
Missouri (St. Louis)	1	1	8	1	958	786
Montana	—	—	2	—	235	55
Nebraska	—	1	3	1	465	194
Nevada	—	—	1	—	63	36
New Hampshire	—	—	1	1	315	102
New Jersey	—	1	9	3	1,868	903
New Mexico	—	1	2	—	154	151
New York (New York)	1	2	30	1	4,941	2,289
North Carolina	—	—	2	2	133	69
North Dakota	—	—	3	3	256	87
Ohio	—	1	8	2	2,086	996
Oklahoma	—	1	1	2	200	73
Oregon	—	1	2	2	250	119
Pennsylvania (Philadelphia)	1	—	15	3	3,243	1,477
Rhode Island	—	—	3	1	393	223
South Carolina	—	—	1	1	86	60
South Dakota	—	—	4	3	202	121
Tennessee	—	—	3	—	132	42
Texas	—	1	14	2	982	910
Utah	—	—	1	1	56	39
Vermont	—	—	1	—	194	63
Virginia	—	—	3	1	191	172
Washington	—	1	3	1	386	310
West Virginia	—	—	1	—	143	71
Wisconsin	—	1	8	3	1,719	823
Wyoming	—	—	—	1	65	7
Eastern Rite Totals	—	3	7	—	523	84
Grand Totals (1971)	8	34	253	54	37,020	21,141

U.S. SEMINARIES AND STUDENTS, 1962–1972

Year	Diocesan Seminaries	Total Diocesan Students	Religious Seminaries Scholasticates	Total Religious Students	Total Seminarians
1962	98	23,662	447	22,657	46,319
1963	107	25,247	454	22,327	47,574
1964	112	26,701	459	22,049	48,750
1965	117	26,762	479	22,230	48,992
1966	126	26,252	481	21,862	48,114
1967	123	24,293	452	21,086	45,379
1968	124	22,232	437	17,604	39,836
1969	122	19,573	407	14,417	33,990
1970	118	17,317	383	11,589	28,906
1971	110	14,987	340	10,723	25,710
1972	106	13,554	326	9,409	22,963

From *The Official Catholic Directory*, in *1973 Catholic Almanac* (Huntington, Ind.: Our Sunday Visitor, Inc., 1973), p. 615

BREAKDOWN

The peak enrollment year for diocesan seminaries was 1965, when they had a total of 26,792 students. The comparative figure at the beginning of 1972 was 13,554, a decrease of more than 50 percent.

The peak year for seminaries of religious institutes was 1962, when the total enrollment was 22,657. The comparative figure at the beginning of 1972 was 9,409, a decrease of 58 percent.

The total all-time high enrollment of 48,992 in 1965 was down to 22,963 at the beginning of 1972, a decrease of 53 percent.

REASONS

Many reasons have been advanced for the decline in the number of candidates for the priesthood and religious life.

Obvious ones are defections from both ways of life; the impact of changes rightly or wrongly attributed to the Second Vatican Council; the slow pace of institutional renewal in the priesthood, the religious life and the Church in general, coupled with confused expectations; opportunities for apostolic service in other vocations; the problem of adjusting personalist strivings with the needs for institutional commitment; the difficulty of submitting oneself to the other- as well as this-worldly demands of these vocations in the contemporary cultural and social climate.

The basic reason, however, is a crisis of faith. So stated Cardinal Gabriel Garrone, prefect of the Congregation for Catholic Education, in a Vatican Radio interview in April, 1972.

He said that the progressive decrease in vocations "is in direct relation to the crisis in the priesthood" and religious life.

This crisis in turn, he added, is "linked to the crisis of faith, and the crisis of faith is linked to the absolutely unprecedented conditions of the present-day life of men and of society."

The Cardinal said: "Our fundamental concern must spring from the fact that we live in a very complex and very new environment; and that we, therefore, run the risk of remaining passive, either through discouragement or cowardice, or else we lose sight of the most fundamental impulse of all in the matter of vocations—faith."

OPINIONS OF U.S. ROMAN CATHOLICS ON KEY ISSUES

Catholics and Divorce: Opinions and Figures

EDITOR'S NOTE:

In a poll of American Catholics by Louis Harris and Associates published in *Newsweek* (March 20, 1967, p. 69):

- Half of the respondents *opposed* the drastic Church laws and position on divorce.
- 65% *favored* papal annulments of marriages for "innocent" partners (*i.e.*, who had been wronged, deserted, "betrayed," etc.).
- 39% favored the *acceptance* of divorce. [LR].

Priests' Poll on Divorce and Remarriage
From *Religion in America 1971*, Gallup Opinion Index, April 1971, Report No. 70, p. 37

A Gallup Poll of Catholic priests in 1970 asked this question: "Do you agree or disagree with the Church's stand that divorced people who remarry are living in sin?" The results are striking:

Catholic Priests	Agree	Disagree	Don't Know
All priests	54%	32%	14%
39 years & below	32	51	17
40 years & over	66	21	13

In 1971, a Gallup Poll for *Newsweek* (published October 4, 1971, pp. 81–88) contained the significant finding that 60 percent of the American Roman Catholics polled did not think that a divorced and remarried Catholic is "living in sin."

For the most recent expression of the official position of the Church, see "What Is a Catholic?," in Part One of this book.

Catholic Rates of Divorce

Sociologists' studies lead to the unmistakable conclusion that the divorce rate among Catholics in the United States is rapidly approaching the national average (above 25 percent of all marriages). Some 20 percent of divorced Catholics do not remarry; 80 percent do. See Part Two, Chapter XV.

Catholics who divorce and remarry can attend Mass, but they may not receive Holy Communion or other sacraments.

Some Catholic theologians predict that the Vatican, perhaps within a decade, will extend grounds for marital *annulment*—to include adultery, insanity, desertion. [LR]

U.S. Catholics: Newsweek's Key Findings
Gallup Poll for Newsweek, October 4, 1971, pp. 81–88

How often do you attend Mass?	*Sundays and Holy Days* 52%	*Less Frequently* 38%	*More Frequently* 10%
How often have you gone to confession in the past eight weeks? (Don't knows omitted)	*Never* 63%	*Once* 24%	*More Than Once* 12%
Can a good Catholic ignore the Pope's condemnation of artificial birth control?	*Yes* 58%	*No* 31%	*Don't Know* 11%
Is a divorced Catholic who remarries living in sin?	*Yes* 28%	*No* 60%	*Don't Know* 12%
If your child decided to leave the church, do you think he could still be saved?	*Yes* 78%	*No* 8%	*Don't Know* 14%
Does your family pray together often?	*Yes* 38%	*No* 61%	*Don't Know* 1%
Do you consider it a sin to miss Mass when you could easily have attended?	*Yes* 58%	*No* 41%	*Don't Know* 1%
Would you like to have more rosary devotions and novenas at your church?	*Yes* 26%	*No* 54%	*Don't Know* 20%

How often do you attend Mass?	Sundays and Holy Days 52%	Less Frequently 38%	More Frequently 10%
How often have you prayed the rosary in the past four weeks? (Don't knows omitted)	Never 58%	Less Than Once a Week 15%	Once a Week or More 25%
Can you name any decisions made by the National Conference of Catholic Bishops that have been important for your life?	No 92%	Yes 7%	Don't Know 1%

Which sources have you found most helpful when you were confused about what to believe as a Christian	Prayer 31%	Catholic Friends 23%	Your Priest 22%	Your Spouse 21%	The Pope 4%	Billy Graham 3%

How much time a week do you spend reading Catholic publications? ("Don't knows" omitted)	None 54%	One Hour or Less 39%	More Than One Hour 6%
Against which of the following should the church take a public stand?	Pornography 52%	Liberalized Abortion Laws 46%	Racial Discrimination 43%
Should sex education be taught in parochial junior high schools?	Yes 73%	No 16%	Don't Know 11%
Should priests be permitted to marry?	Yes 53%	No 36%	Don't Know 11%

ENCYCLICAL OF POPE PAUL VI: "HUMANAE VITAE"

The following are verbatim excerpts from His Holiness' encyclical, printed by the Daughters of Saint Paul, 50 St. Paul's Ave., Jamaica Plain, Boston, Mass. 02130 [Selection made by LR]

ENCYCLICAL LETTER (JULY 25, 1968) OF HIS HOLINESS POPE PAUL VI
ON THE REGULATION OF BIRTH (HUMANAE VITAE)

. . . a reciprocal act of love which jeopardizes the responsibility to transmit life which God the Creator, according to particular laws, inserted therein, is in contradiction with the design constitutive of marriage, and with the will of the Author of life. To use this divine gift destroying, even if only partially, its meaning and its purpose is to contradict the nature both of man and of woman and of their most intimate relationship, and therefore it is to contradict also the plan of God and His will.

. . . just as man does not have unlimited domain over his body in general, so also, with particular reason, he has no such dominion over his generative faculties . . .

. . . we must once again declare that the direct interruption of the generative process already begun, and, above all, directly willed and procured abortion, *even if for therapeutic reasons, are to be absolutely excluded as licit means of regulating birth.* [Italics added.]

. . . Equally to be excluded . . . is direct sterilization, whether perpetual or temporary, whether of the man or of the woman. Similarly excluded is every action which, either in anticipation of the conjugal act, or in its accomplishment . . . proposes, whether as an end or as a means, to render procreation impossible.

. . . it is not licit, even for the gravest reasons, to do evil so that good may follow therefrom . . . even when the intention is to safeguard or promote individual, family or social well-being. Consequently it is an error to think that a conjugal act which is deliberately made infecund and so is intrinsically dishonest could be made honest and right by the ensemble of a fecund conjugal life. . . .

Now, some may ask: in the present case, is it not reasonable in many circumstances to have recourse to artificial birth control if, thereby, we secure the harmony and peace of the family, and better conditions for the education of the children already born? . . .

If, then, there are serious motives to space out births, which derive from the physical or psychological conditions of husband and wife, or from external conditions, the Church teaches that it is then licit to take into account the natural rhythms immanent in the generative functions, for the use of marriage in the infecund periods only, and in this way to regulate birth without offending the moral principles which have been recalled earlier.

. . . The Church is coherent with herself when she considers recourse to the infecund periods to be licit, while at the same time condemning, as being always illicit, the use of means directly contrary to fecundation, even if such use is inspired by reasons which may appear honest and serious.

. . . [consider] the consequences of methods of artificial birth control. Let them consider, first of all, how wide and easy a road would thus be opened towards conjugal infidelity and the general lowering of morality. . . .

. . . men—especially the young, who are so vulnerable on this point— have need of encouragement to be faithful to the moral law, so that they must not be offered some easy means of eluding its observance.

. . . It is also to be feared that the man, growing used to the employment of anti-conceptive practices, may finally lose respect for the woman and . . . may come to the point of considering her as a mere instrument of selfish enjoyment, and no longer as his respected and beloved companion.

. . . Let it be considered also that a dangerous weapon would thus be placed in the hands of those public authorities who take no heed of moral exigencies. Who could blame a government for applying to the solution of the problems of the community those means acknowledged to be licit for married couples in the solution of a family problem? Who will stop rulers from favoring, from even imposing upon their peoples, if they were to consider it necessary, the method of contraception which they judge to be most efficacious? . . .

. . . To dominate instinct by means of one's reason and free will undoubtedly requires ascetical practices [and] . . . the observance of periodic continence. . . .

. . . We are well aware of the serious difficulties experienced by public authorities in this regard, especially in the developing countries. To their legitimate preoccupations we devoted our encyclical letter *Populorum Progressio* (The Development of Peoples). But with our predecessor Pope John XXIII, we repeat: no solution to these difficulties is acceptable "which does violence to man's essential dignity" and is based only on an utterly materialistic conception of man himself and of his life. . . .

The only possible solution to this question is one which envisages the social and economic progress both of individuals and of the whole of human society, and which respects and promotes true human values. Neither can one . . . consider divine providence to be responsible for what depends, instead, on a lack of wisdom in government, on an insufficient sense of social justice, . . . on blame-worthy indolence in confronting the efforts and the sacrifices necessary to ensure the raising of living standards of a people . . .

. . . We do not at all intend to hide the sometimes serious difficulties inherent in the life of Christian married persons; for them as for everyone else, "the gate is narrow and the way is hard, that leads to life."

Let married couples . . . face up to the efforts needed, supported by the faith and hope which "do not disappoint . . . because God's love has been poured into our hearts through the Holy Spirit, who has been given to us." Let them implore divine assistance by persevering prayer; above all, let them draw from the source of grace and charity in the Eucharist. . . .

. . . we are deeply convinced, both for the world and for the Church, since man cannot find true happiness—towards which he aspires with all his being—other than in respect of the laws written by God in his very nature.

—Paulus PP. VI

CLERGY AND ORDERS: PROBLEMS, DEFECTIONS, THE RADICAL NUNS, THE JESUITS

Loss of Priests

EDITOR'S NOTE:

The Roman Catholic Church in the United States is presently losing five priests (through death, retirement, resignations) for every two new seminarians who are ordained—according to a study of the American clergy which was presented to the Vatican in September 1972.

According to the *1970 Catholic Almanac* (p. 142), a survey prepared by offices of the Vatican and published in the Turin daily, *La Stampa*, in June 1969, revealed that in the six-year period 1963–1968 a total of 7,137 priests asked to be dispensed from the obligations of the priesthood and that 5,652 of these requests had been granted.

The figures, which were confirmed by Vatican press officer Msgr. Fausto Villainc, included many cases of priests who had left the priesthood before 1963.

Diocesan priests seeking dispensations numbered 3,330, or 1.28 percent of the total number of diocesan priests in the world.

Requests from priests belonging to religious institutes were more numerous, 3,807, or 2.31 percent of their total number.

According to Gallup Poll estimates (*Religion in America 1971*, p. 1): ". . . perhaps 2,500 Roman Catholic clergymen, or 4 percent of all priests in the U.S., are dropping out annually." [LR]

Catholic Priests' Reasons for Considering Leaving Their Ministry

From *Religion in America 1971*, Gallup Opinion Index, April 1971, Report No. 70, pp. 2–4

"HAVE YOU EVER SERIOUSLY CONSIDERED LEAVING THE RELIGIOUS LIFE?"

Catholic Priests	Yes	No
All priests	23%	77%
39 years & under	37	63
40 years & over	15	85

Reasons (for those priests who answered "yes"): *

"Frustrated-discouraged when cannot communicate"	24%
"To get married"	17
"Religion is irrelevant"	13
"Too many rules, regulations"	13
"Lack of interest, devotion among congregation"	9
"Don't know what's expected (of me)"	8
Other reasons	27
"Cannot live on wages"	1
"Pressure and criticism from outside"	2

Catholic Priests' Opinions on Communication with Laity

From *Religion in America 1971*, Gallup Opinion Index, April 1971, Report No. 70, p. 36.

"DO YOU THINK THERE IS A COMMUNICATIONS GAP BETWEEN THE CATHOLIC HIERARCHY—POPE AND BISHOPS—AND THE PEOPLE?"

Catholic Priests	Yes	No	No Opinion
All priests	69%	27%	4%
39 years & under	90	8	2
40 years & over	56	39	5

"DO YOU THINK THERE IS A COMMUNICATIONS GAP BETWEEN CATHOLIC PRIESTS AND THE PEOPLE?"

Catholic Priests	Yes	No	No Opinion
All priests	56%	37%	7%
39 years & under	76	19	5
40 years & over	44	48	8

Priests' Desire for Greater Authority

From *1973 Catholic Almanac* (Huntington, Ind.: Our Sunday Visitor, Inc., 1973), p. 145

Far-reaching changes in the exercise of episcopal authority in the Catholic Church in the U.S. were recommended in a 31-page "initial report" released Oct. 16, 1972, by the bishops' Ad Hoc Committee for Priestly Life and Ministry. The report, sent to all American bishops, recommended:

Priests and laity should have a far greater say in the selection of bishops.

* Total exceeds 100% because of multiple responses.

- Priests should participate and "have a voice" in meetings of bishops.
- An interdisciplinary committee should be set up to consider a "limited term of office" for bishops.
- The inclusion of more Spanish-speaking and blacks among the hierarchy is "of utmost and immediate concern."
- "Consultation" in the Church must be taken much more seriously, and stronger structures of consultation and due process should be set up in all dioceses.
- Structures for the evaluation of priests in their ministry must be established as an integral part of their personal growth and pastoral accountability.

The recommendations were made after wide consultation by the committee with priests throughout the country.

The New Jesuits: An Essay

EDITOR'S NOTE:

In the Jesuit weekly *America*, John Cogley (now an Episcopalian) made this arresting comment on the crisis in Jesuit circles:

> There are Jesuits left and Jesuits right,
> A pro and con for most any fight,
> So wherever you stand, you stand not alone,
> Every little movement has a Jebbie of its own.

The amusing (and surprising) quatrain calls attention to a movement within the Catholic Church that has teetered on various edges of controversy for at least a decade.

The winds of social upheaval that have affected so many sectors of Roman Catholicism have not passed the Jesuits by. The Vietnam war, for instance, precipitated deep schisms, symbolized on the one hand by the pro-Vietnam Reverend John McLaughlin, who in 1971 entered the White House staff as a writer of speeches for President Nixon, and on the other by Father Daniel Berrigan, who was in prison for eighteen months (then paroled) after his conviction for destroying U.S. draft board records and hiding out from the FBI for a considerable number of months.

On questions of dress, conduct, and celibacy, Jesuit circles and seminaries today are in the midst of remarkable debates and differences. The order whose motto is *Ad majorem Dei gloriam* ("To the greater glory of God") has recently witnessed the formation of

"Christian Marxist" factions (not as surprising as it once would have been, given the Vatican's recent announcement that much of the thought of Mao Tse-tung is close to Catholic values); the rebellion of young Jesuits in Holland who married—yet continue to exercise their ministry; and the publication of a sensational autobiography in December 1972 by Father José Maria Diez-Alegría. The book was entitled *I Believe in Hope*—and was not submitted, in the customary form, for approval by his superiors. The resulting furor in Rome was activated not only by the author's position on the faculty of the great Gregorian Pontifical University but by the book's leftist politics and uncommon candor about the sexual deprivations of celibacy—even hinting at morally justified masturbation. (Father Diez-Alegría was suspended from the Society of Jesus for two years.)

The stringent discipline that Jesuits have traditionally accepted seems to be in a process of relaxation. Today, many seminarians dress not in severe black but, as college students elsewhere, in sport shirts and blue jeans. Some use college dormitories in which both male and female students live. There are vociferous "Third World" Jesuits, who inveigh against the property and wealth of the Church, demand greater efforts to alleviate poverty, adopt leftish positions on social causes, participate in civil rights demonstrations, undertake social work in slums and black ghettos, and argue about celibacy—many urging that marriage be made optional and not forbidden to priests.

More students at Jesuit seminaries have decided to leave their vocation, before ordination, than ever before. This means that those who remain, and then enter the priesthood, are probably more convinced of their mission and vocation—because of the prolonged self-analysis and group debates in which contemporary seminarians are involved.

The Jesuits are the largest formal religious order in world Roman Catholicism: in 1966, 36,000 (priests, brothers, students). By 1972, according to informed estimates, the Jesuits contained fewer than 31,000 members. In the United States, there are some 6,600 Jesuits —but the annual number of novices seems to have dropped from 350 to less than 100. In the United States, the Society of Jesus operates 28 colleges and 52 high schools, as of the date of this writing.

For centuries, the Jesuits were the most "intellectual" order in the Roman Catholic Church. The order was officially recognized by Pope Paul III in 1540, at least six years after Ignatius (Inigo de Onaz y) Loyola, a poor Basque priest who had studied in the Benedictine abbey at Montserrat, took vows of poverty and chastity, along with a handful of clerical friends, in Paris in 1534. Loyola described the society as "soldiers of Jesus" and special servants of the Holy See—adding to the vows of poverty and chastity those of obedience and particular loyalty to the Holy Father.

Perhaps the best note on which to end this commentary is to quote the president of the Jesuit St. Louis University, Father Paul Reinert: "I have been a Jesuit since 1927. Never have I engaged in so much introspection as I have in the past five years" (*Time*, April 23, 1973, p. 45). [LR]

The "Radical" Nuns: An Essay

EDITOR'S NOTE:

In 1971, Pope Paul VI earnestly exhorted nuns not to deviate from "the essential commitments" of religious life. In February 1972, His Holiness forbade nuns to follow a growing movement of wearing dresses, skirts, blouses, blue jeans—instead of their distinctive habits. Behind these two statements lies a small but meaningful movement in American Catholicism.

Vatican II ended in 1965. In the next seven years, it is estimated, the number of nuns in the United States dropped from 180,000 to around 150,000 (*Time*, March 20, 1972, p. 65).

"Radical" nuns have abandoned their orders and formed experimental communities to "pioneer new forms of religious life for the 21st century." (This quotation comes from the Sisters for a Christian Community, founded in 1970, a group that does not consider itself composed or "ex" nuns but opposes the hierarchical authoritarian, traditional Catholic orders.) The new nuns teach, nurse, work in old-age homes or orphanages, pay taxes, live in one or another home, sometimes alone, sometimes shared, do not wear a habit. (Many continue to wear crucifixes.)

In Los Angeles, a group of defectors from the Immaculate Heart of Mary Sisters formed a community that includes married couples and Protestants.

Some "noncanonical" nuns have chosen to marry.

The National Assembly of Women Religious, an organization of 2,300 nuns from various Catholic orders in 47 states, held a weekend conference in mid-August 1973, in New Rochelle, N.Y., attended by over 800 sisters—who wore "brightly colored shirtwaists and sleeveless dresses." The conference theme was "the changing role of women in the church and society." The outgoing head of the National Assembly, Sister Ethne Kennedy, declared: "We have been oppressed for so long that we don't know how to take what's been given to us. We have to educate and stimulate ourselves to become active in the roles that are presently open to us and move toward the development of other roles."

The assembly conducted animated workshops on women in the Church, urged Catholics to boycott stores that do not sell produce farmed by the United Farm Workers Union, and asked the Church to use the considerable purchasing power of parochial schools, convents, and hospitals to buy only such lettuce, grapes, and wine whose containers bore union labels (*The New York Times,* August 20, 1973, p. 32).

Black and Hispanic nuns have formed their own "break-away" sisterhoods.

Women's liberation ideas are reflected in statements such as that of Sister Margaret Traxler, founder of the National Coalition of American Nuns: "We hope to end domination by priests, no matter what their hierarchical status."

(See "What Is a Catholic?" Part One, for a skeptical view of the size and scope of these defections.) [LR]

CELIBACY: THE PROBLEM

EDITOR'S NOTE:

Since the twelfth century, Roman Catholic priests have been forbidden to marry. Any who did so were excommunicated from the Church.

There is no scriptural prohibition: Jesus simply said, "Let them accept it who can." Of the original disciples, some took wives (Peter, for example).

In the 1960s, within the whole broad tumult of social change, rebellion, and assertion of civil liberties, Catholic circles began to teem with a reexamination of the priesthood and the sisterhood. It has been estimated (see below) that within the past decade, some 10,000 petitions to the Vatican from priests have requested a release from their vows of celibacy (not necessarily to be followed by marriage).

In the United States, a small but noteworthy number of Roman Catholic priests abandoned their vows (and their ministry) by marrying (see below).

Students at Catholic seminaries began to drop out in a new and higher proportion, because they found the celibate life—and the prospect of future celibacy—too difficult. [LR]

Polls of Catholic Priests

In 1967, Joseph Fichter, a Jesuit, polled 3,000 priests in the United States: two-thirds said they preferred to be free to choose whether to remain celibate or get married. Perhaps the most startling datum of all is the response of Roman Catholic priests themselves to celibacy, reflected in a Gallup questionnaire survey to which a sample of 850 priests responded.

From *Religion in America 1971*, Gallup Opinion Index, April 1971, Report No. 70, p. 38

"DO YOU THINK CATHOLIC PRIESTS SHOULD BE PERMITTED TO MARRY, OR NOT?"

Catholic Priests	Yes	No	No Opinion
All priests	52%	41%	7%
39 years & under	77	17	6
40 years & over	36	56	8

"DO YOU APPROVE OR DISAPPROVE OF EXCOMMUNICATION OF PRIESTS WHO MARRY?"

Catholic Priests	Approve	Disapprove	No Opinion
All priests	29%	60%	11%
39 years & under	12.	79	9
40 years & over	40	48	12

The National Association for Pastoral Renewal, an unofficial group, polled 8,000 priests in 22 dioceses and found an "overwhelmingly favorable" response favoring optional celibacy. [LR]

Polls of Catholic Laity

The National Opinion Research Center reported on January 11, 1975, that "some 79 percent of American Roman Catholics favor permitting priests to marry." Compare this striking figure to the 48 percent who, in 1967, hoped the Pope would allow priests to marry (*Newsweek*, March 20, 1967, p. 73).

Background to the Papal Statement on Celibacy: February 8, 1970

EDITOR'S NOTE:

In January 1970, the National Pastoral Council (Catholic) of Holland recommended the abolition of compulsory celibacy for Roman Catholic priests.

On February 8, 1970, Pope Paul VI informed Dutch Catholics that the reasons advanced were "not convincing" and that priests who abandon their sacred commitment to remain celibate could not preach and could not administer the sacraments.

His Holiness said that this ruling would "remain inflexible tomorrow as yesterday," but he mentioned the possibility of *ordaining* married men (in regions where there is an acute shortage of priests).

A relaxation of compulsory celibacy entailed a "lowering of the authentic conception of the priesthood," the Pope stated.

In 1971, a Roman Catholic Synod of Bishops in Rome, the third convened by Pope Paul VI, discussed the problems of the priesthood—and by a small margin of the 212 voting members upheld the papal statement of 1970 and the requirement of celibacy among Catholic priests.

The Vatican announced, on February 20, 1973, that the Pope had ordered a fourth Synod of Bishops to convene in October 1974. The theme would be "the evangelization of the contemporary world"—and would embrace the reexamination of celibacy in the priesthood, the possibility of married priests, and a renewed examination of the role of women in the Roman Catholic Church. [LR]

Papal Encyclical on Celibacy

EDITOR'S NOTE:

This long encyclical by Pope Paul VI, (June 23, 1967) is one of the most interesting and thought-provoking documents on celibacy and the priesthood. I have selected those portions that seem most relevant to nontheologians and central to the papal position. The headings and paragraph numbers are in the document itself. The reaffirmation of the statement by the Pope in 1970 follows the encyclical I have excerpted below. [LR]

Taken from the Papal Encyclical Letter on Priestly Celibacy ("Sacerdotalis Caelibatus"), made public June 23, 1967, and reproduced in the 1968 Catholic Almanac (Huntington, Ind.: Our Sunday Visitor, Inc., 1968), pp. 156–175

CONSECRATED CELIBACY TODAY

1. Priestly celibacy has been guarded by the Church for centuries as a brilliant jewel, and retains its value undiminished even in our time when mentality and structures have undergone such profound change.

Amid the modern stirrings of opinion, a tendency has also been manifested, and even a desire expressed, to ask the Church to reexamine this characteristic institution of hers. It is said that in the world of our time its observance has come to be of doubtful value and almost impossible.

. . .

OBJECTIONS TO PRIESTLY CELIBACY

. . .

VIOLENCE TO NATURE?

10. There are also some who strongly maintain that priests by reason of their celibacy find themselves in a situation that is physically and psychologically detrimental to the development of a mature and well-balanced human personality. And so it happens, they say, that priests often become hard and lacking in human warmth; that, excluded from sharing fully the life and destiny of the rest of their brothers, they are obliged to live a life of solitude which leads to bitterness and discouragement.

Is all this perhaps indicative of unwarranted violence to nature and an unjustified disparagement of human values which have their source in the divine work of creation and have been made whole through the work of the redemption accomplished by Christ?

. . .

VALIDITY OF CELIBACY CONFIRMED

14. Hence we consider that the present law of celibacy should today continue to be firmly linked to the ecclesiastical ministry. This law should support the minister in his exclusive, definitive and total choice of the unique and supreme love of Christ; it should uphold him in the entire dedication of himself to the public worship of God and to the service of the Church; it should characterize his state of life both among the faithful and in the world at large.

. . .

MATRIMONY AND CELIBACY IN THE NEWNESS OF CHRIST

20. Matrimony, according to the will of God, continues the work of the first creation (Gen. 2:18); and, considered within the total plan of salvation, it even acquires a new meaning and a new value. Jesus, in fact, has restored its original dignity (Matt. 19:3–8), has honored it (John 2:1–11), and has raised it to the dignity of a sacrament and of a mysterious symbol of his own union with the Church (Eph. 5:32). Thus, Christian couples walk together toward their heavenly fatherland in the exercise of mutual love, in the fulfillment of their particular obligations, and in striving for the sanctity proper to them. But Christ, Mediator of a more excellent Testament (Heb. 8:6), has also opened a new way in which the human creature adheres wholly and directly to the Lord . . .

CELIBACY AND PRIESTHOOD IN CHRIST THE MEDIATOR

21. Christ, the only Son of the Father, by the power of the Incarnation itself was made Mediator between heaven and earth, between the Father and the human race. Wholly in accord with this mission, Christ remained throughout his whole life in the state of celibacy, which signified his total dedication to the service of God and men. This deep connection between celibacy and the priesthood of Christ is reflected in those whose fortune it is to share in the dignity and in the mission of the Mediator and Eternal Priest; this sharing will be more perfect the freer the sacred minister is from the bonds of flesh and blood(7).

CELIBACY FOR THE KINGDOM OF HEAVEN

22. Jesus, who selected the first ministers of salvation, wished them to be introduced to the understanding of the mysteries of the Kingdom of Heaven (Matt. 13:11; Mark 4:11; Luke 8:10), to be co-workers with God under a very special title, and his ambassadors (2 Cor. 5:20). He called them friends and brethren (John 15:15; 20:17), for whom he consecrated himself so that they might be consecrated in truth (John 17:19). He promised a more than abundant recompense to anyone who should leave home, family, wife and children for the sake of the Kingdom

of God (Luke 18:29–30). More than this, in words filled with mystery and hope, he also commended (8) an even more perfect consecration to the Kingdom of Heaven by means of celibacy, as a special gift (Matt. 19:11–12). . . .

. . .

THE CELIBATE PRIEST IN THE COMMUNITY OF THE FAITHFUL

31. In the community of the faithful committed to his charge, the priest is Christ present. Thus, it is most fitting that in all things he should reproduce the image of Christ and follow in particular his example, both in his personal as well as in his apostolic life. To his children in Christ, the priest is a sign and a pledge of that sublime and new reality which is the Kingdom of God, of which he is the dispenser; he possesses it on his own account and to a more perfect degree, and he nourishes the faith and the hope of all Christians who, because they are such, are bound to observe chastity according to their proper state of life.

. . .

CELIBACY AND HUMAN VALUES

. . .

CELIBACY AND LOVE

50. As we said above (no. 10), the Church is not unaware that the choice of consecrated celibacy, since it involves a series of hard renunciations which affect the very depths of a man, presents also grave difficulties and problems to which the men of today are particularly sensitive. In fact, it might seem that celibacy conflicts with the solemn recognition of human values by the Church in the recent council. And yet a more careful consideration reveals that the sacrifice of human love as experienced in a family and as offered by the priest for the love of Christ, is really a singular tribute paid to that superior love. Indeed, it is universally recognized that man has always offered to God what is worthy of both the giver and the receiver.

GRACE AND NATURE

51. On the other hand, the Church cannot and should not set aside the fact that the choice of celibacy—provided that it is made with human and Christian prudence and responsibility—is governed by grace which, far from destroying or doing violence to nature, elevates it and imparts to it supernatural powers and vigor. God, who has created and redeemed man, knows what he can ask of him and gives him everything necessary to be able to do what his Creator and Redeemer asks of him. St. Augustine, who had fully and painfully experienced in himself the nature of man, exclaimed: "Grant what you command, and command what you will" (34).

. . .

CELIBACY IS NOT CONTRARY TO NATURE

53. After what science has now ascertained, it is not just to continue repeating (cf. no. 10) that celibacy is against nature because it runs counter to lawful physical, psychological and affective needs, or to claim that a completely mature human personality demands fulfillment of these needs. Man, created to God's image and likeness (Gen. 1:26–27), is not just flesh and blood. The sexual instinct is not all that he has. Man also, and preeminently, has understanding, choice, freedom. Thanks to these powers, he is, and must remain, superior to the rest of creation; they give him mastery over his physical, psychological and affective appetites.

* * *

CELIBACY AS AN EXALTATION OF MAN

55. The choice of celibacy does not connote ignorance or contempt for the sexual instinct and affectivity. That would certainly do damage to physical and psychological balance. On the contrary, it demands clear understanding, careful self-control and a wise sublimation of the psychological life on a higher plane. In this way celibacy sets the whole man on a higher level and makes an effective contribution to his own perfection.

CELIBACY AND THE DEVELOPMENT OF PERSONALITY

56. The natural and lawful desire a man has to love a woman and to raise a family are renounced by celibacy, but marriage and the family are not said to be the only way for fully developing the human person. In the priest's heart love is by no means extinct. His charity is drawn from the purest source (1 John 4:8–16), is practiced in the imitation of God and Christ, and, no less than any other genuine love, is demanding and real (1 John 3:16–18). It gives the priest a limitless horizon, deepens and gives breadth to his sense of responsibility—a sign of mature personality —and inculcates in him, as a sign of a higher and greater fatherhood, a generosity and refinement of heart (35) which offer a superlative enrichment.

* * *

CHRIST AND THE LONELINESS OF THE PRIEST

59. At times loneliness will weigh heavily on the priest, but not for that reason will he regret having generously chosen it. Christ, too, in the most tragic hours of his life was alone—abandoned by the very ones whom he had chosen as witnesses to and companions of his life, and whom he had loved unto the end (John 13:1). But he stated, "I am not alone, for the Father is with me" (John 16:32). He who has chosen to belong completely to Christ will find, above all, in intimacy with him and in his grace, the power of spirit necessary to banish sadness and regret and to triumph

over discouragement. . . . And if hostility, lack of confidence and the indifference of his fellow men make his solitude quite painful, he will thus be able to share, with dramatic clarity, the very experience of Christ, as an apostle who is not above him by whom he has been sent (John 13:16; 14:18), and as a friend admitted to the most painful and most glorious secret of his divine Friend. . . .

* * *

THE UNFIT

64. Those who are discovered to be unfit—either for physical, psychological or moral reasons—should be quickly removed from the path to the priesthood. Let educators appreciate that this is one of their very grave duties. Let them not abandon themselves to false hopes and to dangerous illusions, and let them not permit the candidate to nourish these hopes in any way, with resultant damage either to himself or to the Church. The life of the celibate priest, which engages the whole man so totally and so delicately, excludes in fact those of insufficient psycho-physical and moral balance. Nor should anyone pretend that grace supplies for the defects of nature in such a man.

* * *

CONSCIOUS CHOICE

69. The complete education of the candidate to the priesthood ought to be directed to help him acquire a tranquil, convinced and free choice of the grave responsibilities which he must assume in conscience before God and the Church. Ardor and generosity are marvelous qualities of youth; illuminated and supported, they merit, along with the blessing of the Lord, the admiration and confidence of the whole Church as well as of all men. None of the real personal and social difficulties which their choice will bring in its train should remain hidden to the young men, so that their enthusiasm will not be superficial and illusory. At the same time it will be right to highlight with at least equal truth and clarity the sublimity of their choice, which on the one hand leads to a certain physical and psychic void, but on the other hand brings with it an interior richness capable of elevating the person to the highest degree.

* * *

THE CHOICE OF CELIBACY AS A GIFT

72. Once moral certainty has been obtained that the maturity of the candidate is sufficiently guaranteed, he will be in a position to take on himself the heavy and sweet burden of sacerdotal chastity as a total gift of himself to the Lord and to his Church.

In this way, the obligation of celibacy, which the Church adds as an objective condition to Holy Orders, becomes the candidate's own accepted personal obligation under the influence of divine grace and with full reflection and liberty. . . .

* * *

TRUE RESPONSIBILITY

83. Now with fatherly love and affection, our heart turns anxiously and with deep sorrow to those unfortunate priests who always remain our dearly beloved brothers and whose misfortune we keenly regret: those who, retaining the sacred character conferred by their priestly ordination, have been or are unfortunately unfaithful to the obligations they accepted when they were ordained.

Their sad state and its consequences to priests and to others move some to wonder if celibacy is not in some way responsible for such dramatic occurrences and for the scandals they inflict on God's People. In fact, the responsibility falls not on consecrated celibacy in itself but on a judgment of the fitness of the candidate for the priesthood, which was not always adequate or prudent at the proper time, or on the way in which sacred ministers live their life of total consecration.

REASONS FOR DISPENSATIONS

84. The Church is very conscious of the sad state of these sons of hers and judges it necessary to make every effort to avert or to remedy the wounds she suffers by their defection. Following the example of our immediate predecessors of holy memory we also have, in cases concerning ordination to the priesthood, been prepared to allow inquiry to extend beyond the provisions of the present canon law (canon 214) to other very grave reasons which give ground for really solid doubts regarding the full freedom and responsibility of the candidate for the priesthood and his fitness for the priestly state. This has been done to free those who, on careful judicial consideration of their cases, are seen to be really unsuited.

* * *

A HEARTRENDING APPEAL

86. If these priests knew how much sorrow, dishonor and unrest they bring to the holy Church of God; if they reflected on the seriousness and beauty of their obligations, and on the dangers to which they are exposed in this life and in the next: there would be greater care and reflection in their decisions, they would pray more assiduously, they would show greater courage and logic in forestalling the causes of their spiritual and moral collapse.

* * *

THE GRANTING OF DISPENSATIONS

88. There are some whose priesthood cannot be saved, but whose serious dispositions nevertheless give promise of their being able to live as

good Christian lay people. To these the Holy See, having studied all the circumstances with their bishops or with their religious superiors, sometimes grants a dispensation, thus letting love conquer sorrow. . . .

. . .

CONCLUSION

. . .

MARY'S INTERCESSION

98. Venerable brothers, pastors of God's flock throughout the world, and dearly beloved priests, our sons and brothers: As we come to the end of this letter which we have addressed to you, we invite you . . . to turn your eyes and hearts with renewed confidence and filial hope to the most loving Mother of Jesus and Mother of the Church, and to invoke for the Catholic priesthood her powerful and maternal intercession. . . . May Mary, Virgin and Mother, obtain for the Church . . . to rejoice always, though with due humility, in the faithfulness of her priests to the sublime gift they have received of holy virginity, and to see it flourishing and appreciated ever more and more in every walk of life . . .

CONFIDENT HOPE OF THE CHURCH

99. The Church proclaims her hope in Christ. She is conscious of the critical shortage of priests when compared with the spiritual necessities of the world's population. But she is confident in her expectation, which is founded on the infinite and mysterious power of grace, that the high spiritual quality of her ministers will bring about an increase in their numbers . . .

U.S. Bishop's Statement on Celibacy: Editor's Extracts

Extracts from the Statement on Celibacy adopted, on November 13, 1969, by the bishops of the United States at the National Conference of Catholic Bishops in Washington, D.C. Reprinted in 1970 Catholic Almanac (Huntington, Ind.: Our Sunday Visitor, Inc., 1970), pp. 133–137

. . . More and more priests have been withdrawing from the ministry and marrying, some without dispensation from their lawful obligations. Small groups have affirmed that they consider themselves free to exercise their priestly ministry even after marriage. Opinion polls are publicized to indicate that significant numbers of American priests and lay people favor "optional celibacy." All these developments receive such sensational coverage in the news media that a calm and objective handling of these problems has become difficult.

. . .

In the western Church, the link between the priesthood and celibacy is not the result merely of theological reasoning, nor of law, but of the life experience of the Church. The decision to require unmarried candidates for the priesthood to commit themselves to celibacy as a condition for ordination emerged only after a long struggle, and only as the Christian consciousness discerned between priesthood and celibacy a certain affinity of major import for the life of the Church. This decision has survived several severe crises and has been reaffirmed with the general support of the faithful.

. . . we presuppose and reaffirm the teaching of the Second Vatican Council of Pope Paul VI in his encyclical "On Priestly Celibacy," and our own earlier statement of November, 1967.

. . .

Nor is it only the celibate vocation which is under grave pressure today. The vocation to marriage is in at least as serious a crisis. The percentage of marriages which end up in separation or divorce is far higher than the percentage of priests or religious who do not persevere in their celibate call.

Celibacy is ordinarily viewed in relation to marriage, and there is a striking parallelism in the changes affecting both forms of life today. In both, there is a shifting from an institutional emphasis towards a personal one. While marriage is still esteemed for its role of continuing the race of man and his traditions, the partners in marriage are more and more regarded from the viewpoint of personal dignity and fulfillment. The celibate vocation likewise is passing from a largely institutional to a more personal emphasis. Its validity for the priest is increasingly seen in the degree to which it enables him to realize himself as a man.

. . .

The priesthood is . . . in a very special way, the Church's witness to the mystery of Christ in the service of the human community. Where charity and love prevail, God's kingdom has already come among men. It is the call of every priest to dedicate his life in sacrifice to promote this coming of the kingdom among his brothers and sisters.

. . .

Celibacy is a way of being human, Christian, priestly. It is a way of loving and hoping and believing. It does not diminish but enlarges the priest's capacity for love. Celibacy does not negate his personality or any of its component parts. The priest's total strength as a man goes into his life of service because he is called to live in the midst of the people in a close and trusting manner.

. . .

Celibacy does not separate the priest from the Christian community; indeed, it is the instrument of his full and rich relationship to it. As a husband pledges his life in faith to his wife, so the priest pledges his life to the Christian people. The celibate vocation also joins the priest to man's struggle for a better life on earth.

And so we ask priests who may be wavering in their adherence to this difficult vocation to consider whether their total availability for the task of building human community will really be enhanced by a more domestic kind of existence.

. . .

The promotion and defense of priestly celibacy cannot be carried on in isolation from other aspects of a priest's life and ministry. If there is a relation, as we believe between celibacy, community, authority and faith itself, then a crisis in one area is bound to affect the others. No one today would doubt the existence of a crisis in each of these areas. . . .

. . .

For many [priests], perhaps for most, the key problem is not celibacy, but rather a joyful and fruitful style of life and work. The priest . . . remains fully a man, and his faithful response to the gift of celibacy must be simultaneously a valid realization of his manhood. . . . Basic human rights and responsibilities must find appropriate realization in the lives of priests. Customs which isolate the priest from the people he serves tend to retard his growth in pastoral identity.

. . .

. . . it is not realistic to expect that a change in the Church's general discipline regarding celibacy is forthcoming. An abandonment of the law of celibacy would clearly raise cultural, economic, educational and pastoral problems of the gravest kind without proportionate gain. And . . . we again affirm our witness to priestly celibacy. We remind all priests, our brothers and co-operators, of the sacredness of our commitment to a celibate life.

We are convinced that the problem of celibacy is often a symptom of deeper problems. In our rapidly changing culture many priests have become confused as to the nature of their priestly service. Some lack a sense of accomplishment. Others feel that they have been inadequately prepared for the new forms of ministry expected of them. . . .

. . .

With regard to our brother priests who are suffering trials and doubts in their celibate commitment, we are ready to render every assistance possible to help them resolve these doubts. We are aware that in the life of every man, especially if he has professional responsibilities, there are times of self-doubt with its consequent dangers.

We shall increase our efforts to provide priests in such circumstances with competent psychological and spiritual counselling.

With regard to those priests who have made a final decision to ask for a dispensation from their priestly obligations, and those who have taken the unfortunate step of entering marriage without a dispensation, certain things should be said. Contrary to a rather widespread impression, bishops have shown compassion in their efforts to help these priests secure dispensations without undue delay or anguish; nor is it necessary for a priest to enter into an invalid marriage in order to obtain a dispensation. . . .

A priest may seek a dispensation from celibacy not only through his own bishop but through any Ordinary.

• • •

With regard to seminarians . . . we ask them to present themselves for ordination only if they feel ready and willing, in full honesty and freedom, to commit themselves to a life-long celibate priesthood.

• • •

This statement on the heritage of priestly celibacy will obviously not be the last word spoken on the subject. We do not anticipate universal agreement with all its positions. Some will find it unduly concessive, others excessively restrictive. We welcome every constructive criticism which may contribute in any way to a better understanding of the gift of priestly celibacy in the life of the Church.

Celibacy: Church Permission to Thirteen American Priests to Leave the Ministry
From 1973 Catholic Almanac (Huntington, Ind.: Our Sunday Visitor, Inc., 1973), p. 70

Ex-Priests and Wives Club—
Thirteen priests who had left the ministry, with permission of the Church, and their wives began formation of a new kind of couples' club with the advice and consent of the Brooklyn diocese.

One purpose of the group was to influence Catholics to think positively about resigned priests rather than regard them as "misguided or emotionally disturbed" clerics whose marriages should be hushed up.

EDITOR'S NOTE:
As the present volume goes to press, Father Leo McLaughlin, Jesuit, former president and chancellor of Fordham University, a Jesuit priest for forty years, announced that he had married a twenty-six-year-old writer, Sari Gombos, in a civil ceremony. Dr. McLaughlin said that he had asked Jesuit authorities almost a year earlier for a dispensation to marry and a return to layman's status. He had not received such permission—hence, he and his wife were, perforce, in the state of excommunication. Dr. McLaughlin, who had celebrated his last Mass more than a year before his marriage, told reporters that it was possible that the Society of Jesus might remove his excommunication, by granting his ten-month-old request for a dispensation and the surrender of his priestly status. [LR]

PAPAL AUTHORITY AND PAPAL INFALLIBILITY: PRIESTS VERSUS BISHOPS

American Priests' Attitudes to Pope's Authority
From *Religion in America 1971*, Gallup Opinion Index, April 1971, Report No. 70, p. 35

"DO YOU BELIEVE IN THE ABSOLUTE AUTHORITY OF THE POPE?"

Catholic Priests	Yes	No	Don't Know
All priests	56%	34%	10%
39 years & under	40	51	9
40 years & over	67	23	10

Vatican Warns Roman Catholic Bishops to Avoid Public Dissent From Papal Views

EDITOR'S NOTE:

On June 20, 1973, the Vatican published a 50,000-word Directory for the Pastoral Ministry of the Bishops. Approved by Pope Paul VI, as he completed the tenth year of his pontificate, the instructions apply to the 4,300 (approximately) bishops of the Roman Catholic Church.

The most important part of the document warns all bishops against any public dissent (presumably, this includes criticism no less than dissent) from the Pope's views—which are held to impose a duty of agreement with the Pontiff on all matters of faith, morals, social practices, and so on. Any disagreements with papal positions should be expressed through "normal channels" of communication with the Vatican and/or other bishops.

The Directory was initiated in Vatican II and ultimately prepared by the Congregation for Bishops. Vatican II, it may be noted, emphasized the doctrine of "collegiality"—that is, joint governing of the Church by the Pope and the bishops, the former as Vicar of Jesus and the latter as successors to the Apostles.

On October 26, 1974, Pope Paul VI addressed the Synod of Bishops, meeting in Rome, to announce that their proposals for greater freedom for local dioceses, without the Vatican's approval, "need to be placed in proper proportion." His Holiness reaffirmed the principle that "the Pope has full, supreme and universal power in the church" (quoting the constitution approved by the Ecumenical Council in the Vatican II meetings of 1962–65).

The theme of the month-long meeting of the Synod (the fourth since Vatican II) was evangelism in the modern world. The Pope characterized recommendations for the expression of faith according to national or cultural modes as "dangerous." "The content of the faith is either Catholic or it is not."

Further: ". . . the successor of Peter is and remains the ordinary pastor of the church in her union and entirety." His Holiness thus reaffirmed his earlier position on the authoritarian relationship between the Apostolic See and Roman Catholic churches around the world.

African bishops especially had asked for a larger degree of diocesan authority—and for commitment to various liberation movements. The Pontiff responded: "Salvation is not to be confused with one or another aspect of liberation. . . . Human advancement, social progress are not to be excessively emphasized on a temporal level to the detriment of the essential meaning that evangelization has for the church of Christ. . . ." He said that hope of progress would be "truly stunted" if certain local communities were exempted from "ecclesiastical authority" or were left in control of "the arbitrary impulse of individuals."

It will be remembered that the first Synod of Bishops convened after Vatican II, in 1967, asked for a larger sharing of the government of the church with the Roman Catholic bishops.

The next Synod is scheduled to be held in 1977. [LR]

Papal Infallibility

EDITOR'S NOTE:

On July 5, 1973, a 4,000-word statement from the Vatican (entitled "Declaration in Defense of the Catholic Doctrine on the Church Against Certain Errors of the Present Day") sternly reminded Roman Catholic prelates and theologians against "dogmatic relativism" that in any way questioned the dogma of papal infallibility. That dogma, proclaimed in 1870 (during the first Vatican council), holds that when the Pope speaks on matters of faith and morals, he does so *ex cathedra* ("from the chair" of Saint Peter)—

and therefore cannot be in error. The doctrine was supported by official statements during Vatican II (1962–1965).

Papal infallibility has been invoked only once, incidentally, in the 103 years since its announcement: in 1950, when Pope Pius XII defined a new dogma pertaining to the actual physical ("bodily") assumption of the Virgin Mary to Heaven.

Papal statements are always held to be authoritative and binding on Roman Catholics—but if not made *ex cathedra* such pronouncements are considered not infallible and therefore may be changed or revoked in the future (for example, Pope Paul VI's condemnation of "artificial" birth control methods or his reaffirmation of clerical celibacy).

The July 5, 1973, statement was clearly aimed at the Rev. Hans Küng, the Swiss professor at Tübingen University (West Germany) who had published a book that created a considerable stir in theological circles throughout the world—both Catholic and Protestant. The book, *Infallible? An Inquiry,* analyzed the history and content of the dogma and concluded that it was meaningless. Father Küng's book took on added importance because he had been one of the more vigorous young "liberal" theologians appointed to serve as one of Vatican II's expert theologians.

The book launched an investigation inside the Vatican, and a spokesman of the Holy See (Most Rev. Joseph Schroffner) revealed that "proceedings against" Father Küng were "pending" in the Vatican's Sacred Congregation for the Doctrine of the Faith (known until 1965 as the Holy Office), the supreme court, as it were, of the Roman Catholic Church. Bishop Schroffner answered that the Sacred Congregation had written to Father Küng about his published views and that the proceedings would be dropped if Küng accepted the "doctrinal statement."

Father Küng had earlier disclosed that he had been summoned to the Vatican to be interrogated but had refused to appear.

On July 8, three days after the Vatican's reassertion of papal infallibility, Küng told reporters he was opposed to "an absolute, totalitarian, authoritarian papacy." He said he would disregard the new doctrinal statement, would not go to Rome for questioning, and doubted that he would be excommunicated. He voiced strong "dismay" over the "antiecumenical spirit" of the Vatican's doctrinal affirmation. To affirm that the Pope cannot err means to "bar progress in interfaith efforts." Father Küng cited the Vatican's refusal to accept Holy Communion by most Christian churches that are not Roman Catholic.

In a singularly pointed remark, Father Küng reminded reporters that the Sacred Congregation was the heir to the Holy Inquisition, the Vatican office that had condemned Galileo, Bruno, and others. "I was always ready to go to Rome—under fair conditions and not as a 'defendant' with no right to examine the record, and no right or possibility of appeal [from the Congregation's judgment]."

Professing affection and respect for Pope Paul VI, Küng said, "How can you prove that you are infallible? To do that, you must already be infallible. And even [the July 5] document does not claim itself to be infallible." [LR]

ON VATICAN II*

From 1974 Catholic Almanac (Huntington, Ind.: Our Sunday Visitor, Inc., 1974), p. 168

VATICAN II

The Second Vatican Council, which was forecast by Pope John XXIII Jan. 25, 1959, was held in four sessions in St. Peter's Basilica.

Pope John convoked it and opened the first session, which ran from Sept. 11 to Dec. 8, 1962. Following John's death June 3, 1963, Pope Paul VI reconvened the council for the other three sessions which ran from Sept. 29 to Dec. 4, 1963; Sept. 14 to Nov. 21, 1964; Sept. 14 to Dec. 8, 1965.

A total of 2,860 Fathers participated in council proceedings, and attendance at meetings varied between 2,000 and 2,500. For various reasons, including the denial of exit from Communist-dominated countries, 274 Fathers could not attend.

The council formulated and promulgated 16 documents—two dogmatic and two pastoral constitutions, nine decrees and three declarations—all of which reflect its basic pastoral orientation toward renewal and reform in the Church. Given below are the Latin and English titles of the documents and their dates of promulgation.

· *Lumen Gentium* (Dogmatic Constitution on the Church), Nov. 21, 1964.
· *Dei Verbum* (Dogmatic Constitution on Divine Revelation), Nov. 18, 1965.

* See also "Ecumenism," Part Two, Chapter XVI.

- *Sacrosanctum Concilium* (Constitution on the Sacred Liturgy), Dec. 4, 1963.
- *Gaudium et Spes* (Pastoral Constitution on the Church in the Modern World), Dec. 7, 1965.
- *Christus Dominus* (Decree on the Bishops' Pastoral Office in the Church), Oct. 28, 1965.
- *Ad Gentes* (Decree on the Church's Missionary Activity), Dec. 7, 1965.
- *Unitatis Redintegratio* (Decree on Ecumenism), Nov. 21, 1964.
- *Orientalium Ecclesiarum* (Decree on Eastern Catholic Churches), Nov. 21, 1964.
- *Presbyterorum Ordinis* (Decree on the Ministry and Life of Priests), Dec. 7, 1965.
- *Optatam Totius* (Decree on Priestly Formation), Oct. 28, 1965.
- *Perfectae Caritatis* (Decree on the Appropriate Renewal of the Religious Life), Oct. 28, 1965.
- *Apostolicam Actuositatem* (Decree on the Apostolate of the Laity), Nov. 18, 1965.
- *Inter Mirifica* (Decree on the Instruments of Social Communication), Dec. 4, 1963.
- *Dignitatis Humanae* (Declaration on Religious Freedom), Dec. 7, 1965.
- *Nostra Aetate* (Declaration on the Relationship of the Church to Non-Christian Religions), Oct. 28, 1965.
- *Gravissimum Educationis* (Declaration on Christian Education), Oct. 28, 1965.

The key documents were the four constitutions, which set the ideological basis for all the others. To date, the documents with the most visible effects are those on the liturgy, the Church, the Church and the world, ecumenism, the renewal of religious life, the life and ministry of priests, the lay apostolate.

CATHOLIC–JEWISH RELATIONS*

EDITOR'S NOTE:

In 1938, Pope Pius XI established a Commission on anti-Semitism and authorized an encyclical attacking anti-Semitic beliefs, teachings, or practices. That encyclical was never published.

In 1969–1970, a committee of the Vatican drafted a plan for the improvement of relations between Christians (particularly Roman Catholics) and Jews. That document has never been released.†

* See also "Prejudice and Religion," Part Two, Chapter XXX.
† A Vatican statement on Catholic–Jewish relations did appear (January 11, 1975) as this book went to press. [LR]

On October 22, 1974, the Vatican formed a Commission for Judaism—attached to the Secretariat for Christian Unity. The Commission will promote and foster "relations of a religious nature" between Roman Catholics and Jews.

Vatican II had denounced anti-Semitism, renounced "all intent of proselytizing and conversion" of Jews by Catholics, emphasized the validity of the Old Testament independent of the New, and referred sympathetically to the State of Israel—at least in its religious aspect.

In January 1973, Father Cornelius Rijk, the Dutch priest who headed the little-publicized Vatican office for Catholic-Jewish relations, resigned from that post. "I was disillusioned," he told at least one reporter, "by the ignorance on both sides—but especially on the Christian side" (*Time*, February 5, 1973, p. 62).

In January 1973, Pope Paul VI received the Prime Minister of Israel, Golda Meir, in the Vatican. The meeting, according to reports, was rather cool on the part of the Pontiff, who is aware of the extreme hostility of Arab states (and, perhaps, the Christian communities within them) to any rapprochement between the Vatican and the State of Israel—which is not recognized by, or represented at, the Holy See. [LR]

CATHOLICS AND BLACKS*

EDITOR'S NOTE:

In a *Newsweek* poll published on March 20, 1967, seven out of ten Catholics said they would be bound by their pastor's advice on abortion laws, 55 percent said they would follow their priest's opinions on which books not to read, but only 21 percent stated that they would respect "a priest's exhortation" to integrate their neighborhoods. Furthermore, 46 percent of the Catholics polled said they would see no sin in refusing to receive Holy Communion from a black priest.

The most memorable comment on the Catholic laity's hostility to certain relationships to blacks was made by Archbishop Robert E. Lucy of San Antonio:

* See also "Black Americans and the Churches" (Part Two, Chapter IX) and "Prejudice and Religion" (Part Two, Chapter XXX).

To admit that there are three persons in God and that Mary is a virgin mother causes the Catholic no inconvenience. But when the pastor says to his people, "You must love colored folks, you must treat Latin-Americans as equals . . . and, worst of all, you must not pay starvation wages to defenseless men and women," too many Catholics declare that the pastor is taking things too far" (*Newsweek, ibid.,* p. 70). [LR]

VATICAN POLICY CHANGE ON COMMUNISM

EDITOR'S NOTE:

The Vatican has been an adamant opponent of "godless" Marxism/Leninism/communism, firmly united to Western Europe and the United States in opposition to the Soviet Union. In communist countries, cardinals, bishops, and priests were often persecuted or imprisoned.

In 1948, Pope Pius XII pronounced his historic excommunication of "atheistic communism." The record appears to bear out the political ineffectiveness of the papal pronunciamento in countries with large Catholic communist constituencies such as France and Italy.

In 1963, Pope John XXIII welcomed Soviet Premier Nikita Khrushchev's daughter and son-in-law to the Vatican.

In 1972, a Vatican publication suggested that the teachings and philosophy of Mao Tse-tung "reflected" Christian values. This surprising statement was noted widely in the world's press.

Soon after, in Geneva, a Vatican diplomat publicly praised the Chinese Communist "social system."

In June 1973, a delegation of ecumenists from the Vatican issued a statement affirming that there "is a strong tendency toward some form of 'socialism' in many parts of the world."

By July 4, 1973, numerous indications surfaced concerning a marked change to, and possible rapprochement with, communism on the part of Pope Paul VI. In public statements, officials of the Vatican explained that Pope Pius XII's 1948 condemnation of communism still governs the Roman Catholic position—especially since communism preaches atheism. Still . . .

It may be that a toning down in Moscow and/or Peking of overt atheism to discreet agnosticism and a relaxation of hostility to Church services will revolutionize Catholic-communist relations. A prelate in Rome, who is said to be familiar with His Holiness' thinking, recently informed reporters that the Pope realizes that the world is entering "an era of multipolar relationships" and is therefore "adapting the Church" to new political balances. The prelate reminded his listeners of the "unique adeptness" of the papacy in contending with political vicissitudes for 2,000 years.

The monsignors in the Pope's Secretariat of State preserve their traditional ambiguity—although it is common knowledge in Rome that various agencies in the Holy See maintain contacts with diplomats or political figures from countries not formally accredited to the Vatican. The Soviet embassy and the Polish embassy (in Italy) pursue unpublicized conversations or negotiations with papal designees. Cuba and Yugoslavia maintain diplomatic relations with the Vatican.

The Soviet Union, for its part, has made conciliatory moves vis-à-vis the Vatican by formally recognizing Pope Paul VI as the "ruler of the State of Vatican City"—and in 1973 invited that state to take part in the conference in Helsinki on European security.

There seems little reason to doubt that the "cold war" stance of both the Vatican and the Kremlin is ended and that the papacy is pursuing an energetic policy to achieve some sort of rapprochement with communist countries. It may be noted that the papal envoy in Havana for the past twelve years (the Most Reverend Cesare Zacchi) is an open admirer of Fidel Castro.

The Vatican has rejected repeated overtures from Israel for diplomatic recognition or relations—because of the considerable Catholic communities in Arab countries. Envoys to the Vatican from these countries (Egypt, Syria, Algeria, Lebanon) have acted as "something like an anti-Israel lobby" (*The New York Times,* July 5, 1973, p. 12). [LR]

CATHOLICISM TODAY

EDITOR'S NOTE:

All of the above data, however striking, must not be taken too hastily to represent enduring convictions, permanent positions, or unalterable trends. The most important fact about storms is that they end.

Within this frame of caution, I think the following generalizations about Catholicism in American *can* be made—because the evidence for them is so strong and is found in so many areas of behavior besides opinion polls.

1. One of the most significant changes among American Roman Catholics—especially significant because of (a) its dramatic departure from the past and (b) its repercussions on Church leadership and laity alike—is the increase in the number and percentage of Catholics attending college. The statistics (from Andrew M. Greeley's *The Catholic Church in America of 1975*, a monograph prepared for the U.S. Army Chaplain Board, Fort Meade, Maryland, November, 1969, p. 31) are striking:

Catholics under 30 years of age attending college (in 1964)	28%
Catholics aged 50–60 who attended college	12%

These figures take on added consequence if we compare them with college attendance among Protestants:

	Under 30	Age 50–60
Catholics	28%	12%
Protestants	29	25

2. The sharp division of opinions, by age groups, of Roman Catholic priests in the United States is certain to produce profound changes in the position of the Church on the following crucial problems (because the under-forty priests will steadily replace the more conservative, traditional, "orthodox" priests over forty in the hierarchy): birth control, divorce, optional celibacy (and perhaps the acceptance of married priests), abortion, greater participation by priests in Church decisions, greater participation by the Catholic laity in the administration and educational "stance" of parochial schools.

The figures in various tables that follow amply illustrate the breadth of the schism between older and younger priests across the spectrum of problems currently agitating both the clergy and the laity in America today.

3. The marked, continuing rise of *income* among Catholic laymen—which means a continuing shift upward in education, occupations, movement from urban centers to suburbs, and so on—appears

likely to support and reinforce the changes predicted in the preceding paragraphs.

4. Both priests and laity are likely to be more critical (or, at least, less accepting) of higher authorities within the Church; the powerful historical leverage of "loyalty to the Church" is likely to sustain its new stance: openly questioning, debating, even challenging hierarchical orthodoxy.

5. This means, in my opinion, that the loyalty of Catholics to hierarchical authority may decline—*without being accompanied by a decline in faith.*

6. Sexual behavior and mores among Catholics is almost certain to be more "free" and less "puritanical" than in the past (on this point, the tables below are extremely illuminating).

7. The attitudes of Catholics, both in the clergy and in the laity, will become more tolerant, and certainly less hostile, vis-à-vis Protestants and Jews. This may well be the most important historical effect of Vatican II (see the "Declaration on the Relationship of the Church to Non-Christian Religions," Chapter XXX below). [LR]

CATHOLIC HOLIDAYS, FEASTS, AND DEVOTIONS

Holidays and Feasts

EDITOR'S NOTE:

In accordance with revised regulations on liturgical observances, some Catholic feasts were either abolished or relegated to observance in particular places by local option. In addition, a new system of classification for feasts was introduced, by which they are ranked according to dignity and manner of observance. The new categories are: Solemnity (highest, corresponding to former Class I), Feast (corresponding to former Class II), and Memorial (corresponding to former Class III). [LR]

From the *National Catholic Almanac,* 1971 (Paterson, New Jersey: St. Anthony's Guild, 1971)

Solemnity of Mary, Mother of God (formerly called **The Circumcision**), January 1, commemorates the circumcision of Christ eight days after His birth, according to the Jewish law, His initiation into the Jewish religion, and His reception of the name Jesus, which Archangel Gabriel had made known to Mary at the Annunciation.

The Epiphany, January 6, commemorates Christ's manifestation of Himself . . . as represented by the Three Kings of the East who, guided by a star, came to adore Him . . . It also marks Christ's manifestations of Himself . . . when He was baptized by John the Baptist and when He performed His first recorded miracle at the marriage feast in Cana.

Presentation of the Lord (formerly called **The Purification**), February 2, commemorates the presentation of Christ in the Temple according to the prescriptions of Leviticus 12:2–8; Exodus 13:2 and the purification of the Blessed Mother forty days after the birth of Christ. The feast is also called **Candlemas,** because candles . . . are blessed on this day and commemoration is made of the fact that Christ is, in the words of Simeon, "A light to the revelation of the Gentiles and the glory of His people Israel."

Ash Wednesday, first day of the penitential season of Lent . . . : "Remember, man, that thou art dust and unto dust thou shalt return." The priest says these words as, with ashes, he makes the sign of the cross on each person's forehead.

The Annunciation, March 25, commemorates the announcement by the Archangel Gabriel to Mary that she was to become the Mother of Christ, the Second Person of the Blessed Trinity made Man.

HOLY WEEK AND EASTER

Palm Sunday in Passiontide, the first day of Holy Week, commemorates Christ's triumphant entry into Jerusalem. It receives its name from the palm branches which the people spread under the feet of Jesus, crying out, "Hosanna to the Son of David! Blessed is He Who comes in the name of the Lord!" On this day palms are blessed and distributed to the faithful.

Holy Thursday, or **Maundy Thursday,** occurs in Holy Week and commemorates the institution of the holy eucharist by Christ at the Last Supper the night before He died. There is only one Mass in each church on this day; white vestments are used because of the joyful commemoration, but at the same time there are certain signs of the mourning proper . . . such as the silencing of the bells. The celebrant consecrates two Hosts, one of which he receives, while the other is placed in a chalice and carried in solemn procession to an altar . . . Here It remains for the adoration of the faithful until Good Friday when It is taken back to the high altar and received by the priest at the communion in the Mass of the Presanctified. After the procession of the Blessed Sacrament on Holy Thursday, the altars are stripped to recall the fact that Christ was stripped of His garments. Then follows the washing of the feet, known as the "Mandatum" . . . whence the name "Maundy" Thursday. Christ washed the feet of the apostles at the Last Supper.

Good Friday commemorates the Passion and Crucifixion of Christ. The liturgy is in every way of an exceptional character, befitting the day of the Great Atonement. The distinctive feature is the **Mass of the Presanctified,** in which there is no Consecration, the Host having been consecrated in the Mass the day before. The service consists of (1) lessons from Holy Scripture and prayers, terminating with the chanting of the Passion; (2) solemn supplication for all conditions of men; (3) veneration of the Holy Cross; (4) procession of the Blessed Sacrament from the Repository and the priest's communion, or the Mass of the Presanctified proper.

Holy Saturday (Easter Vigil) is the day before Easter. . . . The ceremonies begin early in the morning with the blessing of the new fire and the Paschal Candle, which is followed by the reading of the twelve prophecies. The priest then goes in procession to bless the baptismal font, and the water is scattered toward the four quarters of the world to indicate the catholicity of the Church and the world-wide efficacy of her sacraments. Solemn High Mass is then sung, white vestments are used, flowers and candles are set upon the altar, statues are unveiled, the organ is heard, and the bells, silent since Holy Thursday, are joyfully rung. Lent ends officially at noon on this day.

Easter Sunday or **The Resurrection** commemorates Christ's rising from the dead by His own power on the third day after His Crucifixion. The feast occurs on the first Sunday after the first full moon after the vernal equinox, or March 21.

Saint Joseph, March 19, honors Saint Joseph as the spouse of Mary, and the patron and protector of the Universal Church.

The Ascension, forty days after Easter, commemorates Christ's Ascension into heaven from Mount Olivet, in the presence of His Blessed Mother and His apostles and disciples. It is a holy day of obligation in the United States.

Pentecost or **Whitsunday,** fifty days after Easter, commemorates the descent of the Holy Spirit upon the apostles, in the form of fiery tongues. It is the birthday of the Catholic Church. . . .

Most Holy Trinity Sunday, the first Sunday after Pentecost, commemorates the mystery of One God in Three Divine Persons.

Corpus Christi, held on the Sunday after Trinity Sunday in the U.S., is the feast day of the holy eucharist, on which special honor is paid to Christ truly present in this sacrament under the appearances of bread and wine. The purpose of the feast is to make reparation for sins committed against the Blessed Sacrament and to kindle devotion to the eucharist. . . .

Sacred Heart, the Friday after the Octave of Corpus Christi, commemorates the love of the God-Man Christ for men. An act of reparation is recited in all churches on this feast.

SS. Peter and Paul, June 29, honors the Prince of the Apostles and the great Apostle of the Gentiles who were both martyred on this day at Rome.

The Visitation, May 31, commemorates Mary's visit to her cousin Saint Elizabeth after the Annunciation.

The Assumption, August 15, commemorates the taking into heaven of the Blessed Virgin, soul and body, at the end of her life on earth. It is a holy day of obligation in the United States.

The Immaculate Heart of Mary, held on the Saturday following the Solemnity of the Sacred Heart, honors the Blessed Virgin and commemorates the consecration of the world to her Immaculate Heart by Pope Pius XII in 1942.

The Nativity of the Blessed Virgin, September 8, commemorates the birth of Mary.

The Exaltation of the Holy Cross, September 14, commemorates the recovery of the Cross from the Persians by Heraclius, King of Judea.

SS. Michael, Gabriel and **Raphael,** September 29, is a joint feast honoring the three Archangels.

Christ the King, the last Sunday of the liturgical year, commemorates the Kingship of Christ and His rule over the world.

All Saints, November 1, honors all the saints in heaven, especially those who have no set feasts during the year. It is a holy day of obligation in the United States.

All Souls' Day, November 2, is a day set apart for the Church to pray for all the faithful departed in purgatory. All priests may say three Masses on this day.

The Presentation of the Blessed Virgin Mary, November 21, commemorates Mary's presentation in the Temple of Jerusalem by her parents, SS. Joachim and Anne.

The Immaculate Conception, December 8, commemorates the preservation of the Blessed Virgin from the stain of original sin from the moment of her conception. It is . . . a holy day of obligation.

Christmas or **The Nativity,** December 25, commemorates the birth of Christ. It is a holy day of obligation. Priests may say three Masses on this day.

Devotions
From the *National Catholic Almanac*, 1972 (Paterson, New Jersey: St. Anthony's Guild, 1971)

Angelus, The, commemorates the Incarnation of Christ. It consists of three versicles, three Hail Marys, and a special prayer, and recalls the announcement to Mary by the Archangel Gabriel that she was chosen to be the Mother of Christ, her acceptance of the divine will, and the Incarnation. . . .

Benediction is a short exposition of the Blessed Sacrament for adoration by the faithful. At the close of the exposition, the priest makes the Sign of the Cross with the Blessed Sacrament over the people. Benediction closes with recitation of the Divine Praises.

Enthronement of the Sacred Heart, The, in the home is the acknowledgment of the sovereignty of Jesus Christ over the Christian family, expressed by installation of an image or picture of the Sacred Heart in a place of honor, accompanied by a prescribed act of consecration. **Night Adoration** in the home, which consists of one hour of adoration once a month between the hours of 9 P.M. and 6 A.M. . . . is connected with the Enthronement, though distinct from it. Its purpose is to make reparation for the sins of families.

First Friday devotion is the practice of receiving holy communion on the first Friday of nine consecutive months in honor of the Sacred Heart of Jesus and in reparation for sin. . . .

First Saturday devotion had its origin in the promise of Mary at Fatima in 1917 to obtain the graces necessary to salvation for those who . . . would on the first Saturday of five consecutive months receive holy communion, recite five decades of the Rosary, and meditate on the mysteries for fifteen minutes.

Five Wounds, The, of Christ are honored as the channels through which His Precious Blood flowed for the redemption of mankind.

Forty Hours Adoration, The, is the solemn exposition of the Blessed Sacrament for forty hours, in memory of the time Christ's Body lay in the tomb, and for the purpose of making reparation for sin and begging God's graces. . . .

Immaculate Heart of Mary, The, devotion was first propagated by Saint John Eudes (d. 1680), and was revived and increased after the apparitions of Mary at Fatima in 1917. . . . Recitation of the Rosary and observance of the five First Saturdays are elements of this devotion. (*See below and above.*)

Infant Jesus of Prague, The, devotion began in the early seventeenth century in Prague, Bohemia. . . . After recovery of the statue [of the Infant, in Prague] devotions were instituted and became widespread.

Little Office of the Blessed Virgin, The, consists of psalms, lessons, hymns, and prayers in honor of the Blessed Virgin, arranged in seven hours like the Divine Office. . . .

Miraculous Medal, The, devotion owes its origin to apparitions made by Mary to Saint Catharine Laboure in 1830. In the course of the apparitions the Blessed Virgin revealed the form and elements of the Miraculous Medal, which was first struck in 1832. . . .

Mother of Sorrows, The, devotion consists of the recitation of approved prayers, a sermon on the Blessed Virgin, the Via Matris and Benediction of the Most Blessed Sacrament. The **Via Matris,** or Stations of the Cross of Our Sorrowful Mother, represents her seven Sorrows.

Rosary, The, is a form of prayer in honor of Our Lady made up of a series of ten "Hail Marys" or decades, each beginning with an "Our Father" and ending with a "Glory be to the Father." The Apostles' Creed and the Hail, Holy Queen are also recited in the Rosary. The complete Rosary is made up of fifteen decades. While reciting the prayers of each

decade a person meditates on **Mysteries of the Rosary,** which commemorate events in the life of Mary and Christ. The mysteries are **Joyful**—Annunciation, Visitation, Nativity of Christ, Presentation, Finding of the
Christ Child in the Temple; **Sorrowful**—Agony in the Garden, Scourging
at the Pillar, Crowning with Thorns, Carrying the Cross, Crucifixion;
Glorious—Resurrection, Ascension, Descent of the Holy Spirit upon the
Apostles, Assumption, Coronation of Mary as Queen of Heaven. Rosary
beads are used to aid in counting the prayers without distraction. Recitation of the Rosary is highly indulgenced. A common practice is the recitation of five decades daily. The Blessed Virgin confirmed the efficacy of
this devotion by an appearance to Saint Dominic in the thirteenth century . . .

Sacred Heart, The, devotion is directed to the humanity of Christ
which is personally united with His divinity. In adoring the Heart of
Christ, persons adore Christ Himself. The devotion was revealed by
Christ to Saint Margaret Mary Alacoque in the seventh century. . . . The
Holy Hour and the Communion of Reparation on the first Friday of
each month are special manifestations of the devotion. Christ made the
12 Promises of the Sacred Heart to Saint Margaret Mary: I will give
them all the graces necessary in their state of life.—I will establish peace
in their homes.—I will comfort them in all their afflictions.—I will be their
secure refuge during life and above all in death.—I will bestow abundant
blessing upon all their undertakings.—Sinners shall find in My Heart the
source and the infinite ocean of mercy.—By devotion to My Heart tepid
souls shall grow fervent.—Fervent souls shall quickly mount to high perfection.—I will bless every place where a picture of My Heart shall be
set up and honored.—I will give to priests the gift of touching the most
hardened hearts.—Those who promote this devotion shall have their
names written in My Heart, never to be blotted out.—I will grant the
grace of final penitence to those who communicate on the first Friday
of nine consecutive months. (*See* Enthronement of, *above.*)

Seven Sorrows or **Seven Dolors** of the Blessed Virgin Mary is a form
of prayer in honor of the seven Sorrows: prophecy of Simeon, flight into
Egypt, loss of Jesus in the temple of Jerusalem, meeting Jesus on the way
to Calvary, crucifixion, removal of the sacred Body from the Cross, burial
of Jesus. Seven Hail Marys are said during a meditation on each of these
Sorrows . . .

Stations of the Cross, The, is a series of meditations on the sufferings
endured by Christ during His Passion. The subjects of the meditations:
Jesus is condemned to death by Pilate, Jesus carries His Cross, Jesus falls
the first time, Jesus meets His Mother Mary, Simon of Cyrene helps Jesus
carry the Cross, Veronica wipes the face of Jesus, Jesus falls the second
time, Jesus speaks to the women of Jerusalem, Jesus falls the third time,
Jesus is stripped of His garments, Jesus is nailed to the Cross, Jesus dies
upon the Cross, Jesus is taken down from the Cross, Jesus is buried in
the tomb. Depictions of these scenes (pictures or sculptured-pieces sur-

mounted by crosses) are mounted in most churches and chapels. The person making the Way of the Cross passes in succession before each of these stations, pausing at each for the required meditations. Pilgrims to the Holy Land make the Stations by visiting places at which these events of the Passion occurred. The Stations of the Cross is highly indulgenced.

Those at sea, prisoners, the sick, residents of pagan countries, and others who are unable to make the Stations in their ordinary form, may gain all the indulgences provided they hold in their hand a crucifix blessed for this purpose (**Stations Crucifix**), and recite with the proper sentiments Our Father, Hail Mary, and Glory once for each Station, five times in honor of the Wounds of Our Lord, and once for the Pope's intention.

Those whose grave bodily infirmity prevents their making even the shorter Way of the Cross described above, may gain all the indulgences if they contritely kiss, or at least fix their eyes upon, a crucifix blessed for this purpose, and recite if possible some short prayer or ejaculation in memory of the Passion and Death of Christ.

Three Hours' Agony, The, is a devotion practiced on Good Friday in memory of the three hours Christ hung upon the Cross. It usually begins at twelve o'clock, when Christ was nailed to the Cross, includes prayers, hymns, and meditations upon His sufferings and His seven last words, and ends at three o'clock, the hour of His death.

Vespers and Compline are parts of the Divine Office which must be said daily by priests, men in major orders, and solemnly professed religious.

The order of Vespers is as follows: (1) five psalms, each with an antiphon; (2) capitulum, or little chapter; (3) a hymn; (4) versicle and response; (5) the Magnificat, with its antiphon; (6) the prayer; (7) conclusion, after which comes an anthem to the Blessed Virgin. There are four anthems sung according to the season.

The order of Compline is as follows: (1) Confiteor, followed by three psalms with antiphon; (2) hymn "Te Lucis ante Terminum"; (3) a little chapter, with responses; (4) the canticle of Simeon, "Nunc Dimittis"; (5) the prayer, "Visita, Quaesumus"; (6) one of the four anthems used at Vespers.

XI / CHURCH ATTENDANCE IN THE UNITED STATES

CHURCH ATTENDANCE

Gallup Poll, January 13, 1974 (Chicago: Publishers-Hall Syndicate), a 4-page news-release. Verbatim text. [All italics added]

Churchgoing in the United States *leveled off during the last three years*, after having undergone a steady decline in the preceding decade and a half.

In a typical week of 1973, 40 percent of adults attended church or synagogue—the same percentage as recorded in 1972 and in 1971. *Since 1958, however, attendance has dropped a total of 9 percentage points.*

The overall decline since 1958 can be attributed almost entirely to falling attendance among *Catholics*. In 1973, the percentage of Catholics who attended church in a typical week was 55 percent—far below that recorded a decade earlier, in 1964, when the comparable percentage was 71.

In sharp contrast, *Protestant* churchgoing has undergone virtually no change over this same period of time. In 1973, 37 percent of Protestants attended in an average week, compared to 38 percent in 1964.

Attendance among *Jews* at synagogue has also shown little change over the last decade, with 19 percent having attended in a typical week in 1973 compared to 17 percent a decade earlier.

These findings emerge from annual Gallup audits of church attendance. To estimate the average attendance during 1973, surveys of representative samples of the adult population were made in selected weeks during the year to account for seasonal fluctuations. A total of 6,154 people, 18 and older, were interviewed in person in more than 300 scientifically selected sampling localities. This question was asked:

"Did you yourself happen to attend church or synagogue in the last seven days?"

Gallup Poll findings indicate that *the much-discussed decline in church-going in America is a Catholic, not a Protestant, phenomenon.* Catholic church attendance over the last decade declined by 16 percentage points, while Protestant attendance showed virtually no change over this same period of time. The following table compares Protestant and Catholic church attendance year by year since 1964:

Year	Catholic	Protestant
1964	71%	38%
1965	67	38
1966	68	38
1967	66	39
1968	65	38
1969	63	37
1970	60	38
1971	57	37
1972	56	37
1973	55	37

The 1973 national attendance figure projects to approximately *55 million adults who attended church or synagogue in a typical week during 1973.*

Consistent with findings from previous years, *women* were better churchgoers in 1973 than men. The South and Midwest had the best record for attendance, despite the fact that a high proportion of Catholics live in the East. Young adults, 18 to 29, were less likely to attend church in 1973 than older adults . . .

ATTENDED CHURCH DURING AVERAGE WEEK, 1973

Group	Percentage
NATIONAL (projects to 55 million adults)	40%
RELIGION	
Catholic	55
Protestant	37
Jewish*	19
SEX	
Men	35
Women	43
RACE	
White	40
Nonwhite	41
EDUCATION	
College	40
High school	38
Grade school	43

* Since Jews represent about 3 percent of the U.S. population, the number included in the 1973 audit (179) is necessarily small.

Group	Percentage
AGE	
18–29 years	28
30–49 years	41
50 & over	46
REGION	
East	38
Midwest	43
South	44
West	29

SEASONAL FLUCTUATIONS

Annual Gallup audits of church attendance conducted over a period of 19 years—and based on a total of 103 individual national surveys reaching more than 150,000 adults—show attendance to be slightly above average at the beginning of the year. It increases during the Lenten months of February, March and April, but then declines to a low point in midsummer. The peak level is reached in December.

The following table shows average church attendance for each month of the year:

SEASONAL FLUCTUATIONS IN CHURCH ATTENDANCE (1955–1973)

Month	Percentage
January	43%
February*	47
March*	47
April*	48
May	44
June	44
July	43
August	42
September	43
October	46
November	43
December	49
19-year Average	45%

* Lenten months.

CHURCH ATTENDANCE: NATIONAL TREND SINCE 1955
(When Gallup audits started on regular basis)

Year	Percentage
1955	49%
1956	46
1957	47
1958	49
1959	47
1960	47
1961	47
1962	46
1963	46
1964	45
1965	44
1966	44
1967	43
1968	43
1969	42
1970	42
1971	40
1972	40
1973	40
19-year Average	45%

DROP IN CATHOLIC ATTENDANCE AT MASS

EDITOR'S NOTE:

Clergy Report, a study published by the Archdiocese of New York, revealed that attendance at Sunday Mass in the archdiocese had dropped 23 percent in the fifteen years between 1955 and 1970.

The study analyzed attendance at 343 of the 410 parishes in the archdiocese. Figures given:

1965: Attended Mass on typical Sunday 824,475
1970: Attended Mass on typical Sunday 627,235

A survey in 1972–1973 by the National Opinion Research Center reported a sharp decline in Catholic church attendance—not among Catholic youth, as many would assume, but among communicants over thirty years of age (*Time*, November 26, 1973, p. 101). The NORC report for 1974 shows that during the past decade attendance dropped from 71 to 50 percent. [LR]

From *Religion in America 1971*, Gallup Opinion Index, April 1971, Report No. 70, pp. 43–44

- Catholics were more faithful in church attendance than Protestants. In a "typical week":

  > *Attended Church: 1970*
  > Catholics 60%
  > Protestants 38%
  > Jews 19%

- The *decline* in attendance, over the decade 1960–1970, was greater among Roman Catholics than among Protestants:

  > *Roman Catholic Church Attendance*
  > 1964 .... 71%
  > 1970 .... 60%

- The decline was strongest in the Catholic 20–30-year-old age group.

THE CLERGY'S OPINIONS ON CHURCHGOING
From *Religion in America 1971*, Gallup Opinion Index, April 1971, Report No. 70, p. 27

"DO YOU THINK A PERSON CAN BE A GOOD CATHOLIC/PROTESTANT/JEW AND NOT ATTEND CHURCH/TEMPLE REGULARLY?"

Clergy	Yes	No	Don't Know
Protestant ministers	20%	78%	2%
39 years & under	24	74	2
40 years & over	17	81	2
Catholic priests	32	65	3
39 years & under	47	51	2
40 years & over	22	74	4
Jewish rabbis	60	36	4
39 years & under	64	31	5
40 years & over	59	37	4

COMPARISON OF CHURCHGOING IN SEVEN NATIONS

From *Religion in America 1971*, Gallup Opinion Index, April 1971, Report No. 70, p. 44

Church attendance in the U.S. closely parallels that recorded in Canada, and exceeds the rate of churchgoing in five other nations surveyed in a recent Gallup international poll.

The following table shows the percent of adults in each country who attend church in a typical week:

ATTEND CHURCH IN TYPICAL WEEK

Nation	Percentage
Canada	44
United States	42
Holland	36
Greece	26
Australia	25
England	20
Uruguay	18

XII / CHURCH MEMBERSHIP: SEVENTY-NINE DENOMINATIONS

CENSUS OF RELIGIOUS GROUPS IN THE UNITED STATES

From *The World Almanac, 1975* (New York: Newspaper Enterprise Association, 1975). Sources cited: *The World Almanac* Questionnaire and the *Yearbook of American Churches* for 1974. Note: The number of churches is given in parentheses.

Denomination	Members
Adventist Bodies:	480,708
Advent Christian Church (400)	30,969
Primitive Advent Christian Church (10)	551
Seventh Day Adventists (3,278)	449,188
Amana Church Society (7)	735
American Rescue Workers (25)	2,500
Anglican Orthodox Church (37)	2,630
Apostolic Faith (45)	4,100
Armenian Church of America (58)	372,000
Assemblies of God (8,920)	751,818
Baptist Bodies:	27,588,478
American Baptist Assn. (3,361)	1,003,695
American Baptist Convention (6,020)	1,502,759
Baptist General Conference (632)	109,000
Baptist Missionary Assn. of America (1,437)	199,640
Christian Unity Baptist Assn. (5)	345
Conserv. Baptist Assn. of Amer. (1,127)	300,000
Duck River (and kindred) Assns. of Baptists (86)	8,909
Free Will Baptists, Natl. Assn. of (2,350)	225,000
Gen. Assn. of General Baptists (834)	70,000

Denomination	Members
Gen. Assn. of Regular Baptist Chs. (1,473)	214,000
General Baptists (773)	66,640
General Six-Principle Baptists (8)	308
Natl. Baptist Conv. of Amer. (11,398)	2,668,799
Natl. Baptist Conv., U.S.A. (27,396)	6,487,003
Natl. Primitive Baptist Convention (2,198)	1,645,000
No. Amer. Baptist Gen. Conf. (247)	41,563
Progressive Natl. Baptist Conv. (655)	521,692
Regular Bapt. Chs., Gen. Assn. of (1,473)	214,000
Separate Baptists in Christ (84)	7,496
Seventh Day Bapt. Gen. Conf. (68)	5,284
Southern Baptist Convention (34,183)	12,297,346
Berean Fundamental Church (50)	2,530
Bethel Ministerial Association (25)	4,000
Bible Protestant Church (42)	2,254
Bible Way Churches of Our Lord Jesus Christ World Wide (350)	30,000
Brethren (German Baptists):	233,782
Brethren Ch. (Ashland, Ohio) (119)	16,357
Brethren Churches, Natl. Fellowship of (243)	33,514

Denomination	Members
Church of the Brethren (1,037)	179,686
Old German Baptist Brethren (54)	4,225
Brethren, Plymouth (740)	37,500
Brethren (River):	10,607
Brethren in Christ Church (151)	9,730
United Zion Church (16)	877
Buddhist Churches of America (60)	100,000
Christadelphians (850)	15,008
Christian Catholic Church (6)	3,000
Christian Church of N. Amer. Gen. Council (110)	8,500
Christian Church (Disciples of Christ) (4,584)	1,335,458
Christian & Missionary Alliance (1,145)	137,710
Christian Nation Church, U.S.A. (16)	2,000
Christian Union (112)	5,643
Church of Christ (32)	2,400
Church of Christ (Holiness) U.S.A. (159)	9,289
Church of Christ, Scientist (2,350) (membership not recorded)	
The Church of God (2,035)	75,890
Church of God in Christ (4,500)	425,000
Church of Illumination (14)	9,000
Church of the Nazarene (4,717)	417,200
Church of Revelation (5)	750
Churches of Christ (18,000)	2,400,000
Churches of Christ in Christian Union (256)	8,771
Churches of God:	657,531
Church of God (Anderson, Ind.) (2,235)	157,828
Church of God (Cleveland, Tenn.) (4,152)	297,103
Church of God of Prophecy (1,711)	59,535
Church of God, Seventh Day (7)	2,000
Ch. of God, Seventh Day (Denver) (56)	5,500

Denomination	Members
Churches of God, Gen. Conference (353)	34,675
The Church of God (2,035)	75,890
The Original Ch. of God (70)	20,000
The Church of God by Faith (135)	5,000
Churches of the Living God:	47,670
Church of the Living God (276)	45,320
House of God, Which Is the Church of the Living God, the Pillar and Ground of the Truth (107)	2,350
Church of New Jerusalem, Gen. (33)	2,143
Congregational Christian Churches, Natl. Assn. of (346)	75,000
Congregational Holiness Ch. (147)	4,859
Conservative Cong. Christian Conf. (121)	20,400
Eastern Orthodox Churches:	4,420,005
Albanian Orthodox Archdio. in Amer. (13)	62,000
Albanian Orthodox Diocese of Amer. (10)	5,150
American Carpatho-Russian Orthodox Greek Catholic Church (70)	108,400
American Catholic Church (Syro-Antiochian) (5)	495
Antiochian Orthodox Archdiocese of Toledo, O. (18)	16,400
Antiochian Orthodox Christian Archdio. (102)	100,000
Armenian Apostolic Ch. of America (29)	125,000
Diocese of the Armenian Church of Amer. (58)	372,000
Bulgarian Eastern Orthodox Ch. (12)	1,500
Church of the East (Assyrians) (12)	5,000

Denomination	Members
Greek Archdio. of N. and S. America (502)	1,950,000
Holy Orthodox Church in America (Eastern Cath. & Apostolic) (4)	260
Holy Ukrainian Autocephalic Orthodox Ch. in Exile (15)	4,800
Orthodox Church in America (370)	1,000,000
Romanian Orthod. Episc. of Amer. (50)	50,000
Russian Orthodox Church in the U.S.A. Patriarchal Parishes (41)	50,000
Russian Orthodox Church Outside Russia (110)	60,000
Serbian Eastern Orthodox Church (60)	350,000
Syrian Orthodox Church of Antioch (Archdio. of the U.S.A. and Canada) (10)	50,000
Ukrainian Orthodox Ch. of the U.S.A. (95)	79,000
Ukrainian Orthodox Church in Amer. (Ecumenical Patriarchate) (23)	30,000
Ethical Union, American (23)	4,000
Evangelical Christian Churches (119)	21,655
Evangelical Congregational Ch. (160)	29,434
Evangelical Covenant Ch. of America (523)	68,771
Evangelical Free Ch. of America (562)	70,490
Evangelistic Associations:	70,956
Apostolic Christian Chs. of Amer. (78)	9,500
Apostolic Christian Ch. (Nazarean) (54)	3,771
The Christian Congregation (297)	52,585
Pillar of Fire (61)	5,100
Free Christian Zion Ch. of Christ (742)	22,260
Friends:	70,552
Friends United Meeting (515)	68,717

Denomination	Members
Religious Society of Friends (Conservative) (26)	1,835
Holiness Church of God (28)	927
Independent Fundamental Churches of Amer. (602)	77,079
Internatl. Church of the Foursquare Gospel (760)	109,562
Jehovah's Witnesses (6,059)	498,177
Jewish Congregations:	5,500,000
Union of Amer. Hebrew Cong. (686)	1,000,000
Union of Orthodox Jewish Cong. of Amer. (3,000)	3,000,000
United Synagogue of America (835)	1,500,000
Latter-Day Saints:	3,503,758
Church of Jesus Christ (Bickertonites) (50)	2,439
Church of Jesus Christ of Latter-Day Saints (Mormon) (7,524)	3,321,556
Reorganized Church of Jesus Christ of Latter-Day Saints (1,031)	179,763
Lutheran Bodies:	8,658,055
Lutheran Church–Mo. Synod (6,983)	3,055,254
The American Lutheran Church (4,818)	2,464,744
The Lutheran Ch. in Amer. (6,092)	3,138,057
Other Lutheran Churches:	426,892
Church of the Lutheran Brethren of America (97)	9,010
Church of the Lutheran Confession (69)	9,490
Evangelical Lutheran Synod (Norwegian Synod) (96)	17,321
Protestant Conference (Lutheran) (7)	2,660
Wisc. Evangelical Lutheran Synod (1,019)	388,411

Denomination	Members	Denomination	Members
Mennonite Bodies:	170,914	New Apostolic Church of	
Beachy Amish Mennonite		N. America (276)	21,023
Ch. (62)	4,069		
Ch. of God in Christ		Old Catholic Churches:	
(Mennonite) (38)	6,204	American Catholic Church	
Evangelical Mennonite		N.Y. Archdio. (4)	200
Brethren (32)	3,784	N. American Old R.C.	
Evangelical Mennonite		Church (25)	1,290
Church (20)	3,136	Old Roman Catholic Ch.	
Gen. Conference Mennonite		(English Rite) (186)	65,128
Ch. (189)	36,129	Open Bible Standard	
Hutterian Brethren (29)	3,405	Churches (270)	25,000
Mennonite Church (1,054)	90,967		
Old Order Amish Church		Pentecostal Assemblies:	494,518
(368)	14,720	Elim Fellowship (70)	5,000
Old Order (Wisler)		Internatl. Pentecostal	
Mennonite Ch. (38)	8,000	Assemblies (55)	10,000
Reformed Mennonite		Pentecostal Church of	
Church (12)	500	Christ (45)	1,365
Methodist Bodies:	13,303,126	Pentecostal Ch. of God of	
African Meth. Episcopal		Amer. (975)	115,000
Ch. (4,500)	1,500,000	Pentecostal Fire-Baptized	
African M.E. Zion Church		Holiness Ch. (41)	545
(5,994)	1,024,974	Pentecostal Free Will	
Christian Meth. Episcopal		Baptist Ch. (150)	13,500
Ch. (2,598)	466,718	Pentecostal Holiness	
Evangelical Methodist		Church (1,340)	74,108
Church (141)	10,519	United Pentecostal Church	
Free Methodist Ch. of		(2,600)	275,000
N. America (1,058)	65,066	Polish Natl. Catholic Church	
Fundamental Methodist		of Amer. (162)	282,411
Church (14)	722	Presbyterian Bodies:	4,015,524
The United Methodist		Associate Reformed	
Church (39,395)	10,192,265	Presbyt. Church (General	
Primitive Method. Ch.		Synod) (148)	28,711
U.S.A. (86)	11,945	Cumberland Presbyterian	
Reformed Meth. Union		Ch. (821)	87,838
Episc. Ch. (20)	5,000	Orthodox Presbyterian Ch.	
Reformed Zion Union		(123)	14,871
Apostolic Ch. (50)	16,000	Presbyterian Ch. in the	
Southern Methodist		U.S. (4,284)	951,788
Church (150)	9,917	Reformed Presbyterian Ch.	
Missionary Church, The		Evangelical Synod (129)	17,798
(273)	20,078	Reformed Presbyterian	
Moravian Bodies:	62,240	Church of N. Amer. (68)	5,560
Moravian Ch. in Amer.		United Presbyt. Ch. in the	
North Prov. (99)	33,687	U.S.A. (8,732)	2,908,958
Moravian Ch. in Amer.		Protestant Episcopal Church	
South Prov. (49)	22,411	(7,317)	3,198,212
Unity of the Brethren (32)	6,142		

Denomination	Members	Denomination	Members
Reformed Bodies:	668,753	Natl. Spiritual Assn. of Chs. (204)	4,962
Christian Reformed Church (750)	287,114	Triumph the Church and Kingdom of God in Christ (495)	54,307
Hungarian Reformed Ch. in Amer. (27)	11,250		
Reformed Church in America (923)	366,381	Unitarian Universalist Assn. (1,019)	210,648
Reformed Church in the U.S. (24)	4,008	United Brethren:	26,809
Reformed Episcopal Church (66)	6,727	United Brethren in Christ (284)	26,409
Roman Catholic Church (23,880)	48,460,427	United Christian Church (12)	400
		United Church of Christ (6,617)	1,867,810
Salvation Army (1,121)	361,571	United Holy Ch. of America (470)	28,980
The Schwenkfelder Church (5)	2,250		
Social Brethren (31)	1,672	Vedanta Society of New York (13)	1,000
Spiritualists:	16,692	Volunteers of America (571)	30,620
Int. Gen. Assembly of Spiritualists (43)	8,500		
Natl. Spiritual Alliance of the U.S.A. (34)	3,230	Wesleyan Church, The (1,864)	86,854

COMPARATIVE ANNUAL FIGURES

EDITOR'S NOTE:

I call the attention of readers to the fact that although the number of church members in the United States is higher today than will be found in all previous censuses/polls/data, the *proportion* (of the total population) of church members is declining in certain important denominations—or the number is growing more slowly than the country's population as a whole. [LR]

Sources: U.S. Bureau of the Census; figures for 1950, 1960, and 1970 include an estimate of the numbers of Americans in the armed forces overseas. The 1971 figure is for April 1, 1971, published by the Bureau of the Census.

TOTAL NUMBER OF MEMBERS—ALL RELIGIOUS BODIES

1926	1940	1950	1960	1971
54,576,346	64,501,594	86,830,490	114,449,217	128,505,084

ESTIMATED POPULATION OF THE UNITED STATES

1926	1940	1950	1960	1971
117,399,000	131,669,000	151,132,000	180,004,000	205,056,000

From Constant A. Jacquet, Jr., ed., 1972 and 1973 Yearbooks of American Churches (New York: National Council of Churches of Christ in the U.S.A., 1972, 1973), p. 229 and p. 234, respectively

COMPARATIVE FIGURES: 1970, 1971, 1972

Membership	1970	1971	1972
Church membership as a percentage of U.S. population	62.4%	63.2%	62.4%
Membership gain over previous year	35,448	2,540,869	343,689
Percentage of gain over previous year	.03%	1.97%	.26%

CHURCH AFFILIATION AND POPULATION GROWTH: FIGURES AND TRENDS

EDITOR'S NOTE:

All figures given should be considered within the context of the total population of the United States: 205,056,000 (estimate of the U.S. Bureau of the Census, April 1, 1971, published by the Bureau). This figure includes an estimate of the number of Americans serving overseas in our armed forces. [LR]

Comments on Changes in Church Membership

EDITOR'S NOTE:

Total church membership in 1971 in the United States rose to 131 million.

But most major "liberal" Protestant denominations either lost members or did not gain any significant number, compared to 1970.

The United Methodist Church, for instance, which in 1965 reached a high of 11.1 million members, now reports 10.7 million.

The Episcopal Church, which had more than 3,400,000 members in 1964–1967, dropped to 3,286,000. [LR]

Growth Trends in Church Membership

From Constant A. Jacquet, Jr., ed., 1972 Yearbook of American Churches (New York: National Council of Churches of Christ in the U.S.A., 1972), p. 229

SUMMARY OF UNITED STATES CURRENT AND NONCURRENT STATISTICS*

	Bodies Reported	No. of Churches	Inclusive Membership	Full, Communicant or Confirmed Members	No. of Pastors Having Charges	Total No. of Clergy	No. of Sunday or Sabbath Schools	Total Enrollment
1972 YEARBOOK								
Current	140	245,109	115,442,829	52,374,722	178,702	298,988	155,054	40,501,517
Noncurrent	96	83,548	15,603,124	N.R.	56,487	94,838	N.R.	N.R.
Totals	236	328,657	131,045,953		235,189	393,826		
1971 YEARBOOK								
Current	120	222,025	103,726,366	46,370,234	140,740	263,625	148,068	37,650,077
Noncurrent	110	100,063	24,778,718	N.R.	76,620	124,017	N.R.	N.R.
Totals	230	322,088	128,505,084		217,360	387,642		

* "Current" statistics are those reported for the years 1971 and 1970. "Noncurrent" statistics are for the years 1969 and earlier. Only current totals are provided in the following categories: Full, Communicant, or Confirmed Members; Number of Sunday or Sabbath Schools; Total Enrollment.

CENSUS OF WORLD RELIGIOUS GROUPS

From the 1973 *Britannica Book of the Year* (Chicago: Encyclopaedia Britannica, 1973). Note: Readers may wish to compare American figures with comparable data for the world.

WORLD RELIGIOUS POPULATION

Religion	N. America*	S. America	Europe†	Asia	Africa	Oceania‡	Total
Total Christian	224,139,000	176,731,500	415,097,000	85,654,000	107,530,000	14,955,000	1,024,106,500
Roman Catholic	126,205,000	171,125,000	192,142,000	46,121,000	37,890,500	4,150,000	577,633,500
Eastern Orthodox	4,100,000	50,000	92,445,000	1,510,000	25,000,000	80,000	123,185,000
Protestant§	93,834,000	5,556,500	130,510,000	38,023,000	44,639,500	10,725,000	323,288,000
Jewish	6,281,900	769,800	3,996,280	2,664,170	200,500	77,000	13,989,650
Muslim	200,000	85,000	25,065,000	376,269,500	126,735,000	525,000	528,879,500
Zoroastrian	—	—	—	180,000	—	—	180,000
Shinto	25,000	60,000	—	60,000,000	—	—	60,085,000
Taoist‖	15,000	18,000	—	51,850,000	—	—	51,883,000
Confucian‖	90,000	100,000	50,000	305,175,000	—	40,000	305,455,000
Buddhist	300,000	160,000	20,000	267,185,000	—	—	267,665,000
Hindu	60,000	710,000	200,000	475,541,500	772,000	375,000	477,658,500
Totals	231,110,900	178,634,300	444,428,280	1,624,519,170	235,237,500	15,972,000	2,729,902,150

* Includes Central America and the West Indies.   † Includes the USSR where it is difficult to determine religious affiliation.   ‡ Includes Australia, New Zealand.   § Protestant figures include "full members" rather than all baptized persons and are not comparable to those of ethnic religions or churches counting all adherents.   ‖ Statistics for Confucianism and Taoism are undeterminable in China since the Cultural Revolution.

Similar patterns are seen in the American Lutheran Church, the Christian Church (Disciples of Christ), the United Church of Christ, the United Presbyterians, and others.

Some churches are gaining in membership: the Church of Jesus Christ of Latter-day Saints (Mormons) reported that its membership in the United States has increased 50 percent to 2.1 million during the last twelve years.

Statistics show increases of 2–5 percent (during a comparable period) for Southern Baptists, Seventh-day Adventists, Jehovah's Witnesses, the Christian Reformed Church, and various small Pentecostal groups.

Roman Catholic Church membership in the United States has been leveling off since 1968; in 1970, the Roman Catholic Church experienced the first decrease in numbers since its founding in the United States; there was a slight recovery in 1971. [LR]

COMPARISON OF PROTESTANT AND CATHOLIC MEMBERSHIP STATISTICS

EDITOR'S NOTE:

No precise comparison is possible between Protestant and Roman Catholic figures: most Protestant churches enumerate (as members) persons who have reached full membership, usually at age thirteen. Roman Catholics regard all baptized persons, including children, as members. [LR]

CHURCH MEMBERSHIP STATISTICS BY STATES AND REGIONS

EDITOR'S NOTE:

STATISTICS FOR CATHOLICS for the 130 dioceses in the United States are issued yearly in the *Official Catholic Directory* published by P. J. Kenedy and Sons, New York. State figures can be compiled from the diocesan data but not with complete accuracy, for in several cases diocesan boundaries cross state lines. The *Official Catholic Directory* provides statistical information about many sub-

PROTESTANT AND CATHOLIC STATISTICS

Membership	1926	1940	1950	1960	1970*
Membership of all Protestant bodies	31,511,701	37,814,606	51,079,578	63,668,835	69,740,413
Protestants as percentage of total population	27.0%	28.7%	33.8%	35.4%	34.3%
Membership of the Roman Catholic Church	18,605,003	21,284,455	28,634,878	42,104,900	47,872,089
Roman Catholics as percentage of total population	16.0%	16.1%	18.9%	23.6%	23.6%

* U.S. Population (1970 census): 203,235,298

jects, including Roman Catholic Church membership, clergy, educational, health and welfare institutions, and vital statistics on baptisms, marriages, and deaths.

STATISTICS FOR JEWS are given in the annual *American Jewish Year Book*, published jointly by the American Jewish Committee, New York, and the Jewish Publication Society of America, Philadelphia. This book contains yearly estimates, derived from a variety of community surveys, of the Jewish population by communities and states.

STATISTICS FOR PROTESTANTS are not available annually on a state-by-state basis. Although many Protestant churches publish annual reports or yearbooks, Protestant religious bodies as a group do not follow standardized methods of collecting and reporting data on church membership. Definitions of membership vary greatly, and subdivisions of national figures are more frequently made by ecclesiastical units (diocese, synod, conference, congregation, etc.) than by states.

In 1952, a major study entitled *Churches and Church Membership; An Enumeration and Analysis by Counties, States and Regions* was undertaken by the Bureau of Research and Survey of the National Council of Churches of Christ in the U.S.A. The results were reported in a series of eighty bulletins published between 1956 and 1958.

Although the data on which the study *Churches and Church Membership; An Enumeration and Analysis by Counties, States and Regions* is based were collected in the early 1950s, the study is the most recent source available for Protestant statistics by states.

Because of cost, unfortunately, no further studies are planned in the near future. [LR]

SEX AND RACE COMPOSITION

From *Religion in America 1971*, Gallup Opinion Index, April 1971, Report No. 70

Religious Group	Membership (Percentage of Total Population)	Men	Women	White	Nonwhite
Total population	100%	48%	52%	90%	10%
Protestants	66	47	53	87	13
Baptists	21	48	52	73	27
Episcopalians	3	49	51	93	7
Lutherans	7	48	52	99	1
Methodists	14	47	53	89	11
Presbyterians	6	46	54	98	2
Roman Catholics	26	47	53	97	3
Jews	3	49	51	99	1

AGE COMPOSITION

From *Religion in America 1971*, Gallup Opinion Index, April 1971, Report No. 70

Religious Group	21–29 years	30–49 years	50 and Over	Undesignated
Total population	20%	38%	42%	0%
Protestants	18	37	45	0
Baptists	20	39	40	1
Episcopalians	15	36	49	0
Lutherans	18	38	43	1
Methodists	16	37	46	1
Presbyterians	16	35	49	0
Roman Catholics	22	41	36	1
Jews	19	31	47	3

EDUCATION* AND CHURCH AFFILIATION

From *Religion in America 1971*, Gallup Opinion Index, April 1971, Report No. 70

Religious Group	Grade School	High School	College
Total population	25%	52%	23%
Protestants	26	52	22
Baptists	34	54	12
Episcopalians	12	42	47
Lutherans	22	56	22
Methodists	21	55	24
Presbyterians	15	46	39
Roman Catholics	23	57	21
Jews	16	42	42

* See also "Education in Religious Schools in the United States," Part Two, Chapter XVII

OCCUPATION AND CHURCH AFFILIATION

From *Religion in America 1971*, Gallup Opinion Index, April 1971, Report No. 70

Religious Group	Professional and Business	Clerical and Sales	Farmers	Manual	Nonlabor Force
Total population	22%	12%	6%	40%	18%
Protestants	20	11	8	40	21
Baptists	14	10	8	49	19
Episcopalians	38	12	1	25	24
Lutherans	21	12	12	38	17
Methodists	22	12	8	38	20
Presbyterians	31	15	4	26	24
Roman Catholics	22	12	3	45	18
Jews	40	22	1	16	21

INCOME AND CHURCH AFFILIATION
From *Religion in America 1971*, Gallup Opinion Index, April 1971, Report No. 70

Religious Group	Under $3,000	$3,000– $4,999	$5,000– $6,999	$7,000– $9,999	$10,000– $14,999	$15,000 and Over
Total population	12%	13%	16%	21%	23%	14%
Protestants	13	15	17	20	22	12
Baptists	16	19	20	20	18	6
Episcopalians	10	7	10	15	25	32
Lutherans	8	14	13	20	28	15
Methodists	12	14	17	20	23	13
Presbyterians	10	10	13	20	25	21
Roman Catholics	9	10	5	23	27	15
Jews	7	9	11	16	26	30

COMPOSITION BY REGIONS
From *Religion in America 1971*, Gallup Opinion Index, April 1971, Report No. 70

Religious Group	East	Midwest	South	West
Total population	30%	28%	26%	16%
Protestants	20	30	34	16
Baptists	12	22	56	10
Episcopalians	40	16	22	23
Lutherans	21	56	10	14
Methodists	25	31	31	13
Presbyterians	30	26	25	19
Roman Catholics	47	28	11	13
Jews	82	5	5	8

COMMUNITY SIZE AND CHURCH AFFILIATION

From *Religion in America 1971*, Gallup Opinion Index, April 1971, Report No. 70

Religious Group	Under 2,500, Rural	2,500– 49,999	50,000– 499,999	500,000– 999,999	1,000,000 and Over
Total population	29%	15%	23%	13%	20%
Protestants	37	18	22	10	12
Baptists	39	18	22	9	11
Episcopalians	22	16	25	18	20
Lutherans	34	18	22	12	13
Methodists	41	19	21	9	10
Presbyterians	28	18	25	14	16
Roman Catholics	14	10	26	18	31
Jews	1	3	14	18	66

CRITICAL EVALUATION OF STATISTICS ON RELIGION

EDITOR'S NOTE:

A valuable comment on church membership figures is to be found in *Information Service* (a biweekly bulletin, no longer published, from the Department of Research of the National Council of the Churches of Christ) for February 24, 1968. In this bulletin, the editor of the *1968 Yearbook of American Churches* offers some revealing insights. [LR]

Excerpts from Lauris B. Whitman, "The 1968 Yearbook: An Interpretation by Its Editor," *Information Service*, National Council of the Churches of Christ in the U.S.A., February 24, 1968, p. 7

LIMITATIONS

The limitations and weaknesses of church statistics are by now well-known. Several of these problems are stated here as a reminder to those who already know, and as a warning to those who have not yet given attention to the difficulties involved.

1. Church statistics are subject to all the problems that are present in other statistical compilation. They are always incomplete. They pass through many hands, some skilled, others unskilled. They are reported through various channels of bureaucratic structure.

2. They are not always comparable. For example, the definitions of membership vary from denomination to denomination. Jewish congregations estimate the number of Jews in communities having congregations.

Roman Catholics, and a few Protestant bodies, number all baptized persons, including children. Most Protestant bodies include only "adults" or persons 13 years of age or older. There is considerable evidence that some denominations, such as the Southern Baptists, are baptizing children at a much earlier age than previously.

3. Church statistical data does not cover any single year. Not only do the basic fiscal or reporting years differ from denomination to denomination but some do not report regularly and the latest report is actually noncurrent. Any effort to manipulate this combination of current and noncurrent data for purposes of interpretation or projection is hazardous.

4. Many of the more important types of data are simply not available. Church attendance records are rarely kept. There is no over-all data on participation in church activities and programs. There is no general data on patterns of church giving.

5. Increasingly, material from regional and sample surveys and projects is available and can be used to supplement the statistics reported. Clearly, this offers a promising prospect, if over-all data can be adequately improved.

Statistics are important. The value we attach to them is indicated in the way we interpret and use them. Furthermore, it is incumbent on all who are interested in the field to do everything to upgrade and strengthen them.

It is to be hoped that users of church statistics will always look beyond the quantitative to the qualitative aspects of religious life. Certainly the head-count approach will always represent only part of the description and analysis of religious life.

EDITOR'S NOTE:

The ambiguities and lacunae of statistics on church membership have long perplexed students of religion.

The best caveat, and the best analysis of the deficiencies in figures on church affiliation, remains that published by Benson Y. Landis, as "Confessions of a Church Statistician," from which I quote extensively below.

The remarks are all the more pertinent because of Mr. Landis' "inside" view and unimpeachable experience. [LR]

Excerpted from Benson Y. Landis, "Confessions of a Church Statistician," National Council Outlook, National Council of Churches of Christ in the U.S.A., Vol. 7, No. 2 (February 1957), p. 3

For almost forty years I have compiled and studied church statistics on an interdenominational basis. During that time I have been interested in noting the various responses to the publication of my elementary summaries and compilations. They may be grouped under these heads:

(1) Most people who have published comments have, in my opinion, overestimated the value or significance of these products of simple arithmetic and an ordinary adding machine.

(2) Some will have nothing to do with them because they are church statistics. In this group are eminent social scientists.

(3) Others, possibly a small group, have sought to make careful use of church statistics, have tried to understand the nature of the sources, and have engaged in inquiry concerning their meaning.

Since the federal Census of Religious Bodies, 1926, there have been no compilations for U.S.A. by uniform methods, gathered at one time, with the relatively full cooperation of the local churches. The federal census of 1936 was marred because of the non-cooperation of about 20 percent of the local churches. That of 1946 was begun and never completed. In 1956 the executive branch of a government with leaders vocal on religion did not bother to request an appropriation from Congress.*

Many religious bodies make annual reports of the figures that they obtain from their local churches. But it is not even known how many of the 268 religious bodies gather such information annually. Perhaps half of them do.

Thus much of the quality of the reporting is dependent on what the local churches have by way of records and on the willingness of pastors or lay people to make careful accountings. Many of the published figures come from local church records that are apparently not carefully kept, either by clergymen or lay people.

What about those that do not make annual collections of reports from local churches? Some gather figures at irregular intervals, and others simply make crude estimates of their constituencies.

Just as local churches vary in the care of their reporting, so the various religious bodies vary in their conceptions of membership and of the formality with which people are related to their churches. There has never been a compilation of definitions of church membership. In some Protestant denominations it is only by custom, and not by formal action, that many persons are taken into full membership at age 13.

Also, a number of Protestant bodies do count all baptized children, including infants; it is not correct to say that Protestants, of course, only count persons aged 13 years and over. In 1945, I estimated carefully and found 5,000,000 Protestant church members officially reported under age 13.

Roman Catholics include all baptized persons. Jewish congregations include all Jews in communities having congregations. The Eastern Orthodox include all persons in the cultural or nationality or racial group served. The relation of many Negro families to their churches is a very informal one, and it is difficult for these churches to keep records.

The great migrations have brought problems for the churches, one of which may be a higher proportion of non-resident and inactive members than in former years. We may also be getting to a place where duplication of membership is more than negligible. . . .

* No statistics on religion were issued by the Bureau of the Census in 1970.
[LR]

Statistics Not Standardized

Excerpted from Benson Y. Landis, "Trends in Church Membership in the United States," *Annals of the American Academy of Political and Social Science,* Vol. 332 (November 1960) pp. 3–4, 6–8.

Can comparisons be made between the latest information and earlier statistics? What can be said about trends? Between 1890 and 1958 there were thirty compilations of church membership. Five of these were made by the Bureau of the Census according to standardized methods. The other compilations were made by the *Christian Herald,* a periodical published in New York, and by the Federal Council of Churches and the National Council of Churches. The National Council has compiled the latest information annually since 1951. The difficulty is that the private compilations were not made by uniform methods. Because of the lack of uniformity and the irregularity with which figures are reported, there currently are no national statistics compiled by standardized methods. Thus no direct comparisons between religious bodies can be made on a national basis.

The federal religious censuses were made by means of standard forms mailed to the pastors and clerks of local congregations. The figures were summarized by denominations and were distributed by states, counties and cities.

The *Census of Religious Bodies* for 1926 is generally regarded as the most adequate book on church statistics ever published in the United States. The 1936 statistics were much less satisfactory. The Bureau of the Census stated that the census for that year was "incomplete." It seems that about 20 percent of the local churches did not report to the Bureau even after a series of requests. The number of local churches recorded by the census was about 20 percent lower than the number reported that year to the *Christian Herald,* which had collected figures in various previous years.

The 1946 *Census of Religious Bodies* was begun but never completed owing to the refusal of Congress to make an appropriation sufficient for the project. In 1956 no recommendation was made to Congress by the administration concerning the matter, and no member of Congress appears to have been sufficiently interested to raise a question about it, and no official of a religious body appeared before a congressional committee to request an appropriation for the purpose. Officials of religious bodies have occasionally made representations to the Bureau of the Census regarding the value of these projects.

. . .

Two additional sources on religious affiliation should be noted: a church distribution study and a survey of a sample of the civilian population conducted by the Bureau of the Census. Data from 114 religious bodies for the year 1952 were published in a series of eighty bulletins entitled "Churches and Church Membership in the United States" by the National Council of Churches . . .

For several decades there has been an interest in the inclusion of a question on religion in the decennial Census of Population. In 1956, the Bureau of the Census began a consultation among many agencies concerning the inclusion of the question "What is your religion?" in the forthcoming population census of 1960. The question was tried in a few localities, and in March 1957 a sample of persons over 14 years of age in 35,000 households in all parts of the nation were questioned. Officials of the Bureau of the Census indicated that if the question were used in 1960 it would probably be asked only of a sample of 20 percent of the households enumerated.

Considerable discussion of the proposal ensued in church circles and elsewhere during 1957. Roman Catholic officials and press were, with one exception, in favor of the proposal; Jewish press and agencies, again with one exception, were opposed; Protestant officials and press were apparently sharply divided. Religious liberty—the freedom of the individual in relation to the power of the government—was the overriding consideration among those opposed. . . .

After careful study of the discussion, the Director of the Bureau of the Census issued a statement on December 12, 1957, to the effect that the Bureau would not ask a question on religion in the census of 1960. It was recognized at the time that a considerable number of persons would be reluctant to answer and the refusal to answer would be legally punishable. The value of statistics based on the question was not considered great enough to justify overriding such an attitude. Cost factors were also a consideration . . .

Nature and Limitations of the Data*

Quoted from Wilbur Zelinsky, "An Approach to the Religious Geography of the United States: Patterns of Church Membership in 1952," *Annals of the Association of American Geographers,* Vol. 51, No. 2 (June 1961), pp. 141–142

Beginning with the Seventh Census in 1850, information on churches was compiled in connection with each of the decennial enumerations until 1890, although the 1880 material never reached the publication stage. In 1906, the Bureau inaugurated a special Census of Religious Bodies which was continued at ten-year intervals until 1936.†

---

* There is no single comprehensive bibliography of the statistical data and general literature on religion in the United States.

† The basic tabulations appear in the following publications:

Seventh Census of the United States: 1850, Table 14 "Church Property, etc.," 1853.

Eighth Census of the United States: 1860. Statistics of the United States (Including Mortality, Property, etc.) in 1860, 1866.

Ninth Census of the United States: 1870, vol. 1, Tables 40, 41, 42, 1872.

It is generally believed that the 1926 Census was the most complete and successful in the series. The 1850, 1860 and 1870 enumerations resulted in the publication of information on the number and seating capacity of church edifices, as well as a variety of facts about finances, educational, missionary and other activities of the denominations, but not statistics on membership. The earliest figures on number of members (for each denomination, on a county basis) appeared in the reports of the 1890 Census; and this material was published for all the subsequent Censuses of Religious Bodies.

In every instance, the Census canvass involved the procurement of information from the local congregation, at first by direct interrogation by an enumerator and later by means of mailed inquiries. No effort was ever made to ascertain the church affiliation or preference of individuals by including a religious query in the regular census schedule. A single attempt to do so on a sample basis in 1957 proved to be abortive.°

The constitutional doctrine of the separation of church and state had come to be interpreted in many quarters as even prohibiting the collection by a government agency of any information concerning churches, much less any facts regarding the religious status of individuals. It was apparently a growing sensitivity on this issue that led to a marked deterioration in the response to the 1936 canvass and the failure to publish the partial results of the 1946 Census of Religious Bodies or even to initiate one in 1956. . . .

It is highly unlikely that any additional religious statistics will be issued by the Bureau of the Census until 1970, if then.†

Critics of the various Census efforts to tally church membership have unanimously appraised them as seriously defective in terms of completeness, reliability and comparability. These shortcomings stem from the highly variable responses of the thousands of local church officials in-

---

Eleventh Census of the United States: 1890, vol. 9, Report on Statistics of Churches in the United States, 1894.

Religious Bodies: 1906. Part 1, Summary, Part 2, Separate Denominations, 2 vols., 1910.

Religious Bodies: 1916. Part 1, Summary, Part 2, Separate Denominations, 2 vols., 1919.

Religious Bodies: 1926. vol. 1, Summary, vol. 2, Separate Denominations, 2 vols., 1929–1930.

Religious Bodies: 1936. vol. 1, Summary, vol. 2, Statistics, History, Doctrine, Organization, and Work, 2 vols. in 3, 1941.

° Only a portion of the material that had been collected and analyzed had appeared ("Religion Reported by the Civilian Population of the United States; March 1957," *Current Population Reports,* Series P-20, Population Characteristics No. 79, Washington, February 2, 1958) before the Bureau decided to suspend further publication.

† No statistics on religion were issued by the Bureau of the Census in 1970; a question on religious preference was not included in that survey. [LR]

volved and the many different criteria of church membership used by the various denominations.

An additional factor, for which the Census officials are completely blameless, is the frequency with which religious bodies in the United States splinter, merge, change their names, simply vanish, and otherwise make it difficult to keep track of their identity from one enumeration to another.

Comments on Yearbook Figures

From Lauris B. Whitman, "The 1968 Yearbook: An Interpretation by Its Editor," *Information Service*, National Council of Churches of Christ in the U.S.A., February 24, 1968, pp. 1 ff.

The appearance of the *Yearbook of American Churches* [1968] always provokes widespread discussion of church statistics. The quantitative orientation of our society with its emphasis on bigness and growth has also invaded our churches. The result is an absorption with statistics which tends to focus attention upon the statistics of the *Yearbook*.

• • •

Membership data in the 1968 edition of the *Yearbook of American Churches* seems to indicate that the rate of numerical gain which has received so much publicity in recent years is slowing down. Statistics in the new *Yearbook* show a rate of growth over the previous year's figure for U.S. churches, of less than .9 of one percent. At the same time the population increased by better than 1.1%. This may well be an indicator of the changes taking place in the growth pattern of the churches.

There are other indicators in addition to the membership data which seem to point in the same direction, namely a slowing in the growth process. In the area of Christian Education a number of major denominations report serious drops in Sunday School enrollment. . . .

Financial data points in the same direction. The current *Yearbook* reports on more denominations than before. In fact there was an increase of nearly 50% in the number of religious bodies reporting. While church finances reflect to a considerable extent the affluence of our society, they do not begin to keep pace with increases in other types of expenditure. . . .

. . . Quantitative church growth must be seen in relationship to the general growth of the population. Certainly, in a period of sensational growth of the population, many denominations are almost marking time and others are actually losing ground.

XIII / THE CLERGY

STATISTICS FOR FORTY RELIGIOUS GROUPS

From Constant H. Jacquet, Jr., ed., *1973 Yearbook of American Churches** (New York: National Council of Churches of Christ in the U.S.A., 1973). Latest figures for all churches reporting a membership of 50,000 or more.

CLERGY MEMBERSHIP

Religious Body	Total Clergy	Inclusive Membership
Adventists, Seventh-day	3,365	433,906
Baptist Bodies		
American Baptist Association	3,368	869,000
American Baptist Churches in the U.S.A.	8,222	1,562,636
Baptist General Conference	1,032	108,474
Baptist Missionary Association of America	1,800	193,439
Conservative Baptist Association of America	—	300,000
Free Will Baptists	3,374	210,000
General Baptists (General Association of)	1,115	65,000
National Baptist Convention of America	28,574	2,668,799
National Baptist Convention, U.S.A., Inc.	27,500	5,500,000
National Baptist Evangelical Life and Soul Saving Assembly of U.S.A.	137	57,674
National Primitive Baptist Convention, Inc.	601	1,645,000
North American Baptist General Conference	423	54,441
Primitive Baptists	—	72,000
Progressive National Baptist Convention, Inc.	863	521,692
Regular Baptist Churches, General Association of	—	204,357
Southern Baptist Convention	—	11,824,676
United Free Will Baptist Church	784	100,000
Brethren (German Baptists)		
Church of the Brethren	2,011	181,183
Buddhist Churches of America	101	100,000
Christian and Missionary Alliance	1,227	127,353
Christian Church (Disciples of Christ)	6,886	1,386,374
Christian Churches and Churches of Christ	7,314	1,036,288
Christian Congregation	267	51,310
Church of God (Anderson, Ind.)	3,352	152,787
Church of the Nazarene	6,774	394,197
Churches of Christ	6,200	2,400,000
Congregational Christian Churches, National Association of	391	85,000

* Estimates vary somewhat from source to source.

Religious Body	Total Clergy	Inclusive Membership
Eastern Churches		
Albanian Orthodox Archdiocese in America	23	62,000
American Carpatho-Russian Orthodox Greek Catholic Church	67	108,000
Antiochian Orthodox Christian Archdiocese of New York and all North America	110	100,000
Armenian Apostolic Church of America	34	125,000
Armenian Church of North America, Diocese of the (including Diocese of California)	71	300,000
Bulgarian Eastern Orthodox Church	11	86,000
Greek Orthodox Archdiocese of North and South America	675	1,950,000
Orthodox Church in America	448	1,000,000
Romanian Orthodox Episcopate of America	50	50,000
Russian Orthodox Church in the U.S.A., Patriarchal Parishes of the	98	152,973
Russian Orthodox Church Outside Russia	168	55,000
Serbian Eastern Orthodox Church for the U.S.A. and Canada	64	65,000
Ukrainian Orthodox Church in America	131	87,475
Episcopal Church	11,108	3,217,365
Evangelical Covenant Church of America	671	68,428
Evangelical Free Church of America	—	70,490
Friends United Meeting	554	68,773
Independent Fundamental Churches of America	1,231	139,932
Jehovah's Witnesses	None	416,789
Jewish Congregations	6,400	6,060,000
Latter Day Saints		
Church of Jesus Christ of Latter-day Saints	17,272	2,133,072
Reorganized Church of Jesus Christ of Latter Day Saints	14,634	154,481
Lutherans		
American Lutheran Church	6,169	2,521,930
Lutheran Church in America	7,377	3,069,679
Lutheran Church–Missouri Synod	7,041	2,788,110
Wisconsin Evangelical Lutheran Synod	967	383,263
Mennonites		
Mennonite Church	2,335	88,947
Old Order (Wisler) Mennonite Church	101	81,000
Methodists		
African Methodist Episcopal Church	7,089	1,166,301
African Methodist Episcopal Zion Church	5,500	940,000
Christian Methodist Episcopal Church	2,259	466,718
Free Methodist Church of North America	1,740	65,040
United Methodist Church	34,822	10,509,198
Moravian Church in America	217	57,339
North American Old Roman Catholic Church	112	60,098
Old Roman Catholic Church (English Rite)	201	65,128

Religious Body	Clergy Total	Membership Inclusive
Pentecostal Assemblies		
Apostolic Overcoming Holy Church of God	350	75,000
Assemblies of God	12,037	1,078,332
Church of God	2,737	75,890
Church of God (Cleveland, Tenn.)	4,095	287,099
Church of God in Christ	4,500	425,000
Church of God in Christ, International	1,041	501,000
Church of God of Prophecy	—	51,527
International Church of the Foursquare Gospel	2,690	89,215
Pentecostal Church of God of America, Inc.	1,375	115,000
Pentecostal Holiness Church, Inc.	2,422	72,696
United Pentecostal Church	—	250,000
Polish National Catholic Church of America	144	282,411
Presbyterians		
Cumberland Presbyterian Church	633	90,368
Presbyterian Church in the U.S.	4,858	949,857
United Presbyterian Church in the U.S.A.	13,451	3,013,808
Reformed Bodies		
Christian Reformed Church	999	286,094
Reformed Church in America	1,277	369,951
Roman Catholic Church	57,778	48,390,990
Salvation Army	5,180	335,684
Spiritualists, International General Assembly	—	164,072
Triumph the Church and Kingdom of God in Christ	1,375	54,307
Unitarian Universalist Association	868	265,408
United Church of Christ	9,378	1,928,674
Wesleyan Church	2,925	84,499

INCOME OF PROTESTANT MINISTERS

Data from Edgar W. Mills and Janet F. Morse, "Clergy Support in 1968" (pamphlet), *Spectrum Journal**

EDITOR'S NOTE:

In 1968, the research unit of the Department of Ministry of the National Council of Churches conducted a survey on the salaries of the American clergy in twenty different Protestant denominations—and their attitudes to their income.

The sample used for each Protestant denomination ranged from 5 percent of the largest to 25 percent of the smaller.

Almost 8,000 (7,990) lengthy questionnaires were mailed. The response was 57.9 percent.

* This pamphlet may be obtained from the Department of Public Services, N.C.C., 475 Riverside Drive, New York, N.Y. 10027.

The questionnaire was a revision of one used for an earlier study (1963) conducted by Ross P. Scherer. The 1968 questionnaire included seven sections:

1. Professional background and experience
2. Employment information
3. Family situation
4. Financial information
5. Clergymen's preferences and opinions
6. Continuing education
7. Career stress points

One section included a "1968 Compensation Data Sheet" and a "1968 Business Cost Data Sheet." The questionnaire was thirteen pages long. It represented the most complete survey of its kind on the American Protestant clergy. [LR]

SUMMARY OF FINDINGS

1. The median income of full-time American Protestant ministers in 1968 was $8,037, including salary, housing value, utilities allowance, and fees. Half of the ministers received less than this; one of six full-time pastors received less than $6,000. This places ministers far below the averages for most other professionals and below many craftsmen and laborers. It represents an increase of 17% over 1963 income.
2. Ministers averaged $692 in fringe benefits, as compared with $1,822 received in 1967 by employees in nonmanufacturing industries.
3. Clergymen receive relatively little in fees, perquisites, free goods and services, discounts, etc.; and one-fifth of the ministers retain no fees at all.
4. Seven percent of ministers "moonlight" in nonparish jobs to supplement their incomes, but their average net loss on business use of their cars amounts to more than they earn at their second jobs.
5. Clergy income is highest in the northeast and far west. Higher income is reported by ministers with large churches and/or living in large cities or their suburbs.
6. Clergy income tends to increase with increased academic training and with years of pastoral experience, although it declines after the 25th year.
7. Median income varies strikingly between denominations.
8. The minister is subsidizing his ministry by an average of $1,018 because of inadequate reimbursement for business expenses such as automobile use, denominational meetings, and continuing education.
9. Nearly half of the ministers' wives are employed outside the home, about double the number in 1963.
10. About three-fourths of the ministers reported some indebtedness, and

over one-third do not participate in long range savings or investment programs.

11. Slightly more than half of the ministers reported that some group in the congregation reviews the salary with him; 7% of the clergymen received no increase in salary from 1964 to 1968.

CLERGYMEN'S ESTIMATE OF THEIR RELATION TO THE LAITY
From *Religion in America 1971*, Gallup Opinion Index, April 1971, Report No. 70, p. 16

"HOW WOULD YOU DESCRIBE THE RELATIONS BETWEEN THE CLERGY AND LAITY IN YOUR CHURCH?"

CLERGY	FEBRUARY–MARCH, 1971				
	Excellent	Good	Fair	Poor	Don't Know
TOTAL PROTESTANT MINISTERS	34%	48%	14%	2%	2%
39 years & under	33	50	14	2	1
40 years & over	35	47	13	3	2
East	33	43	20	2	2
Midwest	32	53	11	2	2
South	35	48	13	3	1
West	37	45	11	4	3
Have considered leaving religious life	22	50	21	5	2
TOTAL CATHOLIC PRIESTS	17	55	23	4	1
39 years & under	13	47	32	7	1
40 years & over	20	59	17	3	1
East	18	55	23	4	–
Midwest	18	51	26	4	1
South	12	63	18	6	1
West	21	55	20	2	2
Have considered leaving religious life	10	41	40	9	–
TOTAL JEWISH RABBIS	27	47	19	5	2
39 years & under	30	46	18	4	2
40 years & over	27	48	19	4	2
East	27	47	18	5	3
Midwest	26	47	20	7	–
South	30	47	16	4	3
West	27	48	23	1	1
Have considered leaving religious life	19	42	28	8	3

CLERGYMEN'S CRITICISM OF CHURCH PERFORMANCE

From *Religion in America 1971*, Gallup Opinion Index, April 1971, Report No. 70, p. 11

"IN WHAT WAYS DO YOU FEEL RELIGION OR THE CHURCH IS FAILING TO DO THE JOB IT SHOULD?"

Comment	Protestant Ministers	Catholic Priests	Jewish Rabbis
Church's message is wrong, teaching the wrong things	37%	16%	12%
Church does not face issues, problems	14	18	22
Church is old fashioned, behind-the-times	14	16	26
Poor communication between clergy and people	12	16	15
Church too materialistic, too interested in raising money	8	7	10
People have lost interest in religion	7	8	6
Church is too diversified—trying to do too much	6	4	3
Church is conforming too much to society	4	3	2
Need for adult education programs	2	4	6
Don't think church has failed	2	4	3
Others	10	12	8
Don't know, no answer	2	6	3
	118%*	114%*	116%*

* Totals exceed 100% because of multiple responses.

CLERGYMEN'S VOTE ON THE ROLE OF THE CHURCH

EDITOR'S NOTE:

The contrast between the views of Protestant ministers and Catholic priests on the secular activity of the churches is both extraordinary and surprising: one would have expected the positions and percentages to be reversed.

Equally noteworthy is the huge proportion of "Don't know" answers—the largest I have ever encountered in a poll on any subject.

The figures reveal in dramatic form how deep and enduring has been the effect of the political and social turmoil of the 1960s and early 1970s—on the American clergy perhaps more than on the population as a whole. The clergy was confronted by explicit challenges to its moral/religious integrity, its role as the spearhead of the community's conscience, its "obligation" to take a stand on crises ordinarily regarded as secular or political.

The figures below demonstrate how deeply American churchmen as individuals, and American churches as institutions, were shaken by the war in Vietnam, passive disobedience, the civil rights movement, the upsurge of black rebellion, racial conflicts, the repercussions of the New Left, campus revolt, resorts to violence, the women's liberation movement, the public demands of homosexuals for equality of treatment and an end to discrimination, resistance to draft laws, increased agitation for population control, movements to liberalize birth control and abortion laws, and so on.

The question asked clergymen was: "Should churches be concerned mainly with the spiritual life of the individual or should they be concerned mainly with problems of society as a whole?" [LR]

From *Religion in America 1971*, Gallup Opinion Index, April 1971, Report No. 70, p. 17

OPINIONS OF CLERGYMEN

Clergy	Spiritual Life	Problems of Society	Don't Know
Protestant ministers	49%	12%	39%
Catholic priests	35	30	35
Jewish rabbis	15	38	47

PROTESTANT CLERGYMEN'S ATTITUDE: "WOULD YOU ENTER THE CLERGY TODAY?"

From Rodney Stark, et al., *Wayward Shepherds: Prejudice and the Protestant Clergy* (New York: Harper & Row, 1970)

There were 1,580 questionnaire answers from Protestant clergymen of 9 denominations in California to the question "Looking back on things—if you had it to do over—how certain are you that you would enter the ministry?" [LR]

Definitely would	56%
Probably would	27
Not sure	27
Probably would not	5
Definitely would not	5

- In today's ministry, defection is high, probably increasing, whereas recruitment is declining.
- Slightly over half (56%) of the California ministers said that "if they had to do it again" they would enter the ministry. But of this group, only 14% of the "modernists" agreed, as against 75% of the "traditionalists."
- Projecting the trend, Sunday sermons promise to remain the same, "with America's silent majority sitting in the churches, listening to silent sermons."

WOMEN IN THE PROTESTANT MINISTRY: STATISTICS, ATTITUDES, PROBLEMS

EDITOR'S NOTE:

For statements of the latest official posture of each denomination on the present or likely future role of women in the ministry, the reader is referred to the separate essays in Part One. Every denomination was asked to reply to two questions: "What is the position [of your church] on the role of women?" and "May women be ordained as ministers (priests)?"

The best overall survey of women's ordination into the ministry will be found in *What Is Ordination Coming To?*, a report of a Consultation on the Ordination of Women held in Geneva, Switzerland, September 21–26, 1970 (edited by Brigalia Barn, published in 1971 by the World Council of Churches, Department on Cooperation of Men and Women in Church, Family and Society). For a general discussion of the problem, see E. Gibson's *When the Minister Is a Woman* (New York: Holt, Rinehart and Winston, 1970).

The Geneva meeting consisted of twenty-five participants from six continents—including Roman Catholics and one Eastern Orthodox bishop.

The material below is taken from that report. [LR]

Women in the Protestant Ministry Worldwide
From What Is Ordination Coming To? (Geneva: World Council of Churches, 1971), pp. 96, 99

There has been a marked increase of ordained women since the Second World War. Out of the 239 member churches of the WCC, 68 churches now ordain women. It should be noted though that the bulk of our member churches (Anglican and Orthodox Churches) have not changed their views on ordination.

The survey showed that in terms of numbers of ordained women, 39% of those who answered the questionnaire were ordained in the last decade while only 7% were ordained between 1940–1950.

FUNCTIONS

Special attention was directed to the kind of work that ordained women do. The figures below indicate the related priorities according to the actual time spent:

Preaching	70%
Pastoral Visiting	55%
Administration	55%
Teaching	61%
Counselling	44%
Administering the Sacraments	53%
Women's Work	44%
Youth Work	43%
Chaplain to Institution	22%
Urban Industrial Work	4%
Social Work	20%

Between 3 and 9 percent of their time was spent in other forms of ministry.

The Problem of Ordaining Women: Current Arguments
From *What Is Ordination Coming To?* (Geneva: World Council of Churches, 1971), pp. 59–64

1. THE DISCUSSION ON THE ORDINATION OF WOMEN TO THE
MINISTRY HAS CHANGED

a) The number of churches which ordain women to the ministry has considerably increased. While in 1960 a few member churches of the World Council of Churches were ready to ordain women to any of their ministries, the figure has reached in 1970 ca. 70. Some churches have opened new areas of ministry to women.

b) The question has become an issue of serious discussion in a larger number of traditions, while in 1960 in some traditions the question had not even been considered. In theological discussion this is particularly true for the Roman Catholic church (cf. resolution 12 of the Congress of Theologians at Brussels). . . .

c) . . . previously theological arguments from scripture and tradition have been used negatively, but now the weight of the theological arguments in favour of the ordination of women is strongly felt. In an increasing number of churches the burden of proof is with those who are opposed to the ordination . . .

d) The argument has often been used that a change of practice with regard to the ordination of women would threaten the growing unity among the churches. . . . This argument has lost much of its significance. Though it is still felt to be relevant (e.g., Roman Catholic and Eastern Orthodox churches) it is more and more recognised that the ordination does not necessarily threaten the cohesion of the ecumenical fellowship. . . .

2. WHY HAS THE NATURE OF THE DISCUSSION CHANGED?

a) There has been in recent years a more radical emphasis on renewal and the necessity of change in the church. Only a few years ago the reference to the need of unbroken continuity with the past carried more weight than today.

b) All patterns of ministry are being challenged by the development of the contemporary society. Ministers are fulfilling more and more functions they were not originally ordained for. They are fulfilling tasks which are also fulfilled by women though the women have not been ordained. The distinction between ordained and unordained becomes unclear.

c) The experience of churches in which women are ordained is generally positive. None of these churches has found any reason to reconsider its decision.

d) Probably . . . more important than all these reasons is the fact that the understanding and the experience of the relationship of men and women has further changed in many societies. There is less importance attached to preconceived images of the role to be fulfilled by either men or women. It has become more and more a matter of course that women may fulfill the role of leadership.

3. WEIGHT OF ARGUMENT IN FAVOUR OF ORDINATION INCREASINGLY FELT

. . . There is growing consensus that many of the theological arguments which have been used in the past do not carry real weight. Where the churches differ on the question it is mainly because of their different theological attitude to the Tradition. . . .

In the last few decades, among a number of Catholic thinkers (especially but not only women) there has been growing criticism of the traditional view. They refer to Paul's doctrine that in Christ "there is no male and female, but you are all one person in Christ Jesus" (Gal. 3:28).

. . . There is a growing difficulty in refusing ordination to women simply on biblical and theological grounds. . . .

4. POSITIVE CONSIDERATIONS FOR THE ORDINATION OF WOMEN

a) *The basic oneness of man and woman in creation and redemption—* According to the doctrine of creation, man, homo, in the duality of male and female, is made in the image of God, i.e. neither man alone nor woman alone.

• • •

b) *The significance of Baptism*—Both men and women, by virtue of their baptism, are engrafted into Christ and called to be members of His body. This means that all baptised persons share in the royal priesthood of the Church. When considering the . . . ministries based on the total priesthood of the body there is no theological reason for introducing barriers at this point on grounds of sex.

c) *The Calling of women to the historic ordained ministry*—The fact is that in an increasing number of churches some women believe themselves to have been called, and this call has been ratified by the Church and sealed in ordination. In other churches women believe themselves to have been so called and are asking to have this call tested. . . .

d) *The Wholeness of the Church*—The health and effective functioning of the body require the full and free participation of all the members. This is also true within the ministry, which is maimed without the participation of women.

e) *Sociological factors*—In view of sociological developments which have in many cases outpaced the Church, the Church may now be in danger of . . . perpetuating a past concept of freedom . . . the Church may discern in sociological movement the working of the Holy Spirit.

5. PARTIAL SOLUTIONS

The question would be clouded by discussing only that part of the ministry thought to be suitable for women, e.g. the diaconate, orders of women, lectors. Rather, the question must be posed whether there is *any* function in the Church which cannot be fulfilled as well by men as by women.

6. THE DISCUSSION OF THE ORDINATION OF WOMEN OCCURS WHEN ORDINATION ITSELF IS BEING QUESTIONED IN MANY CHURCHES

. . . Our conviction is that the church of our grand-children is as important as the church of our grand-fathers. The church is something given once and for all and it is also moving towards fullness . . . This is a dynamic view in contrast to a static view; it has enabled the thinkers of the Vatican II Council to be loyal to the tradition of their Church and at the same time to give a positive value to other Christian churches.

This fresh approach has consequences for the doctrine of the ministry. The major changes in thinking about ordination in the last 10 years have been seen in the emphasis on . . . the ministry of all Christian people, called by some 'the priesthood of all believers', stress on the ministry of the laity as well as the clergy, and great concern for a variety of ministries . . . Radical changes in society have led to radical changes in the practice of ministry, such as group ministries and specialist ministries.

The ordination of women, if accepted today, would be within a church whose understanding and practice of its ministry is developing. The ordination of women would further this development. The comment of the

Lambeth Conference in this context is apt, "The New Testament does not encourage Christians to think that nothing should be done for the first time." (Lambeth Conference Report, 1968, p. 106). . . . We believe that in the development of the practice and understanding of ministry, women will have an essential role. The Church which seeks to be the people of God . . . must be a body where there is full cooperation between men and women. Today this is only possible if the ordination of women is permitted.

. . . Education of all members of the church is necessary if divisive controversies are to be avoided and changes accepted with goodwill. We believe that the ordination of women may be a part of the joyful renewal to which we are called.

CATHOLICS AND THE ORDINATION OF WOMEN

EDITOR'S NOTE:

Historians of the future will surely mark the movement toward ordination of Roman Catholic women as one of the salient aspects of the women's liberation movement of 1970–1973 and one of the most unexpected events in the history of the Church. (By January 1975, almost a third of American Catholics polled by the National Opinion Research Center would support the ordination of women as priests.)

Below, I have selected the key events that culminated in the declaration (*Ministeria Quaedam*) by Pope Paul VI on September 13, 1972. This brief declaration stated that the Pope would not allow Catholic women to participate in "the sacred orders" of bishops, priests, or deacons. In presenting the declaration to the press, it was emphasized that "it would be inopportune to anticipate or prejudice what might subsequently be established at the end of the study of women's participation in the Church's community life, a study which some bishops requested during the 1971 Synod."

Reactions from Catholic sources to *Ministeria Quaedam* are noted. I have arranged the following items in chronological order.

Bishop's Committee Report

EDITOR'S NOTE:

On December 19, 1972, the Bishop's Committee on Pastoral Research and Practices, the study committee of American Roman Catholic bishops (headquartered in Washington, D.C.), announced that the ordination of women to the Roman Catholic priesthood was a question that had not been studied sufficiently.

The panel held out little hope that a change was likely in Roman Catholic ordination, a change in the wholly male priesthood—at least in the near future.

Roman Catholic women today perform certain liturgical duties (reading of lessons from the Bible, leading a congregation in singing); but the traditional exclusion of women from the Catholic priesthood "is of such a nature as to constitute a clear teaching of the ordinary magisterium of the Church." Hence: "a negative answer to the possible ordination of women is indicated."

Aside from tradition and practice, the commission reported, this central question must be considered: "What is pastorally prudent?"

The commission noted papal statements rejecting discrimination against women and citing women's emancipation as a "positive" trend in modern times.

Neither scripture nor theological writings can, by themselves, give "a clear answer to [the] question," the committee averred. The answer, finally, will come from "the magisterium"—that is, the whole body of teachings that constitute Roman Catholic doctrine.[*]
[LR]

Women in the Church
From *National Catholic Almanac 1971* (Paterson, N.J.: St. Anthony's Guild), p. 129

The liberation of Catholic women to be included in the general changing lifestyle of American women "must be guided by their Christian commitment," according to Margaret Mealey, the executive director of the National Council of Catholic Women.

In an address to the Chicago Archdiocesan Council of Catholic Women Sept. 28, 1970, she said:

"As we become less rigid, less blindly conforming, less traditionally subservient, we will become more free to render the real service that determines how truly Christ-like we are. At the same time, our religious perimeters provide the necessary guidelines to keep liberation from becoming a purely agnostic or humanistic pursuit."

• • •

Miss Mealey, a member of President Nixon's Citizens' Advisory Council on the Status of Women, noted that . . . "Those of us who have spent years in church, community, political and other work can attest that secur-

---

[*] For a summary of the study commission's report, see *The New York Times*, December 20, 1972, p. 16.

ing equal rights and due recognition for women are not new goals, are not spontaneous ideas that have sprung up overnight. . . . What women's lib has done," she added, "is to universalize the concern." . . .

A CANONIST'S VIEW

Clara M. Henning, the only woman member of the Canon Law Society of America, expressed the view Sept. 10, 1970, that "the problem of women's ineffectual status in the Catholic Church can no longer be ignored."

In an interview, Miss Henning told NC News she wanted some changes in canon law regarding what she called "the outrageous and outright discrimination against women." Otherwise, she thought the Church was "going to have to face a problem so potent and so far-reaching as to affect even ecumenism." . . .

DEMANDS

Dr. Elizabeth J. Farians, director of the Joint Committee of Organizations Concerned about the Status of Women in the Catholic Church, told NC News that she met Aug. 20, 1970, with the Liaison Committee of the National Conference of Catholic Bishops to request a voice at its November meeting.

She also wanted to submit demands for:

Opening all liturgical functions to women: "This means the diaconate, the priesthood—everything," Miss Farians said.

An unequivocal statement from the bishops denouncing the immorality of antifeminism in society and in the Church.

Introduction of "women study courses" for men preparing for the priesthood, to help them overcome what Miss Farians called a "bachelor psychosis."

She made a call for creation of a standing committee for women in the United States Catholic Conference.

. . . She said the "real stumbling block to women's full role in the Church is sociological. . . . It is clear "that many persons in the Catholic Church are not ready to accept women in positions of power and authority —especially in liturgical functions."

"This is the result of bad theology which," she contended, "has brainwashed Catholics, clergy and laity alike—both men and women—into thinking that women are ritually impure, intellectually inferior, emotionally unstable, or that they must remain in subjection to the male by divine ordinance."

Discrimination
From National Catholic Almanac 1972, op. cit., p. 95

The Church's former reluctance to let women read the word of God in church was branded narrow and discriminatory in *L'Osservatore della Domenica*. "We must frankly recognize that this legislation shows marks of a narrow outlook and of human discrimination, as if man were superior to woman," wrote Father Gaetano Meaolo. His comment concerned a regulation of the 1969 rubrics for the *Roman Missal*, which stipulated that, in the absence of a suitable man, national or regional bishops' conferences could allow "a well-prepared woman, standing outside the sanctuary, to read the lessons preceding the Gospel." He asserted that the rule implied "discrimination against God's word itself, as if it were no longer the word of God when proclaimed by a woman."

From National Catholic Almanac 1972, op. cit., p. 115

Movements [are] underway for status of equality with men in church law and practice; possibility of ordination as deacons and priests being urged. Evidence of the movements are the years-long activities of the international St. Joan Alliance and of groups formed more recently in this country. One result was the action of the National Conference of Catholic Bishops in setting up, September 1971, a special committee to study problems experienced by women in the church and to serve as a communications link between women and the conference.

Papal Declaration: Ministeria Quaedam
From Catholic Almanac 1973 (Huntington, Ind.: Our Sunday Visitor), p. 106

REVISION OF ORDERS

Two documents issued by Pope Paul [in September, 1972] on his own initiative in the form of apostolic letters clarified the clerical order of deacon (*Ad Pascendum*) and revised the structure of other ministries (*Ministeria Quaedam*). The documents were dated Aug. 15, were released for publication Sept. 14, and were scheduled to go into effect Jan. 1, 1973. . . .

One of the shortest passages in *Ministeria Quaedam* occasioned the loudest comment. It stated: "In accordance with the venerable tradition of the Church, installation in the ministries of lector and acolyte is reserved to men."

Prediction (in October, 1972):
(*Ibid.*, p. 109)

Pope Paul will not allow women to share in the sacred orders of bishop, priest or deacon, but will probably institute an "initiation rite" for installing them in lesser ministries, an informed Vatican source told NC News.

Survey of Present Status of Catholic Problem

From Catholic Almanac 1973, op. cit., p. 111

WOMEN IN THE CHURCH

The most recent protest from champions of women's rights in the Church has been raised against the shortest paragraph in two Vatican documents stating that, in line with longstanding tradition, ordination to holy orders is reserved to men.

Earlier protests, still continuing, have been and are being lodged against what is called second-class citizenship for women in the Church—as well as society in general. Targets of the protests are the Church, theological prejudice—attributed especially to Sts. Paul, Augustine and Thomas Aquinas—and sociological subjection to men.

In response to criticism concerning the restriction of holy orders and of formal installation in minor ministries to men, the Vatican pleaded innocent in October, 1972, to the charge that Pope Paul had demoted women in *Ministeria Quaedam,* a document he issued on his own initiative in September.

Although the document reserved to men the formal office of lector (that is, reader), an official clarification in the Vatican daily, *L'Osservatore Romano,* said that women may still read scriptural lessons at Mass.

. . .

Many of the criticisms of the new regulations complained that they failed to provide for the formal admission of women into various liturgical ministries. The Vatican's clarification, however, said it would be "inopportune to anticipate or prejudice what might subsequently be established at the end of the study on women's participation in the Church's community life."

This was the first public indication that the Vatican had accepted the request of several participants in the 1971 Synod of Bishops for serious theological study of the possibility of ordaining women.

The Vatican statement, after noting that the *motu proprio* had opened to the laity certain ministries previously reserved to the clergy, continued:

"Concerning the exercise by women of some liturgical offices, the *motu proprio* did not intend to make innovations, and stood by the norms then in vigor.

"Furthermore, it would be inopportune to anticipate or prejudice what might subsequently be established at the end of the study of women's participation in the Church's community life, a study which some bishops requested during the 1971 Synod. . . .

"Likewise, according to the norms in existence, the bishops may still seek from the Holy See authorization for women to distribute Holy Communion, as extraordinary ministers."

ORDINATION NOT ANTICIPATED

Informed sources at the Vatican were of the opinion that the commission studying the role of women in the Church would not recommend to Pope Paul the ordination of women, on the grounds that Christ did not ordain women as priests.

JEWISH WOMEN AND THE RABBINATE

EDITOR'S NOTE:

The first woman to lead a Jewish congregation in the United States, Sally Preisand, assumed her duties as a Reform rabbi in 1972. Several other women are completing theological study in order to enter the rabbinate in this country.

The immensity of the change these events signify to the Jewish tradition may be seen from the items below.

American Jewish Congress Women's Convention, 1973

In March 1973, some 500 Jewish women delegates to a convention (Washington, D.C.) of the National Women's Division of the American Jewish Congress called for "a reinterpretation" of the traditional, restrictive aspects of Jewish law and tradition with respect to the activities of women outside of the home (where the wife/mother is charged with paramount duties and obligations in raising the children and imparting the Jewish tradition, mores and ethics).

Women and men are traditionally separated, during religious services, in Orthodox and Conservative congregations. Women may not be called from the congregation to the pulpit to read from the Torah. Nor are women "counted" among the ten needed to form a *minyan* and conduct a religious service.

Mrs. Naomi Levine, executive director of the Congress, said that Jewish law, however much it may exalt the woman's role in bringing up the children and transmitting the Jewish heritage, is "insensitive" to women's rights and dignity. She firmly rejected the position, often voiced by defenders of the Orthodox or traditional view, that women's religious rights in Judaism are of no concern to secular organizations:

I am not black but I am concerned with inequities that blacks suffer. I am not Orthodox but Orthodox law affects us all as Jews and as women. We can no longer accept the status of second-class citizens. [See *The New York Times*, March 27, 1973, p. 24.]

Conservative Rabbinical Assembly Convention, 1972
From Barbara Trecker, New York Post, March 14, 1972, pp. 2, 71

Ten young Jewish women, unable to reconcile their religion with their needs as women, plan to air their complaints today at a Conservative Rabbinical Assembly convention.

Denied permission to speak at the five-day conference, the women plan to attend uninvited, call a caucus and discuss the issue of equality for women in Judaism.

All from Conservative and Orthodox backgrounds, they are members of an organization called Ezrat Nashim . . .

They all participate actively in Jewish life. All have received Jewish educations. One is the daughter of a Conservative rabbi; others are working in synagogues or other Jewish organizations. They are deeply committed to their religion, but they feel there must be change.

"What we want," said Paula Hyman . . . "is full equality of women and men." . . .

Within the synagogue, she said, Ezrat Nashim is protesting the fact that women may not be rabbis or cantors and that women may not be counted toward a minyan (the group of 10 men necessary for formal prayer services).

They are also protesting the fact that, within Jewish law, women are not recognized as witnesses. Nor may they initiate divorce. In the yeshivas (Jewish schools), girls do not study the same curriculum as boys.

In Judaism, Miss Hyman said, "the role of women revolves around their being wives, mothers and homemakers. The things with the most status—the spiritual aspects and study—are reserved for the male."

Among Reform congregations, attitudes towards women are more liberal, but these women reject the entire Reform philosophy. In the Orthodox movement, where women often sit apart from men in synagogues lest their voices and appearance distract the men from prayer, strictures on women are even tighter. "We're directing our demands at the Conservative movement," they said. "But ultimately all of Judaism will have to come around."

LUTHERANS AND THE ROLE OF WOMEN

EDITOR'S NOTE:

On October 15, 1974, the American Lutheran Church convention voted (431 to 307) to establish a panel of twelve, mostly women, which would "monitor" the responsibilities given to women in the governing of the church. [LR]

XIV / DENOMINATIONS AND THEIR "FAMILY" GROUPS

CHURCH GROUPINGS IN THE UNITED STATES

From 1972 Yearbook of American Churches (New York: National Council of Churches of Christ in the U.S.A., 1972), pp. 115–117

The following list of religious bodies . . . shows the "families," or related clusters, into which American religious bodies can be grouped. For example, there are many communions that can be grouped under the heading "Baptist" for historical and theological reasons. It is not to be assumed, however, that all denominations under one family heading are similar in belief or practice. Often, any similarity is purely coincidental. The family clusters tend to represent historical factors more often than theological or practical ones. The family categories provide one of the major pitfalls of church statistics, because of the tendency to combine the statistics by "families" for analytical and comparative purposes. Such combined totals are almost meaningless, although often used as variables for sociological analysis. Religious bodies not grouped under family headings appear alphabetically and are not indented in the following list.

Adventist Bodies
   Advent Christian Church
   Church of God General Conference (Abrahamic Faith)
   Primitive Advent Christian Church
   Seventh-day Adventists
The African Orthodox Church
Amana Church Society
The American Episcopal Church
American Evangelical Christian Churches
American Rescue Workers
The Anglican Orthodox Church of North America
Baha'i Faith
Baptist Bodies
   American Baptist Association
   American Baptist Convention
   Baptist General Conference
   Baptist Missionary Association of America
   Bethel Ministerial Association, Inc.
   Christian Unity Baptist Association
   Conservative Baptist Association of America
   Duck River (and Kindred) Associations of Baptists

Free Will Baptist
The General Association of Regular Baptist Churches
General Conference of the Evangelical Baptist Church, Inc.
General Six-Principle Baptists
National Baptist Convention of America
National Baptist Convention, U.S.A., Inc.
National Baptist Evangelical Life and Soul Saving Assembly of U.S.A.
National Primitive Baptist Convention, Inc.
North American Baptist General Conference
Primitive Baptists
Progressive National Baptist Convention, Inc.
Separate Baptists in Christ
Seventh Day Baptist General Conference
Seventh Day Baptists (German, 1728)
Southern Baptist Convention
United Baptists
The United Free Will Baptist Church
Berean Fundamental Church
Brethren (German Baptists)
Brethren Church (Ashland, Ohio)
Brethren Churches, National Fellowship of
Church of the Brethren
Old German Baptist Brethren
Brethren, River
Brethren in Christ Church
United Zion Church
Buddhist Churches of America
Christadelphians
The Christian and Missionary Alliance
Christian Catholic Church
Christian Church (Disciples of Christ)
Christian Churches and Churches of Christ
Christian Nation Church U.S.A.
Christian Union
Christ's Sanctified Holy Church
Church of Christ (Holiness), U.S.A.
Church of Christ, Scientist
Churches of God
Church of God (Anderson, Ind.)
The Church of God (Seventh Day)
The Church of God (Seventh Day), Denver, Colo.
Church of God and Saints of Christ
Church of God by Faith
Churches of God in North America, General Eldership
The Church of God of the Mountain Assembly
The Church of Illumination

Church of Our Lord Jesus Christ of the Apostolic Faith, Inc.
Church of the Nazarene
The Church of Revelation
Churches of Christ
Churches of Christ in Christian Union
Churches of God, Holiness
Churches of the Living God
   Church of the Living God
   House of God, Which is the Church of the Living God, the Pillar and
     Ground of the Truth, Inc.
Churches of the New Jerusalem
   General Church of the New Jerusalem
   General Convention The Swedenborgian Church
Community Churches
Congregational Christian Churches, National Association of
Conservative Congregational Christian Conference
Eastern Churches
   Albanian Orthodox Archdiocese in America
   Albanian Orthodox Diocese of America
   The American Carpatho-Russian Orthodox Greek Catholic Church
   Antiochian Orthodox Archdiocese of Toledo, Ohio and Dependencies in
    N.A.
   The Antiochian Orthodox Christian Archdiocese of N.Y. and all N.A.
   Armenian Apostolic Church of America
   Armenian Church of North America, Diocese of the (Including Diocese
    of California)
   Bulgarian Eastern Orthodox Church
   Church of the East (Assyrians)
   Eastern Orthodox Catholic Church in America
   Greek Orthodox Archdiocese of North and South America
   Holy Orthodox Church in America
   Holy Ukrainian Autocephalic Orthodox Church in Exile
   The Orthodox Church in America
   Romanian Orthodox Church in America
   The Romanian Orthodox Episcopate of America
   Russian Orthodox Church in the U.S.A., Patriarchal Parishes of the
   The Russian Orthodox Church Outside Russia
   Serbian Eastern Orthodox Church for the U.S.A. and Canada
   Syrian Orthodox Church of Antioch (Archdiocese of the U.S.A. and
    Canada)
   Turkish Orthodox Church in America, Patriarchal Exarchate
   Ukrainian Orthodox Church in America
   Ukrainian Orthodox Church of America (Ecumenical Patriarchate)
The Episcopal Church
Ethical Culture Movement
Evangelical Church of North America

Evangelical Congregational Church
The Evangelical Covenant Church of America
The Evangelical Free Church of America
Evangelistic Associations
    Apostolic Christian Church (Nazarene)
    Apostolic Christian Churches of America
    The Christian Congregation
    Church of Daniel's Band
    The Church of God (Apostolic)
    The Gospel Mission Corps
    The Missionary Church
    Pillar of Fire
Free Christian Zion Church of Christ
Friends
    Evangelical Friends Church, Eastern Region
    Friends United Meeting
    Northwest Yearly Meeting of Friends Churches
    Ohio Yearly Meeting of Friends Church
    Pacific Yearly Meeting of Friends
    Philadelphia Yearly Meeting of the Religious Society of Friends
    Religious Society of Friends (Conservative)
    Religious Society of Friends (General Conference)
    Religious Society of Friends, Kansas City Yearly Meeting
    Rocky Mountain Yearly Meeting of Friends Church
The Holiness Church of God, Inc.
Independent Fundamental Churches of America
Israelite House of David
Jehovah's Witnesses
Jewish Congregations
Kodesh Church of Immanuel
Latter-day Saints
    Church of Christ
    The Church of Jesus Christ (Bickertonites)
    The Church of Jesus Christ of Latter-day Saints
    Reorganized Church of Jesus Christ of Latter Day Saints
Liberal Catholic Church (California)
The Liberal Catholic Church (World Headquarters—London, England)
Lutherans
    The American Lutheran Church
    Apostolic Lutheran Church of America
    Church of the Lutheran Brethren of America
    Evangelical Lutheran Church in America (Eielsen Synod)
    Evangelical Lutheran Synod
    Lutheran Church in America
    The Lutheran Church—Missouri Synod
    The Protestant Conference (Lutheran)
    Wisconsin Evangelical Lutheran Synod

Mennonite Bodies
 Beachy Amish Mennonite Churches
 Church of God in Christ (Mennonite)
 Conservative Mennonite Conference
 Evangelical Mennonite Brethren
 Evangelical Mennonite Church, Conference of the
 General Conference of Mennonite Brethren Churches
 Hutterian Brethren
 Mennonite Church
 Mennonite Church, The General Conference
 Old Order Amish Church
 Old Order (Wisler) Mennonite Church
 Reformed Mennonite Church
Methodist Bodies
 African Methodist Episcopal Church
 African Methodist Episcopal Zion Church
 African Union First Colored Methodist Protestant Church, Inc.
 Bible Protestant Church
 Christian Methodist Episcopal Church
 Cumberland Methodist Church
 Evangelical Methodist Church
 First Congregational Methodist Church of U.S.A.
 Free Methodist Church of North America
 Fundamental Methodist Church, Inc.
 Lumber River Annual Conference of the Holiness Methodist Church
 New Congregational Methodist Church
 Primitive Methodist Church, U.S.A.
 Reformed Methodist Union Episcopal Church
 Reformed Zion Union Apostolic Church
 Southern Methodist Denomination
 Union American Methodist Episcopal Church
 The United Methodist Church
 The United Wesleyan Methodist Church of America
The Metropolitan Church Association
Moravian Bodies
 Moravian Church in America (Unitas Fratrum)
 Unity of the Brethren
Muslims
New Apostolic Church of North America
North American Old Roman Catholic Church
Old Catholic Churches
 The American Catholic Church, Archdiocese of New York
 The American Catholic Church (Syro-Antiochian)
 Christ Catholic Church (Diocese of Boston)
 Christ Catholic Exarchate of Americas and Europe
 North American Old Roman Catholic Church

The Old Roman Catholic Church (English Rite)
Pentecostal Assemblies
   The Apostolic Faith
   Apostolic Overcoming Holy Church of God
   Assemblies of God
   Bible Way Churches of Our Lord Jesus Christ World Wide, Inc.
   Christian Church of North America, General Council
   The Church of God
   Church of God (Cleveland, Tenn.)
   Church of God in Christ
   The Church of God in Christ, International (Evanston, Ill. Body)
   The Church of God of Prophecy
   Congregational Holiness Church
   Elim Missionary Assemblies
   The Fire-Baptized Holiness Church (Wesleyan)
   Independent Assemblies of God, International
   International Church of the Foursquare Gospel
   International Pentecostal Assemblies
   Open Bible Standard Churches
   The (Original) Church of God
   Pentecostal Assemblies of the World, Inc.
   Pentecostal Church of Christ
   Pentecostal Church of God of America, Inc.
   Pentecostal Fire-Baptized Holiness Church
   The Pentecostal Free-Will Baptist Church, Inc.
   Pentecostal Holiness Church
   United Holy Church of America
   United Pentecostal Church, Inc.
Plymouth Brethren
Polish National Catholic Church of America
Presbyterian Bodies
   Associate Reformed Presbyterian Church (General Synod)
   Cumberland Presbyterian Church
   The Orthodox Presbyterian Church
   Presbyterian Church in the U.S.
   Reformed Presbyterian Church, Evangelical Synod
   Reformed Presbyterian Church of North America
   Second Cumberland Presbyterian Church in U.S.
   The United Presbyterian Church in the U.S.A.
Reformed Bodies
   Christian Reformed Church
   Hungarian Reformed Church in America
   Netherlands Reformed Congregations
   Protestant Reformed Churches in America
   Reformed Church in America
   Reformed Church in the U.S.

Reformed Episcopal Church
Roman Catholic Church
The Salvation Army
The Schwenkfelder Church
Social Brethren
Spiritualist Bodies
    International General Assembly of Spiritualists
    The National Spiritual Alliance of the U.S.A.
    National Spiritualist Association of Churches
Triumph the Church and Kingdom of God in Christ
Unitarian Universalist Association
United Brethren Bodies
    United Brethren in Christ
    United Christian Church
United Church of Christ
United Seventh Day Brethren
Vedanta Society of New York
Volunteers of America
The Wesleyan Church

CHURCH MERGERS

Based on data from *Britannica Book of the Year, 1955–1971* (Chicago: *Encyclopaedia Britannica*)
and news reports, 1972

MERGERS AND PROPOSED MERGERS OF
AMERICAN CHURCHES: 1955–1972

Merger Adopted	Name of Merged Church	Date Merger Proposed	Date Proposal Adopted
Congregational Christian Churches Evangelical and Reformed Church	United Church of Christ	1947	1957
Presbyterian Church in the U.S.A. United Presbyterian Church of North America	United Presbyterian Church in the U.S.A.	1955	1958
American Lutheran Church Evangelical Lutheran Church United Evangelical Lutheran Church	The American Lutheran Church	1954	1960
American Unitarian Association Universalist Church of America	Unitarian Universalist Association	1955	1961

Merger Adopted	Merged Church Name of	Date Merger Proposed	Adopted Date Proposal
American Evangelical Lutheran Church	Lutheran Church in America	1955	1962
Augustana Evangelical Lutheran Church			
Finnish Evangelical Lutheran Church of America (Suomi Synod)			
United Lutheran Church in America			
Evangelical United Brethren Church	United Methodist Church	1958	1968
Methodist Church			

Merger Proposed	Name of Merged Church	Date Merger Proposed
African Methodist Episcopal Church	American Protestant Church	1970
African Methodist Episcopal Zion Church		
Christian Churches (Disciples of Christ)		
Christian Methodist Episcopal Church		
Episcopal Church		
Presbyterian Church in the U.S.		
United Church of Christ		
United Methodist Church		
United Presbyterian Church in the U.S.A.		
Presbyterian Church in the U.S.		
United Presbyterian Church in the U.S.A.	(not announced)	1971

Merger Proposed and Rejected	Date Merger Proposed	Date Proposal Rejected
United Presbyterian Church in the U.S.A. Presbyterian Church in the U.S.	1955	1955
Christian Churches (Disciples of Christ) International Council of Community Churches United Church of Christ	1956	
Bible Presbyterian Church Christian Reformed Church Orthodox Presbyterian Church Reformed Presbyterian Church of America	1956 and 1959	
Pilgrim Holiness Church Wesleyan Methodist Church of America	1958	1959

LUTHERAN MERGERS

EDITOR'S NOTE:

Church mergers over the past fifteen years have placed 95 percent of the 9 million Lutherans in North America in three major bodies:

The Lutheran Church in America (LCA)—3.2 million members
The Lutheran Church–Missouri Synod (LC–MS)—2.9 million members
The American Lutheran Church (ALC)—2.6 million members

The Lutheran Church in America was formed in 1962 by a merger of the United Lutheran Church, the Augustana (Swedish) Lutheran Church, and smaller Finnish and Danish-background bodies. Its history traces back to early settlers in the New World. The LCA, the most ecumenical of the Lutheran groups, is a member of the World Council of Churches, the National Council of Churches, and the Lutheran World Federation. Within the framework of the Lutheran confessions, it permits considerable theological freedom to its constituent churches. The LCA is headquartered in New York. It has 7,800 clergy and 6,200 congregations.

The Lutheran Church–Missouri Synod may be called the most conservative of the three major groups. It conducts a vigorous parochial school system. Headquartered in St. Louis, the LC–MS does not belong to any ecumenical organization, although it cooperates in some social service and mission work. It has 7,328 ministers and 6,084 congregations.

The American Lutheran Church was formed in 1960 by a merger of churches of Norwegian, German and Danish background. It cooperates closely in several areas with the LCA (parish education and missions) and holds a similar theological outlook. The ALC has 6,412 ministers and 5,141 congregations.

In 1965 the three major bodies—LCA, LC–MS, and ALC—organized the Lutheran Council in the U.S.A. to act as a common agency for them in various cooperative endeavors that did not compromise their respective theological positions. Service to military personnel, campus ministries, and refugee and relief work are among the areas in which the three bodies cooperate through the council. (A similar agency serves the Canadian branches of the churches.)

The remainder of the Lutherans in the United States are scattered in nine small bodies. The largest is the Wisconsin Evangelical Lutheran Synod (976 ministers, 980 congregations, 380,000 members). Like most of the smaller Lutheran groups, it is marked by conservatism.

Lutheran polity places ultimate authority in its congregations—which, in turn, relinquish some of this authority to the larger bodies. Regional Lutheran groups are known as districts or synods. They elect delegates to national conventions, which then act as the church.

It should be emphasized that despite organizational variances, all Lutheran bodies hold a similar doctrinal basis: They accept the Bible as the Word of God, and their creeds and confessions as a proper explanation of that Word. The chief confessional documents are the Augsburg Confession and Martin Luther's catechisms. These and six other "confessions" are collected into the Book of Concord.

[LR]

CLERGYMEN'S PREFERENCE ON PROTESTANT CHURCH MERGER

EDITOR'S NOTE:

The far greater percentage of Catholic priests favoring "a single Protestant church" (70 percent) than Protestant ministers (32 percent) seems to suggest that those not personally involved in intramural conflicts, and therefore not likely to be personally affected by a settlement of disputes, are more pacific and pacifying in their counsel than those who are emotionally locked in controversy—and committed to separatist positions.

In the longer view, one might point out, Catholics are likely to fare better in a society where there are a multitude of Protestant churches rather than one "monolithic" power, just as Protestants have fared better in countries with large Catholic populations where the political order has been kept officially separated from the Catholic Church (France) than in countries where Catholicism has been the politically sponsored and protected order (Spain). [LR]

From *Religion in America 1971*, Gallup Opinion Index, April 1971, Report No. 70, p. 22

"A PLAN IS BEING CONSIDERED WHEREBY CERTAIN MAJOR PROTESTANT DENOMINATIONS WOULD JOIN TO FORM A SINGLE PROTESTANT CHURCH. WOULD YOU LIKE TO SEE SUCH A PLAN GO INTO EFFECT, OR NOT?"

Clergy	Yes	No	Don't Know
Protestant ministers	32%	61%	7%
Catholic priests	70	11	19

XV / DIVORCE AND RELIGION

DESERTION AS DIVORCE

EDITOR'S NOTE:

I call the reader's attention to a remarkable study, too little known. Although made two decades ago, it presents extremely significant points about desertion as a concealed, unreported aspect of marital disruptions where divorce is not possible or desired.

The study is Thomas P. Monahan and William M. Kephart, "Divorce and Desertion by Religious and Mixed-Religious Groups," *American Journal of Sociology*, March 1954, pp. 454–465.

Monahan and Kephart analyzed over 1,300 cases in Philadelphia for marriages, divorces, and separations. Highlights of that study are given here:

- Protestants in Philadelphia (and in three areas studied by other scholars—Maryland, Washington, and Michigan) show a higher incidence of divorce than Catholics.
- Divorce is increasing among the Catholic population.
- Catholics figure in a disproportionately high number of desertions and nonsupport cases.
- Jews appear least often (of the three major religious groups) in both the divorce and the desertion categories.
- Mixed religious marriages are *not* a factor in desertion—but do appear to account for a higher percentage of divorces.

Monahan and Kephart concluded that "the sizable proportion of divorces among Catholics . . . is surprising. A prior or present divorce for both parties was found in many of the Catholic-Catholic marriages in Philadelphia's desertion cases . . ." Further: ". . . while Catholics were found to contribute less than their share of divorce" they appear "much more frequently than their relative number in the population" in desertion cases. [LR]

NATIONAL DIVORCE FIGURES AND PROJECTIONS

EDITOR'S NOTE:

About one of every three marriages performed in the United States at present will end in divorce, according to statistical/sociological projections. (See *Monthly Vital Statistics Reports,* published by U.S. Department of Health, Education and Welfare, Washington, D.C.)

For the year August 1973–1974, there were 948,000 divorces in the United States—a rise from 892,000 in 1972–1973. The divorce rate (per 1,000 population) now stands at 4.5 percent; in 1971 it was 3.6 percent. (*Ibid.*, "Births, Marriages, Divorces for August 1974," pp. 1–2).

The national divorce rate has risen 85 percent during the past decade. (See "More and More Broken Marriages," *U.S. News and World Report,* August 14, 1972, *passim.*) [LR]

CATHOLIC DIVORCE RATE AND TREND

EDITOR'S NOTE:

The divorce rate among Roman Catholics in the United States is approaching the national average. Sociologists and churchmen estimate the present divorce rate among Catholics as 25 percent (see below).

Some Catholic scholars (Andrew M. Greeley, John Charles Wynn, etc.) assert that when Catholics marry (today), their chances of avoiding a future separation or divorce are only "slightly better" than those of other faiths. (See *Divorce and Remarriage in the Catholic Church,* edited by Reverend Lawrence G. Wrenn, Newman Press, New York, 1973, p. 143; also *Monthly Vital Statistics Report,* May, 1972, published by the U.S. Department of Health, Education and Welfare, Washington, D.C.)

Of those Catholics who divorce, 80 percent remarry; 20 percent do not.

Divorced Catholics who remarry may attend Mass but may not receive Holy Communion or other sacraments.

Some Vatican sources privately predict that the papacy, within a decade, will extend the grounds for annulment of marriages clouded by adultery, desertion, insanity.

The recent comments of a Jesuit priest and teacher are particularly interesting. [LR]

From David S. Toolan, S.J., "Divorce and Remarriage," *Commonweal*, February 22, 1974, p. 505

. . . *whereas in 1971 the marital tribunals of the United States annulled or prepared for dissolution something less than 3,000 apparently valid marriages, during that same year roughly 120,000 Catholics obtained civil divorces.* In 1972 there were more divorces among Catholics in the diocese of Brooklyn than there were tribunal decisions in the entire country. According to Lawrence G. Wrenn, the editor of a valuable collection of studies on this whole subject (*Divorce and Remarriage in the Catholic Church,* New York, Newman Press, 1973), less than 10 percent of the potential petitioners for divorce could expect to gain a hearing from the current [church] system, and this figure will soon reach 1 percent. In order to handle the volume, Wrenn argues, as do a number of the contributors to his anthology, that tribunals should be shifted to the parish level, to the local pastor assisted by a competent board of consultors. [Italics added.]

EDITOR'S NOTE:

For a fascinating discussion by ten Catholics on the Church's tribunal system and its assumption that marriage is "indissoluble" see *Divorce and Remarriage in the Catholic Church, op. cit.,* edited by Reverend Lawrence G. Wrenn, chief judge of the Tribunal of the Archdiocese of Hartford and annual lecturer at The Catholic University of America. The following excerpts from Father Wrenn's summary chapter are of special interest. [LR]

In short, marriage is a changing part of a changing world. Thus *it is very difficult if not impossible for the people of our time to view marriage as something endowed with a kind of ultimate stability. That kind of stability is simply alien to our experience.* It could be argued, of course, that now is precisely the time to emphasize stability and indissolubility, that deep down these are the things our world craves. But that is a tactical approach, and if it comes to that, then most people, I think, will agree that the "Try it, you'll like it" approach can only impress people either as an attempt to impose personal preferences or as a blind adherence to a sterile and anachronistic idol. In either case the Church is bound to lose her audience because they won't even understand what she is talking about. And how then shall we preach the Gospel?

We would do much better, it seems to me, if we would only recognize that ours is an age of turmoil, having much in common with the post-empire days, and that it behooves us therefore to adapt. [Pp. 143–144. Italics added.]

. . . Perhaps *it is time to face the fact that, at least in the United States, the [Church] tribunals are just not equipped to handle or even to summarily review a reasonable percentage of the vast number of cases that deserve attention.* Over the past several years the Canon Law Society of America has done yeoman service in obtaining from Rome the approval of a set of procedural norms that have literally revolutionized the tribunals of the United States and permitted them to operate with considerable efficiency. But with all of that and with all of the hard work and dedication of hundreds of tribunal personnel around the country, *the results have only pointed up the impotence of the system. During 1971 the United States tribunals annulled or prepared for dissolution something less than 3,000 apparently valid marriages. Perhaps twice that many people received a preliminary but probably reasonable hearing as to the merits of their case.* . . . [Pp. 144–145. Italics added.]

Nor is that the whole problem. Obviously those people who did not get a hearing last year do not just disappear. They accumulate. And year after year we get further and further behind, so that in a very few years it is no longer 10% of the people who are getting a hearing but 1%. This is quicksand. The more you struggle, the deeper you sink. . . . We must come soon to the realization that *it is the bond, not the bondage, that is important,* that if we are genuinely interested in making marriage less dissoluble, then the most effective way to do that is *not to insist on the bondage of marriage but to strengthen its bonds.*

Young people, for example, must be made as aware as possible of what they're really doing when they marry, not only so that they can marry in a holy way but so they can marry in a human way. [Pp. 147–148. Italics added.]

CATHOLIC ATTITUDES TOWARD DIVORCE: 1967–1971

Poll of Catholics: 1967
Source: Louis Harris and Associates Poll, Newsweek, March 20, 1967, p. 69

EDITOR'S SUMMARY

- 50 percent opposed drastic Church laws prohibiting divorce.
- 39 percent favored the acceptance of divorce within the Church.
- 65 percent favored papal annulments of marriages where an innocent spouse has been deserted, betrayed, or wronged. [LR]

Poll of Catholics: 1971
Source: Gallup Poll, *Newsweek*, October 4, 1971, pp. 81–88

"IS A DIVORCED CATHOLIC WHO REMARRIES LIVING IN SIN?"

Answer	Percentage
Yes	28%
No	60
Don't know	12

CATHOLIC LAW ON DIVORCE
From *1974 Catholic Almanac* (Huntington, Ind.: Our Sunday Visitor, 1974), p. 280

Civil Divorce: Because of the unity and the indissolubility of marriage, the Church denies that civil divorce can break the bond of a valid marriage whether the marriage involves two Catholics, a Catholic and a non-Catholic, or non-Catholics with each other.

In view of serious circumstances of marital distress, the Church permits an innocent and aggrieved party, whether wife or husband, to seek and obtain a civil divorce for the purpose of acquiring title and right to the civil effects of divorce, such as separate habitation and maintenance, and the custody of children. Permission for this kind of action should be obtained from proper church authority. The divorce, if obtained, does not break the bond of a valid marriage.

Under other circumstances—as would obtain if a marriage was invalid . . . civil divorce is permitted for civil effects and as a civil ratification of the fact that the marriage bond really does not exist.

In the United States, according to a decree of the Third Plenary Council of Baltimore, the penalty of excommunication is automatically incurred by persons who attempt to contract marriage after having obtained a divorce from a valid marriage.

CATHOLIC THEOLOGIANS ON SECOND MARRIAGES
From *1973 Catholic Almanac* (Huntington, Ind.: Our Sunday Visitor, 1973), p. 109

The Church should not always oppose second marriages after the failure of the first, according to a committee of the Catholic Theological Society of America.

Father John R. Connery, committee chairman, reported that "in our judgment the absolute prohibition of a second union in cases of doubt is not a necessary protection of Christian marriage."

The committee statement said: "It would be rash to assert that every first marriage that has failed was invalid from the beginning, but there are serious reasons today, that were either not present or not recognized in the past, to question the validity of many of them."

A JESUIT'S VIEW
From David S. Toolan, S.J., *Commonweal*, pp. 504–505

. . . Current Church policy on divorce is simply unjust to many couples who have sincerely exhausted all available ways of redeeming a crippled relationship. It puts them in a terrible bind, and often forces them out of the Church. And it is a bind for the pastor as well. The very least that can be said about this bind is that it rests on very bad theology, more specifically, on an *ex opere operato* mystification indistinguishable from magic. In fact, tribunal rules are founded on no theology of marriage at all. To follow the letter of the law with regard to most petitioners seeking resolution here would seem to be a quick way to discredit the law, and *if the recent NORC survey of American clergy is any indication, this is precisely what is happening. An increasing number of the lower clergy no longer take Church discipline on this subject seriously, and are resorting to the bypass of the "good conscience solution"*—notwithstanding the recent papal ban of that remedy. As in so many other instances, official Church reform of the substantive law in this matter may amount to little more than an autopsy . . . [Italics added.]

To alter the Church's current divorce law need not represent so great a change as many Catholics might imagine, but like many of our recent changes, a recovery of our authentic tradition. The Lord's sayings regarding divorce are indeed demanding, but they must be seen in context. Jesus' prohibition of divorce occurs first, for instance, in Matthew's Gospel in the context of his most rigorous call to perfection, "even as the Father is perfect," and together with equally stern bans on swearing oaths and resisting violence, neither of which the Church has taken absolutely. And in a later chapter (Mt. 9), when the Apostles express alarm at the hard saying, Jesus remarks that "This teaching does not apply to everyone, but only to those to whom God has given it." (v. 11) . . .

. . . the Christian revelation is seriously deficient if you are looking for a manual on how to convert a marriage into that symbol of the "great mystery" of which Paul eloquently speaks. Paul insisted on the ideal and its possible realization, but he was also a realist, and as 1 Corinthians 7 makes clear, he was not up for turning the Lord's command into an excuse for sado-masochistic duty. In that chapter, he outlines a classic circumstance in which he judges that Christ's command must admit of an exception in the interests of equity: the case of irreconcilable religious differences. And he gives us the counter-value to permanency which should guide our discernment in resolving the conflict of values arising from a dying or dead marriage: "God has called you to live in peace." (1 Cor. 7:15) In Paul's view, apparently, the Christian was not obliged . . . to stick to a killing contract where an exchange of rights substitutes for real mutuality. . . .

The Church's error here seems to be that in the period of classic canonical codification it adhered to the letter of Paul's words, converting what was an *example* of an equitable exception, apt for extension to analogous "irreconcilable differences," into an exclusive *privilege* "in favor of the faith." I think it is time we enlarged the favor to anyone trapped in a dead end.

. . . in view of the Church's current compassionate practice in releasing priests from their ministry and vows of celibacy, certainly an equally serious social commitment, intransigence on the divorce question, seems a clear example of double standard. I know the retort is that the clerical vocation involves a "counsel of perfection," whereas the married vocation implies a universal "command"—and the latter permits of no release. The distinction is neat, but unconvincing.

EPISCOPALIANS LIBERALIZE DIVORCE

EDITOR'S NOTE:

See "What Is an Episcopalian?," Part I, page 105, footnote to question "Does the Episcopal Church Permit Divorce?" [LR]

POLL OF CATHOLICS AND PROTESTANTS ON CHURCH UNIFICATION

Lay Attitudes Toward Protestant-Catholic Unity

EDITOR'S NOTE:

A Gallup Poll (published April 20, 1965) showed huge pessimism concerning Catholic-Protestant union within the next twenty years. The question was formulated: "Looking ahead to 1985—20 years' time—do you think all Catholic and Protestant groups will be united into one church?" [LR]

Answer	Catholics	Protestants
Yes	28%	16%
No	65	75
No Opinion	7	9

The poll continued:

Previous surveys have consistently shown that both Catholics and Protestants hold the view that "in order to unify, the other side must give in."

A major argument cited by Protestants is that Catholics believe in the "infallibility of the Pope" and that they believe the Catholic Church is the "only true church of God."

Catholics, on the other hand, hold that the Protestant denominations are too diversified.

The issue of the unification of Protestant and Catholic churches brings up the question of the number of persons of both faiths who would be involved in such a move. It is estimated that there are roughly a billion Christians in the world today. Roman Catholics have a wide numerical advantage of well over 2-to-1. In addition, the proportion of Catholics in the world is increasing at a faster rate than the proportion of Protestants.

Clergymen's Attitudes Toward Protestant-Catholic Unity

EDITOR'S NOTE:

I, for one, would have thought the percentages below would be reversed—that far fewer Catholic priests wanted unity with Protestant churches than the other way around. We must assume that the 94 percent figure for priests contains a heavy quotient of assumption that the Protestant churches would end their post-Reformation "apostasy" and return to "the one, holy, apostolic" Roman Catholic Church. [LR]

From *Religion in America* 1971, Gallup Opinion Index, April 1971, Report No. 70, p. 18

"HOW DO YOU FEEL ABOUT THE MOVEMENT TOWARD PROTESTANT-CATHOLIC UNITY—DO YOU APPROVE OR DISAPPROVE OF THIS?"

Clergy	Approve	Disapprove	Don't Know
Protestant ministers	56%	39%	5%
Catholic priests	94	4	2

THE ECUMENICAL MOVEMENT: A HISTORICAL SUMMARY

EDITOR'S NOTE:

Many laymen, especially in Protestant and Jewish circles, mistakenly think that the celebrated "Vatican II" was the second ecumenical convocation of the Roman Catholic Church. Vatican II was in fact the twenty-first ecumenical council (see table below).

The summary that follows is designed to indicate the broad range, historical roots, and probable prospects of interfaith ecumenism, which has been acclaimed by theologians as "the Christian miracle of the 1960s." My emphasis, for the purposes of this volume, is on American participation after the eighteenth century.

Roman Catholic Church

"Ecumenical" comes from the Greek *oikoumene*, "the whole world."

To Roman Catholics, an ecumenical council is the prerogative of the Pope, called by him, as an assembly of bishops, serving under his presidency—thus deriving supreme authority in the Church on those problems of faith, worship, morals, and discipline for which the council was convened (*Dogmatic Constitution on the Church,* No. 22).

The assembly of bishops with the Holy Pontiff represents the whole Roman Catholic Church—not, be it noted, as democratic representatives but as successors to and of the Apostles, hence endowed with authority over the whole Roman Catholic Church.

The prototype of Catholic ecumenical councils was the Council of Jerusalem in the year 51, at which time the Apostles, under Peter's leadership, declared that converts to Christian faith were not required to observe all of the Old Testament laws and prescriptions (Acts 15).

By the second century, Christian bishops were holding regional synods, meetings, or councils on doctrinal, pastoral, liturgical, or disciplinary problems.

Emperors were actively involved in convoking the first eight ecumenical councils, for the kings held themselves to be "guardians of the faith." No less important, surely, were the close intertwinings of religious-political-social-economic factors in the state of domestic turmoils or intersovereignty wars.

Ecumenical councils, prior to the Reformation, served as the Church's way of preserving, reforming, or renewing Christian (Catholic) faith and practice. The first eight ecumenical councils were held in the East.

The first ecumenical council was convened by Constantine in 325, at Nicaea, and voted against Arianism—the idea that Jesus was not made of the same "substance" as God but was created, however, exalted above all others.

The Roman Catholic Church has held twenty-one ecumenical councils:

THE ECUMENICAL COUNCILS

Council	Pope	Date
Nicaea I	Sylvester I	May–June 325
Constantinople I	Saint Damascus I	May–July 381
Ephesus	Celestine I	June–July 431
Chalcedon	Saint Leo the Great	Oct.–Nov. 451
Constantinople II	Vigilius	May–June 553
Constantinople III	Saint Agatho; Leo II	Nov. 680–Sept. 681
Nicaea II	Hadrian I	Sept.–Oct. 787
Constantinople IV	Nicholas I; Hadrian II	Oct. 869–Feb. 870
Lateran I	Callistus II	Mar.–Apr. 1123
Lateran II	Innocent II	Apr. 1139
Lateran III	Alexander III	Mar. 1179
Lateran IV	Innocent III	Nov. 1215
Lyons I	Innocent IV	June–July 1245
Lyons II	Gregory X	May–July 1274
Vienne	Clement V	Oct. 1311–May 1312
Constance	Martin V	Nov. 1414–Apr. 1418
Florence	Eugene IV	Dec. 1431–Aug. 1445[?]
Lateran V	Julius II; Leo X	May 1512–Mar. 1517
Trent	Paul III; Pius IV	Dec. 1545–Dec. 1563
Vatican I	Pius IX	Dec. 1869–July 1870
Vatican II	John XXIII; Paul VI	Oct. 1962–Dec. 1965

Protestants

Most ecumenical *movements* have been Protestant (that is, between or among Protestant churches)—since there were so many denominations, churches, sects, creedal variations within the overall rubric "Protestant."

In 1838, a Lutheran named Samuel Schmucker presented his proposal for a federated Protestant church.

"The Second Awakening," a revival movement in the first half of the nineteenth century, resulted in various interdenominational societies. Some promoted temperance, others opposed slavery, some set up foreign missions. Whatever the names adopted (American Bible Society, Home Missionary Society, Board of Commissioners for Foreign Missions), the work entailed interdenominational co-operation.

In 1846, the Evangelical Alliance (of persons, not churches or denominations) was formed in London and became the vehicle for a world-wide movement of an ecumenical character. The alliance stressed prayer, unity through international conferences, world missions, and religious liberty.

In the late 1880s at least six different "world-denominational fellowships" of churches, which sought to bridge their differences, came into being: Anglicans, Baptists, Methodists, Presbyterians, Congregationalists. (The YMCA and YWCA were offshoots of these endeavors.)

In 1893, the Foreign Missions Conference of North America was founded. Later, such groups as the Home Missions Council and the International Council of Religious Education followed.

In 1908, the Federal Council of Churches was established in the United States. Within two years, thirty-one different Protestant denominations had joined.

The year 1910 is often regarded as the bridge between nineteenth- and twentieth-century changes in the ecumenical movement. In that year, the World Missionary Conference met in Edinburgh, Scotland, and the representatives discussed the "scandalous" state of disunity that they, the missionaries themselves, were evangelizing around the world.

In 1921, seventeen different missionary groups formed the International Missionary Council.

In 1925, after the prolonged schisms effected by World War I (churchmen on both sides refused to support Swedish Archbishop Soderblom's eloquent appeal for peace and "Christian fellowship"), the Universal Christian Conference on Life and Work met in Stockholm. Over 600 delegates attended.

In 1927, the First World Conference on Faith and Order in Lausanne, Switzerland, attracted 400 delegates from 108 churches.

In 1928, Pope Pius XI issued a noteworthy encyclical, "Fostering True Religious Union," which declared: "There is only one way in which Christian unity may be fostered, and that is by furthering the return to the one true Church of Christ of those who are separated from it; for from that one true Church they have in the past fallen away." The encyclical greatly distressed Protestant groups who had been dreaming ecumenical dreams.

In 1938, the "Faith and Order" and the "Life and Work" movements joined efforts and produced a committee to set up a World Council of Churches—"a body representative of the churches."

In 1948, after the traumas of World War II, the World Council of

Churches met in Amsterdam, with delegates from 147 separate denominations. "We intend to stay together" was the theme.

In 1950, in the United States, the National Council of Churches was formed: 29 or 30 Protestant denominations, containing a purported membership of 32 million. This event was of great importance for the conception and implementation of ecclesiastical cooperation/unification.

In 1954, the Second Assembly of the World Council convened in Evanston, Illinois. (Cardinal Stritch of Chicago forbade Catholics to attend any sessions of the assembly.)

Vatican II

Until this point, the Roman Catholic Church remained rather unalterable in taking the position that "church unity" was simply a matter of the "defecting" or "schismatic" Christian "sects" returning to the only, the "one true," Mother Church.

The historic turning point came in 1959, when Pope John XXIII called for a Second Vatican Council—nominally to continue and complete the work of the First Vatican Council (1870), which had been "interrupted" by the outbreak of the Franco-Prussian War. His Holiness said: "By God's grace, we shall hold this council [and] shall work hard at whatever it is, on the Catholic side, which most needs to be healed and strengthened—according to the teachings of our Lord."

John XXIII established, within the Vatican, a Secretariat for the Promotion of Christian Unity.

In 1961, for the first time in history, Roman Catholic "observers" attended the assembly of the World Council of Churches in New Delhi—by permission of the Pope.

In October 1962, Vatican II convened in St. Peter's, Rome; representatives from the Eastern Orthodox and various Protestant denominations were allowed to "observe" all sessions—including attendance at all of the closed (to the public) working sessions.

From 1962 through 1965, in autumn sessions of Vatican II, Pope John XXIII and 2,500 of his bishops discussed various aspects of Christian unity.

A 1965 Vatican decree, "On Ecumenism," referred to "separated brethren" (no longer "heretics" or "schismatics") whose "churches were used by the Spirit as a means of salvation."

The decree stated that Catholics, too, were guilty of "sins" vis-à-vis unity with non-Catholics—and asked both to be penitent and move "toward" one another.

"On Ecumenism" overtly encouraged (not merely sanctioned) Catholics to discuss religion and faith with non-Roman Catholics (Anglicans, Eastern Orthodox, Protestants). Roman Catholic priests were urged to enter certain cooperative enterprises. Under special circumstances, they were allowed to join in prayer, in ecumenical services, with non-Roman Catholics.

The decree "On Ecumenism" was clearly a landmark in Catholic-Protestant relations.

In 1963, Paul VI succeeded to the papacy (after John XXIII's death), and stated: "The ecumenical question has been raised by Rome in all of its seriousness [and] countless implications in doctrine and in practice. The question has not been considered merely from time to time [but] has become the object of permanent interest, systematic study, and constant charity."

When Vatican II concluded its sessions, a Joint Working Group was established between the Roman Catholic Church and the World Council of Churches.

In 1974, an historic accord was reached by Roman Catholic and Lutheran theologians on "papal primacy" and reconciliation between the two churches. (See below: "Papal Infallibility Reaffirmed.")

World Council of Churches

At the World Council of Churches Fourth Assembly, in 1968, at Uppsala, Sweden, Roman Catholics were elected, for the first time, to membership in the "Faith and Order Commission" of the World Council.

In Uppsala, the Catholic theologian the Reverend Roberto Tucci, announced: "Roman Catholics no longer regard themselves as outside spectators who are . . . merely curious, [and] still less as severe judges of the ecumenical movement, but as *partners* engaged in the same joint fraternal quest for the unity which is Christ's will for His Church."

The Catholic Church has never "joined" the National Council of Churches; but in recent years, a nun and two Catholic priests have become staff members.

Councils of Church in various *states* contain Catholic dioceses in their membership. Almost thirty state councils work, in one or another way, with Roman Catholic churches. Some councils contain Catholic "observers."

Today, Roman Catholics in nine countries belong to a national Council of Churches.

In August 1963, Catholic priests, Protestant clergymen, and Jewish rabbis participated in the historic March on Washington.

In 1972, a seventeen-member Study Committee, representing both the National Council of Churches and the Roman Catholic Church in America, recommended that the U.S. Catholic Church join the National Council.

The Catholic Church already belongs to eleven state interchurch bodies but not yet to the National Council.

Consultation on Church Union

In the Protestant ranks, the Consultation on Church Union considered the formal merger of nine denominations in the United States that, between them, contain over 25 million adherents.

In 1962, the Consultation on Church Union held its first annual convocation. Represented were these churches:

Protestant Episcopal
United Presbyterian
Methodist
United Church of Christ
African Methodist Episcopal
African Methodist Episcopal Zion
Christian Methodist Episcopal
Christian Churches (Disciples of Christ)
Southern Presbyterian

(In 1968 the United Methodist Church came into being—to include the Evangelical United Brethren.)

In 1968, the Consultation on Church Union met in Dayton, Ohio, and established a commission to draft a working plan of union among its members.

Other Moves Toward Unity

Other important mergers between Protestant bodies are in the offing: for example, the Presbyterian and the Reformed churches; and the African Methodist Episcopalian with the Christian Methodist Episcopal and the American Methodist Episcopal Zion Church (the last three are predominantly black).

. . .

Lutherans in the United States have sharply reduced the number of their separate churches. Today, over 90 percent of the Lutherans in the United States belong to one of three formal groups: the American Lutheran Church, the Lutheran Church in America, and the Lutheran Church–Missouri Synod.

Discussions have taken place between the Lutheran World Federation and the Vatican Secretariat for Promoting Christian Unity— as well as between the U.S. Lutheran Committee and representatives of the Roman Catholic Church in the United States.

"Basic understandings" have apparently been reached on such matters as the reciprocal acceptance (and, therefore, validity) of baptisms.

. . .

In 1963, the civil rights movement, raging on American campuses and streets, led to a joint Catholic-Jewish-Protestant statement—a historic "first."

In 1963, the first Catholic-Jewish-Protestant interfaith conference assembled in Chicago, on the centenary of the Emancipation Proclamation, to consult on the burning issue of race and racism in the United States.

. . .

In June 1963, the National Council of Churches, representing over 30 separate Protestant denominations, claiming a total of over 40 million members, issued a call to "the church," which urged it "to confess her sin of omission and delay and to move forward to witness to her essential belief that every child of God is a brother to every other."

. . .

The Civil Rights Act of 1964 was the result, in part, of intense pressure from religious groups, the black community, and interfaith cooperation.

. . .

In 1964, riots destroyed forty Negro churches in Mississippi—and led to a committee to raise money to rebuild these houses of worship: Southern Baptists, Methodists, Episcopalians, Jews, Disciples of Christ, and many others.

At the 1968 Lambeth Conference, in London, high Anglicans were addressed by Roman Catholics—a historic event for each and both.

The 1968 Latin American Catholic Bishops' Conference observed the singular spectacle of Eastern Orthodox and Protestant theologians addressing the assemblage from the podium.

. . .

At the Ecumenical Center in Geneva, Athenagoras I, Patriarch of Constantinople, attended a "divine liturgy."

Ecumenism and Jews

Only recently has the concept and momentum of ecumenism been widened enough to embrace Jews (see Chapter X). Bishop Stephen Neill has written: "In the opinion of many Christians, far more serious than any division within the Church was the original schism within the People of God, as a result of which Church and Synagogue have gone separate ways."

The late Rabbi Abraham J. Heschel, who received the singular distinction of being appointed Visiting Professor at New York's prestigious Union Theological Seminary, wrote this striking passage:

Both of us [Christians and Jews] must realize that anti-Christianity is anti-Semitism. What unites us? A commitment to the Hebrew Bible as Holy Scripture, faith in the Creator, the God of Abraham, commitment to many of His commandments, to justice and mercy, a sense of contrition, sensitivity to the sanctity of life and to the involvement of God in history, the conviction that without the holy good will be defeated, prayer that history may not end before the end of days, and much more.

Ecumenism and Marxism

In April 1968, the World Council of Churches convened a conference in Geneva, Switzerland, which had invited (and obtained) representatives who were Protestant, Roman Catholic, Eastern Orthodox, and Marxist.

The title of this extraordinary colloquium was "Trends in Christian and Marxist Thinking About the Humanization of Technical and Economic Development." (For the Vatican's shift in attitude vis-à-vis Soviet Russia and Red China, see Part Two, Chapter X.)

Holy Communion

In January 1972, after four centuries of controversy on the nature and meaning of Holy Communion, an "Agreed Statement on Eucharistic Doctrine," approved by Pope Paul VI and the Archbishop of Canterbury (Arthur Michael Ramsey), was released. The declaration was the work of an Anglican-Roman Catholic International Commission.

Although the agreement contained no new theological positions but affirmed traditional viewpoints of the two churches, an official addendum described the joint declaration as "the most important statement since the Reformation for Anglicans and Roman Catholics."

The document avoided the use of the Catholic term "transubstantiation" and seemed to remove one critical obstacle to unity between the Anglican and Roman Catholic churches. Many others (see below) remain. [LR]

LESS OPTIMISTIC ASPECTS

EDITOR'S NOTE:

Pope Paul VI has remarked that it is the papacy—that is, the power, status, and role of the Pope himself—which "undoubtedly [represents] the most grave obstacle in the path of ecumenism." The prophetic power of this statement will be seen below.

In 1968, just a few days before the opening of the momentous Fourth Assembly of the World Council of Churches in Uppsala, Sweden, Pope Paul VI issued a surprising and (to Protestant ecumenists) disturbing pronunciamento—reaffirming some "unalterable" doctrines of the Roman Catholic Church.

A week or so after the assembly in Uppsala had completed its work (and despite a report of Catholic doctors, gynecologists, and associated experts), Pope Paul issued a flat rejection of birth control by "artificial" means (that is, differing from the "rhythm" fertility method).

The Rev. Dr. Eugene Carson Blake, of the World Council of Churches, remarked that the papal statements well deflated "romantic ecumenism, which is to suppose that all that is required for unity in the Church is to be more friendly and tolerant . . ." [LR]

PAPAL INFALLIBILITY REAFFIRMED

EDITOR'S NOTE:

On July 5, 1973, the Vatican forcefully reaffirmed the dogma of papal infallibility.

Paul VI's reassertion of the dogma of papal infallibility not only placed in "dire jeopardy" the future of the ecumenical movement, said the Episcopal canon of the Church of St. John the Divine in New York, Walter D. Dennis, but has probably dealt a "death blow" to the Anglican-Roman Catholic dialogue.

It is the faulty logic of the theory of infallibility, not the institution of the papacy, which I am criticizing . . . most of the Popes never spoke infallibly at all . . . John XXIII, almost certainly the greatest Pope for many centuries, in a few swift years brought the papacy to a height of prestige perhaps unknown since . . . the 13th century [and] never put forth any infallible utterance . . . Why is this questionable dogma reasserted at this time unless it is a signal to end serious ecumenical endeavor? It may very well be that the Roman Curia has decided ecumenical dialogue has reached its outer limits. [The New York Times, July 16, 1973.]

But on December 13, 1973, the prestigious Anglican-Roman Catholic International Commission, a body of twenty-one theologians and historians representing Catholics and Anglicans around the world, published a 3,200-word report, which stated that the commission had reached "basic agreement" on "the nature of the priesthood" in the Christian ministry and on the ministry of laymen.

This historic report seems to resolve a dispute that has separated the two churches for 400 years—and the significance of the document is underlined by the fact that it was released with the approval of Pope Paul VI and the Archbishop of Canterbury, even though the declaration carries only the authority of the commission. Formal permission to Roman Catholics to receive holy communion from Anglican priests must still come from the Pope and from individual Anglican Churches—including the Episcopalian.

The Reverend Herbert Ryan, an American Jesuit who served on the commission, said: "Changes today must come from a consensus of the people themselves. . . . If there is a general acceptance, it can then be ratified by the proper authorities. . . . What we are trying to say is that it's not a question of either-or, but of both-and. Both [Catholic and Anglican] traditions are free to build on either one." (See *The New York Times*, December 13, 1973, p. 58.)

The declaration was promptly characterized as a major ecumenical achievement. At the very least, the accord allows Roman Catholics to accept the validity of the sacraments when administered by Anglican priests. (In 1896, Pope Leo XIII had issued a papal bull that called Anglican orders "absolutely null and utterly void.")

In 1971, the commission had reached a consensus on "the essential" aspects of holy communion.

On March 4, 1974, after a nine-year study and discussion, a joint commission of thirteen Catholic and thirteen Lutheran theologians in the United States declared that "papal primacy" no longer represented an insurmountable barrier to "reconciliation" between their churches. The momentous pronouncement was the first since the Reformation, in the sixteenth century, to offer an area of agreement within the decisive schism.

Although the declaration is not binding on either the Roman Catholic or the Lutheran Church, it appears to eliminate a central obstacle to unity between two great Christian churches. "It is now up to the churches to indicate how far they want to go in implementing [the commission's declaration]," said the Reverend George A. Lindbeck, one of the Lutheran members (see *The New York Times*, March 4, 1974, pp. 1, 25).

Note: "Papal primacy" is by no means synonymous with "papal infallibility"—on which Pope Paul VI has remained adamant. The declaration contains these significant passages:

We do not wish to understate our remaining disagreements. While we have concluded that traditional sharp distinction between divine and human institution are no longer useful, Catholics continue to emphasize that papal primacy is an institution in accordance with God's will. For Lutherans this is a secondary question. The one thing necessary, they insist, is that papal primacy serve the gospel and that its exercise of power not subvert Christian freedom.

There are also differences which we have not yet discussed. We have not adequately explored to what extent the existing forms of the papal office are open to change in the future, nor have we yet touched on the sensitive point of papal infallibility, taught by Vatican Councils I and II.

But the accord has been hailed by theologians and scholars as a feat of consensus that may make agreement about papal infallibility possible within a few years. An editoral in *The New York Times* (March 4, 1974) entitled "Papal Primacy" reads in part:

A monarchial autocracy, no matter how benevolent, would be a high barrier to reconciliation between Rome and other Christian churches. The papacy has already shown an impressive capacity for self-renewal and self-reform; it is a quite different institution than the one against which Martin Luther revolted four hundred years ago or even the one over which Pius IX presided a century ago. The latest Catholic-Lutheran statement of consensus on the papacy's role shows that measurable progress is being made toward that day when the unity of Christendom is restored and the Pope presides over an enlarged community of "sister churches." The determined good will and patient persistence in serious dialogue shown by the theologians may serve as a model for the secular human society, which after several thousand years of civilization is still groping for a genuine human community.

See also "Papal Authority and Papal Infallibility: Priests Versus Bishops," in Part Two, Chapter X, page 415, for polls of the Roman Catholic clergy and important events from January 1973 to October 1974. [LR]

OBSTACLES TO ECUMENISM

EDITOR'S NOTE:

To the objective observer, many mountains block the path of official unity between Roman Catholics and Protestants. One need be no expert to list a dozen extremely sensitive areas in which a reconciliation of views will prove most difficult, if not impossible, for many years:

Papal infallibility
The role of dogma
The Immaculate Conception (as distinguished from the Virgin Birth)
The celebration of the Mass
Birth control
Abortion
Intermarriage
Homosexuality
The relationship of Scripture and tradition (Protestants affirm the primacy
  of the former, Roman Catholics the latter)
The doctrine and worship of the Virgin Mary (the more critical since the
  ex cathedra injunction that Mary ascended bodily into Heaven)
Confession
The teaching of Scripture—the Old Testament as well as the New
Extreme unction
The role of laymen
Women in the ministry

Can a force as immense as Roman Catholicism (half of the world's Christians are Catholic) possibly participate in more unified ecclesiastical endeavors (much less, a formal union) without crushing its partners by the sheer weight of its size, its age, its majestic accretions of symbolism, parochialism, conviction, and dogma?

Some churchmen regard the ecumenical movement as "ecclesiastical vampires, draining the life-blood of religion into internal pursuits when 'secular' problems cry out for solutions the church can help provide" (Lee E. Dirks, *Public Affairs Pamphlet* No. 431, 1969).

The "activist" or "leftist" or avant-garde movement, in whatever denomination, tends to regard ecumenism with skepticism, indifference, or hostility: such "abstract," "theological," "bureaucratic" preoccupations as ecumenism only serve to divert the attention of churchmen from pressing social and political problems.

The Church, to these "liberal" churchmen, is the largest and best force that secular causes can mobilize. Ecumenism, in this context, is "irrelevant," "archaic," "outmoded," "reactionary," "befuddled."

Several final bits of data may suggest the scope of the problems that ecumenism will face in the future and the intensity of the uneasiness these precipitate in various sectors of the theological community.

The Right Reverend Gerald Kennedy, Methodist Bishop of Los Angeles, has said, "We rejoice in the growth of the ecumenical movement and in the development of the ecumenical spirit . . . But we are not sure that God wills the churches of the Reformation to become one organic union. We believe that our pluralism has produced much good fruit, not the least of which has been freedom."

Bishop Stephen Neill commented, "The final and terrible difficulty is that churches cannot unite unless they are willing to die" (see Lee E. Dirks, *ibid.*).

In 1972, the United Presbyterian Church, which had long been a powerful advocate of ecumenism within the Protestant churches, abruptly withdrew from the COCU (Consultation on Church Union), the organization that for over a decade had sought to bring some 25 million American Protestants into some single church.

The COCU contained nine important bodies: the Episcopal Church, the United Methodists, United Church of Christ, Presbyterian Church in the U.S., United Presbyterian Church in the U.S.A., Christian Church (Disciples of Christ), African Methodist Episcopal Church, African Methodist Episcopal Zion Church, and Christian Methodist Episcopal Church.

COCU's secretary, Dr. Paul Crow, Jr., observed that a great many Protestant laymen opposed any ecumenical movement—because they would not abdicate or diminish their local church's power and influence in local congregations. This position, sometimes called "ecumenical populism," has remained an unaltered obstacle to ecumenism from the very outset. There is little reason to anticipate its diminution or demise. [LR]

NOTABLE STUDIES—AND PREDICTIONS

EDITOR'S NOTE:
For detailed information on the history of ecumenism from the beginnings of Protestantism until today, see: *A History of the Ecumenical Movement 1517–1948*, edited by Stephen Charles Neill

and Ruth Rouse (Philadelphia: Westminster Press, 1967); and *A History of the Ecumenical Movement 1948–1968*, Vol. II, edited by Harold E. Fey (Philadelphia: Westminster Press, 1970). The most authoritative book on the famous ecumenical council of 1968 is *The Uppsala Report, 1968: Official Report of the Fourth Assembly of the World Council of Churches* (New York: World Council of Churches, 1968).

A notable study of Protestant-Catholic relations in America is Rodney Stark's "Through a Stained Glass Darkly: Reciprocal Protestant-Catholic Images in America," *Sociological Analysis*, Vol. 25, No. 3 (Fall 1964). This study collected data in four counties on the West Coast (Dr. Stark was working in the Survey Research Center of the University of California at Berkeley).

The conclusions may be summarized:

- Protestants are uneasy about Catholic power.
- Catholics are relatively confident of their power and influence.
- Both Protestants and Catholics agree that they each have "inflicted inequities" upon the other.
- Although Protestants and Catholics appear to view each other with greater ease and comity than in the past, pervasive distrust still prevails.
- Protestants still are "deeply troubled" about Catholicism—and "sizable proportions" of Catholics admit the truth of certain Protestant fears/claims.
- Catholics are still disturbed by Protestant opposition to public tax support for parochial schools.

Although these findings are ten years old, the attitudes are reflected in recent polls, and pessimism about a formal Catholic-Protestant rapprochement has not abated. [LR]

XVII / EDUCATION IN RELIGIOUS SCHOOLS IN THE UNITED STATES

RELIGIOUS INSTRUCTION (DENOMINATIONS OF 100,000 OR MORE)

EDITOR'S NOTE:

The figures for Catholic students in this section refer to elementary school pupils enrolled in *public* schools, for whom special religious instruction classes are held. Data on parochial school enrollment will be found in the next section.

Catholic children who attend public elementary schools receive their religious instruction at various times, depending upon the customs, traditions, and size of the local parish, and the laws of the state in which the diocese is located. If legally permissible, most Catholic children participate in the released-time program of their parish. Otherwise, they receive their instruction after school hours, or on Saturdays, or after Mass on Sunday. All Catholic public school children who are counted in official figures receive at least one hour of instruction per week. [LR]

Source: Constant H. Jacquet, Jr., ed., 1972 *Yearbook of American Churches* (New York: National Council of Churches of Christ in the U.S.A., 1972), pp. 220–228

RELIGIOUS-INSTRUCTION-CLASS ENROLLMENTS (1972)

Name of Religious Body	Total Enrollment
African Methodist Episcopal Zion Church	162,000
American Baptist Association	452,500
American Baptist Convention	741,664
American Lutheran Church	752,822
Assemblies of God	1,064,631
Baptists, General Conference	119,432
Baptist Missionary Association of America	107,406
Christian Churches (Disciples of Christ)	671,404
Christian Churches and Churches of Christ	1,071,788
Christian and Missionary Alliance	165,251
Church of God (Anderson, Indiana)	239,109

Name of Religious Body	Total Enrollment
Church of God (Cleveland, Tennessee)	315,500
Church of the Nazarene	839,943
Free Methodist Church of North America	124,246
Free Will Baptists	151,715
Independent Fundamental Churches of America	161,353
Jewish Congregations	N.R.
Latter-day Saints (Mormons)	2,135,620
Lutheran Church in America	930,686
Lutheran Church–Missouri Synod	857,375
Mennonite Church	110,475
Pentecostal Holiness Church, Inc.	139,508
Presbyterian Church in the U.S.	587,116
Protestant Episcopal Church	737,801
Reformed Church in America	132,789
Roman Catholic Church	10,374,116
Salvation Army	112,108
Seventh Day Baptist General Conference	369,212
Southern Baptist Convention	7,287,937
United Church of Christ	766,244
United Methodist Church	5,924,464
United Presbyterian Church in the U.S.A.	1,303,271
The Wesleyan Church	212,463

For purposes of comparison, statistics on secular elementary and high schools may be helpful. The following data are from the National Center for Educational Statistics' *Management Bulletin* of June 7, 1972, Number 12, published by U.S. Department of Health, Education, and Welfare, Office of Education.

Total public and nonpublic school enrollment was estimated at 51.5 million for the 1971–1972 school year.

Of this total, 46.2 million were enrolled in public schools.

From 1961–1962 to 1971–1972 nonpublic school enrollment decreased 8.1 percent, due chiefly to *a 17 percent decline of Catholic school pupils.* [LR]

CATHOLIC EDUCATION IN THE UNITED STATES

EDITOR'S NOTE:

The data below combine information from the *Official Catholic Directory,* the U.S. Office of Education, the U.S. Bureau of the

Census, and the National Catholic Educational Association—as summarized in *1973 Catholic Almanac* (Huntington, Ind: Our Sunday Visitor, Inc., 1973).

Conclusions

Enrollment in Catholic elementary and high schools has declined steadily since 1965—after a continuing "boom" from 1945 to 1965.

Enrollment in Catholic colleges and universities shows recurring fluctuations in enrollment.

A report of the U.S. Office of Education (September 1972) indicates that enrollment in the *public* schools of the United States increased by 22.5 percent in the decade 1961–1971; nonpublic school enrollment decreased.

The decline in total Catholic school enrollment for the decade 1961–1971 was 17 percent. [LR]

Number of Catholic Schools in the United States

NUMBER OF CATHOLIC ELEMENTARY SCHOOLS

1965	1971	1974
10,931	9,606	8,647

NUMBER OF CATHOLIC HIGH SCHOOLS

1965	1971	1974
2,465	1,954	1,702

The drop—763 schools—since 1965 is striking.

NUMBER OF CATHOLIC COLLEGES AND UNIVERSITIES

1965	1971	1974
304	283	258

School Enrollment Figures

STUDENT ENROLLMENT IN CATHOLIC ELEMENTARY SCHOOLS

1965	1971	1974
4,566,809	3,413,610	2,717,898

Note the loss of 1,848,911 students since 1965.

STUDENT ENROLLMENT IN CATHOLIC HIGH SCHOOLS

1965	1971	1974
1,095,519	1,015,713	911,730

Note the loss of 183,789 since 1965.

College Enrollment Figures

STUDENT ENROLLMENT IN CATHOLIC COLLEGES AND UNIVERSITIES

1965	1969	1971	1974
384,635	435,716	426,205	407,081

Note the gain of 22,446 in 1972 from 1965.

Catholic Teachers in the United States

1974: 174,711
Priests	7,076
Scholastics	551
Brothers	3,735
Sisters	59,759
Lay teachers	103,590

1971: 200,438

Note: Lay teachers in all Catholic schools constituted 64.6 percent of the faculty in 1974—and only 8.25 percent in 1944.

In 1971, lay teachers for the first time outnumbered priests, brothers, and sisters.

Salaries for lay teachers are considerably higher than those of priests and sisters (whose services represent an endowment to education); hence, the costliest item in Catholic education budgets (after construction and maintenance expenses) is the salary sum.

[LR]

Summary: 1972

- Student enrollment in Catholic colleges and universities in 1972 was 428,853. This represents 2,648 more than 1971, and 44,218 more than 1965; but it is lower than the 1969 number: 435,716.
- Enrollment in Catholic colleges and universities decreased from the 1965–1969 level by 4,853 in 1970, and another 4,658 in 1971.
- Student enrollment in Catholic high schools in 1972 was 961,966 (less by 53,717 than in 1971; the decrease since 1965 is 133,523).
- Student enrollment in Catholic elementary schools in 1972 was 3,105,-417. This was 308,193 below 1971—and 1,461,392 less than 1965. [LR]

POLL ON PAROCHIAL SCHOOLS

EDITOR'S NOTE:

A *Newsweek* poll of Catholics, published October 4, 1971, revealed that: (1) almost half of the Catholic adults in the United States are ready to pay more to keep their schools open; and (2) three-fourths of those whose children are now in Catholic schools are willing to pay more.

Both white and black Catholics "see parochial schools as a disciplined alternative to chaotic public classrooms."

Some Catholic educators are urging sharp decentralization, and a commission for the Chicago Archdiocese has recommended that parents be given "radically" more control over local parochial schools.

Note: In June 1970, the 11,350 Catholic schools in the United States (elementary and high) closed for the summer. In September, 800 did not reopen. Catholic schools were closing at the rate of one a day in 1970–1971. [LR]

PAROCHIAL SCHOOLS AND RACIAL INTEGRATION
From *Newsweek*, October 4, 1971, p. 84

Why do Catholics send their children to parochial schools? Aside from religion, most cite either "better education" or "better discipline." Only 7 percent believe that parents send their children to Catholic schools to avoid racial integration. And indeed, in the South, the bishops have closed off registration in many dioceses to avoid an influx of segregationists. . . .

In the troubled inner cities of the North, the popularity of Catholic schools appears to vary with the quality of the available public education. Both black and white Catholics see parochial schools as a disciplined alternative to chaotic public classrooms. "We don't need churches, we need schools," says Joseph Dulin, the militant principal of the all-black St. Martin de Porres High School in Detroit. "Most black people join the Catholic Church so their kids can attend parochial schools."

Enrollment of Minorities in Catholic Schools in the United States

EDITOR'S NOTE:

Data from the National Catholic Education Association indicates that in 1971, 183,844 black students attended Catholic elementary and high schools. This represented 5 percent of the total enrollment.

A larger number (almost 186,000) of Spanish-surname pupils attended Catholic elementary and high schools.

American Indians and Orientals constituted less than 17 percent of the total Catholic school enrollment. [LR]

Teachers From Minority Groups in Catholic Schools in the United States

Over 5,000 teachers in Catholic schools (total number of teachers in 1971: 200,438) came from minority groups.

CRISIS IN PAROCHIAL SCHOOL FINANCING

EDITOR'S NOTE:

A study of the finances and financing of the Roman Catholic Church in the United States (James Gollin, *Worldly Goods*, New

York: Random House, 1971) emphasized the economic plight of the Church and the parochial school system. The Church gives the outward appearance of affluence and superior organization, said Gollin, but is in reality woefully inefficient in financial and investment practices. No less than 90 percent of church money, concluded Gollin, is tied up in nonproductive assets—such as its school system.

It should be stated that some observers hold that it is only the smaller and less efficient units of the Catholic school system that are closing—and are therefore leaving, in the process, a strengthened, not weakened, system. (See, for instance, John M. Swomley, Jr., in the *Christian Century*, January 13, 1972.)

Further, the National Association of Laity, which consists of around 12,000 American "liberal" Catholics, has charged that the Church is exaggerating its poverty because it is seeking public funds for Catholic schools; the association, in a 100-page report issued in 1972, claims that the actual financial statements of most American dioceses are "incomplete . . . misleading" (*The Wall Street Journal*, January 11, 1972). [LR]

PREDICTIONS: PAROCHIAL SCHOOLS

EDITOR'S NOTE:

A study of New York State's 1,900 nonpublic schools, directed by Louis R. Gary for the New York State Board of Regents and the Special Commission appointed by Governor Nelson Rockefeller, predicted that by 1980 at least 70 percent of the Catholic elementary schools in the state, and 50 percent of the Catholic high schools, would be gone (see *The New York Times*, October 3, 1971).

The Social and Religious Sources of the Crisis in Catholic Schools, an interesting study by John Donovan, Donald Erickson, and George Madaus (on a grant from the U.S. Office of Education), reveals the degree to which American Catholics, formerly "isolated" or "deprived" socially and economically, have become assimilated and "acculturated."

Many Catholics question the need for parochial schools. The managing editor of *Commonweal*, for instance, wrote (*The New*

Republic, March 13, 1972) that he felt that parochial schools have served their purpose—and that "they are now a hindrance rather than a help to Catholicism." [LR]

Excerpts from survey and polls conducted by Newsweek, published October 4, 1971, p. 84

. . . after 170 years in the education business, the U.S. [Roman Catholic] church may have to close its schools.

• • •

Catholic schools are closing an average of one a day . . . Without some form of government aid, predicts the National Catholic Education Association, another 2.1 million pupils—nearly half the current Catholic school enrollment—will be sitting in already over-crowded public classrooms by 1975.

• • •

In his latest assessment of the Catholic school crisis, Father Andrew Greeley, a Chicago sociologist with a keen interest in parochial education, argues that the problem of direction and financing of Catholic schools should be turned over entirely to the laity. "It is, after all," Greeley noted, "the laity whose children attend them." And the *Newsweek* poll shows that nearly half of Catholic adults are prepared to pay more to keep their schools open, while fully three-fourths of those who now have children in Catholic schools are willing to make additional financial sacrifices.

ENROLLMENT IN JEWISH SCHOOLS: 1969–1970

EDITOR'S NOTE:

The data below are taken from the *American Jewish Yearbook, 1972,* Vol. 73 (New York: American Jewish Committee and the Jewish Publication Society of America, 1972), especially the tables on pages 196–201.

The material is based on surveys conducted by the Department of Statistical Research and Information of the American Association for Jewish Education.

In most cases, be it noted, because the sampling was limited and the responses incomplete, the "true enrollment in most communities was higher than reported"—because the reporting agencies indicated that their data came only from schools directly affiliated with them.

Because of these and other difficulties, which could not be overcome, "it is not possible to estimate the number of unreported children attending unaffiliated Jewish schools in these communities."

The reader should note that "Jewish schools" does not mean all-day schools. "Jewish schools" mostly offer courses after public school hours.

"All-day" Jewish schools are equivalent to Catholic parochial schools.

Allowing for the admitted limitations of the data (see above) the following conclusions seem justified:

ENROLLMENT IN JEWISH SCHOOLS (DAY AND PART-TIME) IN 33 U.S. CITIES

1966–1967	1970–1971	Percentage Change
319,811	278,508	−12.9

ESTIMATED ENROLLMENT IN ALL-DAY JEWISH SCHOOLS IN THE U.S.

1969–1970	1970–1971
72,478	74,195

Summary

1. In thirty-three reporting communities, overall enrollment in Jewish schools (supplementing public schools *and* all-day schools) declined 12.9 percent from 1966 to 1971—a mean annual drop of 3.3 percent.
2. The twelve largest cities showed a decline of 9 percent in enrollments, from 1966 to 1971, in Jewish schools.
3. The five intermediate (in size) Jewish communities showed a decline of 9.7 percent, but
4. The thirteen smaller communities found an *increase* of 6.9 percent during this period.
5. Enrollment changes varied widely within each group of cities: for example, five of the medium-size cities reporting showed a decline of 14.4 percent; seven of the smaller communities showed an increase of enrollment of 5.5 percent.

The decline in Jewish school enrollment in almost all reporting communities can be attributed to a combination of factors. Responses to a questionnaire addressed to the agencies reporting drastic declines in enrollment pointed to four major causal factors: fewer young couples in the community; reduced Jewish birth rate; lack of parental interest; and Jewish population movement to suburban areas. Of somewhat lesser importance are an increased pupil dropout rate and high congregational membership dues. Also, the growth of congregational schools brought a decrease in communal-school enrollment.

The likelihood is that the decline in Jewish school enrollment is related to all the suggested factors. Yet, additional exploration is required to ascertain whether all variables contributing to the enrollment problem have been identified. Furthermore, the currently available evidence is insufficient to fully verify or explain the respective roles of any of the factors already identified. [Hillel Hochberg, in the *American Jewish Yearbook, 1972,* p. 198.] [LR]

XVIII / FAMILY SIZE AND PLANNING: POLLS AND STATISTICS

DECLINE IN FAMILY SIZE AND BIRTH RATE*

EDITOR'S NOTE:

All the available evidence indicates a strong and striking decline in the desire of Americans—whatever their faith—to produce large families.

Births in the United States for the year August 1973–1974 were 3,117,000. This was a drop from the 3,186,000 of the preceding year. The birth rate (per 1,000 population) was 14.8 percent—as compared with 15.2 percent in 1973 and 17.7 percent in 1971. (*Monthly Vital Statistics, op. cit.,* "Births, Marriages, Divorces for August 1974," pp. 1–4.)

A Gallup Poll published on February 3, 1973 (see *The New York Times,* February 4, 1973, p. 23), reveals that whereas 40 percent of a national survey in 1967 responded that four children constituted an ideal family, only 20 percent thought so in 1973.

The national birth rate in the United States has dropped steadily and in 1973 was at an unprecedented "low." (We cannot yet say whether this trend will continue, rise, or fall further.)

Among Roman Catholic respondents: in 1967, 50 percent regarded four or more children as ideal, but by 1973 this figure had dropped dramatically—to 23 percent.

Among American women as a whole: in 1967, 45 percent favored four or more children; by 1973, this percentage had dropped to 21.

A report of the President's Commission on Population Growth and the American Future contains this significant passage: "Attractive work may effectively compete with childbearing and have the effect of lowering fertility, especially for births beyond the first child." [LR]

* See also Part Two, Chapter I ("Abortion") and Part Two, Chapter VIII ("Birth Control").

POLL TREND ON FAMILY SIZE
From Gallup Poll, February 3, 1973 (1,549 adults)

PERCENTAGE SAYING FOUR OR MORE IS IDEAL
NUMBER OF CHILDREN

	1967	1973	Point Change
NATIONAL	40	20	−20
SEX			
Men	34	18	−16
Women	45	21	−24
AGE			
Under 30 years	34	12	−22
30–49 years	40	22	−18
50 & over	42	24	−18
RELIGION			
Protestants	37	20	−17
Roman Catholics	50	23	−27
EDUCATION			
College	34	12	−22
High school	40	19	−21
Grade school	44	31	−13

CATHOLIC FERTILITY AND BIRTH RATES
IN VARIOUS COUNTRIES
From "Roman Catholic Fertility and Family Planning: A Comparative Review of the Research Literature," *Studies in Family Planning* (New York: Population Council, October 1968), No. 34

FERTILITY PERFORMANCE

In view of the Roman Catholic emphasis on the positive benefits of high fertility, and the ban on all methods of contraception apart from two—abstinence and rhythm—that require a high level of motivation to be practiced effectively, it is to be expected that if most Catholics adhere to the teachings of their Church, their fertility would exceed that of Protestants, Jews, or agnostics. The empirical evidence suggests that this is indeed the case, but *more striking, perhaps, is the fact that the fertility of Catholics, like that of other religious groups, is closely linked to the economic and social development of the country.* [Italics added.]

Catholic countries exhibit birth rates that are among the highest and lowest in the world (in Latin America and in Europe, respectively).[*]

[*] Such sharp differences are not found in Moslem countries, where fertility appears to be universally high. Albania is the only Moslem country showing clear signs of diminishing fertility.

Birth rates in Belgium, France, Austria and Poland are all under 18 per thousand, that is, among the lowest in the world. Admittedly, crude birth rates are a rough measure of fertility, but their evidence is clear: compared with uncontrolled fertility, which yields birth rates of 40 or more per thousand, fertility in the Catholic countries of Europe is very low, at an absolute level that indicates a high degree of control.

. . . in developed countries of Judeo-Christian tradition, Catholic fertility exceeds that of non-Catholic in almost every country and socioeconomic group. . . . [The data] for the U.S., drawn from a series of samples of married women, provide the greatest detail available for any country of the factors related to fertility differentials among religious groups.

Because U.S. Catholics, on average, marry and complete their childbearing later than Protestants, expected completed family size is a more accurate indicator of family size differentials for women still in the reproductive ages than number of children ever born.* The expected completed family size for Catholics at all ages in the 18–39-year age span exceeds that for Protestants by more than 20 percent . . . Moreover, contrary to the expectations of many demographers, these differences now appear to be widening in the younger groups moving up through the childbearing years. . . . In general, the Protestant-Catholic fertility differential "is maintained for a wide variety of socio-economic control variables."†

Within the Catholic population, substantial differences in fertility exist according to socio-economic status, e.g., level of education, ethnic background, degree of religiosity and place of residence. Standardizing for other variables, *Catholics have higher fertility if they are of Irish rather than of Italian extraction, if they receive the sacraments frequently, and if they are city rather than suburban dwellers.* [Italics added.] The relationship between Catholic fertility and measures of education and socioeconomic status tends to be U-shaped. Wives with the lowest and highest educational attainment, with husbands in the lowest and highest income and occupational status groups, tend to have the highest fertility. . . .

Although education is usually related negatively to fertility, this is not so for American Catholic women, among whom the best educated have both the highest actual and highest expected fertility.†† At least part of the explanation apparently lies in the fact that better educated Catholics have closer associational involvement with their faith: they attend church and receive the sacraments more frequently, and are more likely to have attended church-related schools. . . .

* Higher Catholic family size expectations at the younger ages are, in fact, realized at the older ages.

† A recent U.S. study found that Catholics have substantially higher expected family size than non-Catholics in each of thirty different social and economic categories considered.

†† For younger Catholic women, education is related negatively to actual fertility, but this appears to result from later age at marriage of more highly educated women.

Catholics living in the suburbs become assimilated to the "American" or Protestant way of life. Their cautious inference that Catholic-Protestant differentials in the U.S. might narrow as suburbanization proceeds is questionable, however, in view of the widening differentials in expected completed family size observed among younger cohorts.

The data for the other countries in [the table below] are self-explanatory and with one exception . . . (Catholic compared with Afrikaner Protestant fertility in Johannesburg) consistently show higher Catholic fertility. The available data support the following observations:

1. *The crucial variable related to the fertility of a population is its level of socio-economic development, not its religious composition. Catholic countries that are underdeveloped have high fertility; Catholic countries that are developed have low fertility.* [Italics added.]
2. Most Catholic couples in developed countries produce only 2 to 4 children, far fewer than would be expected in a population making no effort to control fertility.
3. This is not to say that Catholicism has no pro-fertility influence in developed countries. *Catholic fertility is normally higher, sometimes substantially higher, than that of Protestants or Jews living in the same country, with or without standardization for socio-economic background.* [Italics added.]
4. The differential between Catholic and non-Catholic fertility in developed countries that are predominantly Judeo-Christian varies rather widely with a modal Catholic excess of from 18 to 30 percent. Within this range, according to the various measures used, are six of the eleven countries included . . . (the U.S., Canada, West Germany, Australia, New Zealand, and probably Great Britain).

. . . Among developed countries, as a rule, the fertility of Catholics in countries where they constitute a distinguishable *minority* of the population exceeds that of Catholics where they constitute a *majority*. . . .

. . . Catholics of different ethnic background exhibit substantial fertility differentials. In both the U.S. and Canada, for example, Catholics of Irish extraction have higher fertility than those of Italian extraction. In Australia, the fertility of Netherlands-born Catholics is far higher, and that of Polish-born Catholics far lower, than that of native-born or Italian-born Catholics. . . .

OPINIONS ON FERTILITY CONTROL: RELIGIOUS GROUPINGS

Data from P. Whelpton, A. A. Campbell, and J. E. Patterson, Fertility and Family Planning in the United States (Princeton: Princeton University Press, 1966, as reproduced in Studies in Family Planning (New York: Population Council, October 1968), No. 34, p. 19

ATTITUDES TOWARD FERTILITY CONTROL

U.S. 1960: WHITE WIVES 18–39	APPROVE			DISAPPROVE		No Opinion or No Answer
	Strongly	Other	Rhythm Only	Mildly	Strongly	
Q. *Attitude toward fertility control*						
Roman Catholic Total (668)	25	27	33	4	5	5
Educational background						
College	14	25	49	1	6	4
High school 4 years	26	29	33	4	3	6
High school 1–3 years	30	28	29	5	5	4
Grade school	25	21	28	6	14	6
Church attendance						
Once/year or less	52	17	10	10	7	3
2–12 times/year	42	39	13	2	3	2
Over once/month	22	27	36	4	5	5
Q. *Would you use a method given by a doctor?*						
Roman Catholic		50		50		0
Protestant		53		47		0
Moslem		37		63		0
Q. *Would you support establishment of family planning clinics?*						
Roman Catholic		51		49		0
Protestant		60		39		0
Moslem		38		61		1

Q. Would you use family planning clinics if they were established?		Yes	Conditional		
Roman Catholic		47	0	53	0
Protestant		48	3	50	0
Moslem		32	1	67	0
	57	34	5	2	1
Protestant Total (1,596)					
Educational background					
College	65	31	3	1	0
High school 4 years	57	36	5	2	1
High school 1–3 years	55	33	7	2	1
Grade school	49	30	8	7	2
Jewish Total (106)	83	15	0	0	1

FERTILITY AND JEWS: A SPECIAL PROBLEM

EDITOR'S NOTE:

Professor (Rabbi) Seymour Siegel, of the Jewish Theological Seminary, the leading center of Conservative Judaism in the United States, has analyzed several aspects of population control and "zero growth" in the United States in a paper, "Group Competition and Survival" (*The Population Crisis and Moral Responsibility*, ed. P. Wogaman, Washington, D.C.: Public Affairs Press, 1973, pp. 62–71).

Rabbi Siegel examines the dilemma that many Jews today confront: the conflict between the dangers of over-population and the implications to the people that lost six million members of its community in the Nazi holocaust. Since the Bible tells us: "Be fruitful and multiply," the problem of the world's dangerous growth in population presents a special problem to the religious. Professor Siegel quotes a liberal rabbi: "When we talk of the population explosion today we . . . are confronted with a dilemma: shall we be 'liberal' and control our birth rate . . . and lead the world into zero growth? Or shall we remember the six million? Shall we first make up for the six million before we join the rest of the world in keeping the level?"

Furthermore, the Government of Israel officially encourages large families and considers them a contribution to the national welfare—especially since the high birth rate existing among Arabs inside Israel makes the problem of increased Jewish population there "a life or death issue" in the eyes of Israelis.

A striking passage by Professor Emil Fackenheim is worth note: "Jews are not permitted to hand Hitler posthumous victories. Jews are committed to survive as Jews, lest their people perish. . . . An obligation toward survival . . . can be fulfilled (only by) being heretic in the size of the Zero Population Growth dogma. . . ."

Professor Siegel takes the position that people or nations who believe that they are over-populated, whether in India, Japan or the United States, should practice whatever limitations on growth they prefer; but those who feel there are too few of "their kind" rather than too many may prefer to observe the Biblical injunction: "Be fruitful and multiply." [LR]

SUPREME COURT RULINGS ON PAROCHIAL SCHOOLS

From A. P. Klauser, "Religion," 1972 Britannica Book of the Year (Chicago: Encyclopaedia Britannica, 1972)

With many parochial school systems in financial difficulty, a number of states attempted to assist them, chiefly on the ground that this would be cheaper than caring for an influx of Roman Catholic children into the public schools. In June, however, the Supreme Court struck down "parochial" laws passed in Pennsylvania and Rhode Island because they caused "excessive entanglement between government and religion." In a related issue, a proposed constitutional amendment that would permit "nondenominational" prayer in public buildings was introduced in Congress, but was defeated.

FEDERAL AID "REVOKED"

EDITOR'S NOTE:

On June 25, 1973, the Supreme Court of the United States ruled that the First Amendment to the Constitution (the "no establishment of religion" clause) prohibits direct federal aid to church-affiliated schools through public funds. The ruling rescinded assistance programs in New York and Pennsylvania. More than thirty states already had such legislation, and ten states prohibited state aid to "private" schools, whether church-affiliated or not.

Roman Catholic schools have been exempted from taxation on real estate in all the states of the union—and since January 1, 1959, "nonprofit" schools, whether parochial or private, have been exempted from certain federal excise taxes.

In some thirty states where state laws prohibit aid to nonpublic schools, the federal government has been making direct money payments for such programs as free school milk and lunch programs and health examinations. Certain programs authorized by the Elementary and Secondary Education Act of 1965 continue.

The 1973 decision of the Supreme Court created a sensation in educational circles because it blanketed growing hopes for public funds, either federal or state, to help financially hard-pressed private/parochial schools. The reaction was particularly strong among Roman Catholic leaders. Thus, from an article by Evan Jenkins in *The New York Times* (June 27, 1973, p. 19):

The Court acted at a time when parochial schools—which enroll about 80 percent of the nonpublic pupils in the nation—face continued decline in both numbers and enrollment.

Against a background of rising costs, changing attitudes among Catholic families and social and economic transformation of cities that had been their main source of students and income, the number of schools has dropped from 12,814 in 1967–68 to 10,514 in the school year just ended. Enrollment is down from a peak of 5.5 million in 1965 to 3.8 million.

Few observers shared the view of Sister Gwenn, Superintendent of Catholic schools in Memphis, that the Court's decisions were a "death blow to nonpublic schools."

Most appeared to agree with the initial assessment of religious-school leaders in New York concerning the rejection of this state's aid program —that while the door to public money was finally closed, their schools would survive with further belt-tightening.

Msgr. William Novicky, Superintendent of the Cleveland diocesan schools, said he would urge his board to do away with tuition and rely instead on donations to churches, which are tax deductible.

That would leave the burden of financing the schools where it has been during the period of sharp decline—on the parishes and particularly pupils' parents.

An aspect of the Catholic problem not often noticed is the fact that Vatican II emphasized that Catholic men and women could serve the Church without taking vows in a religious order. "This let in a hurricane," said one parochial teacher—for by 1965 more than 63,000 out of 177,219 Catholic faculty members were laymen; today the percentage is well over 55.

The *financial* aspect of this transformation is gigantic, since lay teachers are not committed by vows to a life of poverty—hence teachers' salaries in Catholic schools have risen spectacularly (although, on the whole, remaining lower than salaries in public schools). At some parochial schools, faculty salaries consume 80 percent of the budget. Catholic teachers (laymen) are joining unions and setting up picket lines. Tuition costs in all parochial schools have risen dramatically—in some cases doubling within 3–4 years. [LR]

EFFECTS ON CATHOLIC SCHOOLS

EDITOR'S NOTE:

The main facts and problems confronting parochial schools in the United States will be found in Part Two, Chapter XVII, "Education in Religious Schools in the United States."

Here I may call the reader's attention to correlated but less conspicuous phenomena. Catholic families, like others, are moving into the suburbs as their incomes and affluence increase—and as American cities become less and less attractive (to say nothing of more dangerous) to parents concerned about their children's education and safety.

In these suburbs, parochial schools are neither as numerous nor as near as those left behind in once-Catholic neighborhoods.

Tuition costs, added to transportation costs, added to rising property taxes represent new pressures.

Hence the 1973 Supreme Court decision was a severe blow to Catholics who had hoped for federal or state or local financial aid to parochial schools—and at a time when school costs were skyrocketing, chiefly because of the widespread entry of lay teachers (and unions) into schools whose faculties' low salaries had been a form of devotional subsidy. [LR]

XX / HOLY DAYS AND RELIGIOUS OBSERVANCES: ALL FAITHS

CALENDAR AND DESCRIPTION

Compiled from the following sources: the *Information Please Almanac, 1972* (New York: Dan Golenpaul Associates, Simon and Schuster, 1972), pp. 173–175; the *School Calendar;* indicating *Holidays and Holy Days*, prepared by Community Relations Service, The American Jewish Committee, 165 East 56 Street, New York, N.Y.

EDITOR'S NOTE:

In determining church holidays, both the lunar and the solar calendars are used. Dates determined by the lunar calendar are generally movable; those determined by the solar calendar are fixed. Movable holidays are indicated by an asterisk (*). [LR]

New Year's Day, January 1—Protestant and Catholic Holy Day. Ecclesiastically the New Year celebrates the Feast of Circumcision.

Feast of Epiphany, January 6—Falls the twelfth day after Christmas and commemorates the manifestation of Jesus as the Son of God, as represented by the adoration of the Magi, the baptism of Jesus, and the miracle of the wine at the marriage feast at Cana. Epiphany originally marked the beginning of the carnival season preceding Lent, and the evening (sometimes the eve) is known as Twelfth Night.

*Shrove Tuesday—Falls the day before Ash Wednesday and marks the end of the carnival season, which once began on Epiphany but is now usually celebrated the last three days before Lent. In France, the day is known as Mardi Gras (Fat Tuesday), and Mardi Gras celebrations are also held in several American cities, particularly in New Orleans. The day is sometimes called Pancake Tuesday by the English because fats, which were prohibited during Lent, had to be used up.

*Ash Wednesday—The first day of the Lenten season, which lasts forty days. Having its origin sometime before A.D. 1000, it is a day of public penance and is marked in the Roman Catholic Church by the burning of the palms blessed on the previous Palm Sunday. With his thumb, the priest then marks a cross upon the forehead of each worshiper. The Anglican Church and a few Protestant groups in the United States also observe the day, but generally without the use of ashes.

°**Purim (Feast of Esther)**—The Biblical Book of Esther is read in the synagogue and there is general merry-making in the home. Gifts are exchanged and also distributed to the poor.

°**Palm Sunday**—Is observed the Sunday before Easter to commemorate the entry of Jesus into Jerusalem. The procession and the ceremonies introducing the benediction of palms probably had their origin in Jerusalem.

°**Holy Week**—All the days of the week preceding Easter have special connotation as they relate to the events of the last days in Jesus' life. Beginning with Palm Sunday, each of these days takes on a special importance.

°**Holy Thursday (in Holy Week)**—This day is marked by the sacrament of holy communion in remembrance of the Last Supper, which Jesus had with His disciples.

°**Good Friday**—This day commemorates the Crucifixion, which is retold during services from the Gospel according to Saint John. A feature in Roman Catholic churches is the Liturgy of the Passion: there is no Consecration, the Host having been consecrated the previous day. The eating of hot cross buns on this day is said to have started in England.

°**Easter Sunday**—Observed in all Christian churches, Easter commemorates the Resurrection of Jesus. It is celebrated on the first Sunday after the full moon that occurs on or next after March 21 and is therefore celebrated between March 22 and April 25 inclusive. This date was fixed by the Council of Nicaea in 325.

°**First Day of Passover (Pesach)**—Nisan 15—The Feast of the Passover, also called the Feast of Unleavened Bread, commemorates the escape of the first-born of the Jews from the Angel of Death. As the Jews fled Egypt, they ate unleavened bread, and from that time the Jews have allowed no leavening in the house during Passover, bread being replaced by matzoth.

°**Second Day of Passover.**

°**Conclusion and Last Day of Passover** (8th Day).

°**Greek Orthodox Palm Sunday**—Commemorates the triumphal entry of Jesus into Jerusalem. First day of Greek Orthodox Holy Week.

°**Greek Orthodox Holy Thursday**—Commemorates the Last Supper, at which Jesus instituted the sacrament of holy communion.

°**Greek Orthodox Holy Friday** (Good Friday)—Commemorates the Passion and Crucifixion of Jesus.

°**Greek Orthodox Easter.**

° **Ascension Day**—Ascension of Jesus took place in the presence of His apostles forty days after His Resurrection. It is traditionally held to have occurred on Mount Olivet in Bethany.

°**Pentecost (Whitsunday)**—This day commemorates the descent of the Holy Ghost upon the apostles fifty days after the Resurrection. The sermon by the apostle Peter, which led to the baptism of 3,000 who professed belief, originated the ceremonies that have since been followed. "Whitsunday" is believed to have come from "white Sunday" when, among the English, white robes were worn by those baptized on the day.

°**First Day of Shabuoth (Hebrew Pentecost)**—Sivan 6—This festival, sometimes called the Feast of Weeks, or of Harvest, or of the First Fruits, falls fifty days after Passover and originally celebrated the end of the seven-week grain-harvesting season. In later tradition, it also celebrated the giving of the law to Moses on Mt. Sinai, and both aspects have come down to the present.

°**Fast of Ab (Tishah B'ab)**—A day of mourning in memory of the destruction of the Temple.

Feast of the Assumption—August 15—The principal feast of the Blessed Virgin, this holy day commemorates two events: the happy departure of Mary from this life and the assumption of her body into heaven.

°**First Day of Rosh Hashanah (Jewish New Year)**—Tishri 1—This day marks the beginning of the Jewish year and opens the Ten Days of Penitence, closing with Yom Kippur.

°**Yom Kippur (Day of Atonement)**—Tishri 10—This day marks the end of the Ten Days of Penitence that began with Rosh Hashanah and is the holiest day of the Jewish year. It is described in Leviticus as the "Sabbath of Sabbaths," and synagogue services begin the preceding sundown, resume the following morning, and continue through the day to sundown.

° **First Day of Sukkoth (Feast of Tabernacles)**—Tishri 15—this festival, also known as the Feast of the Ingathering, originally celebrated the fruit harvest; the name comes from the booths or tabernacles in which the Jews lived during the harvest, although one tradition traces it to the shelters used by the Jews in their wandering through the wilderness. During the festival many Jews build small huts in their back yards or on the roofs of houses.

*Eighth Day of the Feast of Tabernacles—This marks the climax of the Jewish Holy Day season. Prayers for rain are recited in the synagogue.

*Simhath Torah (Rejoicing of the Law)—The Reading of the Law is concluded and recommenced. Gaiety is the characteristic mood of the day combined with a spirit of reverence.

Reformation Day—October 31—The date that is regarded as the beginning of the Protestant Reformation, observed in many Protestant churches.

All Saints' Day—November 1—This is a Roman Catholic and Anglican holiday celebrating all saints, known and unknown.

*First Sunday in Advent—Advent is the season in which the faithful must prepare themselves for the advent of the Savior on Christmas. The four Sundays before Christmas are marked by special church services.

Feast of the Immaculate Conception—December 8—Catholic Holy Day of Obligation. Celebrating Mary's privilege of freedom from sin from the first moment of her conception as the child of Saint Joachim and Saint Anne.

*First Day of Hanukkah (Festival of Lights)—Kisler 25—This festival was instituted by Judas Maccabeus in 165 B.C. to celebrate the purification of the Temple of Jerusalem, which had been desecrated three years earlier by Antiochus Epiphanes, who set up a pagan altar and offered sacrifices to Zeus Olympius. In Jewish homes, a light is lighted the first night, and on each succeeding night of the eight-day festival another is lighted.

Christmas (Feast of the Nativity)—December 25—The most widely celebrated holiday of the Christian year, Christmas is observed as the anniversary of the birth of Jesus. Christmas customs are centuries old. The mistletoe, for example, comes from the Druids, who, in hanging the mistletoe, hoped for peace and good fortune. Use of such plants as holly comes from the ancient belief that such plants blossomed at Christmas. Comparatively recent is the Christmas tree, first set up in Germany in the seventeenth century, and the use of candles on trees developed from the belief that candles appeared by miracle on the trees at Christmas. Colonial Manhattan Islanders introduced the name Santa Claus, a corruption of the Dutch name for the fourth-century Asia Minor Saint Nicholas.

[LR]

TABLES OF MOVABLE HOLIDAYS: CHRISTIAN AND SECULAR, AND JEWISH: 1974–1982

From 1974 Information Please Almanac (New York: Dan Golenpaul Associates, Simon and Schuster), p. 167.

CHRISTIAN AND SECULAR

Year	Ash Wed.	Easter	Pentecost	Labor Day	Election Day	Thanksgiving	1st Sun. Advent
1974	Feb. 27	Apr. 14	June 2	Sept. 2	Nov. 5	Nov. 28	Dec. 1
1975	Feb. 12	Mar. 30	May 18	Sept. 1	Nov. 4	Nov. 27	Nov. 30
1976	Mar. 3	Apr. 18	June 6	Sept. 6	Nov. 2	Nov. 25	Nov. 28
1977	Feb. 23	Apr. 10	May 29	Sept. 5	Nov. 8	Nov. 24	Nov. 27
1978	Feb. 8	Mar. 26	May 14	Sept. 4	Nov. 7	Nov. 23	Dec. 3
1979	Feb. 28	Apr. 15	June 3	Sept. 3	Nov. 6	Nov. 22	Dec. 2
1980	Feb. 19	Apr. 6	May 25	Sept. 1	Nov. 4	Nov. 28	Nov. 30
1981	Feb. 11	Mar. 29	May 17	Sept. 7	Nov. 3	Nov. 26	Nov. 29
1982	Feb. 24	Apr. 11	May 30	Sept. 6	Nov. 2	Nov. 25	Nov. 28

Shrove Tuesday: 1 day before Ash Wednesday.
Palm Sunday: 7 days before Easter.
Maundy Thursday: 3 days before Easter.
Good Friday: 2 days before Easter.

Holy Saturday: 1 day before Easter.
Ascension Day: 10 days before Pentecost.
Trinity Sunday: 7 days after Pentecost.
Corpus Christi: 11 days after Pentecost.

NOTE: Easter is celebrated on April 14 by the Orthodox Church.

JEWISH

Year	Purim*	1st day Passover†	1st day Shabuoth‡	1st day Rosh Hashana§	Yom Kippur‖	1st day Sukkoth‖	Simhath Torah#	1st day Hanuk-kah**
1974	Mar. 8	Apr. 7	May 27	Sept. 17	Sept. 26	Oct. 1	Oct. 9	Dec. 9
1975	Feb. 25	Mar. 27	May 16	Sept. 6	Sept. 15	Sept. 20	Sept. 28	Nov. 29
1976	Mar. 16	Apr. 15	June 4	Sept. 25	Oct. 4	Oct. 9	Oct. 17	Dec. 17
1977	Mar. 4	Apr. 3	May 23	Sept. 13	Sept. 22	Sept. 27	Oct. 5	Dec. 5
1978	Mar. 23	Apr. 22	June 11	Oct. 2	Oct. 11	Oct. 16	Oct. 24	Dec. 25
1979	Mar. 13	Apr. 12	June 1	Sept. 22	Oct. 1	Oct. 6	Oct. 14	Dec. 15
1980	Mar. 2	Apr. 1	May 21	Sept. 11	Sept. 20	Sept. 25	Oct. 3	Dec. 3
1981	Mar. 20	Apr. 19	June 8	Sept. 29	Oct. 8	Oct. 13	Oct. 21	Dec. 21
1982	Mar. 9	Apr. 8	May 28	Sept. 18	Sept. 27	Oct. 2	Oct. 10	Dec. 11

* Feast of Lots.   † Feast of Unleavened Bread.   ‡ Hebrew Pentecost; or Feast of Weeks, or of Harvest, or of First Fruits.   § Jewish New Year.
‖ Day of Atonement.   ‖ Feast of Tabernacles, or of the Ingathering.   # Rejoicing of the Law.   ** Festival of Lights.

Length of Jewish holidays (O = Orthodox, C = Conservative, R = Reform):

Passover: O & C, 8 days (holy days: first 2 and last 2); R,
   7 days (holy days: first and last).
Shabuoth: O & C, 2 days; R, 1 day.
Rosh Hashana: O & C, 2 days; R, 1 day.
Yom Kippur: All groups, 1 day.

Sukkoth: All groups, 7 days (holy days: O & C, first 2: R,
   first only). O & C observe two additional days: Shemini
   Atsereth (Eighth Day of the Feast) and Simhath Torah.
   R observes Shemini Atsereth but not Simhath Torah.
Hanukkah: All groups, 8 days.

NOTE: All holidays begin on the evening before the date given.

All holidays begin at sundown on the day given.

EXTENDED CATHOLIC CALENDAR: 1974–1999

EDITOR'S NOTE:

This table, which goes to 1999, is an expanded version of the preceding Christian and Secular table. [LR]

From 1971 National Catholic Almanac (Paterson, N.J.: St. Anthony's Guild, 1971), p. 294

Year	Ash Wednesday	Easter†	Ascension	Pentecost	WEEKS OF "SEASON" THROUGH YEAR*				First Sunday of Advent
					Before Lent		After Pent.		
					Week	Ends	Week	Begins	
1974	Feb. 27	Apr. 14	May 23	June 2	7	Feb. 26	9	June 3	Dec. 1
1975	Feb. 12	Mar. 30	May 8	May 18	5	Feb. 11	7	May 19	Nov. 30
1976	Mar. 3	Apr. 18	May 27	June 6	8	Mar. 2	10	June 7	Nov. 28
1977	Feb. 23	Apr. 10	May 19	May 29	7	Feb. 22	9	May 30	Nov. 27
1978	Feb. 8	Mar. 26	May 4	May 14	5	Feb. 7	6	May 15	Dec. 3
1979	Feb. 28	Apr. 15	May 24	June 3	8	Feb. 27	9	June 4	Dec. 2
1980	Feb. 20	Apr. 6	May 15	May 25	6	Feb. 19	8	May 26	Nov. 30
1981	Mar. 4	Apr. 19	May 28	June 7	8	Mar. 3	10	June 8	Nov. 29
1982	Feb. 24	Apr. 11	May 20	May 30	7	Feb. 23	9	May 31	Nov. 28
1983	Feb. 16	Apr. 3	May 12	May 22	6	Feb. 15	8	May 23	Nov. 27
1984	Mar. 7	Apr. 22	May 31	June 10	9	Mar. 6	10	June 11	Dec. 2
1985	Feb. 20	Apr. 7	May 16	May 26	6	Feb. 19	8	May 27	Dec. 1

Year							
1986	Feb. 12	Mar. 30	May 8	May 18	5 Feb. 11	7 May 19	Nov. 30
1987	Mar. 4	Apr. 19	May 28	June 7	9 Mar. 3	10 June 8	Nov. 29
1988	Feb. 17	Apr. 3	May 12	May 22	6 Feb. 16	8 May 23	Nov. 27
1989	Feb. 8	Mar. 26	May 4	May 14	5 Feb. 7	6 May 15	Dec. 3
1990	Feb. 28	Apr. 15	May 24	June 3	8 Feb. 27	9 June 4	Dec. 2
1991	Feb. 13	Mar. 31	May 9	May 19	5 Feb. 12	7 May 20	Dec. 1
1992	Mar. 4	Apr. 19	May 28	May 28	9 Mar. 3	10 June 8	Nov. 29
1993	Feb. 24	Apr. 11	May 20	May 30	7 Feb. 23	9 May 31	Nov. 28
1994	Feb. 16	Apr. 3	May 12	May 22	6 Feb. 15	8 May 23	Nov. 27
1995	Mar. 1	Apr. 16	May 25	June 4	8 Feb. 28	9 June 5	Dec. 3
1996	Feb. 21	Apr. 7	May 16	May 26	7 Feb. 20	8 May 27	Dec. 1
1997	Feb. 12	Mar. 30	May 8	May 18	5 Feb. 11	7 May 19	Nov. 30
1998	Feb. 25	Apr. 12	May 21	May 31	7 Feb. 24	9 June 1	Nov. 29
1999	Feb. 17	Apr. 4	May 13	May 23	6 Feb. 16	8 May 24	Nov. 28

* Weeks between the end of Christmastide and the beginning of Lent, and from the day after Pentecost to the last Sunday of the liturgical year, belong to the Season-through-the-Year. The table indicates the number and terminal date of the week ending the first part, and the number and starting date of the week beginning the second part, of this season. In some years, as in 1978, a week of this season is eliminated because of calendar conditions.

† The second Vatican Council's "Constitution on the Sacred Liturgy" said there would be no objection "If the feast of Easter were assigned to a particular Sunday of the Gregorian calendar, provided that those whom it may concern, especially the brethren who are not in communion with the Apostolic See, give their assent." Agreement has not yet been reached, although Ecumenical Patriarch Athenagoras I has proposed that Easter be celebrated each year on the second Sunday of April. Calendar expert Father Pierre Jounel made this comment on the subject: "There is no change in the new liturgical calendar concerning fixing the date of Easter. . . . It seems there is no way of arriving at a universal agreement on this point for many years, especially until the general council of the Orthodox Church puts the problem on its agenda."

XXI / HOMOSEXUALITY: THE CHURCHES AND PSYCHIATRY

EDITOR'S NOTE:

Each of the major denominations was asked to state its official position on homosexuality. The answers will be found in Part One.

A survey in 1973 by Andrew M. Greeley and William C. McCready (of the National Opinion Research Center), conducted for the *National Catholic Reporter*, polled 1,367 Americans and asked whether they considered homosexual relations "always wrong." The results: 76 percent of the Protestants replied "yes"—as compared with 71 percent of the Catholics and 31 percent of the Jews. (See *The New York Times*, November 14, 1973, p. 22.)

The Gay Activists Alliance has long tried to remove homosexuality from the *Diagnostic and Statistical Manual [of] Mental Disorders*.

On December 15, 1973, the American Psychiatric Association, through its board of trustees, characterized homosexuality "a sexual orientation disturbance"—changing the position, held for almost a century, which listed homosexuality in the category of "a mental disorder."

The New York Times report by Richard D. Lyons (December 16, 1973, pp. 1, 25) of this extraordinary decision contains these passages:

"Sexual orientation disturbance" was then defined by the association's trustees as a category "for individuals whose sexual interests are directed primarily towards people of the same sex and who are either disturbed by, in conflict with, or wish to change their sexual orientation." However, the trustees went on to say: "This diagnostic category is distinguished from homosexuality, which by itself does not necessarily constitute a psychiatric disorder."

Dr. Robert L. Spitzer, who is a psychiatrist at the Columbia College of Physicians and Surgeons, explained that "we're not saying that homosexuality is either 'normal' or 'abnormal.' We're saying that homosexuality per se is not a psychiatric disorder. . . .

Dr. Alfred M. Freedman, president of the A.P.A., noted that the association's official list of mental disorders had classed homosexuality as a "sexual deviation" along with fetishism, voyeurism, pedophilia, exhibitionism, and others.

The American Psychiatric Association announced on April 8, 1974, that it was removing homosexuality from its list of "mental disorders." This action followed a referendum of the membership of around 20,000 psychiatrists. (About half of the membership did not vote on the issue.) The voting was announced as: 5,854 supporting the position of the trustees (see above) and 3,810 opposed. (See *The New York Times,* April 9, 1974, p. 12.)

As for the religious community, the United Methodists have accepted the following declaration (similar in many ways to the stand of other denominations, as the articles in Part One of the present volume amply demonstrate):

In the light of our commitment within the covenant community and our search for greater understanding of sexual development, we call upon local churches to:

a. Extend to all persons, including those of homosexual orientation, the redemptive life of the church community.

b. Provide support and informed understanding to persons and families facing crises in sexual identity; and

c. Work for removal of laws which define as crime sexual acts privately committed by consenting adults, excluding prostitution.

d. Work for the enactment of civil rights legislation prohibiting discrimination because of sexual orientation in employment, housing, or public accommodations.

e. We strongly affirm also that our concern for civil rights of persons does not relieve the church at all levels of its responsibility for teaching Christian sexual attitudes, values and behavior. [*Proceedings of the General Conference of United Methodist Church,* Atlanta, 1972, p. 590.]

The growth in many denominations of pastoral counseling that is psychiatrically/psychoanalytically oriented is a striking phenomenon and seems certain to spread and grow further. The Roman Catholic Church has incorporated many psychiatric points in its own position and in the responses of priests to confessors of homosexual (male or female) desires or experiences. The Vatican's declaration on celibacy (see Part Two, Chapter X) represents a distinct and historic step forward, despite its conclusion, in the consideration of psychiatric factors. [LR]

XXII / HUMANISTS: MANIFESTO II

EDITOR'S NOTE:

The humanist position is set forth in Part One in the article "The 'Unchurched' Americans: What Do They Believe?" by Edward L. Ericson.

On August 26, 1973, 120 philosophers, religious leaders, historians, scientists, authors, and social commentators (from the United States, Canada, and Europe) signed a statement entitled "Manifesto II." Manifesto I had been adopted forty years earlier, in 1933, under the leadership of John Dewey; the appellation "Manifesto II" may have appealed to those who saw it as a counterpart to "Vatican II."

Humanism opposes formal theology, religious dogma, and church authority—by affirming the preeminence of ethics, reason, human experience, social values, and social concern. Humanism draws upon the great ethical teachings of poets and philosophers no less than saints and theologians. It asserts the continuity of compassion—from Confucianism, Greek philosophy, Buddhism, Judaism, Roman philosophy, down to and through Christianity into modern thought.

Manifesto II said: "No deity will save us; we must save ourselves" and asserted that "traditional dogmatic or authoritarian religions that place revelation, God, ritual and creed above human needs and experience do a disservice to the human species."

The manifesto proceeded to say that human beings must by their own reason and ethics solve those problems that threaten the continued existence of the human family on this planet.

Manifesto II advocated the increase of individual freedoms; affirmed the practice of birth control and the right to abortion; and approved sexual freedom and sexual conduct "between consenting adults" (homosexuals), the individual right to suicide and euthanasia ("mercy killings"), increased "participatory democracy," an annual guaranteed minimum income, universal education, and "world law." It proclaimed nationalism obsolete, called for ecological planning on a world-wide scale, and attacked racial or ethnic divisions and "sexual chauvinism—male or female."

Other striking passages deal with Marxism/communism:

Some forms of political doctrine function religiously, reflecting the worst features of orthodoxy and authoritarianism, especially when they sacrifice individuals on the altar of utopian promises.

And with the current wave of cultism:

[Many people today,] faced with apocalyptic prophecies and doomsday scenarios, flee in despair from reason and embrace irrational cults and theologies of withdrawal and retreat.

And, of course, with theology:

As in 1933, humanists still believe that traditional theism, especially faith in the prayer-hearing God, assumed to love and care for persons, to hear and understand their prayers and to be able to do something about them, is an unproved and outmoded faith.

Salvationism based on mere affirmation, still, appears as harmful, diverting people with false hopes of heaven hereafter . . . Reasonable minds look to other means for survival.

The size of the humanist movement is impossible to establish. If the number of Americans who attend no churches at all is accepted, support for the humanist position in one or another of its aspects is very large: after all, only 42 percent of the adult Americans polled by the Gallup organization in 1970–1971 said that they attended church "in a typical week" (*Religion in America 1971*, Gallup Opinion Index, April 1971, Report No. 70, p. 43), and 75 percent said they thought religion "is losing its influence" on American life (*ibid.*, p. 47).

As for formal membership in a humanist group, perhaps 250,000 Americans belong to either the American Humanist Association or the American Ethical Union—the two dominant agencies in the "ethical culture" movement.

Among the 120 signers of Manifesto II were: B. F. Skinner, Sidney Hook, Brand Blanshard, Herman Bondi (London), H. J. Eysenck (London), A. Eustace Haydon, Charles Morris, Karl Nielson (Canada), Chaim Perelman (Brussels), John Herman Randall, Jr., Andrei Sakharov (formerly of the Academy of Sciences in the USSR), Nobel Prize winner Dr. Francis Crick, Lord Ritchie-Calder, Edward Lamb (president, Lamb Communications, Inc.), John Ciardi, Isaac Asimov, Gerald Wendt, Corliss Lamont, Alan F. Guttmacher (Planned Parenthood Association), Hudson Hoagland

(Worcester Foundation of Experimental Biology). Among clergymen: Raymond B. Bragg, J. Harold Hadley, James M. Hutchinson, Billy Joe Nichols, and Rabbi Mordecai Kaplan (founder of the Jewish Reconstructionist movement).

The most significant passages in the manifesto, aside from those already quoted, follow:

Promises of immortal salvation or fear of eternal damnation are both illusory and harmful. They distract humans from present concerns, from self-actualization and from rectifying social injustices.

We affirm that moral values derive their source from human experience. Ethics is autonomous and situational, needing no theological or ideological sanction. Ethics stems from human need and interest. To deny this distorts the whole basis of life.

We strive for the good life, here and now.

Reason and intelligence are the most effective instruments that humankind possesses. There is no substitute: neither faith nor passion suffices in itself. The controlled use of scientific methods . . . must be extended further in the solution of human problems. But reason must be tempered by humility, since no group has a monopoly of wisdom or virtue.

In the area of sexuality, we believe that intolerant attitudes, often cultivated by orthodox religions and puritanical cultures, unduly repress sexual conduct. The right to birth control, abortion and divorce should be recognized. While we do not approve of exploitive, denigrating forms of sexual expression, neither do we wish to prohibit . . . sexual behavior between consenting adults.

To enhance freedom and dignity, the individual must experience a full range of civil liberties in all societies. This includes . . . a recognition of an individual's right to die with dignity, euthanasia and the right to suicide. . . .

We deplore the division of humankind on nationalistic grounds. We have reached a turning point in human history where the best option is to transcend the limits of national sovereignty and to move toward the building of a world community in which all sectors of the human family can participate. Thus we look to the development of a system of world law and a world order based upon transnational federal government.

We must expand communication and transportation across frontiers. . . . We thus call for full international cooperation in culture, science, the arts and technology across ideological borders. '

The commitment to tolerance, understanding and peaceful negotiation does not necessitate acquiescence to the status quo nor the damming up of dynamic and revolutionary forces. The true revolution is occurring and can continue in countless nonviolent adjustments.

XXIII / INFLUENCE OF RELIGION: OPINION POLLS

IS RELIGION LOSING ITS INFLUENCE?

Quoted from *Religion in America 1971*, Gallup Opinion Index, April 1971, Report No. 70, pp. 45, 47

In the 1970 survey on the subject, three adults in every four (75 percent) said religion as a whole was losing its influence on American life. In 1957, when the first of seven surveys on the subject was conducted, the percentage who held this view was only 14 percent.

"At the present time, do you think religion as a whole is increasing its influence on American life, or losing its influence?"

When asked this question over the past 13 years, the American public has responded as shown in the following table:

Year	Losing	Increasing	No Difference	No Opinion
1957	14%	69%	10%	7%
1962	31	45	17	7
1965	45	33	13	9
1967	57	23	14	6
1968	67	18	8	7
1970	75	14	7	4

Little difference is found between the views of men and women, Protestants and Catholics, churchgoers and non-churchgoers.

Young adults are slightly more likely to say religion is losing its influence than are older persons.

Reasons for believing religion is "losing" ground include these:

1. People are changing—religion isn't important any more (31%).
2. The church is not meeting the needs of the people (18%).
3. Religion is no longer being taught in the home (9%).
4. Moral decay in the U.S. (3%).
5. The world has become too materialistic (3%).

NOTE: A Gallup poll published in January 1975 shows that 31 percent now believe that religion is increasing in influence.)

CONFIDENCE IN AND RESPECT FOR THE CHURCH AS COMPARED WITH OTHER INSTITUTIONS

From Gallup Poll, July 1, 1973 (Publishers-Hall Syndicate, Chicago)

"I AM GOING TO READ YOU A LIST OF INSTITUTIONS IN AMERICAN SOCIETY. WOULD YOU TELL ME HOW MUCH RESPECT AND CONFIDENCE YOU, YOURSELF, HAVE IN EACH ONE— A GREAT DEAL, QUITE A LOT, SOME, OR VERY LITTLE?"*

Institution	A Great Deal, Quite a Lot	Some, Very Little, None
The church or organized religion	66%	32%
The public schools	58	38
The Supreme Court	44	45
Congress	42	50
Newspapers	39	58
Television	37	61
Labor unions	30	60
Big business	26	60

* The findings in the table above are based on in-person interviews with 1,531 adults interviewed during the period May 4–7, 1973.

CLERGYMEN'S ESTIMATE OF RELIGION'S INFLUENCE

From *Religion in America 1971*, Gallup Opinion Index, April 1971, Report No. 70, p. 8

Clergy	Increasing Influence	Losing Influence	Staying the Same	Don't Know
Protestant ministers	26%	58%	13%	3%
Catholic priests	24	61	12	3
Jewish rabbis	14	63	20	3

INFLUENCE OF SERMONS: SOCIOLOGISTS' VIEWS

From Rodney Stark, et al., *Wayward Shepherds: Prejudice and the Protestant Clergy* (New York: Harper & Row, 1970), p. 32

EDITOR'S SUMMARY:
· Belief in Christian teachings is often incompatible with concern for Christian ethics.

- Many clergymen say their sermons fall upon "deaf ears."
- Prejudice, hatred and selfishness appear to be unaffected by exhortations from the pulpit.
- Although the sermon is the essential medium for pastoral influence, it appears to be ineffective as a moral guide to the parishioners: many ministers seem to feel unable to fulfill the role of shepherds guiding their flock. [LR]

OPTIMISM REGARDING FUTURE OF RELIGION

From Gallup Poll release April 11, 1971 (Gallup Poll, Religious Surveys Division, Princeton, N.J.). The views of clergymen were recorded in a nationwide mail survey of clergymen of all faiths, conducted in February and March, utilizing random sampling methods. Questionnaires were received from a total of 2517 clergymen, including 1192 Protestants, 845 Catholics, 421 Jews, and 59 of other faiths.

Note: The following are verbatim excerpts from the Gallup summary. [LR]

Turning to the positive side of the balance sheet, some cause for optimism about the future of religion in the U.S. is seen in the views of younger versus older clergymen, as well as in the fact that discontent with the church does not arise out of a weakening of basic religious convictions.

More specifically, here is the evidence:

- Young clergymen of all faiths (those under 40 years of age) are considerably less likely than are older clergymen to say that religion as a whole is *losing* its influence on American life.
- Younger clergymen are considerably more likely than are older clergymen to say that changes presently going on in the church will make it possible for the church to better teach the aims of Christianity.

Younger clergymen, however, are far from ready to kick over all the traces of organized religion. Large majorities of both Protestant and Catholic clergymen under 40 believe a person *cannot* be a good Protestant or Catholic if he does not attend church regularly.

These findings are particularly significant since this younger generation of clergymen, accounting for more than a third of the nation's total, will largely determine the course of religion in the decades ahead.

- The movement toward Protestant-Catholic unity is backed by solid majorities of Protestant and Catholic clergymen of all ages.
- Although many clergymen—particularly the younger ones—express discontent with the church as an institution, there is no evidence of a turning away from God and other basic religious beliefs, even among those clergymen who have at some point considered leaving the religious life.

Nor has any erosion in basic beliefs been found among the public as a whole. Americans have, in fact, held firmly to basic religious beliefs over the last 20 years, while a dramatic decline in beliefs has taken place in many European nations during this period of time.

In sum, discontent among clergy and laity does not arise from a weakening of religious convictions, but from a reluctance to accept certain aspects of institutionalized religion.

Many clergymen call for the church to be more "relevant." At the same time, there is widespread feeling that the spiritual life of the individual should not be neglected at the expense of social involvement.

Protestant ministers by the ratio of 4-to-1 say churches should be mainly concerned with the spiritual life of the individual rather than problems of society as a whole, although many say "both." Catholic priests are evenly divided in their views, while rabbis are nearly 3-to-1 on the side that problems of society as a whole should be the primary concern of churches and synagogues.

XXIV / INTERMARRIAGE—STATISTICS, OPINIONS, AND CONVERSION DATA: CATHOLICS, PROTESTANTS, AND JEWS*

AMERICAN ATTITUDES TOWARD INTERMARRIAGE

EDITOR'S NOTE:

On November 19, 1972, the Gallup Poll published data on the attitudes of American adults to both interfaith and interracial marriages, comparing the findings in 1970 to a similar poll made in 1968.

I have summarized the results below. (See *The New York Times*, November 19, 1972, p. 12.)

APPROVAL OF MARRIAGES BETWEEN PROTESTANTS AND CATHOLICS

1968	63%
1972	72

APPROVAL OF MARRIAGE BETWEEN JEWS AND NON-JEWS

1968	59%
1972	67

APPROVAL OF MARRIAGES BETWEEN WHITES AND BLACKS

1968	20%
1972	29

Increased tolerance was found in all levels and regions of the United States, including the South.

A comparison of American attitudes to those prevailing in twelve other nations showed:

* See also Part Two, Chapter XXV, "Jews."

- Marriages between Catholics and Protestants were more approved by seven other nations, and less approved by five.
- Marriages between Jews and non-Jews were more approved in Sweden, Finland, and France, and less approved in nine other nations. [LR]

OPINIONS ON INTERMARRIAGE: 1969
From *Gallup Opinion Index, February 1969*

The number of Protestants and Catholics who say that they would approve of marriage between the two faiths is about the same as it was ten years before, in 1959.

"DO YOU APPROVE OR DISAPPROVE OF MARRIAGE BETWEEN CATHOLICS AND PROTESTANTS?"

Faith	Approve	Disapprove	No Opinion
Catholics (1959)	72%	23%	5%
Protestants (1959)	58	35	7
Catholics (1969)	79	13	8
Protestants (1969)	57	26	17

Both groups showed slightly more reservation when asked whether they would approve or disapprove of marriage between Jews and non-Jews, though the shift was predominantly to "No Opinion" rather than simple disapproval. The results of the survey are as follows:

"DO YOU APPROVE OR DISAPPROVE OF MARRIAGE BETWEEN JEWS AND NON-JEWS?"

Faith	Approve	Disapprove	No Opinion
Catholics	75%	14%	11%
Protestants	52	25	23

Little variation in response to either mixed marriage situation was noted by age, sex, or education. The overall tendency, however, was for the younger, the men, and the better educated to register somewhat greater approval.

The answers showed little difference with respect to region, except for the South, where mixed marriage met with significantly less approval.

ATTITUDES TOWARD MARRIAGES BETWEEN CHRISTIANS AND JEWS

EDITOR'S NOTE:

A Gallup Poll (November 1972) disclosed the following "general public acceptance" of marriages between Jews and non-Jews (Council of Jewish Federations and Welfare Funds study, *The New York Times,* February 11, 1973, Section 4):

1968	......	59% approved
1972	......	67% approved	[LR]

ATTITUDES OF JEWS TOWARD INTERMARRIAGE

EDITOR'S NOTE:

Among Jews, the approval of intermarriage is slightly less wide. Those opposed to intermarriage between Jews and non-Jews (Gallup Poll data, *Newsweek,* March 1, 1971, p. 57):

1965	......	83% opposed
1971	......	41% opposed	[LR]

CATHOLICS AND INTERMARRIAGE: APOSTOLIC LETTER

EDITOR'S NOTE:

The text on which this apostolic letter was based is *Matrimonia Mixta,* issued by Pope Paul VI on March 31, 1970.

Roman Catholic doctrine on marriage was redefined in several historic aspects (as will be seen below) by a promulgation of Vatican II: *Pastoral Constitution on the Church in the Modern World* (Nos. 48–51). [LR]

Excerpts from a statement (*Implementation of the Apostolic Letter on Mixed Marriages*) approved by the National Conference of Catholic Bishops, November 16, 1970, effective in the United States since January 1, 1971

AIM OF CHURCH

Within marriage the Church seeks always to uphold the strength and stability of marital union and the family which flows from it.

As the Apostolic Letter observes, the "perfect union of mind and full communion of life" to which married couples aspire can be more readily achieved when both partners share the same Catholic belief and life. For this reason, the Church greatly desires that Catholics marry Catholics and generally discourages mixed marriages.

Yet, *recognizing that mixed marriages do occur, the Church, upholding the principles of Divine Law, makes special arrangements for them.* [Italics added.] And, recognizing that these marriages do at times encounter special difficulties, the Church wishes to see that special help and support are extended to the couples concerned.

PASTORAL CONCERN

The Apostolic Letter . . . recognizes that ". . . the canonical discipline on mixed marriages cannot be uniform and must be adapted . . ." and "the pastoral care to be given to the married people and children of marriage" must also be adapted "according to the distinct circumstances of the married couple and the differing degrees of their ecclesiastical communion." Consequently, pastors, in exercising their ministry in behalf of marriages that unite Catholics and others will do so with zealous concern and respect for the couples involved . . .

In such marriages, the conscientious devotion of the Catholic to the Catholic Church is to be safeguarded, and the conscience of the other partner is to be respected. This is in keeping with the principle of religious liberty. (Cf. *Declaration on Religious Freedom.* (No. 30).

VALUES IN MARRIAGE

The sacred character of all valid marriages, including those which the Church does not consider as sacramental, is recognized. [Italics added.]

The broad areas of agreement which unite Christians and Jews in their appreciation of the religious character of marriage should be kept significantly in mind. (Cf. *Joint Statement on Marriage and Family Life in the United States,* issued by the United States Catholic Conference, the National Council of the Churches of Christ, and the Synagogue Council of America, June 8, 1966.)

In this context, it should be clearly noted that, while Catholics are required to observe the Catholic form of marriage for validity, unless dispensed by their bishop, *the Catholic Church recognizes the reality of marriages contracted validly among those who are not Christians and among those Christians separated from us.* [Italics added.]

SACRAMENTAL MARRIAGE

In addition to the sacred character of all valid marriages, still more must be said of *marriages between a Catholic and another baptized Christian. According to our Catholic tradition, we believe such marriages to be truly sacramental.* [Italics added.] The Apostolic Letter states that there exists between the persons united in them a special "communion of spiritual benefits." . . .

MIXED MARRIAGES

Pastoral experience, which the Catholic Church shares with other religious bodies, confirms the fact that marriages of persons of different beliefs involve special problems related to the continuing religious practice of the concerned persons and to the religious education and formation of their children.

. . .

The Catholic party to a mixed marriage is required to declare his (her) intention of continuing practice of the Catholic faith and to promise to do all in his power to share his faith with children born of the marriage by having them baptized and raised as Catholics. *No declarations or promises are required of the non-Catholic party, but he (she) must be informed of the declaration and promise made by the Catholic.* [Italics added.]

. . .

Mixed marriages may take place with a Nuptial Mass.

A non-Catholic minister may not only attend a marriage but may also address, pray with and give his blessing to the couple following the marriage ceremony.

If a dispensation from the canonical form of marriage is granted by a bishop, a non-Catholic minister can officiate at a mixed marriage. [Italics added.]

FORM OF MARRIAGE

A Catholic is required, for validity and lawfulness, to contract marriage —with another Catholic or with a non-Catholic—in the presence of a competent priest or deacon and two witnesses.

There are two exceptions to this law. A Roman Rite Catholic (since Mar. 25, 1967) or an Eastern Rite Catholic (since Nov. 21, 1964) can contract marriage validly in the presence of a priest of a separated Eastern Rite Church, provided other requirements of law are complied with. . . .

With these two exceptions, and aside from cases covered by special permission, the Church *does not regard as valid any marriages involving Catholics which take place before non-Catholic ministers of religion or civil officials.*

An excommunication formerly in force against Catholics who celebrated marriage before a non-Catholic minister was abrogated in a decree issued by the Sacred Congregation for the Doctrine of the Faith on Mar. 18, 1966. [Italics added.]

The ordinary place of marriage is the parish of the bride, of the Catholic party in case of a mixed marriage, or of an Eastern rite groom.

Church law regarding the form of marriage does not affect non-Catholics in marriages among themselves. *The Church recognizes as valid the*

*marriages of non-Catholics before ministers of religion and civil officials,
unless they are rendered null and void on other grounds.* [Italics added.]

IMPEDIMENTS

Impediments to marriage are factors which render a marriage unlawful
or invalid.

Prohibitory Impediments, which make a marriage *unlawful but do not
affect validity:*

- simple vows of virginity, perpetual chastity, celibacy, to enter a religious order or to receive sacred orders;
- difference of religion, which obtains *when one party is a Catholic and
the other is a baptized non-Catholic.*

The impediment of legal relationship is not in force in the U.S. [Italics
added.]

Diriment Impediments, which make a marriage invalid as well as unlawful. . . .

- disparity of worship, which obtains when one party is a Catholic and
the other party is unbaptized . . .
- religious profession of the solemn vow of chastity . . .

* * *

Dispensations from Impediments: Persons hindered by impediments
either may not or cannot marry unless they are dispensed therefrom in
view of reasons recognized in canon law. Local bishops can dispense from
the impediments most often encountered (e.g., difference of religion, disparity of worship) as well as others.

Decision regarding some dispensations is reserved to the Holy See.

* * *

A legitimate and consummated marriage of a baptized and an unbaptized person can be dissolved by the pope in virtue of the Privilege of
Faith, also called the Petrine Privilege.

* * *

DIFFICULTIES

A number of the particular difficulties faced by Catholics and other
Christians in mixed marriages result from the division among Christians.
However successful these marriages may be, they do not erase the pain of
that wider division. Yet this division need not weaken these marriages;
and, given proper understanding, they may lead to a deep spiritual unity
between the spouses.

RELIGIOUS EDUCATION

Beyond this, parents have the right and the responsibility to provide for
the religious education of their children. This right is clearly taught by

Vatican II: "Since the family is a society in its own original right, it has the right freely to live its own domestic religious life under the guidance of parents. Parents, moreover, have the right to determine, in accordance with their own religious beliefs, the kind of religious education that their children are to receive" (*Declaration on Religious Freedom* No. 5).

It is evident that in preparing for a mixed marriage, the couple will have to reach decisions and make specific choices in order to fulfill successfully the responsibility that is theirs toward their children in this respect. It is to be hoped for their own sake that in this matter the couple may reach a common mind.

· · ·

In reaching a concrete decision concerning the baptism and religious education of children, both partners should remember that neither thereby abdicates the fundamental responsibility of parents to see that their children are instilled with deep and abiding religious values.

In this the Catholic partner is seriously bound to act in accord with his faith which recognizes that: "This is the unique Church of Christ which in the Creed we avow as one, holy, catholic and apostolic. . . ."

· · ·

This faith is the source of a serious obligation in conscience on the part of the Catholic, whose conscience in this regard must be respected.

OPINIONS BY GROUPS

EDITOR'S NOTE:

For data and comparisons of how Americans feel about marrying within or outside their own faith, polls were taken in 1965 and 1952, which may be of interest to those who wish to chart such trends as can be discerned. (See Martin Marty, Stuart E. Rosenberg, and Andrew M. Greeley, *What Do We Believe?*, New York: Meredith Press, 1968, pp. 262–263.) [LR]

INTERMARRIAGE IN A DENOMINATIONAL SOCIETY: COMPARISON OF RATES AND RELIGIOUS GROUPS

From Andrew M. Greeley, "Religious Intermarriage in a Denominational Society," National Opinion Research Center (NORC) report, *American Journal of Sociology*, May 1970, pp. 949–952

The evidence in these studies seems to indicate that Jews are the least likely to marry members of other faiths, Catholics most likely, and Protestants somewhere in between. *Approximately four-fifths of the members of each of the four Protestant denominations are married to people whose present religious affiliation is the same as their own.* [Italics added.] Not only are Protestants married to other Protestants, *but they are married to Protestants who share the same denominational affiliation.* [Italics added.]

For Catholics and Jews it is important that one marry within one's own denomination (and far more important for Jews than for Catholics). When Catholics marry into other denominations, the non-Catholic is likely to convert. Protestants may marry across denominational lines, but then denominational change occurs in order to maintain religious homogeneity in the family environment. . . .

In summary, then, one may say that America is still very much a denominational society to the extent that denominational homogeneity in marriage exists for at least three-quarters of the major religious denominations.

INTERMARRIAGE AND CONVERSION:
CATHOLICS, PROTESTANTS, AND JEWS

From Bernard Lazerwitz, "Intermarriage and Conversion: A Guide for Future Research," *Jewish Journal of Sociology*, June 1971, pp. 305–308. This study was made possible by grants from the National Science Foundation and the Florence Heller-Jewish Welfare Board Research Center. *Note:* All italics have been added.

SOURCE OF DATA

The intermarriage data to be presented were gathered as part of a survey of religio-ethnic identification in the Chicago, Illinois, metropolitan area. The survey involved 572 Jewish, 464 white Protestant, and 257 white Catholic interviews. All respondents resided in Cook County (including Chicago) or contiguous areas in eastern DuPage and southern Lake counties in Illinois during 1966 and 1967. A disproportionately selected and multi-stage area probability sample was used to pick respondent housing units within each religio-ethnic community.

The characteristics and consequences of intermarriage and conversion have been long-standing major concerns and "scare" topics among both Jews and Christians. In turn, these concerns have stimulated a large number of research endeavors.

. . .

Collectively the studies of Jewish intermarriages have revealed the following demographic information:

a. *Low, but increasing, intermarriage levels.* The United States Census Bureau's (1958) Current Population Survey, taken in March 1957, reports that 7 percent of existing Jewish marriages were with non-Jews. However, *all researchers agree that in this century the per-*

centage of Jews married to non-Jews rises considerably with number of generations in an industrial diaspora country. For example, the Springfield and Providence surveys by Goldstein (1968: 145–48) and Goldstein and Goldscheider (1968: 155–57) report that 4.4 and 4.5 percent of Jewish households were based on intermarriages but that the children of respondents have intermarriage rates of 9 percent and 6 percent, respectively.

b. Intermarriage rates appear to be *highest in large growing Jewish communities and in the very small ones.* For instance, Rosenthal (1963) reports that a substantial (for the United States) 13 percent of Washington, D.C. Jewish marriages were intermarriages, and that the small Jewish communities of the state of Iowa averaged a 42 percent intermarriage rate between 1953 and 1959.

c. *Many more Jewish men intermarry than do Jewish women.*

d. *The intermarried have a higher proportion who are in their second, or more, marriage. . . .*

e. The typical convert to Judaism is a non-Jewish woman marrying a Jewish man. Furthermore, according to Goldstein and Goldscheider (1968) the conversion rate is on the increase. Among their intermarried couples 60 years old or older, none of the non-Jews had been converted to Judaism. Among those intermarried couples under 40 years, 70 percent of the non-Jews had been so converted.

f. *All students of intermarriage agree that very few Jews are converted to other faiths.*

. . .

Students of *Protestant-Catholic intermarriages* have found:

a. *Rather sizable Catholic intermarriage rates.* For example, Greeley (1964) reports that 12 percent of his respondents in a national sample of Catholics were intermarried. The Current Population Survey of March 1957 reported that 21 percent of married Catholics had non-Catholic spouses and 9 percent of married Protestants had non-Protestant spouses.

b. As in the case of the Jews, Greeley (1964) finds that *the intermarriage rate increases as the proportion of the Catholic population declines.*

c. Unlike the case of the Jews, Greeley (1964) finds that *Catholic women are considerably more likely to intermarry than are Catholic men.* Salisbury (1964) also states that more Protestant women intermarry than do their men.

d. As among Jewish intermarriages, Salisbury (1964) reports *a divorce rate of 14 percent for Protestant–Catholic marriages in contrast to 5 percent for marriages in which both spouses are Catholics and 8 percent when both are Protestants.*

e. As with Jews, most conversions to Catholicism or Protestantism are results of intermarriages. After examining the available research literature, *Salisbury (1964) concludes that there are about equal conversion rates among the Protestant and Catholic religious communities.*

f. Salisbury (1969) observes that Protestant women are converted at a higher rate than Protestant men and Catholic men and women.

. . .

A quantity of intermarriage and conversion data from the Chicago area has just been examined. It is now possible to leap beyond its narrow confines and to set out the following generalizations about the intermarriage process.

A. CONVERTS

1. Converts usually melt successfully into their new religio-ethnic community.
2. They are often religiously and organizationally more active than those born into a religio-ethnic community.
3. They come of parents who were marginally attached to their childhood faiths.
4. Converts have received less religious training and education than other members of their childhood faiths.

B. SPOUSES OF CONVERTS

1. The spouses of converts, too, are quite active religiously and organizationally in their faiths.
2. They have received considerable religious training and education.
3. They have a childhood and adolescent history of activity in their religio-ethnic communities.
4. Hence, as fairly solid members of their religio-ethnic community, it is to be expected that they would only intermarry with marginal members of other faiths.
5. and that such marginal members would regard it as 'the natural thing' to be converted.
6. *Typically, it is the men who become spouses of converts and the women who are the converts. This applies to all groups.* Hence, even among intermarried Jews, it is expected that intermarried Jewish women will often be more remote from Judaism and more frequently converted to other faiths than intermarried Jewish men.

C. RELIGIOUSLY HETEROGENEOUS MARRIAGES

1. Those who intermarry without conversion will frequently be marginal religio-ethnic members marrying marginal members of other religio-ethnic groups.
2. They will frequently come of parents who had reduced, or marginal, religio-ethnic attachments.
3. They will have had less religious training and education than most members of their childhood faiths.

4. After marriage, they and their spouses will frequently further reduce, if not fully eliminate, any involvement with both their childhood faiths.
5. Such people often deliberately seek out marital partners from other religio-ethnic groups. . . . The people falling into this type frequently seek intermarriage or are highly indifferent to religio-ethnic backgrounds.
6. If a marginal man marries a not-so marginal woman, their children will be brought up in the wife's faith, but usually the man will not be converted.
7. Typically, the presence of different, and marginal, faith backgrounds in the same family will neutralize any tendencies towards religio-ethnic activities. If such a situation becomes intolerable with regard to the rearing of children, such a couple will seek out a mutually 'neutral' faith such as Unitarianism in the United States.

D. DENOMINATION CHANGERS

1. This group differ little from most members of their faith.
2. In all probability their change of denomination is frequently a function of geographical or socio-economic mobility rather than meaningful religious change.
3. More traditional denominations will find that *members change to those less traditional denominations which better facilitate adjustment to and activity in modern urban industrial society*. Hence, the children of Orthodox Jews become Reform or Conservative Jews; children of fundamentalist Protestants become members of main-line Protestant denominations. Since the changes from the eastern European orthodox milieu have been so great and abrupt, such denominational changes are considerably more frequent among Jews than among fundamentalist Protestants, who have undergone a lesser and slower rate of social change.

. . .

It is now suggested that contemporary intermarriages in all three religious communities show a greatly reduced percentage of deviants, a moderate reduction in the percentage of those marginal to their religio-ethnic community, and the appearance of a substantial minority of intermarried people who have and maintain religio-ethnic involvement. It is this last group whose spouses are converted.

The tables permit one to contrast the small Jewish intermarriage group with a much larger all-Jewish marriage group whose family members typically rank low on the identification indices. The contrast shows that *the basic threat to Jewish continuity does not stem from intermarriage. Rather, intermarriage (without conversion) is but a symptom of diaspora Jewry's growing dissatisfaction with contemporary Jewish institutions and cultural forms.*

These generalizations, as they apply to Jews, will soon be fully tested on the much larger number of interviews with Jews, intermarried and not, to be obtained by the forthcoming national survey of the United States Jewish population. Most importantly, the prior statement of many of the identity concepts and generalizations guiding this major Jewish survey ensures that the basic advantage of concept testing will be obtained and post hoc formulations reduced.

RESEARCH ON MIXED MARRIAGES

EDITOR'S NOTE:

More recent data than those which follow will be found in the studies cited above made by Bernard Lazerwitz and by Father Andrew M. Greeley, for the National Research Council Center (NORC).

The Judson and Mary Landis observations (below) contain valuable observations and data—some of which have changed dramatically in the decade following publication of their work. These changes may be seen, and their significance appraised, in the preceding pages of this section. [LR]

Excerpts quoted from Judson T. Landis and Mary G. Landis, "Mixed Marriages—Research Finding," Sex Ways—in Fact and Faith: Bases for Christian Family Policy, Evelyn M. Duvall and Sylvanus M. Duvall, eds. (New York: Association Press, 1961), pp. 84–86, 87–89

CATHOLIC-PROTESTANT MARRIAGES

The most common type of mixed religious marriage in the United States is the marriage of Catholic to Protestant. Early in the twentieth century most Catholics, numerically speaking, came as immigrants to the United States; therefore, in many cases Catholic-Protestant marriages were mixed also by nationality and involved differences in ways of living.* . . .

In spite of the fact that Protestants as well as Catholics oppose interfaith marriages, such marriages are very common. *Studies show that today from one-fourth of the Catholics in some dioceses to three-fourths in other dioceses marry outside their faith.* [Italics added.] These figures are surprising to many Protestants who know of the Catholic policy of putting strong pressure on their young people to marry within their own faith. Protestant pressure against mixed marriages is not so strong nor so consistent as is the Catholic.

When university students are questioned about whether they would be willing to marry outside their own faith, Catholic young people report greater willingness than either Protestant or Jewish young people . . .

* But see "Characteristics of the Population by Ethnic Origin," *Current Population Reports*, U.S. Bureau of the Census, No. 221, 1971, p. 20. [LR]

Jews report less willingness than either Catholics or Protestants. Moreover, Catholic young people report that although they would be willing to marry a Protestant, they would not be willing to change to the faith of the mate. Young Protestants express less willingness to make a mixed marriage. But a higher proportion of them report that if they should marry a Catholic, they would be willing also to change to the faith of the mate (from a study of 3,000 University of California students, 1955).

Perhaps one factor underlying the attitude of the Catholic young people is their confidence in the Catholic policy dealing with mixed marriages. The Catholic Church requires that parties to a mixed marriage sign the Antenuptial Agreement, and if the marriage is to be ecclesiastically valid the non-Catholic member must, in addition, take instruction in the Catholic faith. Protestants and Jews have no similar requirements.° . . .

Sociologists interested in the success or failure rate of mixed marriages have made several studies of Catholic-Protestant marriages. The studies have found the following:

- All studies showed that the divorce rate is lowest when Catholics and Protestants marry within their faith group.
- The divorce rate is three to four times higher in Catholic-Protestant mixed marriages which have produced children.
- There is strong evidence to show that spousal differences over the religious training of the children is a major factor causing disharmony in Catholic-Protestant marriages.
- Although couples sign the Antenuptial Agreement, in which they promise to bring up the children in the Catholic faith, in actual practice the children are more often brought up in the faith of the mother, whether she is Catholic or Protestant.
- The divorce rate is by far the highest in mixed marriages in which the wife is Protestant and the husband is Catholic.
- There is some evidence to indicate that the best solution, as far as marital success is concerned, is for one of the couple to accept the faith of the other.
- As to what happens to the religious life of people who make mixed marriages, the studies reveal that these couples seem to follow one of three patterns: one or both drop out of church; both go to their individual churches and try to maintain their separate faiths; or one gives up his faith and accepts the faith of the other. The predominant pattern seems to be the first mentioned, whereby the parents and their children tend to have little to do with organized religion.

. . . Studies show that young people who are strong in their faith and who come from families devout in their religious beliefs are less willing to state that they would make a mixed marriage. This applies to all major faith groups. . . .

Other studies show that those who rate high in religiousness in all of

° But see the new guidelines for Catholics, pp. 551 ff. [LR]

the faith groups have a high happiness rating in marriage and a low divorce rate. Success in marriage is closely related to whether the married couple have religious or non-religious families. In other words, the non-religious are more willing to enter mixed marriages, but the non-religious also have characteristics that are associated with less successful marriage even if their marriages are not across faith lines. . . .

Successful marriages tend to run in families. Children tend to marry into families who have values similar to their own family values; they tend to marry those who come from the same socio-economic-educational-religious backgrounds. . . .

JEWISH-GENTILE MARRIAGES

The Jewish-Gentile marriage is mixed not only in religion but also in other aspects of culture. Differences in food habits, holidays, and days of rest are involved. Because of these cultural differences and because the Jews strongly urge their people to marry within their group, relatively few Jewish-Gentile marriages take place. Various studies have shown that approximately 95 percent of Jewish marriages are within the faith.[*] In the interfaith marriages that do occur, the Jewish man is much more likely to marry outside the faith than the Jewish woman. . . .

[*] This is no longer true: 16.8 percent of American Jews are married to non-Jews. [LR]

"JESUS MOVEMENTS"

See Part Two, Chapter XXVII, "Pentecostal and Charismatic Movements in the 1970s"

XXV / JEWS

POPULATION FIGURES

From the *American Jewish Year Book, 1972*, Vol. 73 (New York: American Jewish Committee and the Jewish Publication Society of America, 1972), pp. 386–387

U.S. population (1971)	206,256,000
Jews in U.S. (1971)	6,059,730
Jews in U.S. (increase over 1970)	285,000

JEWISH POPULATION IN THE UNITED STATES, 1971

State	Estimated Jewish Population	Total Population	Estimated Jewish Percentage of Total
Alabama	9,140	3,479,000	0.26%
Alaska	300	313,000	0.10
Arizona	21,000	1,849,000	1.14
Arkansas	3,030	1,944,000	0.16
California	721,045	20,223,000	3.56
Colorado	26,475	2,283,000	1.16
Connecticut	105,000	3,081,000	3.41
Delaware	9,000	558,000	1.61
Dist. of Col.	15,000	741,000	2.02
Florida	260,000	7,041,000	3.69
Georgia	25,650	4,664,000	0.55
Hawaii	1,500	789,000	0.19
Idaho	630	732,000	0.09
Illinois	284,285	11,196,000	2.54
Indiana	24,275	5,274,000	0.46
Iowa	8,610	2,852,000	0.30
Kansas	2,100	2,258,000	0.09
Kentucky	10,745	3,282,000	0.33
Louisiana	16,115	3,681,000	0.44
Maine	7,295	1,003,000	0.73
Maryland	187,110	4,000,000	4.68
Massachusetts	267,440	5,758,000	4.64
Michigan	93,530	8,997,000	1.04
Minnesota	34,475	3,881,000	0.89
Mississippi	4,125	2,226,000	0.19
Missouri	84,325	4,749,000	1.78
Montana	845	708,000	0.12
Nebraska	8,290	1,512,000	0.55

State	Estimated Jewish Population	Total Population	Estimated Jewish Percentage of Total
Nevada	3,380	507,000	0.67
New Hampshire	4,000	762,000	0.52
New Jersey	412,465	7,300,000	5.65
New Mexico	2,700	1,030,000	0.26
New York	2,535,870	18,391,000	13.79
North Carolina	10,165	5,146,000	0.20
North Dakota	1,250	625,000	0.20
Ohio	158,560	10,778,000	1.47
Oklahoma	5,940	2,610,000	0.23
Oregon	8,785	2,158,000	0.41
Pennsylvania	471,930	11,879,000	3.97
Rhode Island	22,280	960,000	2.32
South Carolina	7,815	2,627,000	0.30
South Dakota	760	670,000	0.11
Tennessee	17,415	3,990,000	0.44
Texas	67,505	11,460,000	0.59
Utah	1,900	1,099,000	0.17
Vermont	1,855	458,000	0.40
Virginia	41,215	4,714,000	0.87
Washington	15,230	3,449,000	0.44
West Virginia	4,880	1,752,000	0.28
Wisconsin	32,150	4,476,000	0.72
Wyoming	345	340,000	0.10
TOTALS	6,059,730	206,256,000	2.94

FAITH AND RELIGIOUS OBSERVANCE

Attendance (Weekly) at Synagogues and Temples
From *Religion in America 1971*, Gallup Opinion Index, April 1971, Report No. 70, p. 43

AVERAGE WEEKLY ATTENDANCE OF JEWS AT A SYNAGOGUE OR TEMPLE

1964	17%
1970	19

Note: This figure is far below national church attendance: in 1970, 42 percent of American adults (all faiths, including Jews) attended a church "in a typical week." [LR]

Profession of Faith

From a survey by Leonard J. Fein of 200 Jewish families, chosen at random, "in the Boston area," and 200 Jewish families, chosen at random, in London. (See digest in *The New York Times*, August 3, 1969, p. 16.)

ARE THE JEWS A CHOSEN PEOPLE, IN ANY SENSE?

Yes	38%
No	58

HOW OFTEN DO JEWS ATTEND RELIGIOUS SERVICES?

Several times a month	23%
Every few months or on major holidays	57
Less than once every few months	20

DO JEWS OBSERVE THE DIETARY (KOSHER) LAWS?

Yes	38%
No	58

From poll in *Newsweek*, March 1, 1971, p. 57

WHAT PERCENTAGE OF JEWS CONSIDER THEMSELVES RELIGIOUS?

43%

EDUCATION

From "The American Jew Today," *Newsweek*, March 1, 1971, p. 40

JEWS AND OTHER AMERICANS

Education	Jews	Total U.S. Population
Elementary school only	29%	40%
High school only	19	25
College graduates	17	7
Graduate school	13	4
College age now in college	80	40

From survey by Council of Jewish Federations and Welfare Funds (*The New York Times*, November 11, 1972, p. 36)

JEWS WHO HAVE BEEN GRADUATED FROM COLLEGE

Graduates	Percentage
MALES	
Age 50–64	34%
Age 25–29	71
FEMALES	
Age 50–64	29
Age 25–29	46

Note: The apparently huge discrepancy between the *Newsweek* poll figures and those of the Council of Jewish Federations may be resolved if one observes that the latter data deal not with percentages of the total Jewish population but with two widely separated generations: the 25–19-year-olds and the 50–64-year-olds. [LR]

CHANGES IN THE STATUS OF JEWISH WOMEN

EDITOR'S NOTE:

In 1973, the Committee on Jewish Law and Standards of the 1,100-member Rabbinical Assembly (Conservative) voted (9–4) that "men and women are to be included equally in the count of a required forum for Jewish public worship." The ruling is not, however, binding on Conservative Rabbis, who remain the authority on Jewish Law within their congregation.

Orthodox and Reform branches of Judaism are not affected by the Conservative action.

The Park Avenue Synagogue (Conservative) in New York, and five other synagogues, have included women in *minyans* for some time.

Reform Judaism has ordained women as rabbis.

The United Synagogue of America, which is an organization of Conservative laymen, voted 2–1 (on November 14, 1973) to allow women to take part in Jewish religious rituals—to be "counted" in a *minyan,* to be called "to read from the Torah," and to enjoy "equal opportunity . . . to assume positions of leadership [and] authority in all phases of congregational activity." [LR]

JEWS AND INTERMARRIAGE

EDITOR'S NOTE:

(See also the polls and data on Intermarriage in Part Two, Chapter XXIV.)

A three-year study sponsored by the Council of Jewish Federations and Welfare Funds, the coordinating organization for more than 235 local groups in North America, analyzed intermarriages in all cities with a Jewish population of 40,000 or more—plus a representative sample of towns or areas with less than that number.

The highlights are given below. (A summary will be found in *The New York Times,* November 11, 1972, p. 36.)

Figures

- Jews married to non-Jews: 16.8 percent. (The Jewish population in the United States is estimated by the American Jewish Council to be 5.8 million.)
- Jewish men married to non-Jewish women: 9.1 percent of the Jewish population.
- Jewish women married to non-Jewish men: 4.4 percent; 3.3 percent reported "no religious" preference or distinction but said that one of the partners "had ancestral Jewish roots."

It should be noted that in all of the figures above, "non-Jew" refers to religious status *at the time the couples first met*—hence, there are no data offered on conversion, before or after marriage, by one or the other spouse, to the faith of the partner. [LR]

- In "most" cases (no figures given) the children of marriage between a Jew and a non-Jew are raised as Jews, but
- When the husband is Jewish, the children are raised as Jews in "some two-thirds" of the total.

The above figures may be matched against those of the U.S. Bureau of the Census data for 1957 (*Current Population Reports,* February 5, 1958, series P-20, No. 79, pp. 2, 8, Table 6), which revealed that 7.2 percent of marriages involving Jews were intermarriages.

Almost one-third of American Jews *who married in the half-decade 1966–1971* took non-Jewish spouses.

This rate is more than twice the rate that prevailed in 1961–1966 —and more than 400 percent over the figures on intermarriage before 1960. (See the study of the Council of Jewish Federations and Welfare Funds, made public in 1972—as reported in *The New York Times,* "News of the Week" section, February 11, 1973.) [LR]

EDITOR'S SUMMARY:
The studies above agree that:

- Jews are least likely to marry members of other faiths, Catholics most likely, Protestants "somewhere in between." [Andrew M. Greeley, "Religious Intermarriage in a Denominational Society, National Opinion Research Center (NORC) report, *American Journal of Sociology,* May 1970, pp. 949–952.]
- Almost one-third of American Jews who married (1966–1971) took non-Jewish spouses. [*The New York Times,* February 11, 1973, Section 4.]
- The above figures are in marked contrast to the Lazerwitz study and the sources he cites, in which 1968 figures show 4.4 to 4.5 percent Jewish intermarriages. [Bernard Lazerwitz, "Intermarriage and Conversion," *Jewish Journal of Sociology,* June 1971, pp. 305–308.]
- More Jewish men than Jewish women marry non-Jews. [*Ibid.*]
- Intermarriage represents a net *gain* in the number of Jews—because of the number of conversions to Judaism by non-Jews marrying Jews and because of the number of children of intermarriages who are reared as Jews. [Leonard Fein study, *The New York Times,* August 3, 1969, p. 16.]
- Few Jews who intermarry are converted to another faith. [Lazerwitz, *op. cit.*]
- Intermarriage rates appear highest in large, growing Jewish communities—or in very small ones. [*Ibid.*]
- Intermarried Jews contain a larger proportion of second (or more) marriages than Jews who marry Jews. [*Ibid.*]
- Children of intermarried parents themselves intermarry more than children both of whose parents are Jews. [*Ibid.*]   [LR]

JEWISH WOMEN AND THE RABBINATE
See Part Two; Chapter XIII.

OPINIONS OF JEWS: ANTI-SEMITISM, PRIDE

From poll in Newsweek, March 1, 1971, p. 57

"IN THE LAST FEW YEARS, DO YOU THINK ANTI-SEMITISM IN THE U.S. HAS INCREASED OR DECREASED?"

Increased	Decreased	Same
34%	16%	41%

From Leonard Fein survey, The New York Times, August 3, 1969, p. 16

HOW DO JEWS EXPLAIN ANTI-SEMITISM?

As the result of teaching	over 33%
Because of ignorance	22
Because of jealousy	25

WHAT REASON IS GIVEN FOR THE RISE IN ANTI-SEMITISM (BY THOSE JEWS WHO BELIEVE IT HAS)?

Militant blacks	over 33%
"New Left" radicals	10
"Right wing" influence	8

From Newsweek poll, op. cit.

"IN THE LAST FEW YEARS, DO YOU THINK JEWS IN THE U.S. HAVE GENERALLY FELT AN INCREASING OR DECREASING SENSE OF PRIDE AS A GROUP?"

Increased	Decreased	Same
61%	5%	27%

DO JEWS VACATION IN PLACES WHERE THEY EXPECT TO FIND LARGE NUMBERS OF JEWS?

No:	80%

"DO YOU APPROVE OF THE EFFORTS OF THE JEWISH DEFENSE LEAGUE TO HELP SOVIET JEWRY BY HARASSING RUSSIAN DIPLOMATS?"

Approve	Qualified Approval	Disapprove
14%	11%	71%

INTERMARRIAGE: OPINIONS

Attitudes of Jews
From Leonard Fein study, *The New York Times*, August 3, 1969, p. 16

DO JEWS OPPOSE INTERMARRIAGE FOR THEIR CHILDREN?

Yes	58%
Yes, but would not interfere	15
Do not care	11
Depends on who	13

Data on Intermarriage
From *Newsweek* poll, March 1, 1971, p. 57

In a survey made six years ago, 83 percent of U.S. Jews were opposed to marriage with non-Jews. But now the opposition to intermarriage has dropped to 41 percent—and two-thirds of those opposed are over the age of 45. Indeed, 64 percent of those in the current poll report the impression that intermarriage has actually been increasing among their own acquaintances.

Ambivalence of Jews Toward Intermarriage

EDITOR'S NOTE:

The Mosaic laws, and Jewish religious and community pressures ever since, have emphasized Judaism's prohibition against the marriage of a Jew to one of another faith.

Current ambivalence about intermarriage (see below) is not so much anti-Gentile but reflects the extreme anxiety (among laymen no less than rabbis) that the very survival of Judaism (after a loss of 6 million Jews in the Nazi holocaust) appears to be threatened by a decline of marriages "within the faith," or an increase of marriages outside it. Rabbi Marc Tanenbaum, director of Interreligious Affairs of the influential American Jewish Committee, remarked recently that intermarriage threatens "Jewish survival, for without the Jewish community there will be no future for Judaism itself" (*The New York Times,* June 30, 1973, p. 36).

The historical and traditional attitude of Jews to intermarriage rests on a strict adherence to the provisions of *Halacha* (the religious laws of Judaism), under which the non-Jewish spouse must undergo a thorough and intensive study of Judaic law, ethics, rituals, dietary requirements, history, and so on, prior to formal conversion. Prospective non-Jewish bridegrooms are, in addition, required to undergo circumcision.

Since the requirements of Reform rabbis are considerably less stringent, and are not as universally applied, the Reform conversion process is not accepted by the Orthodox and Conservative rabbinate of America. [LR]

CONFLICTING ATTITUDES

There are very few issues so troubling to Jewish leaders, so divisive and "passionately polarized," as intermarriage. For at least sixty or seventy years, the marriage of Jews to non-Jews has been debated among the American rabbinate.

The fate and future of Judaism as a viable religious/ethnic/cultural force, with its own identity, lies at the roots of the debate. The implications of intermarriage may be judged by some typical comments from members of different sectors of Judaism:

Intermarriage involves nothing less than Jewish survival, some rabbis hold. "Without a Jewish community there will be no future for Judaism itself" (Rabbi Marc Tanenbaum, American Jewish Committee).

"Mixed marriages are a grave threat to the survival of Judaism" (Central Conference of American Rabbis).

"We live in an age of action. We cannot compel Jews to marry Jews, any more than we can compel Jews to be Jews" (Rabbi Irwin Fishbein).

"Not only has the threat of mixed marriages to Jewish survival increased, but . . . there is a greater danger of disunity within . . . Judaism today . . ." (Rabbi Ronald B. Gettelson).

Mixed marriages "are a signal to young kids that it's okay" (Rabbi Joseph B. Glaser, Central Conference of American Rabbis).

"I reject the survival argument. History shows lots of periods of extensive intermarriage, and we have survived . . . By the time a couple comes to a rabbi, they have already decided to get married. If he (the rabbi) refuses, then he is just driving both (bride and groom) away from the faith" (Rabbi Philip Schecter).

"Intermarriage may be the result rather than the cause of assimilation." The essential problem is the sense of Jewish identity—which is declining; but intermarriage is "not inconsistent with the preservation of Jewish identity": "Jewish behavior" among Jewish families has become "so minimal . . . that intermarrieds are in many cases equally Jewish, or perhaps more Jewish, than the non-intermarried" (George Johnson, Synagogue Council of America). [LR]

STORM WITHIN THE RABBINATE OVER INTERMARRIAGE

EDITOR'S NOTE:

"Intermarriages have reached epidemic proportions and threaten Jewish survival," reads an official resolution (June 26, 1973) of the Rabbinical Council of America—the leading body of Orthodox rabbis in the United States. The council moved to, according to its president, Rabbi Louis Bernstein, "remove ecclesiastical endorsement of spiritual genocide" by passing a strongly worded resolution that censured any rabbi who performed a "mixed marriage," and resolved to exercise pressure on Jewish secular organizations to exclude from their leadership ranks any rabbis who officiate at marriages between Jews and non-Jews—or any Jews who marry outside the faith.

On June 29, 1973, a two-thirds majority of 166 rabbis in the New York Board of Rabbis (a body formed in 1881 and representing 1,000 Orthodox, Conservative and Reform rabbis in the large metropolitan area of New York and its environs) voted to *bar from membership* any rabbis who perform mixed marriages.

The exclusion also includes rabbis who *refer* couples to other rabbis who will officiate at intermarriages.

This "historic" decision, as it was called by Rabbi William Berkowitz, who presided at the meeting, would not affect a barred rabbi from continuing as the spiritual leader of his congregation, nor fulfilling his other pastoral duties and responsibilities (preaching, teaching, education, counseling).

Behind these long-debated and dramatic events lay the ominous report of the Central Conference of American Rabbis, the Reform organization, which revealed that one-fifth of its members had in fact officiated at marriages between Jews and non-Jews.

In 1909, the Central Conference of American Rabbis adopted the view that mixed marriages are contrary to Jewish religious faith and tradition—and that such marriages should be discouraged. *But* the actual performance of mixed marriages was considered to be a matter for individual rabbis to decide, given "special conditions": conversion, circumcision for non-Jews, the promise to rear children as Jews, and so on.

This official stand was reaffirmed by the conference in 1947 and in 1971.

On June 14, 1972, a study of 600 Reform rabbis (out of 1,000 polled) revealed that 41 percent of the Reform rabbis in the United States "defy" tradition, and the explicit recommendations of their Central Conference, and do officiate at marriages between a Jew and a non-Jew.

Of this 41 percent, one-half stated that they do not require a pledge from the non-Jewish spouse to convert or urge the study of Judaism's religion, ethics, history, culture.

In June 1973, after years of intense pressure from the Orthodox and Conservative branches (and many of its most influential laymen), the Central Conference of American Rabbis officially disapproved of those Reform rabbis who perform mixed marriages.

A group of sixty rabbis later announced that they had formed an autonomous group that would "preserve the autonomous role of the rabbi"—that is, the individual rabbi's right to decide for himself whether to perform a mixed marriage. This group adopted an amendment that was "forced through" the Central Conference, many alleged, calling upon the conference to give cognizance to the fact that "historically its members have held and continue to hold divergent interpretations of Jewish tradition."

This amendment, carried by a vote of 209 to 168, received "a resounding ovation" and is taken to mean that the conference will apply no censuring sanctions against those Reform rabbis who continue to ignore its resolution and perform mixed marriages.

The resolution went on to urge that all Reform rabbis "assist fully in educating children of such mixed marriages as Jews," to provide the opportunity for a non-Jewish spouse to be converted to Judaism, and to encourage "a creative and consistent cultivation of involvement [by the partners] in the Jewish community and the synagogue." (See news accounts in *The New York Times* for June 15, 1972, p. 13; June 21, 1973, p. 32; and June 30, 1973, p. 36.) [LR]

FAMILY LIFE AND JUDAISM

EDITOR'S NOTE:

For 4,000 years, the Jewish family has been the very core, mortar, and citadel of Judaism's faith and the central reason for the survival of the Jews as a distinct ethnic culture. The Jewish home is a temple, according to Judaic law, custom, and tradition. "The Jewish family is what has preserved Judaism, while other groups perished" (Yehuda Rosenman, director of the American Jewish Committee's Communal Affairs Department, February 9, 1973, quoted in *The New York Times*).

The tumultuous social forces of our time have sent profound tremors of challenge and change throughout Jewry. The more conspicuous and disturbing of these are cited below.

Intermarriage

The dramatic increase of marriages between Jews and non-Jews, especially within recent decades (from 1966 to 1971, almost one-third of American Jews who married chose non-Jewish mates: see above) has eroded a growing sector of Jewish family life.

Divorce

Sociologists confirm the "staggering" rise in the divorce rate (30–35 percent) among Jews—especially in the years 1966–1973.

Birth Rate

The birth rate among Jews is said to have reached "the point of diminishing returns" and Jews "are not even reproducing themselves" (Rosenman, *ibid.*)

The net increase in the American Jewish population from 1970 to 1971 was only 285,000.

"Counterculture" Phenomena

The 1960s youth movements, which challenged or opposed the prevailing mores and institutions of American society, did not leave Judaism's youth unaffected.

Dramatic changes in sexual behavior, campus violence, "hippie" values, dropouts (whether from schools, accepted values of work and competition, the professions, conventional allegiances to parents, the home, the nation), the use of drugs, the excesses of revolution, the glorification of Castro and Mao Tse-tung—all these shook the Jewish no less than the Protestant or Catholic bastions of America.

Identity and Consciousness

The figures on intermarriage, attendance at temples or synagogues, observance of rituals, observance of the Sabbath, familiarity with Torah or Talmud, familiarity with Jewish history and culture—all these indices show a marked decline in the strength or fervor of Jews' sense of apartness, of their identity as Jews, of their emotional (no less than religious) commitment.

Conclusion

Every student of Judaism—Jewish or not—stresses the singular and central importance of the home in Jewish life, culture, and history. If the bulwark of the Jewish family is weakened, and if the conduit that the family has always been for the transmission of beliefs and values is broken, then the consequences for the future of Judaism are as grave as many of the experts whom I cite are warning us. [LR]

JEWS AND POLITICS

EDITOR'S NOTE:

It is a fact thoroughly documented by political analysts, sociologists, and public-opinion polls that American Jews are by tradition liberal vis-à-vis social legislation, and Democrat in party allegiance (63 percent in 1971; see Chapter XXVIII).

How have the upheavals of the 1960s—the civil rights movement, black protest, campus rebellion, sexual emancipation, women's liberation—affected the current and probable future political stance of American Jewry?

Contrary to the assumptions of many, and contrary to the energetic participation of Jewish youth and leaders in the movements catalogued above, the overriding liberalism of Jewish thought and values is certain *to resist new and extended radicalization* (*or extremism*).

In a thoughtful essay in the December 1970 issue of *Mainstream,* one of the best-informed students of Jewish life in America, Professor Nathan Glazer of Harvard, mobilizes an impressive array of data and insights to support the "new conservatism" (my phrasing) of American Jews. For formidable political and economic reasons, the "pragmatic interests" of American Jewry may be counted upon to draw back from further radicalization in the United States, across the whole broad front of social and economic issues. Let me list the factors:

1. The American Jewish community contains a predominant proportion of businessmen, salesmen, individual entrepreneurs (shopkeepers), small manufacturers, and professionals (teachers, doctors, lawyers, writers, musicians, painters).

2. These socioeconomic groups always suffer, swiftly and drastically, whenever and wherever a political order decreases free-

market activities and increases government power and controls.

3. Wherever radical regimes have introduced radical political/economic programs, Jewish groups have been penalized and driven out of viable occupations consonant with their skills and experience.

4. *All of the above are true even where there is not the slightest official commitment to a policy of anti-Semitism* or to any of its disguised or malignant manifestations. "Jews individually come upon hard times," said Professor Glazer, whenever radical political policies are instituted.

A dramatic illustration is offered in the case of Cuba, where Fidel Castro's regime, putatively committed to the equality and brotherhood of man, forced the Jewish community of Cuba to emigrate, virtually *in toto*. Why? Because Cuba was no longer a country in which businessmen, doctors, lawyers, and journalists could live and work without interference, harassment, or obloquy.

The same effects may be noted in European countries, especially those behind the Iron Curtain, ever since Lenin's short-lived and desperate New Economic Policy. The recent upsurge of Jewish requests for emigration from Soviet Russia (the country with the second largest Jewish population in the world, after the United States) underlines the point.

Professor Irving Kristol, an uncommonly clear-headed analyst of political and social perplexities, recently declared that Jews "have never had it so good as under the status quo" and that "we Jews may as well admit it, if only to ourselves."

To these professorial judgments, I may add that it is in the very nature of "Jewishness" to be antipathetic to governmental controls or politically sponsored indoctrination of what is desirable or good "for the people." For Jews are trained from their infancy to talk, to ask questions, to question and challenge, to debate and argue, to remain skeptical of promises and appraise them against results. Such intellectual reflexes *must* be offensive to any form of that totalitarian orthodoxy, however sugar-coated, which governs the leaders of states committed to socialist or quasi-socialist programs. These programs are of course designed in the hope that they will achieve noble, idealistic goals—by subordinating individual rights and private preferences to lofty, overriding "social" purposes.

I have yet to discover a single system or country dedicated to "social welfare" that has not in fact embraced, or been driven to enforce, programs that in the long run erode or undermine, diminish or doom, that bright exaltation of individual freedoms that was the essence of nineteenth-century conceptions of liberty.

In this context, Jews—whose entire religion and ethos rest on individual rights—find their fate negatively affected by the inevitable aggrandizements of authority by political powers, however altruistic their intentions and however laudable their professed purposes.

Only under a democratic order, and a maximization of individual choices, have the Jews of the world found an ordering of society in which they are granted (or permitted) safety, security, dignity, prospects for betterment—for themselves and their children—and that most invaluable of citizens' rights: recourse to democratic laws.

In defending our freedom, within which Americans are free to work, worship, or choose a life style ungoverned by political controls, Jews have necessarily been driven to reappraise the role of the free market (or "enlightened capitalism") as a guarantor of liberties —as against the promises and performance of socialist or communist states. The arguments in favor of democracy (and a free market) are "at least as strong as the arguments in favor of Socialism and Communism," remarked Professor Nathan Glazer; "the Jews are defending freedom as well as their own interests."

The argument takes on added force when one considers the persistent antagonism to Israel of all nondemocratic countries (Russia, China, the "Third World," African hegemonies). This hostility is so strong, reasons Glazer, that "the notion of a radicalized Jewish community [in the United States] seems very unlikely." Even Israeli Socialists have learned how virulent is the opposition to them by Arab Socialists, Iron Curtain Communists, the New Left in France and Italy, and so on. Nor can Jewish Socialists or liberals soon forget the rise of anti-Israel sentiment on American campuses—among Jewish New Left students.

The United States and Western Europe support Israel. And it is these countries that further and strengthen a society of heterogeneous groups and faiths. The potent impulse of all nonliberal political theorists/parties toward a centrally governed (and therefore homogenized) society bodes ill for ethnic diversity. It is only where and when political states have *not* tried to create homogeneous masses—and have permitted immense diversities of occupation, professions, creeds, and worship—that Jewish communities have been able to breathe and survive. [LR]

JEWISH HOLIDAYS
Extracts from Mordecai Soltes, *The Jewish Holidays* (New York: National Jewish Welfare Board, 1968)

A distinguishing characteristic of the Jewish religion is its emphasis on conduct and character, rather than on belief, faith or dogma. Judaism is synonymous with life and its ceremonial expression therefore embraces cultural and sociological as well as ritualistic elements. . . .

The Jewish calendar differs from the secular in that the former is based on the revolutions of the moon around the earth (lunar), while the latter is solar in character. The day begins and ends with sunset. The day preceding the Sabbath or a Jewish holiday is designated as *Ereb Shabbat* and *Ereb Yom Tob*.

There are twelve months in a normal year consisting of 29 or 30 days each, and their Hebrew names are: *Nisan* (falls about April), *Iyar* (May), *Sivan* (June), *Tammuz* (July), *Ab* (August), *Elul* (September), *Tishri* (October), *Heshvan* (November), *Kislev* (December), *Tebet* (January), *Shebat* (February), *Adar* (March). In a leap year . . . a thirteenth month is added, known as *Adar Sheni*, Second *Adar*. By means of this additional month, the lunar year (consisting of 354 days) is periodically brought into conformity with the solar year (365 days).

ROSH HASHANAH

Rosh Hashanah (literally, "head of the year") is observed in the beginning of the seventh month (*Tishri*), as the Jewish New Year.

Nisan is regarded as the first month of the Jewish calendar, and all the festivals are arranged according to this reckoning.

The first of *Tishri* marks the anniversary of the creation of the world, which occurred, according to tradition, over 5,700 years ago. Hence Jewish chronology begins the year with this day.

The name "*Rosh Hashanah*" does not occur in the Bible. Instead, it is referred to as the Day of the Blowing of the Trumpet, the Day of Memorial or Remembrance, and the Memorial of the Blowing of the *Shofar*. It is also considered the Day of Judgment (*Yom Hadin*), when all mankind is judged by the Creator, and the fate of each individual is inscribed in the Book of Life.

Rosh Hashanah inaugurates the Ten Days of Penitence, the most solemn season in the Jewish calendar, which has been set apart for retrospection and self-examination. The observance of the High Holy Days is characterized by a feeling of solemnity. Jews generally abstain from their daily occupations and participate in communal worship.

The home customs and ceremonies also reflect concern over the fate for the New Year. In addition to the recital of the *Kiddush* (the sanctification prayer) and the kindling of the festive lights, a piece of sweet apple is dipped in honey on the eve of *Rosh Hashanah* . . . "May it be God's will to grant us a good and sweet year." The bread, too, is dipped in honey, symbolizing the hope that . . . the approaching year be only of the most pleasant . . .

An outstanding feature of the synagogue service is the blowing of the *Shofar*, which serves to intensify the spirit of reverence and contributes toward the creation of an atmosphere of solemnity. Sixty to one hundred distinct sounds, arranged in various combinations, are blown . . . The *Shofar* is blown during the morning service before the Scroll is returned to the Holy Ark, and during the Additional Service. . . .

In the afternoon of the first day of *Rosh Hashanah* (if it does not fall on a Sabbath), pious Jews assemble along the banks of a stream, river or seashore, and recite verses from the prophets and appropriate prayers. . . .

The penitential days reach their culmination on the Day of Atonement (*Yom Kippur*), which is . . . regarded as the most sacred day in the Jewish year. It is frequently referred to as the Sabbath of Sabbaths. . . . It is customary to abstain from all food and drink from sunset on the eve of the Day of Atonement until the beginning of night in the following day. A large taper, sufficient to burn throughout the twenty-four hours of the fast, is kindled on the eve of *Yom Kippur*, in memory of the departed ones.

It is deemed appropriate to wear white shrouds on this solemn day, since white is a symbol of purity. The High Priest, in ancient times, wore white garments on *Yom Kippur*.

YOM KIPPUR—SYNAGOGUE SERVICE

The evening service of the Day of Atonement is preceded by the chanting of *Kol Nidre* (literally "all vows") which is repeated three times. It is a formal abrogation of all vows made under the influence of great emotional strain, and is intended to guard against oaths which may remain unfulfilled through negligence or forgetfulness. The dispensation from vows refers only to those which an individual voluntarily assumes for himself alone . . . No oath or promise involving another person, a community, or a court of justice is implied in the *Kol Nidre*.

The ritual of the Day of Atonement is replete with petitions for forgiveness for sins committed by all the worshipers present. In the "Confessions," transgressions are enumerated of which a particular individual may not be guilty. The prayers for pardon are uttered in behalf of all Israel.

According to Jewish tradition, a person will not be forgiven . . . for any sins committed against a fellow being unless he rights the wrong and makes amends . . .

SUKKOTH, THE FESTIVAL OF BOOTHS OR TABERNACLES

This festival was originally pastoral in nature and occurred during the time of the fruit harvest. It was also generally observed as thanksgiving . . . "for the bounties of nature during the previous year."

Sukkoth are temporary structures, especially built either in the yard or on the roof of a home, for the festival, and serve as a protection against the sun. They are not covered from above with board, but with detached branches, sparsely laid, "to allow the stars to shine through the roof." . . .

The *Sukkah* is the emblem of the *Galut* (Exile)—a temporary dwelling, dependent upon God's protection . . .

HANUKKAH, THE FESTIVAL OF DEDICATION

Hanukkah commemorates the successful struggle for religious liberty carried on by a small band of Israelites, led by the brave Maccabees, against the vast army of their Syrian oppressors, under the leadership of Antiochus, which culminated in the recapture of Jerusalem and the re-dedication of the Holy Temple (165 B.C.).

The celebration of *Hanukkah* begins on the twenty-fifth day of *Kislev*, the day on which the Temple was consecrated anew to the service of God, and lasts for eight days . . .

This holiday is also called the Feast of Lights or Illumination, since it is customary to kindle the *Hanukkah* lamp throughout the eight days of the festival. One light is kindled on the first night, and an additional one is lit on each succeeding evening until the last day, when eight lights are burned, exclusive of the "*Shamas*," which is a special candle used in lighting the others. . . .

PURIM

Purim is one of the minor historical festivals of the Jewish calendar, and occurs on the 14th day of *Adar*. Its observance is based on the narrative recorded in one of the five small Biblical scrolls or *Megillot*, known as the Book of Esther.

The events associated with the Feast of *Purim* occurred in Persia during the reign of Ahasuerus (Xerxes, 485–464 B.C.). Haman, haughty prime minister and arch anti-Semite, plotted to exterminate the entire Jewish people because a Jew, Mordecai, refused to bow down to him. His sinister designs were frustrated by the timely intervention of Queen Esther. . . .

It is customary to read *Megillat Esther* (the Scroll of Esther) in the synagogue and at home on the eve of the *Purim* festival, as well as on the following morning. . . . Whenever the reader mentions the name of

Haman, the children are permitted to stamp their feet, whirl their "greggers" or rattles, and resort to other noise-making devices.

Two important customs prevalent on this holiday are the giving of alms to the poor and the mutual exchange of presents between friends and relatives . . .

Exuberant joy is the keynote of the *Purim* festival. . . . Special dainties and sweets are consumed, including the triangular cakes known as *Haman Taschen* (Haman's hat). . . . In the evening all the members of the household are gathered [for a party].

PESACH, THE FESTIVAL OF FREEDOM

Passover (*Pesach*) is associated with the birth of the Jewish nation, the redemption of its ancestors from Egyptian bondage (1200 B.C.)—an epoch-making event in the early history of its people. . . .

During the Passover festival week Jews abstain from partaking of leavened bread or of any food prepared with leaven. Special sets of utensils and dishes are used, and *matzoth* or unleavened cakes are eaten, as a reminder of the Israelites' hurried departure from Egypt, when they had to bake their bread in haste, without permitting the dough to rise. . . .

A special service known as the *Pesach Seder* is conducted at home on the first two evenings of the Passover festival. "*Seder*" means "order," and refers to the order of the service arranged. . . .

The symbols included in the "*Seder*" . . . consist of the following: three *matzoth*, bitter herbs (*marror*), other vegetables—parsley, celery, lettuce (*karpas*), salt water, a combination made of nuts, apples, raisins and wine (*haroset*), a roasted lamb bone (*z'roa*), and a roasted egg.

Four cups of wine are drunk by every member of the family seated around the table, during the *Seder* service.

The *Haggadah* (literally, narrative), which contains the special ritual service of the evening, the story of Israel's exodus from Egypt, as well as some folk songs and ditties (*Had Gadya, Addir Hu*, etc.), is read aloud and sung.

Various phases of the *Seder* have been introduced primarily for the benefit of the children: They ask the "Four Questions" to which the narrative of the *Haggadah* is a reply.

A special goblet or a cup of wine is prepared for Elijah, the Prophet . . . and a child opens the door to admit the eagerly-awaited guest.

. . . The Bible also calls the *matzoth* "Bread of Affliction," reminding us of the affliction of the Israelites while under Pharaoh's yoke. Thus the unleavened bread is a symbol of both slavery and freedom. *Marror* symbolizes the bitter hardships endured in Egypt. *Haroset* resembles the brick and mortar used in Egypt (Exodus 1:14).

SHABUOTH, THE FESTIVAL OF WEEKS

Shabuoth (literally "Weeks") falls on the sixth day of *Sivan*, the third month of the Jewish calendar, which is exactly seven weeks after *Pesach*. . . .

Originally *Shabuoth* was observed as an agricultural feast, and marked the beginning of the wheat harvest. Later, *Shabuoth* served to commemorate . . . the proclamation of the Ten Commandments at Mount Sinai. Since the destruction of the Temple, when the Jews ceased to be primarily an agricultural people, the historical aspect has assumed greater significance.

Shabuoth is observed one day in Palestine and for two days by all pious Jews in other countries. . . .

Pesach marks the time when Israel received its *physical* freedom, while *Shabuoth* commemorates the occasion when Israel received *spiritual* freedom, the consummation of the purpose for which Israel was led forth from Egyptian bondage. . . .

The Scroll of Ruth is read in the synagogue at the *Shabuoth* services, because [of] the story of Ruth embracing Judaism and the charming description of agricultural life in ancient Palestine. . . . Another reason is that King David, who was a descendant of Ruth, was born and passed away, according to tradition, on this holiday.

Pious Jews stay up until midnight or during the entire first night of *Shabuoth*, devoting their time in the synagogue to the study and reading of excerpts from the Pentateuch, Prophets, and rabbinic literature. . . .

TISHAH B'AB

Tishah B'Ab, the ninth day in the Hebrew month of *Ab*, is observed as a fast day. It marks the anniversary of the destruction of the First and Second Temples in Jerusalem by the Babylonians under Nebuchadnezzar (586 B.C.) and the Romans under Titus (70 A.D.), respectively, and the loss of Jewish independence.

Other sad episodes in the life of the Jewish people are associated with this mournful day, among them the suppression of Bar Kokhba's revolt by the Romans in 135 A.D., and the expulsion of the Jews from Spain in 1492.

Grief is the keynote of *Tishah B'Ab*, and the traditional mourning code governs this day. Pious Jews refrain from eating, drinking, bathing, or participating in festive occasions, from sunset to sunset . . . and study only melancholy phases of the Torah, such as the Book of Job, the prophecies of misfortune in Jeremiah, the laws of mourning . . .

. . . the curtain in front of the Holy Ark [in the synagogue] is removed, the latter being draped in black or remaining bare. Worshipers remove their shoes and seat themselves on boxes, low stools, or turned-over chairs or benches . . . and all prayers and scriptural readings are chanted in a low tone, with a weeping intonation.

In the synagogue *Tishah B'Ab* is ushered in at the evening service with the reading of the prophet Jeremiah's Book of Lamentations, in depressed, mournful tones . . .

SABBATH

The observance of the Sabbath is a fundamental precept of Judaism, and for thousands of years has exerted a dominant influence in Jewish life. The admonition to set aside a weekly day of rest from labor is included among the Ten Commandments ("Remember the Seventh day, to keep it holy") . . .

The Sabbath is ushered in at the home Friday before sunset with the kindling of candles by the housewife, with an appropriate benediction and ceremony, and at the synagogue with the recital of the *Kabbalat Shabbat* (welcoming the Sabbath) prayers.

While observant Jews refrain from carrying on their usual work or business on the Sabbath, the traditional rest on that holy day does not imply mere idleness, but rather a change in occupation. Invested by Scripture with a uniquely religious connotation, the Sabbath is dedicated to physical and spiritual relaxation and replenishment. Biblical readings, discussions of contemporary Jewish affairs, the study of *The Ethics of The Fathers*, and other intellectual activities are indulged in . . . On the other hand, strenuous . . . exercise, mourning, fasting, weeping, and other practices which would detract from the quiet contemplation . . . and pleasure that should characterize the Sabbath, are scrupulously avoided.

Among the Sabbath ceremonies which contribute toward the creation of a distinctive atmosphere in the home and synagogue are the recital of the *Kiddush* (sanctification) prayer over sacramental wine or Sabbath white bread before the Friday evening and Sabbath noon repasts, and the *Habdalah* (distinction) blessings at the conclusion of the Sabbath, the singing of Sabbath hymns and melodies at the family table, attendance at public services, central features of which are the reading of the weekly portion of the Pentateuch . . . a corresponding selection from the Prophets, and a discourse by the rabbi. In recent decades it has become customary to conduct, in addition, late Friday evening services and forums.

JEWISH CALENDAR

Day		1974			1975			1976	
New Moon, Shevat	Th	Jan.	24	M	Jan.	13	Sa	Jan.	3
Hamishshah-ʻasar bi-Shevat	Th	Feb.	7	M	Jan.	27	Sa	Jan.	17
New Moon, Adar I, 1st day	F	Feb.	22	T	Feb.	11	S	Feb.	1
New Moon, Adar I, 2nd day	Sa	Feb.	23	W	Feb.	12	M	Feb.	2
New Moon, Adar II, 1st day		——			——		T	Mar.	2
New Moon, Adar II, 2nd day							W	Mar.	3
Fast of Esther	Th	Mar.	7	M	Feb.	24	M	Mar.	15
Purim	F	Mar.	8	T	Feb.	25	T	Mar.	16
Shushan Purim	Sa	Mar.	9	W	Feb.	26	W	Mar.	17
New Moon, Nisan	S	Mar.	24	Th	Mar.	13	Th	Apr.	1
Passover, 1st day	S	Apr.	7	Th	Mar.	27	Th	Apr.	15
Passover, 2nd day	M	Apr.	8	F	Mar.	28	F	Apr.	16
Passover, 7th day	Sa	Apr.	13	W	Apr.	2	W	Apr.	21
Passover, 8th day	S	Apr.	14	Th	Apr.	3	Th	Apr.	22
New Moon, Iyar, 1st day	M	Apr.	22	F	Apr.	11	F	Apr.	30
New Moon, Iyar, 2nd day	T	Apr.	23	S	Apr.	12	Sa	May	1
Lag Ba-ʻomer	F	May	10	T	Apr.	29	T	May	18
New Moon, Siwan	W	May	22	S	May	11	S	May	30
Shavuʻot, 1st day	M	May	27	F	May	16	F	June	4
Shavuʻot, 2nd day	T	May	28	S	May	17	Sa	June	5
New Moon, Tammuz, 1st day	Th	June	20	M	June	9	M	June	28
New Moon, Tammuz, 2nd day	F	June	21	T	June	10	T	June	29
Fast of the 17th of Tammuz	S	July	7	Th	June	26	Th	July	15
New Moon, Av	Sa	July	20	W	July	9	W	July	28
Fast of the 9th of Av	S	July	28	Th	July	17	Th	Aug.	5
New Moon, Elul, 1st day	S	Aug.	18	Th	Aug.	7	Th	Aug.	26
New Moon, Elul, 2nd day	M	Aug.	19	F	Aug.	8	F	Aug.	27

XXVI / LUTHERANS: RECENT CRISES

EDITOR'S SUMMARY:

On July 11, 1973, around 400 Lutheran delegates to the biennial convention in New Orleans of the Lutheran Church–Missouri Synod (about 2.8 million members) marched in protest against the adoption by their church of new creedal definitions (drawn up by the reelected president of the church, Reverend J. A. O. Preus), which require a literal acceptance of the Bible and involve a stricter control of "liberalism" in Lutheran seminaries.

The vote, 562 to 455, indicates the magnitude of the division within the leadership of the denomination. One delegate called the newly adopted document "endorsement of a legalistic church dictatorship" (*The New York Times*, July 12, 1973, p. 14).

The enforcement of conservative Lutheran theology by Reverend Preus was reinforced despite the most bitter debate and opposition to "semi-dictatorial powers." Such a schism is not without irony in a church that was born of Martin Luther's revolt against central, absolutist Church authority.

Like other churches in America, the Lutherans were strongly affected in the 1960s by secular and "liberalizing" movements—and, in the decade before that, by the growth of "the social gospel," the opening up of Biblical interpretation to modern scholarship, new historical emphases, and critical exegesis.

Advances in linguistics, archaeology, comparative religion and Bible analysis led to widespread reinterpretations (or abandonment) of fundamentalism; many episodes recounted in Holy Scripture (the story of Creation, Adam's rib, Jonah and the whale, miracles in both the Old and New Testament) were interpreted as allegorical or folklore—not to be taken literally.

Conservative Lutheran factions began to oppose such "heretical" approaches to "God's word." In 1969, the followers of Reverend Preus won control of various boards within the church—most notably, the supervision of the Concordia Seminary in St. Louis, the seat and generating force of "liberal" or "revisionist" teachings. The new Church leadership insisted upon strict, traditional orthodoxy—and, said their opponents, sought to "purge" or intimidate the faculty of Concordia.

A remarkable aspect of the struggle within the ranks of Lutherans is the fact that 40–45 percent of the delegates to the 1973 New Orleans convention opposed their president and the "hard line" on doctrine, scholarship, the training of ministers, the content of sermons. The president of Concordia Seminary, Reverend John H. Tietjen, publicly remarked that President Preus now "controls the institutions [of the church] but not the people" (*The New York Times,* July 21, 1973, p. 24).

The Reverend John H. Tietjen was suspended by the Board of Control on January 20, 1973, for allegedly teaching false doctrines. On October 15, 1974, Dr. Tietjen was dismissed.

The controversy involved "fundamentalist" as against "modern" or "liberal" interpretations of the Bible. Many members of the Concordia Seminary faculty supported Dr. Tietjen. Many theological students also supported Dr. Tietjen's "liberal" curriculum.

After his suspension, Dr. Tietjen told a press conference: "I do not and will not accept the validity of the Board's decision. I have not been and am not now a teacher of false doctrine, as my responses to the charges have made clear." He stated he would not appeal the ruling. [LR]

MARRIAGE AND RELIGION

See Part Two, Chapters XV, "Divorce and Religion," and XXIV, "Intermarriage"

XXVII / PENTECOSTAL AND CHARISMATIC MOVEMENTS IN THE 1970s

NATURE OF THE MOVEMENTS

EDITOR'S NOTE:

A not insignificant footnote to the religious phenomena of the 1970s is found in many new "pentecostal," "charismatic," "Jesus freaks," and similar movements. They seem to have succeeded the extraordinary, but short-lived, "God is dead" episodes. What cultural historian could have predicted, five years ago, the production and success of a musical entitled *Jesus Christ, Superstar?*

Revivalist meetings in tents, in meadows, on compuses; stickers on automobile bumpers ("Jesus Loves You," "Youth for Christ"); hearty verbal greetings such as "God is Love," "The Lord wants you!" "I have been saved; why not you?"; banners and posters proclaiming "Christ is King"; the signaling of one or another group affiliation by a raised fist (à la communist salute and Black power gesture of the 1960s) except that the index finger points upward to heaven; ecstatic mass chantings and "speaking in tongues"—all around us we today behold testimony, visible and audible, of converts to old faiths via new "baptisms of the Spirit," inner illuminations, and expressed fervors of supernatural rebirth or salvation.

The "charismatic movement" is not limited to young people, as many assume—young people in search of spiritual "cleansing," inner ecstasy, and those shared, communal, "encounter" groups during which mystical revelations, mental "expansion," and supernatural illuminations are experienced. "Jesus is making a great comeback," said one member of the generation of whom John Lennon remarked: "The Beatles are more popular than Jesus Christ."

HOW LARGE ARE THE PENTECOSTAL MOVEMENTS?

It has been estimated that in the United States, 200,000–300,000 Catholics, and some 100,000 Protestants, have become "pentecostal" or "charismatic" and that 2,000 Presbyterian and Episcopalian clergymen have participated in or sponsored "neo-pentecostal" groups.

In June 1973, around 22,000 pentecostalists from various countries and faiths (but predominantly Roman Catholic, and containing many priests and nuns) assembled on the campus of Notre Dame University. For three days, the celebrants heard evangelistic sermons, sang hymns, embraced constantly as "brothers and sisters in the Lord," testified to miraculous cures via faith and a new experiencing of the Holy Spirit, and broke into chants or babblings —interpreted by others as new revelations of passages from the Bible.

In Dallas, Texas, in February 1973, some 300 Episcopalian clergymen attended the First National Episcopal Charismatic Conference. "The stained glass windows of the old Gothic cathedral shook as the clergymen" (nearly all wearing "Roman collars") repeatedly broke into exclamations of ecstasy, lifted their arms, cried, "Praise the Lord! Praise the Lord!," embraced each other, and said they had received a new "baptism" during three eucharistic services. "Thank God we are losing our stiffness and dignity," the bishop-elect of Colorado, the Right Reverend William C. Frey, exclaimed (see *The New York Times*, February 18, 1973).

WHAT IS PENTECOSTALISM?

Pentecostalists (however they describe themselves) believe that they receive "the power of the Holy Ghost" via a "baptism of the Spirit" such as was experienced by the disciples of Jesus on the seventh Sunday after Easter (Pentecost). "When the day of Pentecost had come," says the Acts of the Apostles (2:1–4), "they were all filled with the Holy Spirit and began to speak in other tongues."

To "speak in tongues" (technically known as "glossolalia") was one of the nine special gifts of the Spirit enumerated by the apostle Paul. (The other eight were the gift of prophecy, the new interpretation of passages from the Bible, faith, wisdom, knowledge, the power of healing, the recognition of spirits, and the performance of miracles.)

The phenomena of pentecostal, charismatic, or glossolaliacal experiences are, of course, nothing new. "The old time religion," healing by "laying on hands," miraculous cures, outbursts of prophecy, ecstatic testimonies to being born or reborn or truly baptized by being possessed by the Spirit—these are familiar phenomena in American history (for example, the Holy Rollers) or to any who remember William James' classic *Varieties of Religious Experience*.

Part of the appeal of the new "charisma" groups is the liberating sense of ecumenism; for the first time, Protestants and Catholics (including priests and nuns), ministers and laymen, evangelists and conservative churchgoers, pray together, sing together, embrace, heal by the "laying on of hands," and share in self- and group-induced seizures of spiritual ecstasy. Many celebrate Mass together (though Catholic prelates will not give communion to the non-Catholics present). Even some Jewish students are participating in a small "Jews for Jesus" movement.

CHURCH RESPONSES

Three days after the June 1973 meeting of "charismatics" at Notre Dame, Pope Paul VI was impelled to ask a Vatican audience to reflect seriously upon whether "certain groups in search of the Holy Spirit are on the right road."

And one Catholic psychologist, Father Eugene Kennedy of Loyola University in Chicago, described the new pentecostalism (among young Catholics, at least) as representing the same impulses and emotions "which we see at work in a singles bar or in encounter groups . . . people who have grown up afraid of their own emotions . . . whose feelings have been repressed by the structure of the church . . . now coming together in an ambience that suddenly makes it legitimate for them freely to express those emotions" (*Newsweek,* June 25, 1973, p. 80).

But Archbishop John R. Quinn of Oklahoma City, chairman of a committee of the United States Conference of Bishops that is studying the charismatic movement, recently asserted: "If [pentecostalism] is practiced correctly, it doesn't really differ all that much [sic!] from traditional Catholicism." And Bishop Joseph McKinney of Grand Rapids, one of the small number of Catholic hierarchs actively practicing pentecostalism, states: "It has shown people that a deeper spiritual life is available to everyone, not just people in monasteries." (Both quotations are taken from a comprehensive survey of "Old-Time Religion" in *The Wall Street Journal,* March 12, 1974, pp. 1, 13.)

Father Eugene Kennedy believes that pentecostalism appeals to Catholics who have led "very restrictive emotional lives. . . . [In pentecostalism] they have found a way of experiencing controlled ecstasy" (*ibid.* p. 13).

Reverend Andrew M. Greeley, noted sociologist and priest, affiliated with the National Opinion Research Center at the University of Chicago, describes pentecostalism as "anti-intellectual"—but "the most vital movement within the Catholic Church today" (*ibid.*).

Pentecostal preachers who profess to spread the gospel through mass excitations have aroused both the concern and the hostility of many churchmen. Some Southern Baptist Congregations expel ordained ministers who claim to be possessed by the Holy Spirit or encourage glossolalia in their flock.

FOUR DIFFERENT PENTECOSTAL GROUPS

We should distinguish various sectors in the new pentecostal-apocalyptic-revivalist movement:

1. Interdenominational young and middle-aged worshipers who reach out for shared religious experience and a heightened religious consciousness through evangelical, participatory activities, such as the Campus Crusade for Christ.
2. Roman Catholic pentecostalists, intense and ecstatic in their courting of the Holy Spirit or the acquisition of healing gifts, who seek a

renewal or heightening of faith through mystical experiences akin to those of the apostles.

3. The "Jesus people," who form communes or "Christian houses," of which there are said to be more than 500 throughout the United States. These welcome families of any faith and sometimes include priests and nuns.

4. Aberrant, self-described "Freak groups"—such as "Christian Surfers," who attest to Christ's enhancement of the thrills of surf-boarding; mystical-seeking groups who find fresh, new "vibes" (vibrations) in chanting, shouting, and religious transports; the "Voice of Elijah" and "I Am" missionaries; groups that in "encounters" effected by pressing their bodies together, holding hands, shouting "Praise the Lord!" or "Jesus loves me" or "The Holy Spirit is in my soul!" achieve hallucinations, "visions," intense "inner illuminations," and so on.

PSYCHOLOGY OF PENTECOSTALISM

The emotionally starved or disturbed (*vide* the weaving, chanting street celebrants of "Hare Krishna," reiterated over and over for hours on end) often seem possessed by psychopathological, rather than explicitly religious, aberrations. As Cardinal John Heenan of Westminster compassionately remarked in a pastoral letter (May 27, 1972):

. . . young people enjoy what they regard as religious experiences [which are] sometimes no more than hallucinations . . . It would be no less wrong to laugh at their efforts than to regard them as proof that youth has rediscovered God . . . Their new-found admiration for Christ need not have a religious explanation. It may be that they have merely become disillusioned with their former (pop) heroes. [*Catholic Almanac 1972, op. cit.*, p. 135.]

DRUGS AND PENTECOSTALISM

A valuable diagnosis emerged from the researches of Robert L. Adams and Robert Jon Fox, who studied drug addiction in pentecostal youth groups in the United States and concluded (in the Fall 1972 issue of *Trans-Action*):

Members of the Jesus movement have a high incidence of past drug use, with 62 percent of those over 18, and 44 percent of those under 18, having used dope. Only a few individuals [of those studied] were extremely light users, usually of marijuana.

Adams and Fox reported similar findings for Japan—and a marked ideological swing, politically, from the extreme left to the far right among the new pentecostalists.

Ample evidence supports the concern connecting the consumption of drugs and the solicitation of religious visions. Some young people refer to their pentecostalism as "the Jesus trip" or "Jesus high" or "high on Jesus." One mystic described his new faith-via-hallucination as "a rush—like 'speed' " (amphetamines).

I find both moving and revealing the remarks of a teen-ager, in an addendum to the popular *Whole Earth Catalogue:*

Acid trips in the seventh grade, sex in the eighth, the Vietnam war a daily serial on TV since you were nine, parents and school worse than "irrelevant"—meaningless—no wonder Jesus is making a great comeback. [*Time,* June 24, 1971, p. 59.]

HISTORICAL NOTE

Millenarian, evangelistic, revivalist movements in the United States began back in the 1740s. Jonathan Edwards and George Whitefield hammered away at the sinfulness of man's nature, the horrors of hell and damnation, and so on.

The westbound pioneers, frontier folk, land seekers, home-steaders, gold-rushers attended "camp meetings" in which tub-thumping evangelists worked audiences into spiritual frenzy.

"The Day of Judgment is here" and "The Second Coming of Christ is at hand" are not unfamiliar prophetic slogans to American ears. The names of Dwight L. Moody, Charles Finney, Billy Sunday, Aimee Semple MacPherson, and Oral Roberts attest to the recurring role of missionaries and evangelists in American life.

PREDICTION

No one can predict with confidence how long and how far the pentecostalist movement will spread. But for all its drama (and melodrama), the pentecostal movement, however sincere and urgent, strikes objective observers as likely to follow the path of its predecessors and to fluctuate with social tensions and crises—especially when the institutions of our society, whether political or sociological or theological, fail to satisfy the emotional/psychological/religious hungers of what is, statistically, a relatively small, aberrant fringe of the large, complex, periodically crisis-torn social order. [LR]

A NEW ROMAN CATHOLIC MASS
Adapted from The New York Times, February 26, 1973, p. 7

In Melbourne, Australia, during the fortieth International Eucharistic Congress, on February 25, 1973, solemn parts of the Roman Catholic Mass were replaced (or "interpreted") by ecstatic hand clapping and songs and dances of the Australian aborigines. There was much foot stamping, arm waving, and spontaneous song.

Some twenty cardinals and thousands of prelates and laymen from many countries attended the eight-day services and seminars.

The papal legate to the congress, Lawrence Cardinal Shehan, Archbishop of Baltimore, conducted a Mass before 30,000 celebrants—wearing vestments that had been decorated by an aboriginal artist, featuring a tribal totem in the form of a giant bird.

The holy altar was made of bark and decorated with paintings of kangaroos, snakes, and an emu.

At climactic points in the Mass, the space before the altar became a stage for native dancers, who were accompanied by the tapping of sticks and the sound of a woodwind called the "didgeridoo." These participants had painted their faces and bodies in geometrical patterns of yellow, blue, red, and white. The men wore only breechcloths. The rhythm often became so contagious that the entire audience joined in hand clapping and singing. This display, said one priest, did not make the Mass less sacred as the central sacrament of the Eucharist.

A priest from New Zealand said, "There has never been a Mass like this."

Catholic prelates said that the dramatic "involvement" of Australian aborigines and aboriginal culture was only an extension of Catholic brotherhood. [LR]

XXVIII / POLITICS AND RELIGIOUS AFFILIATION

From *Religion in America 1971*, Gallup Opinion Index, April 1971, Report No. 70

POLITICAL COMPOSITION OF MAJOR UNITED STATES RELIGIOUS GROUPS, 1971

Religious Groups	Republican	Democrat	Independent
Total pop.	28%	43%	28%
Protestants	33	39	26
Baptists	21	52	25
Episcopalians	44	32	23
Lutherans	40	31	27
Methodists	35	36	26
Presbyterians	45	28	25
Roman Catholics	19	52	27
Jews	6	63	29

"THE U.S. SUPREME COURT HAS RULED THAT NO STATE OR LOCAL GOVERNMENT MAY REQUIRE THE READING OF THE LORD'S PRAYER OR BIBLE VERSES IN PUBLIC SCHOOLS. WHAT ARE YOUR VIEWS ON THIS—DO YOU APPROVE OR DISAPPROVE OF THIS?"

Group	Approve	Disapprove	No Opinion
Total	27%	67%	6%
SEX			
Men	28	64	8
Women	26	69	5
RACE			
White	28	66	6
Nonwhite	22	73	5
EDUCATION			
College	45	51	4
High school	21	73	6
Grade school	22	70	8
PROFESSION			
Prof. and Bus.	34	61	5
White collar	27	57	6
Farmers	26	70	4
Manual	23	70	7
AGE			
18–20 years	37	57	5
21–29 years	35	58	7
30–49 years	26	68	6
50 and over	21	74	5
RELIGION			
Protestant	23	72	5
Catholic	26	65	9
Jewish	Total sample too small for analysis		
REGION			
East	27	63	10
Midwest	29	64	7
South	21	77	2
West	32	63	5

XXX / PREJUDICE AND RELIGION

ATTITUDES TOWARD OTHER FAITHS: CATHOLICS, PROTESTANTS, JEWS

EDITOR'S NOTE:

The decline in religious prejudice and the increasing respect for other religious denominations is one of the most marked and heartening aspects of the change in the "psychological profile" of Americans during the past decade.

The striking growth of religious tolerance stems, of course, from a multiplicity of causes and movements, especially the shared experiences of different religious groups in the social upheavals of our time such as the civil rights movement for blacks, Mexicans, Indians; the long and bitter resistance to the war in Vietnam; and the women's liberation movement.

The interfaith movement in our country goes back a long way—as well it should have, given the constitutional rights of freedom of opinion, faith, and worship, quintessential rights upon which the structure of American democracy was founded and upon which it must be based.

The single most dramatic and influential event in the interfaith movement was undoubtedly the historic declaration of Vatican II— that Roman Catholic convocation which for the first time admitted Protestant clergy to witness its deliberations and which extended the conception of the council to consider the attitude of the papacy and its bishops to "non-Christian religions" such as Muslim, Hindu, Buddhist, and Judaic. (The salient parts of the declaration are given in Chapter X.)

But to think that prejudice has disappeared from our country, or that racial and religious intolerance are certain to disappear, is to ignore stubborn, persistently recurring facts.

With all this as background, the polls I now cite on the attitudes of Americans to Americans of a different faith or race offer memorable data on the psychological and sociological underpinnings of prejudice in the United States. [LR]

RELIGIOUS PREJUDICE AND POLITICS: CATHOLIC, JEWISH, BLACK, WOMAN PRESIDENT

Data from the Gallup Opinion Index, *Prejudice in Politics*, Report No. 46, April 1969, and the Gallup Opinion Index, *Vote for Negro for President?*, Report No. 77, November 1971

Attitudes Toward a Catholic President

Within a year after John F. Kennedy's election to the Presidency in 1960, bias against a Catholic in the nation's top political office declined dramatically—from 71 percent of the electorate in 1960 saying they would vote for a qualified Catholic candidate to 82 percent in 1961. This decrease in prejudice has continued since then, to the point where in future elections being a Roman Catholic should not prove controversial.

The fact is, that even prior to the 1960 election, opinion surveys had noted a steady and long trend of lessening prejudice toward a Catholic in the White House. On this evidence alone, Senator Kennedy should have been expected to fare better with the voting public in 1960 than Governor Alfred Smith had over thirty years before.

The following table records the answers given by Americans from 1937–1969 . . .

"IF YOUR PARTY NOMINATED A GENERALLY WELL-QUALIFIED MAN FOR PRESIDENT AND HE HAPPENED TO BE A CATHOLIC, WOULD YOU VOTE FOR HIM?"

Year	Yes	No	No Opinion
1937	64%	28%	8%
1940	62	31	7
1958	68	25	7
1959	69	20	11
1960	71	20	9
1961	82	13	5
1963	84	13	3
1965	87	10	3
1967	89	9	2
1969	88	8	4

A closer look at the latest of the polls taken reveals that the sharpest decline in anti-Catholic sentiment has come largely from Protestant and older voters.

The youngest voters (21–29 years old) and those with the most education tend to be the least prejudiced. There is little difference in spread between men and women or the various regions of the country, except the South where those unwilling to vote for a qualified Roman Catholic make up 15 percent as compared with less than half that for all other parts of the U.S.

Attitudes Toward a Jewish President

Anti-Jewish feeling as it affects the Presidency has been decreasing over the last three decades at a rate which parallels the decline in prejudice toward a Catholic President. It is noteworthy that the greatest downward jump in negative sentiment occurred during the same period for both groups—from 1960–1963—coinciding with the term of the first Roman Catholic President of the United States. It seems safe to assume that as the groundlessness of one prejudice was exposed, unreasonable fears about other groups were allayed as well.

While Americans are still more reluctant to vote for a well-qualified Jew for the Presidency than for a Catholic, the following table suggests that being Jewish would handicap a candidate far less seriously than formerly. It also indicates that the percentage of persons willing to cast their ballots for a Jew is great enough to prevent religion from looming large as a campaign issue.

VOTE FOR A JEW FOR PRESIDENT

Year	Yes	No	No Opinion
1937	46%	46%	8%
1958	62	28	10
1961	68	23	9
1963	77	17	6
1965	80	15	5
1967	82	13	5
1969	86	8	6

Attitudes Toward a Black or Woman President

Although the electorate is far more open-minded than it used to be concerning Negroes and women in high political office, these two groups still experience far greater prejudice than other minorities.

When Gallup first polled a representative sample of the nation's voters in 1958 concerning their willingness to vote for a well-qualified Negro for President, the result was that only 38 percent said that they would. Since then, prospects for a Negro attaining the Presidency have improved tremendously, with 69 percent of the electorate reporting in 1971 that they would vote for a Negro. Here is the trend:

VOTE FOR A BLACK FOR PRESIDENT

Year	Yes	No	No Opinion
1958	38%	53%	9%
1963	47	45	8
1965	59	34	7
1967	54	40	6
1969	67	23	10
1971	69	23	8

In addition to the inquiry about a Negro President, another question was asked in 1971:

"SUPPOSE THE PRESIDENTIAL CANDIDATE OF YOUR CHOICE NEXT YEAR PICKS A NEGRO AS HIS VICE-PRESIDENTIAL RUNNING MATE—WOULD THIS MAKE YOU MORE LIKELY TO VOTE FOR THIS TICKET OR LESS LIKELY?"

More Likely	Less Likely	No Difference	No Opinion
14%	23%	57%	6%

Views about electing a Negro to either of the two offices follow the same pattern. In each case, the candidate's race would be a substantial liability.

Analysis of the polls shows that rejection of a Negro's candidacy would be strongest in the South, among persons over 50, and among those with only a grade school education.

While many more Southerners said that they would be "less likely" to support a ticket with a Negro as Vice-President than took the opposite position, it is interesting that almost half replied that it would make no difference. As a group, only persons under 30 say that they would be more inclined to vote for a Presidential candidate who chose a Negro as his running mate.

A woman, according to Gallup's reports, would find it nearly impossible to be elected President of the U.S. Of those voters polled, 39 percent said they would not vote for a well-qualified woman if she were nominated by their party. Women, it was found, were likely to receive less support from Catholics (47 percent) than from Protestants (55 percent)—which reverses the usual pattern.

VOTE FOR A WOMAN

Year	Yes	No	No Opinion
1936	31%	65%	4%
1958	52	43	5
1967	57	39	4
1969	54	39	7
1969			
Protestant	55	40	5
Catholic	47	41	12

Decline in Prejudice by Population Groups: A Summary

Prejudice toward qualified Catholics, Jews, Negroes, or women who might seek the Presidency has been declining on the whole. However, with respect to Negroes and women, intolerance would still have a decisive role in prohibiting well-qualified candidates from achieving office.

The factors of religion, age, education, and income appear to affect prejudice in politics in much the same way, regardless of which minority group is the focus of attention. An examination of available information indicates that Jews tend to be the least prejudiced, followed by Catholics, and then Protestants (when they are surveyed with no denominational differentiation).

Younger adults and persons with a college education tend to be the most tolerant, as do persons having higher incomes (which, in the U.S., is frequently connected to more formal education).

PREJUDICE AMONG TEEN-AGERS

EDITOR'S NOTE:

An intensive study of teen-agers in three integrated public schools (each with a black student population of around 20 percent of the total), analyzed by the Survey Research Center of the University of California, headed by Professor Charles Y. Glock, has provided fresh insights on reciprocal attitudes.

The three schools were located "within 200 miles of New York City." The survey polled 4,600 pupils in the eighth, tenth, and twelfth grades. In one school, 50 percent of the students were

Jewish; in the second, 23 percent were Jewish; in the third, there were "few Jews."

The highlights of the findings are the following:

- Anti-Semitism among adolescents is closely linked to low family income and poor grades. The more "deprived" a teen-ager is, the more anti-Semitic.
- But black teen-agers, whether deprived or not, were less prejudiced against Jews than were white teen-agers of matched socioeconomic background. This does not appear to reflect pro-Semitic feelings so much as the fact, corroborated by other questions and answers in the survey, that black teen-agers are prejudiced against *whites*, whether Jewish or not.
- In the school where 50 percent of the students were Jewish, 83 percent viewed Jewish teen-agers as "intelligent, ambitious and successful." This was also the opinion of 82 percent of those polled in the school where 23 percent were Jewish, and 75 percent in the school where there were few Jews.
- But 60 percent of the first two schools reported themselves to feel that their Jewish classmates were "selfish" or "conceited" or "bossy."
- The least prejudiced students, whether Jewish or black, were those with some familiarity of the group they were asked to appraise.

The Anti-Defamation League of B'nai Brith, which has financed a series of scholarly analyses of prejudice, tolerance, and anti-Semitism, sponsored the survey by Dr. Glock's center and in announcing the findings said that "little or no effort is being made by the schools to improve inter-group relations and attitudes."

Dr. Glock observed that in the district tested, there were neither courses nor programs that tried "to teach young people what prejudice is and how it comes about."

Since teen-agers are chiefly influenced by their own peers and parents, they are often anti-Semitic or antiblack because of the prejudices they have heard or seen, and emulate. [LR]

CHRISTIAN FAITH AND ANTI-SEMITISM
Excerpts from Oscar Cohen, "Anti-Semitism in the United States," Continuum (pamphlet), pp. 320–325

The first volume in this series [ed. by Charles Y. Glock, University of California], *Christian Beliefs and Anti-Semitism*, was issued in April 1966 to a controversial reception, as anticipated. Until the appearance of this study, behavioral scientists had shed little light on the extent, if any, to which Christian beliefs have fostered antisemitism.

Research on the subject had been fragmentary, involving small samples and showing no definite trend. Dr. Gordon Allport, author of *The Nature of Prejudice*, long a definitive work in this field, concluded that there was no evidence one way or another that religious belief results in antisemitism. This view was widely accepted, not only in religious circles but in the social-science community as well. Among the religious, there was a profound and understandable reluctance to believe that modern Christianity succors anti-Jewish attitudes. It is painful to consider that a religion of love, so precious to its proponents, might help produce something as evil as antisemitism. Moreover, in this age of ecumenism, theologians and top church authorities in the U.S. and throughout the world had been concentrating great energy on this very problem, making enormous strides through definitive reinterpretation of once-damaging doctrines.

The University of California study sets forth for the first time conclusive evidence that certain interpretations of Christian beliefs continue to play a major role in the development and maintenance of anti-Jewish prejudice in this country. In addition, it provides a measure of the depth and prevalence of such prejudices among the American majority.

The authors of this study . . . do not view religion as the sole cause of antisemitism, but their researches have led them to claim it is an extremely important component. Their book concludes:

"Conservatively, these findings would suggest that at least one-fourth of America's anti-Semites have a religious basis for their prejudice, while nearly another fifth have this religious basis in considerable part. Indeed, only 5 percent of Americans with anti-Semitic views lack all rudiments of a religious basis for their prejudice. On these grounds it seems reasonable to say . . . that an impressive proportion, no less than a fourth, of American anti-Semitism is attached to religious sources. In terms of absolute numbers rather than percentages, these data indicate that approximately 17.5 million Americans who hold fairly strong anti-Semitic beliefs would also be classified in the top two categories of the Religious Bigotry Index. *Far from being trivial, religious outlooks and religious images of the modern Jew seem to lie at the root of the anti-Semitism of millions of American adults.*"

The second volume in this study, *The Apathetic Majority*, opened still another window of understanding when it appeared in September 1966. This book probes the impact on the American public of the Eichmann trial. Its major finding is that dramatic, full-scale news reporting of this event in the United States generated a sympathetic response toward Jews, but failed to deepen understanding of the horrors of the Nazi era.

Although this study found a considerable residue of antisemitism among the respondents, antisemitism was not a major factor influencing opinions on details of the trial or on whether or not it was a "good thing." . . .

There are no simple explanations for the complex phenomenon of anti-semitism in the United States, nor can any single group of culprits be singled out for blame or remedial action. The problem we face today does not concern a single, frustrated minority group any more than did the problem we faced in 1960 concern a handful of extremists and vandals. Attention today, as throughout American history, should be focused on the unspectacular, everyday kind of anti-Jewishness and apathy which represents the real danger to our society, particularly in times of crisis. . . .

The extent of anti-Jewish beliefs, as contrasted to discrimination, toward Jews will be revealed in a forthcoming volume of the *Patterns of American Prejudice* series. But it can be reported now, that the incidence of prejudice is unexpectedly high. About one-third of the American population is highly prejudiced, and perhaps only one-third or less is unprejudiced. This means that there exists a large reservoir of misunderstanding, stereotyping and outright hatred, as it affects American Jews. It would be absurd to think that Jews are in any immediate danger. But the backlog of prejudice represents a potential which could have dreadful consequences.

It was H. A. Overstreet who wrote some years ago in the *Saturday Review of Literature* that "it is the mild and gentle people of prejudice who must bear the burden of the moral guilt. They have given the green light, and the legion of low hostilities has broken through on the run." The enduring difficulties stem not only from those who carry out actions against the Jews, but from those who acquiesce in them. The bystanders are not innocent.

CATHOLICS AND JEWS

EDITOR'S NOTE:

In March 1973, almost eight years after Vatican II removed the catastrophic stigma of deicide from the Jews (see below), two prominent Catholics, addressing a symposium (of educators, heads of theological seminaries, and specialists on religious studies, curriculums and textbooks), remarked upon the "marked change" in the teaching materials used by Roman Catholics in parochial schools vis-à-vis the "image" of Jews and Judaism.

Most Catholic texts, revised since the Vatican II declaration, now portray Jews in an undiabolic and "positive" light and no longer contain traditional "denunciations of Jews and Judaism," reported Father John T. Pawlikowski, author of the new book *Catechetics and Prejudice* and professor of social ethics at the Catholic Theological Union of Chicago. Father Pawlikowski is a member of the Catholic Bishops Secretariat on Catholic-Jewish Relations, itself a byproduct of Vatican II.

Sister Rose Thering of the Institute of Judeo-Christian Studies at Seton Hall University stated: "No longer are Jews depicted as guilty of deicide and therefore condemned to wander over the face of the earth . . . Now most religion texts present the Jewish people as God's beloved people."

Sister Rose informed the seminar that new texts for Catholic schools depicted Jesus as living and preaching his mission within the Jewish community of his time. Such texts sought to describe the crucifixion in a historically correct manner. (It may be noted that crucifixion was a Roman custom, utterly alien to the Jews as a form of punishment and death, and not once mentioned in legal documents, memoirs, letters, or other data pertaining to Jewish history, religious practices, or community regulations.) Sister Rose said that some new textbooks for Catholics would now tell the story of the anti-Semitic horrors that accompanied the Crusades and were part and parcel of the Spanish Inquisition.

Both Father Pawlikowski and Sister Rose Thering deplored the great paucity of material, in Catholic texts and schools, about the Nazi regime and its mass murder of Jews, and of the historical episodes involved in the creation of the State of Israel.

A report of the seminar may be obtained from the American Jewish Committee, 165 E. 56 Street, New York, N.Y. [LR]

PAPAL DECLARATION ON ANTI-SEMITISM AND HISTORICAL BACKGROUND

Papal Declaration

Excerpts from "Declaration on the Relationship of the Church to Non-Christian Religions," 1973 Catholic Almanac (Huntington, Ind.: Our Sunday Visitor, Inc., 1973), pp. 341–342

SPIRITUAL BOND

As this sacred Synod searches into the mystery of the Church, it recalls the spiritual bond linking the people of the New Covenant with Abraham's stock.

For the Church of Christ acknowledges that, according to the mystery of God's saving design, the beginnings of her faith and her election are already found among the patriarchs, Moses and the prophets. She professes that all who believe in Christ, Abraham's sons according to faith . . . are included in the same patriarch's call, and likewise that the salvation of the Church was mystically foreshadowed by the Chosen People's exodus from the land of bondage.

The Church, therefore, cannot forget that she received the revelation of the Old Testament through the people with whom God in His inexpressible mercy deigned to establish the Ancient Covenant. Nor can she forget that she draws sustenance from the root of that good olive tree onto which have been grafted the wild olive branches of the Gentiles (cf. Rom. 11:17–24). Indeed, the Church believes that by His cross Christ, our Peace, reconciled Jew and Gentile, making them both one in Himself (cf. Eph. 2:14–16).

. . . The Jews still remain most dear to God because of their fathers, for He does not repent of the gifts He makes nor of the calls He issues (cf. Rom. 11:28–29). In company with the prophets and the same Apostle [Paul], the Church awaits that day, known to God alone, on which all peoples will address the Lord in a single voice and "serve him with one accord" (Zeph. 3:9; cf. Is. 66:23; Ps. 65–4; Rom. 11:11–32).

Since the spiritual patrimony common to Christians and Jews is thus so great, this sacred Synod wishes to foster and recommend that mutual understanding and respect which is the fruit above all of biblical and theological studies, and of brotherly dialogues.

NO ANTI-SEMITISM

True, authorities of the Jews and those who followed their lead pressed for the death of Christ (cf. Jn. 19:6); still, what happened in His passion cannot be blamed upon all the Jews then living, without distinction, nor upon the Jews of today. Although the Church is the new People of God, the Jews should not be presented as repudiated or cursed by God, as if such views followed from the holy Scriptures. All should take pains, then, lest in catechetical instruction and in the preaching of God's Word they teach anything out of harmony with the truth of the gospel and the spirit of Christ.

The Church repudiates all persecutions against any man. Moreover, mindful of her common patrimony with the Jews, and motivated by the gospel's spiritual love and by no political considerations, she deplores the hatred, persecutions, and displays of anti-Semitism directed against the Jews at any time and from any source . . .

. . . The Church rejects, as foreign to the mind of Christ, any discrimination against men or harassment of them because of their race, color, condition of life, or religion . . .

Historical Background of Vatican Declaration

By Robert A. Graham, S.J., from *The Documents of Vatican II*, ed. Walter M. Abbott, S.J., trans. Monsignor Joseph Gallagher (Geoffrey Chapman, 1966), pp. 656–659

The history of the Declaration on the Relationship of the Church to Non-Christian Religions begins with Pope John XXIII. He wanted the Council to make a statement on the Jews, and he asked Cardinal Bea to see to it. Between that beginning and the outcome there is perhaps the most dramatic story of the Council. It was certainly a story of suspense in the world's newspaper coverage of the Council.

Originally, the material of this Declaration was Chapter 4 in the schema of the Decree on Ecumenism. The early material on religious freedom was contained in Chapter 5. During the second session of the Council, the Moderators called for a vote on the schema's first three chapters; the other two were held over (for lack of time, Cardinal Bea stated).

Just before that decision of the Moderators, Cardinal Bea, on November 19, 1963, in his address to the Council introducing Chapter 4, revealed that Pope John himself had ordered preparation of a text concerning the Jews. Pope John had, in fact, approved the basic lines of the document some months before he died.

A number of bishops, before and after Cardinal Bea's talk, urged that the topic of Catholic-Jewish relations was outside the scope of the ecumenism schema. They advocated that it should be the subject of a separate document. Some, especially patriarchs of the Eastern Churches, did not want the Council to say anything about the Jews, for fear the statement would be considered by Arab governments as a political move favoring recognition of the State of Israel, and the Christian minorities in Arab countries would be made to suffer in reprisal.

During the period between the second and third sessions, the secretariat headed by Cardinal Bea worked out a new draft on the Jews and other non-Christians. The contents became known throughout the world; the text was published in various newspapers. It put an end to the idea held by some Christians through the centuries that the Jews were a "deicide" people.

When the Council Fathers returned to Rome for the third session it was not this text that was presented to them. In the new text, rejection of the charge of deicide had disappeared; the section on non-Christians other than Jews had been extended; special attention was given to Moslems.

Cardinal Liénart began the discussion by insisting that the deleted passages about the Jews be restored—a remarkable development, since he was the senior member of the Coordinating Commission that was said to have made all the changes. He was followed by a long line of cardinals from around the world who, with the exception of Cardinal Tappouni, made the same request—Léger of Canada; Cushing, Meyer, and Ritter of the United States; Frings of Germany; et al.

. . .

The whole story, with its details about the week end when it seemed the statement on the Jews might become only one sentence, and some newspapers carried headlines announcing that the whole Declaration had been shelved, would take many pages in a history of the Council. Suffice it to say here that in the important voting on the sections of the document in October, 1965, there were 2,080 Fathers voting on the proposition that the Jews are not to be regarded as repudiated or cursed by God. There were 1,821 affirmative, 245 negative, and 14 invalid votes. One may perhaps legitimately add to this summary that on the proposition concerning universal brotherhood and exclusion of all discrimination (Article 5) there were 2,128 votes cast: 2,064 affirmative, 58 negative, and 6 invalid.

It has often been said, and rightly so, that if the present document had not been preceded by the earlier one, it would have been universally welcomed as one of the most important advances of the Council. The document certainly ends a sad chapter in Christian history.

. . .

Bishops from the whole world, meeting together and learning the full scope of the Church's concerns, had their horizons considerably widened. The bishops of Europe had some experience of what Cardinal Bea touched upon when he admitted in an address to the Council that anti-Jewish ideas in Christian history had helped Nazism. Bishops from heavily Jewish parts of the United States were proximately aware of the need to clarify true Christian attitudes toward Jews.

. . . Now, in this historic document, the Church affirms that all peoples of the earth with their various religions form one community; the Church respects the spiritual, moral, and cultural values of Hinduism, Buddhism, and Islam. A few, like Dr. W. A. Visser 't Hooft, general secretary of the World Council of Churches, have found this part of the document "very, very weak" because it failed to "come to grips with essential questions raised by these religions" and "confined itself to making polite remarks" about them. Perhaps many readers will find this section of the Declaration rather general and abstruse. However, some historical perspective can be provided by the recollection that it is the first time an Ecumenical Council has expressed such an open approach to the other great faiths of the world.

SUMMARY: CATHOLIC-JEWISH RELATIONS SINCE VATICAN II
From 1973 Catholic Almanac (Huntington, Ind.: Our Sunday Visitor, Inc., 1973), pp. 341–342

The American hierarchy's first move toward implementation of the Vatican II *Declaration on the Relationship of the Church to Non-Christian Religions*° was to establish, in 1965, a Subcommission for Catholic-Jewish Relations in the framework of its Commission for Ecumenical and Interreligious Affairs. This subcommission was reconstituted and given the title of secretariat in September 1967. Its moderator is Bishop Francis J. Mugavero of Brooklyn. The executive director is Father Edward Flannery. The Secretariat for Catholic-Jewish Relations is located at 1312 Massachusetts Ave. N.W., Washington, D.C. 20005.

According to the key norm of a set of guidelines issued by the secretariat Mar. 16, 1967: "The general aim of all Catholic-Jewish meetings (and relations) is to increase our understanding both of Judaism and the Catholic faith, to eliminate sources of tension and misunderstanding, to initiate dialogue or conversations on different levels, to multiply intergroup meetings between Catholics and Jews, and to promote cooperative social action."

Developments in recent years, in the view of Rabbi Marc H. Tanenbaum, director of interreligious affairs of the American Jewish Committee, have reflected a growing commitment by Christian leaders "to lay a foundation for constructive relations between Christians and Jews in this country."

Even so, progress toward better Christian-Jewish relations appears to be greater on the theological and scholarly levels than among local church organizations and synagogue communities. There are indications that some strides forward are being made there as well, however, in mutual discussion programs, temple visits by Catholics, interest in the rituals and observances of Judaism, and the involvement of Catholics and Jews in social action projects.

RELATIONS IMPROVING

Rabbi Marc H. Tanenbaum reported evidence of steadily improving Jewish-Christian relations at the five day 66th annual meeting of the American Jewish Committee early in May, 1972, in New York City.

The evidence emerged from an analysis of statements from a variety of Catholic and other sources. Among the findings, as reported in *The New York Times,* were:

- "A growing and positive shift in Christian sentiment about Israel, 'including a balanced perspective on the rights of Palestinians and the future of a unified Jerusalem, in which Christian churches are begin-

° See page 610.

ning to see their role as one of promoting reconciliation rather than polarization.' "

- "Recognition of Judaism as a source of 'fundamental truth' to its adherents and a repudiation of the use of interfaith dialogues for purposes of conversion."
- "Widespread sensitivity to the plight of Soviet Jews and recognition of the fact that their struggle for justice is 'inextricably linked to the denial of human rights to Christians and various national communities in the Soviet Union.' "

ANTI-SEMITISM AMONG LUTHERANS

From Merton P. Strommen, ed., A Study of Generation (Minneapolis: Augsburg Publishing House, 1972). See also The New York Times, June 18, 1972, p. 45

EDITOR'S NOTE:

This is a survey of 4,745 Lutherans, age fifteen to sixty-five, conducted by the Youth Research Center of Minneapolis under the direction of Dr. Merton P. Strommen. The study was financed and sponsored by the Lutheran Brotherhood, an insurance society.

The 4,745 Lutherans were described as a scientific sample cross-section of the 6 million "confirmed members" of the three major Lutheran bodies: the American Lutheran Church, the Lutheran Church of America, and the Lutheran Church–Missouri Synod.

The chief significance of the study appears to lie in its direct challenge to the earlier researches of Drs. Charles Y. Glock and Rodney Stark, of the University of California, who, in their exhaustive survey, Christian Beliefs and Anti-Semitism (New York: Harper & Row, 1966), found a direct relationship—indeed, "cause" —between contemporary Christian teachings and anti-Semitic attitudes.

The highlights of A Study of Generation are offered below.

- Anti-semitism "is not a separate entity, but just one facet of generalized prejudice."
- One out of five Lutherans was found to hold prejudices against Jews.
- Two out of five Lutherans tend to "reject" persons who differ from them—in belief, values, or "life style" (notably communists, homosexuals, hippies, student radicals, drug takers).
- Anti-Semitism is not a consequence of "Christian orthodoxy" but, like other prejudices, is found among those (Lutherans) who feel threatened by diversity or change, and rigidly adhere to "religious law"—

instead of those who "reflect an awareness of a personal God who cares for them in Jesus Christ," feel "open to renewal and change," and believe the clergy should adapt to broad social changes.

· Those Lutherans who "overemphasize" the "divinity of Christ" are more prejudiced (to others, including Jews) than those who stress "the humanity of Jesus."

· There is no significant difference in attitudes (prejudice) between most Lutheran adults and young people; indeed, the gap between Lutheran clergy and laymen is greater than that between age groups in the laity. [LR]

XXXI / RELIGION IN U.S. HISTORY

CHRONOLOGY: HIGHLIGHTS

Condensed from Richard B. Morris, ed., *Encyclopedia of American History* (New York: Harper & Row, 1965, rev. ed.)

1609. Church of England was established by law in Virginia. A statute (1610), re-enacted when Virginia became a royal colony, but never rigidly enforced, provided for compulsory church attendance. The Anglican Church was also established in the lower counties of New York (1693), and in Maryland (1702), South Carolina (1706), North Carolina (nominally, 1711), and Georgia (1758). . . .

1620. Congregational Churches were introduced by the Pilgrims in Plymouth (1620) and by the Puritans in Massachusetts Bay (1630). The principal difference was that the former (Independents) repudiated the Church of England; the latter (Nonconformists) did not openly break with the Established Church. . . . The *Halfway Covenant* (1647–62), which admitted to baptism the children of baptized persons who themselves had not experienced conversion, served to erase the distinction between the "elect" and all others.

1628. Dutch Reformed Church (a Calvinist, Presbyterian group) was organized in New Amsterdam, by Reverend *Jonas Michaëlius* (1628). . . .

1633. Roman Catholic Church had previously been established in North America as a result of Spanish and French missionary activity, but the first group of Catholics to arrive in the English colonies came to Maryland, which had been founded (1632) to provide refuge for that denomination. . . . The Revolution of 1689 in Maryland, leading to Protestant ascendancy, resulted in the passage of anti-Catholic legislation (1) imposing poll tax on Irish Catholic immigrant servants; (2) requiring that children of mixed marriages be reared as Protestants; (3) imposing a fine for sending children to Catholic schools abroad. . . . In the beginning of the eighteenth century, Rhode Island and Pennsylvania were the only colonies in which Roman Catholics enjoyed religious and civil rights. . . . By 1775, public worship by Roman Catholics was confined to Pennsylvania.

1639. Baptists (opposed to infant baptism and stressing the separation of Church and State) were organized as a church by *Roger Williams* at Providence, Rhode Island, followed by Newport (1644). . . .

1640. Lutheran Church. Reverend *Reorus Torkillus,* first Lutheran minister to serve in the New World, arrived in New Sweden (spring 1640). The first synod was not organized until 1748. . . .

1654. Jews. Despite the efforts of Stuyvesant to deprive them of civil rights, the first group of Jews, arriving in New Amsterdam (1654) from Curaçao, induced the Dutch West India Company (7 Jews were among the 167 stockholders) to permit them to reside and engage in wholesale trade (1655–56). In 1657, they were admitted to the retail trades. In 1685, they demanded the right of public worship, denied under Dutch rule, and a synagogue (Shearith Israel, "Remnant of Israel") was known to exist in New York City in 1695. . . . The Jews prior to 1789 were mainly *Sephardim* (of Spanish, Portuguese and Dutch origin).

1656. Quakers (Society of Friends), founded by *George Fox*, stressed "inner light," separation of Church and State, opposition to war and oaths. Except in Rhode Island, they were persecuted in the period 1656–70. Expansion of this sect is attributed to the visit of Fox to America (1671) and to Penn's "Holy Experiment" (1681). . . .

1683. Mennonites, led by *Francis Daniel Pastorius* (1651–*c*. 1720), settled in Germantown, Pennsylvania. They advocated separation of Church and State, religious liberty, adult baptism, a church of the elect, pacifism, refusal to take oaths, and drew up the first protest against slavery (1688). Most conservative of this group were the *Amish*.

1706. Presbyterians. The first presbytery was organized in Philadelphia by *Francis Makemie* (1658–1708); the first synod in 1718. The Adoption Act, the first constitution of American Presbyterianism, was adopted (1729).

1723. Dunkards, or German Baptists, were organized under the leadership of *Alexander Mack*. Their distinctive features were triple immersion, pacifism and agape feasts.

1726–56. Great Awakening, a series of revivals. . . . Leadership in the movement was assumed by *Jonathan Edwards,* beginning with his sermons of 1734. . . . The Methodist phase . . . reached its climax, 1775–85. Among Presbyterians, the Great Awakening led to a schism between "New Side" (revivalists, who organized an independent synod, 1745) and "Old Side" (conservatives), which was healed in 1758. . . .

1735. Moravians, or United Brethren, comprising Hussites and German Pietists, came to Georgia in 1735, and . . . founded a settlement at Bethlehem, Pennsylvania (1741).

1766. Methodism began in America, as in England, as a movement within the Church of England. It appeared first in New York City (1766).

1775–83. Churches and the Revolution. The Anglican clergy throughout the colonies were Loyalist, the Southern laity overwhelmingly Patriot. The Congregational and Presbyterian clergy took a Patriot stand. The Methodist missionaries were Loyalist. Lutherans and Roman Catholics were divided in loyalty. The Quakers, officially neutral, leaned toward the Loyalists. . . .

1776–89. Disestablishment. Under the leadership of Baptists and Presbyterians the movement for religious freedom and separation of Church and State gained headway in Virginia in the Revolutionary period. . . .

An Act of 1776 suspending payment of tithes . . . really disestablished the Church of England [in Virginia]. Elsewhere the church was disestablished: 1776—Pennsylvania, Delaware and New Jersey; 1777—New York, North Carolina, and Georgia (partially, completely in 1789); 1790—South Carolina. 1818—Connecticut constitution disestablished the Congregational Church; 1833—Massachusetts disestablished the (Congregational) Church.

1780. Universalists. The first American Universalist church, built . . . in Gloucester, Massachusetts, favored separation of Church and State.

1782. First Parochial School erected by St. Mary's Church, Philadelphia ("Mother School"). The system was officially sanctioned in Baltimore (1829). By 1840, there were 200 parochial schools in the U.S.

1784. Theological Schools. The first theological college in the U.S. was established at New Brunswick, New Jersey. Other important seminaries were Andover (founded to oppose Unitarian trends at Harvard, 1808), Princeton (1812), General (1817) . . . and Union Theological (1836).

1789. Protestant Episcopal Church, depleted by Loyalist emigration, now independent of the Church of England, was organized at its first triennial convention in Philadelphia. . . . By 1792, five bishops had been named.

1790. Roman Catholic Episcopate was established with the consecration of Reverend *John Carroll* (1735–1815); nominated, 1788. . . . Political discrimination against Catholics continued until 1835 (North Carolina).

1792. Russian Orthodox Church began missionary activities in Alaska, with a resident bishop at Sitka, 1798. The episcopal see was moved to San Francisco (1872), and in 1905 to New York City.

1794. Deism gained ground after the publication of Tom Paine's *Age of Reason.* . . . Deism's most influential exponent in America was *Elihu Palmer,* ex-Baptist preacher, whose *Principles of Nature* (1797) attacked the orthodox tenets of Christianity. . . .

1797. Great Revivals began on the frontier with the preaching of *James McGready* (*c.* 1758–1817). . . . In New England the revival was led by the *Edwardeans* who were opposed by (1) the *old covenant theologians, Timothy Dwight* and *Lyman Beecher* and (2) by the *rationalists and Unitarians.*

1808. Methodist Church adopted a constitution.

1810. Organization of the *American Board of Commissioners for Foreign Missions* (Congregational), which became interdenominational (1812), marked the beginning of American missionary interest. The American Bible Society (1816), the Home Missionary Society (1826) and the American Tract Society (1825) followed.

Disciples of Christ, a group of progressive Presbyterians opposed to open communion, founded the Independent Church of Christ at *Brush Run,* Pennsylvania.

1813–17. Large Negro groups formed independent churches, including

African Methodist Episcopal Church (Philadelphia, 1816). The first Negro Baptist church was founded in Georgia (1773). In 1861, there were 200,000 Negro members of the Methodist Episcopal Church, South; 150,000 Negro Baptists.

1819. Unitarian Church (stressing unity of God and denying Trinitarianism) founded by *William Ellery Channing.*

1824–50. Revivalism in Pennsylvania, New York and Massachusetts led by *Charles G. Finney,* licensed to preach as a Presbyterian. . . .

1829–54. Anti-Catholic Agitation, following the founding of the Society for the Propagation of the Faith (Lyons, France, 1822) and the Leopold Association (Vienna, 1829) to promote Roman Catholic missions in America, resulted in . . . anti-Catholic sermons by Reverend *Lyman Beecher* and . . . acts of violence, such as the burning of the Ursuline Convent at Charlestown, Massachusetts (August 11, 1834).

1830. Latter-day Saints, or Mormons owe their origin to the publication of the *Book of Mormon,* based on a revelation claimed by *Joseph Smith* (1805–44), followed by the founding of the Church at Fayette, New York. . . . As a result of opposition, the Mormons left New York (1831) for Kirkland, Ohio, and Independence, Missouri. Expelled from Missouri, they settled at Nauvoo, Illinois. Violence followed them, culminating in the lynching of Smith in the jail at Carthage. Driven from Nauvoo (1846), the Saints settled in the valley of the Great Salt Lake in Utah (1848) under the leadership of *Brigham Young.*

1832–69. Slavery and the Churches. The issue of abolitionism came to a head when *Theodore Dwight Weld,* a student at Lane Theological Seminary, Cincinnati, withdrew from that institution when the trustees suppressed an anti-slavery society. In the North abolitionism quickly became part of revivalism. The issue divided the Protestant churches. The Southern Baptists withdrew (1843) to organize the Southern Baptist Convention. The Methodist Church, South, set up a separate organization (1844). An abolitionist group of New School Presbyterians organized the Synod of Free Presbyterian Churches, Ohio (1847), followed by a major schism in the New School (1857), when the United Synod of the South was established. Old School Presbyterians split (1861), and the Presbyterian Church in the Confederate States was founded. The Ohio Synod and the New School Presbyterians united in 1862. In 1864, the Southern groups united as the Presbyterian Church in the U.S. The Northern groups united as the Presbyterian Church in the U.S.A. (1869). Division on this issue was avoided in the Protestant Episcopal Church.

1840–60. Reform and Conservative Judaism. Rabbi *Isaac Mayer Wise* . . . advocated the idea of reform. In 1873, he organized the Union of American Hebrew Congregations, followed (1875) by Hebrew Union College in Cincinnati. . . . A conservative movement in opposition was headed by Rabbis *Isaac Leeser* and *Sabato Morais* of Philadelphia. The Jewish Theological Seminary (conservative) was founded (1886).

1843. Millerism, an Adventist movement, resulted from the preaching of *William Miller* (1782–1849), who prophesied the second coming of Christ between 1843–44. His followers founded the Adventist Church (1845). The *Seventh-Day Adventists* separated from the parent body (1846).

1875–86. Archbishop *John McClosky* became the first American cardinal. Archbishop *James Gibbons* was elected to the same rank (1886). The Catholic University of America was founded at Washington, D.C. (1884).

1875–92. Christian Science textbook, *Science and Health,* by *Mary Baker Eddy* was published and the Christian Science Association organized. The first church was established at Boston, 1879; reorganized, 1892.

1876. Society for Ethical Culture established in New York by *Felix Adler.*

1880. Salvation Army, evangelistic organization, after being first established by General *William Booth* in England, was organized in the U.S.

1895. National Baptist Convention of the U.S.A., representing merger of Negro Baptist groups, formed at Atlanta; incorporated (1915). The National Baptist Convention of America separated (1916).

1905. The Federal Council of Churches of Christ in America, first major interdenominational organization, was founded; succeeded (1950) by the National Council of Churches of Christ in the U.S.A.

1908. Home Missions Council established to direct noncompetitive missionary activity.

1909–25. Fundamentalist Reaction, inspired by such traveling evangelists as *William Jennings Bryan, William A. ("Billy") Sunday,* and *John Alexander Dowie,* reached its climax at Dayton, Tennessee (July 10–21, 1925), in the trial and conviction of *John Scopes,* a Tennessee schoolteacher, for teaching evolution. Scopes was opposed by Bryan; defended by Clarence Darrow and Dudley Field Malone.

1918. United Lutheran Church in U.S. formed, placing 45 synods on the same doctrinal basis.

1931. Jehovah's Witnesses, under the leadership of Judge *J. F. Rutherford* . . . were incorporated (1939) as The Watch Tower Bible and Tract Society.

c.1935. Neo-Orthodoxy, a synthesis of the socio-economic liberalism of the Social Gospel . . . with stress on the fall of man and the judgment of God, secured a wide following among American Protestants under the leadership of *Reinhold Niebuhr.*

1939. Methodist Episcopal Church, Methodist Episcopal Church, South, and the Methodist Protestant Church were reunited.

1950–60. Protestant Church Unity Trend. National Council of the Churches of Christ in the U.S.A. formed November 29, 1950 by 25 Protestant denominations and 5 Eastern Orthodox bodies embracing 37 million church members. Congregational Christian Churches and the Evangelical Reformed Church united (June 1957) to form the United

Church of Christ. Presbyterian Church in the U.S.A. and United Presbyterian Church joined May 28, 1958 to form the United Presbyterian Church in the U.S.A. . . .

1960–1970. Continuation of the Protestant Church Unity Trend. In 1960 the American Lutheran Church joined with the Evangelical and United Evangelical Lutheran Churches to form the American Lutheran Church. The American Unitarian Association merged with the Universalist Church of America in 1961 to become the Unitarian Universalist Association. The United Methodist Church was formed in 1968 when the Methodist Church and Evangelical United Brethren Church united.

RELIGIOUS AFFILIATION OF PRESIDENTS
OF THE UNITED STATES

Listing of Presidents from the 1972 *Information Please Almanac* (New York: Dan Golenpaul Associates, Simon and Schuster, 1972), pp. 771–772

Baptist
Warren Gamaliel Harding
Harry S Truman

Congregationalist
Calvin Coolidge

Deist
Thomas Jefferson

Disciples of Christ
James Abram Garfield
Lyndon Baines Johnson

Dutch Reformed
Martin Van Buren
Theodore Roosevelt

Episcopalian
George Washington
James Madison
James Monroe
William Henry Harrison
John Tyler
Zachary Taylor
Franklin Pierce
Chester Alan Arthur
Franklin Delano Roosevelt
Gerald Ford

Friends (Quakers)
Herbert Clark Hoover
Richard Milhous Nixon

Liberal
Abraham Lincoln

Methodist
Ulysses Simpson Grant
Rutherford B. Hayes
William McKinley
James Knox Polk

Presbyterian
Andrew Jackson
James Buchanan
Grover Cleveland
Benjamin Harrison
Woodrow Wilson
Dwight D. Eisenhower

Roman Catholic
John Fitzgerald Kennedy

Unitarian
John Adams
John Quincy Adams
Millard Fillmore
William Howard Taft

No Specific Denomination
Andrew Johnson

EDITOR'S NOTE:

Some exceptions and amplifications of the above list follow: (1) Madison was not a church member, according to William W. Sweet. Madison "accepted the ministrations of the Episcopal Church, but was never a communicant."* (2) Hayes attended the Methodist Church but never joined it, according to the 1970 *World Almanac*.† (3) According to the *Dictionary of American Biography*, Polk's "wife was an ardent Presbyterian, and he accompanied her regularly to the church of her choice. But his 'opinions and predilections' were in favor of the Methodists, with whom he united just before his death."‡ (4) Sweet describes Jefferson in the same terms as Madison (see note 1 above). The 1970 *World Almanac* says: "Jefferson was a member of the Episcopal Church, but in later life became a deist, described himself as a 'disciple of the doctrines of Jesus' and commended Unitarianism."§ (5) Andrew Johnson, according to the 1972 *Information Please Almanac*, "was not a professed church member; however, he admired the Baptist principles of church government."¶ Johnson is listed as a Methodist by the 1970 *World Almanac*.‖ (6) The *Dictionary of American Biography* makes two relevant statements concerning Lincoln. As a youth, he "shunned the vociferous camp meetings of his time, and avoided membership in the church." "Though never identifying himself with any ecclesiastical denomination, he was not lacking in the religious sense; and in his public papers he expressed with sincerity the spiritual aspirations of his people."# The 1970 *World Almanac* gives this note: "Lincoln attended Presbyterian services in Washington but was not a member."** *Facts about the Presidents* lists Lincoln as having "No Religious Affiliation."†† [LR]

* *Religion in Colonial America* (New York: Scribner, 1942), p. 337. † 1970 *World Almanac* (New York: Newspaper Enterprise Association, Inc., 1970), p. 415. ‡ Eds., Allen Johnson and Dumas Malone, *Dictionary of American Biography* (New York: Scribner, 1928–1937). § *Ibid.*, p. 415. ¶ 1972 *Information Please Almanac* (New York: Dan Golenpaul Associates, Simon and Schuster, 1971), p. 772. ‖ *Ibid.*, p. 415. # *Ibid.* ** *Ibid.* †† Joseph Nathan Kane, *Facts about the Presidents* (New York: H. W. Wilson, 1959), p. 235.

RELIGIOUS AFFILIATION OF JUSTICES OF THE SUPREME COURT

Listing of Justices from the 1972 *Information Please Almanac* (New York: Dan Golenpaul Associates, Simon and Schuster, 1972), pp. 834–836

EDITOR'S NOTE:

The religious affiliation of the 15 men who have served as Chief Justice is as follows:

Baptist	2	Presbyterian	1
Church of England	1	Protestant	1
Congregational	1	Roman Catholic°	2
Episcopalian	5	Unitarian	1
Methodist	1		

The religious affiliation of the 89 Associate Justices appointed before 1972 is as follows:

Protestant	78	Jewish	5
Catholic	5	No denomination	1

[LR]

RELIGIOUS AFFILIATION OF COLONIAL LEADERS

Quoted from William W. Sweet, *Religion in the Development of American Culture, 1765–1840* (New York: Scribner, 1952), p. 85

The framers of the Constitution represented a cross-section of the American religious bodies of that day. Of them, nineteen were Episcopalians, eight were Congregationalists, seven were Presbyterians, two were Roman Catholics, two were Quakers, one a Methodist, one a Dutch Reformed while Edmund Randolph was a deist, though he later became a communicant of the Episcopal Church.

Quoted from William W. Sweet, *Religion in Colonial America* (New York: Scribner, 1942), pp. 336–339

A considerable proportion of the most important leaders in the fight for religious liberty in America were not church members; Madison, Jefferson and Franklin serve as good examples. None of them were communicants of a church; all of them were interested in religion as such; all were philosophical liberals, with little in common with the orthodox churches

° The first Catholic Chief Justice was Roger B. Taney (served 1836–1864), who presided over the Court in the Dred Scott case (1857).

of their time. Madison was a graduate of the College of New Jersey and remained a year after graduation to pursue further study in Hebrew and Ethics under the sturdy Presbyterian president John Witherspoon, who not only presided over his formal studies, but imbued him with his own antipathy for a state-controlled church. Madison had been reared as an Episcopalian, but was never a communicant. Jefferson had little liking for formal Christianity as expressed in the priesthood and dogma, though he was a believer in deity and accepted the ministrations of the Episcopal Church. He was a liberal contributor to many denominations and many clergymen of various churches were his friends, but he abhorred any connection between church and state. . . . Certain it is that the principal leaders of Revolutionary America were latitudinarian in their religious views, with no strong predilection for any one religious body. . . . Thus, the political and religious liberalism of seventeenth- and eighteenth-century England and France was mediated to the American Colonies through a group of unchurched leaders, whose unattached position made them the more responsive to these liberal voices.

WOMEN AND RELIGION

Data on women are included in various chapters of Part
One; see Almanac above for polls, statistics, material on
the clergy, different denominations, etc., especially Chapter XIII.

XXXII / YOUTH AND RELIGION*

EDITOR'S NOTE:
In the preceding pages, statistics on virtually all aspects of religion (faith, self-identification, church attendance, attitudes to God, heaven, hell, life after death, and so on) have been broken down by age groupings, wherever possible.

The reader is therefore referred to these Part Two materials by the subject of particular interest.

A brief summary of the salient facts about the opinions of American youth on selected aspects of faith, the church, the clergy, and so on is offered below. The data are mostly taken, by permission, from the excellent and comprehensive *Religion in America 1971* (Gallup Opinion Index, April 1971, Report No. 70), edited by George Gallup, Jr., and John O. Davies, III. The size of the sample used and the yearly continuity serve to make this volume an invaluable source on many fundamental aspects of American religion. [LR]

COLLEGE STUDENTS: RELEVANCE OF RELIGION
From *Religion in America 1971*, Gallup Opinion Index, April 1971, Report No. 70, p. 52

"IS ORGANIZED RELIGION A RELEVANT PART OF YOUR LIFE AT THE PRESENT TIME, OR NOT?"

Group	Yes	No
AGE		
18 years & under	51%	49%
19 years	43	57
20 years	39	61
21–23 years	38	62
24 years & over	41	59
TYPE OF COLLEGE		
Public	39	61
Private	38	62
Denominational	69	31

* Also see various chapters, by topic, for age groups.

Group	Yes	No
RELIGIOUS PREFERENCE		
Protestant	51	49
Catholic	57	43
PARENTS' INCOME		
$15,000 & over	32	68
$10,000–$14,999	42	58
$ 7,000–$ 9,999	49	51
Under $7,000	56	44

EDITOR'S NOTE:

In 1974 there was a drop in the percentage of students entering American colleges and responding "None" to questions about their religious self-identification or preference. This drop followed a steady rise since 1966 in student opinion. The 1974 increase showed a growing number of college entrants expressing a preference for Protestant, Roman Catholic, and Jewish identification. (These conclusions are based on studies conducted by the American Council on Education and the Higher Education Laboratory, Graduate School of Education, University of California at Los Angeles. See *The New York Times*, February 3, 1974, p. 43.) [LR]

COLLEGE STUDENTS: RELIGION AND TODAY'S PROBLEMS

From *Religion in America 1971*, Gallup Opinion Index, April 1971, Report No. 70, p. 53.
(This poll continues the trend shown in the previous poll.)

"DO YOU BELIEVE THAT RELIGION CAN ANSWER ALL OR MOST OF TODAY'S PROBLEMS—OR IS IT LARGELY OLD FASHIONED AND OUT OF DATE?"

Group	Can Answer	Out of Date	Don't Know
NATIONAL	40%	39%	21%
SEX			
Male	37	43	20
Female	45	33	22

Group	Can Answer	Out of Date	Don't Know
AGE			
18 years & under	39	40	21
19 years	40	41	19
20 years	42	38	20
21–23 years	37	39	24
24 years & over	31	51	18
RELIGION			
Protestant	55	24	21
Catholic	40	34	26
PARENTS' INCOME			
$15,000 & over	32	51	17
$10,000–$14,999	42	38	20
$ 7,000–$ 9,999	39	32	29
Under $7,000	58	27	15

BASED ON THE 40 PERCENT OF STUDENTS WHO SAY (ABOVE) THAT RELIGION CAN ANSWER TODAY'S PROBLEMS

	Percentage
Religion has spiritual significance; "I believe in God"	38%
Religion can give people direction; helps to de-emphasize materialism	37
Religion has helped me solve personal problems	20
Religion is love and more love is needed these days	7
Belief in religion can help bring peace in the world	7
Others	6
Don't know, no answer	6
	121%*

* Total is more than 100% because of multiple responses.

COLLEGE STUDENTS: CHURCH ATTENDANCE

From special *Report on Religion*, Gallup Opinion Index, February 1969, p. 9

"DID YOU, YOURSELF, HAPPEN TO ATTEND CHURCH IN THE LAST SEVEN DAYS?"*

Group	Yes	No
AGE		
18 and under	49%	57%
19	50	50
20	52	48
21–23	40	60
24 and older	47	53
PARENTS' INCOME		
$15,000 & over	33	67
$10,000–$14,999	55	45
$ 7,000–$ 9,999	54	46
Under $7,000	54	46

* Poll taken in May 1968.

YOUTH ATTITUDES: BIRTH CONTROL, ABORTION, DIVORCE

Quoted from "Change—Yes, Upheaval, No," *Life* Magazine, January 1971

LIFE [magazine] commissioned Louis Harris Associates to interview a national cross section of the 26 million Americans who are between the ages of 15 and 21. Their views on a broad range of social questions are remarkably moderate, even conservative. In sum, they describe a rather tolerant, relaxed group whose attitudes and expectations on a great many subjects differ very little from their parents'. As Harris reports, "The majority of youth listens to the rhetoric of dissent, picks what it wants, then slowly weaves it into the dominant social pattern."

Within the cross section, college students on almost every issue are strikingly more skeptical and "progressive" than their younger brothers and sisters in high school. But even here the responses do not forecast a radical future: "Change, yes. Revolution, no."

Some results of the poll appear below:

Is it important to limit the number of children you have?	Yes	77%
Catholics only	Yes	71
How many children do you want?		
Two or less		58
Three		21
Four or more		17

Should a couple be free to divorce simply if they are unhappy
together?   Yes   62
    Catholics only   Yes   57
Is this true even if they have children?   Yes   51
How does divorce affect children?
    Causes serious damage   36
    Upsets them but has no serious effect   43
Should any girl who wants an abortion be allowed to have one?   Yes   46
    No   45

HIGH-SCHOOL RESPONSE TO "RIGHT AND WRONG"

From "The Climate of the High School," *Purdue Opinion Panel,* Report No. 92, July 1971, Question 64

"WHICH ONE OF THESE HAS BEEN MOST IMPORTANT IN SHAPING YOUR OWN FEELINGS OF RIGHT AND WRONG, OR WHAT IS GOOD OR BAD?"

	POLL 74	POLL 92
	1965	*1971*
Teachings by my parents	57%	39%
Teachings by the school	2	5
Religious teachings	13	12
Man-made laws, like those of govt.	3	4
My own experience	26	44
	101%	104%

* Total is more than 100% because of multiple responses.

INTERPRETATION OF DATA ON YOUTH AND RELIGION

George Gallup, in *Religion in America 1971,* Gallup Opinion Index, April 1971, Report No. 70, p. iv

Surveys have indicated that many young people today have been spiritually deprived—they have not had the chance to know what religion can do for them—they have not had an opportunity to know God. Few know how to pray or what prayer is capable of bringing to their lives.

THREE IMPORTANT FACTS ABOUT YOUTH TODAY

In seeking to appeal to youth, the clergyman should keep in mind three facts about youth today.

1. The anti-establishment mood prevalent among some students today is not directed solely at the church, but at many other institutions as well.
2. The levels of religious belief among young adults today are extremely high, despite their disenchantment with the forms of religion; in addition, they manifest a new interest in finding out the meaning of life (for example, the "Jesus cult," and current interest in mysticism and meditation); and
3. Young people are eager to serve others. Surveys have shown that a majority of college students have done at least some work among the poor and underprivileged—a far cry from earlier years. Earning money and "getting ahead" have lost some of their charm.

One of the goals of the religious leader, therefore, could be viewed as that of trying to link the will to believe among young people with their desire to help others.

EDITOR'S NOTE:

The Reverend Andrew Greeley, a Roman Catholic priest and sociologist, in a report of the National Opinion Research Center, states: "Religious devotion among adolescents was substantially higher than their parents'." The NORC report, published January 11, 1975, notes that "64 percent of teenagers [now] attend Mass every week, and 42 percent receive communion weekly." [LR]

REFERENCE AIDS

HEADQUARTERS OF DENOMINATIONS
WITH MEMBERSHIP OF 100,000 OR MORE

Condensed from Constant H. Jacquet, Jr., ed., the 1973 Yearbook of American Churches
(New York: National Council of the Churches of Christ in the U.S.A., 1973), pp. 21–108

Adventists, Seventh-day
6840 Eastern Avenue, N.W.
Washington, D.C. 20012

Armenian Apostolic Church of
America
411 East 53rd Street
New York, New York 10022

Armenian Church of North
America, Diocese of the (including Diocese of California)
630 Second Avenue
New York, New York 10016

Assemblies of God
1445 Boonville Avenue
Springfield, Missouri 65802

BAPTIST GROUPS

American Baptist Association
214 East Broad Street
Texarkana, Texas 75501

American Baptist Convention
Valley Forge,
Pennsylvania 19481

Baptist General Conference
5750 North Ashland Avenue
Chicago, Illinois 60626

Conservative Baptist Association of
America
Geneva Road, P.O. Box 66
Wheaton, Illinois 60187

Free Will Baptists
1134 Murfreesboro Road
Nashville, Tennessee 37217

General Association of Regular
Baptist Churches
1800 Oakton Boulevard
Des Planes, Illinois 60018

National Baptist Convention of
America
1058 Hogan Street
Jasksonville, Florida 32202

National Baptist Convention,
U.S.A., Inc.
405 East 31st Street
Chicago, Illinois 60616

National Primitive Baptist Convention, Inc.
2116 Clinton Avenue, W.
Huntsville, Alabama 35805

North American Baptist Association
Conway, Arkansas 72032

Progressive National Baptist
Convention, Inc.
630 Glenwood Avenue
Cincinnati, Ohio 45229

Southern Baptist Convention
1707 San Jacinto
Dallas, Texas 75210

United Free Will Baptist Church
Kinston College
1000 University Street
Kinston, North Carolina 28501

Buddhist Churches of America
1710 Octavia Street
San Francisco, California 94109

The Christian and Missionary
 Alliance
 260 West 44th Street
 New York, New York 10036
Christian Churches (Disciples of
 Christ)
 International Convention
 222 South Downey Avenue
 Indianapolis, Indiana 46219
Church of the Brethren
 1451 Dundee Avenue
 Elgin, Illinois 60120
Church of Christ, Scientist
 107 Falmouth Street
 Boston, Massachusetts 02115
Church of God in Christ
 938 Mason Street
 Memphis, Tennessee 38126
Church of the Nazarene
 6401 The Paseo
 Kansas City, Missouri 64131
Churches of Christ
 (strictly congregational with no
 general headquarters)

CHURCHES OF GOD

Church of God (Anderson, Indiana)
 Box 2420
 Anderson, Indiana 46011
Church of God (Cleveland,
 Tennessee)
 Keith Street at 25th, N.W.
 Cleveland, Tennessee 37311

EASTERN ORTHODOX CHURCHES

American Carpatho-Russian Ortho-
 dox Greek Catholic Church
 Johnstown, Pennsylvania 15906
Antiochian Orthodox Christian
 Archdiocese of New York and
 North America
 239 85th Street
 Brooklyn, New York 11209
Exarchate of the Russian Orthodox
 Church in North and South
 America
 15 East 97th Street
 New York, New York 10029

Greek Archdiocese of North and
 South America
 10 East 79th Street
 New York, New York 10021
The Orthodox Church in America
 59 East 2nd Street
 New York, New York 10003
Serbian Eastern Orthodox Diocese
 for the U.S.A. and Canada
 8347 West Summerdale Avenue
 Chicago, Illinois 60656

FRIENDS

Friends United Meeting
 7148 West Thompson Road
 Indianapolis, Indiana 46251
Religious Society of Friends
 (General Conference)
 1520 Race Street
 Philadelphia, Pennsylvania 19102

Independent Fundamental
 Churches of America
 145 North Washington Street
 Wheaton, Illinois 60187
Jehovah's Witnesses
 124 Columbia Heights
 Brooklyn, New York 11201

JEWISH CONGREGATIONS

Central Conference of American
 Rabbis
 790 Madison Avenue
 New York, New York 10021
Rabbinical Alliance of America
 156 Fifth Avenue
 New York, New York 10011
Rabbinical Assembly of America,
 Inc.
 3080 Broadway
 New York, New York 10027
Rabbinical Council of America, Inc.
 84 Fifth Avenue
 New York, New York 10011
Synagogue Council of America
 235 Fifth Avenue
 New York, New York 10001

Union of American Hebrew
Congregations
838 Fifth Avenue
New York, New York 10021
Union of Orthodox Jewish Congre-
gations of America
84 Fifth Avenue
New York, New York 10011
Union of Orthodox Rabbis of the
United States and Canada
235 East Broadway
New York, New York 10002
United Synagogue of America
3080 Broadway
New York, New York 10027

LATTER-DAY SAINTS (MORMONS)

Church of Jesus Christ of Latter-
day Saints
47 East South Temple Street
Salt Lake City, Utah 84111
Reorganized Church of Jesus Christ
of Latter-day Saints
The Auditorium
Independence, Missouri 64051

LUTHERAN CHURCHES

American Lutheran Church
422 South 5th Street
Minneapolis, Minnesota 55415
Lutheran Church in America
231 Madison Avenue
New York, New York 10016
Lutheran Church–Missouri Synod
The Lutheran Building
210 North Broadway
St. Louis, Missouri 63102
Wisconsin Evangelical Lutheran
Synod
3512 West North Avenue
Milwaukee, Wisconsin 53208

METHODIST BODIES

African Methodist Episcopal
Church
1212 Fountain Drive, S.W.
Atlanta, Georgia 30314

African Methodist Episcopal
Zion Church
1328 U Street, N.W.
Washington, D.C. 20009
Christian Methodist Episcopal
Church
6432 South Green Street, Apt. 1
Chicago, Illinois 60621
United Methodist Church
1115 South Fourth Street
Louisville, Kentucky 40203

PENTECOSTAL ASSEMBLIES

Pentecostal Church of God of
America, Inc.
312–316 Joplin Avenue
Joplin, Missouri 64801
United Pentecostal Church, Inc.
3645 South Grand Boulevard
St. Louis, Missouri 63118

Polish National Catholic Church of
America
529 East Locust Street
Scranton, Pennsylvania 18505

PRESBYTERIAN BODIES

Presbyterian Church in the U.S.
341 Ponce de Leon Avenue, N.E.
Atlanta, Georgia 30308
United Presbyterian Church in
the U.S.A.
475 Riverside Drive
New York, New York 10027

Protestant Episcopal Church
815 Second Avenue
New York, New York 10017

REFORMED BODIES

Christian Reformed Church
2850 Kalamazoo Avenue, S.E.
Grand Rapids, Michigan 49506
Reformed Church in America
475 Riverside Drive
New York, New York 10027

ROMAN CATHOLIC CHURCH

Apostolic Delegation
  3339 Massachusetts Avenue,
    N.W.
  Washington, D.C. 20008
Archdiocese of Boston
  2121 Commonwealth Avenue
  Brighton, Massachusetts 02135
Archdiocese of Chicago
  211 East Chicago Avenue
  Chicago, Illinois 60611
Archdiocese of Los Angeles
  1531 West 9th Street
  Los Angeles, California 90015

Archdiocese of New York
  451 Madison Avenue
  New York, New York 10022
Archdiocese of St. Louis
  4445 Lindell Boulevard
  St. Louis, Missouri 63108

Unitarian Universalist Association
  25 Beacon Street
  Boston, Massachusetts 02108
United Church of Christ
  297 Park Avenue South
  New York, New York 10010

GLOSSARY OF RELIGIOUS TERMS

The following definitions are adapted from two sources: Frank S. Mead, *Handbook of Denominations in the U.S.* (Nashville: Abingdon-Cokesbury Press, 1961); and *Webster's New International Dictionary of the English Language* (Springfield, Mass. G. & C. Merriam Company, 1940) [LR]

absolution—The remission of guilt and penalty for sin, by a priest, following confession.

Adventism—The doctrine that the second coming of Christ and the end of the world (or age) are near at hand.

agnostic—One who believes in the doctrine that neither the existence nor the nature of God, nor the ultimate origin of the universe, is known or knowable.

Anabaptist—One of a party arising in 1523 in Zurich which rejected infant baptism, held the church to be composed of true Christians baptized on confession of faith, and advocated separation of church and state.

anathema—A solemn ban or curse pronounced by ecclesiastical authority and accompanied by excommunication.

Annunciation—The announcement by the angel Gabriel to the Virgin Mary that she was to be the mother of Christ.

anointing—The act of consecrating by the application of oil, used in consecrating sacred objects or persons, as preparation for death or in completing the efficacy of baptism.

Apocalypse—The last book of the New Testament, otherwise called the Revelation of Saint John the Divine.

apocalyptical—Anything viewed as a prophetic revelation.

Apocrypha—(1) Commonly, the fourteen books of the Old Testament in the Vulgate (Latin) that were taken from the Septuagint (Greek version) but are not found in Hebrew; now excluded from the Authorized Version. (2) Christian gospels, epistles, and apocalypses of fictitious authorship, not admitted to the New Testament.

apocryphal—Not canonical, unauthentic, spurious.

apologetics—Systematic argumentative discourse in defense, especially of the divine origin and authority of Christianity.

apostle—One of the twelve disciples of Christ sent forth to preach the gospel. The original twelve included: Simon Peter, Andrew, James and John (sons of Zebedee), Philip, Bartholomew, Matthew (or Levi),

Thomas (or Didymus), James (son of Alphaeus), Jude (or Thaddeus), Simon the Cananaean, and Judas Iscariot. Matthias was chosen by lot to take the place of Judas. Paul, though not one of the twelve, was equal with them in office and dignity. Barnabas, the companion of Paul on his first missionary journey, is sometimes called an apostle.

Apostles' Creed—A widely used creed, formerly ascribed to the twelve apostles, beginning "I believe in God the Father Almighty, maker [creator] of heaven and earth: and in Jesus Christ his only Son our Lord."

apostolic succession—The doctrine of an unbroken line of succession in the episcopacy from the apostles to the present time, maintained in Greek, Roman, and Anglican churches.

Arminian—A follower of Arminius (1560–1609), a Dutch Protestant theologian. Arminius denied Calvin's doctrine of unconditional predestination, limited atonement, and irresistible grace, and stood for universal salvation for all. The theology of the Wesleyans of Great Britain and the Methodists of America is Arminian.

Athanasian—A follower of Athanasius (293–373), who defended the orthodox view of the divinity of Christ: that the son of God was of the same essence or substance with the Father. He opposed and won over Arius at the council of Nicaea; Arius held that Christ was created by, but was essentially different from, the Father.

atheist—(1) One who holds to atheism, disbelief in or denial of the existence of a God, or Supreme Being. (2) A godless person.

atonement—The reconciliation of the sinner with God through the sufferings of Jesus Christ.

ban—A sentence by the church, which amounts to excommunication or outlawry, upon those guilty of an act or speech forbidden by the church.

baptism—Act or ceremony of baptizing; specifically, a sacrament by whose reception one becomes a Christian or a member of a Christian church.

Bible—(1) The book of writings accepted by Christians as inspired by God and of divine authority. (2) Also, the book made up of writings similarly accepted by the Jews. (3) The Scriptures of the Old and New Testament.

Calvary—(1) The place outside the ancient city of Jerusalem where Christ was crucified. (2) A representation of the crucifixion of Christ.

Calvinism—The doctrines of the French theologian John Calvin (1509–1564), including election or predestination, limited atonement, total depravity, irresistibility of grace, and the perseverance of the saints. Calvinism especially emphasizes the sovereignty of God in the bestowal of grace.

canon—An ecclesiastical decree, code, or constitution.

catechism—A manual or guide for catechizing or oral instruction, especially for moral and religious instruction.

Christ—(1) The Messiah, or (Lord's) Anointed, whose coming was prophesied and expected by the Jews. (2) Jesus; Christ as the person who fulfilled this prophecy and expectation.

Communion—(1) The sacrament of the Eucharist; the celebration of the Lord's Supper. (2) The act of partaking of the sacrament.

communion—A body of Christians having one common faith and discipline.

concordance—An alphabetical index of the principal words in a book, citing the passages in which they occur.

concordat—An agreement made between the Pope and a sovereign or government for the regulation of ecclesiastical matters.

confession—(1) Acknowledgment of sins or sinfulness, especially in a prescribed form in public worship; specifically, the act of disclosing sins or faults to a priest or minister to obtain sacramental absolution. (2) A confession of faith.

confirmation—The initiatory rite by which persons are inducted into the church.

consecrate—To set apart as sacred certain persons, animals, places, objects, or times.

covenant—A solemn compact between members of a church to maintain its faith, discipline, and so on.

creed—An authoritative summary or formula of the essential articles of a faith; for the Christian faith, especially the Apostles' Creed, the Nicene Creed, and the Athanasian Creed.

deism—Belief in a personal God who exerts no influence on men or on the world he has created.

denomination—A class, or society of individuals, called by the same name; a sect.

diocese—(1) The territory of a church under the jurisdiction of a bishop. (2) An archdiocese is the diocese of an archbishop.

disciple—One who receives instruction from another; specifically, a professed follower of Christ in his lifetime, especially one of the twelve apostles.

doctrine—That which is taught as the belief of a church.

dogma—(1) That which is held as an opinion, especially, a definite tenet; also a code of such tenets. (2) A doctrine or body of doctrines of theology and religion formally stated and authoritatively proclaimed by a church or sect, especially the Roman Catholic Church.

ecclesiastical—Pertaining to the church or the clergy.

ecumenical (or **oecumenical**)—General; universal; representing the whole Christian Church.

episcopal—Having to do with bishops, or governed by bishops.

Eucharist—The sacrament of the Lord's Supper; the solemn act or ceremony of commemorating the death of Christ, in the use of bread and wine as the symbols.

evangelical—A word used to denote primary loyalty to the gospel of Christ, in contrast to ecclesiastical or rationalistic types of Christianity; spiritual-mindedness and zeal for Christian living, as distinguished from ritualism, and so on.

excommunication—An ecclesiastical censure whereby one is, for the time, cast out of the communion of the church.

fundamentalist—One who believes in the infallibility of the Bible as inspired by God, and that it should be accepted literally, as distinguished from the *modernist,* who interprets the Bible in accordance with more modern scholarship or scientific knowledge.

Gospel—The story or record of Christ's life and doctrines, contained in the first four books of the New Testament; especially, one of the four New Testament books containing narratives of the life and death of Jesus Christ ascribed respectively to Matthew, Mark, Luke and John.

gospel—The good news concerning Christ, the Kingdom of God, and salvation; hence, the teachings of Christ and the apostles; the Christian faith, revelation, or dispensation.

grace—The gift of God to man of the Divine favor and inner power necessary to salvation.

hierarchy—Government by priests or prelates, as in the Roman Catholic Church.

Holy Ghost—The third person of the Trinity.

holy orders—The ranks, or orders, of the Christian ministry.

homiletics—The art of preaching; that branch of theology which treats of homilies or sermons.

icon—(1) An image or representation. (2) In the Eastern church, an image of Christ, the Virgin Mary or a saint.

Immaculate Conception—In the Roman Catholic Church, the miraculous conception by which the Virgin Mary was herself conceived, without original sin; or the doctrine proclaimed a dogma in 1854, which affirms this.

immersion—Baptism by complete submersion in water.

impanation—A doctrine that the body of Christ is present in the eucharistic bread and wine without any change in their substance.

infallibility—The authority of the Scriptures as incapable of error.

kosher—Sanctioned by Jewish law, especially designating food that may be eaten as ritually clean.

laity—The people, as distinguished from the clergy; laymen.

lay—Of or pertaining to the laity, as distinct from the clergy.

laying on of hands—A form used in consecrating to office, in the rite of confirmation, and in blessing persons. The hands are put upon the head of the recipient.

liturgy, liturgical—(1) A prescribed form or collection of forms for public worship; in "liturgical" churches, rite and ceremony are more prominent than the emphasis on preaching or evangelism. (2) The public rites and services of the Christian church, specifically, the eucharistic rite called the Liturgy (also Divine Liturgy) in the Eastern, the Mass in the Western, church.

Mass—The central worship service of the Roman Catholic Church, consisting of prayers and ceremonies.

Messiah—(1) The expected king and deliverer of the Hebrews. (2) The Christ, the divinely sent Savior of the world.

mezuzah—A tiny piece of parchment bearing the passages Deuteronomy 6:4–9 and 11:13–21 written in twenty-two lines. It is rolled up in a wooden, metal or glass case or tube and attached to the doorpost, by Orthodox Jews, as both the passages command.

missal—The book containing that which is said or sung at Mass for each and every day of the year.

monotheism—The doctrine or belief that there is but one God.

New Testament—The covenant of God with man embodied in the coming of Christ and the teaching of Christ and his followers as set forth in the Bible. Hence, usually, that portion of the Bible in which this covenant is contained.

Nicene (Nicean) Creed—(1) A confession formulated and decreed by the First Council of Nicaea, A.D. 325, settling the controversy concerning the persons of the Trinity. (2) An expanded form of the foregoing read at the Council of Chalcedon (A.D. 451) as the creed of the Council of Constantinople—hence, also called the Niceno-Constantinopolitan Creed. (3) A form now in use in the Western church identical with the preceding except for one extra clause inserted at a church council in A.D. 589.

Old Testament—The covenant of God with the Hebrews as set forth in the Bible. Also the canonical books including the Law, Prophets, and Hagiographa, and (Roman Catholic Church) the books except two of the Apocrypha of Protestants.

ordain, ordination—To invest with ministerial or sacerdotal functions; to introduce into the office of Christian ministry.

order—To admit to holy orders; to ordain.

original sin—In theology, the innate sin, or depravity, inherited from our parents, and the source of all actual sins. It originated in the first sin of Adam, the father of the human race.

orthodoxy—Belief in doctrine considered correct and sound, or holding the commonly accepted faith.

papal infallibility—In the Roman Catholic Church, the dogma adopted by the Ecumenical Council in Rome in 1870 that the Pope cannot, when speaking in his official character of supreme pontiff, err in defining a doctrine of Christian faith or rule of morals to be held by the Church.

parochial—Of or pertaining to a parish; as, parochial clergy, or parochial school.

patriarch—A bishop of highest rank, standing above metropolitans and ruling patriarchates.

penance—An ecclesiastical punishment inflicted for sin, or a sacrament of the Christian Church.

Pentecost—(1) A solemn festival of the Jews celebrated on the fiftieth day (seven weeks) after the second day of the Passover. (2) A Christian festival commemorating on the seventh Sunday after Easter the descent of the Holy Spirit on the apostles; hence, Whitsunday.

Pentecostal—The religious experience of conversion based upon the descent of the Holy Ghost upon the apostles at the Jewish Pentecost.

polity—Form or constitution of the government of a state, or of any institution or organization, such as a church, similarly administered.

presbytery—A church court or assembly having the ecclesiastical or spiritual rule and oversight of a district, or the district itself.

proselyte, proselytize—To convert, especially to some religious sect.

reredos—A screen or partition wall, usually ornamental, behind an altar.

Resurrection—The rising of Christ from the dead.

revelation—(1) God's disclosure or manifestation of himself or of his will to man, as through some act, oracular words, signs, laws, etc.; that which is revealed by God to man. (2) The Revelation of Saint John the Divine: the last of the canonical books of the Bible; the Apocalypse.

rubric—A rule for the conduct of a liturgical service; as, the rubrics of the Mass.

sabbatarian—One who favors a strict observance of the Sabbath; specifically, one who would make compulsory by law abstinence on the Sabbath from all secular occupations or recreations.

Sabbath—A season or day of rest from labor, specifically: (1) The seventh day of the week in the Jewish calendar, now called *Saturday,* the observance of which as a day of rest was enjoined in the Decalogue.

(2) The first day of the week, Sunday, kept by most Christians as a day of rest and worship.

sacerdotal—A term denoting a religious system in which everything is valued in relation to the ministrations of the priestly order.

sacrament—One of certain religious ceremonies distinguished in Christian rites as instituted or recognized by Christ. The Roman Catholic and the Eastern churches recognize seven sacraments, *viz.*, baptism, confirmation, the Eucharist, penance, extreme unction, holy orders and matrimony; Protestants, only baptism and the Lord's Supper.

salvation—The rescue of man from evil or guilt by God's power, that he may obtain blessedness.

sanctify—(1) To set apart to a sacred office or to religious use or observance; to hallow. (2) To render productive of holiness or piety.

Scripture—The books of the Old and the New Testament, or of either of them; the Bible.

sect—(1) A group having in common a leader or a distinctive doctrine. (2) In religion, (a) a party dissenting from an established or parent church; (b) one of the organized bodies of Christians, a denomination.

sectarian—(1) Of or pertaining to, or characteristic of a sect; one of a sect, especially a religious sect. (2) A narrow or bigoted denominationalist.

secular—Of or pertaining to the worldly or temporal, as distinguished from the spiritual or eternal; specifically, (a) not under church control; nonecclesiastical; (b) not sacred; profane, as secular music.

see—The local seat from which a bishop, archbishop, or the Pope exercises jurisdiction.

Septuagint—The Greek version of the Old Testament, still in use in the Eastern Church.

synagogue—(1) A local assembly of Jews organized for public worship. (2) The building or place of assembly used by Jewish communities primarily for religious worship.

syncretism—(1) The reconciliation or union of conflicting beliefs, especially religious beliefs, or a movement or effort intending such. (2) In the development of a religion, the process of growth through coalescence of different forms of faith and worship or through accretions of tenets, rites, and so on from those religions which are being superseded.

synod—An ecclesiastical council, either of regular standing or appointed as needed.

Talmud—The collected body of Jewish civil and canonical law, consisting of the combined Mishnah, or text, and Gemara, or commentary.

tithe—To pay or give a tenth part of, especially for the support of the church.

torah, Torah—(1) In Jewish literature, a law; precept; divine instruction; revelation. (2) The Pentateuch, or "Law of Moses" (Torah).

total depravity—The equivalent of original sin, every human faculty having an innate evil taint.

trine immersion—A form of baptism in which the candidate is immersed three successive times, in the name of the Father, Son, and Holy Ghost.

Trinitarian—A believer in the Trinity—that there is a union of Father, Son and Holy Ghost in one divine nature.

unction—A ceremonial anointing with oil, as in extreme unction, in case of death or imminent death.

Uniat—Persons or churches acknowledging the supremacy of the Pope, but maintaining their own liturgies or rites.

Unitarian—One who denies the doctrine of the Trinity, believing that God exists only in one person; also one of a denomination of Christians holding this belief.

virgin birth—The doctrine that Jesus was miraculously begotten of God and born of a virgin mother.

Vulgate—A Latin version of the Scriptures—in the main, the work of Saint Jerome in the fourth century—used as a standard for services of the Roman Catholic Church.

INDEX

Abortion, 309–23
    attitudes toward, survey data on, 313–16
    Baptists and, 32–33
    blacks and, 320–21
    Catholics and, 55, 238, 313–21
    Christian Scientists and, 80
    Disciples of Christ and, 92
    effects of legalization of, in New York City, 323
    Episcopalians and, 107–8
    Jehovah's Witnesses and, 139
    Judaism and, 153
    Lutherans and, 168, 322–23
    Methodists and, 181
    Mormons and, 194
    Orthodoxy and, 125
    performance of, data on, 320–21
        for Catholics, 321
    Presbyterians and, 210–11
    Quakers and, 238
    Seventh-day Adventists and, 252
    Supreme Court decision on, 309–312
        state laws and, 313
    Unitarian Universalists and, 271
    United Church of Christ and, 279
    youth polled on, 628–29
Absolution, Catholic, 44, 45
Activism, church membership and, 324–28
Adam, 49
Adams, John, 275, 620
Adams, John Quincy, 275, 620
Adams, Robert L., 594–95
Adler, Felix, 619

Advent, 535
Adventist Church, 619
Africa, Baptists in, 35
Agnostics, 285–95
    atheists distinguished from, 285–286
    as "Christians," 288–89
    communism and, 294
    good and evil for, 286–87, 291
    on the hereafter, 290
    on Jesus Christ, 288
    man's "soul" and, 289
    sexual morality and, 292
    trinitarian doctrine and, 288
    as Unitarian Universalists, 265
    view of Bible of, 287–88
    Virgin Birth and, 288
    See also "Unchurched," the
Albanian Orthodox Archdiocese in America, 113
"Alien baptism," 29
All Saints, 427, 535
All Souls' Day, 427
"Amendment, purpose of," 44
American Baptist Board of Education and Publication, 37
American Baptist Churches in the U.S.A., 25, 27, 32, 38
    See also American Baptist Convention
American Baptist Convention, 25, 26, 31, 33, 34, 38, 375
    on abortion, 32–33
    ecumenical movement and, 33, 34
    membership figures for, 35

American Baptist Foreign Missionary Society, 37
American Baptist Home Missionary Society, 37
American Baptist News Service, 25
American Bible Society, 33, 617
American Carpatho-Russian Orthodox Greek Catholic Church, 131
American Civil Liberties Union, 317
American Ethical Union, 258, 261, 543
American Friends Service Committee, 239
American Friends of the World Council of Churches, 25
American Humanist Association, 258, 261, 543
American Jewish Committee, 572, 612
American Jewish Congress, 474
American Law Institute, 32–33
American Lutheran Church (ALC), 157, 166, 168, 444, 485–486
American Missionary Association, 280
American Orthodox Church, 113, 131
American Psychiatric Association, homosexuality and, 540–41
American Quaker Fellowship, see Quakers
American Revolution, church allegiances in, 616
American Sunday School Union, 33
American Theological Society, 96
American Tract Society, 617
Amish, 616
Ancient Oriental churches, 129
Angelus, The, 427
Anglican Church, see Church of England
Anglican Communion, 97, 98, 107, 109, 110
  membership of, 110–11

Anglican-Roman Catholic International Commission, 98n, 506–7
Anglicans
  agreement with Catholics of, on Eucharist, 62
  origins of Methodism and, 172–173
  See also Protestant Episcopalian Church in the U.S.
Annunciation Day, 115, 425
Anti-Defamation League of B'nai Brith, 605
Anti-Semitism
  Christian beliefs and, 605–7
  Jews polled on, 570
  Lutherans and, 613–14
  papal declaration on, 609–13
  Presidential candidates and, 602
  among teen-agers, 604–5
  Vatican II on, 420, 607, 608–13
Apostles' Creed, 99, 158, 201, 204
Aquinas, Saint Thomas, 49
Archbishop of Canterbury, 505
  Episcopalians' relation to, 97, 107
Archbishop of Constantinople, as leader of world Orthodoxy, 114
Archdiocese of New York, 39
Armenian Church, 129
Ascension, The, 426, 534
Ash Wednesday, 51, 425, 532
Asia, Baptists in, 35
Associated Church Press, 25
Assumption, The, feast of, 427, 534
Assumption of Mary, 30
  in Catholic view, 48
  Orthodoxy on, 115
  Presbyterians on, 204
Atheists, 285–86
  as Unitarian Universalists, 265
Athenagoras I, Patriarch of Constantinople, 114, 126, 130, 504

Atonement
Day of, *see* Yom Kippur
Quaker view of, 232–33
Attendance, church, *see* Church attendance
Augsburg Confession, 158, 163–64, 486
Augustana Evangelical Lutheran Church, 157, 485

Ballou, Hosea, 274
Baptism, observance of
Baptist, 26, 28–29, 36
Catholic, 41, 48–49, 54, 116
by Christian Scientists, 72
by Disciples of Christ, 86
Episcopalian, 98
for infants
Baptists and, 26, 29
Jehovah's Witnesses and, 136–137
Jehovah's Witnesses and, 136–37
Lutherans and, 162
Methodist, 175, 176, 178–79
Mormon, 191
Orthodox, 116
Presbyterian, 202, 203
Quaker, 228, 231
Seventh-day Adventists and, 247–48
Baptist Union for Great Britain and Ireland, 36
Baptist World Alliance, 33, 35
Baptist World Alliance Congress, 26
Baptists, 25–38
abortion and, 32–33
baptism and, 26, 28–29, 36
Bible and, 26–27
birth control and, 32
blacks and, 31, 374–75
communion service of, 28
as "denomination," not "church," 26–27
different denominations of, 34–35
divorce and, 31

Baptists (*cont.*)
ecumenical movement and, 33–34
heaven and, 30
hell and, 30
history of, 35–39, 615, 619
homosexuality and, 33
membership figures for, 34–35
organization of, 26–27, 37
on racism, 31
Sacraments and, 28
salvation and, 30, 36
trinitarian doctrine and, 30
Virgin Birth of Christ and, 29–30
on women, 31–32
Barclay, Robert, 225, 241
Bayne, Stephen F., 96
Bea, Cardinal, 610, 611
Beacon Press, 275
Bede, 350
Beecher, Lyman, 617, 618
Benediction, 427
Benezet, Anthony, 239
Berkowitz, William, 574
Bernardin, Joseph, 387–88
Bernstein, Louis, 573
Berrigan, Daniel, 399
Bible, The, 345–55
agnostic views of, 287–88
Baptists and, 27–28
Catholic vs. Protestant view of, 41
Catholic versions of, 752–53
Christian Scientists and, 71
Disciples of Christ and, 87–88
Ecumenical Edition of (1973), 345–46
Episcopalians and, 102
highlights in history of, 350–52
Jehovah's Witnesses and, 135
Methodist view of, 172
Mormon view of, 189
Quaker view of, 225–26
in schools, 64
Seventh-day Adventists and, 246
summary of facts about, 346–48

Bible, The (*cont.*)
  translations of, in progress, 348
  Unitarian Universalists and, 266
  United Church of Christ and, 279
  versions of, 345–46, 350–53
    relative popularity of, in U.S., 354–55
Bible reading in U.S., 354–55
Bickertonites, 187
Bingham, Walter D., 90
Birth control, 356–73
  Baptists and, 32
  Catholics and, 41–42, 52–53, 356–73, 393, 394–96, 523, 526–27
  Catholic priests polled on, 370–371
  Christian Scientists and, 79–80
  Disciples of Christ and, 91–92
  Episcopalians and, 107
  Jehovah's Witnesses and, 139
  Lutherans and, 167–68
  Methodists and, 177
  Mormons and, 193
  Moslem attitudes toward, 523, 526–27
  Orthodoxy and, 125
  Pope's warning to U.N. on, 372–373
  practice of
    by Catholic women, 359–65
    by Catholics world-wide, 357–359
    preferred methods for, Catholic and non-Catholic, 364–365, 369–70
  Presbyterians and, 207
  Quakers and, 237
  Unitarian Universalists and, 270
  United Church of Christ and, 279
  U.S. attitudes toward, poll results on, 366–68, 526–27
  U.S. national statistics on, 356–357
  youth polled on, 29

Birth rates, 522–28
Black Catholic Clergy Caucus, 376–377
Black Manifesto, Disciples of Christ and, 95
Black Muslims, 380–85
  creed of, 381–82
  history of, 380–81
  membership of, 382
  property of, 383
  sects of, 380–81, 382–83
  violence and, 384
Blackmun, Harry A., 310
Blacks, 374–85
  abortion and, 321–22
  affirmation of religious identity by, 329, 330, 334
  attitudes toward
    Baptist, 31
    Catholic, 58–59, 420–21
    Christian Scientist, 79
    of Disciples of Christ, 90, 93, 95
    Episcopalian, 108, 379
    of Jehovah's Witnesses, 137–138
    of Judaism, 151
    Lutheran, 168
    Methodist, 179–80
    Mormon, 194–96
    Orthodox, 123–24
    Presbyterian, 210, 379
    Quaker, 238–39
    of Seventh-day Adventists, 251
    Unitarian Universalist, 269
    of United Church of Christ, 280, 379
  Catholic schools and, 378, 517
  Church membership of
    Baptist, 34–35, 374–75
    comparative statistics on, 374–376
    among Disciples of Christ, 89–90
    Episcopalian, 108–9
    Orthodox, 124

Blacks (*cont.*)
  early U.S. churches of, 385, 617–618
  political prejudice against, 602
  Roman Catholic, data on, 377–378, 379
  See also Black Muslims
Blake, Eugene Carson, 506
Blanchard, Roger W., 326
Blanshard, Brand, 543
Bohr, Niels, 299, 300–301
Bokeleale, I. B., 93
Bondi, Herman, 543
Bonnell, John S., 200
Book of Common Prayer, 99–100
  on the Trinity, 101
  on women's duties, 105–6
Book of Concord, 158
Book of Mormon, 189–90
Booth, William, 619
Bottoms, Lawrence W., 379
Bragg, Raymond B., 544
Brown, Olympia, 270
Bryan, William Jennings, 619
Buddhism, 257
  Catholic view of, 40, 600, 611
Bulgarian Eastern Orthodox Church, 113, 131
Butler University (Indianapolis), 93
Byzantine Rite, 129

Calendar, church
  for all faiths, 532–35
  Catholic, 424–27, 538–39
  Christian and secular, 536
  Jewish, 537, 580–86
Calvin, John, 35
  Presbyterianism and, 207, 208
Calvinism
  of Particular Baptists, 36
  Quakers and, 223
  Universalist challenge to, 274
Candlemas, 425
Canon Law Society of America, 471, 491
Carroll, John, 617

Castro, Fidel, 422, 578
Cathedral College of the Immaculate Conception, 39
Catholic Bishops Secretariat on Catholic-Jewish Relations, 608, 612
Catholics, *see* Roman Catholics
Celibacy
  Catholics and, 56–57, 116, 402–414
    Paul VI on, 404–11
    Priests polled on, 403–4
    U.S. bishops on, 411–14
  Episcopalians and, 104
  Lutherans and, 165
  Orthodoxy and, 116
Censorship, Catholics and, 51
Central America, Baptists in, 35
Central Conference of American Rabbis, 572, 574
Challoner, Richard, 351, 352
Channing, George, 69
Channing, William Ellery, 274, 618
Charismatic Renewal, 63
Charismatics, 590–91, 592
  See also Pentecostalists
Charles II, King of England, 36, 229
Chastity, *see* Celibacy
Chrismation, 116
Christ, *see* Jesus Christ
Christ the King, feast of, 427
Christian Church, *see* Disciples of Christ
Christian churches, "independent," 84–85
Christian Reformed Church, 445
Christian Science Committees on Publication, 69
Christian Scientists, 69–81, 619
  abortion and, 80
  attitude toward other religions of, 81
  baptism and, 72
  basic premise of, 70
  belief in sin of, 78

Christian Scientists (*cont.*)
  birth control and, 79–80
  blacks and, 79
  Christianity of, 70
  on death, 78–79, 80–81
  definition of, 69
  Eucharist and, 72
  evil's existence and, 77–78
  funeral services and, 81
  healing and, 69, 73–77, 80
  "health" for, 71
  heaven and hell for, 78
  homosexuality and, 81
  on Jesus, 72
  Man-God relationship for, 70–71
  medical science and, 74–77
  prayer and, 73
  as Protestants, 81
  psychiatry and, 80
  sacraments and, 72
  salvation and, 72
  "scientific" nature of doctrine of, 70
  service of, 71
  trinitarian doctrine and, 72
  vaccination opposed by, 79
  women's status and, 79
Christian Surfers, 594
Christmas, 427, 535–36
Church of Abyssinia, 124, 129
Church affiliation
  of American Presidents, 620–21
  of colonial leaders, 622–23
  community size and, 451
  educational level and, 449
  income and, 450
  by occupation, 449
  population growth and, 442–44
  by region, 450
  of Supreme Court Justices, 622
  See also Church membership
Church in the Americas, 127
Church attendance, 431–36
  clergy polled on, 435
  college students polled on, 628
  Jewish, 431, 432, 435, 565, 566
  in seven nations, 436

Church attendance (*cont.*)
  in U.S., data on, 431–35
"Church of Christ"
  Catholic Church as, 40
  Disciples of Christ as, 83*n*
Church of Christ, Scientist, *see* First Church of Christ, Scientist
Church of Christ, Temple Lot, 186–87
Church of Constantinople, 114
Church of Cyprus, 113
Church of England, 36, 97
  establishment of, in U.S., 615
  See also Anglicans
Church of Greece, 113, 127
Church of Jesus Christ of Latter-day Saints, *see* Mormons
Church of the Larger Fellowship, 275
Church of Malabar, 129
Church membership, 437–56
  affirmation of religious identity and, 329–34
  by age, 448
  changes in, in U.S., 442–45
  comparative U.S. annual figures for, 441–42
  criticism of statistics on, 451–457
  growth trends in, for U.S., 444
  Protestant and Catholic, compared, 445–46
  by race, 448
  by sex, 448
  social activism and, 324–28
  by state and region, sources of data on, 445–47
  of U.S. denominations, listed, 437–40
  worldwide figures for, 443
  See also Church affiliation; *and specific denominations*
Church of the United Brethren in Christ, 171
Chworowsky, Karl M., 263
Circumcision, The, 424–25

Citizens' Advisory Council on the Status of Women, 470
Clarke, John, 37
Clergy
  polling of
    on church performance, 463
    on church role, 463–64
    on Protestant-Catholic unity, 496
    on Protestant church merger, 487
    on relation to laity, 462
    on religion's future, 547–48
    on religion's influence, 546
  Protestant
    on entering clergy today, 464
    income of, 460–62
    size of, comparative listings on, 458–60
  women as, 465–76
    See also Women–ordination of
Cody, John, 318
Cogley, John 39, 399
Colgate-Rochester Divinity School, 25
College students, polling of
  on church attendance, 628
  on relevance of religion, 625–27
Colonial leaders, religious affiliation of, 622
Columbia University, 39
Communion, observance of
  Anglican-Roman discussion on, 98n, 505
  Baptist, 28
  Catholic, 116, 120
    Mass distinguished from, 41–42
  among Disciples of Christ, 86, 87
  Episcopalian, 98n, 99, 101–2
  Lutheran, 161–62
  Methodist, 175
  Mormon, 191
  Orthodox, 120
  Presbyterian, 202–3

Communion (cont.)
  Unitarian Universalists and, 266–267
  See also Eucharist
Communism
  ecumenical movement and, 505
  humanists on, 543
  Vatican and, 421–22
Compline, 430
Concordia Seminary (St. Louis), 587–88
Confession
  Catholic, 44–46, 204
  Eastern Orthodox, 120–24
  Episcopalians and, 102, 204
  Lutheran, 163
  Methodists and, 174
  by Pope, 43
  Presbyterians and, 204
Confirmation
  Catholics and, 116
  Episcopalians and, 98
  Lutherans and, 162–63
  Orthodoxy and, 116
Congregationalism, 36
  introduced by Pilgrims, 615
  Mary Baker Eddy's background of, 71
Congregationalists, see United Church of Christ
Connery, John R., 493
Conscientious objection
  Jehovah's Witnesses and, 134–135
  Quakers and, 229, 230
  "selective," Lutherans on, 164–165
  Unitarian Universalists and, 273
Consultation on Church Union, 90, 93, 184, 282
  composition of, 502, 510
  withdrawal of United Presbyterian Church from, 510
Contraception, see Birth control
Contrition, Act of, 44
Conversion, intermarriage and, 556–60

Cooke, Cardinal, 318–19
Coptic Church, 129
Corpus Christi, 426
Council of Jerusalem, 497
Council of Jewish Federation and Welfare Funds, 568
Council of Nicaea, 117, 127, 497, 498
Council of Trent, 50
Coverdale, Miles, 351
Craig, James E., 83
Crick, Francis, 543
Cromwell, Oliver, 215, 229
Crow, Paul A., Jr. 93, 510
Cushing, Cardinal, 64
Cutlerites, 187

Darrow, Clarence, 619
Dead Sea Scrolls, 347
Deicide, Jews and, 42n, 607, 609
Deists, 259, 617
   Jefferson and, 620, 621
Demetrios I, Patriarch of Constantinople, 114
Dennis, Walter D., 506
Denominations, U.S.
   by "families," listed, 477–83
   headquarters of, listed, 633–36
Desertion, 488
Devil, the, 50
   belief in, poll data on, 343
   Catholic conception of, 49
Devotions of Catholics, listed, 427–430
Dewey, John, 542
Diez-Alegría, José Maria, 400
Dinwoodey, Dean, 326
Disciples of Christ, 83–95
   abortion and, 92
   attitude toward Catholics of, 92
   baptism observance of, 86
   Bible and, 87–88
   birth control and, 91–92
   blacks and, 89–90, 93, 95
   Churches of Christ distinguished from, 84–85
   communion of, 86

Disciples of Christ (cont.)
   distribution of, 84, 93
   divorce and, 91
   ecumenism and, 85, 87, 92–93, 95
   fundamentalists and liberals among, 88
   General Assembly of, 85, 94
   on heaven and hell, 88–89
   higher education and, 93
   history of, 84, 617
   homosexuality and, 92
   independent Christian Churches distinguished from, 84–85
   Lord's Supper observed by, 86
   membership figures for, 84, 93, 445
   membership requirements of, 86
   organizational structure of, 93–94
   origin of name of, 84
   other Protestants distinguished from, 87
   overseas work of, 93
   sacraments observed by, 86
   service of, 86
   on sin and salvation, 88–89
   social activism and, 95
   trinitarian doctrine and, 88
   use of creed rejected by, 85
   on Virgin Birth, 88
   women as, 90–91
Disestablishment in U.S., 616–17
Divino Afflante Spiritu (encyclical), 61
Divorce, 488–94
   Baptists and, 31
   Catholics and, 41–42, 51, 392–393, 488, 489–94
   Disciples of Christ and, 91
   Episcopalians and, 105
   incidence of, 488–89
   intermarriage and, 561
   Jehovah's Witnesses and, 139
   Judaism and, 149, 152–53
   Lutherans on, 166–67
   Mormons and, 193

Divorce (*cont.*)
Orthodoxy and, 116, 125
Presbyterians and, 207
Quakers and, 237
Seventh-day Adventists and, 252
Unitarian Universalists and, 270
youth polled on, 628–29
Doctrinal Statement of the Basis of
Union of Presbyterian
Churches, 204
Dorcas Societies, 253
Douropulos, Arthur, 112
Dowie, John Alexander, 619
Drake University (Des Moines),
93
Drinking
Catholics and, 63
Episcopalians and, 106–7
Mormons and, 192
Seventh-day Adventists and, 251
Duck River and Kindred Associa-
tions of Baptists, 35
Dulin, Joseph, 379, 517
Dunkards, 616
Dutch Reformed Church, 615
Dutch West India Company, 616
Dwight, Timothy, 617

Easter, date of, 127–28, 536, 538–
539
Easter Sunday, 426, 533
Easter Vigil, 426
Eastern Orthodox Church, 112–31
abortion and, 125
on Assumption of Mary, 115
baptism and, 116
birth control and, 125
branches of, 113, 131
canonization of saints in, 127
celibacy and, 116
church architecture of, 128–29
communion observance of, 120
confession and, 120–21
creed of, 117
date of Easter for, 127–28
divorce and, 116, 125
ecumenism of, 114, 126, 129–30

Eastern Orthodox Church (*cont.*)
Eucharist and, 116
on "filioque" clause, 115
Greek Orthodox Church as identical with, 112–13
history of, 112, 113, 114, 126–
127, 130
homosexuality and, 125–26
icons venerated by, 121
on Immaculate Conception, 115
interfaith marriage and, 123
Jesus as conceived by, 117, 124
Julian calendar used by, 127
liturgy of, 116, 118, 119–20, 128
missionary work of, 126–27
monks and nuns in, 122
orders of ministry in, 121–22
Patriarchates of, 113, 114
priests in
beards of, 122
marriage of, 123
vestments of, 122
proselytizing disapproved of by,
126
purgatory rejected by, 115
relics venerated by, 121
Roman Catholic Church and
differences in practices of, 116,
121
doctrinal differences between,
115–16
history of split between, 114,
130
relations between, 62, 126
sacraments recognized by, 118
saints not recognized by, 116
structure of, 113–14
synod system of, 113
trinitarian doctrine of, 117
on Virgin Mary, 121
women and, 124
Ecumenical Councils, 497–98
Ecumenical movement, 495–510
Baptists and, 33–34
bibliography on, 510–11
Catholics and, 40, 58, 495–98,
500–2, 505–9, 511

Ecumenical movement (*cont.*)
communism and, 505
Disciples of Christ and, 85, 87, 92–93, 95
Eastern Orthodoxy and, 114, 126, 129–30
Episcopalians and, 110, 512
historical summary of, 496–505
Jews and, 504
Lutherans and, 157, 164, 165, 503
Methodists in, 184, 502
obstacles to, 505–6, 509–10
Presbyterians and, 212, 502
Protestants and, 498–500, 503–4
the "unchurched" and, 261
United Church of Christ in, 282, 502
Ecumenical Patriarchate of Constantinople, 113, 114, 126, 127, 130
Eddy, Mary Baker, 71, 78, 81, 619
biography of, 71–72
Christian Science defined by, 69
on healing, 80
on Jesus, 72
on medical attention, 77
Education
Catholic, 62–67, 513–19
abortion and, 320
basic statistics on, 514–16
black control and, 378
decline of, 513, 514–16, 518, 530
history of, 63–64
integration and, 517
public aid to, 65–67, 529–31
in public schools, 512–13
Disciples of Christ and, 93
Episcopalians and, 109
Jewish, 519–21
Lutherans and, 157
Mormon attitude toward, 197–198
Presbyterians and, 208
Unitarian Universalists on, 268
See also Public schools

Edwardeans, 617
Edwards, Jonathan, 595, 616
Enthronement of the Sacred Heart, The, 428
Epiphany, 425, 532
Episcopalians, 96–111
as Pentecostalists, 591
in Scotland, 97
in U.S., *see* Protestant Episcopal Church in the U.S.
Ericson, Edward L., 255
Ethical Culture Societies, 255, 258, 259, 261, 543, 619
Eucharist, 46, 47, 58
Catholic-Anglican agreement on, 62
Christian Scientists and, 72
Episcopalian service of, 99, 101
Orthodoxy and, 116, 129
See also Communion
Evangelical Alliance, 498
Evangelical Church, 171
Evangelical Friends Alliance, 220
Evangelical Reformed Church, 619
Evangelical United Brethren Church, 170, 620
Evans, Richard L., 186
Evolution, theory of, Episcopalians and, 102
Exaltation of the Holy Cross, The, 427
Eysenck, H. J., 543
Ezrat Nashim, 475

Faith healing, *see* Healing
Falashas, 151
Family planning, *see* Birth control
Family size, 522–28
Fard, W. D., 380
Farians, Elizabeth J., 471
Fast of Ab, 534, 584–85
Feast of Esther, 533, 582–83
Feast of Tabernacles, 534–35, 582
Feasts, *see* Holidays
Federal Council of Churches of Christ in America, 34, 87
foundation of, 499, 619

Federal Religious Census (1906), 85

Festival of Dedication (Hanukkah), 535, 582

Festival of Lights (Hanukkah), 535, 582

Fichter, Joseph, 403

"Filioque" clause, 115

Finney, Charles G., 595, 618

First Church of Christ, Scientist
  as church of laymen, 71
  See also Christian Scientists

First Church of Christ, Scientist (Boston), 69, 73

First National Episcopal Charismatic Conference, 591

Fishbein, Irwin, 572

Folk, Jean Wool, 90

Foreign Policy Association, 25

Forty Hours' Adoration, The, 428

Fox, George, 215, 216, 217, 219, 220, 221, 229, 230, 616

Fox, Robert Jon, 594–95

Free School Society, 63, 64

Free Will Baptists, 35

Freedman, Alfred M., 541

Frey, William C., 591

Friedly, Robert L., 83

Friends, see Quakers

"Friends Churches," 220, 221n

Friends General Conference, 213, 219–20

Friends Service Council (London), 239

Friends United Meeting, 220

Frings, Cardinal, 611

Fundamentalist Reaction, 619

Funeral services, Christian Scientists and, 81

Gambling
  Catholics and, 63
  Episcopalians and, 106–7

Gandhi, M. K., 241

Garrone, Gabriel, 391–92

Gay Activists Alliance, 540

"General Baptists," 36

General Six Principle Baptists, 35

General Theological Seminary (New York), 96

General Tract Society, 37

German Baptists, 616

Gettelson, Ronald B., 573

Gibbons, James, 619

"Gift of tongues," 62, 591–92

Glaser, Joseph B., 573

Glazer, Nathan, 577, 578, 579

Glock, Charles E., 604–5, 613

Glossolalia, 62, 591–92

God, belief in, poll data on, 337–40

Golden Gate Association of California, 280

Gollin, James, 517–18

Good Friday, 425–26, 533

Grace
  Catholic view of, 49
  Quaker view of, 223–24

"Graven images," Catholics and, 50

Gray, Darius, 195

Great Awakening, 616

Great Revivals, 617

Greek Catholic Church, 129

Greek Orthodox Diocese of North and South America, 112, 131

Greek Orthodoxy, see Eastern Orthodox Church

Greeley, Andrew M., 489, 519, 540, 593

Gregory the Great, Pope, 61

Guttmacher, Alan F., 543

Hadley, J. Harold, 544

Hanukkah, 535, 582

Hare Krishna celebrants, psychopathology of, 594

Haydon, A. Eustace, 543

Haywood, Margaret A., 379–80

Healing, Christian Scientists and, 69, 73–77, 80

Heaven
  agnostics and, 290
  Baptists and, 30
  belief in, poll results on, 341–43

Heaven (*cont.*)
  Catholic view of, 48
    unbaptized children and, 48–49
  Christian Scientists and, 78
  Disciples of Christ and, 88–89
  Episcopalians and, 103
  Jehovah's Witnesses and, 136
  Judaism's view of, 146
  Lutherans and, 163
  Methodists and, 174
  Mormons and, 192
  Presbyterians and, 202
  Quakers and, 233
  Seventh-day Adventists and, 247
  Unitarian Universalists and, 267
  United Church of Christ and, 279
Hebrew Union College–Jewish Institute of Religion, 152
Heenan, John, 594
Heisenberg, Werner, 299, 300
Hell
  agnostics and, 290
  Baptists and, 30
  belief in, poll data on, 342
  Catholics and, 49
  Christian Scientists and, 78
  Disciples of Christ and, 88–89
  Episcopalians and, 103
  Jehovah's Witnesses and, 135–136
  Jesus in, 135
  Judaism's view of, 146
  Lutherans and, 163
  Methodists and, 174
  Mormons and, 192
  Presbyterians and, 202
  Quakers and, 233
  Seventh-day Adventists and, 247
  Unitarian Universalists and, 267
  United Church of Christ and, 279
Helwys, Thomas, 36
Hendricks, Donald W., 39
Henning, Clara N., 471

Henry VIII, King of England, 101
Henschel, Walter G., 132
Heschel, Abraham J., 504
"High" church as distinct from "low," 100
Hinduism, 260
  Catholic attitude toward, 40, 600, 611
Hitler, Adolf, 42, 164
Hoagland, Hudson, 543–44
Hobart and William Smith Colleges, 109
Holidays
  for all faiths, listed, 532–35
  Catholic, 424–27, 538–39
  Jewish, 532–35, 536, 580–85
  movable, tabulated, 536–39
Holy Club, 173
Holy Communion, *see* Communion, observance of
Holy Cross Orthodox Theological School of Hellenic College (Brookline, Mass.), 124, 131
Holy days, *see* Holidays
Holy Friday, Greek Orthodox, 533
Holy Orders, 41, 104
Holy Rollers, 592
Holy Saturday, 426
Holy Thursday, 425, 533
Holy Trinity, *see* Trinity, doctrine of
Holy Water, 50
Holy Week, 533
Home Missionary Society, 617
Home Missions Council, 619
Homosexuality, 540–41
  Baptists and, 33
  Catholics and, 59, 540, 541
  Christian Scientists and, 80
  Disciples of Christ and, 92
  Episcopalians and, 108
  Jehovah's Witnesses and, 140
  Judaism and, 154
  Lutherans and, 168
  Methodists and, 181–82, 541

Homosexuality (*cont.*)
  Mormons on, 196
  Orthodoxy and, 125–26
  Presbyterians and, 211
  Quakers and, 239
  Seventh-day Adventists and, 253
  Unitarian Universalists and, 271–272
  United Church of Christ and, 279–80
Hook, Sidney, 543
House, Francis, 129–30
Humanae Vitae (encyclical), 52, 372
  extracts from, 394–96
Humanists, 257–58, 261, 265
  death and, 259
  Manifesto II of, 542–44
Hussites, 616
Hutchinson, Anne, 217
Hutchinson, James M., 544
Hyman, Paula, 475

Iakoros, Archbishop, 123, 131
Icons, Eastern Orthodoxy and, 121
Immaculate Conception, 30, 47
  Catholics and, 47–48, 115
  feast of, 427, 535
  Orthodoxy on, 115
  Presbyterians on, 204
Immaculate Heart of Mary, The, 427, 428
Immersion, 28–29, 36, 86, 116, 136
Incarnation
  Episcopalians and, 101
  Judaism and, 145
Independent Christian Churches, 84–85
Independent Church of Christ (Brush Run, Pa.), 617
Indulgences, 116
Infallibility, papal, *see* Papal infallibility
Infant Jesus of Prague, The, 428
Inge, William Ralph, 218–19

Intermarriage, 549–62
  attitudes toward
    American, 549, 550–51, 555
    in other nations, 549–50
  Catholics and, 54, 551–62
  Jew-Gentile, 556–57, 562, 568–569
    attitudes toward, 549, 550, 551, 571–73
  Judaism and, 146, 571–75
  Orthodoxy and, 123
  Protestant-Catholic, 560–62
    attitudes toward, 549, 550
    Catholic view of, 552–53
  rates of, compared, 555–59
  of whites and nonwhites, 376
    attitudes toward, 549
International Eucharistic Congress (1973), 596–97
International Humanist and Ethical Union, 261
Islam
  Catholic view of, 40–41, 600, 611
  See also Black Muslims; Moslems
Israel, 579
  Arabs in, 528
  meaning of, for Jews, 155
  Vatican and, 420, 422
Issenman, Clarence, 320

James, William, 216, 592
Jefferson, Thomas, 259, 275, 620, 621
Jehovah's Witnesses, 132–41, 619
  abortion and, 139
  baptism and, 136–37
  birth control and, 139
  blacks and, 137–38
  blood transfusions and, 139–40
  on divorce, 139
  editions of Bible used by, 135
  government of, 141
  government authority and, 134
  homosexuality and, 140
  membership of, 445
  national flags and, 134

Jehovah's Witnesses (*cont.*)
ordination of, 137
origin of name of, 132
persecution of, 141
service exemption and, 134–35
trinitarian doctrine and, 133
view of heaven of, 136
view of hell of, 135–36
Virgin Birth and, 133
on women, 138–39
Jesuits, 399–401, 414
on divorce, 490, 493–94
Jesus Christ
agnostics and, 288
"brothers" of, 47
Catholic idea of, 42
Christian Scientists' view of, 72
Episcopalians' view of, 101
Jehovah's Witnesses on, 133
Jewish conception of, 144
miracles of, 72
Mormon idea of, 189
Orthodox view of, 117, 124n
Presbyterian view of, 203
Quaker view of, 226–27
resurrection of, *see* Resurrection
Saint Peter and, 45
second coming of, 249–51
Unitarian Universalists on, 263–264, 267
virgin birth of, *see* Virgin Birth
"Jesus people," 594–95
Jewish Defense League, 571
Jewish Theological Seminary, 618
Jews, 564–86
birth rate among, 576
calendar of, 537, 580–86
Catholic relations with, 419–20, 607–13
Catholics compared with, 42
definition of, 142–43
dietary-law observance and, 566
divorce rate among, 576
ecumenical movement and, 504
educational level of, 566–67
fertility control and, 525, 528

Jews (*cont.*)
holidays of, 532–35, 536, 580–585
intermarriage and, 549, 550, 551, 555–62, 568–69, 571–575
meaning of Israel for, 155
opinions of
on anti-Semitism, 570
on "chosen people" claim, 566
on homosexuality, 540
on intermarriage, 571–73
on Jewish Defense League, 571
politics and, 577–80
population figures for, by state, 564–65
prejudice against, *see* Anti-Semitism
schools run by, 519–21
synagogue attendance of, 431, 432, 435, 565, 566
Vatican II on, 42n, 420, 607, 608–13
See also Judaism
Jews for Jesus, 592
John the Baptist, 28
John XXIII, Pope, 396, 421, 610
Vatican II called by, 39–40, 418, 500
Johnson, George, 573
Judaism, 142–55
abortion and, 153, 314
affirmation of, as religious identity, 329–34
blacks and, 151
calendar of, 537, 580–86
Catholic view of, 40–41, 419–20
Christianity compared with, 144–145
Conservative, 147, 149, 151, 153, 525, 567, 618
divorce and, 149, 152–53, 576
as family religion, 148–49, 575–577
festivals of, described, 580–85
homosexuality and, 154

Judaism (*cont.*)
    intermarriage and, 146, 571–75
    on Jesus, 144
    kosher laws of, 149–50, 566
    Liberal, 147, 149, 151, 152
    New Testament reading and, 145
    Orthodox, 147, 149, 153
    principal tenets of, 143–44
    proselytizing and, 145–46
    rabbi's role in, 148
    Reform, 147, 149, 151, 152, 572
        history of, 618
        intermarriage and, 574–75
    Rosh Hashanah in, 154, 580–81
    sects of, 147–48
    Talmud and, 150–51
    Torah and, 150
    view of heaven and hell of, 146
    wearing of skullcaps in, 149
    women's status in, 151–53, 474–475, 567
    Yom Kippur in, 154, 581–82
    See also Jews
Judson, Ann and Adoniram, 37
Justices of U.S. Supreme Court, religious affiliation of, 622

Kaplan, Mordecai, 143, 544
Kelley, M., 326
Kennedy, Ethne, 402
Kennedy, Eugene, 592–93
Kennedy, Gerald, 510
Kennedy, John F., 601, 620
Kenyon College, 109
Kertzer, Morris N., 142
Khaalis, Hamaas Abdul, 383
King, Martin Luther, Jr., 90, 123
Knox, John, 35, 207, 208
Kol, Cardinal, 319
Kosher laws, 149–50, 566
Küng, Hans, 417–18

Lamb, Edward, 543
Lambeth Conference, 107, 504
    on women's ordination, 468–69
Lamont, Corliss, 543

Last Judgment, purgatory and, 47
Last Supper, 46, 129
Latter-day Saints, *see* Mormons
Lay priests, *see* Priesthood—lay
Lee, Harold B., 194–95
Leeser, Isaac, 618
Léger, Cardinal, 611
Lent, 51
Leo XIII, Pope, 507
Leopold Association, 618
Levine, Naomi, 474
Liénart, Cardinal, 610
Life after death, belief in, 343–44
Lincoln, Abraham, 259–60, 620, 621
Lindbeck, George A., 507
Lipphard, William B., 25
Liquor, *see* Drinking
Little Office of the Blessed Virgin, The, 428
Liturgy, Orthodox, 116, 118
    performance of, 119–20
    types of, 120
Lollards, 350
Lord's Supper
    Baptists' observance of, 28
    Disciples of Christ and, 86, 92
    discussion of, between Disciples of Christ and Catholics, 92
    Episcopalians and, 101–2
    Lutherans and, 161, 163
    Methodists and, 175
    See also Communion, observance of
Lost Found Nation of Islam in the Wilderness of North America, *see* Black Muslims
"Low" church as distinct from "high," 100
Lucy, Robert E., 420–21
Luther, Martin, 35, 158, 159, 160, 163, 165
    Bible translation of, 350
    catechisms of, 158, 162
Lutheran Church in America (LCA), 157, 166, 167, 168, 485–86

Lutheran Church–Missouri Synod (LC–MS), 157, 166, 168, 485–86
  power struggles in, 587–88
Lutheran Council in the U.S.A., 157, 486
Lutheran World Federation, 157, 164, 485, 503
Lutherans, 156–69
  abortion and, 168, 322–23
  anti-Semitism among, 613–14
  attitude toward Luther of, 160
  attitude toward Roman Catholics of, 163–64, 503
  attitude toward saints of, 160
  baptism and, 162
  belief in life after death of, 343
  birth control and, 167–68
  blacks and, 168
  catechism of, 158, 159
  church mergers among, 485–86, 620
  on church and state, 164–65
  confession practiced by, 163
  divorce and, 166–67
  ecumenism and, 157, 164, 165, 503
  education and, 157
  government of, 165–66
  groupings of, in U.S., 157, 485–486, 503
  on heaven and hell, 163
  history of, 158, 615
  homosexuality and, 168
  international distribution of, 169
  liberal-conservative power struggles and, 587–88
  Lord's Supper and, 161, 163
  marriage of pastors and, 165
  membership figures for, 169, 445
  other Protestants distinguished from, 159–60
  sacraments of, 161–62
  salvation for, 161
  sin for, 160–61
  tenets of, 158

Lutherans (*cont.*)
  trinitarian doctrine and, 162
  women and, 166, 474

McCloskey, John, 619
McGovern, George, on abortion, 314
McGready, James, 617
Mack, Alexander, 616
McKinney, Joseph, 593
McLaughlin, John, 399
McLaughlin, Leo, 414
MacPherson, Aimee Semple, 595
Madison, James, 110, 275, 620, 621
Maimonides, 146, 153
Makemie, Francis, 616
Malcolm X, 380, 384
Malone, Dudley Field, 619
Manifesto II, 542–44
Mann, Horace, 64, 275
Mardi Gras, 532
Mark, Saint, 30
Marriage
  Catholic view of, 54, 551–55
    Disciples of Christ and, 92
  interfaith, *see* Intermarriage
  Judaism and, 152, 153
  Mormons and, 193
  of priests
    Catholics and, *see* Celibacy
    Episcopalians and, 104
    Orthodoxy and, 123
  Quakers and, 235–36
Martin, Wayne A., 244
Marxism, *see* Communism
Mary
  Assumption of, *see* Assumption of Mary
  Catholic view of, 47–48, 56
  Eastern Orthodoxy and, 115, 121
  Immaculate Conception of, 30, 47–48, 115, 204
  Presbyterian view of, 204
Maryland, Catholicism in, 615
Mass, Catholic, 92, 116
  communion compared with, 41–42

Mass (*cont.*)
  meaning of, 46–47
Maundy Thursday, 425
Maxwell, Arthur S., 244
Mealey, Margaret, 470–71
Meaolo, Gaetano, 472
Meir, Golda, 420
Mennonites, 220, 241
  history of, 616
Mergers of American churches,
    503, 619–20
  list of (1955–72), 483–85
  Lutheran, 485–86, 503
  Protestant, clergy polled on, 487
Methodism, history of, 171, 172–
    173, 616, 617
Methodist Church, 170, 620
  See also United Methodist
    Church
Methodist Episcopal Church, 171,
    173, 619
Methodist Episcopal Church South,
    171, 385, 619
Methodist Protestant Church, 171,
    619
Methodists, *see* United Methodist
    Church
Metropolia, the, 113
Meyer, Cardinal, 611
Michaëlius, Jonas, 615
Miller, Richmond P., 213
Miller, William, 248, 618–19
Millerism, 618–19
Miracles of Jesus, Christian Science
    on, 72
Miraculous Medal, The, 428
Mixed marriages, *see* Intermarriage
Monophysite churches, 124*n*, 129
Moody, Dwight L., 595
Morais, Sabato, 618
Moravians, 616
Mormons, 186–99
  abortion and, 194
  baptism and, 191
  Bible and, 189
  birth control and, 193
  blacks and, 194–96

Mormons (*cont.*)
  communion observed by, 191
  confirmation and, 191
  definition of, 187
  divorce and, 193
  on education, 197–98
  financing of, 197
  government of, 197
  groupings of, 186–87
  on heaven and hell, 192
  history of, 186, 187–88, 618
  homosexuality and, 196
  immortality and, 190
  on Jesus Christ, 189
  lay priesthood of, 192–93
  on liquor, 192
  marriage and, 193
  membership figures for, 199, 444
  philosophy of freedom of, 198
  polygamy and, 186, 190–91
  proselytizing and, 196–97
  temples of, 196
  on tobacco, 192
  trinitarian doctrine and, 189
  women and, 194
Morris, Charles, 543
Moslems
  fertility and, 523, 526–27
  See also Black Muslims
Mother Church, The, *see* First
    Church of Christ, Scientist
    (Boston)
Mother of Sorrows, The, 428
Movable holidays, tabulated, 536–
    539
Muhammad, Elijah, 380, 381, 383,
    384
Murray, John, 274

Nation of Islam, *see* Black Muslims
National Association of Laity, 518
National Baptist Convention,
    U.S.A., 34–35, 619
National Baptist Convention of
    America, 35, 619
National Council of Catholic
    Women, 470

National Council of Churches of
Christ in the U.S.A., 25, 83,
87, 112, 503, 619
Baptists in, 33, 34
Catholics and, 502
Disciples of Christ in, 87, 90, 93
formation of, 500, 619
Lutherans in, 157, 485
Methodists in, 184
Orthodoxy and, 130
Unitarian Universalists and, 266
United Church of Christ and,
282
National Fertility Study, 356–57
Nativity of the Blessed Virgin, The,
427
Neill, Stephen, 504, 510
Neo-Orthodoxy, 619
Newport Church of Rhode Island,
36–37
New Year's Day, 532
Jewish, *see* Rosh Hashanah
New York, Archdiocese of, 39
New York Board of Rabbis, 573
New York City, effects of legal
abortion in, 323
Nicene (Nicaean) Creed
Episcopalians and, 99
Orthodoxy's use of, 117, 201
Nichols, Billy Joe, 544
Niebuhr, Reinhold, 619
Nielson, Karl, 543
Nixon, Richard M., 314, 620
Northern Baptist Convention, 38
Notre Dame University, 591, 593
Nuns, "radical," 401–2

Ordination
of Jehovah's Witnesses, 137
of women, *see* Women—ordination of
Original sin
Disciples of Christ on, 89
Judaism on, 145
Quaker view of, 232
the unbaptized and, in Catholic
view, 48–49

Orthodox Churches in America,
113
Orthodox churches, *see* Eastern
Orthodox Church
Oxford University, 173

Pacifism of Quakers, 229–30
Paine, Thomas, 259, 275, 617
Palm Sunday, 425, 533
Greek Orthodox, 533
Palmer, Elihu, 617
Pantheists, 260
Papal infallibility, 43, 115
American priests on, 415
Lutheran-Catholic discussion of,
163n, 507–8
"papal primacy" and, 501, 507,
508
Paul VI's reassertion of, 506
Vatican defense of, 415–18, 506,
508
"Papal primacy," 501, 507, 508
Park Avenue Synagogue (New
York City), 567
Parochial schools, Catholic, 64–67,
514–19
black control and, 378
crisis of, 516–19, 530
integration and, 516
poll of Catholics on, 516
public aid and, 65–67, 529–31
teaching on Jews in, 607–8
Particular Baptists, 36
Paschal Sacrifice, 46
Passover, 533, 583
Pastorius, Francis Daniel, 616
Patriarchates of Eastern Orthodoxy,
113, 114, 125
Paul, Saint, 70
on virginity, 57
Paul VI, Pope, 47, 126, 420
on birth control, 52, 372–73,
394–96
on celibacy, 404–11
on ecumenism, 501, 505–6
on Mary, 48

Paul VI (*cont.*)
  on mixed marriages, 551
  on non-Christian religions, 608–613
  on papal authority, 415–16, 505, 506
  on women's ordination, 469, 472, 473
Pawlikowski, John T., 607–8
Penance, sacrament of, 44–46
Penn, William, 230, 231
Pentecost, 426, 534
  Jewish, 534, 584
Pentecostalists, 590–96
  definition of, 591–92
  four types of, 593–94
  number of, estimated, 591
  Roman Catholics as, 62–63, 591, 592–94
Perelman, Chaim, 543
Pesach, 533, 583
Philadelphia Baptist Association, 37
Pietists, 616
Pilgrims, 36
Pittenger, W. Norman, 96
Pius IX, Pope, 508
Pius XI, Pope, 419
  on Judaism, 42
  on religious unity, 499
Pius XII, Pope, 30, 61, 421
  on Assumption, 48, 115
"Plain dress" of Quakers, 230–31
Politics
  of American Jews, 577–80
  religious affiliation and, 324–28, 598
Polygamy, Mormons and, 186, 190–91
Poole, Elijah, *see* Muhammad, Elijah
Pope, the
  authority of, and Vatican II, 61–62
  "infallibility" of, *see* Papal infallibility

Pope (*cont.*)
  Lutheran attitude toward, 163–164
  as "Patriarch of the West," 114
  Reformation and, 97, 100
  See also individual popes
Pope, Liston, 375
Prayer in public schools, opinion poll on, 599
Predestination, 206
Preisand, Sally J., 152, 474
Prejudice, 600–614
  against blacks, *see* Blacks; Racism
  decline in, 600, 601–4
  against Jews, *see* Anti-Semitism
  among teen-agers, 604–5
  religious
    against Catholics, 601–2
    politics and, 601–2, 604
Presbyterian Church in the United States, 206, 212, 620
Presbyterians, 200–212
  on Assumption of Mary, 204
  Bible and, 201
  birth control and, 207
  blacks and, 210, 379
  courts of, 209
  definition of, 200–201
  divorce and, 207
  ecumenism of, 212
  education and, 208
  government of, 208
  on heaven and hell, 202
  history of, 616, 618
  on homosexuality, 211
  Immaculate Conception and, 204
  on Jesus, 203
  membership figures for, 209, 212
  organization of, 201–2, 208–9
  as Pentecostalists, 591
  Resurrection and, 205, 206
  in Revolutionary War, 209–10
  sacraments observed by, 202–3
  salvation and, 203, 204–5
  in Scotland, 205, 207, 208, 209
  symbolism in worship of, 205–6

Presbyterians (*cont.*)
  trinitarian doctrine and, 203
  Virgin Birth and, 204
  women and, 210
Presentation of the Blessed Virgin
    Mary, The, 427
Presentation of the Lord, The, 425
Presidents, U.S., religious affiliation
    of, 275, 620–21
Preus, J. A. O., 587–88
Priesthood
  absence of, among Christian
      Scientists, 71
  Anglican-Roman discussion on,
      98n
  Catholic vs. Protestant view of,
      41
  in Episcopal Church, 104
  lay
    among Disciples of Christ, 85
    among Mormons, 192–93
    among Quakers, 234–35
  Orthodox, 121–23
Priestley, Joseph, 274
Primitive Baptists, 35
Proselytizing
  Disciples of Christ and, 92
  Judaism and, 145–46
  Mormons and, 196–97
  Orthodoxy and, 126
  Unitarian Universalists and, 268
Protestant Episcopal Church in the
    U.S., 96–111
  abortion and, 107–8
  as Anglican church, 97, 110
  baptism and, 98
  Bible's role for, 102
  birth control and, 107
  blacks and, 379
  as Catholic church, 97, 98
  communion and, 98n, 99
  confession and, 102
  creeds of, 99
  divorce and, 105
  drinking and, 106–7
  education and, 109

Protestant Episcopal Church
    (*cont.*)
  evolution and, 102–3
  gambling and, 106–7
  General Convention of, 106, 108,
      109
  on heaven and hell, 103
  homosexuality and, 108
  on Jesus Christ, 101
  marriage of ministers and, 104
  membership figures for, 110–11,
      442
  Methodists and, 178
  missionary work of, 109–10
  monks and nuns in, 104
  organization of, 109
  origin of name of, 97
  overseas dioceses of, 110
  Prayer Book and, 97, 99–100
  priesthood in, 104
  the Resurrection and, 103
  role in American history of, 110
  Roman Catholicism and, 98, 100
  sacraments and, 98
  salvation and, 103
  trinitarian doctrine and, 101
  Virgin Birth and, 101
  women's status and, 105–6
Protestantism
  Catholicism contrasted with, 41–
      42
  Quakerism and, 218, 220, 241–
      242
  in U.S. schools, 64
  See also Protestants
Protestants
  Christian Scientists as, 81
  ecumenism of, 498–500, 503–4
  homosexuality and, 540
  intermarriage and, 549–50, 555–
      562
  Lutherans as, 158
  membership figures for
    affirmation of religious identity
        and, 329
    U.S., 445–51
    world-wide, 443

Protestants (*cont.*)
  proposed merger of, 487, 619–620
    See also Mergers of American churches
  slavery and divisions in, 618
  women's ordination and, 465–469
  See also specific denominations
Providence Baptist Church, 36–37
Psychiatry
  Christian Science on, 80
  churches and, 540–41
Public School Society, 64
Public schools
  prayer in, Supreme Court ruling on, 598
  religious instruction in, 512–13
Purgatory
  Catholic view of, 47
  Jehovah's Witnesses and, 136
  Methodists and, 175
  Orthodoxy and, 165
  Quakers and, 233
Purification, The, 425
Purim, 533, 582–83
Puritans, 35, 36, 615
  origins of Quakerism and, 216–217

Quakers, 213–43
  abortion and, 238
  American groupings of, 219–20
  atonement and, 232–33
  baptism and, 228, 231
  basic tenets of, 218–19
  Bible and, 225–26
  birth control and, 237
  blacks and, 238–39
  on church's mission, 240–42
  "Conservative," 219, 220, 241
  definition of, 214–15
  divorce and, 237
  eschatology of, 233
  on evil, 233–34
  form of worship of, 220–21
  history of, 215–17, 219, 616

Quakers (*cont.*)
  homosexuality and, 239
  "Inward Light" of, 223
  on Jesus, 226–27
  lay priesthood of, 234–35
  "liberal," 219–20, 241
  marriage and, 235–36
  "meetings for business" of, 224–225
  membership figures for, 243
  oathtaking and, 235
  origin of name of, 215
  pacifism of, 229–30, 240
  Pentecostal tendencies of, 220, 242
  "plain dress" of, 230–31
  "plain language" and, 231–32
  as Protestants, 218, 220, 241–42
  "Queries" of, 222
  Reconstructionist view of, 216, 218, 220, 241
  Reformation and, 216–17
  reunionist movement among, 217–18, 241
  sacraments eschewed by, 227–228, 241
  sin and, 223–24, 232
  trinitarian doctrine and, 227
  Vietnam War and, 230, 240
  Virgin Birth and, 227
  "witness" and, 222–23
  women and, 226, 237–38
  work ethic and, 226
  working class and, 228–29
Quinn, John R., 593
Quisling, Vidkun, 164

Rabbi, definition of, 148
Rabbinical Council of America, 573
Racism
  attitudes toward a black president and, 602
  Baptists and, 31
  Catholics and, 58–59
  Episcopalians and, 108
  Methodists on, 180

Racism (*cont.*)
  among teen-agers, 604–5
  See also Anti-Semitism; Blacks;
      Prejudice
Raible, Christopher Gist, 263
Ramsey, Arthur Michael, Arch-
      bishop of Canterbury, 505
Randall, John Herman, Jr., 543
Rassoull, Abass, 381–82
Rauf, Muhammad Abdul, 384–85
Reformation, 35, 158, 161
  Episcopalians and, 97
  Quakers and, 216
  Seventh-day Adventists and,
      244–45
Reformation Day, 535
Reinert, Paul, 401
Relics, Eastern Orthodoxy and, 121
Religious instruction in public
      schools, enrollment figures
      for, 512–13
Religious Society of Friends, *see*
      Quakers
Reorganized Church of Jesus Christ
      of Latter-day Saints, 186,
      199
Resurrection
  Episcopalian view of, 103
  feast of, 426
  Presbyterians and, 205, 206
  Unitarian Universalists on, 267
Revelation, papal infallibility and,
      43
Revivalism, 618
Rhode Island, Baptists in, 36–37
Rijk, Cornelius, 420
Ritchie-Calder, Lord, 543
Ritter, Cardinal, 611
Roberts, Oral, 595
Rockefeller, Nelson, 518
Roman Catholic Church, 36
  anti-Semitism and, 420, 607–13
  attitude toward blacks of, 58–
      59, 420–21
  authoritarianism of, 60–62, 398–
      399

Roman Catholic Church (*cont.*)
  authoritarianism of (*cont.*)
    American challenge to, 386–
        388, 423–24
    See also Papal infallibility
  as "Church of Christ," 40
  on communism, 421–22
  as custodian of Bible, 41
  defection from, among priests
      and nuns, 57–58, 391–92,
      397–98, 401–2
  as defined by Vatican II, 40
  distinctive marks of, 42
  Eastern Orthodoxy and, 62, 114–
      117, 126, 130, 504
  ecumenism and, 40, 58, 495–98,
      500–502, 505–9, 511
  General Council of, Twenty-
      first, *see* Vatican II
  on homosexuality, 59–60, 541
  on intermarriage, 551–55
  membership of, 327
    affirmation of religious
        identity and, 329–34
    in U.S., 329–31, 334, 441,
        445, 446
    world-wide, 443
  Methodists' relations with, 184
  on non-Christian religions, 40–
      41, 420, 600, 608–13
  priesthood of, 41
    decline in, 391–92, 397–98
  relations with Jews of, 419–20,
      607–13
  in U.S.
    Episcopate established, 617
    statistical summary of data on,
        388–92
  women and, 55–56, 469–74
  See also Roman Catholics; Vati-
      can II
Roman Catholics, 39–67, 386–430
  abortion and, 55, 238, 313–21
  attitude of Disciples of Christ
      toward, 92
  attitude toward homosexuality of,
      540

Roman Catholics (*cont.*)
  baptism and, 41, 48–49, 54
  birth control and, 52–53, 356–
     373, 393, 394–96, 523,
     526–27
  blacks, data on, 377–78
  calendar of, 424–27, 532–35,
     538–39
  celibacy and, 56–57, 116, 402–
     414
  censorship and, 51
  changing attitudes of, in U.S.,
     386–88, 392–94
    summary of, 422–24
  church attendance of, 431, 432,
     434–35
  confession and, 44–46
  devotions of, listed, 427–30
  divorce and, 41–42, 51, 392–93,
     488, 489–94
  drinking and, 63
  Episcopalians distinguished from,
     97, 98
  family size desired by, 522, 523
  fasting and, 50–51
  fertility of, 523–35
  gambling and, 63
  "graven images" and, 50
  heaven and, 48–49, 341
  hell and, 49
  history of, in U.S., 615, 617, 618
  holy water and, 50
  holidays of
    lists of, 424–27, 532–35
    movable, tabulated, 538–39
  intermarriage and, 54, 551–62
  interreligious services and, 58
  Jesus as seen by, 42
  Lutherans and, 161–62, 163–64
  Mary and, 47–48
  Mass and, 46–47
  as Pentecostalists, 62–63, 591,
     592–94
  political prejudice against, 600,
     601–2
  Pope's infallibility and, *see* Papal
    infallibility

Roman Catholics (*cont.*)
  Protestants compared with, 41–
    42
  purgatory and, 47
  Quaker affinity for, 238
  religious tolerance and, 60
  salvation and, 40–41, 48–49
  Satan as seen by, 49
  schools run by, 63–67, 513–19
    attendance of, 65, 513, 514–
     516
    basic statistics on, 514–16
    black control and, 378
    history of, 63–64
    public aid to, 65–67, 529–31
    teaching on Jews on, 607–8
  See also Roman Catholic Church
Rosary, The, 428
Rosh Hashanah, 154, 534, 580–81
Routh, Porter W., 326
Rowntree, John Wilhelm, 233
Ruff, G. Elson, 156
Rumanian Orthodox Episcopate of
    America, 131
Russell, Bertrand, 284–85, 294–95
Russell, Charles Taze, 132
Russian Orthodox Greek Catholic
    Church of America, 113,
    131, 617
Russian Patriarchate of Moscow,
    113, 131
Ryan, Herbert, 507

Sabbath
  Jewish, 585
  Seventh-day Adventists and,
    245–46
Sacraments
  Baptists and, 28
  Christian Scientists and, 72
  Disciples of Christ and, 86
  Episcopalians and, 97
  Lutheran, 161–62
  Methodist, 175
  Mormon, 191
  Orthodox, 118
  Presbyterians and, 202–3

Sacraments (*cont.*)
  Quaker view of, 227–28
  Unitarian Universalists and, 266–267
  United Church of Christ and, 278
  Vatican II on, 44–45
  See also specific sacraments
Sacred Heart, 426, 429
Saint Joseph, feast of, 426
Sakharov, Andrei, 543
Salanter, Israel, 154
Salvation
  Baptists and, 30, 36
  Catholic view of, 40–41, 48–49
  Christian Scientists and, 72
  Disciples of Christ and, 89
  Episcopalians and, 103–4
  Judaism and, 145
  Lutherans on, 161
  Methodists on, 175–76
  Mormons on, 192
  Presbyterians on, 203, 204–5
  Seventh-day Adventists on, 248
  United Church of Christ on, 278
Salvation Army, 619
Sancto-Caro, Hugo de, 346
Satan, *see* Devil, the
Schechter, Philip, 573
Schmucker, Samuel, 498
Schoffner, Joseph, 417
SCOBA, 130–31
Scopes, John, 619
Scott, Walter, 89
Second Vatican Council, *see* Vatican II
Secretariat on Catholic-Jewish Relations, 608, 612
Secularists, 257
Selma demonstration, 123
Separatists, 35, 36
Septuagint, 350
Serbian Eastern Orthodox Church, 131
Sermons, social irrelevance of, 327–328
Servetus, Michael, 274

Seton, Elizabeth, 64
Seven Sorrows, The, 429
Seventh-day Adventist World Service (AWS), 253
Seventh-day Adventists, 244–54
  abortion and, 252–53
  baptism and, 247
  Bible and, 246
  divorce and, 252
  on drinking, 251
  eschatology of, 247
  on heaven and hell, 247
  history of, 248, 618–19
  homosexuality and, 253
  membership figures for, 254, 445
  missionary work of, 253
  as Protestants, 244–45
  religious liberty and, 254
  Sabbath of, 245–46
  salvation and, 248
  second coming and, 249–51
  on smoking, 251
  Trinity and, 247
  virgin birth and, 247
  welfare work and, 253
  women and, 251–52
Seventh-day Baptists, 35, 248
Shabuoth, 534, 584
Sharp, Frank A., 25–26
Shehan, Lawrence, 596
Shrove Tuesday, 532
Siegel, Seymour, 525, 528
Simhath Torah, 535
Sin
  agnostic view of, 286–87
  Disciples of Christ and, 89
  Judaism's view of, 145
  Lutherans and, 160–61
  Quakers on, 223–24, 232
  Unitarian Universalist view of, 267–68
  United Church of Christ on, 278
  See also Original sin; Salvation
Skinner, B. F., 543
Slavery, church divisions over, 618
Smith, Joseph, 187–88, 190, 198, 618

Smyth, John, 36
Society of Friends, *see* Quakers
Society for the Propagation of the Faith, 618
Sockman, Ralph W., 170
Solemnity of Mary, Mother of God, 424–25
Southern Baptist Convention, 26, 34, 375, 445
  formation of, 37
Southern Presbyterian Church, *see* Presbyterian Church in the U.S.
St. John-Stevas, Norman, 53
Standing Conference of Orthodox Bishops in the Americas (SCOBA), 130–31
Stark, Rodney, 328, 511, 613
Stations of the Cross, The, 427
Stauderman, Albert P., 156
Stokes, J. Burroughs, 69
Strangites, 187
Strommen, Merton P., 613
Stuyvesant, Peter, 616
Sukkoth, 534–35, 582
Sunday, William A. ("Billy"), 595, 619
Supreme Court, U.S.
  abortion decision of, 309–12
  aid to Catholic schools and, 66, 67, 529–31
  justices of, religious affiliation of, 622
  on prayer in public schools, 599
Suzuki, D. T., 260
Sweazey, George E., 326
Synod of Bishops (1971), 57, 59, 60, 415, 416
Syrian Orthodox Church, 131

Talmud, the, 150–51
Tanenbaum, Marc H., 572, 612
Taoism, 260
Texas Christian University (Fort Worth), 93
Thering, Rose, 608
Three Hours' Agony, The, 429

Tietjen, John H., 588
Tietze, Christopher, 323
Tishah B'ab, 534, 584–85
Toolan, David S., 386
Torah, The, 150, 352
Torkillus, Reorus, 615
Traxler, Margaret, 402
Trevelyan, George Macaulay, 221–22
Triennial Baptist Convention, 37, 38
Trinity, doctrine of
  agnostics and, 288
  Baptists and, 30
  Christian Scientists and, 72
  Disciples of Christ and, 88
  Episcopalians and, 101
  Methodists and, 173–74
  Mormons and, 189
  Orthodoxy and, 117
  Jehovah's Witnesses and, 133
  Lutherans and, 162
  Presbyterians and, 203
  Quakers and, 227
  Seventh-day Adventists and, 247
  Unitarian Universalists and, 263
  United Church of Christ and, 278
Trinity Sunday, 426
Tucci, Roberto, 501
Tucker, R. W., 213, 214
Two-Seed-in-the-Spirit Predestinarian Baptists, 35
Tyndale, William, 350–51

Ukrainian Orthodox Church, 131
"Unchurched," the, 255–62
Uniate Church, 129
Unitarian Universalist Association, 264, 271–72, 275
  See also Unitarian Universalists
Unitarian Universalist Service Committee, 273
Unitarian Universalists, 263–76
  abortion and, 271
  belief in God and, 265
  belief in prayer and, 265

Unitarian Universalists (*cont.*)
Bible and, 266
birth control and, 270
blacks and, 269
as Christians, 265
on church and state, 272–73
conscientious objection and, 273
definition of, 263–64
divorce and, 270
education of children and, 268
on heaven and hell, 267
history of, 264, 274–75, 620
homosexuality and, 271–72
on Jesus' divinity, 267
organization of, 275
origin of name of, 264
political activity and, 273
proselytizing and, 268
on the Resurrection, 267
on sacraments, 266–67
services of, 268–69
on sex, 269
on sin, 267–68
Virgin Birth and, 267
women and, 270–71
Unitarians, 264, 274–75, 617, 618
United Brethren, 171, 616
United Church Board for Homeland Ministries, 280
United Church of Christ, 277–83,
619–20
abortion and, 279
Bible and, 279
birth control and, 279
blacks and, 280, 379
creed of, 277
ecumenism and, 282
on heaven and hell, 279
homosexuality and, 279–80
membership figures for, 445
organization of, 281
other Protestants distinguished
from, 281
role in U.S. history of, 283
sacraments and, 278
on salvation, 278
services of, 281

United Church of Christ (*cont.*)
on sin, 278
trinitarian doctrine and, 278
Virgin Birth and, 278
women and, 280–81
United Lutheran Church, 157, 485,
619
United Methodist Church, 170–85
abortion and, 181
on amusements, 176–77
on anti-Semitism, 180
baptism and, 175, 176, 178–79
Bible and, 172
birth control and, 177
blacks and, 179–80
creed eschewed by, 176
distinctive traits of, compared
with other Protestants, 178–
179
divorce and, 178–79
ecumenism and, 184
foundation of 170, 171
on heaven and hell, 174
history of, 171, 172–73
on homosexuality, 181–82, 541
membership figures for, 185, 442
organization of, 179, 183–84
on praying to saints, 174
on purgatory, 175
sacraments of, 175
on salvation, 175–76
social commitment of, 179
social creed of, 183
source books of, 173
"theologizing" and, 182–83
trinitarian doctrine and, 173–74
Virgin Birth and, 174
women's status in, 181
United Presbyterian Church,
U.S.A., 206, 212, 620
membership figures for, 212, 444
withdrawal from COCU of, 510
See also Presbyterians
United Presbyterian Church of
North America, 206
Universalists, 264, 274–75, 617
See also Unitarian Universalists

University of Pittsburgh, 25
University of the South, 109

Vaccination, Christian Scientists' position on, 79
Vatican, *see* Roman Catholic Church; Vatican II
Vatican Commission for Nonbelievers, 261
Vatican Congregation for Divine Worship, 45
Vatican Council, First (1870), 500
Vatican Council, Second, *see* Vatican II
Vatican Secretariat for Promoting Christian Unity, 164
Vatican II, 39–40, 126, 388
  on anti-Semitism, 420, 607, 608–613
  authoritarianism and, 60–62
  on baptism and original sin, 48
  Catholic Church defined by, 40
  confession and, 44–46
  deacons revived by, 57
  documents produced by, listed, 418–19
  on ecumenism, 58, 500–501
  on Jews, 42*n*
  on the Mass, 46
  on non-Christian religions, 40–41, 420, 600, 608–13
  on priesthood, 41, 56, 57
  purposes of, 39–40
  on reciprocal forms of service, 60
  on religious tolerance, 60
  on sacraments, 44–45
  summary of facts on, 418–19
  on Virgin Mary, 48
Vespers, 429
Vietnam War, Quakers and, 230, 240
Virgin Birth, 47
  agnostics and, 288
  Baptists and, 29–30
  Disciples of Christ and, 88
  Episcopalians and, 101

Virgin Birth (*cont.*)
  Jehovah's Witnesses and, 133
  Methodist view of, 174
  Mormons and, 189
  Presbyterians and, 204
  Quakers and, 227
  Seventh-day Adventists and, 247
  Unitarian Universalists and, 267
  United Church of Christ and, 278
Visitation, The, 427
Visser 't Hooft, W. A., 611
Vulgate Bible, 350

Washburn, Paul A., 170, 171
Washington, George, 110, 258, 620
Watch Tower Bible and Tract Society, 132, 141, 619
Weaver, Warren, 296
Weld, Theodore Dwight, 618
Wendt, Gerald, 543
Wesley, Charles, 173
Wesley, John, 171, 172–73, 176, 177, 179
Wesleyans, *see* United Methodist Church
Westminster Confession of Faith, 201, 202–3, 204, 206
White, Byron R., 67, 310, 312
Whitefield, George, 595
Whitsunday, 426, 534
Williams, Roger, 36–37, 615
Wisconsin Evangelical Lutheran Synod, 157, 486
Wise, Isaac Mayer, 618
Witherspoon, John, 210
Women
  attitude toward
    Baptist, 31–32
    Catholic, 55–56
    Christian Scientist, 79
    of Disciples of Christ, 90
    Episcopalian, 105–6
    of Jehovah's Witnesses, 138
    of Judaism, 151–52, 153, 474–475, 567
    Lutheran, 166, 474

Women (*cont.*)
  attitude (*cont.*)
    Methodist, 181
    Mormon, 194
    Orthodox, 124
    Presbyterian, 210
    Quaker, 226, 237–38
    of Seventh-day Adventists
      251–52
    Unitarian Universalist, 270–271
  of United Church of Christ, 280
  Catholic, contraception used by, 357–65
  as clergy, 465–76
    Protestants and, 465–69
  ordination of
    Baptist, 32
    Catholics and, 55–56, 469–74
    Christian Scientists and, 79
    among Disciples of Christ, 91
    Episcopalians and, 106
    Jehovah's Witnesses and, 138–139
    Judaism and, 152, 474–75
    Lutherans and, 166
    Methodist, 181
    Mormons and, 194
    Orthodoxy and, 124
    Presbyterians and, 210
    Protestant discussions on, 465–469
    Seventh-day Adventists and, 252
    Unitarian Universalists and, 270–71
  political prejudice against, 602, 603–4

Woodruff, Wilford, 191
World Alliance of Reformed Churches, 282
World Conference on Church and Society (1968), 25–26
World Council of Churches, 25, 26, 96, 129
  Baptists in, 33, 34
  Catholics in, 501
  Disciples of Christ in, 86, 93
  formation of, 499–500
  Lutherans in, 157, 165, 485
  Orthodoxy and, 130
  Program to Combat Racism of, 374
  United Church of Christ and, 282
World Methodist Council, 184, 185
World Missionary Conference, 499
Wrenn, Lawrence G., 489, 490–91
Wright, Harold Louis, 379
Wyclif, John, 350
Wynn, John Charles, 489

Yale University, 25
YMCA, 499
Yoga, 260
Yom Kippur, 154, 534, 581–82
Young, Brigham, 186, 188, 618
Youth, results of polls of, 625–30
YWCA, 499

Zacchi, Cesare, 422
Zaire
  Baptists in, 35
  Disciples of Christ in, 93
Zen Buddhists, 220, 260
Zwingli, Ulrich, 35